THE BASTIAT COLLECTION

THE BASTIAT COLLECTION

FRÉDÉRIC BASTIAT

SECOND EDITION

MISESINSTITUTE
AUBURN, ALABAMA

Published by Ludwig von Mises Institute
518 West Magnolia Avenue
Auburn, Alabama 36832
Mises.org

ISBN: 978-1-61016-200-5

CONTENTS

INTRODUCTION

And now I would appeal with confidence to men of all schools, who prefer truth, justice, and the public good to their own systems. Economists! Like you, I am the advocate of LIBERTY; and if I succeed in shaking some of these premises which sadden your generous hearts, perhaps you will see in this an additional incentive to love and to serve our sacred cause.

Bastiat, "To the Youth of France,"
Economic Harmonies, p. 14

Claude Frédéric Bastiat was born in Bayonne, France on June 29th, 1801. He was orphaned at age 9 and raised by relatives. He worked in his uncle's accounting firm and then became a farmer when he inherited his grandfather's farm. After the middle-class Revolution of 1830, Bastiat became politically active and was elected Justice of the Peace in 1831 and to the Council General (county-level assembly) in 1832. He was elected to the national legislative assembly after the French Revolution of 1848. Bastiat was inspired by and routinely corresponded with Richard Cobden and the English Anti-Corn Law League and worked with free-trade associations in France. Bastiat wrote sporadically starting in the 1830s, but in 1844 he launched his amazing publishing career when an article on the effects of protectionism on the French and English people was published in the *Journal des Economistes* which was held to critical acclaim.[1] The bulk of his remarkable writing career that so inspired the early generation of English translators—and so many more—is contained in this collection.

If we were to take the greatest economists from all ages and judge them on the basis of their theoretical rigor, their influence on economic education, and their impact in support of the free-market economy, then Frédéric Bastiat would be at the top of the list. As Murray N. Rothbard noted:

> Bastiat was indeed a lucid and superb writer, whose brilliant and witty essays and fables to this day are remarkable and devastating demolitions of protectionism and of all forms of government subsidy and control. He was a truly scintillating advocate of an untrammeled free market.[2]

This book brings together his greatest works and represents the early generation of English translations. These translators were like Bastiat himself, people from the private sector who had a love of knowledge and truth and who altered their careers to vigorously pursue intellectual ventures, scholarly publishing, and advocacy of free trade.

This collection represents some of the best economics ever written. He was the first, and one of the very few, to be able to convincingly communicate the basic propositions of economics. The vast majority of people who have learned anything about economics have relied on Bastiat or publications that were influenced

---

[1]For biographical material on Bastiat see George Roche's *Frédéric Bastiat: A Man Alone* (New Rochelle, N.Y.: Arlington House, 1971) and Dean Russell's *Frédéric Bastiat: Ideas and Influences* (Irvington-on-Hudson, N.Y.: Foundation for Economic Education, 1969).

[2]Murray N. Rothbard, *Classical Economics: An Austrian Perspective on the History of Economic Thought,* vol. II (1995; Auburn, Ala.: Ludwig von Mises Institute, 2006), p. 444.

by his work. This collection—possibly more than anything ever written about economics—is the antidote for economic illiteracy regarding such things as the inadvisability of tariffs and price controls, and everyone from the novice to the Ph.D. economist will benefit from reading it.

The collection consists of three sections, the first of which contains his best-known essays. In "That Which is Seen, and That Which is Not Seen," Bastiat equips the reader to become an economist in the first paragraph and then presents the story of the broken window where a hoodlum is thought to create jobs and prosperity by breaking windows. Bastiat solves the quandary of prosperity via destruction by noting that while the apparent prosperity is seen, what is unseen is that which would have been produced had the windows not been broken. According to Rothbard:

> In this way, the "economist," Bastiat's third-level observer, vindicates common sense and refutes the apologia for destruction of the pseudo-sophisticate. He considers what is not seen as well as what is seen. Bastiat, the economist, is the truly sophisticated analyst.[3]

Professor Jörg Guido Hülsmann credits Bastiat for discovering this counterfactual method, which allowed Bastiat to show that destruction (and a variety of government policies) is actually the path to poverty, not prosperity. This lesson is then applied to a variety of more complex cases and readers will never be able to deny that scarcity exists and will always—hopefully—remember that every policy has an opportunity cost. If nothing else, they will not believe—as is often claimed—that earthquakes, hurricanes, and wars lead to prosperity. The remaining essays cover the important institutions of society—law, government, money, and capital—where Bastiat explains the nature of these institutions and

---

[3]Ibid., p. 445.

disabuses the reader of all the common misconceptions regarding them.

The second section is Bastiat's *Economic Sophisms*, a collection of 35 articles on the errors of protectionism broadly conceived. Here Bastiat shows his mastery of the methods of argumentation—using basic logic and taking arguments to their logical extreme—to demonstrate and ridicule them as obvious fallacies. In his "Negative Railroad" Bastiat argues that if an artificial break in a railroad causes prosperity by creating jobs for boatmen, porters, and hotel owners, then there should be not one break, but many, and indeed the railroad should be just a series of breaks—a negative railroad. In his article "An Immense Discovery!" he asks, would it not be easier and faster simply to lower the tariff between points A and B rather than building a new railroad to transport products at a lower cost? His "Petition of the Candle-makers" argues in jest that a law should be passed to require that all doors and windows be closed and covered during the day to prevent the sun from unfairly competing with the makers of candles and that if such a law were passed it would create high-paying jobs in candle and candlestick making, oil lamps, whale oil, etc. and that practically everyone would profit as a result.

The third section is Bastiat's *Economic Harmonies* which was hastily written before his death in 1850 and is considered incomplete. Here he demonstrates that the interests of everyone in society are in harmony to the extent that property rights are respected. Because there are no inherent conflicts in the market, government intervention is unnecessary. The borrower wants lenders to thrive so that loans will be available and the lender wants borrowers to thrive in order to collect interest on savings and to be paid back the loan principal. This book is the basis of charges that critics have levied against Bastiat, claiming that he made theoretical errors and failed to extend the corpus of theory. I have shown elsewhere that these criticisms must represent a misreading of Bastiat, and Rothbard showed that Bastiat made the vital contribution of returning economics to a focus on wants, exchange, and consumption correcting the errors of British political economy.[4]

In a more recent and very important reappraisal of Bastiat, Professor Hülsmann has shown my suspicions to be correct.[5] He demonstrates that Bastiat's *Harmonies* is an important theoretical innovation that was widely dismissed by interventionists and attacked by equilibrium theorists. Interventionists dismissed it because the analysis proves that society can thrive without any government intervention in the economy. Equilibrium theorists saw Bastiat's conception of harmony as competition for their own concept of equilibrium—and rightly so—because while equilibrium is at best a useful fiction, harmony is an accurate conception of what actually exists in a free-market world. Therefore, the equilibrium approach can in some cases mimic or equal harmony, but it can also be applied to misleading ends and is inapplicable for others. Hülsmann also brilliantly shows how critics have misread and therefore misunderstood Bastiat's concept of value and service and that their criticisms are invalid. The Hülsmann reappraisal smashes the critics and their echoes and is therefore an important primer for this section. Also see the important article by Joseph T. Salerno who shows that the marginalization of Bastiat and the French school involved a long process of deliberate distortion by their doctrinal enemies among the Anglo-American economists.[6]

Patrick James Stirling translated Bastiat's *Economic Harmonies* (1860) and *Economic Sophisms* (1863) which are reproduced in this collection. Stirling was a student of Thomas Chalmers, an important Scottish economist of the first half of the

---

[4]Mark Thornton, "Frédéric Bastiat was an Austrian Economist," *Journal des Economistes et des Etudes Humaines* 11, no. 2/3 (June/September 2001): 387–98.

[5]Jörg Guido Hülsmann, "Bastiat's Legacy in Economics," *Quarterly Journal of Austrian Economics* 4, no. 4 (Winter 2000) pp. 55–70.

[6]Joseph T. Salerno, "The Neglect of Bastiat's School by English-Speaking Economists: A Puzzle Resolved," *Journal des Économistes et des Etudes Humaines* 11, no. 2/3 (June/September 2001), pp. 451–95.

nineteenth century and leader of the Free Kirk schism from the Church of Scotland. Stirling was the author of *The Philosophy of Trade*, in which he provided a theory of prices and profits and examined the principles that determine the relative value of goods, labor, and money.[7] In *The Australian and Californian Gold Discoveries and their Probable Consequences* he examined the impact of the large nineteenth-century gold discoveries and the laws that determined the value and distribution of money and where he exhibited a proto-Austrian theory of the business cycle.[8] Stirling has recently resurfaced in the economics literature as the author of the oldest known undergraduate essay in economics.[9] We remain uncertain regarding the early translations of the essays in the first section of this volume (many translations of this period were unsigned), but what we do know seems to reinforce the Scottish connection to Bastiat. William Ballantyne Hodgson, who held a Chair in Political Economy at the University of Edinburgh, translated the essays from "Things Seen and Things Not Seen" for publication in newspapers and were later published as a booklet[10] and *Economic Sophisms* was first translated by Mrs. Louisa McCord (a Scottish surname) from Charleston, South Carolina.[11]

---

[7]Patrick James Stirling, *The Philosophy of Trade* (Edinburgh: Oliver & Boyd, 1846); or outlines of a theory of profits and prices, including an examination of the principles which determine the relative value of corn, labor, and currency.

[8]*The Australian and Californian Gold Discoveries and Their Probable Consequences: An Inquiry Into The Laws which Determine the Value and Distribution of the Precious Metals with Historical Notices of the Effects of the American Mines on European Prices in the Sixteenth, Seventeenth and Eighteenth Centuries* (Oliver and Boyd, 1853).

[9]A.M.C. Waterman, "The Oldest Extant Undergraduate Essay in Economics?" *Journal of the History of Economic Thought* 27, no. 4 (December 2005): 359–73.

[10]William Ballantyne Hodgson, "Things Seen and Things Not Seen" (London: Cassel & Company Limited, 1910), abridged from the translation by Dr. Hodgson in 1852.

[11]Louisa S. McCord, *Sophisms of the Protective Policy* (New York: Wiley and Putnam, 1848). McCord wrote widely on economics and politics

The first section is based on the David Wells (also a Scottish surname) edition of the essays which contained the long out-of-print essay, "What is Money?"[12]

This collection of early translations is dedicated to improving economic literacy and eliminating the frustration of economic teachers everywhere. No one is better to do so, and in such a forceful and entertaining way, than Bastiat. Enjoy.

Mark Thornton
May 2007

---

anonymously because her contemporaries would consider it inappropriate for a woman to be writing on such controversial matters.

[12]David A. Wells, *Essays on Political Economy* (New York: G.P. Putnam's Sons, 1877). Wells was a successful writer, publisher, and inventor. He opposed the income tax and supported free trade and the gold standard. He was appointed chairman of the national revenue commission after the Civil War and is said to have placed the U.S. on a scientific revenue system.

I.

THAT WHICH IS SEEN,
AND THAT WHICH IS NOT SEEN[1]

In the economy, an act, a habit, an institution, a law, gives birth not only to an effect, but to a series of effects. Of these effects, the first only is immediate; it manifests itself simultaneously with its cause—it is seen. The others unfold in succession—they are not seen: it is well for us if they are foreseen. Between a good and a bad economist this constitutes the whole difference—the one takes account of the visible effect; the other takes account both of the effects which are seen and also of those which it is necessary to foresee. Now this difference is enormous, for it almost always happens that when the immediate consequence is favorable, the ultimate consequences are fatal, and the converse. Hence it follows that the bad economist pursues a small present good, which will be followed by a great evil to come, while the true economist pursues a great good to come, at the risk of a small present evil.

---

[1]First published in 1850.

In fact, it is the same in the science of health, arts, and in that of morals. It often happens, that the sweeter the first fruit of a habit is, the more bitter are the consequences. Take, for example, debauchery, idleness, prodigality. When, therefore, a man, absorbed in the effect which is seen, has not yet learned to discern those which are not seen, he gives way to fatal habits, not only by inclination, but by calculation.

This explains the fatally grievous condition of mankind. Ignorance surrounds its cradle: then its actions are determined by their first consequences, the only ones which, in its first stage, it can see. It is only in the long run that it learns to take account of the others. It has to learn this lesson from two very different masters—experience and foresight. Experience teaches effectually, but brutally. It makes us acquainted with all the effects of an action, by causing us to feel them; and we cannot fail to finish by knowing that fire burns, if we have burned ourselves. For this rough teacher, I should like, if possible, to substitute a more gentle one. I mean Foresight. For this purpose I shall examine the consequences of certain economical phenomena, by placing in opposition to each other those which are seen, and those which are not seen.

1. The Broken Window

Have you ever witnessed the anger of the good shopkeeper, John Q. Citizen, when his careless son happened to break a pane of glass? If you have been present at such a scene, you will most assuredly bear witness to the fact, that every one of the spectators, were there even 30 of them, by common consent apparently, offered the unfortunate owner this invariable consolation: "It is an ill wind that blows nobody good. Everybody must live, and what would become of the glaziers if panes of glass were never broken?"

Now, this form of condolence contains an entire theory, which it will be well to show up in this simple case, seeing that it is precisely the same as that which, unhappily, regulates the greater part of our economical institutions. Suppose it cost six francs to repair the damage, and you say that the accident brings six francs to the glazier's trade—that it encourages that trade to the amount of six francs—I grant it; I have not a word to say against it; you reason justly. The glazier comes, performs his task, receives his six francs, rubs his hands, and, in his heart, blesses the careless child. All this is that which is seen.

But if, on the other hand, you come to the conclusion, as is too often the case, that it is a good thing to break windows, that it causes money to circulate, and that the encouragement of industry in general will be the result of it, you will oblige me to call out, "Stop there! Your theory is confined to that which is seen; it takes no account of that which is not seen."

It is not seen that as our shopkeeper has spent six francs upon one thing, he cannot spend them upon another. It is not seen that if he had not had a window to replace, he would, perhaps, have replaced his old shoes, or added another book to his library. In short, he would have employed his six francs in some way which this accident has prevented.

Let us take a view of industry in general, as affected by this circumstance. The window being broken, the glazier's trade is encouraged to the amount of six francs: this is that which is seen.

If the window had not been broken, the shoemaker's trade (or some other) would have been encouraged to the amount of six francs: this is that which is not seen.

And if that which is not seen is taken into consideration, because it is a negative fact, as well as that which is seen, because it is a positive fact, it will be understood that neither industry in general, nor the sum total of national labor, is affected, whether windows are broken or not.

Now let us consider John Q. Citizen himself. In the former supposition, that of the window being broken, he spends six francs, and has neither more nor less than he had before, the enjoyment of a window. In the second, where we suppose the window not to have been broken, he would have spent six francs in shoes, and would have had at the same time the enjoyment of a pair of shoes and of a window. Now, as John Q. Citizen forms a part of society, we must come to the conclusion that, taking it all together, and making an estimate of its enjoyments and its labors, it has lost the value of the broken window.

Whence we arrive at this unexpected conclusion: "Society loses the value of things which are uselessly destroyed;" and we must assent to a maxim which will make the hair of protectionists stand on end—To break, to spoil, to waste, is not to encourage national labor; or, more briefly, "destruction is not profit."

What will you say, *Moniteur Industriel*? what will you say, disciples of good M.F. Chamans, who has calculated with so much precision how much trade would gain by the burning of Paris, from the number of houses it would be necessary to rebuild?

I am sorry to disturb these ingenious calculations, as far as their spirit has been introduced into our legislation; but I beg him to begin them again, by taking into the account that which is not seen, and placing it alongside of that which is seen.

The reader must take care to remember that there are not two persons only, but three concerned in the little scene which I have submitted to his attention. One of them, John Q. Citizen, represents the consumer, reduced, by an act of destruction, to one enjoyment instead of two. Another, under the title of the glazier, shows us the producer, whose trade is encouraged by the accident. The third is the shoemaker (or some other tradesman), whose labor suffers proportionally by the same cause. It is this third person who is always kept in the shade, and who, personifying that which is not seen, is a necessary element of the problem. It is he who shows us how absurd it is to think we see a profit in an act of destruction. It is he who will soon teach us that it is not less absurd to see a profit in a restriction, which is, after all, nothing else than a partial destruction. Therefore, if you will only go to the root of all the arguments which are adduced in its favor, all you will find will be the paraphrase of this naive question— What would become of the glaziers, if nobody ever broke windows?

2. THE DISBANDING OF TROOPS

It is the same with a people as it is with a man. If it wishes to give itself some gratification, it naturally considers whether it is worth what it costs. To a nation, security is the greatest of advantages. If, in order to obtain it, it is necessary to have an army of a hundred thousand men, I have nothing to say against it. It is an enjoyment bought by a sacrifice. Let me not be misunderstood upon the extent of my position. A member of the assembly proposes to disband a hundred thousand men, for the sake of relieving the tax-payers of a hundred million.

If we confine ourselves to this answer, "The hundred thousand men, and these hundred million of money, are indispensable to the national security: it is a sacrifice; but without this sacrifice, France would be torn by factions or invaded by some foreign power"—I have nothing to object to this argument, which may be true or false in fact, but which theoretically contains nothing which militates against economics. The error begins when the sacrifice itself is said to be an advantage because it profits somebody.

Now I am very much mistaken if, the moment the author of the proposal has taken his seat, some orator will not rise and say, "Disband a hundred thousand men! Do you know what you are saying? What will become of them? Where will they get a living? Don't you know that work is scarce everywhere? That every field is overstocked? Would you turn them out of doors to increase competition and to weigh upon the rate of wages? Just now, when it is a hard matter to live at all, it would be a pretty thing if the State must find bread for a hundred thousand individuals! Consider, besides, that the army consumes wine, arms, clothing—that it promotes the activity of manufactures in garrison towns—that it is, in short, the godsend of innumerable purveyors. Why, anyone must tremble at the bare idea of doing away with this immense industrial stimulus."

This discourse, it is evident, concludes by voting the maintenance of a hundred thousand soldiers, for reasons drawn from the necessity of the service, and from economical considerations. It is these economical considerations only that I have to refute.

A hundred thousand men, costing the taxpayers a hundred million of money, live and bring to the purveyors as much as a hundred million can supply. This is that which is seen.

But, a hundred million taken from the pockets of the tax-payers, ceases to maintain these taxpayers and their purveyors, as far as a hundred million reaches. This is that which is not seen. Now make your calculations. Add it all up, and tell me what profit there is for the masses?

I will tell you where the loss lies; and to simplify it, instead of speaking of a hundred thousand men and a hundred million of money, it shall be of one man and a thousand francs.

We will suppose that we are in the village of A. The recruiting sergeants go their round, and take off a man. The tax-gatherers go their round, and take off a thousand francs. The man and the sum of money are taken to Metz, and the latter is destined to support the former for a year without doing anything. If you consider Metz only, you are quite right; the measure is a very advantageous one: but if you look toward the village of A, you will judge very differently; for, unless you are very blind indeed, you will see that that village has lost a worker, and the thousand francs which would remunerate his labor, as well as the activity which, by the expenditure of those thousand francs, it would spread around it.

At first sight, there would seem to be some compensation. What took place at the village, now takes place at Metz, that is all. But the loss is to be estimated in this way: At the village, a man dug and worked; he was a worker. At Metz, he turns to the right about and to the left about; he is a soldier. The money and the circulation are the same in both cases; but in the one there were three hundred days of productive labor, in the other there are three hundred days of unproductive labor, supposing, of course, that a part of the army is not indispensable to the public safety.

Now, suppose the disbanding to take place. You tell me there will be a surplus of a hundred thousand workers, that competition will be stimulated, and it will reduce the rate of wages. This is what you see.

But what you do not see is this. You do not see that to dismiss a hundred thousand soldiers is not to do away with a hundred million of money, but to return it to the tax-payers. You do not see that to throw a hundred thousand workers on the market, is to throw into it, at the same moment, the hundred million of money needed to pay for their labor: that, consequently, the same act that increases the supply of hands, increases also the demand; from which it follows, that your fear of a reduction of wages is unfounded. You do not see that, before the disbanding as well as after it, there are in the country a hundred million of money corresponding with the hundred thousand men. That the whole difference consists in this: before the disbanding, the country gave the hundred million to the hundred thousand men for doing nothing; and that after it, it pays them the same sum for working. You do not see, in short, that when a taxpayer gives his money either to a soldier in exchange for nothing, or to a worker in exchange for something, all the ultimate consequences of the circulation of this money are the same in the two cases; only, in the second case the taxpayer receives something, in the former he receives nothing. The result is—a dead loss to the nation.

The sophism which I am here combating will not stand the test of progression, which is the touchstone of principles. If, when every compensation is made, and all interests satisfied, there is a national profit in increasing the army, why not enroll under its banners the entire male population of the country?

3. Taxes

Have you never chanced to hear it said: "There is no better investment than taxes. Only see what a number of families it maintains, and consider how it reacts upon industry: it is an inexhaustible stream, it is life itself."

In order to combat this doctrine, I must refer to my preceding refutation. Political economy knew well enough that its arguments were not so amusing that it could be said of them, repetitions please.

It has, therefore, turned the proverb to its own use, well convinced that, in its mouth, repetitions teach.

The advantages which officials advocate are those that are seen. The benefit that accrues to the dispensers is still that which is seen. This blinds all eyes.

But the disadvantages which the taxpayers have to bear are those that are not seen. And the injury that results from it to the providers is still that which is not seen, although this ought to be self-evident.

When an official spends for his own account an extra hundred sous, it implies that a taxpayer spends for his account a hundred sous less. But the expense of the official is seen, because the act is performed, while that of the taxpayer is not seen, because, alas! he is prevented from performing it.

You compare the nation, perhaps to a parched tract of land, and the tax to a fertilizing rain. So be it. But you ought also to ask yourself where are the sources of this rain, and whether it is not the tax itself which draws away the moisture from the ground and dries it up?

Again, you ought to ask yourself whether it is possible that the soil can receive as much of this precious water by rain as it loses by evaporation?

There is one thing very certain, that when John Q. Citizen counts out a hundred sous for the tax-gatherer, he receives nothing in return. Afterwards, when an official spends these hundred sous, and returns them to John Q. Citizen, it is in exchange for an equal value in corn or labor. The final result is a loss to John Q. Citizen of five francs.

It is very true that often, perhaps very often, the official performs for John Q. Citizen an equivalent service. In this case there is no loss on either side; there is merely an exchange. Therefore, my arguments do not at all apply to useful functionaries. All I say is—if you wish to create an office, prove its utility. Show that its value to John Q. Citizen, by the services which it performs for him, is equal to what it costs him. But, apart from this intrinsic utility, do not bring forward as an argument the benefit that it confers upon the official, his family, and his providers; do not assert that it encourages labor.

When John Q. Citizen gives a hundred sous to a Government officer for a really useful service, it is exactly the same as when he gives a hundred sous to a shoemaker for a pair of shoes.

But when John Q. Citizen gives a hundred sous to a Government officer, and receives nothing for them unless it be annoyances, he might as well give them to a thief. It is nonsense to say that the Government officer will spend these hundred sous to the great profit of national labor; the thief would do the same; and so would John Q. Citizen, if he had not been stopped on the road by the extra-legal parasite, nor by the lawful sponger.

Let us accustom ourselves, then, to avoid judging of things by what is seen only, but to judge of them by that which is not seen. Last year I was on the Committee of Finance, for under the constituency the members of the Opposition were not systematically excluded from all the Commissions: in that the constituency acted wisely. We have heard Mr. Thiers say, "I have passed my life in opposing the legitimist party and the priest party. Since the common danger has brought us together, now that I associate with them and know them, and now that we speak face to face, I have found out that they are not the monsters I used to imagine them."

Yes, distrust is exaggerated, hatred is fostered among parties who never mix; and if the majority would allow the minority to be present at the Commissions, it would perhaps be discovered that the ideas of the different sides are not so far removed from each other; and, above all, that their intentions are not so perverse as is supposed. However, last year I was on the Committee of Finance. Every time that one of our colleagues spoke of fixing at a moderate figure the maintenance of the President of the Republic, that of the ministers, and of the ambassadors, it was answered:

"For the good of the service, it is necessary to surround certain offices with splendor and dignity, as a means of attracting men of merit to them. A vast number of unfortunate persons apply to the President of the Republic, and it would be placing him in a very painful position to oblige him to be constantly refusing them. A certain style in the ministerial salons is a part of the machinery of constitutional Governments."

Although such arguments may be controverted, they certainly deserve a serious examination. They are based upon the public interest, whether rightly estimated or not; and as far as I am concerned, I have much more respect for them than many of our Catos have, who are actuated by a narrow spirit of parsimony or of jealousy. But what revolts the economical part of my conscience, and makes me blush for the intellectual resources of my country, is when this absurd relic of feudalism is brought forward, which it constantly is, and it is favorably received too:

"Besides, the luxury of great Government officers encourages the arts, industry, and labor. The head of the State and his ministers cannot give banquets and soirées without causing life to circulate through all the veins of the social body. To reduce their means, would starve Parisian industry, and consequently that of the whole nation."

I must beg you, gentlemen, to pay some little regard to arithmetic, at least; and not to say before the National Assembly in France, lest to its shame it should agree with you, that an addition gives a different sum, according to whether it is added up from the bottom to the top, or from the top to the bottom of the column.

For instance, I want to agree with a drainer to make a trench in my field for a hundred sous. Just as we have concluded our arrangement the tax-gatherer comes, takes my hundred sous, and sends them to the Minister of the Interior; my bargain is at end, but the minister will have another dish added to his table. Upon what ground will you dare to affirm that this official expense helps the national industry? Do you not see, that in this there is only a reversing of satisfaction and labor? A minister has his table better covered, it is true; but it is just as true that an agriculturist has his field worse drained. A Parisian tavern-keeper has gained a hundred sous, I grant you; but then you must grant me that a drainer has been prevented from gaining a hundred sous. It all comes to this—that the official and the tavern-keeper being satisfied, is that which is seen; the field undrained, and the drainer deprived of his job, is that which is not seen. Dear me! how much trouble there is in proving that two and two make four; and if you succeed in proving it, it is said "the thing is so plain it is quite tiresome," and they vote as if you had proved nothing at all.

4. Theaters and Fine Arts

Ought the State to support the arts?

There is certainly much to be said on both sides of this question. It may be said, in favor of the system of voting supplies for this purpose, that the arts enlarge, elevate, and harmonize the soul of a nation; that they divert it from too great an absorption in material occupations; encourage in it a love for the beautiful; and thus act favorably on its manners, customs, morals, and even on its industry. It may be asked, what would become of music in France without her Italian theater and her Conservatoire; of the dramatic art, without her Théâtre-Français; of painting and sculpture, without our collections, galleries, and museums? It might even be asked, whether, without centralization, and consequently the support of the fine arts, that exquisite taste would be developed which is the noble appendage of French labor, and which introduces its productions to the whole world. In the face of such results, would it not be the height of imprudence to renounce this moderate contribution from all her citizens, which, in fact, in the eyes of Europe, realizes their superiority and their glory?

To these and many other reasons, whose force I do not dispute, arguments no less forcible may be opposed. It might first of all be said, that there is a question of distributive justice in it. Does the right of the legislator extend to abridging the wages of the artisan, for the sake of adding to the profits of the artist? Mr. Lamartine said, "If you cease to support the theater, where will you stop? Will you not necessarily be led to withdraw your support from your colleges, your museums, your institutes, and your libraries? It might be answered, if you desire to support everything which is good and useful, where will you stop? Will you not necessarily be led to form a civil list for agriculture, industry, commerce, benevolence, education? Then, is it certain that Government aid favors the progress of art? This question is far from being settled, and we see very well that the theatres which prosper are those which depend upon their own resources. Moreover, if we come to higher considerations, we may observe that wants and desires arise the one from the other, and originate in regions which are more and more refined in proportion as the public wealth allows of their being satisfied; that Government ought not to take part in this correspondence, because in a certain condition of present fortune it could not by taxation stimulate the arts of necessity without checking those of luxury, and thus interrupting the natural course of civilization. I may observe, that these artificial transpositions of wants, tastes, labor, and population, place the people in a precarious and dangerous position, without any solid basis.

These are some of the reasons alleged by the adversaries of State intervention in what concerns the order in which citizens think their wants and desires should be satisfied, and to which, consequently, their activity should be directed. I am, I confess, one of those who think that choice and impulse ought to come from below and not from above, from the citizen and not from the legislator; and the opposite doctrine appears to me to tend to the destruction of liberty and of human dignity.

But, by a deduction as false as it is unjust, do you know what economists are accused of? It is, that when we disapprove of government support, we are supposed to disapprove of the thing itself whose support is discussed; and to be the enemies of every kind of activity, because we desire to see those activities, on the one hand free, and on the other seeking their own reward in themselves. Thus, if we think that the State should not interfere by subsidies in religious affairs, we are atheists. If we think the State ought not to interfere by subsidies in education, we are hostile to knowledge. If we say that the State ought not by subsidies to give a fictitious value to land, or to any particular branch of industry, we are enemies to property and labor. If we think that the State ought not to support artists, we are barbarians, who look upon the arts as useless.

Against such conclusions as these I protest with all my strength. Far from entertaining the absurd idea of doing away with religion, education, property, labor, and the arts, when we say that the State ought to protect the free development of all these kinds of human activity, without helping some of them at the expense of others—we think, on the contrary, that all these living powers of society would develop themselves more harmoniously under the influence of liberty; and that, under such an influence no one of them would, as is now the case, be a source of trouble, of abuses, of tyranny, and disorder.

Our adversaries consider that an activity which is neither aided by supplies, nor regulated by government, is an activity destroyed. We think just the contrary. Their faith is in the legislator, not in mankind; ours is in mankind, not in the legislator.

Thus Mr. Lamartine said, " Upon this principle we must abolish the public exhibitions, which are the honor and the wealth of this country." But I would say to Mr. Lamartine—According to your way of thinking, not to support is to abolish; because, setting out upon the maxim that nothing exists independently of the will of the State, you conclude that nothing lives but what the State causes to live. But I oppose to this assertion the very example which you have chosen, and beg you to note, that the grandest and noblest of exhibitions, one which has been conceived in the most liberal and universal spirit—and I might even make use of the term humanitarian, for it is no exaggeration—is the exhibition now preparing in London; the only one in which no government is taking any part, and which is being paid for by no tax.

To return to the fine arts. There are, I repeat, many strong reasons to be advanced, both for and against the system of government assistance: The reader must see that the object of this work leads me neither to explain these reasons, nor to decide in their favor, nor against them.

But Mr. Lamartine has advanced one argument which I cannot pass by in silence, for it is closely connected with this economic study. "The economical question, as regards theatres, is comprised in one word—labor. It matters little what is the nature of this labor; it is as fertile, as productive a labor as any other kind of labor in the nation. The theatres in France, you know, feed and salary no less than 80,000 workmen of different kinds; painters, masons, decorators, costumers, architects, etc., which constitute the very life and movement of several parts of this capital, and on this account they ought to have your sympathies." Your sympathies! Say rather your money.

And further on he says: "The pleasures of Paris are the labor and the consumption of the provinces, and the luxuries of the rich are the wages and bread of 200,000 workmen of every description, who live by the manifold industry of the theatres on the surfeit of the republic, and who receive from these noble pleasures, which render France illustrious, the sustenance of their lives and the necessities of their families and children. It is to them that you will give 60,000 francs." (Very well; very well. Great applause.) For my part I am constrained to say, "Very bad! very bad!" confining this opinion, of course, within the bounds of the economical question which we are discussing.

Yes, it is to the workmen of the theatres that a part, at least, of these 60,000 francs will go; a few bribes, perhaps, may be abstracted on the way. Perhaps, if we were to look a little more closely into the matter, we might find that the cake had gone another way, and that those workmen were fortunate who had come in for a few crumbs. But I will allow, for the sake of argument, that the entire sum does go to the painters, decorators, etc.

This is that which is seen. But whence does it come? This is the other side of the question, and quite as important as the former. Where do these 60,000 francs spring from? and where would they go, if a vote of the legislature did not direct them first toward the Rue Rivoli and thence toward the Rue Grenelle? This is what is not seen. Certainly, nobody will think of maintaining that the legislative vote has caused this sum to be hatched in a ballot urn; that it is a pure addition made to the national wealth; that but for this miraculous vote these 60,000 francs would have been forever invisible and impalpable. It must be admitted that all that the majority can do is to decide that they shall be taken from one place to be sent to another; and if they take one direction, it is only because they have been diverted from another.

This being the case, it is clear that the taxpayer, who has contributed one franc, will no longer have this franc at his own disposal. It is clear that he will be deprived of some gratification to the amount of one franc; and that the workman, whoever he may be, who would have received it from him, will be deprived of a benefit to that amount. Let us not, therefore, be led by a childish illusion into believing that the vote of the 60,000 francs may add anything whatever to the well-being of the country, and to national labor. It displaces enjoyments, it transposes wages—that is all.

Will it be said that for one kind of gratification, and one kind of labor, it substitutes more urgent, more moral, more reasonable gratifications and labor? I might dispute this; I might say, by taking 60,000 francs from the taxpayers, you diminish the wages of laborers, drainers, carpenters, blacksmiths, and increase in proportion those of the singers.

There is nothing to prove that this latter class calls for more sympathy than the former. Mr. Lamartine does not say that it is so. He himself says that the labor of the theatres is as fertile, as productive as any other (not more so); and this may be doubted; for the best proof that the latter is not so fertile as the former lies in this, that the other is to be called upon to assist it.

But this comparison between the value and the intrinsic merit of different kinds of labor forms no part of my present subject. All I have to do here is to show, that if Mr. Lamartine and those persons who commend his line of argument have seen on one side the salaries gained by the providers of the comedians, they ought on the other to have seen the salaries lost by the providers of the taxpayers: for want of this, they have exposed themselves to ridicule by mistaking a displacement for a gain. If they were true to their doctrine, there would be no limits to their demands for government aid; for that which is true of one franc and of 60,000 is true, under parallel circumstances, of a hundred million francs.

When taxes are the subject of discussion, you ought to prove their utility by reasons from the root of the matter, but not by this unfortunate assertion: "The public expenses support the working classes." This assertion disguises the important fact, that public expenses always supersede private expenses, and that therefore we bring a livelihood to one workman instead of another, but add nothing to the share of the working class as a whole. Your arguments are fashionable enough, but they are too absurd to be justified by anything like reason.

5. PUBLIC WORKS

Nothing is more natural than that a nation, after having assured itself that an enterprise will benefit the community, should have it executed by means of a general assessment. But I lose patience, I confess, when I hear this economic blunder advanced in support of such a project: "Besides, it will be a means of creating labor for the workmen."

The State opens a road, builds a palace, straightens a street, cuts a canal, and so gives work to certain workmen—this is what is seen: but it deprives certain other workmen of work—and this is what is not seen.

The road is begun. A thousand workmen come every morning, leave every evening, and take their wages—this is certain. If the road had not been decreed, if the supplies had not been voted, these good people would have had neither work nor salary there; this also is certain.

But is this all? Does not the operation, as a whole, contain something else? At the moment when Mr. Dupin pronounces the emphatic words, "The Assembly has adopted," do the millions descend miraculously on a moonbeam into the coffers of Misters

Fould and Bineau? In order that the evolution may be complete, as it is said, must not the State organize the receipts as well as the expenditure? Must it not set its tax-gatherers and taxpayers to work, the former to gather and the latter to pay?

Study the question, now, in both its elements. While you state the destination given by the State to the millions voted, do not neglect to state also the destination which the taxpayer would have given, but cannot now give, to the same. Then you will understand that a public enterprise is a coin with two sides. Upon one is engraved a laborer at work, with this device, that which is seen; on the other is a laborer out of work, with the device, that which is not seen.

The sophism which this work is intended to refute is the more dangerous when applied to public works, inasmuch as it serves to justify the most wanton enterprises and extravagance. When a railroad or a bridge are of real utility, it is sufficient to mention this utility. But if it does not exist, what do they do? Recourse is had to this mystification: "We must find work for the workmen."

Accordingly, orders are given that the drains in the Champ-de-Mars be made and unmade. The great Napoleon, it is said, thought he was doing a very philanthropic work by causing ditches to be made and then filled up. He said, therefore, "What signifies the result? All we want is to see wealth spread among the laboring classes."

But let us go to the root of the matter. We are deceived by money. To demand the cooperation of all the citizens in a common work, in the form of money, is in reality to demand a concurrence in kind; for every one procures, by his own labor, the sum to which he is taxed. Now, if all the citizens were to be called together, and made to execute, in conjunction, a work useful to all, this would be easily understood; their reward would be found in the results of the work itself.

But after having called them together, if you force them to make roads which no one will pass through, palaces which no one will inhabit, and this under the pretext of finding them work, it would be absurd, and they would have a right to argue, "With this labor we have nothing to do; we prefer working on our own account."

A proceeding which consists in making the citizens cooperate in giving money but not labor, does not, in any way, alter the general results. The only thing is, that the loss would react upon all parties. By the former, those whom the State employs, escape their part of the loss, by adding it to that which their fellow-citizens have already suffered.

There is an article in our constitution which says: "Society favors and encourages the development of labor—by the establishment of public works, by the State, the departments, and the parishes, as a means of employing persons who are in want of work."

As a temporary measure, on any emergency, during a hard winter, this interference with the taxpayers may have its use. It acts in the same way as insurance. It adds nothing either to labor or to wages, but it takes labor and wages from ordinary times to give them, at a loss it is true, to times of difficulty.

As a permanent, general, systematic measure, it is nothing else than a ruinous mystification, an impossibility, which shows a little excited labor which is seen, and hides a great deal of prevented labor, which is not seen.

6. The Intermediaries

Society is the total of the forced or voluntary services that men perform for each other; that is to say, of public services and private services.

The former, imposed and regulated by the law, which it is not always easy to change, even when it is desirable, may survive with the law their own usefulness, and still preserve the name of public services, even when they are no longer services at all, but rather public annoyances. The latter belong to the sphere of the will, of individual responsibility. Everyone gives and receives what he wishes, and what he can, after due consideration. They have always the presumption of real utility, in exact proportion to their comparative value.

This is the reason why the former description of services so often become stationary, while the latter obey the law of progress.

While the exaggerated development of public services, by the waste of strength that it involves, fastens upon society a fatal sycophancy, it is a singular thing that several modern movements, attributing this vice to free and private services, are endeavoring to transform professions into functions.

These sects violently oppose what they call intermediaries. They would gladly suppress the capitalist, the banker, the speculator, the promoter, the merchant, and the trader, accusing them of interposing between production and consumption, to extort from both, without giving either anything in return. Or rather, they would transfer to the State the work that they accomplish, for this work cannot be done without.

The sophism of the Socialists on this point is, showing to the public what it pays to the intermediaries in exchange for their services, and concealing from it what is necessary to be paid to the State. Here is the usual conflict between what is before our eyes and what is perceptible to the mind only; between what is seen and what is not seen.

It was at the time of the scarcity, in 1847, that the Socialist schools attempted and succeeded in popularizing their lethal theory. They knew very well that the most absurd notions have always a chance with people who are suffering; *malisunda fames*.

Therefore, by the help of the fine words, " trafficking in men by men, speculation on hunger, monopoly," they began to blacken commerce, and to cast a veil over its benefits.

"What can be the use," they say, "of leaving to the merchants the care of importing food from the United States and the Crimea? Why do not the State, the departments, and the towns, organize a service for provisions and a magazine for stores? They would sell at a just price, and the people, poor things, would be exempted from the tribute which they pay to free, that is, to greedy, selfish, and anarchical commerce."

The tribute paid by the people to commerce is that which is seen. The tribute which the people would pay to the State, or to its agents, in the Socialist system, is what is not seen.

In what does this pretended tribute, which the people pay to commerce, consist? In this: that two men render each other a mutual service, in all freedom, and under the pressure of competition and reduced prices.

When the hungry stomach is at Paris, and corn which can satisfy it is at Odessa, the suffering cannot cease till the corn is brought into contact with the stomach. There are three means by which this contact may be effected. First, the famished men may go themselves and fetch the corn. Second, they may leave this task to those to whose trade it belongs. Third, they may club together, and give the office in charge to public functionaries. Which of these three methods possesses the greatest advantages? In every time, in all countries, and the more free, enlightened, and experienced they are, men have voluntarily chosen the second. I confess that this is sufficient, in my opinion, to justify this choice. I cannot believe that mankind, as a whole, is deceiving itself upon a point which touches it so nearly. But let us now consider the subject.

For 36 million citizens to go and fetch the corn they want from Odessa is a manifest impossibility. The first means, then, goes for nothing. The consumers cannot act for themselves. They must, of necessity, have recourse to intermediaries, officials or agents.

But observe, that the first of these three means would be the most natural. In reality, the hungry man has to fetch his corn. It is a task which concerns himself, a service due to himself. If another person, on whatever ground, performs this service for him, takes the task upon himself, this latter has a claim upon him for a compensation. I mean by this to say that intermediaries contain in themselves the principle of remuneration.

However that may be, since we must refer to what the Socialists call a parasite, I would ask, which of the two is the most exacting parasite, the merchant or the official?

Commerce (free, of course, otherwise I could not reason upon it), commerce, I say, is led by its own interests to study the seasons, to give daily statements of the state of the crops, to receive information from every part of the globe, to foresee wants, to take precautions beforehand. It has vessels always ready, correspondents everywhere; and it is its immediate interest to buy at the lowest possible price, to economize in all the details of its operations, and to attain the greatest results by the smallest efforts. It is not the French merchants only who are occupied in procuring provisions for France in time of need, and if their interest leads them irresistibly to accomplish their task at the smallest possible cost, the competition which they create amongst each other leads them no less irresistibly to cause the consumers to partake of the profits of those realized savings. The corn arrives: it is to the interest of commerce to sell it as soon as possible, so as to avoid risks, to realize its funds, and begin again at the first opportunity.

Directed by the comparison of prices, it distributes food over the whole surface of the country, beginning always at the highest price, that is, where the demand is the greatest. It is impossible to imagine an organization more completely calculated to meet the interest of those who are in want; and the beauty of this organization, unperceived as it is by the Socialists, results from the very fact that it is free. It is true, the consumer is obliged to reimburse commerce for the expenses of conveyance, freight, store-room, commission, etc.; but can any system be devised in which he who eats corn is not obliged to defray the expenses, whatever they may be, of bringing it within his reach? The remuneration for the service performed has to be paid also; but as regards its amount, this is reduced to the smallest possible sum by competition; and as regards its justice, it would be very strange if the merchants of Paris would not work for the artisans of Marseilles, when the merchants of Marseilles work for the artisans of Paris.

If, according to the Socialist invention, the State were to stand in the stead of commerce, what would happen? I should like to be informed where the saving would be to the public. Would it be in the price of purchase? Imagine the delegates of 40,000 parishes arriving at Odessa on a given day, and on the day of need: imagine the effect upon prices. Would the saving be in the expenses? Would fewer vessels be required; fewer sailors, fewer transports, fewer sloops? or would you be exempt from the payment of all these things? Would it be in the profits of the merchants? Would your officials go to Odessa for nothing? Would they travel and work on the principle of fraternity? Must they not live? Must not they be paid for their time? And do you believe that these expenses would not exceed a thousand times the two or three percent that the merchant gains, at the rate at which he is ready to treat?

And then consider the difficulty of levying so many taxes, and of dividing so much food. Think of the injustice, of the abuses inseparable from such an enterprise. Think of the responsibility that would weigh upon the Government.

The Socialists who have invented these follies, and who, in the days of distress, have introduced them into the minds of the masses, take to themselves literally the title of superior men; and it is not without some danger that custom, that tyrant of tongues, authorizes the term, and the sentiment that it involves. Superior! This supposes that these gentlemen can see further than the common people; that their only fault is that they are too ahead of their times; and if the time is not yet come for suppressing certain free services, pretended parasites, the fault is to be attributed to the public, which hasn't caught onto Socialism. I say, from my soul and my conscience, the reverse is the truth; and I know not to what barbarous age we should have to go back, if we were to sink to the level of Socialist knowledge on this subject. These modern zealots incessantly distinguish association from actual society. They overlook the fact that society, free of regulation, is a true association, far superior to any of those that proceed from their fertile imaginations.

Let me illustrate this by an example. Before a man, when he gets up in the morning, can put on a coat, ground must have been enclosed, broken up, drained, tilled, and sown with a particular kind of plant; flocks must have been fed, and have given their wool; this wool must have been spun, woven, dyed, and converted into cloth; this cloth must have been cut, sewed, and made into a garment. And this series of operations implies a number of others; it supposes the employment of instruments for plowing, etc., sheepfolds, sheds, coal, machines, carriages, etc.

If society were not a perfectly real association, a person who wanted a coat would be reduced to the necessity of working in solitude; that is, of performing for himself the innumerable parts of this series, from the first stroke of the pickaxe to the last stitch which concludes the work. But, thanks to the sociability which is the distinguishing character of our race, these operations are distributed amongst a multitude of workers; and they are further subdivided, for the common good, to an extent that, as the consumption becomes more active, one single operation is able to support a new trade.

Then comes the division of the profits, which operates according to the constituent value which each has brought to the entire work. If this is not association, I should like to know what is.

Observe, that as no one of these workers has obtained the smallest particle of matter from nothingness, they are confined to performing for each other mutual services, and to helping each other in a common object, and that all may be considered, with respect to others, intermediaries. If, for instance, in the course of the operation, the conveyance becomes important enough to occupy one person, the spinning another, the weaving another, why should the first be considered a parasite more than the other two? The conveyance must be made, must it not? Does not he who performs it devote to it his time and trouble? and by so doing does he not spare that of his colleagues? Do these do more or other than this for him? Are they not equally dependent for remuneration, that is, for the division of the produce, upon the law of reduced price? Is it not in all liberty, for the common good, that this separation of work takes place, and that these arrangements are entered into? What do we want with a Socialist then, who, under pretense of organizing for us, comes despotically to break up our voluntary arrangements, to check the division of labor, to substitute isolated efforts for combined ones, and to send civilization back? Is association, as I describe it here, in itself less association, because everyone enters and leaves it freely, chooses his place in it, judges and bargains for himself on his own responsibility, and brings with him the motivation and assurance of personal interest? That it may deserve this name, is it necessary that a pretended reformer should come and impose upon us his plan and his will, and, as it were, to concentrate mankind in himself?

The more we examine these advanced schools, the more do we become convinced that there is but one thing at the root of them: ignorance proclaiming itself infallible, and claiming despotism in the name of this infallibility.

I hope the reader will excuse this digression. It may not be altogether useless, at a time when declamations, springing from St. Simonian, Phalansterian, and Icarian books, are invoking the press and the tribune, and which seriously threaten the liberty of labor and commercial transactions.

7. Protectionism

Mr. Protectionist (it was not I who gave him this name, but Mr. Charles Dupin) devoted his time and capital to converting the ore found on his land into iron. As nature had been more lavish toward the Belgians, they furnished the French with iron cheaper than Mr. Protectionist; which means, that all the French, or France, could obtain a given quantity of iron with less labor by buying it of the honest Flemings. Therefore, guided by their own interest, they did not fail to do so; and every day there might be seen a multitude of nail-smiths, blacksmiths, cartwrights, machinists, farriers, and laborers, going themselves, or sending intermediaries, to supply themselves in Belgium. This displeased Mr. Protectionist exceedingly.

At first, it occurred to him to put an end to this abuse by his own efforts: it was the least he could do, for he was the only sufferer. "I will take my carbine," said he; " I will put four pistols into my belt; I will fill my cartridge box; I will gird on my sword, and go thus equipped to the frontier. There, the first blacksmith, nail-smith, farrier, machinist, or locksmith, who presents himself to do his own business and not mine, I will kill, to teach him how to live." At the moment of starting, Mr. Protectionist made a few reflections which calmed down his warlike ardor a little. He said to himself, "In the first place, it is not absolutely impossible that the purchasers of iron, my countrymen and enemies, should take the thing ill, and, instead of letting me kill them, should kill me instead; and then, even were I to call out all my servants, we should not be able to defend the passages. In short, this proceeding would cost me very dear, much more so than the result would be worth."

Mr. Protectionist was on the point of resigning himself to his sad fate, that of being only as free as the rest of the world, when a ray of light darted across his brain. He recollected that at Paris there is a great factory of laws. "What is a law?" said he to himself. "It is a measure to which, when once it is decreed, be it good or bad, everybody is bound to conform. For the execution of the same a public force is organized, and to constitute the said public force, men and money are drawn from the whole nation. If, then, I could only get the great Parisian manufactory to pass a little law, 'Belgian iron is prohibited,' I should obtain the following results: The Government would replace the few valets that I was going to send to the frontier by 20,000 of the sons of those refractory blacksmiths, farriers, artisans, machinists, locksmiths, nail-smiths, and laborers. Then to keep these 20,000 custom-house officers in health and good humor, it would distribute among them 25,000,000 francs taken from these blacksmiths, nail-smiths, artisans, and laborers. They would guard the frontier much better; would cost me nothing; I should not be exposed to the brutality of the brokers; should sell the iron at my own price, and have the sweet satisfaction of seeing our great people shamefully mystified. That would teach them to proclaim themselves perpetually the harbingers and promoters of progress in Europe. Oh! it would be a capital joke, and deserves to be tried."

So Mr. Protectionist went to the law factory. Another time, perhaps, I shall relate the story of his underhanded dealings, but now I shall merely mention his visible proceedings. He brought the following consideration before the view of the legislating gentlemen.

"Belgian iron is sold in France at ten francs, which obliges me to sell mine at the same price. I should like to sell at fifteen, but cannot do so on account of this Belgian iron, which I wish was at the bottom of the Red Sea. I beg you will make a law that no more Belgian iron shall enter France. Immediately I raise my price five francs, and these are the consequences:

"For every hundred-weight of iron that I shall deliver to the public, I shall receive fifteen francs instead of ten; I shall grow rich more rapidly, extend my traffic, and employ more workmen. My workmen and I shall spend much more freely, to the great advantage of our tradesmen for miles around. These latter, having more custom, will furnish more employment to trade, and activity on both sides will increase in the country. This fortunate piece of money, which you will drop into my strong-box, will, like a stone thrown into a lake, give birth to an infinite number of concentric circles."

Charmed with his discourse, delighted to learn that it is so easy to promote, by legislating, the prosperity of a people, the law-makers voted the restriction. "Talk of labor and economy," they said, "what is the use of these painful means of increasing the national wealth, when all that is wanted for this object is a decree?"

And, in fact, the law produced all the consequences announced by Mr. Protectionist: the only thing was, it produced others which he had not foreseen. To do him justice, his reasoning was not false, but only incomplete. In endeavoring to obtain a privilege, he had taken cognizance of the effects which are seen, leaving in the background those which are not seen. He had pointed out two personages, whereas there are three concerned in the affair. It is for us to supply this involuntary or premeditated omission.

It is true, the crown-piece, thus directed by law into Mr. Protectionist's strong-box, is advantageous to him and to those whose labor it would encourage; and if the Act had caused the pot of gold to descend from the moon, these good effects would not have been counterbalanced by any corresponding evils. Unfortunately, the mysterious gold does not come from the moon, but from the pocket of a blacksmith, or a nail-smith, or a cartwright, or a farrier, or a laborer, or a shipwright; in a word, from John Q. Citizen, who gives it now without receiving a grain more of iron than when he was paying ten francs. Thus, we can see at a glance that this very much alters the state of the case; for it is very evident that Mr. Protectionist's profit is compensated by John Q. Citizen's loss, and all that Mr. Protectionist can do with the pot of gold, for the encouragement of national labor, John Q. Citizen might have done himself. The stone has only been thrown upon one part of the lake, because the law has prevented it from being thrown upon another.

Therefore, that which is not seen supersedes that which is seen, and at this point there remains, as the residue of the operation, a piece of injustice, and, sad to say, a piece of injustice perpetrated by the law!

This is not all. I have said that there is always a third person left in the background. I must now bring him forward, that he may reveal to us a second loss of five francs. Then we shall have the entire results of the transaction.

John Q. Citizen is the possessor of fifteen francs, the fruit of his labor. He is now free. What does he do with his fifteen francs? He purchases some article of fashion for ten francs, and with it he pays (or the intermediary pays for him) for the hundredweight of Belgian iron. After this he has five francs left. He does not throw them into the river, but (and this is what is not seen) he gives them to some tradesman in exchange for some enjoyment; to a bookseller, for instance, for Bossuet's "Discourse on Universal History."

Thus, as far as national labor is concerned, it is encouraged to the amount of fifteen francs, viz.: ten francs for the Paris article, five francs to the bookselling trade.

As to John Q. Citizen, he obtains for his fifteen francs two gratifications, viz.:

First, a hundred-weight of iron.

Second, a book.

The decree is put in force. How does it affect the condition of John Q. Citizen? How does it affect the national labor?

John Q. Citizen pays every centime of his five francs to Mr. Protectionist, and therefore is deprived of the pleasure of a book, or of some other thing of equal value. He loses five francs. This must be admitted; it cannot fail to be admitted, that when protectionism raises the price of things, the consumer loses the difference.

But, then, it is said, national labor is the gainer.

No, it is not the gainer; for since the Act, it is no more encouraged than it was before, to the amount of fifteen francs.

The only thing is that, since the Act, the fifteen francs of John Q. Citizen go to the metal trade, while before it was put in force, they were divided between the ironmonger and the bookseller.

The violence used by Mr. Protectionist on the frontier, or that which he causes to be used by the law, may be judged very differently in a moral point of view. Some persons consider that plunder is perfectly justifiable, if only sanctioned by law. But, for myself, I cannot imagine anything more aggravating. However it may be, the economical results are the same in both cases.

Look at the thing as you will; but if you are impartial, you will see that no good can come of legal or illegal plunder. We do not deny that it affords Mr. Protectionist, or his trade, or, if you will, national industry, a profit of five francs. But we affirm that it causes two losses, one to John Q. Citizen, who pays fifteen francs where he otherwise would have paid ten; the other to national industry, which does not receive the difference. Take your choice of these two losses, and compensate with it the profit which we allow. The other will prove a dead loss either way. Here is the moral: To take by violence is not to produce, but to destroy. Truly, if taking by violence was producing, this country of ours would be a little richer than she is.

8. MACHINERY

"A curse on machines! Every year, their increasing power relegates millions of workmen to pauperism, by depriving them of work, and therefore of wages and bread. A curse on machines!"

This is the cry which is raised by vulgar prejudice, and echoed in the journals.

But to curse machines is to curse the spirit of humanity!

It puzzles me to conceive how any man can feel any satisfaction in such a doctrine.

For, if true, what is its inevitable consequence? That there is no activity, prosperity, wealth, or happiness possible for any people, except for those who are stupid and inert, and to whom God has not granted the fatal gift of knowing how to think, to observe, to combine, to invent, and to obtain the greatest results with the smallest means. On the contrary, rags, mean huts, poverty, and inanition, are the inevitable lot of every nation which seeks and finds in iron, fire, wind, electricity, magnetism, the laws of chemistry and mechanics, in a word, in the powers of nature, an assistance to its natural powers. We might as well say with Rousseau—"Every man that thinks is a depraved animal."

This is not all. If this doctrine is true, all men think and invent, since all, from first to last, and at every moment of their existence, seek the cooperation of the powers of nature, and try to make the most of a little, by reducing either the work of their hands or their expenses, so as to obtain the greatest possible amount of gratification with the smallest possible amount of labor. It must follow, as a matter of course, that the whole of mankind is rushing toward its decline, by the same mental aspiration toward progress, which torments each of its members.

Hence, it ought to be revealed by statistics, that the inhabitants of Lancashire, abandoning that land of machines, seek for work in Ireland, where they are unknown; and, by history, that barbarism darkens the epochs of civilization, and that civilization shines in times of ignorance and barbarism.

There is evidently in this mass of contradictions something which revolts us, and which leads us to suspect that the problem contains within it an element of solution which has not been sufficiently disengaged.

Here is the whole mystery: behind that which is seen lies something which is not seen. I will endeavor to bring it to light. The demonstration I shall give will only be a repetition of the preceding one, for the problems are one and the same.

Men have a natural propensity to make the best bargain they can, when not prevented by an opposing force; that is, they like to obtain as much as they possibly can for their labor, whether advantage is obtained from a foreign producer or a skillful mechanical producer.

The theoretical objection which is made to this propensity is the same in both cases. In each case it is reproached with the apparent inactivity which it causes to labor. Now, labor rendered available, not inactive, is the very thing that motivates it. And, therefore, in both cases, the same practical obstacle—force—is opposed to it also.

The legislator prohibits foreign competition, and forbids mechanical competition. For what other means can exist for arresting a propensity which is natural to all men, but that of depriving them of their liberty?

In many countries, it is true, the legislator strikes at only one of these competitions, and confines himself to grumbling at the other. This only proves one thing, that is, that the legislator is inconsistent.

We need not be surprised at this. On a wrong road, inconsistency is inevitable; if it were not so, mankind would be sacrificed. A false principle never has been, and never will be, carried out to the end.

Now for our demonstration, which shall not be a long one.

John Q. Citizen had two francs with which he paid two workmen; but it occurs to him that an arrangement of ropes and weights might be made which would diminish the labor by half. Therefore he obtains the same advantage, saves a franc, and discharges a workman.

He discharges a workman: this is that which is seen.

And seeing this only, it is said, "See how misery attends civilization; this is the way that liberty is fatal to equality. The human mind has made a conquest, and immediately a workman is cast into the gulf of pauperism. John Q. Citizen may possibly employ the two workmen, but then he will give them only half their wages, for they will compete with each other, and offer themselves at the lowest price. Thus the rich are always growing richer, and the poor, poorer. Society needs remodeling." A very fine conclusion, and worthy of the preamble.

Happily, preamble and conclusion are both false, because, behind the half of the phenomenon which is seen, lies the other half which is not seen.

The franc saved by John Q. Citizen is not seen, no more are the necessary effects of this saving.

Since, in consequence of his invention, John Q. Citizen spends only one franc on hand labor in the pursuit of a determined advantage, another franc remains to him.

If, then, there is in the world a workman with unemployed arms, there is also in the world a capitalist with an unemployed franc. These two elements meet and combine, and it is as clear as daylight, that between the supply and demand of labor, and between the supply and demand of wages, the relation is in no way changed.

The invention and the workman paid with the first franc now perform the work that was formerly accomplished by two workmen. The second workman, paid with the second franc, realizes a new kind of work.

What is the change, then, that has taken place? An additional national advantage has been gained; in other words, the invention is a gratuitous triumph—a gratuitous profit for mankind.

From the form that I have given to my demonstration, the following inference might be drawn: "It is the capitalist who reaps all the advantage from machinery. The working class, if it suffers only temporarily, never profits by it, since, by your own showing, they displace a portion of the national labor, without diminishing it, it is true, but also without increasing it."

I do not pretend, in this slight treatise, to answer every objection; the only end I have in view is to combat a vulgar, widely spread, and dangerous prejudice. I want to prove that a new machine only causes the discharge of a certain number of hands, when the remuneration that pays them is confiscated by force. These hands and this remuneration would combine to produce what it was impossible to produce before the invention; whence it follows that the final result is an increase of advantages for equal labor.

Who is the gainer by these additional advantages?

First, it is true, the capitalist, the inventor; the first who succeeds in using the machine; and this is the reward of his genius and courage. In this case, as we have just seen, he effects a saving upon the expense of production, which, in whatever way it may be spent (and it always is spent), employs exactly as many hands as the machine caused to be dismissed.

But soon competition obliges him to lower his prices in proportion to the saving itself; and then it is no longer the inventor who reaps the benefit of the invention—it is the purchaser of what is produced, the consumer, the public, including the workman; in a word, mankind.

And that which is not seen is, that the saving thus procured for all consumers creates a fund whence wages may be supplied, and which replaces that which the machine has exhausted.

Thus, to recur to the aforementioned example, John Q. Citizen obtains a profit by spending two francs in wages. Thanks to his invention, the hand labor costs him only one franc. So long as he sells the thing produced at the same price, he employs one workman less in producing this particular thing, and that is what is seen; but there is an additional workman employed by the franc that John Q. Citizen has saved. This is that which is not seen.

When, by the natural progress of things, John Q. Citizen is obliged to lower the price of the thing produced by one franc, then he no longer realizes a saving; then he has no longer a franc to dispose of to procure for the national labor a new production. But then another gainer takes his place, and this gainer is mankind. Whoever buys the thing he has produced pays a franc less, and necessarily adds this saving to the fund of wages; and this, again, is what is not seen.

Another solution, founded upon facts, has been given of this problem of machinery.

It was said, machinery reduces the expense of production, and lowers the price of the thing produced. The reduction of the price causes an increase of consumption, which necessitates an increase of production; and, finally, the hiring of as many workmen, or more, after the invention as were necessary before it. As a proof of this, printing, weaving, etc., are instanced.

This demonstration is not a scientific one. It would lead us to conclude, that if the consumption of the particular production of which we are speaking remains stationary, or nearly so, machinery must injure labor. This is not the case.

Suppose that in a certain country all the people wore hats. If, by machinery, the price could be reduced half, it would not necessarily follow that the consumption would be doubled.

Would you say that in this case a portion of the national labor had been thrown out of work? Yes, according to the vulgar demonstration; but, according to mine, No; for even if not a single hat more should be bought in the country, the entire fund of wages would not be the less secure. That which failed to go to the hat-making trade would be found to have gone to the economy realized by all the consumers, and would thence serve to pay for all the labor that the machine had rendered useless, and to excite a new development of all the trades. And thus it is that things go on. I have known newspapers to cost 80 francs, now we pay 48: here is a saving of 32 francs to the subscribers. It is not certain, or at least necessary, that the 32 francs should take the direction of the journalist trade; but it is certain, and necessary too, that if they do not take this direction they will take another. One makes use of them for taking in more newspapers; another, to get better living; another, better clothes; another, better furniture. It is thus that the trades are bound together. They form a vast whole, whose different parts communicate by secret channels: what is saved by one, profits all. It is very important for us to understand that savings never take place at the expense of labor and wages.

9. CREDIT

In all times, but more especially of late years, attempts have been made to extend wealth by the extension of credit.

I believe it is no exaggeration to say that since the revolution of February, the Parisian presses have issued more than 10,000 pamphlets, advocating this solution of the social problem.

The only basis, alas! of this solution, is an optical illusion—if, indeed, an optical illusion can be called a basis at all.

The first thing done is to confuse cash with products, then paper money with cash; and from these two confusions it is pretended that a reality can be drawn.

It is absolutely necessary in this question to forget money, coin, bills, and the other instruments by means of which products pass from hand to hand. Our business is with the products themselves, which are the real objects of the loan; for when a farmer borrows fifty francs to buy a plow, it is not, in reality, the fifty francs that are lent to him, but the plow; and when a merchant borrows 20,000 francs to purchase a house, it is not the 20,000 francs that he owes, but the house. Money only appears for the sake of facilitating the arrangements between the parties.

Peter may not be disposed to lend his plow, but James may be willing to lend his money. What does William do in this case? He borrows money of James, and with this money he buys the plow of Peter.

But, in point of fact, no one borrows money for the sake of the money itself; money is only the medium by which to obtain possession of products. Now, it is impossible in any country to transmit from one person to another more products than that country contains.

Whatever may be the amount of cash and of paper which is in circulation, the whole of the borrowers cannot receive more plows, houses, tools, and supplies of raw material, than the lenders all together can furnish; for we must take care not to forget that every borrower supposes a lender, and that what is once borrowed implies a loan.

This granted, what advantage is there in institutions of credit? It is, that they facilitate, between borrowers and lenders, the means of finding and treating with each other; but it is not in their power to cause an instantaneous increase of the things to be borrowed and lent. And yet they ought to be able to do so, if the aim of the reformers is to be attained, since they aspire to nothing less than to place plows, houses, tools, and provisions in the hands of all those who desire them.

And how do they intend to effect this?

By making the State security for the loan.

Let us try and fathom the subject, for it contains something which is seen, and also something which is not seen. We must endeavor to look at both.

We will suppose that there is but one plow in the world, and that two farmers apply for it.

Peter is the possessor of the only plow which is to be had in France; John and James wish to borrow it. John, by his honesty, his property, and good reputation, offers security. He inspires confidence; he has credit. James inspires little or no confidence. It naturally happens that Peter lends his plow to John.

But now, according to the Socialist plan, the State interferes, and says to Peter, "Lend your plow to James, I will be security for its return, and this security will be better than that of John, for he has no one to be responsible for him but himself; and I, although it is true that I have nothing, dispose of the fortune of the taxpayers, and it is with their money that, in case of need, I shall pay you the principal and interest." Consequently, Peter lends his plow to James: this is what is seen.

And the Socialists rub their hands, and say, "See how well our plan has answered. Thanks to the intervention of the State, poor James has a plow. He will no longer be obliged to dig the ground; he is on the road to make a fortune. It is a good thing for him, and an advantage to the nation as a whole."

Indeed, it is no such thing; it is no advantage to the nation, for there is something behind which is not seen.

It is not seen, that the plow is in the hands of James, only because it is not in those of John.

It is not seen, that if James farms instead of digging, John will be reduced to the necessity of digging instead of farming.

That, consequently, what was considered an increase of loan, is nothing but a displacement of loan. Besides, it is not seen that this displacement implies two acts of deep injustice.

It is an injustice to John, who, after having deserved and obtained credit by his honesty and activity, sees himself robbed of it.

It is an injustice to the taxpayers, who are made to pay a debt which is no concern of theirs.

Will any one say, that Government offers the same facilities to John as it does to James? But as there is only one plow to be had, two cannot be lent. The argument always maintains that, thanks to the intervention of the State, more will be borrowed than there are things to be lent; for the plow represents here the bulk of available capital.

It is true, I have reduced the operation to the most simple expression of it, but if you submit the most complicated Government institutions of credit to the same test, you will be convinced that they can have but one result; viz., to displace credit, not to augment it. In one country, and in a given time, there is only a certain amount of capital available, and all is employed. In guaranteeing the non-payers, the State may, indeed, increase the number of borrowers, and thus raise the rate of interest (always to the prejudice of the taxpayer), but it has no power to increase the number of lenders, and the importance of the total of the loans.

There is one conclusion, however, which I would not for the world be suspected of drawing. I say, that the law ought not to favor, artificially, the power of borrowing, but I do not say that it ought not to restrain them artificially. If, in our system of mortgage, or in any other, there be obstacles to the diffusion of the application of credit, let them be got rid of; nothing can be better or more just than this. But this is all that is consistent with liberty, and it is all that any who are worthy of the name of reformers will ask.

10. ALGERIA

Here are four orators disputing for the platform. First, all the four speak at once; then they speak one after the other. What have they said? Some very fine things, certainly, about the power and the grandeur of France; about the necessity of sowing, if we would reap; about the brilliant future of our gigantic colony; about the advantage of diverting to a distance the surplus of our population, etc., etc. Magnificent pieces of eloquence, and always adorned with this conclusion: "Vote 50 million, more or less, for making ports and roads in Algeria; for sending emigrants there; for building houses and breaking up land. By so doing, you will relieve the French workman, encourage African labor, and give a stimulus to the commerce of Marseilles. It would be profitable every way."

Yes, it is all very true, if you take no account of the fifty million until the moment when the State begins to spend them; if you only see where they go, and not where they come from; if you look only at the good they are to do when they come out of the tax-gatherer's bag, and not at the harm which has been done, and the good that has been prevented, by putting them into it. Yes, at this limited point of view, all is profit. The house that is built in Barbary is that which is seen; the harbor made in Barbary is that which is seen; the work caused in Barbary is what is seen; a few less hands in France is what is seen; a great stir with goods at Marseilles is still that which is seen.

But, besides all this, there is something that is not seen. The fifty million expended by the State cannot be spent, as they otherwise would have been, by the taxpayers. It is necessary to deduct, from all the good attributed to the public expenditure that has been effected, all the harm caused by the prevention of private expense, unless we say that John Q. Citizen would have done nothing with the money that he had gained, and of which the tax had deprived him; an absurd assertion, for if he took the trouble to earn it, it was because he expected the satisfaction of using it. He would have repaired the palings in his garden, which he cannot now do, and this is that which is not seen. He would have manured his field, which now he cannot do, and this is what is not seen. He would have added another story to his cottage, which he cannot do now, and this is what is not seen. He might have increased the number of his tools, which he cannot do now, and this is what is not seen. He would have been better fed, better clothed, have given a better education to his children, and increased his daughter's dowry, this is what is not seen. He would have become a member of the Mutual Assistance Society, but now he cannot; this is what is not seen. On one hand, are the enjoyments of which he has been deprived, and the means of action which have been destroyed in his hands; on the other, are the labor of the drainer, the carpenter, the smith, the tailor, the village schoolmaster, which he would have encouraged, and which are now prevented—all this is what is not seen.

Much is hoped from the future prosperity of Algeria; be it so. But the drain to which France is being subjected ought not to be kept entirely out of sight. The commerce of Marseilles is pointed out to me; but if this is to be brought about by means of taxation, I shall always show that an equal commerce is destroyed thereby in other parts of the country. It is said, "There is an emigrant transported into Barbary; this is a relief to the population which remains in the country," I answer, "How can that be, if, in transporting this emigrant to Algiers, you also transport two or three times the capital which would have served to maintain him in France?"[2] The only object I have in view is to make it evident to the reader that in every public expense, behind the apparent benefit, there is an evil which it is not so easy to discern. As far as in me lies, I would make him form a habit of seeing both, and taking account of both.

When a public expense is proposed, it ought to be examined in itself, separately from the pretended encouragement of labor that results from it, for this encouragement is a delusion. Whatever is done in this way at the public expense, private expense would have done all the same; therefore, the interest of labor is always out of the question.

It is not the object of this treatise to criticize the intrinsic merit of the public expenditure as applied to Algeria, but I cannot withhold a general observation. It is that the presumption is always unfavorable to collective expenses by way of tax. Why? For this reason: First, justice always suffers from it in some degree. Since John Q. Citizen had labored to gain his money, in the hope of receiving a gratification from it, it is to be regretted that the exchequer should interpose, and take from John Q. Citizen this gratification, to bestow it upon another. Certainly, it behooves the exchequer, or those who regulate him, to give good reasons for this. It has been shown that the State gives a very provoking one, when it says, "With this money I shall employ workmen;" for John Q. Citizen (as soon as he sees it) will be sure to answer, "It is all very fine, but with this money I might employ them myself."

Apart from this reason, others present themselves without disguise, by which the debate between the exchequer and poor John becomes much simplified. If the State says to him, "I take

---

[2]The Minister of War has lately asserted that every individual transported to Algeria has cost the State 8,000 francs. Now it is certain that these poor creatures could have lived very well in France on a capital of 4,000 francs. I ask, how the French population is relieved, when it is deprived of a man, and of the means of subsistence of two men?

your money to pay the gendarme, who saves you the trouble of providing for your own personal safety; for paving the street that you are passing through every day; for paying the magistrate who causes your property and your liberty to be respected; to maintain the soldier who maintains our frontiers," John Q. Citizen, unless I am much mistaken, will pay for all this without hesitation. But if the State were to say to him, "I take this money that I may give you a little prize in case you cultivate your field well; or that I may teach your son something that you have no wish that he should learn; or that the Minister may add another to his score of dishes at dinner; I take it to build a cottage in Algeria, in which case I must take more money every year to keep an emigrant in it, and another to maintain a soldier to guard this emigrant, and yet more to maintain a general to guard this soldier," etc., etc., I think I hear poor James exclaim, "This system of law is very much like a system of cheat!" The State foresees the objection, and what does it do? It jumbles all things together, and brings forward just that provoking reason which ought to have nothing whatever to do with the question. It talks of the effect of this money upon labor; it points to the cook and purveyor of the Minister; it shows an emigrant, a soldier, and a general, living upon the money; it shows, in fact, what is seen, and if John Q. Citizen has not learned to take into the account what is not seen, John Q. Citizen will be duped. And this is why I want to do all I can to impress it upon his mind, by repeating it over and over again.

As the public expenses displace labor without increasing it, a second serious presumption presents itself against them. To displace labor is to displace laborers, and to disturb the natural laws which regulate the distribution of the population over the country. If 50,000,000 francs are allowed to remain in the possession of the taxpayers since the taxpayers are everywhere, they encourage labor in the 40,000 parishes in France. They act like a natural tie, which keeps everyone upon his native soil; they distribute themselves amongst all imaginable laborers and trades. If the State, by drawing off these 50,000,000 francs from the citizens, accumulates them, and expends them on some given point, it attracts to this point a proportional quantity of displaced labor, a corresponding number of laborers, belonging to other parts; a fluctuating population, which is out of its place, and I venture to say dangerous when the fund is exhausted. Now here is the consequence (and this confirms all I have said): this feverish activity is, as it were, forced into a narrow space; it attracts the attention of all; it is what is seen. The people applaud; they are astonished at the beauty and facility of the plan, and expect to have it continued and extended. That which they do not see is that an equal quantity of labor, which would probably be more valuable, has been obliterated over the rest of France.

11. Frugality and Luxury

It is not only in the public expenditure that what is seen eclipses what is not seen. Setting aside what relates to political economy, this phenomenon leads to false reasoning. It causes nations to consider their moral and their material interests as contradictory to each other. What can be more discouraging or more dismal?

For instance, there is not a father of a family who does not think it his duty to teach his children order, system, the habits of carefulness, of economy, and of moderation in spending money.

There is no religion which does not thunder against pomp and luxury. This is as it should be; but, on the other hand, how frequently do we hear the following remarks:

"To hoard is to drain the veins of the people."

"The luxury of the great is the comfort of the little."

"Prodigals ruin themselves, but they enrich the State."

"It is the superfluity of the rich that makes bread for the poor."

Here, certainly, is a striking contradiction between the moral and the social idea. How many eminent spirits, after having made the assertion, repose in peace. It is a thing I never could understand, for it seems to me that nothing can be more distressing than to discover two opposite tendencies in mankind. Why, it comes to degradation at each of the extremes: economy brings it to misery; prodigality plunges it into moral degradation. Happily, these vulgar maxims exhibit economy and luxury in a false light, taking account, as they do, of those immediate consequences that are seen, and not of the remote ones, which are not seen. Let us see if we can rectify this incomplete view of the case.

Mondor and his brother Aristus, after dividing the parental inheritance, have each an income of 50,000 francs. Mondor practices the fashionable philanthropy. He is what is called a squanderer of money. He renews his furniture several times a year; changes his carriages every month. People talk of his ingenious contrivances to bring them sooner to an end: in short, he surpasses the extravagant lives of Balzac and Alexander Dumas.

Thus everybody is singing his praises. It is, "Tell us about Mondor! Mondor forever! He is the benefactor of the workman; a blessing to the people. It is true, he revels in dissipation; he splashes the pedestrians; his own dignity and that of human nature are lowered a little; but what of that? He does good with his fortune, if not with himself. He causes money to circulate; he always sends the tradespeople away satisfied. Is not money made round that it may roll?"

Aristus has adopted a very different plan of life. If he is not an egotist, he is, at any rate, an individualist, for he considers expense, seeks only moderate and reasonable enjoyments, thinks of his children's prospects, and, in fact, he economizes.

And what do people say of him? "What is the good of a rich fellow like him? He is a skinflint. There is something imposing, perhaps, in the simplicity of his life; and he is humane, too, and benevolent, and generous, but he calculates. He does not spend his income; his house is neither brilliant nor bustling. What good does he do to the paperhangers, the carriage makers, the horse dealers, and the confectioners?"

These opinions, which are fatal to morality, are founded upon what strikes the eye: the expenditure of the prodigal; and another, which is out of sight, the equal and even superior expenditure of the economizer.

But things have been so admirably arranged by the Divine inventor of social order that in this, as in everything else, political economy and morality, far from clashing, agree; and the wisdom of Aristus is not only more dignified, but still more profitable, than the folly of Mondor. And when I say profitable, I do not mean only profitable to Aristus, or even to society in general, but more profitable to the workmen themselves—to the trade of the time.

To prove it, it is only necessary to turn the mind's eye to those hidden consequences of human actions, which the bodily eye does not see.

Yes, the prodigality of Mondor has visible effects in every point of view. Everybody can see his landaus, his phaetons, his berlins, the delicate paintings on his ceilings, his rich carpets, the brilliant effects of his house. Everyone knows that his horses run at the race track. The dinners which he gives at the Hotel de Paris attract the attention of the crowds on the Boulevards; and it is said, "That is a generous man; far from saving his income, he is very likely breaking into his capital." That is what is seen.

It is not so easy to see, with regard to the interest of workers, what becomes of the income of Aristus. If we were to trace it carefully, however, we should see that the whole of it, down to the last farthing, affords work to the laborers, as certainly as the fortune of Mondor. Only there is this difference: the wanton extravagance of Mondor is doomed to be constantly decreasing, and to come to an end without fail; while the wise expenditure of Aristus will go on increasing from year to year. And if this is the case, then, most assuredly, the public interest will be in unison with morality.

Aristus spends upon himself and his household 20,000 francs a year. If that is not sufficient to content him, he does not deserve to be called a wise man. He is touched by the miseries which oppress the poorer classes; he thinks he is bound in conscience to afford them some relief, and therefore he devotes 10,000 francs to acts of benevolence. Amongst the merchants, the manufacturers, and the agriculturists, he has friends who are suffering under temporary difficulties; he makes himself acquainted with their situation, that he may assist them with prudence and efficiency, and to this work he devotes 10,000 francs more. Then he does not forget that he has daughters to portion, and sons for whose prospects it is his duty to provide, and therefore he considers it a duty to lay by and put out to interest 10,000 francs every year.

The following is a list of his expenses:

1st, Personal expenses . . . . .20,000 fr.
2nd, Benevolent objects 10,000
3rd, Offices of friendship 10,000
4th, Saving 10,000

Let us examine each of these items, and we shall see that not a single farthing escapes the national labor.

1. Personal expenses: These, as far as workpeople and tradesmen are concerned, have precisely the same effect as an equal sum spent by Mondor. This is self-evident, therefore we shall say no more about it.

2. Benevolent objects: The 10,000 francs devoted to this purpose benefit trade in an equal degree; they reach the butcher, the baker, the tailor, and the carpenter. The only thing is, that the bread, the meat, and the clothing are not used by Aristus, but by those whom he has made his substitutes. Now, this simple substitution of one consumer for another in no way affects trade in general. It is all one, whether Aristus spends a crown or desires some unfortunate person to spend it instead.

3. Offices of friendship: The friend to whom Aristus lends or gives 10,000 francs does not receive them to bury them; that would be against the hypothesis. He uses them to pay for goods, or to discharge debts. In the first case, trade is encouraged. Will anyone pretend to say that it gains more by Mondor's purchase of a thoroughbred horse for 10,000 francs than by the purchase of 10,000 francs' worth of goods by Aristus or his friend? For if this sum serves to pay a debt, a third person appears, viz., the creditor, who will certainly employ them upon something in his trade, his household, or his farm. He forms another medium

between Aristus and the workmen. The names only are changed, the expense remains, and also the encouragement to trade.

4. Saving: There remains now the 10,000 francs saved; and it is here, as regards the encouragement to the arts, to trade, labor, and the workmen, that Mondor appears far superior to Aristus, although, in a moral point of view, Aristus shows himself, in some degree, superior to Mondor.

I can never look at these apparent contradictions between the great laws of nature without a feeling of physical uneasiness which amounts to suffering. Were mankind reduced to the necessity of choosing between two parties, one of whom injures his interest, and the other his conscience, we should have nothing to hope from the future. Happily, this is not the case; and to see Aristus regain his economical superiority, as well as his moral superiority, it is sufficient to understand this consoling maxim, which is no less true from having a paradoxical appearance, "To save is to spend."

What is Aristus's object in saving 10,000 francs? Is it to bury them in his garden? No, certainly; he intends to increase his capital and his income; consequently, this money, instead of being employed upon his own personal gratification, is used for buying land, a house, etc., or it is placed in the hands of a merchant or a banker. Follow the progress of this money in any one of these cases, and you will be convinced, that through the medium of vendors or lenders, it is encouraging labor quite as certainly as if Aristus, following the example of his brother, had exchanged it for furniture, jewels, and horses.

For when Aristus buys lands or mortgages for 10,000 francs, he is motivated by the consideration that he does not want to spend this money. This is why you complain of him.

But, at the same time, the man who sells the land or the mortgage, is motivated by the consideration that he does want to spend the 10,000 francs in some way; so that the money is spent in any case, either by Aristus or by others in his stead.

With respect to the working class, to the encouragement of labor, there is only one difference between the conduct of Aristus and that of Mondor. Mondor spends the money himself, and around him, and therefore the effect is seen. Aristus, spending it partly through intermediate parties, and at a distance, the effect is not seen. But, in fact, those who know how to attribute effects to their proper causes, will perceive, that what is not seen is as certain as what is seen. This is proved by the fact that in both cases the money circulates, and does not lie in the iron chest of the wise man, any more than it does in that of the spendthrift. It is, therefore, false to say that economy does actual harm to trade; as described above, it is equally beneficial with luxury.

But how far superior is it, if, instead of confining our thoughts to the present moment, we let them embrace a longer period!

Ten years pass away. What is become of Mondor and his fortune and his great popularity? Mondor is ruined. Instead of spending 60,000 francs every year in the social body, he is, perhaps, a burden to it. In any case, he is no longer the delight of shopkeepers; he is no longer the patron of the arts and of trade; he is no longer of any use to the workmen, nor are his heirs, whom he has brought to want.

At the end of the same ten years Aristus not only continues to throw his income into circulation, but he adds an increasing sum from year to year to his expenses. He enlarges the national capital, that is, the fund that supplies wages, and as it is upon the extent of this fund that the demand for hands depends, he assists in progressively increasing the remuneration of the working class; and if he dies, he leaves children whom he has taught to succeed him in this work of progress and civilization. In a moral point of view, the superiority of frugality over luxury is indisputable. It is consoling to think that it is so in political economy to everyone who, not confining his views to the immediate effects of phenomena, knows how to extend his investigations to their final effects.

12. He Who Has a Right to Work Has a Right to Profit

"Brethren, you must club together to find me work at your own price." This is the right to work; i.e., elementary socialism of the first degree.

"Brethren, you must club together to find me work at my own price." This is the right to profit; i.e., refined socialism, or socialism of the second degree.

Both of these live upon such of their effects as *are seen*. They will die by means of those effects *that are not seen*.

That *which is seen* is the labor and the profit excited by social combination. *That which is not seen* is the labor and the profit to which this same combination would give rise if it were left to the taxpayers.

In 1848, the right to labor for a moment showed two faces. This was sufficient to ruin it in public opinion.

One of these faces was called national workshops. The other, forty-five centimes. Millions of francs went daily from the Rue Rivoli to the national workshops. This was the fair side of the medal.

And this is the reverse. If millions are taken out of a cash-box, they must first have been put into it. This is why the organizers of the right to public labor apply to the taxpayers.

Now, the peasants said, "I must pay forty-five centimes; then I must deprive myself of clothing. I cannot manure my field; I cannot repair my house."

And the country workmen said, "As our townsman deprives himself of some clothing, there will be less work for the tailor; as he does not improve his field, there will be less work for the drainer; as he does not repair his house, there will be less work for the carpenter and mason."

It was then proved that two kinds of meal cannot come out of one sack, and that the work furnished by the Government was done at the expense of labor, paid for by the taxpayer. This was the death of the right to labor, which showed itself as much a chimera as an injustice. And yet, the right to profit, which is only an exaggeration of the right to labor, is still alive and flourishing.

Ought not the protectionist to blush at the part he would make society play?

He says to it, "You must give me work, and, more than that, lucrative work. I have foolishly fixed upon a trade by which I lose

ten percent. If you impose a tax of twenty francs upon my countrymen, and give it to me, I shall be a gainer instead of a loser.
Now, profit is my right; you owe it to me." Now, any society that
would listen to this sophist, burden itself with taxes to satisfy him,
and not perceive that the loss to which any trade is exposed is no
less a loss when others are forced to make up for it—such a society, I say, would deserve the burden inflicted upon it.

Thus we learn by the numerous subjects that I have treated,
that, to be ignorant of political economy is to allow ourselves to
be dazzled by the immediate effect of a phenomenon; to be
acquainted with it is to embrace in thought and in forethought the
whole compass of effects.

I might subject a host of other questions to the same test; but
I shrink from the monotony of a constantly uniform demonstra-
tion, and I conclude by applying to political economy what
Chateaubriand says of history:

"There are," he says,

> two consequences in history; an immediate one, which is
> instantly recognized, and one in the distance, which is not
> at first perceived. These consequences often contradict each
> other; the former are the results of our own limited wis-
> dom, the latter, those of that wisdom which endures. The
> providential event appears after the human event. God rises
> up behind men. Deny, if you will, the supreme counsel; dis-
> own its action; dispute about words; designate, by the term,
> force of circumstances, or reason, what the vulgar call Prov-
> idence; but look to the end of an accomplished fact, and you
> will see that it has always produced the contrary of what
> was expected from it, if it was not established at first upon
> morality and justice.[3]

---

[3]Chateaubriand's *Posthumous Memoirs*.

II.

THE LAW[1]

The law perverted! The law—and, in its wake, all the collective forces of the nation—the law, I say, not only diverted from its proper direction, but made to pursue one entirely contrary! The law become the tool of every kind of avarice, instead of being its check! The law guilty of that very iniquity which it was its mission to punish! Truly, this is a serious fact, if it exists, and one to which I feel bound to call the attention of my fellow citizens.

We hold from God the gift that, as far as we are concerned, contains all others, Life—physical, intellectual, and moral life.

But life cannot support itself. He who has bestowed it, has entrusted us with the care of supporting it, of developing it, and of perfecting it. To that end, He has provided us with a collection of wonderful faculties; He has plunged us into the midst of a variety of elements. It is by the application of our faculties to these elements that the phenomena of assimilation and of appropriation, by which life pursues the circle that has been assigned to it are realized.

---

[1]First published in 1850.

Existence, faculties, assimilation—in other words, personality, liberty, property—this is man.

It is of these three things that it may be said, apart from all demagogic subtlety, that they are anterior and superior to all human legislation.

It is not because men have made laws, that personality, liberty, and property exist. On the contrary, it is because personality, liberty, and property exist beforehand, that men make laws. What, then, is law? As I have said elsewhere, it is the collective organization of the individual right to lawful defense.

Nature, or rather God, has bestowed upon every one of us the right to defend his person, his liberty, and his property, since these are the three constituent or preserving elements of life; elements, each of which is rendered complete by the others, and that cannot be understood without them. For what are our faculties, but the extension of our personality? and what is property, but an extension of our faculties?

If every man has the right of defending, even by force, his person, his liberty, and his property, a number of men have the right to combine together to extend, to organize a common force to provide regularly for this defense.

Collective right, then, has its principle, its reason for existing, its lawfulness, in individual right; and the common force cannot rationally have any other end, or any other mission, than that of the isolated forces for which it is substituted. Thus, as the force of an individual cannot lawfully touch the person, the liberty, or the property of another individual—for the same reason, the common force cannot lawfully be used to destroy the person, the liberty, or the property of individuals or of classes.

For this perversion of force would be, in one case as in the other, in contradiction to our premises. For who will dare to say that force has been given to us, not to defend our rights, but to annihilate the equal rights of our brethren? And if this be not true of every individual force, acting independently, how can it be true of the collective force, which is only the organized union of isolated forces?

Nothing, therefore, can be more evident than this: The law is the organization of the natural right of lawful defense; it is the substitution of collective for individual forces, for the purpose of acting in the sphere in which they have a right to act, of doing what they have a right to do, to secure persons, liberties, and properties, and to maintain each in its right, so as to cause justice to reign over all.

And if a people established upon this basis were to exist, it seems to me that order would prevail among them in their acts as well as in their ideas. It seems to me that such a people would have the most simple, the most economical, the least oppressive, the least to be felt, the most restrained, the most just, and, consequently, the most stable Government that could be imagined, whatever its political form might be.

For under such an administration, everyone would feel that he possessed all the fullness, as well as all the responsibility of his existence. So long as personal safety was ensured, so long as labor was free, and the fruits of labor secured against all unjust attacks, no one would have any difficulties to contend with in the State. When prosperous, we should not, it is true, have to thank the State for our success; but when unfortunate, we should no more think of taxing it with our disasters than our peasants think of attributing to it the arrival of hail or of frost. We should know it only by the inestimable blessing of Safety.

It may further be affirmed, that, thanks to the non-intervention of the State in private affairs, our wants and their satisfactions would develop themselves in their natural order. We should not see poor families seeking for literary instruction before they were supplied with bread. We should not see towns peopled at the expense of rural districts, nor rural districts at the expense of towns. We should not see those great displacements of capital, of labor, and of population, that legislative measures occasion; displacements that render so uncertain and precarious the very sources of existence, and thus enlarge to such an extent the responsibility of Governments.

Unhappily, law is by no means confined to its own sphere. Nor is it merely in some ambiguous and debatable views that it has left its proper sphere. It has done more than this. It has acted in direct opposition to its proper end; it has destroyed its own object; it has been employed in annihilating that justice which it ought to have established, in effacing amongst Rights, that limit which it was its true mission to respect; it has placed the collective force in the service of those who wish to traffic, without risk and without scruple, in the persons, the liberty, and the property of others; it has converted plunder into a right, that it may protect it, and lawful defense into a crime, that it may punish it.

How has this perversion of law been accomplished? And what has resulted from it?

The law has been perverted through the influence of two very different causes—naked greed and misconceived philanthropy.

Let us speak of the former. Self-preservation and development is the common aspiration of all men, in such a way that if every one enjoyed the free exercise of his faculties and the free disposition of their fruits, social progress would be incessant, uninterrupted, inevitable.

But there is also another disposition which is common to them. This is to live and to develop, when they can, at the expense of one another. This is no rash imputation, emanating from a gloomy, uncharitable spirit. History bears witness to the truth of it, by the incessant wars, the migrations of races, sectarian oppressions, the universality of slavery, the frauds in trade, and the monopolies with which its annals abound. This fatal disposition has its origin in the very constitution of man—in that primitive, and universal, and invincible sentiment that urges it toward its well-being, and makes it seek to escape pain.

Man can only derive life and enjoyment from a perpetual search and appropriation; that is, from a perpetual application of his faculties to objects, or from labor. This is the origin of property.

But also he may live and enjoy, by seizing and appropriating the productions of the faculties of his fellow men. This is the origin of plunder.

Now, labor being in itself a pain, and man being naturally inclined to avoid pain, it follows, and history proves it, that wherever plunder is less burdensome than labor, it prevails; and neither religion nor morality can, in this case, prevent it from prevailing.

When does plunder cease, then? When it becomes more burdensome and more dangerous than labor. It is very evident that the proper aim of law is to oppose the fatal tendency to plunder with the powerful obstacle of collective force; that all its measures should be in favor of property, and against plunder.

But the law is made, generally, by one man, or by one class of men. And as law cannot exist without the sanction and the support of a preponderant force, it must finally place this force in the hands of those who legislate.

This inevitable phenomenon, combined with the fatal tendency that, we have said, exists in the heart of man, explains the almost universal perversion of law. It is easy to conceive that, instead of being a check upon injustice, it becomes its most invincible instrument.

It is easy to conceive that, according to the power of the legislator, it destroys for its own profit, and in different degrees amongst the rest of the community, personal independence by slavery, liberty by oppression, and property by plunder.

It is in the nature of men to rise against the injustice of which they are the victims. When, therefore, plunder is organized by law, for the profit of those who perpetrate it, all the plundered classes tend, either by peaceful or revolutionary means, to enter in some way into the manufacturing of laws. These classes, according to the degree of enlightenment at which they have arrived, may propose to themselves two very different ends, when they thus attempt the attainment of their political rights; either they may wish to put an end to lawful plunder, or they may desire to take part in it.

Woe to the nation where this latter thought prevails amongst the masses, at the moment when they, in their turn, seize upon the legislative power!

Up to that time, lawful plunder has been exercised by the few upon the many, as is the case in countries where the right of legislating is confined to a few hands. But now it has become universal, and the equilibrium is sought in universal plunder. The injustice that society contains, instead of being rooted out of it, is generalized. As soon as the injured classes have recovered their political rights, their first thought is not to abolish plunder (this would suppose them to possess enlightenment, which they cannot have), but to organize against the other classes, and to their own detriment, a system of reprisals—as if it was necessary, before the reign of justice arrives, that all should undergo a cruel retribution—some for their iniquity and some for their ignorance.

It would be impossible, therefore, to introduce into society a greater change and a greater evil than this—the conversion of the law into an instrument of plunder.

What would be the consequences of such a perversion? It would require volumes to describe them all. We must content ourselves with pointing out the most striking.

In the first place, it would efface from everybody's conscience the distinction between justice and injustice. No society can exist unless the laws are respected to a certain degree, but the safest way to make them respected is to make them respectable. When law and morality are in contradiction to each other, the citizen finds himself in the cruel alternative of either losing his moral sense, or of losing his respect for the law—two evils of equal magnitude, between which it would be difficult to choose.

It is so much in the nature of law to support justice that in the minds of the masses they are one and the same. There is in all of us a strong disposition to regard what is lawful as legitimate, so much so that many falsely derive all justice from law. It is sufficient, then, for the law to order and sanction plunder, that it may appear to many consciences just and sacred. Slavery, protection, and monopoly find defenders, not only in those who profit by them, but in those who suffer by them. If you suggest a doubt as to the morality of these institutions, it is said directly—"You are a dangerous experimenter, a utopian, a theorist, a despiser of the laws; you would shake the basis upon which society rests."

If you lecture upon morality, or political economy, official bodies will be found to make this request to the Government:

> That henceforth science be taught not only with sole reference to free exchange (to liberty, property, and justice), as has been the case up to the present time, but also, and especially, with reference to the facts and legislation (contrary to liberty, property, and justice) that regulate French industry.

> That, in public lecterns salaried by the treasury, the professor abstain rigorously from endangering in the slightest degree the respect due to the laws now in force.[2]

So that if a law exists that sanctions slavery or monopoly, oppression or plunder, in any form whatever, it must not even be mentioned—for how can it be mentioned without damaging the respect that it inspires? Still further, morality and political economy must be taught in connection with this law—that is, under the supposition that it must be just, only because it is law.

Another effect of this deplorable perversion of the law is that it gives to human passions and to political struggles, and, in general, to politics, properly so called, an exaggerated importance.

I could prove this assertion in a thousand ways. But I shall confine myself, by way of an illustration, to bringing it to bear upon a subject which has of late occupied everybody's mind: universal suffrage.

Whatever may be thought of it by the adepts of the school of Rousseau, which professes to be very far advanced, but which I consider 20 centuries behind, universal suffrage (taking the word

---

[2]General Council of Manufactures, Agriculture, and Commerce, 6th of May, 1850.

in its strictest sense) is not one of those sacred dogmas with respect to which examination and doubt are crimes.

Serious objections may be made to it.

In the first place, the word universal conceals a gross sophism. There are, in France, 36,000,000 inhabitants. To make the right of suffrage universal, 36,000,000 electors should be reckoned. The most extended system reckons only 9,000,000. Three persons out of four, then, are excluded; and more than this, they are excluded by the fourth. Upon what principle is this exclusion founded? Upon the principle of incapacity. Universal suffrage, then, means: universal suffrage of those who are capable. In point of fact, who are the capable? Are age, sex, and judicial condemnations the only conditions to which incapacity is to be attached?

On taking a nearer view of the subject, we may soon perceive the reason why the right of suffrage depends upon the presumption of incapacity; the most extended system differing from the most restricted in the conditions on which this incapacity depends, and which constitutes not a difference in principle, but in degree.

This motive is, that the elector does not stipulate for himself, but for everybody.

If, as the republicans of the Greek and Roman tone pretend, the right of suffrage had fallen to the lot of every one at his birth, it would be an injustice to adults to prevent women and children from voting. Why are they prevented? Because they are presumed to be incapable. And why is incapacity a reason for exclusion? Because the elector does not reap alone the responsibility of his vote; because every vote engages and affects the community at large; because the community has a right to demand some assurances, as regards the acts upon which its well-being and its existence depend.

I know what might be said in answer to this. I know what might be objected. But this is not the place to settle a controversy of this kind. What I wish to observe is this, that this same controversy (in common with the greater part of political questions) that agitates, excites, and unsettles the nations, would lose almost all its importance if the law had always been what it ought to be.

In fact, if law were confined to causing all persons, all liberties, and all properties to be respected—if it were merely the organization of individual right and individual defense—if it were the obstacle, the check, the chastisement opposed to all oppression, to all plunder—is it likely that we should dispute much, as citizens, on the subject of the greater or lesser universality of suffrage? Is it likely that it would compromise that greatest of advantages, the public peace? Is it likely that the excluded classes would not quietly wait for their turn? Is it likely that the enfranchised classes would be very jealous of their privilege? And is it not clear, that the interest of all being one and the same, some would act without much inconvenience to the others?

But if the fatal principle should come to be introduced, that, under pretense of organization, regulation, protection, or encouragement, the law may take from one party in order to give to another, help itself to the wealth acquired by all the classes that it may increase that of one class, whether that of the agriculturists, the manufacturers, the ship owners, or artists and comedians; then certainly, in this case, there is no class which may not try, and with reason, to place its hand upon the law, that would not demand with fury its right of election and eligibility, and that would overturn society rather than not obtain it. Even beggars and vagabonds will prove to you that they have an incontestable title to it. They will say:

> We never buy wine, tobacco, or salt, without paying the tax, and a part of this tax is given by law in perquisites and gratuities to men who are richer than we are. Others make use of the law to create an artificial rise in the price of bread, meat, iron, or cloth.

> Since everybody traffics in law for his own profit, we should like to do the same. We should like to make it produce the right to assistance, which is the poor man's plunder. To effect this, we ought to be electors and legislators, that we may organize, on a large scale, alms for our own class, as you have organized, on a large scale, protection for yours.

Don't tell us that you will take our cause upon yourselves,
and throw to us 600,000 francs to keep us quiet, like giving
us a bone to pick. We have other claims, and, at any rate, we
wish to stipulate for ourselves, as other classes have stipulated for themselves!

How is this argument to be answered? Yes, as long as it is admitted that the law may be diverted from its true mission, that it may
violate property instead of securing it, everybody will be wanting
to manufacture law, either to defend himself against plunder, or
to organize it for his own profit. The political question will
always be prejudicial, predominant, and absorbing; in a word,
there will be fighting around the door of the Legislative Palace.
The struggle will be no less furious within it. To be convinced of
this, it is hardly necessary to look at what passes in the Chambers
in France and in England; it is enough to know how the question
stands.

Is there any need to prove that this odious perversion of law
is a perpetual source of hatred and discord, that it even tends to
social disorganization? Look at the United States. There is no
country in the world where the law is kept more within its proper
domain—which is, to secure to everyone his liberty and his property. Therefore, there is no country in the world where social
order appears to rest upon a more solid basis. Nevertheless, even
in the United States, there are two questions, and only two, that
from the beginning have endangered political order. And what
are these two questions? That of slavery and that of tariffs; that
is, precisely the only two questions in which, contrary to the general spirit of this republic, law has taken the character of a plunderer. Slavery is a violation, sanctioned by law, of the rights of the
person. Protection is a violation perpetrated by the law upon the
rights of property; and certainly it is very remarkable that, in the
midst of so many other debates, this double legal scourge, the sorrowful inheritance of the Old World, should be the only one
which can, and perhaps will, cause the rupture of the Union.
Indeed, a more astounding fact, in the heart of society, cannot be
conceived than this: That law should have become an instrument
of injustice. And if this fact occasions consequences so formidable

to the United States, where there is but one exception, what must it be with us in Europe, where it is a principle—a system?

Mr. Montalembert, adopting the thought of a famous proclamation of Mr. Carlier, said, "We must make war against socialism." And by socialism, according to the definition of Mr. Charles Dupin, he meant plunder. But what plunder did he mean? For there are two sorts: extralegal and legal plunder.

As to extralegal plunder, such as theft, or swindling, which is defined, foreseen, and punished by the penal code, I do not think it can be adorned by the name of socialism. It is not this that systematically threatens the foundations of society. Besides, the war against this kind of plunder has not waited for the signal of Mr. Montalembert or Mr. Carlier. It has gone on since the beginning of the world; France was carrying it on long before the revolution of February—long before the appearance of socialism—with all the ceremonies of magistracy, police, gendarmerie, prisons, dungeons, and scaffolds. It is the law itself that is conducting this war, and it is to be wished, in my opinion, that the law should always maintain this attitude with respect to plunder.

But this is not the case. The law sometimes takes its own part. Sometimes it accomplishes it with its own hands, in order to save the parties benefited the shame, the danger, and the scruple. Sometimes it places all this ceremony of magistracy, police, gendarmerie, and prisons, at the service of the plunderer, and treats the plundered party, when he defends himself, as the criminal. In a word, there is a legal plunder, and it is, no doubt, this that is meant by Mr. Montalembert.

This plunder may be only an exceptional blemish in the legislation of a people, and in this case, the best thing that can be done is, without so many speeches and lamentations, to do away with it as soon as possible, notwithstanding the clamors of interested parties. But how is it to be distinguished? Very easily. See whether the law takes from some persons that which belongs to them, to give to others what does not belong to them. See whether the law performs, for the profit of one citizen, and, to the injury of others, an act that this citizen cannot perform without committing a crime. Abolish this law without delay; it is not merely an iniquity—it is a fertile source of iniquities, for it invites reprisals; and if you do not take care, the exceptional case will extend, multiply, and become systematic. No doubt the party benefited will exclaim loudly; he will assert his acquired rights. He will say that the State is bound to protect and encourage his industry; he will plead that it is a good thing for the State to be enriched, that it may spend the more, and thus shower down salaries upon the poor workmen. Take care not to listen to this sophistry, for it is just by the systematizing of these arguments that legal plunder becomes systematized.

And this is what has taken place. The delusion of the day is to enrich all classes at the expense of each other; it is to generalize plunder under pretense of organizing it. Now, legal plunder may be exercised in an infinite multitude of ways. Hence come an infinite multitude of plans for organization; tariffs, protection, perquisites, gratuities, encouragements, progressive taxation, free public education, right to work, right to profit, right to wages, right to assistance, right to instruments of labor, gratuity of credit, etc., etc. And it is all these plans, taken as a whole, with what they have in common, legal plunder, that takes the name of socialism.

Now socialism, thus defined, and forming a doctrinal body, what other war would you make against it than a war of doctrine? You find this doctrine false, absurd, abominable. Refute it. This will be all the easier, the more false, absurd, and abominable it is. Above all, if you wish to be strong, begin by rooting out of your legislation every particle of socialism which may have crept into it—and this will be no light work.

Mr. Montalembert has been reproached with wishing to turn brute force against socialism. He ought to be exonerated from this reproach, for he has plainly said: "The war that we must make against socialism must be one that is compatible with the law, honor, and justice."

But how is it that Mr. Montalembert does not see that he is placing himself in a vicious circle? You would oppose law to socialism. But it is the law that socialism invokes. It aspires to legal, not extralegal plunder. It is of the law itself, like monopolists of all kinds, that it wants to make an instrument; and when once it has the law on its side, how will you be able to turn the law against it? How will you place it under the power of your tribunals, your gendarmes, and of your prisons? What will you do then? You wish to prevent it from taking any part in the making of laws. You would keep it outside the Legislative Palace. In this you will not succeed, I venture to prophesy, so long as legal plunder is the basis of the legislation within.

It is absolutely necessary that this question of legal plunder should be determined, and there are only three solutions of it:

1. When the few plunder the many.
2. When everybody plunders everybody else.
3. When nobody plunders anybody.

Partial plunder, universal plunder, absence of plunder, amongst these we have to make our choice. The law can only produce one of these results.

Partial plunder. This is the system that prevailed so long as the elective privilege was partial; a system that is resorted to, to avoid the invasion of socialism.

Universal plunder. We have been threatened by this system when the elective privilege has become universal; the masses having conceived the idea of making law, on the principle of legislators who had preceded them.

Absence of plunder. This is the principle of justice, peace, order, stability, conciliation, and of good sense, which I shall proclaim with all the force of my lungs (which is very inadequate, alas!) till the day of my death.

And, in all sincerity, can anything more be required at the hands of the law? Can the law, whose necessary sanction is force, be reasonably employed upon anything beyond securing to every one his right? I defy anyone to remove it from this circle without perverting it, and consequently turning force against right. And as this is the most fatal, the most illogical social perversion that can possibly be imagined, it must be admitted that the true solution, so much sought after, of the social problem, is contained in these simple words—LAW IS ORGANIZED JUSTICE.

Now it is important to remark, that to organize justice by law, that is to say by force, excludes the idea of organizing by law, or by force any manifestation whatever of human activity—labor, charity, agriculture, commerce, industry, instruction, the fine arts, or religion; for any one of these organizings would inevitably destroy the essential organization. How, in fact, can we imagine force encroaching upon the liberty of citizens without infringing upon justice, and so acting against its proper aim?

Here I am taking on the most popular prejudice of our time. It is not considered enough that law should be just, it must be philanthropic. It is not sufficient that it should guarantee to every citizen the free and inoffensive exercise of his faculties, applied to his physical, intellectual, and moral development; it is required to extend well-being, instruction, and morality, directly over the nation. This is the fascinating side of socialism.

But, I repeat it, these two missions of the law contradict each other. We have to choose between them. A citizen cannot at the same time be free and not free. Mr. de Lamartine wrote to me one day thus: "Your doctrine is only the half of my program; you have stopped at liberty, I go on to fraternity." I answered him: "The second part of your program will destroy the first." And in fact it is impossible for me to separate the word fraternity from the word voluntary. I cannot possibly conceive fraternity legally enforced, without liberty being legally destroyed, and justice legally trampled under foot. Legal plunder has two roots: one of them, as we have already seen, is in human greed; the other is in misconceived philanthropy.

Before I proceed, I think I ought to explain myself upon the word plunder.

I do not take it, as it often is taken, in a vague, undefined, relative, or metaphorical sense. I use it in its scientific acceptation, and as expressing the opposite idea to property. When a portion of wealth passes out of the hands of him who has acquired it, without his consent, and without compensation, to him who has not created it, whether by force or by artifice, I say that property is violated, that plunder is perpetrated. I say that this is exactly what the law ought to repress always and everywhere. If the law itself performs the action it ought to repress, I say that plunder is still perpetrated, and even, in a social point of view, under aggravated circumstances. In this case, however, he who profits from the plunder is not responsible for it; it is the law, the lawgiver, society itself, and this is where the political danger lies.

It is to be regretted that there is something offensive in the word. I have sought in vain for another, for I would not wish at any time, and especially just now, to add an irritating word to our disagreements; therefore, whether I am believed or not, I declare that I do not mean to impugn the intentions nor the morality of anybody. I am attacking an idea that I believe to be false—a system that appears to me to be unjust; and this is so independent of intentions, that each of us profits by it without wishing it, and suffers from it without being aware of the cause.

Any person must write under the influence of party spirit or of fear, who would call into question the sincerity of protectionism, of socialism, and even of communism, which are one and the same plant, in three different periods of its growth. All that can be said is, that plunder is more visible by its partiality in protectionism,[3] and by its universality in communism; whence it follows that, of the three systems, socialism is still the most vague, the most undefined, and consequently the most sincere.

Be that as it may, to conclude that legal plunder has one of its roots in misconceived philanthropy, is evidently to put intentions out of the question.

---

[3] If protection were only granted in France to a single class, to the engineers, for instance, it would be so absurdly plundering, as to be unable to maintain itself. Thus we see all the protected trades combine, make common cause, and even recruit themselves in such a way as to appear to embrace the mass of the national labor. They feel instinctively that plunder is slurred over by being generalized.

With this understanding, let us examine the value, the origin, and the tendency of this popular aspiration, which pretends to realize the general good by general plunder.

The Socialists say, since the law organizes justice, why should it not organize labor, instruction, and religion?

Why? Because it could not organize labor, instruction, and religion, without disorganizing justice.

For remember, that law is force, and that consequently the domain of the law cannot properly extend beyond the domain of force.

When law and force keep a man within the bounds of justice, they impose nothing upon him but a mere negation. They only oblige him to abstain from doing harm. They violate neither his personality, his liberty, nor his property. They only guard the personality, the liberty, the property of others. They hold themselves on the defensive; they defend the equal right of all. They fulfill a mission whose harmlessness is evident, whose utility is palpable, and whose legitimacy is not to be disputed. This is so true that, as a friend of mine once remarked to me, to say that the aim of the law is to cause justice to reign, is to use an expression that is not rigorously exact. It ought to be said, the aim of the law is to prevent injustice from reigning. In fact, it is not justice that has an existence of its own, it is injustice. The one results from the absence of the other.

But when the law, through the medium of its necessary agent—force—imposes a form of labor, a method or a subject of instruction, a creed, or a worship, it is no longer negative; it acts positively upon men. It substitutes the will of the legislator for their own will, the initiative of the legislator for their own initiative. They have no need to consult, to compare, or to foresee; the law does all that for them. The intellect is for them a useless encumbrance; they cease to be men; they lose their personality, their liberty, their property.

Try to imagine a form of labor imposed by force, that is not a violation of liberty; a transmission of wealth imposed by force, that is not a violation of property. If you cannot succeed in reconciling this, you are bound to conclude that the law cannot organize labor and industry without organizing injustice.

When, from the seclusion of his office, a politician takes a view of society, he is struck with the spectacle of inequality that presents itself. He mourns over the sufferings that are the lot of so many of our brethren, sufferings whose aspect is rendered yet more sorrowful by the contrast of luxury and wealth.

He ought, perhaps, to ask himself whether such a social state has not been caused by the plunder of ancient times, exercised in the way of conquests; and by plunder of more recent times, effected through the medium of the laws? He ought to ask himself whether, granting the aspiration of all men to well-being and improvement, the reign of justice would not suffice to realize the greatest activity of progress, and the greatest amount of equality compatible with that individual responsibility that God has awarded as a just retribution of virtue and vice?

He never gives this a thought. His mind turns toward combinations, arrangements, legal or factitious organizations. He seeks the remedy in perpetuating and exaggerating what has produced the evil.

For, justice apart, which we have seen is only a negation, is there any one of these legal arrangements that does not contain the principle of plunder?

You say, "There are men who have no money," and you apply to the law. But the law is not a self-supplied fountain, whence every stream may obtain supplies independently of society. Nothing can enter the public treasury, in favor of one citizen or one class, but what other citizens and other classes have been forced to send to it. If everyone draws from it only the equivalent of what he has contributed to it, your law, it is true, is no plunderer, but it does nothing for men who want money—it does not promote equality. It can only be an instrument of equalization as far as it takes from one party to give to another, and then it is an instrument of plunder. Examine, in this light, the protection of tariffs, subsidies, right to profit, right to labor, right to assistance, free public education, progressive taxation, gratuitousness of credit, social workshops, and you will always find at the bottom legal plunder, organized injustice.

You say, "There are men who want knowledge," and you apply to the law. But the law is not a torch that sheds light that originates within itself. It extends over a society where there are men who have knowledge, and others who have not; citizens who want to learn, and others who are disposed to teach. It can only do one of two things: either allow a free operation to this kind of transaction, i.e., let this kind of want satisfy itself freely; or else pre-empt the will of the people in the matter, and take from some of them sufficient to pay professors commissioned to instruct others for free. But, in this second case there cannot fail to be a violation of liberty and property—legal plunder.

You say, "Here are men who are wanting in morality or religion," and you apply to the law; but law is force, and need I say how far it is a violent and absurd enterprise to introduce force in these matters?

As the result of its systems and of its efforts, it would seem that socialism, notwithstanding all its self-complacency, can scarcely help perceiving the monster of legal plunder. But what does it do? It disguises it cleverly from others, and even from itself, under the seductive names of fraternity, solidarity, organization, association. And because we do not ask so much at the hands of the law, because we only ask it for justice, it alleges that we reject fraternity, solidarity, organization, and association; and they brand us with the name of individualists.

We can assure them that what we repudiate is not natural organization, but forced organization.

It is not free association, but the forms of association that they would impose upon us.

It is not spontaneous fraternity, but legal fraternity.

It is not providential solidarity, but artificial solidarity, which is only an unjust displacement of responsibility.

Socialism, like the old policy from which it emanates, confounds Government and society. And so, every time we object to a thing being done by Government, it concludes that we object to its being done at all. We disapprove of education by the State—then we are against education altogether. We object to a State religion—then we would have no religion at all. We object to an equality which is brought about by the State then we are against equality, etc., etc. They might as well accuse us of wishing men not to eat, because we object to the cultivation of corn by the State.

How is it that the strange idea of making the law produce what it does not contain—prosperity, in a positive sense, wealth, science, religion—should ever have gained ground in the political world? The modern politicians, particularly those of the Socialist school, found their different theories upon one common hypothesis; and surely a more strange, a more presumptuous notion, could never have entered a human brain.

They divide mankind into two parts. Men in general, except one, form the first; the politician himself forms the second, which is by far the most important.

In fact, they begin by supposing that men are devoid of any principle of action, and of any means of discernment in themselves; that they have no initiative; that they are inert matter, passive particles, atoms without impulse; at best a vegetation indifferent to its own mode of existence, susceptible of assuming, from an exterior will and hand an infinite number of forms, more or less symmetrical, artistic, and perfected.

Moreover, every one of these politicians does not hesitate to assume that he himself is, under the names of organizer, discoverer, legislator, institutor or founder, this will and hand, this universal initiative, this creative power, whose sublime mission it is to gather together these scattered materials, that is, men, into society.

Starting from these data, as a gardener according to his caprice shapes his trees into pyramids, parasols, cubes, cones, vases, espaliers, distaffs, or fans; so the Socialist, following his chimera, shapes poor humanity into groups, series, circles, subcircles, honeycombs, or social workshops, with all kinds of variations. And as the gardener, to bring his trees into shape, needs hatchets, pruning hooks, saws, and shears, so the politician, to bring society into shape, needs the forces which he can only find in the laws; the law of tariffs, the law of taxation, the law of assistance, and the law of education.

It is so true, that the Socialists look upon mankind as a subject for social experiments, that if, by chance, they are not quite certain of the success of these experiments, they will request a portion of mankind, as a subject to experiment upon. It is well known how popular the idea of trying all systems is, and one of their chiefs has been known seriously to demand of the Constituent Assembly a parish, with all its inhabitants, upon which to make his experiments.

It is thus that an inventor will make a small machine before he makes one of the regular size. Thus the chemist sacrifices some substances, the agriculturist some seed and a corner of his field, to make trial of an idea.

But think of the difference between the gardener and his trees, between the inventor and his machine, between the chemist and his substances, between the agriculturist and his seed! The Socialist thinks, in all sincerity, that there is the same difference between himself and mankind.

No wonder the politicians of the nineteenth century look upon society as an artificial production of the legislator's genius. This idea, the result of a classical education, has taken possession of all the thinkers and great writers of our country.

To all these persons, the relations between mankind and the legislator appear to be the same as those that exist between the clay and the potter.

Moreover, if they have consented to recognize in the heart of man a capability of action, and in his intellect a faculty of discernment, they have looked upon this gift of God as a fatal one, and thought that mankind, under these two impulses, tended fatally toward ruin. They have taken it for granted that if abandoned to their own inclinations, men would only occupy themselves with religion to arrive at atheism, with instruction to come to ignorance, and with labor and exchange to be extinguished in misery.

Happily, according to these writers, there are some men, termed governors and legislators, upon whom Heaven has bestowed opposite tendencies, not for their own sake only, but for the sake of the rest of the world.

Whilst mankind tends to evil, they incline to good; whilst mankind is advancing toward darkness, they are aspiring to enlightenment; whilst mankind is drawn toward vice, they are attracted by virtue. And, this granted, they demand the assistance of force, by means of which they are to substitute their own tendencies for those of the human race.

It is only needful to open, almost at random, a book on philosophy, politics, or history, to see how strongly this idea—the child of classical studies and the mother of socialism—is rooted in our country; that mankind is merely inert matter, receiving life, organization, morality, and wealth from power; or, rather, and still worse—that mankind itself tends toward degradation, and is only arrested in its tendency by the mysterious hand of the legislator. Classical conventionalism shows us everywhere, behind passive society, a hidden power, under the names of Law, or Legislator (or, by a mode of expression which refers to some person or persons of undisputed weight and authority, but not named), which moves, animates, enriches, and regenerates mankind.

We will give a quotation from Bossuet:

> One of the things which was the most strongly impressed (by whom?) upon the mind of the Egyptians, was the love of their country. . . . Nobody was allowed to be useless to the State; the law assigned to every one his employment, which descended from father to son. No one was permitted to have two professions, nor to adopt another. . . . But there was one occupation which was obliged to be common to all, this was the study of the laws and of wisdom; ignorance of religion and the political regulations of the country was excused in no condition of life. Moreover, every profession had a district assigned to it (by whom?). . . . Amongst good laws, one of the best things was, that everybody was taught to observe them (by whom?). Egypt abounded with wonderful inventions, and nothing was neglected which could render life comfortable and tranquil.

Thus men, according to Bossuet, derive nothing from themselves; patriotism, wealth, inventions, husbandry, science—all
come to them by the operation of the laws, or by kings. All they
have to do is to be passive. It is on this ground that Bossuet takes
exception when Diodorus accuses the Egyptians of rejecting
wrestling and music. "How is that possible," says he, "since these
arts were invented by Trismegistus?"

It is the same with the Persians:

> One of the first cares of the prince was to encourage agri-
> culture. . . . As there were posts established for the regula-
> tion of the armies, so there were offices for the superintend-
> ing of rural works. . . . The respect with which the Persians
> were inspired for royal authority was excessive.

The Greeks, although full of mind, were no less strangers to
their own responsibilities; so much so, that of themselves, like
dogs and horses, they would not have ventured upon the most
simple games. In a classical sense, it is an undisputed thing that
everything comes to the people from without.

> The Greeks, naturally full of spirit and courage, had been
> early cultivated by kings and colonies who had come from
> Egypt. From them they had learned the exercises of the
> body, foot races, and horse and chariot races. . . . The best
> thing that the Egyptians had taught them was to become
> docile, and to allow themselves to be formed by the laws for
> the public good.

FÉNELON—Reared in the study and admiration of antiquity
and a witness of the power of Louis XIV, Fenelon naturally
adopted the idea that mankind should be passive, and that its misfortunes and its prosperities, its virtues and its vices, are caused by
the external influence that is exercised upon it by the law, or by
the makers of the law. Thus, in his Utopia of Salentum, he brings
the men, with their interests, their faculties, their desires, and
their possessions, under the absolute direction of the legislator.
Whatever the subject may be, they themselves have no voice in
it—the prince judges for them. The nation is just a shapeless mass,

of which the prince is the soul. In him resides the thought, the foresight, the principle of all organization, of all progress; on him, therefore, rests all the responsibility.

In proof of this assertion, I might transcribe the whole of the tenth book of *Telemachus*. I refer the reader to it, and shall content myself with quoting some passages taken at random from this celebrated work, to which, in every other respect, I am the first to render justice.

With the astonishing credulity that characterizes the classics, Fénelon, against the authority of reason and of facts, admits the general felicity of the Egyptians, and attributes it, not to their own wisdom, but to that of their kings:

> We could not turn our eyes to the two shores, without perceiving rich towns and country seats, agreeably situated; fields that were covered every year, without intermission, with golden crops; meadows full of flocks; laborers bending under the weight of fruits that the earth lavished on its cultivators; and shepherds who made the echoes around repeat the soft sounds of their pipes and flutes. "Happy," said Mentor, "is that people who is governed by a wise king.". . . Mentor afterwards desired me to remark the happiness and abundance that was spread over all the country of Egypt, where twenty-two thousand cities might be counted. He admired the excellent police regulations of the cities; the justice administered in favor of the poor against the rich; the good education of the children, who were accustomed to obedience, labor, and the love of arts and letters; the exactness with which all the ceremonies of religion were performed; the disinterestedness, the desire of honor, the fidelity to men, and the fear of the gods, with which every father inspired his children. He could not sufficiently admire the prosperous state of the country. "Happy" said he, "is the people whom a wise king rules in such a manner."

Fénelon's idyll on Crete is still more fascinating. Mentor is made to say:

> All that you will see in this wonderful island is the result of the laws of Minos. The education that the children receive renders the body healthy and robust. They are accustomed,

from the first, to a frugal and laborious life; it is supposed that all the pleasures of sense enervate the body and the mind; no other pleasure is presented to them but that of being invincible by virtue, that of acquiring much glory . . . there they punish three vices that go unpunished amongst other people—ingratitude, dissimulation, and avarice. As to pomp and dissipation, there is no need to punish these, for they are unknown in Crete. . . . No costly furniture, no magnificent clothing, no delicious feasts, no gilded palaces are allowed.

It is thus that Mentor prepares his scholar to mould and manipulate, doubtless with the most philanthropic intentions, the people of Ithaca, and, to confirm him in these ideas, he gives him the example of Salentum.

So we receive our first political notions. We are taught to treat men very much as Oliver de Serres teaches farmers to manage and to mix the soil.

MONTESQUIEU—

To sustain the spirit of commerce, it is necessary that all the laws should favor it; that these same laws, by their regulations in dividing the fortunes in proportion as commerce enlarges them, should place every poor citizen in sufficiently easy circumstances to enable him to work like the others, and every rich citizen in such mediocrity that he must work, in order to retain or to acquire.

Thus the laws are to dispose of all fortunes.

Although in a democracy, real equality be the soul of the State, yet it is so difficult to establish that an extreme exactness in this matter would not always be desirable. It is sufficient that a census be established to reduce or fix the differences to a certain point, after which, it is for particular laws to equalize, as it were, the inequality by burdens imposed upon the rich and reliefs granted to the poor.

Here, again, we see the equalization of fortunes by law, that is, by force.

There were, in Greece, two kinds of republics. One was military, as Sparta; the other commercial, as Athens. In the one it was wished (by whom?) that the citizens should be idle: in the other, the love of labor was encouraged.

It is worth our while to pay a little attention to the extent of genius required by these legislators, that we may see how, by confounding all the virtues, they showed their wisdom to the world. Lycurgus, blending theft with the spirit of justice, the hardest slavery with extreme liberty, the most atrocious sentiments with the greatest moderation, gave stability to his city. He seemed to deprive it of all its resources, arts, commerce, money, and walls; there was ambition without the hope of rising; there were natural sentiments where the individual was neither child, nor husband, nor father. Chastity even was deprived of modesty. By this road Sparta was led on to grandeur and to glory.

The phenomenon that we observe in the institutions of Greece has been seen in the midst of the degeneracy and corruption of our modern times. An honest legislator has formed a people where probity has appeared as natural as bravery among the Spartans. Mr. Penn is a true Lycurgus, and although the former had peace for his object, and the latter war, they resemble each other in the singular path along which they have led their people, in their influence over free men, in the prejudices which they have overcome, the passions they have subdued.

Paraguay furnishes us with another example. Society has been accused of the crime of regarding the pleasure of commanding as the only good of life; but it will always be a noble thing to govern men by making them happy.

Those who desire to form similar institutions will establish community of property, as in the republic of Plato, the same reverence as he enjoined for the gods, separation from strangers for the preservation of morality, and make the city and not the citizens create commerce: they should give our arts without our luxury, our wants without our desires.

Vulgar infatuation may exclaim, if it likes, "It is Montesquieu! magnificent! sublime!" I am not afraid to express my opinion, and to say:

> What! You have the gall to call that fine? It is frightful! It is abominable! And these extracts, which I might multiply, show that according to Montesquieu, the persons, the liberties, the property, mankind itself, are nothing but grist for the mill of the sagacity of lawgivers.

ROUSSEAU—Although this politician, the paramount authority of the Democrats, makes the social edifice rest upon the general will, no one has so completely admitted the hypothesis of the entire passiveness of human nature in the presence of the lawgiver:

> If it is true that a great prince is a rare thing, how much more so must a great lawgiver be? The former has only to follow the pattern proposed to him by the latter. This latter is the engineer who invents the machine; the former is merely the workman who sets it in motion.

And what part have men to act in all this? That of the machine, which is set in motion; or rather, are they not the brute matter of which the machine is made? Thus, between the legislator and the prince, between the prince and his subjects, there are the same relations as those that exist between the agricultural writer and the agriculturist, the agriculturist and the clod. At what a vast height, then, is the politician placed, who rules over legislators themselves and teaches them their trade in such imperative terms as the following:

> Would you give consistency to the State? Bring the extremes together as much as possible. Suffer neither wealthy persons nor beggars.

> If the soil is poor and barren, or the country too much confined for the inhabitants, turn to industry and the arts, whose productions you will exchange for the provisions which you require. . . . On a good soil, if you are short of inhabitants, give all your attention to agriculture, which multiplies men, and banish the arts, which only serve to

depopulate the country. . . . Pay attention to extensive and convenient coasts. Cover the sea with vessels, and you will have a brilliant and short existence. If your seas wash only inaccessible rocks, let the people be barbarous, and eat fish; they will live more quietly, perhaps better, and most certainly more happily. In short, besides those maxims which are common to all, every people has its own particular circumstances, which demand a legislation peculiar to itself.

It was thus that the Hebrews formerly, and the Arabs more recently, had religion for their principal object; that of the Athenians was literature; that of Carthage and Tyre, commerce; of Rhodes, naval affairs; of Sparta, war; and of Rome, virtue. The author of the "Spirit of Laws" has shown the art by which the legislator should frame his institutions towards each of these objects. . . . But if the legislator, mistaking his object, should take up a principle different from that which arises from the nature of things; if one should tend to slavery, and the other to liberty; if one to wealth, and the other to population; one to peace, and the other to conquests; the laws will insensibly become enfeebled, the Constitution will be impaired, and the State will be subject to incessant agitations until it is destroyed, or becomes changed, and invincible Nature regains her empire.

But if Nature is sufficiently invincible to regain its empire, why does not Rousseau admit that it had no need of the legislator to gain its empire from the beginning? Why does he not allow that by obeying their own impulse, men would of themselves apply agriculture to a fertile district, and commerce to extensive and commodious coasts without the interference of a Lycurgus, a Solon, or a Rousseau, who would undertake it at the risk of deceiving themselves?

Be that as it may, we see with what a terrible responsibility Rousseau invests inventors, institutors, conductors, and manipulators of societies. He is, therefore, very exacting with regard to them.

He who dares to undertake the institutions of a people, ought to feel that he can, as it were, transform every individual, who is by himself a perfect and solitary whole, receiving his life and being from a larger whole of which he forms a part; he must feel that he can change the constitution of man, to fortify it, and substitute a social and moral existence for the physical and independent one that we have all received from nature. In a word, he must deprive man of his own powers, to give him others that are foreign to him.

Poor human nature! What would become of its dignity if it were entrusted to the disciples of Rousseau?

RAYNAL—

The climate, that is, the air and the soil, is the first element for the legislator. His resources prescribe to him his duties. First, he must consult his local position. A population dwelling upon maritime shores must have laws fitted for navigation. . . . If the colony is located in an inland region, a legislator must provide for the nature of the soil, and for its degree of fertility. . . .

It is more especially in the distribution of property that the wisdom of legislation will appear. As a general rule, and in every country, when a new colony is founded, land should be given to each man, sufficient for the support of his family. . . .

In an uncultivated island, which you are colonizing with children, it will only be needful to let the germs of truth expand in the developments of reason! . . . But when you establish old people in a new country, the skill consists in only allowing it those injurious opinions and customs which it is impossible to cure and correct. If you wish to prevent them from being perpetuated, you will act upon the rising generation by a general and public education of the children. A prince or legislator ought never to found a colony without previously sending wise men there to instruct the youth.... In a new colony, every facility is open to the precautions of the legislator who desires to purify the tone and the manners of the people. If he has genius and virtue, the lands and the men that are at his disposal will inspire his soul with a plan of society that a writer can only vaguely trace, and in a way that would be subject to the instability of all hypotheses, which are varied and complicated by an infinity of circumstances too difficult to foresee and to combine.

One would think it was a professor of agriculture who was saying to his pupils

> The climate is the only rule for the agriculturist. His resources dictate to him his duties. The first thing he has to consider is his local position. If he is on a clayey soil, he must do so and so. If he has to contend with sand, this is the way in which he must set about it. Every facility is open to the agriculturist who wishes to clear and improve his soil. If he only has the skill, the manure which he has at his disposal will suggest to him a plan of operation, which a professor can only vaguely trace, and in a way that would be subject to the uncertainty of all hypotheses, which vary and are complicated by an infinity of circumstances too difficult to foresee and to combine.

But, oh! sublime writers, deign to remember sometimes that this clay, this sand, this manure, of which you are disposing in so arbitrary a manner, are men, your equals, intelligent and free beings like yourselves, who have received from God, as you have, the faculty of seeing, of foreseeing, of thinking, and of judging for themselves!

MABLY—(He is supposing the laws to be worn out by time and by the neglect of security, and continues thus):

> Under these circumstances, we must be convinced that the bonds of Government are slack. Give them a new tension (it is the reader who is addressed), and the evil will be remedied. . . . Think less of punishing the faults than of encouraging the virtues that you want. By this method you will bestow upon your republic the vigor of youth. Through ignorance of this, a free people has lost its liberty! But if the evil has made so much way that the ordinary magistrates are unable to remedy it effectually, have recourse to an extraordinary magistracy, whose time should be short, and its power considerable. The imagination of the citizens requires to be impressed.

In this style he goes on through twenty volumes.

There was a time when, under the influence of teaching like this, which is the foundation of classical education, everyone was for placing himself beyond and above mankind, for the sake of arranging, organizing, and instituting it in his own way.

CONDILLAC—

> Take upon yourself, my lord, the character of Lycurgus or of Solon. Before you finish reading this essay, amuse yourself with giving laws to some wild people in America or in Africa. Establish these roving men in fixed dwellings; teach them to keep flocks. . . . Endeavor to develop the social qualities that nature has implanted in them. . . . Make them begin to practice the duties of humanity. . . . Cause the pleasures of the passions to become distasteful to them by punishments, and you will see these barbarians, with every plan of your legislation, lose a vice and gain a virtue.

> All these people have had laws. But few among them have been happy. Why is this? Because legislators have almost always been ignorant of the object of society, which is to unite families by a common interest.

> Impartiality in law consists in two things, in establishing equality in the fortunes and in the dignity of the citizens. . . . In proportion to the degree of equality established by the laws, the dearer will they become to every citizen. How can avarice, ambition, dissipation, idleness, sloth, envy, hatred, or jealousy agitate men who are equal in fortune and dignity, and to whom the laws leave no hope of disturbing their equality?

> What has been told you of the republic of Sparta ought to enlighten you on this question. No other State has had laws more in accordance with the order of nature or of equality.

It is not to be wondered at that the seventeenth and eighteenth centuries should have looked upon the human race as inert matter, ready to receive everything—form, figure, impulse, movement, and life, from a great prince, or a great legislator, or a great genius. These ages were reared in the study of antiquity; and antiquity presents everywhere—in Egypt, Persia, Greece, and Rome, the spectacle of a few men molding mankind according to their fancy, and mankind to this end enslaved by force or by imposture. And what does this prove? That because men and society are improvable, error, ignorance, despotism, slavery, and superstition must be more prevalent in early times. The mistake of the writers quoted above is not that they have asserted this fact, but that they have proposed it as a rule for the admiration and imitation of future generations. Their mistake has been, with an inconceivable absence of discernment, and upon the faith of a puerile conventionalism, that they have admitted what is inadmissible, viz., the grandeur, dignity, morality, and well-being of the artificial societies of the ancient world; they have not understood that time produces and spreads enlightenment; and that in proportion to the increase of enlightenment, right ceases to be upheld by force, and society regains possession of herself.

And, in fact, what is the political work that we are endeavoring to promote? It is no other than the instinctive effort of every people toward liberty. And what is liberty, whose name can make every heart beat, and which can agitate the world, but the union of all liberties, the liberty of conscience, of education, of association, of the press, of movement, of labor, and of exchange; in other words, the free exercise, for all, of all the inoffensive faculties; and again, in other words, the destruction of all despotisms, even of legal despotism, and the reduction of law to its only rational sphere, which is to regulate the individual right of legitimate defense, or to repress injustice?

This tendency of the human race, it must be admitted, is greatly thwarted, particularly in our country, by the fatal disposition, resulting from classical teaching and common to all politicians, of placing themselves beyond mankind, to arrange, organize, and regulate it, according to their fancy.

For whilst society is struggling to realize liberty, the great men who place themselves at its head, imbued with the principles of the seventeenth and eighteenth centuries, think only of subjecting it to the philanthropic despotism of their social inventions, and making it bear with docility, according to the expression of Rousseau, the yoke of public felicity as pictured in their own imaginations.

This was particularly the case in 1789. No sooner was the old system destroyed than society was to be submitted to other artificial arrangements, always with the same starting point—the omnipotence of the law.

SAINT-JUST—

> The legislator commands the future. It is for him to will for the good of mankind. It is for him to make men what he wishes them to be.

ROBESPIERRE—

> The function of Government is to direct the physical and moral powers of the nation toward the object of its institution.

BILLAUD VARENNES—

> A people who are to be restored to liberty must be formed anew. Ancient prejudices must be destroyed, antiquated customs changed, depraved affections corrected, inveterate vices eradicated. For this, a strong force and a vehement impulse will be necessary. . . . Citizens, the inflexible austerity of Lycurgus created the firm basis of the Spartan republic. The feeble and trusting disposition of Solon plunged Athens into slavery. This parallel contains the whole science of Government.

LEPELLETIER—

> Considering the extent of human degradation, I am convinced—of the necessity of effecting an entire regeneration of the race, and, if I may so express myself, of creating a new people.

Men, therefore, are nothing but raw material. It is not for them to will their own improvement. They are not capable of it; according to Saint-Just, it is only the legislator who is. Men are merely to be what he wills that they should be. According to Robespierre, who copies Rousseau literally, the legislator is to begin by assigning the aim of the institutions of the nation. After this, the Government has only to direct all its physical and moral forces toward this end. All this time the nation itself is to remain perfectly passive; and Billaud Varennes would teach us that it ought to have no prejudices, affections, nor wants, but such as are authorized by the legislator. He even goes so far as to say that the inflexible austerity of a man is the basis of a republic.

We have seen that, in cases where the evil is so great that the ordinary magistrates are unable to remedy it, Mably recommends a dictatorship, to promote virtue. "Have recourse," says he, "to an extraordinary magistracy, whose time shall be short, and his power considerable. The imagination of the people requires to be impressed." This doctrine has not been neglected. Listen to Robespierre:

> The principle of the Republican Government is virtue, and the means to be adopted, during its establishment, is terror. We want to substitute, in our country, morality for self-indulgence, probity for honor, principles for customs, duties for decorum, the empire of reason for the tyranny of fashion, contempt of vice for contempt of misfortune, pride for insolence, greatness of soul for vanity, love of glory for love of money, good people for good company, merit for intrigue, genius for wit, truth for glitter, the charm of happiness for the weariness of pleasure, the greatness of man for the littleness of the great, a magnanimous, powerful, happy people, for one that is easy, frivolous, degraded; that is to say, we would substitute all the virtues and miracles of a republic for all the vices and absurdities of monarchy.

At what a vast height above the rest of mankind does Robespierre place himself here! And observe the arrogance with which he speaks. He is not content with expressing a desire for a great renovation of the human heart, he does not even expect such a result from a regular Government. No; he intends to effect it himself, and by means of terror. The object of the discourse from which this puerile and laborious mass of antithesis is extracted, was to exhibit the principles of morality that ought to direct a revolutionary Government. Moreover, when Robespierre asks for a dictatorship, it is not merely for the purpose of repelling a foreign enemy, or of putting down factions; it is that he may establish, by means of terror and as a preliminary to the operation of the Constitution, his own principles of morality. He pretends to nothing short of extirpating from the country by means of terror, self-interest, honor, customs, decorum, fashion, vanity, the love of money, good company, intrigue, wit, luxury, and misery. It is not until after he, Robespierre, shall have accomplished these miracles, as he rightly calls them, that he will allow the law to regain her empire. Truly it would be well if these visionaries, who think so much of themselves and so little of mankind, who want to renew everything, would only be content with trying to reform themselves, the task would be arduous enough for them. In general, however, these gentlemen, the reformers, legislators, and politicians, do not desire to exercise an immediate despotism over mankind. No, they are too moderate and too philanthropic for that. They only contend for the despotism, the absolutism, the omnipotence of the law. They aspire only to make the law.

To show how universal this strange disposition has been in France, I had need not only to have copied the whole of the works of Mably, Raynal, Rousseau, Fenelon, and to have made long extracts from Bossuet and Montesquieu, but to have given the entire transactions of the sittings of the Convention. I shall do no such thing, however, but merely refer the reader to them.

No wonder this idea suited Bonaparte so well. He embraced it with ardor, and put it in practice with energy. Playing the part of a chemist, Europe was to him the material for his experiments. But this material reacted against him. More than half undeceived, Bonaparte, at St. Helena, seemed to admit that there is an initiative in every people, and he became less hostile to liberty. Yet this did not prevent him from giving this lesson to his son in his will—"To govern is to diffuse morality, education, and well-being."

After all this, I hardly need show, by fastidious quotations, the opinions of Morelly, Babeuf, Owen, Saint Simon, and Fourier. I shall confine myself to a few extracts from Louis Blanc's book on the organization of labor.

"In our project, society receives the impulse of power."

In what does the impulse that power gives to society consist? In imposing upon it the project of Mr. Louis Blanc.

On the other hand, society is the human race. The human race, then, is to receive its impulse from Mr. Louis Blanc.

It is at liberty to do so or not, it will be said. Of course the human race is at liberty to take advice from anybody, whoever it may be. But this is not the way in which Mr. Louis Blanc understands the thing. He means that his project should be converted into law, and consequently forcibly imposed by power.

> In our project, the State has only to give a legislation to labor, by means of which the industrial movement may and ought to be accomplished in all liberty. It (the State) merely places society on an incline (that is all) that it may descend, when once it is placed there, by the mere force of things, and by the natural course of the established mechanism.

But what is this incline? One indicated by Mr. Louis Blanc. Does it not lead to an abyss? No, it leads to happiness. Why, then, does not society go there of itself? Because it does not know what it wants, and it requires an impulse. What is to give it this impulse? Power. And who is to give the impulse to power? The inventor of the machine, Mr. Louis Blanc.

We shall never get out of this circle—mankind passive, and a great man moving it by the intervention of the law. Once on this incline, will society enjoy something like liberty? Without a doubt. And what is liberty?

> Once for all: liberty consists not only in the right granted, but in the power given to man to exercise, to develop his faculties under the empire of justice, and under the protection of the law.
>
> And this is no vain distinction; there is a deep meaning in it, and its consequences are imponderable. For when once it is admitted that man, to be truly free, must have the power to exercise and develop his faculties, it follows that every member of society has a claim upon it for such education as shall enable his faculties to display themselves, and for the tools of labor, without which human activity can find no

scope. Now, by whose intervention is society to give to each
of its members the requisite education and the necessary
tools of labor, unless by that of the State?

Thus, liberty is power. In what does this power consist? In
possessing education and tools of labor. Who is to give education
and tools of labor? Society, who owes them. By whose intervention is society to give tools of labor to those who do not possess
them? By the intervention of the State. From whom is the State to
obtain them?

It is for the reader to answer this question, and to notice
whither all this tends.

One of the strangest phenomena of our time, and one that
will probably be a matter of astonishment to our descendants, is
the doctrine which is founded upon this triple hypothesis: the
radical passiveness of mankind—the omnipotence of the law—
the infallibility of the legislator: this is the sacred symbol of the
party that proclaims itself exclusively democratic.

It is true that it professes also to be social.

So far as it is democratic, it has an unlimited faith in mankind.

So far as it is social, it places mankind beneath the mud.

Are political rights under discussion? Is a legislator to be chosen? Oh, then the people possess science by instinct: they are
gifted with an admirable discernment; their will is always right;
the general will cannot err. Suffrage cannot be too universal.
Nobody is under any responsibility to society. The will and the
capacity to choose well are taken for granted. Can the people be
mistaken? Are we not living in an age of enlightenment? What!
Are the people to be forever led about by the nose? Have they not
acquired their rights at the cost of effort and sacrifice? Have they
not given sufficient proof of intelligence and wisdom? Are they
not arrived at maturity? Are they not in a state to judge for themselves? Do they not know their own interest? Is there a man or a
class who would dare to claim the right of putting himself in the
place of the people, of deciding and of acting for them? No, no;
the people would be free, and they shall be so. They wish to conduct their own affairs, and they shall do so.

But when once the legislator is duly elected, then indeed the style of his speech alters. The nation is sent back into passiveness, inertness, nothingness, and the legislator takes possession of omnipotence. It is for him to invent, for him to direct, for him to impel, for him to organize. Mankind has nothing to do but to submit; the hour of despotism has struck. And we must observe that this is decisive; for the people, just before so enlightened, so moral, so perfect, have no inclinations at all, or, if they have any, these all lead them downward toward degradation. And yet they ought to have a little liberty! But are we not assured by Mr. Considerant that liberty leads fatally to monopoly? Are we not told that liberty is competition? and that competition, according to Mr. Louis Blanc, is a system of extermination for the people, and of ruination for trade? For that reason people are exterminated and ruined in proportion as they are free—take, for example, Switzerland, Holland, England, and the United States? Does not Mr. Louis Blanc tell us again that competition leads to monopoly, and that, for the same reason, cheapness leads to exorbitant prices? That competition tends to drain the sources of consumption, and diverts production to a destructive activity? That competition forces production to increase, and consumption to decrease—whence it follows that free people produce for the sake of not consuming; that there is nothing but oppression and madness among them; and that it is absolutely necessary for Mr. Louis Blanc to see to it?

What sort of liberty should be allowed to men? Liberty of conscience?—But we should see them all profiting by the permission to become atheists. Liberty of education?—But parents would be paying professors to teach their sons immorality and error; besides, if we are to believe Mr. Thiers, education, if left to the national liberty, would cease to be national, and we should be educating our children in the ideas of the Turks or Hindus, instead of which, thanks to the legal despotism of the universities, they have the good fortune to be educated in the noble ideas of the Romans. Liberty of labor? But this is only competition, whose effect is to leave all products unconsumed, to exterminate the people, and to ruin the tradesmen. The liberty of exchange? But it is well known that the protectionists have shown, over and over again, that a man will inevitably be ruined when he exchanges freely, and that to become rich it is necessary to exchange without liberty. Liberty of association? But according to the socialist doctrine, liberty and association exclude each other, for the liberty of men is attacked just to force them to associate.

You must see, then, that the socialist democrats cannot in conscience allow men any liberty, because, by their own nature, they tend in every instance to all kinds of degradation and demoralization.

We are therefore left to conjecture, in this case, upon what foundation universal suffrage is claimed for them with so much importunity.

The pretensions of organizers suggest another question, which I have often asked them, and to which I am not aware that I ever received an answer: Since the natural tendencies of mankind are so bad that it is not safe to allow them liberty, how comes it to pass that the tendencies of organizers are always good? Do not the legislators and their agents form a part of the human race? Do they consider that they are composed of different materials from the rest of mankind? They say that society, when left to itself, rushes to inevitable destruction, because its instincts are perverse. They presume to stop it in its downward course, and to give it a better direction. They have, therefore, received from heaven, intelligence and virtues that place them beyond and above mankind: let them show their title to this superiority. They would be our shepherds, and we are to be their flock. This arrangement presupposes in them a natural superiority, the right to which we are fully justified in calling upon them to prove.

You must observe that I am not contending against their right to invent social combinations, to propagate them, to recommend them, and to try them upon themselves, at their own expense and risk; but I do dispute their right to impose them upon us through the medium of the law, that is, by force and by public taxes.

I would not insist upon the Cabetists, the Fourierists, the Proudhonians, the Academics, and the Protectionists renouncing their own particular ideas; I would only have them renounce the idea that is common to them all—viz., that of subjecting us by force to their own categories and rankings to their social laboratories, to their ever-inflating bank, to their Greco-Roman morality, and to their commercial restrictions. I would ask them to allow us the faculty of judging of their plans, and not to oblige us to adopt them if we find that they hurt our interests or are repugnant to our consciences.

To presume to have recourse to power and taxation, besides being oppressive and unjust, implies further, the pernicious assumption that the organized is infallible, and mankind incompetent.

And if mankind is not competent to judge for itself, why do they talk so much about universal suffrage?

This contradiction in ideas is unhappily to be found also in facts; and whilst the French nation has preceded all others in obtaining its rights, or rather its political claims, this has by no means prevented it from being more governed, and directed, and imposed upon, and fettered, and cheated, than any other nation. It is also the one, of all others, where revolutions are constantly to be dreaded, and it is perfectly natural that it should be so.

So long as this idea is retained, which is admitted by all our politicians, and so energetically expressed by Mr. Louis Blanc in these words—"Society receives its impulse from power," so long as men consider themselves as capable of feeling, yet passive—incapable of raising themselves by their own discernment and by their own energy to any morality, or well-being, and while they expect everything from the law; in a word, while they admit that their relations with the State are the same as those of the flock with the shepherd, it is clear that the responsibility of power is immense. Fortune and misfortune, wealth and destitution, equality and inequality all proceed from it. It is charged with everything, it undertakes everything, it does everything; therefore it has to answer for everything. If we are happy, it has a right to claim our gratitude; but if we are miserable, it alone must bear the blame. Are not our persons and property in fact, at its disposal?

Is not the law omnipotent? In creating the educational monopoly, it has undertaken to answer the expectations of fathers of families who have been deprived of liberty; and if these expectations are disappointed, whose fault is it?

In regulating industry, it has undertaken to make it prosper, otherwise it would have been absurd to deprive it of its liberty; and if it suffers, whose fault is it? In pretending to adjust the balance of commerce by the game of tariffs, it undertakes to make commerce prosper; and if, so far from prospering, it is destroyed, whose fault is it? In granting its protection to maritime armaments in exchange for their liberty, it has undertaken to render them self-sufficient; if they become burdensome, whose fault is it?

Thus, there is not a grievance in the nation for which the Government does not voluntarily make itself responsible. Is it any wonder that every failure threatens to cause a revolution? And what is the remedy proposed? To extend indefinitely the dominion of the law, i.e., the responsibility of Government. But if the Government undertakes to raise and to regulate wages, and is not able to do it; if it undertakes to assist all those who are in want, and is not able to do it; if it undertakes to provide work for every laborer, and is not able to do it; if it undertakes to offer to all who wish to borrow, easy credit, and is not able to do it; if, in words that we regret should have escaped the pen of Mr. de Lamartine, "the State considers that its mission is to enlighten, to develop, to enlarge, to strengthen, to spiritualize, and to sanctify the soul of the people"—if it fails in this, is it not obvious that after every disappointment, which, alas! is more than probable, there will be a no less inevitable revolution?

I shall now resume the subject by remarking, that immediately after the economical part[4] of the question, and before the political part, a leading question presents itself. It is the following:

---

[4]Political economy precedes politics: the former has to discover whether human interests are harmonious or antagonistic, a fact which must be settled before the latter can determine the prerogatives of Government.

What is law? What ought it to be? What is its domain? What are its limits? Where, in fact, does the prerogative of the legislator stop?

I have no hesitation in answering, Law is common force organized to prevent injustice—in short, Law is Justice.

It is not true that the legislator has absolute power over our persons and property, since they pre-exist, and his work is only to secure them from injury.

It is not true that the mission of the law is to regulate our consciences, our ideas, our will, our education, our sentiments, our works, our exchanges, our gifts, our enjoyments. Its mission is to prevent the rights of one from interfering with those of another, in any one of these things.

Law, because it has force for its necessary sanction, can only have the domain of force, which is justice.

And as every individual has a right to have recourse to force only in cases of lawful defense, so collective force, which is only the union of individual forces, cannot be rationally used for any other end.

The law, then, is solely the organization of individual rights that existed before law.

Law is justice.

So far from being able to oppress the people, or to plunder their property, even for a philanthropic end, its mission is to protect the people, and to secure to them the possession of their property.

It must not be said, either, that it may be philanthropic, so long as it abstains from all oppression; for this is a contradiction. The law cannot avoid acting upon our persons and property; if it does not secure them, then it violates them if it touches them.

The law is justice.

Nothing can be more clear and simple, more perfectly defined and bounded, or more visible to every eye; for justice is a given quantity, immutable and unchangeable, and which admits of neither increase or diminution.

Depart from this point, make the law religious, fraternal, equalizing, industrial, literary, or artistic, and you will be lost in vagueness and uncertainty; you will be upon unknown ground, in a forced Utopia, or, what is worse, in the midst of a multitude of contending Utopias, each striving to gain possession of the law, and to impose it upon you; for fraternity and philanthropy have no fixed limits, as justice has. Where will you stop? Where is the law to stop? One person, Mr. de Saint Cricq, will only extend his philanthropy to some of the industrial classes, and will require the law to slight the consumers in favor of the producers. Another, like Mr. Considerant, will take up the cause of the working classes, and claim for them by means of the law, at a fixed rate, clothing, lodging, food, and everything necessary for the support of life. A third, Mr. Louis Blanc, will say, and with reason, that this would be an incomplete fraternity, and that the law ought to provide them with tools of labor and education. A fourth will observe that such an arrangement still leaves room for inequality, and that the law ought to introduce into the most remote hamlets luxury, literature, and the arts. This is the high road to communism; in other words, legislation will be—as it now is—the battlefield for everybody's dreams and everybody's covetousness.

Law is justice.

In this proposition we represent to ourselves a simple, immovable Government. And I defy anyone to tell me whence the thought of a revolution, an insurrection, or a simple disturbance could arise against a public force confined to the repression of injustice. Under such a system, there would be more well-being, and this well-being would be more equally distributed; and as to the sufferings inseparable from humanity, no one would think of accusing the Government of them, for it would be as innocent of them as it is of the variations of the temperature. Have the people ever been known to rise against the court of appeals, or assail the justices of the peace, for the sake of claiming the rate of wages, free credit, tools of labor, the advantages of the tariff, or the social workshop? They know perfectly well that these matters are beyond the jurisdiction of the justices of the peace, and they would soon learn that they are not within the jurisdiction of the law quite as much.

But if the law were to be made upon the principle of fraternity, if it were to be proclaimed that from it proceed all benefits and all evils—that it is responsible for every individual grievance and for every social inequality—then you open the door to an endless succession of complaints, irritations, troubles, and revolutions.

Law is justice.

And it would be very strange if it could properly be anything else! Is not justice right? Are not rights equal? With what show of right can the law interfere to subject me to the social plans of Misters. Mimerel, de Melun, Thiers, or Louis Blanc, rather than to subject these gentlemen to my plans? Is it to be supposed that Nature has not bestowed upon me sufficient imagination to invent a Utopia too? Is it for the law to make choice of one amongst so many fancies, and to make use of the public force in its service?

Law is justice.

And let it not be said, as it continually is, that the law, in this sense, would be atheistic, individual, and heartless, and that it would mold mankind in its own image. This is an absurd conclusion, quite worthy of the governmental infatuation which sees mankind in the law.

What then? Does it follow that if we are free, we shall cease to act? Does it follow that if we do not receive an impulse from the law, we shall receive no impulse at all? Does it follow that if the law confines itself to securing to us the free exercise of our faculties, our faculties will be paralyzed? Does it follow, that if the law does not impose upon us forms of religion, modes of association, methods of education, rules for labor, directions for exchange, and plans for charity, we shall plunge headlong into atheism, isolation, ignorance, misery, and greed? Does it follow, that we shall no longer recognize the power and goodness of God; that we shall cease to associate together, to help each other, to love and assist our unfortunate brethren, to study the secrets of nature, and to aspire after perfection in our existence?

Law is justice.

And it is under the law of justice, under the reign of right, under the influence of liberty, security, stability, and responsibility, that every man will attain to the fullness of his worth, to all the dignity of his being, and that mankind will accomplish with order and with calmness—slowly, it is true, but with certainty— the progress ordained for it.

I believe that my theory is correct; for whatever be the question upon which I am arguing, whether it be religious, philosophical, political, or economical; whether it affects well-being, morality, equality, right, justice, progress, responsibility, property, labor, exchange, capital, wages, taxes, population, credit, or Government; at whatever point of the scientific horizon I start from, I invariably come to the same thing—the solution of the social problem is in liberty.

And have I not experience on my side? Cast your eye over the globe. Which are the happiest, the most moral, and the most peaceable nations? Those where the law interferes the least with private activity; where the Government is the least felt; where individuality has the most scope, and public opinion the most influence; where the machinery of the administration is the least important and the least complicated; where taxation is lightest and least unequal, popular discontent the least excited and the least justifiable; where the responsibility of individuals and classes is the most active, and where, consequently, if morals are not in a perfect state, at any rate they tend incessantly to correct themselves; where transactions, meetings, and associations are the least fettered; where labor, capital, and production suffer the least from artificial displacements; where mankind follows most completely its own natural course; where the thought of God prevails the most over the inventions of men; those, in short, who realize the most nearly this idea that within the limits of right, all should flow from the free, perfectible, and voluntary action of man;

nothing be attempted by the law or by force, except the administration of universal justice.

I cannot avoid coming to this conclusion—that there are too many great men in the world; there are too many legislators, organizers, institutors of society, conductors of the people, fathers of nations, etc., etc. Too many persons place themselves above mankind, to rule and patronize it; too many persons make a trade of looking after it. It will be answered—"You yourself are occupied upon it all this time." Very true. But it must be admitted that it is in another sense entirely that I am speaking; and if I join the reformers it is solely for the purpose of inducing them to relax their hold.

I am not doing as Vaucauson did with his automaton, but as a physiologist does with the human frame; I would study and admire it.

I am acting with regard to it in the spirit that animated a celebrated traveler. He found himself in the midst of a savage tribe. A child had just been born, and a crowd of soothsayers, magicians, and quacks were around it, armed with rings, hooks, and bandages. One said—"This child will never smell the perfume of a calumet, unless I stretch his nostrils." Another said—"He will be without the sense of hearing, unless I draw his ears down to his shoulders." A third said—"He will never see the light of the sun, unless I give his eyes an oblique direction." A fourth said—"He will never be upright, unless I bend his legs." A fifth said—"He will not be able to think, unless I press his brain." "Stop!" said the traveler. "Whatever God does, is well done; do not pretend to know more than He; and as He has given organs to this frail creature, allow those organs to develop themselves, to strengthen themselves by exercise, use, experience, and liberty."

God has implanted in mankind also all that is necessary to enable it to accomplish its destinies. There is a providential social physiology, as well as a providential human physiology. The social organs are constituted so as to enable them to develop harmoniously in the grand air of liberty. Away, then, with quacks and organizers! Away with their rings, and their chains, and their hooks, and their pincers! Away with their artificial methods! Away with their social laboratories, their governmental whims, their centralization, their tariffs, their universities, their State religions, their inflationary or monopolizing banks, their limitations, their restrictions, their moralizations, and their equalization by taxation! And now, after having vainly inflicted upon the social body so many systems, let them end where they ought to have begun—reject all systems, and try liberty—liberty, which is an act of faith in God and in His work.

III.

GOVERNMENT[1]

I wish someone would offer a prize—not of a hundred francs, but of a million, with crowns, medals and ribbons—for a good, simple and intelligible definition of the word "Government."

What an immense service it would confer on society!

The Government! What is it? Where is it? what does it do? what ought it to do? All we know is, that it is a mysterious personage; and assuredly, it is the most solicited, the most tormented, the most overwhelmed, the most admired, the most accused, the most invoked, and the most provoked, of any personage in the world.

I have not the pleasure of knowing my reader, but I would stake ten to one that for six months he has been making Utopias, and if so, that he is looking to Government for the realization of them.

And should the reader happen to be a lady, I have no doubt that she is sincerely desirous of seeing all the evils of suffering

---

[1]First published in 1848.

humanity remedied, and that she thinks this might easily be done, if Government would only undertake it.

But, alas! that poor unfortunate personage, like Figaro, knows not to whom to listen, nor where to turn. The hundred thousand mouths of the press and of the speaker's platform cry out all at once:

"Organize labor and workmen."

"Do away with greed."

"Repress insolence and the tyranny of capital."

"Experiment with manure and eggs."

"Cover the country with railways."

"Irrigate the plains."

"Plant the hills."

"Make model farms."

"Found social laboratories."

"Colonize Algeria."

"Nourish children."

"Educate the youth."

"Assist the aged."

"Send the inhabitants of towns into the country."

"Equalize the profits of all trades."

"Lend money without interest to all who wish to borrow."

"Emancipate Italy, Poland, and Hungary."

"Rear and perfect the saddle-horse."

"Encourage the arts, and provide us with musicians and dancers."

"Restrict commerce, and at the same time create a merchant navy."

"Discover truth, and put a grain of reason into our heads. The mission of Government is to enlighten, to develop, to extend, to fortify, to spiritualize, and to sanctify the soul of the people."

"Do have a little patience, gentlemen," says Government in a beseeching tone. "I will do what I can to satisfy you, but for this I must have resources. I have been preparing plans for five or six taxes, which are quite new, and not at all oppressive. You will see how willingly people will pay them."

Then comes a great exclamation: "No! indeed! Where is the merit of doing a thing with resources? Why, it does not deserve the name of a Government! So far from loading us with fresh taxes, we would have you withdraw the old ones. You ought to suppress:

"The salt tax,

"The tax on liquors,

"The tax on letters,

"Custom-house duties,

"Patents."

In the midst of this tumult, and now that the country has two or three times changed its Government, for not having satisfied all its demands, I wanted to show that they were contradictory. But what could I have been thinking about? Could I not keep this unfortunate observation to myself?

I have lost my character for I am looked upon as a man without *heart* and without *feeling*—a dry philosopher, an individualist, a plebeian—in a word, an economist of the English or American school. But, pardon me, sublime writers, who stop at nothing, not even at contradictions. I am wrong, without a doubt, and I would willingly retract. I should be glad enough, you may be sure, if you had really discovered a beneficent and inexhaustible being, calling itself the Government, which has bread for all mouths, work for all hands, capital for all enterprises, credit for all projects, salve for all wounds, balm for all sufferings, advice for all perplexities, solutions for all doubts, truths for all intellects, diversions for all who want them, milk for infancy, and wine for old age—which can provide for all our wants, satisfy all our curiosity, correct all our errors, repair all our faults, and exempt us henceforth from the necessity for foresight, prudence, judgment, sagacity, experience, order, economy, temperance and activity.

What reason could I have for not desiring to see such a discovery made? Indeed, the more I reflect upon it, the more do I see that nothing could be more convenient than that we should all of us have within our reach an inexhaustible source of wealth and enlightenment—a universal physician, an unlimited pocketbook, and an infallible counselor, such as you describe Government to be. Therefore I want to have it pointed out and defined, and a prize should be offered to the first discoverer of the will-o-the-wisp. For no one would think of asserting that this precious discovery has yet been made, since up to this time everything presenting itself under the name of the Government is immediately overturned by the people, precisely because it does not fulfill the rather contradictory requirements of the program.

I will venture to say that I fear we are in this respect the dupes of one of the strangest illusions that have ever taken possession of the human mind.

Man recoils from trouble—from suffering; and yet he is condemned by nature to the suffering of privation, if he does not take the trouble to work. He has to choose then between these two evils. What means can he adopt to avoid both? There remains now, and there will remain, only one way, which is, *to enjoy the labor of others*. Such a course of conduct prevents the trouble and the enjoyment from assuming their natural proportion, and causes all the trouble to become the lot of one set of persons, and all the enjoyment that of another. This is the origin of slavery and of plunder, whatever its form may be—whether that of wars, taxes, violence, restrictions, frauds, etc.—monstrous abuses, but consistent with the thought that has given them birth. Oppression should be detested and resisted—it can hardly be called trivial.

Slavery is subsiding, thank heaven! and on the other hand, our disposition to defend our property prevents direct and open plunder from being easy.

One thing, however, remains—it is the original inclination that exists in all men to divide the lot of life into two parts, throwing the trouble upon others, and keeping the satisfaction for themselves. It remains to be shown under what new form this sad tendency is manifesting itself.

The oppressor no longer acts directly and with his own powers upon his victim. No, our discretion has become too refined for that. The tyrant and his victim are still present, but there is an intermediate person between them, which is the Government—that is, the Law itself. What can be better calculated to silence our scruples, and, which is perhaps better appreciated, to overcome all resistance? We all, therefore, put in our claim under some pretext or other, and apply to Government. We say to it,

> I am dissatisfied at the proportion between my labor and my enjoyments. I should like, for the sake of restoring the desired equilibrium, to take a part of the possessions of others. But this would be dangerous. Could not you facilitate the thing for me? Could you not find me a good place? or check the industry of my competitors? or, perhaps, lend me gratuitously some capital, which you may take from its possessor? Could you not bring up my children at the public expense? or grant me some subsidies? or secure me a pension when I have attained my fiftieth year? By this means I shall gain my end with an easy conscience, for the law will have acted for me, and I shall have all the advantages of plunder, without its risk or its disgrace!

As it is certain, on the one hand, that we are all making some similar request to the Government; and as, on the other, it is proved that Government cannot satisfy one party without adding to the labor of the others, until I can obtain another definition of the word Government, I feel authorized to give my own. Who knows but it may obtain the prize?

Here it is:

> Government *is that great fiction, through which everybody endeavors to live at the expense of everybody else.*

For now, as formerly, everyone is more or less for profiting by the labors of others. No one would dare to profess such a sentiment; he even hides it from himself; and then what is done? A medium is thought of; Government is applied to, and every class in its turn comes to it, and says, "You, who can take justifiably and honestly, take from the public, and we will partake." Alas! Government is only too much disposed to follow this diabolical advice, for it is composed of ministers and officials—of men, in short, who, like all other men, desire in their hearts, and always seize every opportunity with eagerness, to increase their wealth and influence. Government is not slow to perceive the advantages it may derive from the part that is entrusted to it by the public. It is glad to be the judge and the master of the destinies of all; it will take much, for then a large share will remain for itself; it will multiply the number of its agents; it will enlarge the circle of its privileges; it will end by appropriating a ruinous proportion.

But the most remarkable part of it is the astonishing blindness of the public through it all. When successful soldiers used to reduce the vanquished to slavery, they were barbarous, but they were not irrational. Their object, like ours, was to live at other people's expense, and they did not fail to do so. What are we to think of a people who never seem to suspect that *reciprocal plunder* is no less plunder because it is reciprocal; that it is no less criminal because it is executed legally and with order; that it adds nothing to the public good; that it diminishes it, just in proportion to the cost of the expensive medium which we call the Government?

And it is this great chimera that we have placed, for the edification of the people, as a frontispiece to the Constitution. The following is the beginning of the preamble:

> France has constituted itself a republic for the purpose of raising all the citizens to an ever-increasing degree of morality, enlightenment, and well-being.

Thus it is France, or an abstraction, that is to raise the French, or flesh-and-blood *realities*, to morality, well-being, etc. Is it not by yielding to this strange delusion that we are led to expect everything from an energy not our own? Is it not announcing that there is, independently of the French, a virtuous, enlightened, and rich being, who can and will bestow upon them its benefits? Is not this supposing, and certainly very presumptuously, that there are between France and the French—between the simple, abridged, and abstract denomination of all the individualities, and these individualities themselves—relations as of father to son, tutor to his pupil, professor to his scholar? I know it is often said, metaphorically, "the country is a tender mother." But to show the inanity of the constitutional proposition, it is only needed to show that it may be reversed, not only without inconvenience, but even with advantage. Would it be less exact to say,

> The French have constituted themselves a Republic, to raise France to an ever-increasing degree of morality, enlightenment, and well-being.

Now, where is the value of an axiom where the subject and the attribute may change places without inconvenience? Everybody understands what is meant by this, "The mother will feed the child." But it would be ridiculous to say, "The child will feed the mother."

The Americans formed a different idea of the relations of the citizens with the Government when they placed these simple words at the head of their Constitution:

> We, the people of the United States, for the purpose of forming a more perfect union, of establishing justice, of securing interior tranquility, of providing for our common defense, of increasing the general well-being, and of securing the benefits of liberty to ourselves and to our posterity, decree, etc.

Here there is no chimerical creation, no *abstraction*, from which the citizens may demand everything. They expect nothing except from themselves and their own energy.

If I may be permitted to criticize the first words of our Constitution, I would remark that what I complain of is something more than a mere metaphysical allusion, as might seem at first sight.

I contend that this deification of Government has been in past times, and will be hereafter, a fertile source of calamities and revolutions.

There is the public on one side, Government on the other, considered as two distinct beings; the latter bound to bestow upon the former, and the former having the right to claim from the latter, all imaginable human benefits. What will be the consequence?

In fact, Government is not impotent, and cannot be so. It has two hands—one to receive and the other to give; in other words, it has a rough hand and a smooth one. The activity of the second is necessarily subordinate to the activity of the first. Strictly, Government may take and not restore. This is evident, and may be explained by the porous and absorbing nature of its hands, which always retain a part, and sometimes the whole, of what they touch. But the thing that never was seen, and never will be seen or conceived, is, that Government can restore more to the public than it has taken from it. It is therefore ridiculous for us to appear before it in the humble attitude of beggars. It is radically impossible for it to confer a particular benefit upon any one of the individualities which constitute the community, without inflicting a greater injury upon the community as a whole.

Our requisitions, therefore, place it in a dilemma.

If it refuses to grant the requests made to it, it is accused of weakness, ill-will, and incapacity. If it endeavors to grant them, it is obliged to load the people with fresh taxes—to do more harm than good, and to bring upon itself from another quarter the general displeasure.

Thus, the public has two hopes, and Government makes two promises—*many benefits and no taxes*. Hopes and promises that, being contradictory, can never be realized.

Now, is not this the cause of all our revolutions? For between the Government, which lavishes promises which it is impossible to perform, and the public, which has conceived hopes which can never be realized, two classes of men interpose—the ambitious and the Utopians. It is circumstances which give these their cue. It is enough if these vassals of popularity cry out to the people— "The authorities are deceiving you; if we were in their place, we would load you with benefits and exempt you from taxes."

And the people believe, and the people hope, and the people make a revolution!

No sooner are their friends at the head of affairs, than they are called upon to redeem their pledge. "Give us work, bread, assistance, credit, education, colonies," say the people; "and at the same time protect us, as you promised, from the taxes."

The new *Government* is no less embarrassed than the former one, for it soon finds that it is much easier to promise than to perform. It tries to gain time, for this is necessary for maturing its vast projects. At first, it makes a few timid attempts: on one hand it institutes a little elementary instruction; on the other, it makes a little reduction in the liquor tax (1850). But the contradiction is forever rearing its ugly head; if it would be philanthropic, it must raise taxes; if it neglects its taxing, it must abstain from being philanthropic.

These two promises are forever clashing with each other; it cannot be otherwise. To live upon credit, which is the same as exhausting the future, is certainly a present means of reconciling them: an attempt is made to do a little good now, at the expense of a great deal of harm in future. But such proceedings call forth the specter of bankruptcy, which puts an end to credit. What is to be done then? Why, then, the new Government takes a bold step; it unites all its forces in order to maintain itself; it smothers opinion, has recourse to arbitrary measures, repudiates its former maxims, declares that it is impossible to conduct the administration except at the risk of being unpopular; in short, it proclaims itself *governmental*. And it is here that other candidates for popularity are waiting for it. They exhibit the same illusion, pass by the same way, obtain the same success, and are soon swallowed up in the same gulf.

We had arrived at this point in February.[2] At this time, the illusion that is the subject of this article had made more headway than at any former period in the ideas of the people, in connection with Socialist doctrines. They expected, more firmly than ever, that *Government,* under a republican form, would open in grand style the source of benefits and close that of taxation. "We have often

---

[2]This was written in 1849.

been deceived," said the people; "but we will see to it ourselves this time, and take care not to be deceived again!"

What could the Provisional Government do? Alas! Just that which always is done in similar circumstances—make promises, and gain time. It did so, of course; and to give its promises more weight, it announced them publicly thus:

> Increase of prosperity, diminution of labor, assistance, credit, free education, agricultural colonies, cultivation of waste land, and, at the same time, reduction of the tax on salt, liquor, letters, meat; all this shall be granted when the National Assembly meets.

The National Assembly meets, and, as it is impossible to realize two contradictory things, its task, its sad task, is to withdraw, as gently as possible, one after the other, all the decrees of the Provisional Government. However, in order somewhat to mitigate the cruelty of the deception, it is found necessary to negotiate a little. Certain engagements are fulfilled, others are, in a measure, begun, and therefore the new administration is compelled to contrive some new taxes.

Now I transport myself in thought to a period a few months hence and ask myself with sorrowful forebodings, what will come to pass when the agents of the new Government go into the country to collect new taxes upon legacies, revenues, and the profits of agricultural traffic? It is to be hoped that my presentiments may not be verified, but I foresee a difficult part for the candidates for popularity to play.

Read the last manifesto of the Montagnards—that which they issued on the occasion of the election of the President. It is rather long, but at length it concludes with these words: "*Government ought to give a great deal to the people, and take little from them.*" It is always the same tactics, or, rather, the same mistake.

"Government is bound to give gratuitous instruction and education to all the citizens."

It is bound to give "A general and appropriate professional education, as much as possible adapted to the wants, the callings, and the capacities of each citizen."

It is bound "To teach every citizen his duty to God, to man, and to himself; to develop his sentiments, his tendencies, and his faculties; to teach him, in short, the scientific part of his labor; to make him understand his own interests, and to give him a knowledge of his rights."

It is bound "To place within the reach of all, literature and the arts, the patrimony of thought, the treasures of the mind, and all those intellectual enjoyments which elevate and strengthen the soul."

It is bound "To give compensation for every accident, from fire, inundation, etc., experienced by a citizen." (The *et cetera* means more than it says.)

It is bound "To attend to the relations of capital with labor, and to become the regulator of credit."

It is bound "To afford important encouragement and efficient protection to agriculture."

It is bound "To purchase railroads, canals, and mines; and, doubtless, to transact affairs with that industrial capacity which patronizes it."

It is bound "To encourage useful experiments, to promote and assist them by every means likely to make them successful. As a regulator of credit, it will exercise such extensive influence over industrial and agricultural associations as shall ensure them success."

Government is bound to do all this, in addition to the services to which it is already pledged; and further, it is always to maintain a menacing attitude toward foreigners; for, according to those who sign the program, "Bound together by this holy union, and by the precedents of the French Republic, we carry our wishes and hopes beyond the boundaries that despotism has placed between nations. The rights that we desire for ourselves, we desire for all those who are oppressed by the yoke of tyranny;

we desire that our glorious army should still, if necessary, be the army of liberty."

You see that the *gentle hand* of Government—that good hand that gives and distributes, will be very busy under the government of the Montagnards. You think, perhaps, that it will be the same with the rough hand—that hand which dives into our pockets. Do not deceive yourselves. The aspirants after popularity would not know their trade if they had not the art, when they show the gentle hand, to conceal the rough one.

Their reign will assuredly be the jubilee of the tax-payers.

"It is superfluities, not necessities," they say "that ought to be taxed."

Truly, it will be a happy day when the treasury, for the sake of loading us with benefits, will content itself with curtailing our superfluities!

This is not all. The Montagnards intend that "taxation shall lose its oppressive character, and be only an act of fraternity." Good heavens! I know it is the fashion to thrust fraternity in everywhere, but I did not imagine it would ever be put into the hands of the tax-gatherer.

To come to the details: Those who sign the program say, "We desire the immediate abolition of those taxes that affect the absolute necessities of life, such as salt, liquors, etc., etc.

"The reform of the tax on landed property, customs, and patents.

"Gratuitous justice—that is, the simplification of its forms, and reduction of its expenses," (This, no doubt, has reference to stamps.)

Thus, the tax on landed property, customs, patents, stamps, salt, liquors, postage, all are included. These gentlemen have discovered the secret of giving an excessive activity to the gentle hand of Government, while they entirely paralyze its *rough hand*.

Well, I ask the impartial reader, is it not childishness, and worse, dangerous childishness? Is it not inevitable that we shall have revolution after revolution, if there is a determination never to stop till this contradiction is realized: "To give nothing to Government and to receive much from it?"

If the Montagnards were to come into power, would they not become the victims of the means that they employed to take possession of it?

Citizens! In all times, two political systems have been in existence, and each may be maintained by good reasons. According to one of them, Government ought to do much, but then it ought to take much. According to the other, this twofold activity ought to be little felt. We have to choose between these two systems. But as regards the third system, which partakes of both the others, and which consists in exacting everything from Government, without giving it anything, it is chimerical, absurd, childish, contradictory, and dangerous. Those who proclaim it, for the sake of the pleasure of accusing all Governments of weakness, and thus exposing them to your attacks, are only flattering and deceiving you, while they are deceiving themselves.

For ourselves, we consider that Government is and ought to be nothing whatever but *common force* organized, not to be an instrument of oppression and mutual plunder among citizens; but, on the contrary, to secure to everyone his own, and to cause justice and security to reign.

IV.

WHAT IS MONEY?[1]

"Hateful money! Hateful money!" cried F——, the economist, despairingly, as he came from the Committee of Finance, where a project of paper money had just been discussed.

"What's the matter?" I said. "What is the meaning of this sudden dislike to the most extolled of all the divinities of this world?"

F. Hateful money! Hateful money!

B. You alarm me. I hear peace, liberty, and life cried down, and Brutus went so far even as to say, "Virtue! Thou art but a name!" But what can have happened?

F. Hateful money! Hateful money!

B. Come, come, exercise a little philosophy. What has happened to you? Has Croesus been affecting you? Has Jones been playing you false? Or has Smith been libeling you in the papers?

---

[1]First published in 1849.

F. I have nothing to do with Croesus; my character, by its insignificance, is safe from any slanders of Smith; and as to Jones——

B. Ah! Now I have it. How could I be so blind? You, too, are the inventor of a social reorganization—of the F—— system. In fact, your society is to be more perfect than that of Sparta, and, therefore all money is to be strictly banished from it. And the thing that troubles you is how to persuade your people to throw away the contents of their purses. What would you have? This is the rock on which all reorganizers split. Anyone could do wonders if he could contrive to overcome all resisting influences, and if all mankind would consent to become soft wax in his fingers; but men are resolved not to be soft wax; they listen, applaud, or reject and—go on as before.

F. Thank heaven I am still free from this fashionable mania. Instead of inventing social laws, I am studying those which it has pleased Providence to invent, and I am delighted to find them admirable in their progressive development. This is why I exclaim, "Hateful money! Hateful money!"

B. You are a disciple of Proudhon, then? Well, there is a very simple way for you to satisfy yourself. Throw your purse into the river, only reserving a small draft on the Bank of Exchange.

F. If I cry out against money, is it likely I should tolerate its deceitful substitute?

B. Then I have only one more guess to make. You are a new Diogenes, and are going to belabor me with a discourse on the contempt of riches.

F. Heaven preserve me from that! For riches, don't you see, are not a little more or a little less money. They are bread for the hungry, clothes for the naked, fuel to warm you, oil to lengthen the day, a career open to your son, a certain portion for your daughter, a day of rest after fatigue, a cordial for the faint, a little assistance slipped into the hand of a poor man, a shelter from the storm, a diversion for a brain worn by thought, the incomparable pleasure of making those happy who are dear to us. Riches are education, independence, dignity, confidence, charity; they are progress and civilization. Riches are the admirable civilizing result of two admirable agents, more civilizing even than riches themselves—labor and exchange.

B. Well! Now you seem to be singing the praises of riches, when, a moment ago, you were loading them with imprecations!

F. Why, don't you see that it was only the whim of an economist? I cry out against money, just because everybody confounds it, as you did just now, with riches, and that this confusion is the cause of errors and calamities without number. I cry out against it because its function in society is not understood, and very difficult to explain. I cry out against it because it jumbles all ideas, causes the means to be taken for the end, the obstacle for the cause, the alpha for the omega; because its presence in the world, though in itself beneficial, has nevertheless introduced a fatal notion, a perversion of principles, a contradictory theory which in a multitude of forms, has impoverished mankind and deluged the earth with blood. I cry out against it, because I feel that I am incapable of contending against the error to which it has given birth, otherwise than by a long and fastidious dissertation to which no one would listen. Oh! if I could only find a patient and right-thinking listener!

B. Well, it shall not be said that for want of a victim you remain in the state of irritation in which you now are. I am listening; speak, lecture, do not restrain yourself in any way.

F. You promise to take an interest?

B. I promise to have patience.

F. That is not much.

B. It is all that I can give. Begin, and explain to me, at first, how a mistake on the subject of money, if mistake there be, is to be found at the root of all economical errors?

F. Well, now, is it possible that you can conscientiously assure me that you have never happened to confound wealth with money?

B. I don't know; but, after all, what would be the consequence of such a confusion?

F. Nothing very important. An error in your brain, which would have no influence over your actions; for you see that, with respect to labor and exchange, although there are as many opinions as there are heads, we all act in the same way.

B. Just as we walk based on the same principle, although we are not agreed upon the theory of equilibrium and gravitation.

F. Precisely. A person who argued himself into the opinion that during the night our heads and feet changed places, might write very fine books upon the subject, but still he would walk about like everybody else.

B. So I think. Nevertheless, he would soon suffer the penalty of being too much of a logician.

F. In the same way, a man would die of hunger who, having decided that money is real wealth, should carry out the idea to the end. That is the reason that this theory is false, for there is no true theory but such as results from facts themselves, as manifested at all times and in all places.

B. I can understand, that practically, and under the influence of personal interest, the injurious effects of the erroneous action would tend to correct an error. But if that of which you speak has so little influence, why does it disturb you so much?

F. Because, when a man, instead of acting for himself, decides for others, personal interest, that ever watchful and sensible sentinel, is no longer present to cry out, "Stop! The responsibility is misplaced." It is Peter who is deceived, and John suffers; the false system of the legislator necessarily becomes the rule of action of whole populations. And observe the difference. When you have money, and are very hungry, whatever your theory about money may be, what do you do?

B. I go to a baker's and buy some bread.

F. You do not hesitate about using your money?

B. The only use of money is to buy what one wants.

F. And if the baker should happen to be thirsty, what does he do?

B. He goes to the wine merchant's, and buys wine with the money I have given him.

F. What! Is he not afraid he shall ruin himself?

B. The real ruin would be to go without eating or drinking.

F. And everybody in the world, if he is free, acts in the same manner?

B. Without a doubt. Would you have them die of hunger for the sake of saving up pennies?

F. So far from it, that I consider they act wisely, and I only wish that the theory was nothing but the faithful image of this universal practice. But, suppose now, that you were the legislator, the absolute king of a vast empire, where there were no gold mines.

B. Sounds good to me.

F. Suppose, again, that you were perfectly convinced of this,—that wealth consists solely and exclusively of money; to what conclusion would you come?

B. I should conclude that there was no other means for me to enrich my people, or for them to enrich themselves, but to draw away the money from other nations.

F. That is to say, to impoverish them. The first conclusion, then, to which you would arrive would be this—a nation can only gain when another loses.

B. This axiom has the authority of Bacon and Montaigne.

F. It is not the less sorrowful for that, for it implies that progress is impossible. Two nations, no more than two men, cannot prosper side by side.

B. It would seem that such is the result of this principle.

F. And as all men are ambitious to enrich themselves, it follows that all are desirous, according to a law of Providence, of ruining their fellow-creatures.

B. This is not Christianity, but it is political economy.

F. Such a doctrine is detestable. But, to continue, I have made you an absolute king. You must not be satisfied with reasoning; you must act. There is no limit to your power. How would you treat this doctrine—wealth is money?

B. It would be my endeavor to increase, incessantly, among my people the quantity of money.

F. But there are no mines in your kingdom. How would you set about it? What would you do?

B. I should do nothing: I should merely forbid, on pain of death, that a single dollar should leave the country.

F. And if your people should happen to be hungry as well as rich?

B. Never mind. In the system we are discussing, to allow them to export dollars would be to allow them to impoverish themselves.

F. So that, by your own confession, you would force them to act upon a principle equally opposite to that upon which you would yourself act under similar circumstances. Why so?

B. Because only my own hunger touches me, and the hunger of a nation does not touch legislators.

F. Well, I can tell you that your plan would fail, and that no superintendence would be sufficiently vigilant, when the people were hungry, to prevent the dollars from going out and the grain from coming in.

B. If so, this plan, whether erroneous or not, would effect nothing; it would do neither good nor harm, and therefore requires no further consideration.

F. You forget that you are a legislator. A legislator must not be disheartened at trifles, when he is making experiments on others. The first measure not having succeeded, you ought to take some other means of attaining your end.

B. What end?

F. You must have a bad memory. Why, that of increasing, in the midst of your people, the quantity of money, which is presumed to be true wealth.

B. Ah! To be sure; I beg your pardon. But then you see, as they say of music, a little is enough; and this may be said, I think, with still more reason, of political economy. I must consider. But really I don't know how to contrive——

F. Ponder it well. First, I would have you observe that your first plan solved the problem only negatively. To prevent the dollars from going out of the country is the way to prevent the wealth from diminishing, but it is not the way to increase it.

B. Ah! Now I am beginning to see . . . the grain which is allowed to come in . . . a bright idea strikes me . . . the contrivance is ingenious, the means infallible; I am coming to it now.

F. Now, I, in turn, must ask you—to what?

B. Why, to a means of increasing the quantity of money.

F. How would you set about it, if you please?

B. Is it not evident that if the heap of money is to be constantly increasing, the first condition is that none must be taken from it?

F. Certainly.

B. And the second, that additions must constantly be made to it?

F. To be sure.

B. Then the problem will be solved, either negatively or positively; if on the one hand I prevent the foreigner from taking from it, and on the other I oblige him to add to it.

F. Better and better.

B. And for this there must be two simple laws made, in which money will not even be mentioned. By the one, my subjects will be forbidden to buy anything abroad; and by the other, they will be required to sell a great deal.

F. A well-advised plan.

B. Is it new? I must take out a patent for the invention.

F. You need do no such thing; someone has beaten you to it. But you must take care of one thing.

B. What is that?

F. I have made you an absolute king. I understand that you are going to prevent your subjects from buying foreign productions. It will be enough if you prevent them from entering the country. Thirty or forty thousand custom-house officers will do the trick.

B. It would be rather expensive. But what does that signify? The money they receive will not go out of the country.

F. True; and in this system it is the grand point. But to insure a sale abroad, how would you proceed?

B. I should encourage it by bounties, obtained by means of some good taxes laid upon my people.

F. In this case, the exporters, constrained by competition among themselves, would lower their prices in proportion, and it would be like making a present to the foreigner of the prizes or of the taxes.

B. Still, the money would not go out of the country.

F. Of course. That is understood. But if your system is beneficial, the governments of other countries will adopt it. They will make similar plans to yours; they will have their custom-house officers, and reject your products; so that with them, as with you, the heap of money may not be diminished.

B. I shall have an army and force down their barriers.

F. They will have an army and force down yours.

B. I shall arm vessels, make conquests, acquire colonies, and create consumers for my people, who will be obliged to eat our corn and drink our wine.

F. The other governments will do the same. They will dispute your conquests, your colonies, and your consumers; then on all sides there will be war, and all will be uproar.

B. I shall raise my taxes, and increase my custom-house officers, my army, and my navy.

F. The others will do the same.

B. I shall redouble my exertions.

F. The others will redouble theirs. In the meantime, we have no proof that you would succeed in selling to a great extent.

B. It is but too true. It would be well if the commercial efforts would neutralize each other.

F. And the military efforts also. And, tell me, are not these custom-house officers, soldiers, and vessels, these oppressive taxes, this perpetual struggle towards an impossible result, this permanent state of open or secret war with the whole world, are they not the logical and inevitable consequence of the legislators having adopted an idea that you admit is acted upon by no man who is his own master, that "wealth is money; and to increase the amount of money is to increase wealth?"

B. I grant it. Either the axiom is true, and then the legislator ought to act as I have described, although universal war should be the consequence; or it is false; and in this case men, in destroying each other, only ruin themselves.

F. And, remember, that before you became a king, this same axiom had led you by a logical process to the following maxims— That which one gains, another loses. The profit of one is the loss of the other—which maxims imply an intractable antagonism amongst all men.

B. It is only too certain. Whether I am a philosopher or a legislator, whether I reason or act upon the principle that money is wealth, I always arrive at one conclusion, or one result:—universal war. It is well that you pointed out the consequences before beginning a discussion upon it; otherwise, I should never have had the courage to follow you to the end of your economical dissertation, for, to tell you the truth, it is not much to my taste.

F. What do you mean? I was just thinking of it when you heard me grumbling against money! I was lamenting that my countrymen have not the fortitude to study what it is so important that they should know.

B. And yet the consequences are frightful.

F. The consequences! As yet I have only mentioned one. I might have told you of others still more fatal.

B. You make my hair stand on end! What other evils can have been caused to mankind by this confusion between money and wealth?

F. It would take me a long time to enumerate them. This doctrine is one of a very numerous family. The eldest, whose acquaintance we have just made, is called the prohibitive system; the next, the colonial system; the third, hatred of capital; the last and worst, paper money.

B. What! Does paper money proceed from the same error?

F. Yes, directly. When legislators, after having ruined men by war and taxes, persevere in their idea, they say to themselves, "If the people suffer, it is because there is not money enough. We must make some." And as it is not easy to multiply the precious metals, especially when the pretended resources of prohibition have been exhausted, they add, "We will make fictitious money, nothing is more easy, and then every citizen will have his pocket-book full of it, and they will all be rich."

B. In fact, this proceeding is more expeditious than the other, and then it does not lead to foreign war.

F. No, but it leads to domestic disaster.

B. You are a grumbler. Make haste and dive to the bottom of the question. I am quite impatient, for the first time, to know if money (or its sign) is wealth.

F. You will grant that men do not satisfy any of their wants immediately with coined dollars, or dollar bills. If they are hungry, they want bread; if naked, clothing; if they are ill, they must have remedies; if they are cold, they want shelter and fuel; if they would learn, they must have books; if they would travel, they must have conveyances—and so on. The riches of a country consist in the abundance and proper distribution of all these things. Hence you may perceive and rejoice at the falseness of this gloomy maxim of Bacon's, "What one people gains, another necessarily loses"—a maxim expressed in a still more discouraging manner by Montaigne, in these words: "The profit of one is the loss of another." When Shem, Ham, and Japhet divided amongst themselves the vast solitudes of this earth, they surely might each of them build, drain, sow, reap, and obtain improved lodging, food and clothing, and better education, perfect and enrich themselves—in short, increase their enjoyments, without causing a necessary diminution in the corresponding enjoyments of their brothers. It is the same with two nations.

B. There is no doubt that two nations, the same as two men, unconnected with each other, may, by working more, and working better, prosper at the same time, without injuring each other. It is not this that is denied by the axioms of Montaigne and Bacon. They only mean to say, that in the transactions that take place between two nations or two men, if one gains, the other must lose. And this is self-evident, as exchange adds nothing by itself to the mass of those useful things of which you were speaking; for if, after the exchange, one of the parties is found to have gained something, the other will, of course, be found to have lost something.

F. You have formed a very incomplete, nay, a false idea of exchange. If Shem is located upon a plain that is fertile in corn, Japhet upon a slope adapted for growing the vine, Ham upon a rich pasturage—the distinction of their occupations, far from hurting any of them, might cause all three to prosper more. It must be so, in fact, for the distribution of labor, introduced by exchange, will have the effect of increasing the mass of corn, wine, and meat that is produced, and that is to be shared. How can it be otherwise, if you allow liberty in these transactions? From the moment that any one of the brothers should perceive that labor in company, as it were, was a permanent loss, compared to solitary labor, he would cease to exchange. Exchange brings with it its claim to our gratitude. The fact of its being accomplished proves that it is a good thing.

B. But Bacon's axiom is true in the case of gold and silver. If we admit that at a certain moment there exists in the world a given quantity, it is perfectly clear that one purse cannot be filled without another being emptied.

F. And if gold is considered to be riches, the natural conclusion is that displacements of fortune take place among men, but no general progress. It is just what I said when I began. If, on the contrary, you look upon an abundance of useful things, fit for satisfying our wants and our tastes, as true riches, you will see that simultaneous prosperity is possible. Money serves only to facilitate the transmission of these useful things from one to another, which may be done equally well with an ounce of rare metal like gold, with a pound of more abundant material as silver, or with a hundredweight of still more abundant metal, as copper. According to that, if a country like the United States had at its disposal as much again of all these useful things, its people would be twice as rich, although the quantity of money remained the same; but it would not be the same if there were double the money, for in that case the amount of useful things would not increase.

B. The question to be decided is whether the presence of a greater number of dollars has not the effect, precisely, of augmenting the sum of useful things?

F. What connection can there be between these two terms? Food, clothing, houses, fuel, all come from nature and from labor, from more or less skillful labor exerted upon a more or less liberal nature.

B. You are forgetting one great force, which is exchange. If you acknowledge that this is a force, as you have admitted that dollars facilitate it, you must also allow that they have an indirect power of production.

F. But I have added that a small quantity of rare metal facilitates transactions as much as a large quantity of abundant metal; from which it follows that a people is not enriched by being forced to give up useful things for the sake of having more money.

B. Thus, it is your opinion that the treasures discovered in California will not increase the wealth of the world?

F. I do not believe that, on the whole, they will add much to the enjoyments, to the real satisfactions of mankind. If the Californian gold merely replaces in the world that which has been lost and destroyed, it may have its use. If it increases the amount of money, it will depreciate it. The gold diggers will be richer than they would have been without it. But those who possess the gold at the moment of its depreciation, will obtain a smaller gratification for the same amount. I cannot look upon this as an increase, but as a reallocation of true riches, as I have defined them.

B. All that is very plausible. But you will not easily convince me that I am not richer (all other things being equal) if I have two dollars, than if I had only one.

F. I do not deny it.

B. And what is true of me is true of my neighbor, and of the neighbor of my neighbor, and so on, from one to another, all over the country. Therefore, if every citizen of the United States has more dollars, the United States must be more rich.

F. And here you fall into the common mistake of concluding that what affects one affects all, and thus confusing the individual with the general interest.

B. Why, what can be more conclusive? What is true of one, must be so of all. What are all, but a collection of individuals? You might as well tell me that every American could suddenly grow an inch taller, without the average height of all the Americans being increased.

F. Your reasoning is apparently sound, I grant you, and that is why the illusion it conceals is so common. However, let us examine it a little. Ten persons were gambling. For greater ease, they had adopted the plan of each taking ten chips, and against these they each placed a hundred dollars under a candlestick, so that each chip corresponded to ten dollars. After the game the winnings were adjusted, and the players drew from under the candlestick as many dollars as would represent the number of chips. Seeing this, one of them, a great arithmetician perhaps, but an indifferent reasoner, said: "Gentlemen, experience invariably teaches me that, at the end of the game, I find myself a gainer in proportion to the number of my chips. Have you not observed the same with regard to yourselves? Thus, what is true of me must be true of each of you, and what is true of each must be true of all. We should, therefore, all of us gain more, at the end of the game, if we all had more chips. Now, nothing can be easier; we have only to distribute twice the number of chips." This was done; but when the game was finished, and they came to adjust the winnings, it was found that the money under the candlestick had not been miraculously multiplied, according to the general expectation. They had to be divided accordingly, and the only result obtained (chimerical enough) was this: every one had, it is true, his double number of chips, but every chip, instead of corresponding to ten dollars, only represented five. Thus it was clearly shown that what is true of each is not always true of all.

B. I see; you are supposing a general increase of chips, without a corresponding increase of the sum placed under the candlestick.

F. And you are supposing a general increase of dollars, without a corresponding increase of things, the exchange of which is facilitated by these dollars.

B. Do you compare the dollars to chips?

F. In any other point of view, certainly not; but in the case you place before me, and which I have to argue against, I do. Consider one thing. In order that there be a general increase of dollars in a country, this country must have mines, or its commerce must be such as to give useful things in exchange for money. Apart from these two circumstances, a universal increase is impossible, the dollars only changing hands; and in this case, although it may be very true that each one, taken individually, is richer in proportion to the number of dollars that he has, we cannot draw the inference which you drew just now, because a dollar more in one purse implies necessarily a dollar less in some other. It is the same as with your comparison of the average height. If each of us grew only at the expense of others, it would be very true of each, taken individually, that he would be a taller man if he had the chance, but this would never be true of the whole taken collectively.

B. Be it so: but, in the two suppositions that you have made, the increase is real, and you must allow that I am right.

F. To a certain point, gold and silver have a value. To obtain this value, men consent to give other useful things that have a value also. When, therefore, there are mines in a country, if that country obtains from them sufficient gold to purchase a useful thing from abroad—a locomotive, for instance—it enriches itself with all the enjoyments that a locomotive can procure, exactly as if the machine had been made at home. The question is whether it spends more efforts in the former proceeding than in the latter? For if it did not export this gold, it would depreciate, and something worse would happen than what did sometimes happen in California and in Australia, for there, at least, the precious metals are used to buy useful things made elsewhere. Nevertheless, there is still a danger that they may starve on heaps of gold; as it would be if the law prohibited the exportation of gold. As to the second supposition—that of the gold that we obtain by trade—it is an advantage, or the reverse, according as the country stands more or less in need of it, compared to its wants of the useful things that must be given up in order to obtain it. It is not for the law to judge of this, but for those who are concerned in it; for if the law should start upon this principle, that gold is preferable to useful things, whatever may be their value, and if it should act effectually in this sense, it would tend to put every country adopting the law in the curious position of having a great deal of cash to spend, and nothing to buy. It is the very same system that is represented by Midas, who turned everything he touched into gold, and was in consequence in danger of dying of starvation.

B. The gold that is imported implies that a useful thing is exported, and in this respect there is a satisfaction withdrawn from the country. But is there not a corresponding benefit? And will not this gold be the source of a number of new satisfactions, by circulating from hand to hand, and stimulating labor and industry, until at length it leaves the country in its turn, and causes the importation of some useful thing?

F. Now you have come to the heart of the question. Is it true that a dollar is the principal that causes the production of all the objects whose exchange it facilitates? It is very clear that a piece of coined gold or silver stamped as a dollar is only worth a dollar; but we are led to believe that this value has a particular character: that it is not consumed like other things, or that it is exhausted very gradually; that it renews itself, as it were, in each transaction; and that, finally this particular dollar has been worth a dollar as many times as it has accomplished transactions—that it is of itself worth all the things for which it has been successively exchanged; and this is believed because it is supposed that without this dollar these things would never have been produced. It is said the shoemaker would have sold fewer shoes, and consequently he would have bought less of the butcher; the butcher would not have gone so often to the grocer, the grocer to the doctor, the doctor to the lawyer, and so on.

B. No one can dispute that.

F. This is the time, then, to analyze the true function of money, independently of mines and importations. You have a dollar. What does it imply in your hands? It is, as it were, the witness and proof that you have, at some time or other, performed some labor, which, instead of turning to your advantage, you have bestowed upon society as represented by your client (employer or debtor). This coin testifies that you have performed a service for society, and moreover it shows the value of it. It bears witness, besides, that you have not yet obtained from society a real equivalent service, to which you have a right. To place you in a condition to exercise this right, at the time and in the manner you please, society, as represented by your client, has given you an acknowledgment, a title, a privilege from the republic, a token, a title to a dollar's worth of property in fact, which only differs from executive titles by bearing its value in itself; and if you are able to read with your mind's eye the inscriptions stamped upon it you will distinctly decipher these words: "Pay the bearer a service equivalent to what he has rendered to society, the value received being shown, proved, and measured by that which is represented by me." Now, you give up your dollar to me. Either my title to it is gratuitous, or it is a claim. If you give it to me as payment for a service, the following is the result: your account with society for real satisfactions is enumerated, balanced, and closed. You had rendered it a service for a dollar, you now restore the dollar for a service; as far as you are concerned you are clear. As for me, I am now in the position in which you were previously. It is I who am now in advance to society for the service which I have just rendered it in your person. I have become its creditor for the value of the labor that I have performed for you, and that I might have devoted to myself. It is into my hands then, that the title of this credit—the proof of this social debt—ought to pass. You cannot say that I am any richer; if I am entitled to receive, it is because I have given. Still less can you say that society is a dollar richer because one of its members has a dollar more and another has one less. For if you let me have this dollar gratis, it is certain that I shall be so much the richer, but you will be so much the poorer for it; and the social fortune, taken in a mass, will have undergone no change, because as I have already said, this fortune consists in real services, in effective satisfactions, in useful things. You were a creditor to society; you made me a substitute to your rights, and it signifies little to society, which owes a service, whether it pays the debt to you or to me. This is discharged as soon as the bearer of the claim is paid.

B. But if we all had a great number of dollars we should obtain from society many services. Would not that be very desirable?

F. You forget that in the process that I have described, and that is a picture of the reality, we only obtain services from society because we have bestowed some upon it. Whoever speaks of a service speaks at the same time of a service received and returned, for these two terms imply each other, so that the one must always be balanced by the other. It is impossible for society to render more services than it receives, and yet a belief to the contrary is the chimera which is being pursued by means of the multiplication of coins, of paper money, etc.

B. All that appears very reasonable in theory, but in practice I cannot help thinking, when I see how things go, that if by some fortunate circumstance the number of dollars could be multiplied in such a way that each of us could see his little property doubled, we should all be more at our ease; we should all make more purchases, and trade would receive a powerful stimulus.

F. More purchases! And what should we buy? Doubtless, useful articles—things likely to procure for us substantial gratification—such as food, clothing, houses, books, pictures. You should begin, then, by proving that all these things create themselves; you must suppose the Mint melting ingots of gold that have fallen from the moon; or that the printing presses be put in action at the Treasury Department; for you cannot reasonably think that if the quantity of corn, cloth, ships, hats, and shoes remains the same, the share of each of us can be greater because we each go to market with a greater amount of real or fictitious money. Remember the players. In the social order the useful things are what the players place under the candlestick, and the dollars that circulate from hand to hand are the chips. If you multiply the dollars without multiplying the useful things, the only result will be that more dollars will be required for each exchange, just as the players required more chips for each deposit. You have the proof of this in what passes for gold, silver, and copper. Why does the same exchange require more copper than silver, more silver than gold? Is it not because these metals are distributed in the world in different proportions? What reason have you to suppose that if gold were suddenly to become as abundant as silver, it would not require as much of one as of the other to buy a house?

B. You may be right, but I should prefer your being wrong. In the midst of the sufferings that surround us, so distressing in themselves, and so dangerous in their consequences, I have found some consolation in thinking that there was an easy method of making all the members of the community happy.

F. Even if gold and silver were true riches, it would be no easy matter to increase the amount of them in a country where there are no mines.

B. No, but it is easy to substitute something else. I agree with you that gold and silver can do but little service, except as a mere means of exchange. It is the same with paper money, bank notes, etc. Then, if we had all of us plenty of the latter, which it is so easy to create, we might all buy a great deal, and should lack nothing. Your cruel theory dissipates hopes, illusions, if you will, whose principle is assuredly very philanthropic.

F. Yes, like all other barren dreams formed to promote universal felicity. The extreme facility of the means that you recommend is quite sufficient to expose its hollowness. Do you believe that if it were merely needful to print bank notes in order to satisfy all our wants, our tastes, and desires, that mankind would have been contented to go on till now without having recourse to this plan? I agree with you that the discovery is tempting. It would immediately banish from the world not only plunder, in its diverse and deplorable forms, but even labor itself, except in the National

Printing Bureau. But we have yet to learn how greenbacks are to purchase houses, that no one would have built; corn, that no one would have raised; textiles that no one would have taken the trouble to weave.

B. One thing strikes me in your argument. You say yourself that if there is no gain, at any rate there is no loss in multiplying the instrument of exchange, as is seen by the instance of the players, who were entirely unaffected by a very mild deception. Why, then, refuse the philosopher's stone, which would teach us the secret of changing base material into gold, or what is the same thing, converting paper into money? Are you so blindly wedded to logic that you would refuse to try an experiment where there can be no risk? If you are mistaken, you are depriving the nation, as your numerous adversaries believe, of an immense advantage. If the error is on their side, no harm can result, as you yourself say, beyond the failure of a hope. The measure, excellent in their opinion, in yours is merely negative. Let it be tried, then, since the worst that can happen is not the realization of an evil, but the nonrealization of a benefit.

F. In the first place, the failure of a hope is a very great misfortune to any people. It is also very undesirable that the government should announce the abolition of several taxes on the faith of a resource that must infallibly fail. Nevertheless, your remark would deserve some consideration, if after the issue of paper money and its depreciation, the equilibrium of values should instantly and simultaneously take place in all things and in every part of the country. The measure would tend, as in my example of the players, to a universal mystification, in respect to which the best thing we could do would be to look at one another and laugh. But this is not in the course of events. The experiment has been made, and every time a government—be it King or Congress—has altered the money. . . .

B. Who says anything about altering the money?

F. Why, to force people to take in payment scraps of paper that have been officially baptized dollars, or to force them to receive, as weighing an ounce, a piece of silver that weighs only half an ounce but that has been officially named a dollar, is the same thing, if not worse; and all the reasoning that can be made in favor of paper money has been made in favor of legal false-coined money. Certainly, looking at it as you did just now, and as you appear to be doing still, if it is believed that to multiply the instruments of exchange is to multiply the exchanges themselves as well as the things exchanged, it might very reasonably be thought that the most simple means was to mechanically divide the coined dollar, and to cause the law to give to the half the name and value of the whole. Well, in both cases, depreciation is inevitable. I think I have told you the cause. I must also inform you that this depreciation which, with paper might go on till it came to nothing, is effected by continually making dupes; and of these, poor people, simple persons, workmen and farmers are the chief.

B. I see; but stop a little. This dose of Political Economy is rather too strong for once.

F. Be it so. We are agreed, then, upon this point—that wealth is the mass of useful things we produce by labor; or, still better, the result of all the efforts we make for the satisfaction of our wants and tastes. These useful things are exchanged for each other according to the convenience of those to whom they belong. There are two forms in these transactions; one is called barter: in this case a service is rendered for the sake of receiving an equivalent service immediately. In this form transactions would be exceedingly limited. In order that they may be multiplied, and accomplished independently of time and space amongst persons unknown to each other, and by infinite fractions, an intermediate agent has been necessary—this is money. It gives occasion for exchange, which is nothing else but a complicated bargain. This is what has to be noted and understood. Exchange decomposes itself into two bargains, into two departments, sale and purchase—the reunion of which is needed to complete it. You sell a service, and receive a dollar—then, with this dollar you buy a service. Then only is the bargain complete; it is not till then that your effort has been followed by a real satisfaction. Evidently you only work to satisfy the wants of others, that others may work to satisfy yours. So long as you have only the dollar that has been given you for your work, you are only entitled to claim the work of another person. When you have done so, the economical evolution will be accomplished as far as you are concerned, since you will only then have obtained, by a real satisfaction, the true reward for your trouble. The idea of a bargain implies a service rendered, and a service received. Why should it not be the same with exchange, which is merely a bargain in two parts? And here there are two observations to be made. First: It is a very unimportant circumstance whether there be much or little money in the world. If there is much, much is required; if there is little, little is wanted, for each transaction: that is all. The second observation is this: Because it is seen that money always reappears in every exchange, it has come to be regarded as the sign and the measure of the things exchanged.

B. Will you still deny that money is the sign of the useful things of which you speak?

F. A gold eagle is no more the sign of a barrel of flour, than a barrel of flour is the sign of a gold eagle.

B. What harm is there in looking at money as the sign of wealth?

F. The inconvenience is this: it leads to the idea that we have only to increase the sign, in order to increase the things signified; and we are in danger of adopting all the false measures that you took when I made you an absolute king. We should go still further. Just as in money we see the sign of wealth, we see also in paper money the sign of money; and thence conclude that there is a very easy and simple method of procuring for everybody the pleasures of fortune.

B. But you will not go so far as to dispute that money is the measure of values?

F. Yes, certainly, I do go as far as that, for that is precisely where the illusion lies. It has become customary to refer the value of everything to that of money. It is said, this is worth five, ten, or twenty dollars, as we say this weighs five, ten, or twenty grains;

this measures five, ten, or twenty yards; this ground contains five, ten, or twenty acres; and hence it has been concluded that money is the measure of values.

B. Well, it appears as if it was so.

F. Yes, it appears so, and it is this appearance I complain of, and not of the reality. A measure of length, size, surface, is a quantity agreed upon, and unchangeable. It is not so with the value of gold and silver. This varies as much as that of corn, wine, cloth, or labor, and from the same causes, for it has the same source and obeys the same laws. Gold is brought within our reach, just like iron, by the labor of miners, the investments of capitalists, and the combination of merchants and seamen. It costs more or less, according to the expense of its production, according to whether there is much or little in the market, and whether it is much or little in request; in a word, it undergoes the fluctuations of all other human productions. But one circumstance is singular, and gives rise to many mistakes. When the value of money varies, the variation is attributed by language to the other products for which it is exchanged. Thus, let us suppose that all the circumstances relative to gold remain the same, and that the wheat harvest has failed. The price of wheat will rise. It will be said, "The barrel of flour that was worth five dollars is now worth eight;" and this will be correct, for it is the value of the flour that has varied, and language agrees with the fact. But let us reverse the supposition: let us suppose that all the circumstances relative to flour remain the same, and that half of all the gold in existence is swallowed up; this time it is the price of gold that will rise. It would seem that we ought to say, "This gold eagle that was worth ten dollars is now worth twenty." Now, do you know how this is expressed? Just as if it was the other objects of comparison which had fallen in price, it is said: "Flour that was worth ten dollars is now only worth five."

B. It all comes to the same thing in the end.

F. No doubt; but only think what disturbances, what cheatings are produced in exchanges when the value of the medium varies without our becoming aware of it by a change in the name.

Coins or notes are issued bearing the name of five dollars, and which will bear that name through every subsequent depreciation. The value will be reduced a quarter, a half, but they will still be called coins or notes of five dollars. Clever persons will take care not to part with their goods unless for a larger number of notes— in other words, they will ask ten dollars for what they would formerly have sold for five; but simple persons will be taken in. Many years must pass before all the values will find their proper level. Under the influence of ignorance and custom, the day's pay of a country laborer will remain for a long time at a dollar while the salable price of all the articles of consumption around him will be rising. He will sink into destitution without being able to discover the cause. In short, since you wish me to finish, I must beg you, before we separate, to fix your whole attention upon this essential point: Once false money (under whatever form it may take) is put into circulation, depreciation will ensue, and manifest itself by the universal rise of everything that is capable of being sold. But this rise in prices is not instantaneous and equal for all things. Sharp men, brokers, and men of business, will not suffer by it; for it is their trade to watch the fluctuations of prices, to observe the cause, and even to speculate upon it. But little tradesmen, farm workers, and workmen will bear the whole weight of it. The rich man is not any the richer for it, but the poor man becomes poorer by it. Therefore, expedients of this kind have the effect of increasing the distance that separates wealth from poverty, of paralyzing the social tendencies that are incessantly bringing men to the same level, and it will require centuries for the suffering classes to regain the ground they have lost in their advance towards equality of condition.

B. Well, I've got to go. I will meditate on the lecture you have been giving me.

F. Have you finished your own dissertation? As for me, I have scarcely begun mine. I have not yet spoken of the popular hatred of capital, of gratuitous credit (loans without interest)—a most unfortunate notion, a deplorable mistake, which takes its rise from the same source.

B. What! Does this frightful commotion of the populace against capitalists arise from money being confounded with wealth?

F. It is the result of different causes. Unfortunately, certain capitalists have arrogated to themselves monopolies and privileges that are quite sufficient to account for this feeling. But when the theorists of democracy have wished to justify it, to systematize it, to give it the appearance of a reasonable opinion, and to turn it against the very nature of capital, they have had recourse to that false political economy at whose root the same confusion is always to be found. They have said to the people: "Take a dollar; put it under a glass; forget it for a year; then go and look at it, and you will be convinced that it has not produced ten cents, nor five cents, nor any fraction of a cent. Therefore, money produces no interest." Then, substituting for the word money, its pretended sign, capital, they have made it by their logic undergo this modification: "Then capital produces no interest." Then follows this series of consequences: "Therefore he who lends capital ought to obtain nothing from it; therefore he who lends you capital, if he gains something by it, is robbing you; therefore all capitalists are robbers; therefore wealth, which ought to serve gratuitously those who borrow it, belongs in reality to those to whom it does not belong; therefore there is no such thing as property, therefore everything belongs to everybody; therefore..."

B. This is very serious; the more so from the syllogism being so admirably formed. I should very much like to be enlightened on the subject. But, alas! I can no longer command my attention. There is such a confusion in my head of the words coin, money, services, capital, interest, that really I hardly know where I am. We will, if you please, resume the conversation another day.

F. In the meantime here is a little work entitled *Capital and Rent*. It may perhaps remove some of your doubts. Just look at it when you are in want of a little amusement.

B. To amuse me?

F. Who knows? One nail drives in another; one wearisome thing drives away another.

B. I have not yet made up my mind that your views on money and political economy in general are correct. But, from your conversation, this is what I have gathered: That these questions are of the highest importance; for peace or war, order or anarchy, the union or the antagonism of citizens, are at the root of the answer to them. How is it that in France and most other countries that regard themselves as highly civilized, a science that concerns us all so nearly, and the diffusion of which would have so decisive an influence upon the fate of mankind, is so little known? Is it that the State does not teach it sufficiently?

F. Not exactly. For, without knowing it, the State applies itself to loading everybody's brain with prejudices, and everybody's heart with sentiments favorable to the spirit of disorder, war, and hatred; so that, when a doctrine of order, peace, and comity presents itself, it is in vain that it has clearness and truth on its side; it cannot gain admittance.

B. Decidedly you are a frightful grumbler. What interest can the State have in mystifying people's intellects in favor of revolutions, and civil and foreign wars? There must certainly be a great deal of exaggeration in what you say.

F. Consider. At the period when our intellectual faculties begin to develop themselves, at the age when impressions are liveliest, when habits of mind are formed with the greatest ease—when we might look at society and understand it—in a word, as soon as we are seven or eight years old, what does the State do? It puts a blindfold over our eyes, takes us gently from the midst of the social circle that surrounds us, to plunge us, with our susceptible faculties, our impressible hearts, into the midst of Roman society. It keeps us there for ten years at least, long enough to make an indelible impression on the brain. Now observe, that Roman society is directly opposed to what our society ought to be. There they lived upon war; here we ought to hate war; there they hated labor; here we ought to live upon labor. There the means of subsistence were founded upon slavery and plunder; here they should be drawn from free industry. Roman society was organized in consequence of its principle. It necessarily admired what made it prosper. There they considered as virtue what we look upon as vice. Its poets and historians had to exalt what we ought to despise. The very words liberty, order, justice, people, honor, influence, etc., could not have the same signification at Rome as they have, or ought to have, at Paris. How can you expect that all these youths who have been at university or conventual schools with Livy and Quintus Curtius for their catechism, will not understand liberty like the Gracchi, virtue like Cato, patriotism like Caesar? How can you expect them not to be factious and warlike? How can you expect them to take the slightest interest in the mechanism of our social order? Do you think that their minds have been prepared to understand it? Do you not see that in order to do so they must get rid of their present impressions, and receive others entirely opposed to them?

B. What do you conclude from that?

F. I will tell you. The most urgent necessity is not that the State should teach, but that it should allow education. All monopolies are detestable, but the worst of all is the monopoly of education.

V.

CAPITAL AND INTEREST

1. INTRODUCTION

My object in this treatise is to examine the real nature of the Interest on Capital, for the purpose of proving that it is lawful and explaining why it should be perpetual. This may appear a radical proposition, and yet, I confess, I am more afraid I may weary the reader by a series of mere truisms. But it is no easy matter to avoid this danger, when the facts with which we have to deal are known to every one by personal, familiar, and daily experience.

But then you will say, "What is the use of this treatise? Why explain what everybody knows?"

But, although this problem appears at first sight so very simple, there is more in it than you might suppose. I shall endeavor to prove this by an example. Thomas lends a tool today that will be entirely consumed in a week, yet the investment will not produce an unchanging amount of interest to Thomas and his heirs, through all eternity. Reader, can you honestly say that you understand the reason of this?

It would be a waste of time to seek any satisfactory explanation from the writings of economists. They have not thrown much light upon the reasons of the existence of interest. For this they are not to be blamed; for at the time they wrote, its lawfulness was not called in question. Now, however, times are altered; the case is different. Men who consider themselves to be in advance of their times, have organized an active crusade against capital and interest; it is the productiveness of capital that they are attacking; not certain abuses in the administration of it, but the principle itself.

Some years ago a journal was established in Paris by Mr. Proudhon especially to promote this crusade, which for a time is reported to have had a very large circulation. The first number that was issued contained the following declaration of its principles: "The productiveness of capital, which is condemned by Christianity under the name of usury, is the true cause of misery, the true origin of destitution, the eternal obstacle to the establishment of a true Republic."

Another French journal, *La Ruche Populaire*, also thus expresses its views on this subject: "But above all, labor ought to be free; that is, it ought to be organized in such a manner *that money-lenders and owners or controllers of capital should not be paid* for granting the opportunity to labor, and for which privilege they charge as high a price as possible." The only thought that I notice here, is that expressed by the words in the italics, which imply a denial of the right to charge interest.

A noted leader among the French Socialists, Mr. Thoré, also thus expresses himself:

> The revolution will always have to be recommenced, so long as we occupy ourselves with consequences only, without having the logic or the courage to attack the principle itself. This principle is capital, false property, interest, and usury, which by old custom is made to weigh upon labor.

> Ever since the aristocrats invented the incredible fiction, *that capital possesses the power of reproducing itself*, the workers have been at the mercy of the idle.

At the end of a year, will you find an additional dollar in a bag of one hundred dollars? At the end of fourteen years will your dollars have doubled in your bag?

Will a work of industry or of skill produce another, at the end of fourteen years?

Let us begin, then, by demolishing this fatal fiction.

I have quoted the above merely for the sake of establishing the fact that many persons consider the productiveness of capital a false, a fatal, and an iniquitous principle. But quotations are superfluous; it is well known that large numbers of poor people attribute their poverty to what they call the *tyranny of capital*; meaning thereby the unwillingness of the owners of capital to allow others to use it without security for its safe return and compensation for its use.

I believe there is not a man in the world who is aware of the whole importance of this question:

"Is the interest of capital natural, just, and lawful, and as useful to the borrower who pays, as to the lender who receives?"

You answer, No; I answer, Yes. Then we differ entirely; but it is of the utmost importance to discover which of us is in the right, otherwise we shall incur the danger of making a false solution of the question, a matter of opinion. If the error is on my side, however, the evil would not be so great. It must be inferred that I know nothing about the true interests of the masses, or the march of human progress; and that all my arguments are but as so many grains of sand, by which the train of the revolution will certainly not be arrested.

But if, on the contrary, men like Proudhon and Thoré in France (John Ruskin in England, and others in the United States) are deceiving themselves, it follows that they are leading the people astray—that they are showing them evil where it does not exist; and thus giving a false direction to their ideas, to their antipathies, to their dislikes, and to their attacks. It follows that the misguided people are rushing into a horrible and pointless struggle, in which victory would be more fatal than defeat; since according to this supposition, the result would be the realization of universal evils, the destruction of every means of emancipation, the consummation of its own misery.

This is just what Mr. Proudhon has acknowledged, with perfect good faith. "The foundation stone," he told me, "of my system is the *availability of free credit*. If I am mistaken in this, Socialism is a vain dream." I add, it is a dream in which the people are tearing themselves to pieces. Will it, therefore, be a cause for surprise if, when they awake, they find themselves mangled and bleeding? Such a danger as this is enough to justify me fully, if, in the course of the discussion, I allow myself to be led into some trivialities and some prolixity.

2. Ought Capital to Produce Interest?

I address this treatise to working men, more especially to those who have enrolled themselves under the banner of Socialist democracy. I proceed to consider these two questions:

First. Is it consistent with the nature of things, and with justice, that capital should bear interest?

Second. Is it consistent with the nature of things, and with justice, that the interest of capital should be perpetual?

The working men everywhere will certainly acknowledge that a more important subject could not be discussed. Since the world began, it has been allowed, at least in part, that capital ought to produce interest. But latterly it has been affirmed that herein lies the very social error that is the cause of pauperism and inequality; it is, therefore, most essential to know now on what ground we stand.

For if levying interest from capital is a sin, the workers have a right to revolt against social order, as it exists. It is in vain to tell them that they ought to have recourse to legal and peaceful means: it would be a hypocritical recommendation. When on the one side there is a strong man, poor, and a victim of robbery—on the other, a weak man, but rich, and a robber—it is ridiculous that we should say to the former, with a hope of persuading him, "Wait till your oppressor voluntarily renounces oppression, or till it shall cease of itself." This cannot be; and those who tell us that capital is by nature unproductive ought to know that they are provoking a terrible and disastrous struggle.

If, on the contrary, the interest of capital is natural, lawful, consistent with the general good, as favorable to the borrower as to the lender, the economists who deny it, the writers who grieve over this pretended social wound, are leading the workmen into a senseless and unjust effort which can have no other issue than the misfortune of all. In fact, they are arming labor against capital. So much the better, if these two powers are really antagonistic; and may the struggle soon be ended! But, if they are in harmony, the struggle is the greatest evil that can be inflicted on society. You see then, workmen, that there is not a more important question than this: "Is the interest of capital rightful or not?" In the former case, you must immediately renounce the struggle to which you are being urged; in the second, you must carry it on resolutely, and to the end.

Productiveness of capital—perpetuity of interest. These are difficult questions. I must endeavor to make myself clear. And for that purpose I shall have recourse to example rather than to demonstration; or rather, I shall place the demonstration in the example. I begin by acknowledging that, at first sight, it may appear strange that capital should pretend to a remuneration, and above all to a perpetual remuneration. You will say, "here are two men. One of them works from morning till night, from one year's end to another; and if he consumes all that he has gained, even by superior energy, he remains poor. When Christmas comes he is in no better condition than he was at the beginning of the year, and has no other prospect but to begin again. The other man does nothing, either with his hands or his head; or at least, if he makes use of them at all, it is only for his own pleasure; it is allowable for him to do nothing, for he has an income. He does not work, yet he lives well; he has everything in abundance; delicate dishes, sumptuous furniture, elegant equipages; nay, he even consumes, daily, things that the workers have been obliged to produce by the sweat of their brow, for these things do not make themselves;

and, as far as he is concerned, he has had no hand in their production. It is the workmen who have caused this corn to grow, decorated this furniture, woven these carpets; it is our wives and daughters who have spun, cut out, sewed, and embroidered these materials. We work, then, for him and for ourselves; for him first, and then for ourselves, if there is anything left.

"But here is something more striking still. If the former of these two men, the worker, consumes within the year any profit that may have been left him in that year, he is always at the point from which he started, and his destiny condemns him to move incessantly in a perpetual circle, and in a monotony of exertion. Labor, then, is rewarded only once. But if the other, the 'gentleman,' consumes his yearly income in the year, he has, the year after, in those which follow, and through all eternity, an income always equal, inexhaustible, *perpetual*. Capital, then, is remunerated, not only once or twice, but an indefinite number of times! So that, at the end of a hundred years, a family that has placed 20,000 francs, at five percent will have had 100,000 francs; and this will not prevent them from having 100,000 francs more in the following century. In other words, for 20,000 francs, which represents its labor, it will have levied, in two centuries, a tenfold value on the labor of others. In this social arrangement is there not a monstrous evil to be reformed? And this is not all. If it should please this family to curtail its enjoyments a little—to spend, for example, only 900 francs, instead of 1,000—it may, without any labor, without any other trouble beyond that of investing 100 francs a year, increase its capital and its income in such rapid progression that it will soon be in a position to consume as much as a hundred families of industrious workmen. Does not all this go to prove that society itself has in its bosom a hideous cancer, which ought to be eradicated at the risk of some temporary suffering?"

These are, it appears to me, the sad and unsettling reflections that must be excited in your minds by the active and notorious crusade that is being carried on against capital and interest. On the other hand, there are moments in which, I am convinced, doubts are awakened in your minds, and scruples in your conscience. You say to yourselves sometimes: "But to assert that capital ought not to produce interest is to say that he who has created tools, or materials, or provisions of any kind, ought to yield them up without compensation. Is that just? And then, if it is so, who would lend these tools, these materials, these provisions? Who would take care of them? Who would even create them? Everyone would consume his proportion, and the human race would not advance a step. Capital would be no longer accumulated, since there would be no interest in accumulating it. It would become exceedingly scarce. This would be a most peculiar step for the obtaining of loans gratuitously! A peculiar means of improving the condition of borrowers, to make it impossible for them to borrow at any price! What would become of labor itself? For there will be no money advanced, and not one single kind of labor can be mentioned, not even hunting, that can be pursued without capital of some kind. And, as for ourselves, what would become of us? What! We are not to be allowed to borrow, in order to work in the prime of life, nor to lend, that we may enjoy repose in its decline? The law will rob us of the prospect of laying by a little property, because it will prevent us from gaining any advantage from it. It will deprive us of all stimulus to save at the present time, and of all hope of repose for the future. It is useless to exhaust ourselves with fatigue; we must abandon the idea of leaving our sons and daughters a little property, since the new views render it useless, for we should become traffickers in the toil of men if we were to lend it at interest. Alas! the world that these persons would open before us, as an imaginary good, is still more dreary and desolate than that which they condemn, for hope, at any rate, is not banished from the latter." Thus, in all respects, and in every point of view, the question is a serious one. Let us hasten to arrive at a solution.

The French civil code has a chapter entitled, "On the manner of transmitting property." When a man by his labor has made some useful things—in other words, when he has created a value—it can only pass into the hands of another by one of the following modes: *as a gift, by the right of inheritance, by exchange, loan, or theft*. One word upon each of these, except the last, although it plays a greater part in the world than we may think. A *gift* needs no definition. It is essentially voluntary and spontaneous. It depends exclusively upon the giver, and the receiver cannot be said to have any right to it. Without a doubt, morality and religion make it a duty for men, especially the rich, to deprive themselves voluntarily of that which they possess in favor of their less fortunate brethren. But this is an entirely moral obligation. If it were to be asserted on principle, admitted in practice, sanctioned by law, that every man has a right to the property of another, the gift would have no merit—charity and gratitude would be no longer virtues. Besides, such a doctrine would suddenly and universally arrest labor and production, as severe cold congeals water and suspends animation; for who would work if there was no longer to be any connection between labor and the satisfying of our wants? Political economy has not considered the matter of gifts. This has led people to conclude that it is opposed to such things and that it is therefore a science devoid of heart. This is a ridiculous accusation. That science which treats of the laws resulting from the reciprocity of services had no business to inquire into the consequences of generosity with respect to him who receives, nor into its effects, perhaps even more beneficial, on him who gives. Such considerations belong evidently to the science of morals. We must allow the sciences to have limits; above all, we must not accuse them of denying or undervaluing what they look upon as foreign to their department.

The right of inheritance, against which so much has been objected of late, is one of the forms of *gift*, and assuredly the most natural of all. That which a man has produced, he may consume, exchange, or give. What can be more natural than that he should give it to his children? It is this power, more than any other, that inspires him with the drive to labor and to save. Do you know why the principle of right of inheritance is thus called in question? Because it is imagined that the property thus transmitted is plundered from the masses. This is a fatal error. Political economy demonstrates, in the most peremptory manner, that all value produced is a creation which does no harm to any person whatever. For that reason it may be consumed, and, still more, transmitted, without hurting anyone; but I shall not pursue these reflections, which do not belong to the subject.

Exchange is the principal department of political economy, because it is by far the most frequent method of transmitting property, according to the free and voluntary acquiescence in the laws and effects of which this science treats.

Properly speaking, exchange is the reciprocity of services. The parties say between themselves, "Give me this, and I will give you that" or, "Do this for me, and I will do that for you." It is well to remark (for this will throw a new light on the notion of value) that the second form is always implied in the first. When it is said, "Do this for me, and I will do that for you," an exchange of service for service is proposed. Again, when it is said, "Give me this, and I will give you that," it is the same as saying, "I yield to you what I have done, yield to me what you have done." The labor is past, instead of present; but the exchange is not the less governed by the comparative valuation of the two services; so that it is quite correct to say that the principle of value is in the services rendered and received on account of the products exchanged, rather than in the products themselves.

In reality, services are scarcely ever exchanged directly. There is a medium that is termed *money*. Paul has completed a coat, for which he wishes to receive a little bread, a little wine, a little oil, a visit from a doctor, a ticket for the play, etc. The exchange cannot be effected in kind, so what does Paul do? He first exchanges his coat for some money, which is called selling; then he exchanges this money again for the things he wants, which is called purchasing; and now, only, has the reciprocity of service completed its circuit; now, only, the labor and the compensation are balanced in the same individual—"I have done this for society, it has done that for me." In a word, it is only now that the exchange is actually accomplished. Thus, nothing can be more correct than this observation of J.B. Say: "Since the introduction of money, every exchange is resolved into two elements, *sale* and *purchase*. It is the reunion of these two elements which renders the exchange complete."

We must note, also, that the constant appearance of money in every exchange has overturned and misled all our ideas: men have ended in thinking that money was true riches, and that to multiply it was to multiply services and products. Hence the protectionist system; hence paper money; hence the celebrated aphorism, "What one gains the other loses;" and of the errors that have impoverished the earth, and imbrued it with blood. After much investigation it has been found, that in order to make the two services exchanged of equivalent value, and in order to render the exchange *equitable*, the best means was to allow it to be free. However plausible at first sight, the intervention of the State might be, it was soon perceived that it is always oppressive to one or other of the contracting parties. When we look into these subjects, we are always compelled to reason upon this maxim, that *equal value* results from liberty. We have, in fact, no other means of knowing whether, at a given moment, two services are of the same value but that of examining whether they can be readily and freely exchanged. Allow the State, which is the same thing as force, to interfere on one side or the other, and from that moment all the means of evaluation will be complicated and entangled, instead of becoming clear. It ought to be the part of the State to prevent, and, above all, to repress artifice and fraud; that is, to secure liberty, and not to violate it. I have enlarged a little upon exchange, although loan is my principal object: my excuse is that I conceive that there is in a loan an actual exchange, an actual service rendered by the lender, and that makes the borrower liable to an equivalent service—two services whose comparative value can only be appreciated, like that of all possible services, in freedom. Now, if it is so, the perfect rightfulness of what is called house-rent, farm-rent, interest, will be explained and understood. Let us consider what is involved in a *loan*.

Suppose two men exchange two services or two objects, whose equal value is beyond all dispute. Suppose, for example,

Peter says to Paul, "Give me ten ten-cent pieces, I will give you a silver dollar." We cannot imagine an equal value more unquestionable. When the bargain is made, neither party has any claim upon the other. The exchanged services are equal. Then it follows that if one of the parties wishes to introduce into the bargain an additional clause advantageous to himself but unfavorable to the other party, he must agree to a second clause, which shall reestablish the equilibrium, and the law of justice. It would be absurd to deny the justice of a second clause of compensation. This granted, we will suppose that Peter, after having said to Paul, "Give me ten ten-cent pieces, I will give you a dollar," adds, "You shall give me the ten ten-cent pieces *now*, and I will give you the silver dollar in *a year*;" it is very evident that this new proposition alters the claims and advantages of the bargain; that it alters the proportion of the two services. Does it not appear plainly enough, in fact, that Peter asks of Paul a new and an additional service; one of a different kind? Is it not as if he had said, "Render me the service of allowing me to use for my profit, for a year, the dollar that belongs to you, and that you might have used for yourself?" And what good reason have you to maintain that Paul is bound to render this especial service gratuitously; that he has no right to demand anything more in consequence of this requisition; that the State ought to interfere to force him to submit? Is it not incomprehensible that the economist, who preaches such a doctrine to the people, can reconcile it with his principle of the *reciprocity of service*? Here I have introduced money; I have been led to do so by a desire to place, side by side, two objects of exchange, of a perfect and indisputable equality of value. I was anxious to be prepared for objections; but, on the other hand, my demonstration would have been more striking still if I had illustrated my principle by an agreement for exchanging of services or commodities directly.

Suppose, for example, a house and a vessel of a value so perfectly equal that their proprietors are disposed to exchange them even-handed, without excess or abatement. In fact let the bargain be settled by a lawyer. At the moment of each taking possession,

the ship-owner says to the house-owner, "Very well; the transaction is completed, and nothing can prove its perfect equity better
than our free and voluntary consent. Our conditions thus fixed, I
will propose to you a little practical modification. You shall let me
have your house today, but I will not put you in possession of my
ship for a year; and the reason I make this demand of you is that
during this year of *delay,* I wish to use the vessel." That we may
not be embarrassed by considerations relative to the deterioration
of the thing lent, I will suppose the ship-owner to add, "I will
engage, at the end of the year, to hand over to you the vessel in
the state in which it is today." I ask of every candid man, if the
house-owner has not a right to answer, "The new clause that you
propose entirely alters the proportion or the equal value of the
exchanged services. By it I shall be deprived for the space of a
year, both at once of my house and of your vessel. By it you will
make use of both. If in the absence of this clause the bargain was
just, for the same reason the clause is injurious to me. It stipulates
a loss to me, and a gain to you. You are requiring of me a new
service; I have a right to refuse, or to require of you, as a compensation, an equivalent service." If the parties are agreed upon
this compensation, the principle of which is incontestable, we can
easily distinguish two transactions in one, two exchanges of service in one. First, there is the exchange of the house for the vessel;
after this, there is the delay granted by one of the parties, and the
compensation corresponding to this delay yielded by the other.
These two new services take the generic and abstract names of
credit and *interest.* But names do not change the nature of things;
and I defy any one to disprove that there exists here, when all is
done, a service for a service, or a reciprocity of services. To say
that one of these services does not challenge the other, to say that
the first ought to be rendered gratuitously, without injustice, is to
say that injustice consists in the reciprocity of service—that justice
consists in one of the parties giving and not receiving, which is a
contradiction in terms.

But to give an idea of interest and its mechanism, allow me to make use of two or three anecdotes. But first, I must say a few words upon capital.

3. What Is Capital?

There are some persons who imagine that capital is money, and this is precisely the reason why they deny its productiveness; for, as John Ruskin and others say, dollars are not endowed with the power of reproducing themselves. But it is not true that capital and money are the same thing.

Before the discovery of the precious metals, there were capitalists in the world; and I venture to say that at that time, as now, everybody was a capitalist, to a certain extent.

What is capital, then? It is composed of three things:

First, of the materials upon which men operate, when these materials have already a value communicated by human effort, which has bestowed upon them the property of exchangeability—wool, flax leather, silk, wood, etc.

Second, instruments that are used for working—tools, machines, ships, carriages, etc.

Third, provisions that are consumed during labor—victuals, fabrics, houses, etc.

Without these things the labor of man would be unproductive and almost void; yet these very things have required much work, especially at first. This is the reason that so much value has been attached to the possession of them, and also that it is perfectly lawful to exchange and to sell them, to make a profit off them if used, to gain remuneration from them if lent. Now for my anecdotes.

4. The Sack of Corn

William, in other respects as poor as Job, and obliged to earn his bread by day-labor, became, nevertheless, by some inheritance, the owner of a fine piece of uncultivated land. He was exceedingly anxious to cultivate it. "Alas!" said he, "to make

ditches, to raise fences, to break the soil, to clear away the bram-
bles and stones, to plow it, to sow it, might bring me a living in a
year or two; but certainly not today, or tomorrow. It is impossible to set about farming it, without previously saving some provisions for my subsistence until the harvest; and I know by experience that preparatory labor is indispensable in order to render
present labor productive."

The good William was not content with making these reflections. He resolved to work by the day, and to save something
from his wages to buy a spade and a sack of corn, without which
things he must give up his agricultural projects. He acted so well,
was so active and steady, that he soon saw himself in possession
of the wished-for sack of corn. "I shall have enough to live upon
till my field is covered with a rich harvest." Just as he was starting, David came to borrow his accumulation of food of him. "If
you will lend me this sack of corn," said David, "you will do me
a great service; for I have some very lucrative work in view, which
I cannot possibly undertake for want of provisions to live upon
till it is finished." "I was in the same situation," answered
William; "and if I have now secured bread for several months, it
is at the expense of my arms and my stomach. Upon what principle of justice can it be devoted to the carrying out of your enterprise instead of *mine*?"

You may well believe that the bargain was a long one. However, it was finished at length, and on these conditions:

First—David promised to give back, at the end of the year, a
sack of corn of the same quality, and of the same weight, without
missing a single grain. "This first clause is perfectly just," said he,
"for without it William would *give*, and not *lend*."

Second—He further engaged to deliver *one-half bushel of
corn for every five bushels originally borrowed, when the loan was
returned*. "This clause is no less just than the other," thought he;
"for unless William would do me a service without compensation,
he would inflict upon himself a privation—he would renounce his
cherished enterprise—he would enable me to accomplish mine—
he would cause me to enjoy for a year the fruits of his savings, and

all this gratuitously. Since he delays the cultivation of his land, since he enables me to prosecute a lucrative employment, it is quite natural that I should let him partake, in a certain proportion, of the profits that I shall gain by the sacrifice he makes of his own profits."

On his side, William, who was something of a scholar, made this calculation: "Since by virtue of the first clause, the sack of corn will return to me at the end of a year," he said to himself, "I shall be able to lend it again; it will return to me at the end of the second year; I may lend it again, and so on, to all eternity. However, I cannot deny that it will have been eaten long ago."

It is singular that I should be perpetually the owner of a sack of corn, although the one I have lent has been consumed forever. But this is explained thus: It will be consumed in the service of David. It will enable David to produce a greater value; and consequently, David will be able to restore me a sack of corn, or the value of it, without having suffered the slightest injury; but on the contrary, having gained from the use of it. And as regards myself, this value ought to be my property, as long as I do not consume it myself. If I had used it to clear my land, I should have received it again in the form of a fine harvest. Instead of that, I lend it, and shall recover it in the form of repayment.

"From the second clause, I gain another piece of information. At the end of the year I shall be in possession of one bushel of corn for every ten that I may lend. If, then, I were to continue to work by the day, and to save part of my wages, as I have been doing, in the course of time I should be able to lend two sacks of corn; then three; then four; and when I should have gained a sufficient number to enable me to live on these additions of a half a bushel over and above and on account of every ten bushels lent, I shall be at liberty to take a little repose in my old age. But how is this? In this case, shall I not be living at the expense of others? No, certainly, for it has been proved that in lending I perform a service; I make more profitable the labor of my borrowers, and only deduct a trifling part of the excess of production, due to my lendings and savings. It is a marvelous thing that a man may thus realize a leisure that injures no one, and for which he cannot be reproached without injustice."

5. THE HOUSE

Again, Thomas had a house. In building it, he had extorted nothing from any one whatever. He obtained it by his own personal labor, or, which is the same thing, by the labor of others justly rewarded. His first care was to make a bargain with a handyman, in virtue of which, on condition of the payment of a hundred dollars a year, the latter engaged to keep the house in constant good repair. Thomas was already congratulating himself on the happy days he hoped to spend in this pleasant home, which our laws declared to be his own exclusive property. But Richard wished to use it also as his residence.

"How can you think of such a thing?" said Thomas to Richard. "It is I who have built it; it has cost me ten years of painful labor, and now you would come in and take it for your enjoyment?" They agreed to refer the matter to judges. They chose no profound economists—there were none such in the country. But they found some just and sensible men; it all comes to the same thing; political economy, justice, good sense, are all the same thing. And here is the decision made by the judges: If Richard wishes to occupy Thomas's house for a year, he is bound to submit to three conditions. The first is to quit at the end of the year, and to restore the house in good repair, saving the inevitable decay resulting from mere duration. The second, to refund to Thomas the one hundred dollars Thomas pays annually to the handyman to repair the injuries of time; for these injuries taking place while the house is in the service of Richard, it is perfectly just that he should bear the expense. The third, that he should render to Thomas a service equivalent to that which he receives. And as to what shall constitute this equivalence of services, this must be left for Thomas and Richard to mutually agree upon.

6. The Plane

One further illustration to the same ethic. A very long time ago there lived in a poor village, a carpenter, who was a philosopher, as all my heroes are in their way. James worked from morning till night with his two strong arms, but his brain was not idle for all that. He was fond of reviewing his actions, their causes, and their effects. He sometimes said to himself, "With my hatchet, my saw, and my hammer, I can make only coarse furniture, and can only get the pay for such. If I only had a plane, I should please my customers more, and they would pay me more. But this is all right; I can only expect services proportioned to those which I render myself. Yes! I am resolved, I will make myself a *plane*."

However, just as he was setting to work, James reflected further: "I work for my customers 300 days in the year. If I give ten to making my plane, supposing it lasts me a year, only 290 days will remain for me to make my furniture. Now, in order that I be not the loser in this matter, I must earn henceforth, with the help of the plane, as much in 290 days as I now do in 300. I must even earn more; for unless I do so, it would not be worth my while to venture upon any innovations," James began to calculate. He satisfied himself that he should sell his finished furniture at a price which would amply compensate him for the ten days devoted to the plane; and when no doubt remained in his mind on this point, he set to work. I beg the reader to note, that the power that exists in the tool to increase the productiveness of labor, is the basis for the successful solution of the experiment that James the carpenter proposed to make.

At the end of ten days, James had in his possession an admirable plane, which he valued all the more for having made it himself. He danced for joy—for like the girl with her basket of eggs, he reckoned in anticipation all the profits he expected to derive from the ingenious instrument; but, more fortunate than she, he was not reduced to the necessity of saying good-by, when the eggs were smashed, to the expected calf, cow, pig, as well as the eggs, together. He was building his fine castles in the air, when he was interrupted by his acquaintance William, a carpenter in the neighboring village. William having admired the plane, was struck with the advantages that might be gained from it. He said to James:

W. You must do me a service.

J. What service?

W. Lend me the plane for a year.

As might be expected, James at this proposal did not fail to cry out, "How can you think of such a thing, William? But if I do you this service, what will you do for me in return?"

W. Nothing. Don't you know that John Ruskin says a loan ought to be gratuitous? Don't you know that Proudhon and other notable writers and friends of the laboring classes assert that capital is naturally unproductive? Don't you know that all the new school of liberal advanced writers say we ought to have perfect fraternity among men? If you only do me a service for the sake of receiving one from me in return, what merit would you have?

J. William, my friend, fraternity does not mean that all the sacrifices are to be on one side; if so, I do not see why they should not be on yours. Whether a loan should be gratuitous I don't know but I do know that if I were to lend you my plane for a year it would be giving it you. To tell you the truth, that was not what I made it for.

W. Well, we will say nothing about the modern maxims discovered by the friends of the working classes. I ask you to do me a service; what service do you ask me in return?

J. First, then, in a year the plane will be used up, it will be good for nothing. It is only just that you should let me have another exactly like it; or that you should give me money enough to get it repaired; or that you should supply me the ten days which I must devote to replacing it.

W. This is perfectly just. I submit to these conditions. I engage to return it, or to let you have one like it, or the value of the same. I think you must be satisfied with this, and can require nothing further.

J. I think otherwise. I made the plane for myself, and not for you. I expected to gain some advantage from it, by my work being better finished and better paid; by improving my condition. What reason is there that I should make the plane, and you should gain the profit? I might as well ask you to give me your saw and hatchet! What a confusion! Is it not natural that each should keep what he has made with his own hands, as well as his hands themselves? To use without recompense the hands of another, I call slavery; to use without recompense the plane of another, can this be called fraternity?

W. But, then, I have agreed to return it to you at the end of a year, as well polished and as sharp as it is now.

J. We have nothing to do with next year; we are speaking of this year. I have made the plane for the sake of improving my work and condition: if you merely return it to me in a year, it is you who will gain the profit of it during the whole of that time. I am not bound to do you such a service without receiving anything from you in return; therefore, if you wish for my plane, independently of the entire restoration already bargained for, you must do me a service which we will now discuss; you must grant me remuneration.

And this was what the two finally agreed upon: William granted a remuneration calculated in such a way that, at the end of the year, James received his plane quite new, and in addition a new plank, as a compensation for the advantages of which he had deprived himself in lending the plane to his friend.

It was impossible for anyone acquainted with the transaction to discover the slightest trace in it of oppression or injustice.

The singular part of it is, that, at the end of the year, the plane came into James's possession, and he lent it again; recovered it, and lent it a third and fourth time. It has passed into the hands of his son, who still lends it. Poor plane! How many times has it changed, sometimes its blade, sometimes its handle. It is no longer the same plane, but it has always the same value, at least for James's posterity. Workmen; let us examine further these little stories.

I maintain, first of all, that the *sack of corn* and the *plane* are here the type, the model, a faithful representation, the symbol of all capital; as the half bushel of corn and the plank are the type, the model, the representation, the symbol of all interest. This granted, the following are, it seems to me, a series of consequences, the justice of which it is impossible to dispute.

First. If the yielding of a plank by the borrower to the lender is a natural, equitable, lawful remuneration, the just price of a real service, we may conclude that, as a general rule, it is in the nature of capital when loaned or used to produce interest. When this capital, as in the foregoing examples, takes the form of an *instrument of labor*, it is clear enough that it ought to bring an advantage to its possessor, to him who has devoted to it his time, his brains, and his strength. Otherwise, why should he have made it? No necessity of life can be immediately satisfied with instruments of labor; no one eats planes or drinks saws, unless, of course, he is a magician. If a man determines to spend his time in the production of such things, he must have been led to it by the consideration of the increased power these instruments give to him; of the time which they save him; of the perfection and rapidity they give to his labor; in a word, of the advantages they procure for him. Now these advantages, which have been obtained by labor, by the sacrifice of time that might have been used for other purposes, are we bound, as soon as they are ready to be enjoyed, to confer them gratuitously upon another? Would it be an advance in social order if the law so stated, and citizens should pay officials for enforcing such a law by force? I venture to say that there is not one amongst you who would support it. It would be to legalize, to organize, to systematize injustice itself, for it would be proclaiming that there are men born to render, and others born to receive, gratuitous services. Grant, then, that interest is just, natural, and expedient.

Second. A second consequence, not less remarkable than the former, and, if possible, still more conclusive, to which I call your attention, is this: *Interest is not injurious to the borrower.* I mean to say, the obligation in which the borrower finds himself, to pay a remuneration for use of capital, cannot do any harm to his condition. Observe, in fact, that James and William are perfectly free, as regards the transaction to which the plane gave occasion. The transaction cannot be accomplished without the consent of one as well as of the other. The worst that can happen is that James may ask too much; and in this case, William, refusing the loan, remains as he was before. By the fact of his agreeing to borrow, he proves that he considers it an advantage to himself; he proves that after every calculation, whatever may be the remuneration or interest required of him, he still finds it more profitable to borrow than not to borrow. He only determines to do so because he has compared the inconveniences with the advantages. He has calculated that the day on which he returns the plane, accompanied by the remuneration agreed upon, he will have effected more work, with the same labor, thanks to this tool. A profit will remain to him, otherwise he would not have borrowed. The two services of which we are speaking are exchanged according to the law that governs all exchanges, the law of supply and demand. The demands of James have a natural and impassable limit. This is the point at which the remuneration demanded by him would absorb all the advantage that William might find in making use of a plane. In this case, the borrowing would not take place. William would be bound either to make a plane for himself, or do without one, which would leave him in his original condition. He borrows because he gains by borrowing. I know very well what will be told me. You will say, William may be deceived, or, perhaps, he may be governed by necessity, and be obliged to submit to a harsh law.

It may be so. As to errors in calculation, they belong to the infirmity of our nature, and to argue from this against the transaction in question, is objecting to the possibility of loss in all imaginable transactions, in every human act. Error is an accidental fact, which is incessantly remedied by experience. In short, everybody must guard against it. As far as those hard necessities are concerned that force persons to borrow under onerous conditions, it is clear that these necessities existed previously to the borrowing.

If William is in a situation in which he cannot possibly do without a plane, and must borrow one at any price, does this situation result from James having taken the trouble to make the tool? Does it not exist independently of this circumstance? However harsh, however severe James may be, he will never render the supposed condition of William worse than it is. Morally, it is true, the lender will be to blame if he demands more than is just; but in an economical point of view, the loan itself can never be considered responsible for previous necessities, which it has not created, and which it relieves to a certain extent. But this proves something to which I shall return. It is evidently for the interest of William, representing here the borrowers, that there shall be many Jameses and planes, or, in other words, lenders and capitals. It is very evident that if William can say to James, "Your demands are exorbitant; there is no lack of planes in the world;" he will be in a better situation than if James's plane was the only one he could borrow. Assuredly, there is no maxim more true than this—service for service. But let us not forget that no service has a fixed and absolute value compared with others. The contracting parties are free. Each pushes his advantage to the farthest possible point, and the most favorable circumstance for these advantages is the absence of rivalship. Hence it follows that if there is a class of men more interested than any other in the creation, multiplication, and abundance of capital goods, it is mainly that of the borrowers. Now, since capital goods can only be formed and increased by the stimulus and the prospect of remuneration, let this class understand the injury they are inflicting on themselves when they deny the lawfulness of interest, when they proclaim that credit should be gratuitous, when they declaim against the pretended tyranny of capital, when they discourage saving, thus forcing capital to become scarce, and consequently interest to rise.

Third. The anecdote I have just related enables you to explain this apparently objectionable phenomenon, which is termed the duration or perpetuity of interest. Since, in lending his plane, James has been able, very lawfully, to make it a condition that it should he returned to him at the end of a year in the same state in which it was when he lent it, is it not evident that he may, at the expiration of the term, lend it again on the same conditions? If he resolves upon the latter plan, the plane will return to him at the end of every year, and that without end. James will then be in a condition to lend without end; that is, he may derive from it a perpetual interest. It will be said that the plane will be worn out. That is true; but it will be worn out by the hand and for the profit of the borrower. The latter has taken this gradual wear into account and taken upon himself, as he ought, the consequences. He has reckoned that he shall derive from this tool an advantage that will allow him to restore it to its original condition after having realized a profit from it. As long as James does not use this capital himself, or for his own advantage—as long as he renounces the advantages that allow it to be restored to its original condition—he will have an incontestable right to have it restored, and that independently of interest.

Observe besides that if, as I believe I have shown, James, far from doing any harm to William, has done him a service in lending him his plane for a year; for the same reason, he will do no harm to a second, a third, a fourth borrower, in the subsequent periods. Hence you may understand that the interest from capital is as natural, as lawful, as useful, in the thousandth year, as in the first. We may go still further. It may happen that James lends more than a single plane. It is possible, that by means of working, of saving, of privations, of discipline, of activity, he may come to be able to lend a multitude of planes and saws; that is to say, to do a multitude of services.

I insist upon this point—that if the first loan has been a social good, it will be the same with all the others; for they are all similar, and based upon the same principle. It may happen, then, that the amount of all the remunerations received by our honest operative, in exchange for services rendered by him, may suffice to maintain him. In this case, there will be a man in the world who has a right to live without working. I do not say that he would be doing right to give himself up to idleness—but I say that he has a right to do so; and if he does so, it will be at nobody's expense, but quite the contrary. If society at all understands the nature of things, it will acknowledge that this man subsists on services that he receives certainly (as we all do), but that he receives lawfully in exchange for other services, that he himself has rendered, that he continues to render, and that are real services, inasmuch as they are freely and voluntarily accepted.

And here we have a glimpse of one of the finest harmonies in the social world. I allude to *leisure*: not that leisure that the war-like and tyrannical classes arrange for themselves by the plunder of the workers, but that leisure which is the lawful and innocent fruit of past activity and economy.

In expressing myself thus, I know that I shall shock many received ideas. But see! Is not leisure an essential spring in the social machine? Without it the world would never have had a Newton, a Pascal, a Fênelon; mankind would have been ignorant of all arts, sciences, and of those wonderful inventions prepared originally by investigations of mere curiosity; thought would have been inert—man would have made no progress.[4] On the other hand, if leisure could only be explained by plunder and oppression—if it were a benefit that could only be enjoyed unjustly, and at the expense of others, there would be no middle path between these two evils; either mankind would be reduced to the necessity of stagnating in a vegetable and stationary life in eternal ignorance from the absence of wheels to its machine—or else it would

---

[4]Of all the results that are produced among a people by their climate, food, and soil, the accumulation of wealth (capital) is the earliest, and in many respects the most important. For although the progress of knowledge eventually accelerates the increase of wealth, it is nevertheless certain that, in the first formation of society, the wealth must accumulate before the knowledge can begin. As long as every man is engaged in collecting the materials necessary for his own subsistence, there will be neither leisure nor taste for higher pursuits. But if the produce is greater than consumption, a surplus arises by means of which men can use what they did not produce, and are thus enabled to devote themselves to subjects for which at an earlier period the pressure of their daily wants would have left them no time."—*Buckle's History of Civilization*.

have to acquire these wheels at the price of inevitable injustice, and would necessarily present the sad spectacle, in one form or other, of the ancient classification of human beings into masters and slaves. I defy anyone to show me, in this case, any other alternative. We should be compelled to contemplate the Divine plan that governs society with the regret of thinking that it presents a deplorable chasm. The stimulus of progress would be forgotten or, which is worse, this stimulus would be no other than injustice itself. But no! God has not left such a chasm in His work of love. We must take care not to disregard His wisdom and power; for those whose imperfect meditations cannot explain the lawfulness of leisure, are very much like the astronomer who said, at a certain point in the heavens there ought to exist a planet that will be at last discovered, for without it the celestial world is not harmony, but discord.

Therefore I say that, if well understood, the history of my humble plane, although very modest, is sufficient to raise us to the contemplation of one of the most consoling but least understood of the social harmonies.

It is not true that we must choose between the denial or the unlawfulness of leisure; thanks to rent and its natural duration, leisure may arise from labor and saving. It is a pleasing prospect, which everyone may have in view; a noble recompense, to which each may aspire. It makes its appearance in the world; it distributes itself proportionately to the exercise of certain virtues; it opens all the avenues to intelligence; it ennobles, it raises the morals; it spiritualizes the soul of humanity, not only without laying any weight on those of our brethren whose lot in life makes severe labor necessary, but it relieves them gradually from the heaviest and most repugnant part of this labor. It is enough that capital should be formed, accumulated, multiplied; should be lent on conditions less and less burdensome; that it should descend, penetrate into every social circle, and that by an admirable progression, after having liberated the lenders from onerous toil, it should bring a similar liberation to the borrowers themselves. For that end, the laws and customs ought all to be favorable to economy, the source of capital. It is enough to say, that the first of all these conditions is not to alarm, to attack, to deny that which is the stimulus of saving and the reason of its existence—interest.

As long as we see nothing passing from hand to hand, in the operations of loan, but *provisions, materials, instruments,* things indispensable to the productiveness of labor itself, the ideas thus far exhibited will not find many opponents. Who knows, even, that I may not be reproached for having made a great effort to burst what may be said to be an open door. But as soon as money makes its appearance as the subject of the transaction (and it is this which appears almost always), immediately a crowd of objections are raised. Money, it will be said, will not reproduce itself, like your *sack of corn*; it does not assist labor, like your *plane*; it does not afford an immediate satisfaction, like your *house*. It is incapable, by its nature, of producing interest, of multiplying itself, and the remuneration it demands is a positive extortion.

Who cannot see the sophistry of this? Who does not see that money is only an instrumentality that men use to represent other *values*, or real objects of usefulness, for the sole object of facilitating their exchanges of commodities or services? In the midst of social complications, the man who is in a condition to lend scarcely ever has the exact thing the borrower wants. James, it is true, has a plane; but, perhaps, William wants a saw. They cannot negotiate; the transaction favorable to both cannot take place, and then what happens? It happens that James first exchanges his plane for money; he lends the money to William, and William exchanges the money for a saw. The transaction is no longer a simple one; it is resolved into two transactions, as I explained above in speaking of exchange. But for all that, it has not changed its nature; it still contains all the elements of a direct loan. James has parted with a tool which was useful to him; William has at the same time received an instrument that facilitates his work and increases his profits; there is still a service rendered by the lender, which entitles him to receive an equivalent service from the borrower; and this just balance is not the less established by free mutual bargaining. The obvious natural obligation to restore at the end of the term the *entire value* of what was borrowed still constitutes the principle of the rightfulness of interest.

At the end of a year, says Mr. Thoré, will you find an additional dollar in a bag of a hundred dollars?

No, certainly if the borrower puts the bag of one hundred dollars on the shelf. In such a case, neither the plane nor the sack of corn would reproduce themselves. But it is not for the sake of leaving the money in the bag, nor the plane on the shelf, that they are borrowed. The plane is borrowed to be used, or the money to procure a plane. And if it is clearly proved that this tool enables the borrower to obtain profits he could not have made without it; if it is proved that the lender has given up the opportunity of creating for himself this excess of profits, we may understand how the stipulation of a part of this excess of profits in favor of the lender is equitable and lawful.

Ignorance of the true part money plays in human transactions is the source of the most fatal errors. From what we may infer from the writings of Mr. Proudhon, that which has led him to think that gratuitous credit was a logical and definite consequence of social progress, is the observation of the phenomenon that interest seems to decrease almost in direct proportion to the progress of civilization. In barbarous times it is, in fact, a hundred percent, and more. Then it descends to eighty, sixty, fifty, forty, twenty, ten, eight, five, four and three percent. In Holland, it has even been as low as two percent. Hence it is concluded that "in proportion as society comes to perfection, the rate of interest will diminish and finally run down to zero, or nothing, by the time civilization is complete. In other words, that which characterizes social perfection is the gratuitousness of credit. When, therefore, we shall have abolished interest, we shall have reached the last step of progress." This is mere sophistry, and as such false arguing may contribute to render popular the unjust, dangerous, and destructive dogma that credit should be gratuitous, by representing it as coincident with social perfection, with the reader's permission I will examine in a few words this new view of the question.

7. What Regulates Interest?

What is *interest*? It is the service rendered, after a free bargain, by the borrower to the lender, in remuneration for the service he has received by or from the loan. By what law is the rate of these remunerative services established? By the general law that regulates the equivalent of all services; that is, by the law of supply and demand.

The more easily a thing is procured, the smaller is the service rendered by yielding it or lending it. The man who gives me a glass of water among the springs of the mountains does not render me so great a service as he who allows me one in the desert of Sahara. If there are many planes, sacks of corn, or houses, in a country, the use of them is obtained, other things being equal, on more favorable conditions than if they were few, for the simple reason that the lender renders in this case a smaller *relative service*.

It is not surprising, therefore, that the more abundant capital is, the lower is the interest. Is this saying that it will ever reach zero? No; because, I repeat it, the principle of a remuneration is in the loan. To say that interest will be annihilated, is to say that there will never be any motive for saving, for denying ourselves, in order to form new capitals, nor even to preserve the old ones. In this case, the waste would immediately create a void, and interest would soon reappear.

In that, the nature of the services of which we are speaking does not differ from any other. Thanks to industrial progress, a pair of stockings, which used to be worth six shillings, has successively been worth only four, three, and two. No one can say to what point this value will descend; but we can affirm that it will never reach zero, unless the stockings finish by producing themselves spontaneously. Why? Because the principle of remuneration is in labor; because he who works for another renders a service, and ought to receive a service. If no one paid for stockings they would cease to be made; and, with the scarcity, the price would not fail to reappear.

The sophism I am now combating has its root in the infinite divisibility that belongs to *value*, as it does to matter.

It may appear at first paradoxical, but it is well known to all mathematicians, that, through all eternity, fractions may be taken from a weight without the weight ever being annihilated. It is sufficient that each successive fraction be less than the preceding one, in a determined and regular proportion.

There are countries where people apply themselves to increasing the size of horses, or diminishing in sheep the size of the head. It is impossible to say precisely to what point they will arrive in this. No one can say that he has seen the largest horse or the smallest sheep's head that will ever appear in the world. But he may safely say that the size of horses will never attain to infinity, nor the heads of sheep be reduced to nothing. In the same way, no one can say to what point the price of stockings nor the interest of capital will come down; but we may safely affirm, when we know the nature of things, that neither the one nor the other will ever arrive at zero, for labor and capital can no more live without recompense than a sheep without a head. The arguments of Mr. Proudhon reduce themselves, then, to this: Since the most skillful agriculturists are those who have reduced the heads of sheep to the smallest size, we shall have arrived at the highest agricultural perfection when sheep have no longer any heads. Therefore, in order to realize the perfection, let us behead them.

I have now done with this wearisome discussion. Why is it that the breath of false doctrine has made it needful to inquire into the innate nature of interest? I must not leave off without remarking upon a beautiful moral which may be drawn from this law: "The reduction in the rate of interest is proportional to the abundance of capital." This law being granted, if there is a class of men to whom it is more important than to any other that stocks of capital should accumulate, multiply, abound, and superabound, it is certainly the class that borrows capital directly or indirectly; it is those men who operate upon *materials*, who gain assistance by *tools*, who live upon accumulations produced and saved by other men.

Imagine, in a vast and fertile country, a population of a thousand inhabitants, destitute of all capital as thus defined. It will assuredly perish by the pangs of hunger. Let us suppose a case hardly less cruel. Let us suppose that ten of these savages (for persons without capital are savages) are provided with tools and provisions sufficient to work and to live themselves until harvest time, as well as to remunerate the services of ninety laborers. The inevitable result will be the death of nine hundred human beings. It is clear, then, that since 990 men, urged by want, will crowd upon the supports that would only maintain a hundred, the ten capitalists will be masters of the market. They will obtain labor on the hardest conditions, for they will put it up to auction or the highest bidder. And observe this—if these capitalists entertain such pious sentiments as would induce them to impose personal privations on themselves, in order to diminish the sufferings of some of their brethren, this generosity, which attaches to morality, will be as noble in its principle as useful in its effects. But if, duped by that false philosophy that persons wish so inconsiderately to mingle with economic laws, they take to remunerating labor in excess of what it is worth, and in excess of what they are able to pay, far from doing good, they will do harm. They will give double wages, it may be. But then, forty-five men will be better provided for, while forty-five others from the diminution in the supply of capital, will augment the number of those who are sinking into the grave. Upon this supposition, it is not the deprivation of wages that primarily works the mischief, but the scarcity of capital. Low wages are not the cause, but the effect of the evil. I may add that they are to a certain extent the remedy. It acts in this way: it distributes the burden of suffering as much as it can, and saves as many lives as a limited quantity of available sustenance permits.

Suppose now, that instead of ten capitalists, there should be a hundred, two hundred, five hundred—is it not evident that the condition of the whole population, and, above all, that of the mass of the people will be more and more improved? Is it not evident that, apart from every consideration of generosity, they would obtain more work and better pay for it?—that they themselves will be in a better condition to accumulate capital, without being able to fix the limits to this ever-increasing facility of realizing equality and well-being? Would it not be madness in them to accept and act upon the truth of such doctrines as Proudhon and John Ruskin teach, and to act in a way that would reduce the source of wages, and paralyze the activity and stimulus of saving? Let them learn this lesson, then. Accumulations of capital are good for those who possess them: who denies it? But they are also useful to those who have not yet been able to form them; and it is important to those who have them not that others should have them.

Yes, if the laboring classes knew their true interests, they would seek to know with the greatest earnestness what circumstances are, and what are not favorable to saving, in order to encourage the former and to discourage the latter. They would sympathize with every measure that encourages the rapid accumulation of capital. They would be enthusiastic promoters of peace, liberty, order, security; the unity of classes and peoples, economy, moderation in public expenses, simplicity in the machinery of government; for it is under the sway of all these circumstances that saving does its work, brings plenty within the reach of the masses, invites those persons to become the owners of capital who were formerly under the necessity of borrowing under hard terms. They would repel with energy the war-like spirit, which diverts from its true course so large a part of human labor; the monopolizing spirit, that deranges the equitable distribution of riches, in the way by which liberty alone can realize it; the multitude of public services which attack our purses only to check our liberty; and, in short, those subversive, hateful, thoughtless doctrines, that alarm capital, prevent its formation, oblige it to flee, and finally to raise its price, to the especial disadvantage of the workers, who bring it into existence.

Take for example the revolution that overthrew the government of France, and disturbed society in February, 1848, is it not
a hard lesson? Is it not evident that the insecurity it has thrown
into the world of business on the one hand; and, on the other, the
advancement of the fatal theories to which I have alluded, and
which, from the clubs, have almost penetrated into the regions of
the legislature, have everywhere raised the rate of interest? Is it
not evident that from that time the laboring classes of France have
found greater difficulty in procuring those materials, tools, and
provisions, without which labor is impossible? Is it not that which
has caused stagnation of business; and does not paralysis of industry in turn lower wages? Thus there is a deficiency of work to
those who need to labor, from the same cause that loads the
objects they consume with an increase of price, in consequence of
the rise of interest. High interest and low wages signify in other
words that the same article preserves its price, but that the remuneration of the capitalist has invaded, without profiting himself,
that of the workman.

A friend of mine, commissioned to make inquiry into Parisian
industry, has assured me that the manufacturers have revealed to
him a very striking fact that proves, better than any reasoning can,
how much insecurity and uncertainty injure the formation of capital. It was noted that during the most distressing period of this
revolution the popular expenditures for personal gratification did
not diminish. The small theatres, the public-houses, and tobacco
depots, were as much frequented as in prosperous times. On
inquiry, the operatives themselves explained this phenomenon as
follows: "What is the use of economizing? Who knows what will
happen to us? Who knows that interest will not be abolished?
Who knows but that the State will become a universal and gratuitous lender, and that it will annihilate all the fruits that we might
expect from our savings?" Well! I say that if such ideas could prevail during two single years, it would be enough to turn our beautiful France into a Turkey—misery would become general and
endemic, and, most assuredly, the poor would be the first upon
whom it would fall.

Laboring men! They talk to you a great deal of the *artificial* organization of labor; do you know why they do so? Because they are ignorant of the laws of its *natural* organization; that is, of the wonderful organization that results from liberty. You are told that liberty gives rise to what is called the radical antagonism of classes; that it creates, and makes to clash, two opposite interests—that of the capitalists and that of the laborers. But we ought to begin by proving that the antagonism exists *by* a law of nature; and afterwards it would remain to be shown how far the arrangements for intervention are superior to those of liberty, for between liberty and intervention I see no middle path. Again, it would remain to be proved that intervention would always operate to your advantage, and to the prejudice of the rich. But, no; this radical antagonism, this natural opposition of interests, does not exist. It is only an evil dream of perverted and intoxicated imaginations. No; a plan so defective has not proceeded from the Divine Mind. To affirm it, we must begin by denying the existence of God. And see how, by means of social laws, and because men exchange amongst themselves their labors and their products, a harmonious tie attaches the different classes of society one to the other! There are the landowners; what is their interest? That the soil be fertile, and the sun beneficent: and what is the result? That wheat abounds, that it falls in price, and the advantage turns to the profit of those who have had no patrimony. There are the manufacturers—what is their constant thought? To perfect their labor, to increase the power of their machines, to procure for themselves, upon the best terms, the raw material. And to what does all this tend? To the abundance and the low price of produce; that is, all the efforts of the manufacturers, and without their suspecting it, result in a profit to the public consumer, of which each of you is one. It is the same with every profession. Now, the capitalists are not exempt from this law. They are very busy making schemes, economizing, and turning them to their advantage. This is all very well; but the more they succeed, the more do they promote the abundance of capital, and, as a necessary consequence, the reduction of interest. Now, who is it that profits by the reduction of interest? Is it not the borrower first, and finally, the consumers of the things the capital contributes to produce?

It is therefore certain that the final result of the efforts of each class is the common good of all.

You are told that capital tyrannizes over labor. I do not deny that each one endeavors to draw the greatest possible advantage from his situation; but in this sense, he realizes only that which is possible. Now, it is never more possible for capitalists to tyrannize over labor, than when capital is scarce; for then it is they who make the law—it is they who regulate the rate of sale. Never is this tyranny more impossible to them than when capital and capitalists are abundant; for in that case, it is labor which has the command. [Where there is one to sell and two to buy, the seller fixes the price; where there are two to sell and one to buy, the buyer always has the advantage.—*Editor.*]

Away, then, with the jealousies of classes, ill-will, unfounded hatreds, unjust suspicions. These depraved passions injure those who nourish them in their heart. This is no declamatory morality; it is a chain of causes and effects, which is capable of being rigorously, mathematically demonstrated. It is not the less sublime in that it satisfies the intellect as well as the feelings.

I shall sum up this whole dissertation with these words: Workmen, laborers, destitute and suffering classes, will you improve your condition? You will not succeed by strife, insurrection, hatred, and error. But there are three things that always result in benefit and blessing to every community and to every individual who helps to compose it; and these things are—peace, liberty, and security.

VI.

ECONOMIC SOPHISMS— FIRST SERIES

INTRODUCTION[1]

My design in this little volume is to refute some of the arguments that are urged against the Freedom of Trade.

I do not propose to engage in a contest with the protectionists; but rather to instill a principle into the minds of those who hesitate because they sincerely doubt.

I am not one of those who say that Protection is founded on men's interests. I am of the opinion rather that it is founded on errors, or, if you will, upon incomplete truths. Too many people fear liberty to permit us to conclude that their apprehensions are not sincerely felt.

It is perhaps aiming too high, but my wish is, I confess, that this little work should become, as it were, the Manual of those whose business it is to pronounce between the two principles. Where men have not been long accustomed and familiarized to the doctrine of liberty, the fallacies of protection, in one shape or another, are constantly coming back upon them. In order to disabuse them of such errors when they recur, a long process of

---

[1]The first series of the *Sophismes Economiques* appeared at the end of 1845; the second series in 1848.

analysis becomes necessary; and everyone has not the time required for such a process—legislators less than others. This is my reason for endeavoring to present the analysis and its results cut and dried.

But it may be asked: Are the benefits of liberty so hidden as to be discovered only by professional Economists?

We must confess that our adversaries have a marked advantage over us in the discussion. In very few words they can announce a half-truth; and in order to demonstrate that it is incomplete, we are obliged to have recourse to long and dry dissertations.

This arises from the nature of things. Protection concentrates on one point the good which it produces, while the evils it inflicts are spread over the masses. The one is visible to the naked eye; the other only to the eye of the mind. In the case of liberty, it is just the reverse.

In the treatment of almost all economic questions we find it to be so.

You say: Here is a machine that has turned thirty workmen onto the street.

Or: Here is a spendthrift who encourages every branch of industry.

Or: The conquest of Algeria has doubled the trade of Marseilles.

Or: The budget secures subsistence for a hundred thousand families.

You are understood at once and by all. Your propositions are in themselves clear, simple, and true. What are your deductions from them?

Machinery is an evil.

Luxury, conquests, and heavy taxation are productive of good.

And your theory receives wide support in that you are in a situation to support it by reference to undoubted facts.

On our side, we must decline to confine our attention to the cause and its direct and immediate effect. We know that this very effect in its turn becomes a cause. To judge correctly of a measure, then, we must trace it through the whole chain of effects to its final result. In other words, we are forced to reason upon it.

But then clamour gets up: You are theorists, metaphysicians, idealists, Utopian dreamers, doctrinarians; and all the prejudices of the popular mind are roused against us.

What, under such circumstances, are we to do? We can only invoke the patience and good sense of the reader, and set our deductions, if we can, in a light so clear that truth and error must show themselves plainly, openly, and without disguise; and that the victory, once gained, may remain on the side of intervention or on that of freedom.

And here I must set down an essential observation.

Some extracts from this little volume have already appeared in the *Journal des Economistes*.

In a criticism, in other respects very favorable, from the pen of Viscount de Romanet, he supposes that I demand the suppression of customs. He is mistaken. I demand the suppression of the protectionist system. We don't refuse taxes to the Government, but we desire, if possible, to dissuade the governed from taxing one another. Napoleon said that "the customhouse should not be made an instrument of revenue, but a means of protecting industry." We maintain the contrary, and we contend that the customhouse ought not to become in the hands of the working classes an instrument of reciprocal rapine, but that it may be used as an instrument of revenue as legitimately as any other. So far are we—or, to speak only for myself, so far am I—from demanding the suppression of customs, that I see in that branch of revenue our future anchor of safety. I believe our resources are capable of yielding to the Treasury immense returns; and, to speak plainly, I must add that, seeing how slow is the spread of sound economic doctrines, and so rapid the increase of our budgets, I am disposed to count more upon the necessities of the Treasury than on the force of enlightened opinion for furthering the cause of commercial reform.

You ask me, then: What is your conclusion? And I reply, that here there is no need to arrive at a conclusion. I combat fallacies; that is all.

But you rejoin that it is not enough to pull down—it is also necessary to build up. True; but to destroy an error is to build up the truth that stands opposed to it.

After all, I have no repugnance to declare what my wishes are. I desire to see public opinion led to sanction a law of customs conceived nearly in these terms—

Articles of primary necessity to pay a duty, *ad valorem*, of 5 percent. Articles of convenience, 10 percent.

Articles of luxury, 15 to 20 percent.

These distinctions, I am aware, belong to an order of ideas that are quite foreign to Political Economy strictly so called, and I am far from thinking them as just and useful as they are commonly supposed to be. But this subject does not fall within the compass of my present design.

1

Abundance—Scarcity

Which is best for man and for society, abundance or scarcity? What! you exclaim, can that be a question? Has anyone ever asserted, or is it possible to maintain, that scarcity is at the foundation of human well-being?

Yes, this has been asserted, and is maintained every day; and I do not hesitate to affirm that the theory of scarcity is the most popular by far. It is the life of conversation, of the newspapers, of books, and of political oratory; and, strange as it may seem, it is certain that Political Economy will have fulfilled its practical mission when it has established beyond question, and widely disseminated, this very simple proposition: "The wealth of men consists in the abundance of commodities."

Do we not hear it said every day: "The foreigner is about to inundate us with his products?" Then we fear abundance.

Did not Mr. Saint-Cricq exclaim: "Production is excessive"? Then he feared abundance.

Do workmen break machines? Then they fear an excess of production, or abundance.

Has not Mr. Bugeaud pronounced these words: "Let bread be dear, and agriculturists will get rich"? Now, bread can only be dear because it is scarce. Therefore Mr. Bugeaud extols scarcity.

Does not Mr. d'Argout urge as an argument against sugar-growing the very productiveness of that industry? Does he not say: "Beetroot has no future, and its culture cannot be extended, because a few acres devoted to its culture in each department would supply the whole consumption of France"? Then, in his eyes, good lies in sterility, in dearth, and evil in fertility and abundance.

La Presse, *Le Commerce*, and the greater part of the daily papers, have one or more articles every morning to demonstrate to the Legislative Chamber and the Government that it is sound policy to raise legislatively the price of all things by means of tariffs. And do the Chamber and the Government not obey the injunction? Now tariffs can raise prices only by diminishing the supply of commodities in the market! Then the journals, the Chamber, and the Minister put into practice the theory of scarcity, and I am justified in saying that this theory is by far the most popular.

How does it happen that in the eyes of workmen, of publicists, and statesmen abundance should appear a thing to be dreaded and scarcity advantageous? I propose to trace this illusion to its source.

We remark that a man grows richer in proportion to the return yielded by his exertions, that is to say, in proportion as he sells his commodity at a higher price. He sells at a higher price in proportion to the rarity, to the scarcity, of the article he produces. We conclude from this that, as far as he is concerned at least, scarcity enriches him. Applying successively the same reasoning to all other producers, we construct the theory of scarcity. We next proceed to apply this theory and, in order to favor producers generally, we raise prices artificially, and cause a scarcity of all commodities, by prohibition, by intervention, by the suppression of machinery, and other analogous means.

The same thing holds of abundance. We observe that when a product is plentiful, it sells at a lower price, and the producer gains less. If all producers are in the same situation, they are all poor. Therefore it is abundance that ruins society. And as theories are soon reduced to practice, we see the law struggling against the abundance of commodities.

This fallacy in its more general form may make little impression, but applied to a particular order of facts, to a certain branch of industry, to a given class of producers, it is extremely specious; and this is easily explained. It forms a syllogism that is not false, but incomplete. Now, what is true in a syllogism is always and necessarily present to the mind. But incompleteness is a negative quality, an absent datum, which it is very possible, and indeed very easy, to leave out of account.

Man produces in order to consume. He is at once producer and consumer. The reasoning I have just explained considers him only in the first of these points of view. Had the second been taken into account, it would have led to an opposite conclusion. In effect, may it not be said:

The consumer is richer in proportion as he purchases all things cheaper; and he purchases things cheaper in proportion to their abundance; therefore it is abundance that enriches him. This reasoning, extended to all consumers, leads to the theory of plenty.

It is the notion of exchange imperfectly understood that leads to these illusions. If we consider our personal interest, we recognize distinctly that it is two-sided. As sellers we have an interest in dearness, and consequently in scarcity; as buyers, in cheapness, or what amounts to the same thing, in the abundance of commodities. We cannot, then, found our reasoning on one or the other of these interests before inquiring which of the two coincides and is identified with the general and permanent interest of mankind at large.

If man were a solitary animal, if he labored exclusively for himself, if he consumed directly the fruit of his labor—in a word, if he did not exchange—the theory of scarcity would never have appeared in the world. It is too evident that in that case, abundance would be advantageous, from whatever quarter it came, whether from the result of his industry, from ingenious tools, from powerful machinery of his invention, or whether due to the fertility of the soil, the liberality of nature, or even to a mysterious invasion of products brought by the waves and left by them upon the shore. No solitary man would ever have thought that in order to encourage his labor and render it more productive, it was necessary to break in pieces the instruments that lessened it, to neutralize the fertility of the soil, or give back to the sea the good things it had brought to his door. He would perceive at once that labor is not an end, but a means; and that it would be absurd to reject the result for fear of doing injury to the means by which the result was accomplished. He would perceive that if he devotes two hours a day to providing for his wants, any circumstance (machinery, fertility, gratuitous gift, no matter what) that saves him an hour of that labor, the result remaining the same, puts that hour at his disposal, and that he can devote it to increasing his enjoyments; in short, he would see that to save labor is nothing else than progress.

But exchange disturbs our view of a truth so simple. In the social state, and with the separation of employments to which it leads, the production and consumption of a commodity are not mixed up and confounded in the same individual. Each man comes to see in his labor no longer a means but an end. In relation to each commodity, exchange creates two interests, that of the producer and that of the consumer; and these two interests are always directly opposed to each other.

It is essential to analyze them, and examine their nature.

Take the case of any producer whatever, what is his immediate interest? It consists of two things; first, that the fewest possible number of persons should devote themselves to his branch of industry; second, that the greatest possible number of persons should be in quest of the article he produces. Political economy explains it more succinctly in these terms: Supply very limited, demand very extended; or, in other words still, Competition limited, demand unlimited.

What is the immediate interest of the consumer? That the supply of the product in question should be extended, and the demand restrained.

Seeing, then, that these two interests are in opposition to each other, one of them must necessarily coincide with social interests in general, and the other be antagonistic to them.

But which of them should legislation favor, as identical with the public good—if, indeed, it should favor either?

To discover this, we must inquire what would happen if the secret wishes of men were granted.

In as far as we are producers, it must be allowed that the desire of every one of us is antisocial. Are we vinedressers? It would give us no great regret if hail should shower down on all the vines in the world except our own: this is the theory of scarcity. Are we iron-masters? Our wish is that there should be no other iron in the market but our own, however much the public may be in want of it; and for no other reason than this want, keenly felt and imperfectly satisfied, shall ensure us a higher price: this is still the theory of scarcity. Are we farmers? We say with Mr. Bugeaud: Let bread be dear, that is to say, scarce, and agriculturists will thrive: always the same theory, the theory of scarcity.

Are we physicians? We cannot avoid seeing that certain physical ameliorations, improving the sanitary state of the country, the development of certain moral virtues, such as moderation and temperance, the progress of knowledge tending to enable each man to take better care of his own health, the discovery of certain simple remedies of easy application, would be so many blows to our professional success. In so far as we are physicians, then, our secret wishes would be antisocial. I do not say that physicians form these secret wishes. On the contrary, I believe they would hail with joy the discovery of a universal panacea; but they would not do this as physicians, but as men and as Christians. By a noble abnegation of self, the physician places himself in the consumer's point of view. But as practicing a profession, from which he derives his own and his family's subsistence, his desires, or, if you will, his interests, are antisocial.

Are we manufacturers of cotton goods? We desire to sell them at the price most profitable to ourselves. We should consent willingly to an interdict being laid on all rival manufactures; and if we could venture to give this wish public expression, or hope to realize it with some chance of success, we should attain our end, to some extent by indirect means; for example, by excluding foreign fabrics in order to diminish the supply, and thus produce, forcibly and to our profit, a scarcity of clothing.

In the same way, we might pass in review all other branches of industry, and we should always find that the producers, as such, have antisocial views. "The shopkeeper," says Montaigne, "thrives only by the irregularities of youth; the farmer by the high price of corn, the architect by the destruction of houses, the officers of justice by lawsuits and quarrels. Ministers of religion derive their distinction and employment from our vices and our death. No physician rejoices in the health of his friends, nor soldiers in the peace of their country; and so of the rest."

Hence it follows that if the secret wishes of each producer were realized, the world would retrograde rapidly toward barbarism. The sail would supersede steam, the oar would supersede the sail, and general traffic would be carried on by the carrier's wagon; the latter would be superseded by the mule, and the mule by the peddler. Wool would exclude cotton, cotton in its turn would exclude wool, and so on until the dearth of all things had caused man himself to disappear from the face of the earth.

Suppose for a moment that the legislative power and the public force were placed at the disposal of Mineral's committee, and that each member of that association had the privilege of bringing in and sanctioning a favorite law, is it difficult to divine to what sort of industrial code the public would be subjected?

If we now proceed to consider the immediate interest of the consumer, we shall find that it is in perfect harmony with the general interest, with all that the welfare of society calls for. When the purchaser goes to market he desires to find it well stocked. Let the seasons be propitious for all harvests; let inventions, more and more marvellous, bring within reach a greater and greater number of products and enjoyments; let time and labor be saved; let distances be effaced by the perfection and rapidity of transit; let the spirit of justice and of peace allow of a diminished weight of taxation; let barriers of every kind be removed—in all this the interest of the consumer runs parallel with the public interest. The consumer may push his secret wishes to a chimerical and absurd length, without these wishes becoming antagonistic to the public welfare. He may desire that food and shelter, the hearth and the roof, instruction and morality, security and peace, power and health, should be obtained without exertion and without measure, like the dust of the highways, the water of the brook, the air that we breathe; and yet the realization of his desires would not be at variance with the good of society.

It might be said that, if these wishes were granted, the work of the producer would become more and more limited, and would end with being stopped for want of sustenance. But why? Because on this extreme supposition, all imaginable wants and desires would be fully satisfied. Man, like Omnipotence, would create all things by a simple act of volition. Well, on this hypothesis, what reason should we have to regret the stoppage of industrial production?

I made the supposition not long ago of the existence of an assembly composed of workmen, each member of which, in his capacity of producer, should have the power of passing a law embodying his secret wish, and I said that the code that would emanate from that assembly would be monopoly systematized, the theory of scarcity reduced to practice.

In the same way, a chamber in which each should consult exclusively his own immediate interest as a consumer, would tend to systematize liberty, to suppress all restrictive measures, to overthrow all artificial barriers—in a word, to realize the theory of plenty.

Hence it follows:

That to consult exclusively the immediate interest of the producer is to consult an interest that is antisocial;

That to take for basis exclusively the immediate interest of the consumer would be to take for basis the general interest.

Let me enlarge on this view of the subject a little, at the risk of being prolix.

A radical antagonism exists between seller and buyer.

The former desires that the subject of the bargain should be scarce, its supply limited, and its price high.

The latter desires that it should be abundant, its supply large, and its price low.

The laws, which should be at least neutral, take the part of the seller against the buyer, of the producer against the consumer, of dearness against cheapness, of scarcity against abundance.

They proceed, if not intentionally, at least logically, on this datum: a nation is rich when it is in want of everything.

For they say, it is the producer that we must favor by securing him a good market for his product. For this purpose it is necessary to raise the price, and in order to raise the price we must restrict the supply; and to restrict the supply is to create scarcity.

Just let us suppose that at the present moment, when all these laws are in full force, we make a complete inventory, not in value but in weight, measure, volume, quantity, of all the commodities existing in the country, that are fitted to satisfy the wants and tastes of its inhabitants—corn, meat, cloth, fuel, colonial products, etc.

Suppose, again, that next day all the barriers that oppose the introduction of foreign products are removed.

Lastly, suppose that in order to test the result of this reform they proceed three months afterwards to make a new inventory.

Is it not true that there will be found in France more corn, cattle, cloth, linen, iron, coal, sugar, etc., at the date of the second than at the date of the first inventory?

So true is this that our protective tariffs have no other purpose than to hinder all these things from reaching us, to restrict the supply, and prevent low prices and abundance.

Now I would ask, Are the people who live under our laws better fed because there is less bread, meat, and sugar in the country? Are they better clothed because there is less cloth and linen? Better warmed because there is less coal? Better assisted in their labor because there are fewer tools and less iron, copper, and machinery?

But it may be said, If the foreigner inundates us with his products he will carry away our money.

And what does it matter? Men are not fed on money. They do not clothe themselves with gold, or warm themselves with silver. What does it matter whether there is more or less money in the country if there is more bread on our sideboards, more meat in our larders, more linen in our wardrobes, more firewood in our cellars.

Restrictive laws always land us in this dilemma: Either you admit that they produce scarcity, or you do not. If you admit it, you avow by the admission that you inflict on the people all the injury in your power. If you do not admit it, you deny having restricted the supply and raised prices, and consequently you deny having favored the producer.

What you do is either hurtful or profitless, injurious or ineffectual. It never can bring any useful result.

2

OBSTACLE—CAUSE

The obstacle mistaken for the cause—scarcity mistaken for abundance—this is the same fallacy under another aspect; and it is well to study it in all its phases.

Man is originally destitute of everything.

Between this destitution and the satisfaction of his wants there exist a multitude of obstacles that labor enables us to surmount. It is of interest to inquire how and why these very obstacles to his material prosperity have come to be mistaken for the cause of that prosperity.

I want to travel a hundred miles. But between the starting-point and the place of my destination, mountains, rivers, marshes, impenetrable forests, brigands—in a word, obstacles—interpose themselves; and to overcome these obstacles it is necessary for me to employ many efforts, or, what comes to the same thing, that others should employ many efforts for me, the price of which I must pay them. It is clear that I should have been in a better situation if these obstacles had not existed.

On his long journey through life, from the cradle to the grave, man has need to assimilate to himself a prodigious quantity of alimentary substances, to protect himself against the inclemency of the weather, to preserve himself from a number of ailments, or cure himself of them. Hunger, thirst, disease, heat, cold, are so many obstacles strewn along his path. In a state of isolation he must overcome them all by hunting, fishing, tillage, spinning, weaving, building; and it is clear that it would be better for him that these obstacles were less numerous and formidable, or, better still, that they did not exist at all. In society he does not combat these obstacles personally, but others do it for him; and in return he employs himself in removing one of those obstacles that are encountered by his fellow men.

It is clear also, considering things in the gross, that it would be better for men in the aggregate, or for society, that these obstacles should be as few and feeble as possible.

But when we come to scrutinize the social phenomena in detail, and men's sentiments as modified by the introduction of exchange, we soon perceive how men have come to confound wants with wealth, the obstacle with the cause.

The separation of employments, the division of labor, which results from the faculty of exchanging, causes each man, instead of struggling on his own account to overcome all the obstacles that surround him, to combat only one of them; he overcomes that one not for himself but for his fellow men, who in turn render him the same service.

The consequence is that this man, in combating this obstacle that it is his special business to overcome for the sake of others, sees in it the immediate source of his own wealth. The greater, the more formidable, the more keenly felt this obstacle is, the greater will be the remuneration that his fellow men will be disposed to accord him; that is to say, the more ready will they be to remove the obstacles that stand in his way.

The physician, for example, does not bake his own bread, or manufacture his own instruments, or weave or make his own coat. Others do these things for him, and in return he treats the diseases with which his patients are afflicted. The more numerous, severe, and frequent these diseases are, the more others consent, and are obliged, to do for his personal comfort. Regarding it from this point of view, disease, that general obstacle to human happiness, becomes a cause of material prosperity to the individual physician. The same argument applies to all producers in their several departments. The shipowner derives his profits from the obstacle called distance; the agriculturist from that called hunger; the manufacturer of cloth from that called cold; the schoolmaster lives upon ignorance; the lapidary upon vanity; the attorney on cupidity; the notary upon possible bad faith—just as the physician lives upon the diseases of men. It is quite true, therefore, that each profession has an immediate interest in the continuation, nay, in the extension, of the special obstacle which it is its business to combat.

Observing this, theorists make their appearance, and, founding a system on their individual sentiments, tell us: Want is wealth, labor is wealth, obstacles to material prosperity are prosperity. To multiply obstacles is to support industry.

Then statesmen intervene. They have the disposal of the public force; and what more natural than to make it available for developing and multiplying obstacles, since this is developing and multiplying wealth? They say, for example: If we prevent the importation of iron from places where it is abundant, we place an obstacle in the way of its being procured. This obstacle, keenly felt at home, will induce men to pay in order to be set free from it. A certain number of our fellow citizens will devote themselves to combating it, and this obstacle will make their fortune. The greater the obstacle is—that is, the scarcer, the more inaccessible, the more difficult to transport, the more distant from the place where it is to be used, the mineral sought for becomes—the more hands will be engaged in the various ramifications of this branch of industry. Exclude, then, foreign iron, create an obstacle, for you thereby create the work that is to overcome it.

The same reasoning leads to the proscription of machinery.

Here, for instance, are men who are in want of casks for the storage of their wine. This is an obstacle; and here are other men whose business it is to remove that obstacle by making the casks that are wanted. It is fortunate, then, that this obstacle should exist, since it gives employment to a branch of national industry, and enriches a certain number of our fellow citizens. But then we have ingenious machinery invented for felling the oak, cutting it up into staves, and forming them into the wine-casks that are wanted. By this means the obstacle is lessened, and so are the gains of the cooper. Let us maintain both at their former elevation by a law, and ban the machinery.

To get at the root of this sophism it is necessary only to reflect that human labor is not the end, but the means. It never remains unemployed. If one obstacle is removed, it does battle with another; and society is freed from two obstacles by the same amount of labor that was formerly required for the removal of one. If the labor of the cooper is rendered unnecessary in one department, it will soon take another direction. But how and from what source will it be remunerated? From the same source exactly from which it is remunerated at present; for when a certain amount of labor becomes disposable by the removal of an obstacle, a corresponding amount of remuneration becomes disposable also. To maintain that human labor will ever come to want employment, would be to maintain that the human race will cease to encounter obstacles. In that case labor would not only be impossible; it would be superfluous. We should no longer have anything to do, because we should be omnipotent; and we should only have to pronounce our fiat in order to ensure the satisfaction of all our desires and the supply of all our wants.

3

EFFORT—RESULT

We have just seen that between our wants and the satisfaction of these wants, obstacles are interposed. We succeed in overcoming these obstacles, or in diminishing their force, by the employment of our faculties. We may say, in a general way, that industry is an effort followed by a result.

But what constitutes the measure of our prosperity, or of our wealth? Is it the result of the effort? Or is it the effort itself? A relation always subsists between the effort employed and the result obtained. Progress consists in the relative enhancement of the second or of the first term of this relation.

Both theses have been maintained; and in political economy they have divided the region of opinion and of thought.

According to the first system, wealth is the result of labor, increasing as the relative proportion of result to effort increases. Absolute perfection, of which God is the type, consists in the infinite distance interposed between the two terms—in this sense, effort is nil, result infinite.

The second system teaches that it is the effort itself that constitutes the measure of wealth. To make progress is to increase the relative proportion which effort bears to result. The ideal of this system may be found in the sterile and eternal efforts of Sisyphus.[1]

The first system naturally welcomes everything which tends to diminish pains and augment products; powerful machinery that increases the forces of man, exchange that allows him to derive greater advantage from natural resources distributed in various proportions over the face of the earth, intelligence that discovers, experience that proves, competition that stimulates, etc.

Logically, the second invokes everything which has the effect of increasing pains and diminishing products; privileges, monopolies, restrictions, prohibitions, suppression of machinery, barrenness, etc.

It is well to remark that the universal practice of mankind always points to the principle of the first system. We have never seen, we shall never see, a man who labors in any department, be he agriculturist, manufacturer, merchant, artificer, soldier, author, or philosopher, who does not devote all the powers of his mind to work better, to work with more rapidity, to work more economically—in a word, to effect more with less.

The opposite doctrine is in favor only with theorists, legislators, journalists, statesmen, ministers—men, in short, born to make experiments on the social body.

At the same time, we may observe that in what concerns themselves personally they act as everyone else does, on the

---

[1]For this reason, and for the sake of conciseness, the reader will pardon us for designating this system in the sequel by the name of sisyphism. (Sisyphus in Greek mythology was condemned, as a punishment for his wickedness in this life, to roll a large stone from the bottom to the top of a high hill, which, whenever it reached the top, rolled down again, and thus made his task unending.)

principle of obtaining from labor the greatest possible amount of useful results.

Perhaps I may be thought to exaggerate, and there are no true sisyphists.

If it be argued that in practice they do not press their principle to its most extreme consequences, I willingly grant it. This is always the case when one sets out with a false principle. Such a principle soon leads to results so absurd and so mischievous that we are obliged to stop short. This is the reason why practical industry never admits sisyphism; punishment would follow error too closely not to expose it. But in matters of speculation, such as theorists and statesmen deal in, one may pursue a false principle a long time before discovering its falsity by the complicated consequences to which men were formerly strangers; and when at last its falsity is found out, the authors take refuge in the opposite principle, turn round, contradict themselves, and seek their justification in a modern maxim of incomparable absurdity: in political economy there is no inflexible rule, no absolute principle.

Let us see, then, if these two opposite principles that I have just described do not predominate by turns, the one in practical industry, the other in industrial legislation.

I have already noticed the saying of Mr. Bugeaud that "when bread is dear agriculturists become rich"; but in Mr. Bugeaud are embodied two separate characters, the agriculturist and the legislator.

As an agriculturist, Mr. Bugeaud directs all his efforts to two ends—to save labor, and obtain cheap bread. When he prefers a good plough to a bad one; when he improves his pastures; when, in order to pulverize the soil, he substitutes as much as possible the action of the weather for that of the harrow and the hoe; when he calls to his aid all the processes of which science and experiment have proved the efficacy—he has but one object in view, viz. to diminish the proportion of effort to result. We have indeed no other test of the ability of a cultivator, and the perfection of his processes, than to measure to what extent they have lessened the one and added to the other. And as all the farmers in the world act upon this principle we may assert that the effort of mankind at large is to obtain, for their own benefit undoubtedly, bread and all other products cheaper, to lessen the labor needed to procure a given quantity of what they want.

This incontestable tendency of mankind once established should, it would seem, reveal to the legislator the true principle, and point out to him in what way he should aid industry (in so far as it falls within his province to aid it); for it would be absurd to assert that human laws should run counter to the laws of Providence.

And yet we have heard Mr. Bugeaud, as a legislator, exclaim: "I understand nothing of this theory of cheapness; I should like better to see bread dearer and labor more abundant." And following out this doctrine, the representative of the Dordogne votes legislative measures, the effect of which is to hamper exchanges, for the very reason that they procure us indirectly what direct production could procure us only at greater expense.

Now, it is very evident that Mr. Bugeaud's principle as a legislator is directly opposed to the principle on which he acts as an agriculturist. To act consistently he should vote against all legislative restriction, or else import into his farming operations the principle that he proclaims from the tribune. We should then see him sow his corn in his most barren fields, for in this way he would succeed in working much to obtain little. We should see him throwing aside the plough, since hand-culture would satisfy his double wish for dearer bread and more abundant labor.

Intervention has for its avowed object, and its acknowledged effect, to increase labor.

It has also for its avowed object, and its acknowledged effect, to cause dearness, which means simply scarcity of products; so that, carried out to its extreme limits, it is pure sisyphism, such as we have defined it—labor infinite; product nil.

Baron Charles Dupin, the light of the peerage, it is said, on economic science, accuses railways of injuring navigation; and it is certain that it is of the nature of a better means of conveyance to reduce the use of a worse means of conveyance. But railways cannot hurt navigation except by attracting traffic; and they cannot attract traffic but by conveying goods and passengers more cheaply; and they cannot convey them more cheaply but by diminishing the proportion that the effort employed bears to the result obtained, seeing that that is the very thing that constitutes cheapness. When, then, Baron Dupin deplores this diminution of the labor employed to effect a given result, it is the doctrine of sisyphism he preaches. Logically, since he prefers the ship to the rail, he should prefer the cart to the ship, the pack-saddle to the cart, and the pannier to all other known means of conveyance, for it is the latter that exacts the most labor with the least result.

"Work constitutes the wealth of a people," said Mr. de Saint-Cricq, that Minister of Commerce who has imposed so many restrictions upon trade. We must not suppose that this was an elliptical expression, meaning, "The results of work constitute the wealth of a people." No, this economist distinctly intended to affirm that it is the intensity of labor that is the measure of wealth, and the proof of it is that, from consequence to consequence, from one restriction to another, he induced France (and in this he thought he was doing her good) to expend double the amount of labor, in order, for example, to provide herself with an equal quantity of iron. In England iron was then at eight francs, while in France it cost sixteen francs. Taking a day's labor at one franc, it is clear that France could, by means of exchange, procure a quintal of iron by subtracting eight days' work from the aggregate national labor. In consequence of the restrictive measures of Mr. de Saint-Cricq, France was obliged to expend sixteen days' labor in order to provide herself with a quintal of iron by direct production. Double the labor for the same satisfaction, hence double the wealth. Then it follows that wealth is not measured by the result, but by the intensity of the labor. Is not this sisyphism in all its purity?

And in order that there may be no mistake as to his meaning, the Minister takes care afterwards to explain more fully his ideas; and as he had just before called the intensity of labor wealth, he goes on to call the more abundant results of that labor, or the more abundant supply of things proper to satisfy our wants, poverty. "Everywhere," he says, "machinery has taken the place of manual labor; everywhere production superabounds; everywhere the equilibrium between the faculty of producing and the means of consuming is destroyed." We see, then, to what, in Mr. de Saint-Cricq's estimation, the critical situation of the country was owing: it was to having produced too much, and her labor being too intelligent, and too fruitful. We were too well fed, too well clothed, too well provided with everything; a too rapid production surpassed all our desires. It was necessary, then, to put a stop to the evil, and for that purpose to force us, by restrictions, to labor more in order to produce less.

I have referred likewise to the opinions of another Minister of Commerce, Mr. d'Argout. They deserve to be dwelt upon for an instant. Desiring to strike a formidable blow at beet-root culture, he says, "Undoubtedly, the cultivation of beet-root is useful, but this utility is limited. The developments attributed to it are exaggerated. To be convinced of this it is sufficient to observe that this culture will be necessarily confined within the limits of consumption. Double, triple, if you will, the present consumption of France, you will always find that a very trifling portion of the soil will satisfy the requirements of that consumption." (This is surely rather a singular subject of complaint!) "Do you desire proof of this? How many hectares had we under beet-root in 1828?—3,130, which is equivalent to 1-10540th of our arable land. At the present time, when indigenous sugar supplies one-third of our consumption, how much land is devoted to that culture?—16,700 hectares, or 1-1978th of the arable land, or 45 centiares in each commune. Suppose indigenous sugar already supplied our whole consumption we should have only 48,000 hectares under beet-root, or 1-689th of the arable land."[2]

There are two things to be remarked upon in this quotation—the facts and the doctrine. The facts tend to prove that little land,

---

[2]1 hectare = 2 acres, 1 rood, 35 perches.

little capital, and little labor are required to produce a large quantity of sugar, and that each commune of France would be abundantly provided by devoting to beet-root cultivation one hectare of its soil. The doctrine consists in regarding this circumstance as adverse, and in seeing in the very power and fertility of the new industry, a limit to its utility.

I do not mean to constitute myself here the defender of beet-root culture, or a judge of the strange facts advanced by Mr. d'Argout; but it is worthwhile to scrutinize the doctrine of a statesman to whom France for a long time entrusted the care of her agriculture and of her commerce.

I remarked at the outset that a variable relation exists between an industrial effort and its result; that absolute imperfection consists in an infinite effort without any result; absolute perfection in an unlimited result without any effort; and perfectibility in the progressive diminution of effort compared with the result.

But Mr. d'Argout tells us there is death where we think we perceive life, and that the importance of any branch of industry is in direct proportion to its powerlessness. What are we to expect, for instance, from the cultivation of beet-root? Do you not see that 48,000 hectares of land, with capital and manual labor in proportion, are sufficient to supply all France with sugar? Then, this is a branch of industry of limited utility; limited, of course, with reference to the amount of labor it demands, the only way in which, according to the ex-Minister, any branch of industry can be useful. This utility would be still more limited if, owing to the fertility of the soil and the richness of the beet-root, we could reap from 24,000 hectares what at present we only obtain from 48,000. Oh! Were only twenty times, a hundred times, more land, capital and labor necessary to yield us the same result, so much the better. We might build some hopes on this new branch of industry, and it would be worthy of state protection, for it would offer a vast field to our national industry. But to produce much with little! That is a bad example, and it is time for the law to interfere.

But what is true with regard to sugar cannot be otherwise with regard to bread. If, then, the utility of any branch of industry is to be estimated not by the amount of satisfaction it is fitted to procure us with a determinate amount of labor, but, on the contrary, by the amount of labor it exacts in order to yield us a determinate amount of satisfactions, what we ought evidently to desire is, that each acre of land should yield less corn, and each grain of corn less nourishment; in other words, that our land should be comparatively barren; for then the quantity of land, capital, and manual labor that would be required for the maintenance of our population would be much more considerable; we could then say that the demand for human labor would be in direct proportion to this barrenness. The aspirations of Misters Bugeaud, Saint-Cricq, Dupin, and d'Argout would then be satisfied; bread would be dear, labor abundant, and France rich—rich at least in the sense in which these gentlemen understand the word.

What we should desire also is that human intelligence should be enfeebled or extinguished; for as long as it survives, it will be continually endeavoring to augment the proportion that the end bears to the means, and that the product bears to the labor. It is in that precisely that intelligence consists.

Thus, it appears that sisyphism has been the doctrine of all the men who have been entrusted with our industrial destinies. It would be unfair to reproach them with it. This principle guides Ministers only because it is predominant in the Chambers; and it predominates in the Chambers only because it is sent there by the electoral body, and the electoral body is imbued with it only because public opinion is saturated with it.

I think it right to repeat here that I do not accuse men such as Misters Bugeaud, Dupin, Saint-Cricq, and d'Argout of being absolutely and under all circumstances sisyphists. They are certainly not so in their private transactions; for in these they always desire to obtain by way of exchange what would cost them dearer to procure by direct production; but I affirm they are sisyphists when they hinder the country from doing the same thing.

4

TO EQUALIZE THE CONDITIONS OF PRODUCTION

It has been said—but in case I should be accused of putting fallacies into the mouths of the protectionists, I shall allow one of their most vigorous champions to speak for them.

> It has been thought that protection in our case should simply represent the difference that exists between the cost price of a commodity that we produce and the cost price of the same commodity produced by our neighbors. . . . A protective duty calculated on this basis would only ensure free competition . . . free competition exists only when there is equality in the conditions and in the charges. In the case of a horse-race, we ascertain the weight each horse has to carry, and so Equalize the conditions; without that there could be no fair competition. In the case of trade, if one of the sellers can bring his commodity to market at less cost, he ceases to be a competitor, and becomes a monopolist. . . . Do away with this protection that represents the difference of cost

> price, and the foreigner invades our markets and acquires a
> monopoly.[1]

> Everyone must wish, for his own sake, as well as for the sake
> of others, that the production of the country should be pro-
> tected against foreign competition whenever the latter can
> furnish products at a lower price.[2]

This argument recurs continually in works of the protectionist school. I propose to examine it carefully, and I solicit earnestly
the reader's patience and attention. I shall consider, first of all,
the inequalities attributable to nature, and afterwards those which
are attributable to differences in taxation.

In this, as in other cases, we shall find protectionist theorists
viewing their subject from the producer's standpoint, while we
advocate the cause of the unfortunate consumers, whose interests
they studiously keep out of sight. They institute a comparison
between the field of industry and a horse race. But as regards the
latter, the race is at once the means and the end. The public feel
no interest in the competition beyond the competition itself.
When you start your horses, your end, your object, is to find out
which is the swiftest runner, and I see your reason for equalizing
the weights. But if your end, your object, were to secure the
arrival of some important and urgent news at the finish line,
could you, without inconsistency, throw obstacles in the way of
anyone who should offer you the best means of expediting your
message? This is what you do in commercial affairs. You forget
the end, the object sought to be attained, which is material prosperity; you disregard it, you sacrifice it to a veritable *petitio principii*; in plain language, you are begging the question.

But since we cannot bring our opponents to our point of view,
let us place ourselves in theirs, and examine the question in its
relations with production.

I shall endeavor to prove:

---

[1]Viscount de Romanet.

[2]Matthieu de Dombasle.

First—That to level and Equalize the conditions of labor is to attack exchange in its essence and principle.

Second—That it is not true that the labor of a country is neutralized by the competition of more favored countries.

Third—That if that were true, protective duties would not Equalize the conditions of production.

Fourth—That liberty, freedom of trade, levels these conditions as much as they can be levelled.

Fifth—That the least favored countries gain most by exchange.

1. To level and Equalize the conditions of labor is not simply to cramp exchanges in certain branches of trade; it is to attack exchange in its principle, for its principle rests upon that very diversity, upon those very inequalities of fertility, aptitude, climate, and temperature, that you desire to efface. If Guiènne sends wine to Brittany, and if Brittany sends corn to Guiènne, it arises from their being situated under different conditions of production. Is there a different law for international exchanges? To urge against international exchanges that inequality of conditions that gives rise to them and explains them, is to argue against their very existence. If protectionists had on their side sufficient logic and power, they would reduce men, like snails, to a state of absolute isolation. Moreover, there is not one of their fallacies which, when submitted to the test of rigorous deductions, does not obviously tend to destruction and annihilation.

2. It is not true, in point of fact, that inequality of conditions existing between two similar branches of industry entails necessarily the ruin of that which is less favorably situated. On the race track, if one horse gains the prize, the other loses it; but when two horses are employed in useful labor, each produces a beneficial result in proportion to its powers; and if the more vigorous renders the greater service, it does not follow that the other renders no service at all. We cultivate wheat in all the departments of France, although there are between them enormous differences of fertility; and if there be any one department that does not cultivate wheat, it is because it is not profitable to engage in that

species of culture in that locality. In the same way, analogy shows us that under the regime of liberty, in spite of similar differences, they produce wheat in all the countries of Europe; and if there be one that abandons the cultivation of that grain, it is because it is found more for its interest to give another direction to the employment of its land, labor, and capital. And why should the fertility of one department not paralyze the agriculturist of a neighboring department less favorably situated? Because the economic phenomena have a flexibility, an elasticity, levelling powers, so to speak, that appear to have altogether escaped the notice of the protectionist school. That school accuses us of being dogmatic; but it is the protectionists who are systematic in the last degree, if dogmatism consists in bolstering up arguments that rest upon one fact instead of upon an aggregation of facts. In the example which I have given, it is the difference in the value of lands that compensates the difference in their fertility. Your field produces three times more than mine. Yes, but it has cost you ten times more, and I can still compete with you. This is the whole mystery. And observe that superiority in some respects leads to inferiority in others. It is just because your land is more fertile that it is dearer; so that it is not accidentally, but necessarily, that the equilibrium is established, or tends to be established; and it cannot be denied that liberty is the system that is most favorable to this tendency.

I have referred to a branch of agricultural industry; I might as well have referred to industry in a different department. There are tailors at Quimper, and that does not hinder there being tailors also in Paris, though the latter pay a higher rent, and live at much greater expense. But then they have a different set of customers, and that serves not only to redress the balance, but to make it incline to their side.

When we speak, then, of equalizing the conditions of labor, we must examine whether liberty gives us what we seek from an arbitrary system.

This natural levelling power of the economic phenomena is so important to the question we are considering, and at the same time so fitted to inspire us with admiration of the providential wisdom that presides over the equitable government of society, that I must ask permission to dwell upon it for a little.

The protectionist gentlemen tell us: Such or such a people have over us an advantage in the cheapness of coal, of iron, of machinery, of capital—we cannot compete with them.

We shall examine the proposition afterwards under all its aspects. At present, I confine myself to the inquiry whether, when a superiority and an inferiority are both present, they do not possess in themselves, the one an ascending, the other a descending force, which must ultimately bring them back to a just equilibrium.

Suppose two countries, A and B. A possesses over B all kinds of advantages. You infer from this that every sort of industry will concentrate itself in A, and that B is powerless. A, you say, sells much more than it buys; B buys much more than it sells. I might dispute this, but I will allow your hypothesis.

On this hypothesis, labor is much in demand in A, and will soon rise in price there.

Iron, coal, land, food, capital are much in demand in A, and they will soon rise in price there.

Contemporaneously with this, labor, iron, coal, land, food, capital are in little request in B, and will soon fall in price there. Nor is this all. While A is always selling, and B is always buying, money passes from B to A. It becomes abundant in A, and scarce in B.

But abundance of money means that we must have plenty of it to buy everything else. Then in A, to the real dearness that arises from a very active demand, there is added a nominal dearness, which is due to an excess of money.

Scarcity of money means that little is required for each purchase. Then in B a nominal cheapness comes to be combined with real cheapness.

In these circumstances, industry will have all sorts of motives—motives, if I may say so, carried to the highest degree of intensity—to desert A and establish itself in B.

Or, to come nearer what would actually take place under such circumstances, we may affirm that sudden displacements being so repugnant to the nature of industry, such a transfer would not have been so long delayed, but that from the beginning, under the free system, it would have gradually and progressively shared and distributed itself between A and B, according to the laws of supply and demand—that is to say, according to the laws of justice and utility.

And when I assert that if it were possible for industry to concentrate itself upon one point, that very circumstance would set in motion an irresistible decentralizing force, I indulge in no idle hypothesis.

Let us listen to what was said by a manufacturer in addressing the Manchester Chamber of Commerce (I omit the figures by which he supported his demonstration):

"Formerly we exported woven goods; then that exportation gave place to that of yarns, which are the raw material of woven goods; then to that of machines, which are the instruments for producing yarn, afterwards to the exportation of the capital with which we construct our machines; finally to that of our workmen and our industrial skill, which are the source of our capital. All these elements of labor, one after the other, are set to work wherever they find the most advantageous opening, wherever the expense of living is cheaper and the necessaries of life are most easily procured; and at the present day, in Prussia, in Austria, in Saxony, in Switzerland, in Italy, we see manufactures on an immense scale founded and supported by English capital, worked by English operatives, and directed by English engineers."

You see very clearly, then, that nature, or rather that Providence, more wise, more far-seeing than your narrow and rigid theory supposes, has not ordered this concentration of industry, this monopoly of all advantages upon which you found your reasoning as upon a fact that is unalterable and without remedy. Nature has provided, by means as simple as they are infallible, that there should be dispersion, diffusion, coordination, simultaneous progress; all constituting a state of things that your restrictive laws paralyze as much as they can; for the tendency of such laws is, by isolating communities, to render the diversity of condition much more marked, to prevent equalization, hinder integration, neutralize countervailing circumstances, and segregate nations, whether in their superiority or in their inferiority of condition.

3. In the third place, to contend that by a protective duty you Equalize the conditions of production, is to give currency to an error by a deceptive form of speech. It is not true that an import duty equalizes the conditions of production. These remain, after the imposition of the duty, the same as they were before. At most, all that such a duty equalizes are the conditions of sale. It may be said, perhaps, that I am playing upon words, but I throw back the accusation. It is for my opponents to show that production and sale are synonymous terms; and if they cannot do this, I am warranted in fastening upon them the reproach, if not of playing on words, at least of mixing them up and confusing them.

To illustrate what I mean by an example: I suppose some Parisian speculators to devote themselves to the production of oranges. They know that the oranges of Portugal can be sold in Paris for a penny apiece, while they, on account of the frames and hot-houses that the colder climate would render necessary, could not sell them for less than a shilling as a remunerative price. They demand that Portuguese oranges should have a duty of elevenpence imposed upon them. By means of this duty, they say, the conditions of production will be equalized; and the Chamber, giving effect, as it always does, to such reasoning, inserts in the tariff a duty of elevenpence upon every foreign orange.

Now, I maintain that the conditions of production are in no way changed. The law has made no change on the heat of the sun in Lisbon, or on the frequency and intensity of the frosts of Paris. The ripening of oranges will continue to go on naturally on the banks of the Tagus, and artificially on the banks of the Seine—that is to say, much more human labor will be required in the one country than in the other. The conditions of sale are what have been equalized. The Portuguese must now sell us their oranges at a shilling, elevenpence of which goes to pay the tax. That tax will be paid, it is evident, by the French consumer. And look at the nonsensical result. Upon each Portuguese orange consumed, the country will lose nothing, for the extra elevenpence charged to the consumer will be paid into the treasury. This will cause displacement, but not loss. But upon each French orange consumed there will be a loss of elevenpence, or nearly so, for the purchaser will certainly lose that sum, and the seller as certainly will not gain it, seeing that by the hypothesis he will only have received the cost price. I leave it to the protectionists to draw the inference.

4. If I dwelt upon this distinction between the conditions of production and the conditions of sale, a distinction that the protectionists will no doubt pronounce paradoxical, it is because it leads me to impose on them another, and a much stranger, paradox, which is this: Would you Equalize effectually the conditions of production, leave exchange free?

Now, really, it will be said, this is too much; you must be making fun of us. Well, then, were it only for curiosity, I entreat the gentlemen protectionists to follow me on to the conclusion of my argument. It will not be long. I revert to my former illustration.

Let us suppose for a moment that the average daily wage that a Frenchman earns is equal to a shilling, and it follows incontestably that to produce directly an orange in France, a day's work, or its equivalent, is required: while to produce the value of a Portuguese orange only a twelfth of that day's labor would be necessary; which means exactly this, that the sun does at Lisbon what human labor does at Paris. Now, is it not very evident that if I can produce an orange or, what comes to the same thing, the means of purchasing one, with a twelfth part of a day's labor, I am placed, with respect to this production, under exactly the same conditions as the Portuguese producer himself, excepting the carriage, which must be at my expense. It is certain, then, that liberty equalizes the conditions of production direct or indirect, as far as they can be equalized, since it leaves no other difference but the inevitable one arising from the expense of transport.

I add that liberty equalizes also the conditions of enjoyment, of satisfaction, of consumption, with which the Protectionists never concern themselves, and which are yet the essential consideration, consumption being the end and object of all our industrial efforts. In virtue of Free Trade we enjoy the sun of Portugal like the Portuguese themselves. The inhabitants of Havre and the citizens of London are put in possession, and on the same conditions, of all the mineral resources that nature has bestowed on Newcastle.

5. Gentlemen protectionists, you find me in a paradoxical mood; and I am disposed to go further still. I say, and I sincerely think, that if two countries are placed under unequal conditions of production, it is that one of the two that is least favored by nature that has most to gain by Free Trade. To prove this, I must depart a little from the usual form of such a work as this. I shall do so nevertheless, first of all, because the entire question lies there, and also because it will afford me an opportunity of explaining an economic law of the highest importance, and which, if rightly understood, appears to me to be fitted to bring back to the science all those sects who in our day seek in the land of chimeras that social harmony which they fail to discover in nature. I refer to the law of consumption, which it is perhaps to be regretted that the majority of economists have neglected.

Consumption is the end and final cause of all the economic phenomena, and it is in consumption consequently that we must expect to find their ultimate and definitive solution.

Nothing, whether favorable or unfavorable, can abide permanently with the producer. The advantages that nature and society bestow upon him, the inconveniences he may experience, pass through him, so to speak, and are absorbed and mixed up with the community in so far as the community represents consumers. This is an admirable law both in its cause and in its effects, and he who shall succeed in clearly describing it is entitled, in my opinion, to say, "I have not passed through life without paying my debt to society."

Everything that favors the work of production is welcomed with joy by the producer, for the immediate effect of it is to put him in a situation to render greater service to the community, and to exact from it a greater remuneration. Every circumstance that retards or interrupts production gives pain to the producer, for the immediate effect of it is to circumscribe his services, and consequently his remuneration. Immediate good or ill circumstances—fortunate or unfortunate—necessarily fall upon the producer, and leave him no choice but to accept the one and eschew the other.

In the same way, when a workman succeeds in discovering an improved process in manufactures, the immediate profit from the improvement results to him. This was necessary in order to give his labor an intelligent direction; and it is just, because it is fair that an effort crowned with success should carry its recompense along with it.

But I maintain that these good or bad effects, though in their own nature permanent, are not permanent as regards the producer. If it had been so, a principle of progressive, and therefore of indefinite, inequality would have been introduced among men, and this is the reason why these good or evil effects become very soon absorbed in the general destinies of the human race.

How is this brought about? I shall show how it takes place by some examples.

Let us go back to the thirteenth century. The men who then devoted themselves to the art of copying received for the service they rendered a remuneration regulated by the general rate of profits. Among them there arose one who discovered the means of multiplying copies of the same work rapidly. He invented printing.

In the first instance, one man was enriched, and many others were impoverished. At first sight, marvellous as the invention proves itself to be, we hesitate to decide whether it is hurtful or useful. It seems to introduce into the world, as I have said, an indefinite element of inequality. Gutenberg profits by his invention, and extends his invention with its profits indefinitely, until he has ruined all the copyists. As regards the public, in the capacity of consumer, it gains little; for Gutenberg takes care not to lower the price of his books, but just enough to undersell his rivals.

But the intelligence that has introduced harmony into the movements of the heavenly bodies has implanted it also in the internal mechanism of society. We shall see the economic advantages of the invention when it has ceased to be individual property, and has become forever the common patrimony of the masses.

At length the invention comes to be known. Gutenberg is no longer the only printer; others imitate him. Their profits at first are large. They are thus rewarded for having been the first to imitate the invention; and it is right that it should be so, for this higher remuneration was necessary to induce them to concur in the grand definite result that is approaching. They gain a great deal, but they gain less than the inventor, for competition now begins its work. The price of books goes on falling. The profit of imitators goes on diminishing in proportion as the invention becomes of older date; that is to say, in proportion as the imitation becomes less meritorious. . . . The new branch of industry at length reaches its normal state; in other words, the remuneration of printers ceases to be exceptionally high, and comes, like that of the copyists, to be regulated by the ordinary rate of profits. Here we have production, as such, brought back to the point from which it started. And yet the invention is not the less an acquisition; the saving of time, of labor, of effort to produce a given result, that is, to produce a determinate number of copies is not the less realized. But how does it show itself? In the cheapness of books. And to whose profit? To the profit of the consumer, of society, of the human race. The printers, who have thenceforth no exceptional merit, no longer receive exceptional remuneration. As men, as consumers, they undoubtedly participate in the advantages that the invention has conferred upon the community. But that is all. As printers, as producers, they have returned to the ordinary condition of the other producers of the country. Society pays them for their labor, and not for the utility of the invention. The latter has become the common and gratuitous heritage of mankind at large.

I confess that the wisdom and the beauty of these laws call forth my admiration and respect. I see in them Saint-Simonianism: To each according to his capacity; to each capacity according to its works. I see in them communism; that is, the tendency of products to become the common heritage of men; but a Saint-Simonianism, a communism, regulated by infinite prescience, and not abandoned to the frailties, the passions, and the arbitrary will of men.

What I have said of the art of printing may be affirmed of all the instruments of labor, from the nail and the hammer to the locomotive and the electric telegraph. Society becomes possessed of all through its more abundant consumption, and it enjoys all gratuitously, for the effect of inventions and discoveries is to reduce the price of commodities; and all that part of the price which has been annihilated, and which represents the share invention has in production evidently renders the product gratuitous to that extent. All that remains to be paid for is the human labor, the immediate labor, and it is paid for without reference to the result of the invention, at least when that invention has passed through the cycle I have just described—the cycle it is designed to pass through. I send for a workman to my house; he comes and brings his saw with him. I pay him two shillings for his day's work, and he saws me twenty-five boards. Had the saw not been invented, he would probably not have been able to furnish me with one, and I should have had to pay him the same wages for his day's work. The utility produced by the saw is then, as far as I am concerned, a gratuitous gift of nature, or, rather, it is a part of that inheritance that, in common with all my brethren, I have received from my ancestors. I have two workmen in my field. The one handles the plough, the other the spade. The result of their labor is very different, but the day's wages are the same, because the remuneration is not proportioned to the utility produced, but to the effort, the labor, that is exacted.

I entreat the reader's patience, and beg him to believe that I have not lost sight of Free Trade. Let him only have the goodness to remember the conclusion at which I have arrived: Remuneration is not in proportion to the utilities the producer brings to market, but to his labor.[3]

I have drawn my illustrations as yet from human inventions. Let us now turn our attention to natural advantages.

In every branch of production nature and man concur. But the portion of utility that nature contributes is always gratuitous. It is only the portion of utility contributed by human labor that forms the subject of exchange and, consequently, of remuneration. The latter varies, no doubt, very much in proportion to the intensity of the labor, its skill, its promptitude, its suitableness, the need there is of it, the temporary absence of rivalry, etc. But it is not the less true, in principle, that the concurrence of natural laws, which are common to all, counts for nothing in the price of the product.

We do not pay for the air we breathe, although it is so useful to us that, without it, we could not live two minutes. We do not pay for it, nevertheless, because nature furnishes it to us without the aid of human labor. But if, for example, we should desire to separate one of the gases of which it is composed to make an experiment, we must make an exertion; or if we wish another to make that exertion for us we must sacrifice for that other an equivalent amount of exertion, although we may have embodied it in another product. Whence we see that pains, efforts, and exertions are the real subjects of exchange. It is not, indeed, the oxygen gas that I pay for, since it is at my disposal everywhere, but the labor necessary to disengage it, labor that has been saved me, and that must be recompensed. Will it be said that there is something else to be paid for, materials, apparatus, etc? Still, in

---

[3]It is true that labor does not receive a uniform remuneration. It may be more or less Intense, dangerous, skilled, etc. Competition settles the usual or current price in each department—and this is the fluctuating price of which I speak.

paying for these I pay for labor. The price of the coal employed, for example, represents the labor necessary to extract it from the mine and to transport it to the place where it is to be used.

We do not pay for the light of the sun, because it is a gift of nature. But we pay for gas, tallow, oil, wax, because there is here human labor to be remunerated; and it will be noted that, in this case, the remuneration is proportioned, not to the utility produced, but to the labor employed, so much so, that it may happen that one of these kinds of artificial light, though more intense, costs us less, and for this reason that the same amount of human labor affords us more of it.

Were the porter who carries water to my house to be paid in proportion to the absolute utility of water, my whole fortune would be insufficient to remunerate him. But I pay him in proportion to the exertion he makes. If he charges more, others will do the work, or, if necessary, I will do it myself. Water, in truth, is not the subject of our bargain, but the labor of carrying it. This view of the matter is so important, and the conclusions that I am about to deduce from it throw so much light on the question of the freedom of international exchanges, that I deem it necessary to elucidate it by other examples.

The alimentary substance contained in potatoes is not very costly, because we can obtain a large amount of it with comparatively little labor. We pay more for wheat, because the production of it costs a greater amount of human labor. It is evident that if nature did for the one what it does for the other, the price of both would tend to equality. It is impossible that the producer of wheat should permanently gain much more than the producer of potatoes. The law of competition would prevent it.

If by happy miracle the fertility of all arable lands should come to be augmented, it would not be the agriculturist but the consumer who would reap advantage from that phenomenon, for it would resolve itself into abundance and cheapness. There would be less labor incorporated in each quarter of corn, and the cultivator could exchange it only for a smaller amount of labor worked up in some other product. If, on the other hand, the fertility of the soil came all at once to be diminished, nature's part in the process of production would be less, that of human labor would be greater, and the product dearer. I am, then, warranted in saying that it is in consumption, in the human element, that all the economic phenomena come ultimately to resolve themselves. The man who has failed to regard them in this light, to follow them out to their ultimate effects, without stopping short at immediate results, and viewing them from the producer's standpoint, can no more be regarded as an economist than the man who should prescribe a draught, and, instead of watching its effect on the entire system of the patient, should inquire only how it affected the mouth and throat, could be regarded as a physician.

Tropical regions are very favorably situated for the production of sugar and of coffee. This means that nature does a great part of the work, and leaves little for human labor to do. But who reaps the advantage of this liberality of nature? Not the producing countries, for competition causes the price barely to remunerate the labor. It is the human race that reaps the benefit, for the result of nature's liberality is cheapness, and cheapness benefits everybody.

Imagine a temperate region where coal and iron-ore are found on the surface of the ground, where one has only to stoop down to get them. That, in the first instance, the inhabitants would profit by this happy circumstance, I allow. But competition would soon intervene, and the price of coal and iron-ore would go on falling, till the gift of nature became free to all, and then the human labor employed would be alone remunerated according to the general rate of earnings.

Thus, the liberality of nature, like improvements in the processes of production, is, or continually tends to become, under the law of competition, the common and gratuitous patrimony of consumers, of the masses, of mankind in general. Then, the countries that do not possess these advantages have everything to gain by exchanging their products with those countries that possess them, because the subject of exchange is labor, apart from the consideration of the natural utilities worked up with that labor;

and the countries that have incorporated in a given amount of their labor the greatest amount of these natural utilities, are evidently the most favored countries. Their products, which represent the least amount of human labor, are the least profitable; in other words, they are cheaper; and if the whole liberality of nature resolves itself into cheapness, it is evidently not the producing but the consuming country that reaps the benefit.

Hence we see the enormous absurdity of consuming countries that reject products for the very reason that they are cheap. It is as if they said, "We want nothing that nature gives us. You ask me for an effort equal to two in exchange for a product that I cannot create without an effort equal to four; you can make that effort, because in your case nature does half the work. If that is the case, I reject your offer, and I shall wait until your climate, having become more inclement, will force you to demand from me an effort equal to four, in order that I may treat you on a footing of equality."

A is a favored country. B is a country to which nature has been less bountiful. I maintain that exchange benefits both, but benefits B especially; because exchange is not an exchange of utilities for utilities, but of value for value. Now A includes a greater amount of utility in the same value, seeing that the utility of a product includes what nature has put there as well as what labor has put there; whilst value includes only what labor has put there. Then B makes quite an advantageous bargain. In recompensing the producer of A for his labor only it receives into the bargain a greater amount of natural utility than it has given.

This enables us to lay down the general rule: Exchange is a barter of values; value under the action of competition being made to represent labor, exchange becomes a barter of equal labor. What nature has imparted to the products exchanged is on both sides given gratuitously and into the bargain; whence it follows necessarily that exchanges effected with countries the most favored by nature are the most advantageous.

The theory of which in this chapter I have endeavored to trace the outlines would require great developments. I have glanced at it only in as far so it bears upon my subject of Free Trade. But perhaps the attentive reader may have perceived in it the fertile germ which in the fullness of its maturity will not only smother Protection, but along with it Fourierism, Saint-Simonianism, communism, and all those schools whose object it is to exclude from the government of the world the law of COMPETITION. Regarded from the producer's point of view, competition no doubt frequently clashes with our immediate and individual interests; but if we change our point of view and extend our regards to industry in general, to universal prosperity—in a word, to consumption—we shall find that competition in the moral world plays the same part that equilibrium does in the material world. It lies at the root of true communism, of true socialism, of that equality of conditions and of happiness so much desired in our day; and if so many sincere publicists and well-meaning reformers seek after the arbitrary, it is for this reason—that they do not understand liberty.

5

OUR PRODUCTS ARE
BURDENED WITH TAXES

We have here, again, the same fallacy. We demand that foreign products should be taxed to neutralize the effect of the taxes that weigh upon our national products. The object, then, still is to equalize the conditions of production. We have only a word to say, and it is this: That the tax is an artificial obstacle that produces exactly the same result as a natural obstacle, its effect is to enhance prices. If this enhancement reach a point that makes it a greater loss to create the product for ourselves than to procure it from abroad by producing a counter value, let well alone. Of two evils, private interest will manage to choose the least. I might then simply refer the reader to the preceding demonstration; but the fallacy we have here to combat recurs so frequently in the lamentations and demands—I might say in the challenges—of the protectionist school as to merit a special discussion.

If the question relates to one of those exceptional taxes that are imposed on certain products, I grant readily that it is reasonable to impose the same duty on the foreign product. For example, it would be absurd to exempt foreign salt from duty; not that, in an economical point of view, France would lose anything by doing so, but the reverse. Let them say what they will, principles are always the same; and France would gain by the exemption as she must always gain by removing a natural or artificial obstacle. But in this instance the obstacle has been interposed for purposes of revenue. These purposes must be attained; and were foreign salt sold in our market duty free, the Treasury would lose its hundred millions of francs (four millions sterling), and must raise that sum from some other source. There would be an obvious inconsistency in creating an obstacle, and failing in the object. It might have been better to have had recourse at first to another tax than upon French salt. But I admit that there are certain circumstances in which a tax may be laid on foreign commodities, provided it is not protective, but fiscal.

But to pretend that a nation, because she is subjected to heavier taxes than her neighbors, should protect herself by tariffs against the competition of her rivals, in this is a fallacy, and it is this fallacy that I intend to attack.

I have said more than once that I propose only to explain the theory, and lay open, as far as possible, the sources of protectionist errors. Had I intended to raise a controversy, I should have asked the protectionists why they direct their tariffs chiefly against England and Belgium, the most heavily taxed countries in the world? Am I not warranted in regarding their argument only as a pretext? But I am not one of those who believe that men are protectionists from self-interest, and not from conviction. The doctrine of protection is too popular not to be sincere. If the majority had faith in liberty, we should be free. Undoubtedly it is self-interest that makes our tariffs so heavy; but conviction is at the root of it. "The will," says Pascal, "is one of the principal organs of belief." But the belief exists nevertheless, although it has its root in the will, and in the insidious suggestions of selfishness.

Let us revert to the fallacy founded on taxation.

The State may make a good or a bad use of the taxes it levies. When it renders to the public services that are equivalent to the value it receives, it makes a good use of them. And when it dissipates its revenues without giving any service in return, it makes a bad use of them.

In the first case, to affirm that the taxes place the country that pays them under conditions of production more unfavorable than those of a country that is exempt from them, is a fallacy. We pay twenty millions of francs for justice and police; but then we have them, with the security they afford us, and the time they save us; and it is very probable that production is neither more easy nor more active in those countries, if there are any such, where the people take the business of justice and police into their own hands. We pay many hundreds of millions of francs for roads, bridges, harbors, and railways. Granted; but then we have the benefit of these roads, bridges, harbors, and railways; and whether we make a good or a bad bargain in constructing them, it cannot be said that they render us inferior to other nations, who do not indeed support a budget of public works, but who have no public works. And this explains why, while accusing taxation of being a cause of industrial inferiority, we direct our tariffs especially against those countries that are the most heavily taxed. Their taxes, well employed, far from harming, have improved the conditions of production in these countries. Thus we are continually arriving at the conclusion that protectionist fallacies are not only not true, but are the very reverse of true.

If taxes are unproductive, suppress them, if you can; but assuredly the strangest mode of neutralizing their effect is to add individual to public taxes. Fine compensation truly! You tell us that the State taxes are too much; and you give that as a reason why we should tax one another!

A protective duty is a tax directed against a foreign product; but we must never forget that it falls back on the home consumer. Now the consumer is the tax-payer. The agreeable language you address to him is this: "Because your taxes are heavy, we raise the price of everything you buy; because the State lays hold of one part of your income, we hand over another to the monopolist."

But let us penetrate a little deeper into this fallacy that is in such repute with our legislators, although the extraordinary thing is that it is the very people who maintain unproductive taxes who attribute to them our industrial inferiority, and in that inferiority find an excuse for imposing other taxes and restrictions.

It appears evident to me that the nature and effects of protection would not be changed, were the State to levy a direct tax and distribute the money afterwards in premiums and indemnities to the privileged branches of industry.

Suppose that while foreign iron cannot be sold in our market below eight francs, French iron cannot be sold for less than twelve francs.

On this hypothesis, there are two modes in which the State can secure the home market to the producer.

The first mode is to lay a duty of five francs on foreign iron. It is evident that that duty would exclude it, since it could no longer be sold under thirteen francs, namely, eight francs for the cost price and five francs for the tax, and at that price it would be driven out of the market by French iron, the price of which we suppose to be only twelve francs. In this case, the purchaser, the consumer, would bear the whole cost of the protection.

Or again, the State might levy a tax of five francs from the public, and give the proceeds as a premium to the ironmaster. The protective effect would be the same. Foreign iron would in this case be equally excluded; for our ironmaster can now sell his iron at seven francs, which, with the five francs premium, would make up to him the remunerative price of twelve francs. But with home iron at seven francs, the foreigner could not sell his for eight, which by the supposition is his lowest remunerative price.

Between these two modes of going to work, I can see only one difference. The principle is the same; the effect is the same: but in the one, certain individuals pay the price of protection; in the other, it is paid for by the nation at large.

I frankly avow my predilection for the second mode. It appears to me more just, more economical, and more honorable; more just, because if society desires to give largess to some of its members, all should contribute; more economical, because it would save much expense in collecting, and get us rid of many restrictions; more honorable, because the public would then see clearly the nature of the operation, and act accordingly.

But if the protectionist system had taken this form, it would have been laughable to hear men say: "We pay heavy taxes for the army, for the navy, for the administration of justice, for public works, for the university, the public debt, etc., in all exceeding a milliard (£40,000,000 sterling). For this reason, the State should take another milliard from us to relieve these poor ironmasters, these poor shareholders in the coalmines of Anzin, these unfortunate proprietors of forests, these useful men who supply us with cod-fish."

Look at the subject closely, and you will be satisfied that this is the true meaning and effect of the fallacy we are combating. It is all in vain; you cannot give money to some members of the community but by taking it from others. If you desire to ruin the tax-payer, you may do so. But at least do not banter him by saying: "In order to compensate your losses, I take from you again as much as I have taken from you already."

To expose fully all that is false in this fallacy would be an endless work. I shall confine myself to three observations.

You assert that the country is overburdened with taxes, and on this fact you found an argument for the protection of certain branches of industry. But we have to pay these taxes in spite of protection. If, then, a particular branch of industry presents itself, and says, "I share in the payment of taxes; that raises the cost price of my products, and I demand that a protecting duty should also raise their selling price," what does such a demand amount to? It amounts simply to this, that the tax should be thrown over on the rest of the community. The object sought for is to be reimbursed the amount of the tax by a rise of prices. But as the Treasury requires to have the full amount of all the taxes, and as the

masses have to pay the higher price, it follows that they have to
bear not only their own share of taxation but that of the particular branch of industry that is protected. But we mean to protect
everybody, you will say. I answer, in the first place, that that is
impossible; and, in the next place, that if it were possible, there
would be no relief. I would pay for you, and you would pay for
me; but the tax must be paid all the same.

You are thus the dupes of an illusion. You wish in the first
instance to pay taxes in order that you may have an army, a navy,
a church, a university, judges, highways, etc., and then you wish
to free from taxation first one branch of industry, then a second,
then a third, always throwing back the burden upon the masses.
You do nothing more than create interminable complications,
without any other result than these complications themselves.
Show me that a rise of price caused by protection falls upon the
foreigner, and I could discover in your argument something specious. But if it be true that the public pays the tax before your law,
and that after the law is passed it pays for protection and the tax
into the bargain, truly I cannot see what is gained by it.

But I go further, and maintain that the heavier our taxes are,
the more we should hasten to throw open our ports and our frontiers to foreigners less heavily taxed than ourselves. And why? In
order to throw back upon them a greater share of our burden. Is
it not an incontestable axiom in political economy that taxes ultimately fall on the consumer? The more, then, our exchanges are
multiplied, the more will foreign consumers reimburse us for the
taxes incorporated and worked up in the products we sell them;
while we in this respect will have to make them a smaller restitution, seeing that their products, according to our hypothesis, are
less heavily burdened than ours.

Finally, have you never asked yourselves whether these heavy
burdens on which you found your argument for a prohibitory system are not caused by that very system? If commerce were free,
what use would you have for your great standing armies and powerful navies? . . . But this belongs to the domain of politics.

6

BALANCE OF TRADE

Our adversaries have adopted tactics that are rather embarrassing. Do we establish our doctrine? They admit it with the greatest possible respect. Do we attack their principle? They abandon it with the best grace in the world. They demand only one thing—that our doctrine, which they hold to be true, should remain relegated to books, and that their principle, which they acknowledge to be vicious, should reign paramount in practical legislation. Resign to them the management of tariffs, and they will give up all dispute with you in the domain of theory.

"Assuredly," said Mr. Gauthier de Rumilly, on a recent occasion, "no one wishes to resuscitate the antiquated theories of the balance of trade." Very right, Mr. Gauthier, but please remember that it is not enough to give a passing slap to error, and immediately afterwards and for two hours at a time, reason as if that error were truth.

Let me speak of Mr. Lestiboudois. Here we have a consistent reasoner, a logical disputant. There is nothing in his conclusions that is not to be found in his premises. He asks nothing in practice but what he justifies in theory. His principle may be false; that is open to question. But at any rate, he has a principle. He believes, and he proclaims it aloud, that if France gives ten, in order to receive fifteen, she loses five; and it follows, of course, that he supports laws that are in keeping with this view of the subject.

"The important thing to attend to," he says, "is that the amount of our importations goes on augmenting, and exceeds the amount of our exportations—that is to say, France every year purchases more foreign products, and sells less of her own. Figures prove this. What do we see? In 1842 imports exceeded exports by 200 million. These facts appear to prove in the clearest manner that national industry is not sufficiently protected, that we depend upon foreign labor for our supplies, that the competition of our rivals oppresses our industry. The present law appears to me to recognize the fact that the economists are wrong in saying that when we purchase we necessarily sell a corresponding amount of commodities. It is evident that we can purchase, not with our usual products, not with our revenue, not with the results of permanent labor, but with our capital, with products that have been accumulated and stored up, those intended for reproduction—that is to say, that we may expend, that we may dissipate, the proceeds of previous economies, that we may impoverish ourselves, that we may proceed on the road to ruin, and consume entirely the national capital. This is exactly what we are doing. Every year we give away 200 million francs to the foreigner."

Well, here is a man with whom we can come to an understanding. There is no hypocrisy in this language. The doctrine of the balance of trade is openly avowed. France imports 200 million more than she exports. Then we lose 200 millions a year. And what is the remedy? To place restrictions on importation. The conclusion is unexceptionable.

It is with Mr. Lestiboudois, then, that we must deal, for how can we argue with Mr. Gauthier? If you tell him that the balance of trade is an error, he replies that that was what he laid down at the beginning. If you say that the balance of trade is a truth, he will reply that that is what he proves in his conclusions.

The economist school will blame me, no doubt, for arguing with Mr. Lestiboudois. To attack the balance of trade, it will be said, is to fight with a windmill.

But take care. The doctrine of the balance of trade is neither so antiquated, nor so sick, nor so dead as Mr. Gauthier would represent it, for the entire Chamber—Mr. Gauthier himself included—has recognized by its votes the theory of Mr. Lestiboudois.

I shall not fatigue the reader by proceeding to probe that theory, but content myself with subjecting it to the test of facts.

We are constantly told that our principles do not hold good, except in theory. But tell me, gentlemen, if you regard the books of merchants as holding good in practice? It appears to me that if there is anything in the world that should have practical authority when the question regards profit and loss, it is commercial accounts. Have all the merchants in the world come to an understanding for centuries to keep their books in such a way as to represent profits as losses, and losses as profits? It may be so, but I would much rather come to the conclusion that Mr. Lestiboudois is a bad economist.

Now, a merchant of my acquaintance having had two transactions, the results of which were very different, I felt curious to compare the books of the counting-house with the books of the Customhouse, as interpreted by Mr. Lestiboudois to the satisfaction of our six hundred legislators.

M.T. dispatched a ship from Havre to the United States, with a cargo of French goods, chiefly those known as articles from Paris, amounting to 200,000 francs. This was the figure declared at the Customhouse. When the cargo arrived at New Orleans it was charged with 10 percent freight and 30 percent duty, making a total of 280,000 francs. It was sold with 20 percent profit, or 40,000 francs, and produced a total of 320,000 francs, which the consignee invested in cottons. These cottons had still for freight, insurance, commission, etc., to bear a cost of 10 percent; so that when the new cargo arrived at Havre it had cost 352,000 francs, which was the figure entered in the Customhouse books. Finally M.T. realized upon this return cargo 20 percent profit, or 70,400 francs; in other words, the cottons were sold for 422,400 francs.

If Mr. Lestiboudois desires it, I shall send him an extract from the books of M.T. He will there see at the credit of the profit and loss account—that is to say, as profits—two entries, one of 40,000 another of 70,400 francs, and M.T. is very sure that his accounts are accurate.

And yet, what do the Customhouse books tell Mr. Lestiboudois regarding this transaction? They tell him simply that France exported 200,000 francs' worth, and imported to the extent of 352,000 francs; from which the honorable deputy concludes "that she had expended and dissipated the profits of her previous economies, that she is impoverishing herself, that she is on the high road to ruin, and has given away to the foreigner 152,000 francs of her capital."

Some time afterwards, M.T. dispatched another vessel with a cargo also of the value of 200,000 francs, composed of the products of our native industry. This unfortunate ship was lost in a gale of wind after leaving the harbor, and all M.T. had to do was to make two short entries in his books, to this effect:

"Sundry goods due to X, 200,000 francs, for purchases of different commodities dispatched by the ship N."

"Profit and loss owed to sundry goods, 200,000 francs, in consequence of definitive and total loss of the cargo."

At the same time, the Customhouse books bore an entry of 200,000 francs in the list of exportations; and as there was no corresponding entry to make in the list of importations, it follows that Mr. Lestiboudois and the Chamber will see in this shipwreck a clear and net profit for France of 200,000 francs.

There is still another inference to be deduced from this, which is that according to the theory of the balance of trade, France has a very simple means of doubling her capital at any moment. It is enough to pass them through the Customhouse, and then pitch them into the sea. In this case the exports will represent the amount of her capital, the imports will be nil, and impossible as well, and we shall gain all that the sea swallows up.

This is a joke, the protectionists will say. It is impossible we could give utterance to such absurdities. You do give utterance to them, however, and, what is more, you act upon them and impose them on your fellow-citizens to the utmost of your power.

The truth is, it would be necessary to take the balance of trade backwards (*au rebours*), and calculate the national profits from foreign trade by the excess of imports over exports. This excess, after deducting costs, constitutes the real profit. But this theory, which is true, leads directly to Free Trade. I make you a present of it, gentlemen, as I do of all the theories in preceding chapters. Exaggerate it as much as you please—it has nothing to fear from that test. Suppose, if that amuses you, that the foreigner inundates us with all sorts of useful commodities without asking in return—that our imports are infinite and exports nil, I defy you to prove to me that we should be poorer on that account.

7

PETITION OF THE MANUFACTURERS OF CANDLES, WAXLIGHTS, LAMPS, CANDLELIGHTS, STREET LAMPS, SNUFFERS, EXTINGUISHERS, AND THE PRODUCERS OF OIL, TALLOW, RESIN, ALCOHOL, AND, GENERALLY, OF EVERYTHING CONNECTED WITH LIGHTING

To the Members of the Chamber of Deputies. GENTLEMEN—You are on the right road. You reject abstract theories, and have little consideration for cheapness and plenty. Your chief care is the interest of the producer. You desire to protect him from foreign competition and reserve the national market for national industry.

We are about to offer you an admirable opportunity of applying your—what shall we call it?—your theory? No; nothing is more deceptive than theory—your doctrine? your system? your principle? But you dislike doctrines, you abhor systems, and as for principles you deny that there are any in social economy. We shall say, then, your practice—your practice without theory and without principle.

We are suffering from the intolerable competition of a foreign rival, placed, it would seem, in a condition so far superior to ours for the production of light that he absolutely inundates our national market with it at a price fabulously reduced. The moment he shows himself our trade leaves us—all consumers apply to him; and a branch of native industry, having countless ramifications, is all at once rendered completely stagnant. This rival, who is no other than the sun, wages war mercilessly against us, and we suspect that he has been raised up by perfidious Albion (good policy nowadays); inasmuch as he displays toward that haughty island a circumspection with which he dispenses in our case.

What we pray for is that it may please you to pass a law ordering the shutting up of all windows, skylights, dormer-windows, outside and inside shutters, curtains, blinds, bull's-eyes; in a word, of all openings, holes, chinks, clefts, and fissures, by or through which the light of the sun has been in use to enter houses, to the prejudice of the meritorious manufactures with which we flatter ourselves we have accommodated our country—a country that, in gratitude, ought not to abandon us now to a strife so unequal.

We trust, gentlemen, that you will not regard this our request as a satire, or refuse it without at least first hearing the reasons which we have to urge in its support.

And, first, if you shut up as much as possible all access to natural light, and create a demand for artificial light, which of our French manufactures will not be encouraged by it?

If more tallow is consumed, then there must be more oxen and sheep; and, consequently, we shall behold the multiplication of meadows, meat, wool, hides, and above all, manure, which is the basis and foundation of all agricultural wealth.

If more oil is consumed, then we shall have an extended cultivation of the poppy, of the olive, and of rape. These rich and soil-exhausting plants will come at the right time to enable us to avail ourselves of the increased fertility that the rearing of additional cattle will impart to our lands.

Our heaths will be covered with resinous trees. Numerous swarms of bees will, on the mountains, gather perfumed treasures, now wasting their fragrance on the desert air, like the flowers from which they emanate. No branch of agriculture but will then exhibit a cheering development.

The same remark applies to navigation. Thousands of vessels will proceed to the whale fishery; and in a short time, we shall possess a navy capable of maintaining the honor of France, and gratifying the patriotic aspirations of your petitioners, the undersigned candlemakers and others.

But what shall we say of the manufacture of articles de Paris? Henceforth you will behold gildings, bronzes, crystals, in candlesticks, in lamps, in lustres, in candelabra, shining forth in spacious showrooms, compared with which those of the present day can be regarded but as mere shops.

No poor resinier from his heights on the seacoast, no coalminer from the depth of his sable gallery, but will rejoice in higher wages and increased prosperity.

Only have the goodness to reflect, gentlemen, and you will be convinced that there is perhaps no Frenchman, from the wealthy coalmaster to the humblest vendor of lucifer matches, whose lot will not be ameliorated by the success of this our petition.

We foresee your objections, gentlemen, but we know that you can oppose to us none but such as you have picked up from the effete works of the partisans of Free Trade. We defy you to utter a single word against us which will not instantly rebound against yourselves and your entire policy.

You will tell us that, if we gain by the protection we seek, the country will lose by it, because the consumer must bear the loss.

We answer:

You have ceased to have any right to invoke the interest of the consumer; for, whenever his interest is found opposed to that of the producer, you sacrifice the former. You have done so for the purpose of encouraging labor and increasing employment. For the same reason you should do so again.

You have yourselves obviated this objection. When you are told that the consumer is interested in the free importation of iron, coal, corn, textile fabrics—yes, you reply, but the producer is interested in their exclusion. Well, be it so; if consumers are interested in the free admission of natural light, the producers of artificial light are equally interested in its prohibition.

But, again, you may say that the producer and consumer are identical. If the manufacturer gain by protection, he will make the agriculturist also a gainer; and if agriculture prosper, it will open a vent to manufactures. Very well; if you confer upon us the monopoly of furnishing light during the day, first of all we shall purchase quantities of tallow, coals, oils, resinous substances, wax, alcohol—besides silver, iron, bronze, crystal—to carry on our manufactures; and then we, and those who furnish us with such commodities, having become rich will consume a great deal, and impart prosperity to all the other branches of our national industry.

If you urge that the light of the sun is a gratuitous gift of nature, and that to reject such gifts is to reject wealth itself under pretense of encouraging the means of acquiring it, we would caution you against giving a death-blow to your own policy. Remember that hitherto you have always repelled foreign products, because they approximate more nearly than home products the character of gratuitous gifts. To comply with the exactions of other monopolists, you have only half a motive; and to repulse us simply because we stand on a stronger vantage-ground than others would be to adopt the equation $+ \times + = -$; in other words, it would be to heap absurdity upon absurdity.

Nature and human labor cooperate in various proportions (depending on countries and climates) in the production of commodities. The part nature executes is always gratuitous; it is the part executed by human labor that constitutes value, and is paid for.

If a Lisbon orange sells for half the price of a Paris orange, it is because natural, and consequently gratuitous, heat does for one what artificial, and therefore expensive, heat must do for the other.

When an orange comes to us from Portugal, we may conclude that it is furnished in part gratuitously, in part for an onerous consideration; in other words, it comes to us at half price as compared with those of Paris.

Now, it is precisely the gratuitous half (pardon the word) that we contend should be excluded. You say, How can national labor sustain competition with foreign labor, when the former has all the work to do, and the latter only does one-half, the sun supplying the remainder? But if this half, being gratuitous, determines you to exclude competition, how should the whole, being gratuitous, induce you to admit competition? If you were consistent, you would, while excluding as hurtful to native industry what is half gratuitous, exclude a fortiori and with double zeal, that which is altogether gratuitous.

Once more, when products such as coal, iron, corn, or textile fabrics are sent us from abroad, and we can acquire them with less labor than if we made them ourselves, the difference is a free gift conferred upon us. The gift is more or less considerable in proportion as the difference is more or less great. It amounts to a quarter, a half, or three-quarters of the value of the product, when the foreigner only asks us for three-fourths, a half, or a quarter of the price we should otherwise pay. It is as perfect and complete as it can be, when the donor (like the sun in furnishing us with light) asks us for nothing. The question, and we ask it formally, is this: Do you desire for our country the benefit of gratuitous consumption, or the pretended advantages of onerous production? Make your choice, but be logical; for as long as you exclude, as you do, coal, iron, corn, foreign fabrics, in proportion as their price approximates to zero, what inconsistency it would be to admit the light of the sun, the price of which is already at zero during the entire day!

8

Differential Duties—Tariffs

A poor vine-dresser of the Gironde had trained with fond enthusiasm a slip of vine, which, after much fatigue and much labor, yielded him at length a tun of wine; and his success made him forget that each drop of this precious nectar had cost his brow a drop of sweat. "I shall sell it," said he to his wife, "and with the price I shall buy fabrics sufficient to enable you to furnish a trousseau for our daughter." The honest countryman repaired to the nearest town, and met a Belgian and an Englishman. The Belgian said to him: "Give me your cask of wine, and I will give you in exchange fifteen parcels of fabric." The Englishman said: "Give me your wine, and I will give you twenty parcels of fabric; for we English can manufacture the fabric cheaper than the Belgians." But a Customhouse officer, who was present interposed, and said: "My good friend, exchange with the Belgian if you think proper, but my orders are to prevent you from making an exchange with the Englishman." "What!" exclaimed the countryman; "you wish me to be content with fifteen parcels of stuff that have come from Brussels when I can get twenty parcels that have come from Manchester?" "Certainly;

don't you see that France would be a loser if you received twenty parcels instead of fifteen?" "I am at a loss to understand you," said the vine-dresser. "And I am at a loss to explain it," rejoined the Customhouse official; "but the thing is certain, for all our deputies, ministers, and journalists agree in this, that the more a nation receives in exchange for a given quantity of its products, the more it is impoverished." The peasant found it necessary to conclude a bargain with the Belgian. The daughter of the peasant got only three-quarters of her trousseau; and these simple people are still asking themselves how it happens that one is ruined by receiving four instead of three; and why a person is richer with three dozen towels than with four dozen.

9

IMMENSE DISCOVERY

At a time when everybody is bent on bringing about a saving in the expense of transport—and when, in order to effect this saving, we are forming roads and canals, improving our steamers, and connecting Paris with all our frontiers by a network of railways—at a time, too, when I believe we are ardently and sincerely seeking a solution of the problem, how to bring the prices of commodities, in the place where they are to be consumed, as nearly as possible to the level of their prices in the place where they were produced—I should think myself remiss to my country, to my age, and to myself if I kept any longer secret the marvellous discovery which I have just made.

The illusions of inventors are proverbial, but I am positively certain that I have discovered an infallible means of bringing products from every part of the world to France, and vice versa, at a considerable reduction of cost.

Infallible, did I say? Its being infallible is only one of the advantages of my invention.

It requires neither plans, estimates, preparatory study, engineers, mechanists, contractors, capital, shareholders, or Government aid!

It presents no danger of shipwreck, explosion, fire, or collision!

It may be brought into operation at any time!

Moreover—and this must undoubtedly recommend it to the public—it will not add a penny to the Budget, but the reverse. It will not increase the staff of functionaries, but the reverse. It will interfere with no man's liberty, but the reverse.

It is observation, not chance, which has put me in possession of this discovery, and I will tell you what suggested it.

I had at the time this question to resolve:

"Why does an article manufactured at Brussels, for example, cost dearer when it comes to Paris?"

I soon perceived that it proceeds from this: That between Paris and Brussels obstacles of many kinds exist. First of all, there is distance, which entails loss of time, and we must either submit to this ourselves, or pay another to submit to it. Then come rivers, marshes, accidents, bad roads, which are so many difficulties to be surmounted. We succeed in building bridges, in forming roads, and making them smoother by pavements, iron rails, etc. But all this is costly, and the commodity must be made to bear the cost. Then there are robbers who infest the roads, and a body of police must be kept up, etc.

Now, among these obstacles there is one which we have ourselves set up, and at no little cost, too, between Brussels and Paris. There are men who lie in ambuscade along the frontier, armed to the teeth, and whose business it is to throw difficulties in the way of transporting merchandise from one country to the other. They are called Customhouse officers, and they act in precisely the same way as ruts and bad roads. They retard, they trammel commerce, they augment the difference we have noted between the price paid by the consumer and the price received by the producer—that very difference, the reduction of which, as far as possible, forms the subject of our problem.

That problem is resolved in three words: Reduce your tariff.

You will then have done what is equivalent to constructing the Northern Railway without cost, and will immediately begin to put money in your pocket.

In truth, I often seriously ask myself how anything so whimsical could ever have entered into the human brain, as first of all to lay out many millions for the purpose of removing the natural obstacles that lie between France and other countries, and then to lay out many more millions for the purpose of substituting artificial obstacles, which have exactly the same effect; so much so, indeed, that the obstacle created and the obstacle removed neutralize each other, and leave things as they were before, the residue of the operation being a double expense.

A Belgian product is worth at Brussels 20 francs, and the cost of carriage would raise the price at Paris to 30 francs. The same article made in Paris costs 40 francs. And how do we proceed?

In the first place, we impose a duty of 10 francs on the Belgian product, in order to raise its cost price at Paris to 40 francs; and we pay numerous officials to see the duty stringently levied, so that, on the road, the commodity is charged 10 francs for the carriage and 10 francs for the tax.

Having done this, we reason thus: The carriage from Brussels to Paris, which costs 10 francs, is very dear. Let us expend two or three hundred millions (of francs) in railways, and we shall reduce it by one-half. Evidently all that we gain by this is that the Belgian product would sell in Paris for 35 francs, viz:

20 francs, its price at Brussels. 10 francs duty. 5 francs reduced carriage by railway.

Total, 35 francs, representing cost price at Paris. Now, I ask, would we not have attained the same result by lowering the tariff by 5 francs. We should then have—20 francs, the price at Brussels. 5 francs reduced duty. 10 francs carriage by ordinary roads.

Total, 35 francs, representing cost price at Paris. And by this process we should have saved the 200 millions which the railway cost, plus the expense of Customhouse surveillance, for this last would be reduced in proportion to the diminished encouragement held out to smuggling.

But it will be said that the duty is necessary to protect Parisian industry. Be it so; but then you destroy the effect of your railway.

For if you persist in desiring that the Belgian product should cost at Paris 40 francs, you must raise your duty to 15 francs, and then you have—20 francs, the price at Brussels. 15 francs protecting duty. 5 francs railway carriage.

Total, 40 francs, being the equalized price.

Then, I venture to ask, what, under such circumstances, is the good of your railway?

In sober earnestness, let me ask, is it not humiliating that the nineteenth century should make itself a laughingstock to future ages by such puerilities, practiced with such imperturbable gravity? To be the dupe of other people is not very pleasant, but to employ a vast representative apparatus in order to dupe, and double dupe, ourselves—and that, too, in an affair of arithmetic—should surely humble the pride of this age of enlightenment.

10

Reciprocity

We have just seen that whatever increases the expense of conveying commodities from one country to another—in other words, whatever renders transport more onerous—acts in the same way as a protective duty; or if you prefer to put it in another shape, that a protective duty acts in the same way as more onerous transport.

A tariff, then, may be regarded in the same light as a marsh, a rut, an obstruction, a steep declivity—in a word, it is an obstacle, the effect of which is to augment the difference between the price the producer of a commodity receives and the price the consumer pays for it. In the same way, it is undoubtedly true that marshes and quagmires are to be regarded in the same light as protective tariffs.

There are people (few in number, it is true, but there are such people) who begin to understand that obstacles are not less obstacles because they are artificial, and that our mercantile prospects have more to gain from liberty than from protection, and exactly for the same reason that makes a canal more favorable to traffic than a steep, roundabout, and inconvenient road.

But they maintain that this liberty must be reciprocal. If we remove the barriers we have erected against the admission of Spanish goods, for example, Spain must remove the barriers she has erected against the admission of ours. They are, therefore, the advocates of commercial treaties, on the basis of exact reciprocity, concession for concession; let us make the sacrifice of buying, say they, to obtain the advantage of selling.

People who reason in this way, I am sorry to say, are, whether they know it or not, protectionists in principle; only, they are a little more inconsistent than pure protectionists, as the latter are more inconsistent than absolute prohibitionists.

The following apologue will demonstrate this:

STULTA AND PUERA

There were, no matter where, two towns called Stulta and Puera. They completed at great cost a highway from the one town to the other. When this was done, Stulta said to herself: "See how Puera inundates us with her products; we must see to it." In consequence, they created and paid a body of obstructives, so called because their business was to place obstacles in the way of traffic coming from Puera. Soon afterwards Puera did the same.

At the end of some centuries, knowledge having in the interim made great progress, the common sense of Puera enabled her to see that such reciprocal obstacles could only be reciprocally hurtful. She therefore sent an envoy to Stulta, who, laying aside official phraseology, spoke to this effect: "We have made a highway, and now we throw obstacles in the way of using it. This is absurd. It would have been better to have left things as they were. We should not, in that case, have had to pay for making the road in the first place, nor afterwards have incurred the expense of maintaining obstructives. In the name of Puera, I come to propose to you, not to give up opposing each other all at once—that would be to act upon a principle, and we despise principles as much as you do—but to lessen somewhat the present obstacles, taking care to estimate equitably the respective sacrifices we make for this purpose." So spoke the envoy. Stulta asked for time to consider the proposal, and proceeded to consult, in succession, her manufacturers and agriculturists. At length, after the lapse of some years, she declared that the negotiations were broken off.

On receiving this intimation, the inhabitants of Puera held a meeting. An old gentleman (they always suspected he had been secretly bought by Stulta) rose and said: The obstacles created by Stulta injure our sales, which is a misfortune. Those we have ourselves created injure our purchases, which is another misfortune. With reference to the first, we are powerless; but the second rests with ourselves. Let us, at least, get rid of one, since we cannot rid ourselves of both evils. Let us suppress our obstructives without requiring Stulta to do the same. Some day, no doubt, she will come to know her own interests better.

A second counselor, a practical, matter-of-fact man, guiltless of any acquaintance with principles, and brought up in the ways of his forefathers, replied: "Don't listen to that Utopian dreamer, that theorist, that innovator, that economist, that Stultomaniac. We shall all be undone if the stoppages of the road are not equalized, weighed, and balanced between Stulta and Puera. There would be greater difficulty in going than in coming, in exporting than in importing. We should find ourselves in the same condition of inferiority relatively to Stulta as Havre, Nantes, Bordeaux, Lisbon, London, Hamburg, and New Orleans are with relation to the towns situated at the sources of the Seine, the Loire, the Garonne, the Tagus, the Thames, the Elbe, and the Mississippi, for it is more difficult for a ship to ascend than to descend a river. (A Voice: Towns at the mouths of rivers prosper more than towns at their source.) This is impossible. (Same Voice: But it is so.) Well, if it be so, they have prospered contrary to rules." Reasoning so conclusive convinced the assembly, and the orator followed up his victory by talking largely of national independence, national honor, national dignity, national labor, inundation of products, tributes, murderous competition. In short, he carried the vote in favor of the maintenance of obstacles; and if you are at all curious on the subject, I can point out to you countries where you will see with your own eyes Road-makers and

Obstructives working together on the most friendly terms possible, under the orders of the same legislative assembly, and at the expense of the same taxpayers, the one set endeavoring to clear the road, and the other set doing their utmost to render it impassable.

11

Nominal Prices

Do you desire to be in a situation to decide between liberty and protection? Do you desire to appreciate the impact of an economic phenomenon? Inquire into its effects upon the abundance or scarcity of commodities, and not upon the rise or fall of prices. Distrust nominal prices; they will only land you in an inextricable labyrinth.

Mr. Matthieu de Dombasle, after having shown that Protection raises prices, adds:

"The enhancement of prices increases the expense of living, and consequently the price of labor, and each man receives, in the enhanced price of his products, compensation for the higher prices he has been obliged to pay for the things he has occasion to buy. Thus, if everyone pays more as a consumer, everyone receives more as a producer."

It is evident that we could reverse this argument, and say:

"If everyone receives more as a producer, everyone pays more as a consumer."

Now, what does this prove? Nothing but this, that Protection displaces wealth uselessly and unjustly. In so far, it simply perpetrates spoliation.

Again, to conclude that this vast apparatus leads to simple compensations, we must stick to the "consequently" of Mr. de Dombasle, and make sure that the price of labor will not fail to rise with the price of the protected products. This is a question of fact that I remit to Mr. Moreau de Jonnes, that he may take the trouble to find out whether the rate of wages advances along with the price of shares in the coal mines of Anzin. For my own part, I do not believe that it does; because, in my opinion, the price of labor, like the price of everything else, is governed by the relation of supply to demand. Now, I am convinced that restriction diminishes the supply of coal, and consequently enhances its price; but I do not see so clearly that it increases the demand for labor, so as to enhance the rate of wages; and that this effect should be produced is all the less likely, because the quantity of labor demanded depends on the available capital. Now, Protection may indeed displace capital, and cause its transference from one employment to another, but it can never increase it by a single farthing.

But this question, which is one of the greatest interest and importance, will be examined in another place. I return to the subject of nominal price; and I maintain that it is not one of those absurdities that can be rendered specious by such reasonings as those of Mr. de Dombasle.

Put the case of a nation that is isolated, and possesses a given amount of specie, and that chooses to amuse itself by burning each year one-half of all the commodities that it possesses. I undertake to prove that, according to the theory of Mr. de Dombasle, it will not be less rich.

In fact, in consequence of the fire, all things will be doubled in price, and the inventories of property, made before and after the destruction, will show exactly the same nominal value. But then what will the country in question have lost? If John buys his cloth dearer, he also sells his corn at a higher price; and if Peter loses on his purchase of corn, he retrieves his losses by the sale of his cloth. "Each recovers, in the extra price of his products, the extra expense of living he has been put to; and if everybody pays as a consumer, everybody receives a corresponding amount as a producer."

All this is a jingling quibble, and not science. The truth, in plain terms, is this: That men consume cloth and corn by fire or by using them, and that the effect is the same as regards money, but not as regards wealth, for it is precisely in the use of commodities that wealth or material prosperity consists.

In the same way, restriction, while diminishing the abundance of things, may raise their price to such an extent that each party shall be, pecuniarily speaking, as rich as before. But to set down in an inventory three measures of corn at 20s., or four measures at 15s., because the result is still 60s.—would this, I ask, come to the same thing with reference to the satisfaction of men's wants?

It is to this, the consumer's point of view, that I shall never cease to recall the Protectionists, for this is the end and design of all our efforts, and the solution of all problems. I shall never cease to say to them: Is it, or is it not, true that restriction by impeding exchanges, by limiting the division of labor, by forcing labor to connect itself with difficulties of climate and situation, diminishes ultimately the quantity of commodities produced by a determinate amount of efforts? And what does this signify, it will be said, if the smaller quantity produced under the regime of Protection has the same nominal value as that produced under the regime of liberty? The answer is obvious. Man does not live upon nominal values, but upon real products, and the more products there are, whatever be their price, the richer he is.

In writing what precedes, I never expected to meet with an anti-economist who was enough of a logician to admit, in so many words, that the wealth of nations depends on the value of things, apart from the consideration of their abundance. But here is what I find in the work of Mr. de Saint-Chamans (p. 210):

> If fifteen million worth of commodities, sold to foreigners, are taken from the total production, estimated at fifty millions, the thirty-five million worth of commodities remaining,

not being sufficient to meet the ordinary demand, will increase in price, and rise to the value of fifty millions. In that case the revenue of the country will represent a value of fifteen million additional. . . . There would then be an increase of the wealth of the country to the extent of fifteen million, exactly the amount of specie imported.

This is a pleasant view of the matter! If a nation produces in one year, from its agriculture and commerce, a value of fifty million it has only to sell a quarter of it to the foreigner to be a quarter richer! Then if it sells the half, it will be one-half richer! And if it should sell the whole, to its last tuft of wool and its last grain of wheat, it would bring up its revenue to one hundred million. What a way of getting rich, by producing infinite dearness by absolute scarcity!

Again, would you judge of the two doctrines? Submit them to the test of exaggeration.

According to the doctrine of Mr. de Saint-Chamans, the French would be quite as rich—that is to say, quite as well supplied with all things—had they only a thousandth part of their annual products, because they would be worth a thousand times more.

According to our doctrine, the French would be infinitely rich if their annual products were infinitely abundant, and consequently, without any value at all.

12

Does Protection Raise Wages?

Let us inquire whether injustice is not done you by fixing legislatively the people from whom you are to purchase the things you have need of—bread, meat, linens, or cloth; and in dictating, if I may say so, the artificial scale of prices which you are to adopt in your dealings.

Is it true that protection, which admittedly makes you pay dearer for everything, and entails a loss upon you in this respect, raises proportionately your wages?

On what does the rate of wages depend?

One of your own class has put it forcefully, thus: When two workmen run after one master, wages fall; they rise when two masters run after one workman.

For the sake of brevity, allow me to make use of this formula, more scientific, although, perhaps, not quite so clear. The rate of wages depends on the proportion that the supply of labor bears to the demand for it.

Now, on what does the supply of labor depend?

On the number of men waiting for employment; and on this first element protection can have no effect.

On what does the rate of wages depend?

On the disposable capital of the nation. But does the law which says: We shall no longer receive such or such a product from abroad, we shall make it at home, augment the capital? Not in the least degree. It may force capital from one employment to another, but it does not increase it by a single farthing. It does not then increase the demand for labor.

We point with pride to a certain manufacture. Is it established or maintained with capital that has fallen from the moon? No; that capital has been withdrawn from agriculture, from shipping, from the production of wines. And this is the reason why, under the system of protective tariffs, there are more workmen in our mines and in our manufacturing towns, and fewer sailors in our ports, and fewer laborers in our fields and vineyards. I could expatiate at length on this subject, but I prefer to explain what I mean by an example.

A countryman was possessed of twenty acres of land, which he worked with a capital of £400. He divided his land into four parts and established the following rotation of crops: 1st, corn; 2nd, wheat; 3rd, clover; 4th, rye. He required for his own family only a moderate portion of the grain, meat, and milk that his farm produced, and he sold the surplus to buy oil, flax, wine, etc. His whole capital was expended each year in wages, hires, and small payments to the working classes in his neighborhood. This capital was returned to him in his sales, and even went on increasing year by year; and our countryman, knowing very well that capital produces nothing when it is unemployed, benefited the working classes by devoting the annual surplus to enclosing and clearing his land, and to improving his agricultural implements and farm buildings. He had even some savings in the neighboring town with his banker, who, of course, did not let the money lie idle in his till, but lent it to shipowners and contractors for public works, so that these savings were always resolving themselves into wages.

At length the countryman died, and his son, who succeeded him, said to himself: "My father was a dupe all his life. He purchased oil, and so paid tribute to Provence, whilst our own land, with some pains, can be made to grow the olive. He bought cloth, wine, and oranges, and thus paid tribute to Brittany, Medoc, and Hyeres, while we can cultivate hemp, the vine, and the orange tree with more or less success. He paid tribute to the miller and the weaver, while our own domestics can weave our linen and grind our wheat. In this way he ruined himself, and spent among strangers that money which he might have spent at home."

Misled by such reasoning, the restive youth changed his rotation of crops. His land he divided into twenty divisions. In one he planted olives, in another mulberry trees, in a third he sowed flax, in a fourth he had vines, in a fifth wheat, and so on. By this means he succeeded in supplying his family with what they required, and felt himself independent. He no longer drew anything from the general circulation, nor did he add anything to it.

Was he the richer for this? No; for the soil was not adapted for the cultivation of the vine, and the climate was not fitted for the successful cultivation of the olive; and he was not long in finding out that his family was less plentifully provided with all the things they wanted than in the time of his father, who procured them by exchanging his surplus produce.

As regarded his workmen, they had no more employment than formerly. There were five times more fields, but each field was five times smaller; they produced oil, but they produced less wheat; he no longer purchased linens, but he no longer sold rye. Moreover, the farmer could expend in wages only the amount of his capital, and his capital went on constantly diminishing. A great part of it went for buildings, and the various implements needed for the more varied cultivation in which he had engaged. In short, the supply of labor remained the same, but as the means of remunerating that labor fell off, the ultimate result was a forcible reduction of wages.

On a greater scale, this is exactly what takes place in the case of a nation that isolates itself by adopting a prohibitive system. It multiplies its branches of industry, I grant, but they become of diminished scale; it adopts, so to speak, a more complicated industrial rotation, but it is not so productive, because its capital and labor have now to struggle with natural difficulties. A greater proportion of its circulating capital, which forms the wages fund, must be converted into fixed capital. What remains may have more varied employment, but the total mass is not increased. It is like distributing the water of a pond among a multitude of shallow reservoirs—it covers more ground, and presents a greater surface to the rays of the sun, and it is precisely for this reason that it is all the sooner absorbed, evaporated, and lost.

The amount of capital and labor being given, they create a smaller amount of commodities in proportion as they encounter more obstacles. It is beyond doubt that when international obstructions force capital and labor into channels and localities where they meet with greater difficulties of soil and climate, the general result must be, fewer products created—that is to say, fewer enjoyments for consumers. Now, when there are fewer enjoyments upon the whole, will the workman's share of them be augmented? If it were augmented, as is asserted, then the rich—the men who make the laws—would find their own share not only subject to the general diminution, but that diminished share would be still further reduced by what was added to the laborers' share. Is this possible? Is it credible? I advise you, workmen, to reject such suspicious generosity.

13

THEORY—PRACTICE

As advocates of Free Trade, we are accused of being theorists, and of not taking practice sufficiently into account. "What fearful prejudices were entertained against Mr. Say," says Mr. Ferrier,[1]

> by that long train of distinguished administrators, and that imposing phalanx of authors who dissented from his opinions; and Mr. Say was not unaware of it. Hear what he says: It has been alleged in support of errors of long standing that there must have been some foundation for ideas which have been adopted by all nations. Ought we not to distrust observations and reasonings which run counter to opinions which have been constantly entertained down to our own time, and which have been regarded as sound by so many men remarkable for their enlightenment and their good intentions? This argument, I allow, is calculated to make a

---

[1] *De l'Administration Commerciale opposee a l'Economie Politique*, p. 5.

profound impression, and it might have cast doubt upon
points which we deem the most incontestable, if we had not
seen, by turns, opinions the most false, and now generally
acknowledged to be false, received and professed by everybody during a long series of ages. Not very long ago all
nations, from the rudest to the most enlightened, and all
men, from the street-porter to the savant, admitted the existence of four elements. No one thought of contesting that
doctrine, which, however, is false; so much so that even the
greenest assistant in a naturalist's class-room would be
ashamed to say that he regarded earth, water and fire as elements.

On this Mr. Ferrier remarks:

If Mr. Say thinks to answer thus the very strong objection
which he brings forward he is singularly mistaken. That
men, otherwise well informed, should have been mistaken
for centuries on certain points of natural history is easily
understood, and proves nothing. Water, air, earth and fire,
whether elements or not, are not the less useful to man. . . .
Such errors are unimportant: they lead to no popular com-
motions, no uneasiness in the public mind; they run counter
to no pecuniary interest; and this is the reason why without
any felt inconvenience they may endure for a thousand
years. The physical world goes on as if they did not exist.
But of errors in the moral world can the same thing be said?
Can we conceive that a system of administration, found to
be absolutely false and therefore hurtful, should be followed
out among many nations for centuries, with the general
approval of all well-informed men? Can it be explained how
such a system could coexist with the constantly increasing
prosperity of nations? Mr. Say admits that the argument
which he combats is fitted to make a profound impression.
Yes, indeed; and the impression remains; for Mr. Say has
rather deepened than done away with it.

Let us hear what Mr. de Saint-Chamans says on the same subject:

It was only in the middle of the last century, of that eighteenth century which handed over all subjects and all principles without exception to free discussion, that these speculative purveyors of ideas, applied by them to all things

without being really applicable to anything, began to write upon political economy. There existed previously a system of political economy not to be found in books, but which had been put in practical operation by governments. Colbert, it is said, was the inventor of it, and it was adopted as a rule by all the nations of Europe. The singular thing is that, in spite of contempt and maledictions, in spite of all the discoveries of the modern school, it still remains in practical operation. This system, which our authors have called the mercantile system, was designed to . . . impede, by prohibitions or import duties, the entry of foreign products which might ruin our own manufactures by their competition. Economic writers of all schools[2] have declared this system untenable, absurd, and calculated to impoverish any country. It has been banished from all their books, and forced to take refuge in the practical legislation of all nations. They cannot conceive why, in measures relating to national wealth, governments should not follow the advice and opinions of learned authors, rather than trust to their experience of the tried working of a system which has been long in operation. Above all, they cannot conceive why the French government should in economic questions obstinately set itself to resist the progress of enlightenment, and maintain in its practice those ancient errors, which all our economic writers have exposed. But enough of this mercantile system, which has nothing in its favor but facts, and is not defended by any speculative writer.[3]

Such language as this would lead one to suppose that in demanding for everyone the free disposal of his property, economists were propounding some new system, some new, strange and chimerical social order, a sort of phalanstere, coined in the mint of their own brain, and without precedent in the annals of the human race. To me it would seem that if we have here anything

---

[2]Might we not say, that it is a "fearful prejudice" against Misters Ferrier and Saint-Chamans, that "economists of all schools," that is to say, everybody who has studied the question, should have arrived at the conclusion, that, after all, liberty is better than constraint, and the laws of God wiser than those of Colbert.

[3]*Du Systeme de l'Impot*, by Mr. le Vicomte de Saint-Chamans, p. II.

factitious or contingent, it is to be found, not in liberty, but in protection; not in the free power of exchanging, but in customs duties employed to overturn artificially the natural course of remuneration.

But our business at present is not to compare, or pronounce between, the two systems; but to inquire which of the two is founded on experience.

The advocates of monopoly maintain that the facts are on their side, and that we have on our side only theory.

They flatter themselves that this long series of public acts, this old experience of Europe, which they invoke, has presented itself as something very formidable to the mind of Mr. Say; and I grant that he has not refuted it with his characteristic sagacity. For my own part, I am not disposed to concede to the monopolists the domain of facts, for they have only in their favor facts that are forced and exceptional; and we oppose to these, facts that are universal, the free and voluntary acts of mankind at large.

What do we say; and what do they say?

We say—

"You should buy from others what you cannot make for yourself but at a greater expense."

And they say—

"It is better to make things for yourself, although they cost you more than the price at which you could buy them from others."

Now, gentlemen, throwing aside theory, argument, demonstration—all which seem to affect you with nausea—which of these two assertions has on its side the sanction of universal practice?

Visit your fields, your workshops, your forges, your warehouses; look above, below, and around you; look at what takes place in your own houses; note your own everyday acts; and say what is the principle that guides these laborers, artisans and merchants; say what is your own personal practice.

Does the farmer make his own clothes? Does the tailor produce the corn he consumes? Does your housekeeper continue to have your bread made at home, after she finds she can buy it cheaper from the baker? Do you resign the pen for the brush to save your paying tribute to the shoeblack? Does the entire economy of society not rest upon the separation of employments, the division of labor—in a word, upon exchange? And what is exchange but a calculation which we make with a view to discontinuing direct production in every case in which we find that possible, and in which indirect acquisition enables us to effect a saving in time and in effort?

It is not you, therefore, who are the men of practice, since you cannot point to a single human being who acts upon your principle.

But you will say, we never intended to make our principle a rule for individual relations. We perfectly understand that this would be to break up the bond of society, and would force men to live like snails, each in his own shell. All that we contend is that our principle regulates de facto the relations that obtain between the different agglomerations of the human family.

Well, I affirm that this principle is still erroneous. The family, the commune, the canton, the department, the province, are so many agglomerations, which all, without any exception, reject practically your principle, and have never dreamt of acting on it. All procure themselves, by means of exchange, those things that it would cost them dearer to procure by means of production. And nations would do the same, did you not hinder them by force.

We, then, are the men of practice and of experience; for we oppose to the restriction you have placed exceptionally on certain international exchanges the practice and experience of all individuals and of all agglomerations of individuals, whose acts are voluntary and can consequently be adduced as evidence. But you begin by constraining, by hindering, and then you lay hold of acts that are forced or prohibited, as warranting you to exclaim, "We have practice and experience on our side!"

You inveigh against our theory, and even against theories in general. But when you lay down a principle in opposition to ours you perhaps imagine you are not proceeding on theory. Clear your heads of that idea. You, in fact, form a theory as we do; but between your theory and ours there is this difference:

Our theory consists merely in observing universal facts, universal opinions, calculations and ways of proceeding that universally prevail; and in classifying these and rendering them co-ordinate, with a view to their being more easily understood.

Our theory is so little opposed to practice that it is nothing else but practice explained. We observe men acting as they are moved by the instinct of self-preservation and a desire for progress, and what they thus do freely and voluntarily we denominate political or social economy. We can never help repeating that each individual man is practically an excellent economist, producing or exchanging according as he finds it more to his interest to produce or to exchange. Each, by experience, educates himself in this science; or, rather, the science itself is only this same experience accurately observed and methodically explained.

But on your side you construct a theory in the worst sense of the word. You imagine, you invent, a course of proceeding that is not sanctioned by the practice of any living man under the canopy of heaven; and then you invoke the aid of constraint and prohibition. It is quite necessary that you should have recourse to force, for you desire that men should be made to produce those things that they find it more advantageous to buy; you desire that they should renounce this advantage, and act upon a doctrine that implies a contradiction in terms.

I defy you to take the doctrine, which you acknowledge would be absurd in the relations of individuals, and extend it, even in speculation, to transactions between families, communities, or provinces. By your own admission it is only applicable to international relations.

This is the reason why you are forced to keep repeating:

"There are no absolute principles, no inflexible rules. What is good for an individual, a family, a province, is bad for a nation. What is good in detail—namely, to purchase rather than produce, when purchasing is more advantageous than producing—that same is bad in the gross. The political economy of individuals is not that of nations"; and other nonsense of the same kind.

And to what does all this tend? Look at it a little closer. The intention is to prove that we, the consumers, are your property!—that we are yours body and soul!—that you have an exclusive right over our stomachs and our limbs!—that it belongs to you to feed and clothe us on your own terms, whatever be your ignorance, incapacity or rapacity!

No, you are not men of practice; you are men of abstraction—and of extortion.

14

CONFLICT OF PRINCIPLES

There is one thing that confounds me; and it is this: Sincere publicists, studying the economy of society from the producer's point of view, have laid down this double formula:

"Governments should order the interests of consumers who are subject to their laws, in such a way as to be favorable to national industry."

"They should bring distant consumers under subjection to their laws, for the purpose of ordering their interests in a way favorable to national industry."

The first of these formulas gets the name of protection; the second we call outlets, or the creating of markets, or vents, for our produce.

Both are founded on what we call the Balance of Trade:

"A nation is impoverished when it imports; enriched when it exports."

For if every purchase from a foreign country is a tribute paid and a national loss, it follows, of course, that it is right to restrain, and even prohibit, importations.

And if every sale to a foreign country is a tribute received, and a national profit, it is quite right and natural to create markets for our products even by force.

The system of protection and the colonial system are, then, only two aspects of one and the same theory. To hinder our fellow-citizens from buying from foreigners, and to force foreigners to buy from our fellow-citizens, are only two consequences of one and the same principle.

Now, it is impossible not to admit that this doctrine, if true, makes general utility to repose on monopoly or internal spoliation, and on conquest or external spoliation.

I enter a cottage on the French side of the Pyrenees.

The father of the family has received but slender wages. His half-naked children shiver in the icy north wind; the fire is extinguished, and there is nothing on the table. There are wool, firewood, and corn on the other side of the mountain; but these good things are forbidden to the poor day-laborer, for the other side of the mountain is not in France. Foreign firewood is not allowed to warm the cottage hearth; and the shepherd's children can never know the taste of Biscayan wheat,[1] and the wool of Navarre can never warm their benumbed limbs. General utility has so ordered it. Be it so; but let us agree that all this is in direct opposition to the first principles of justice. To dispose legislatively of the interests of consumers, and postpone them to the supposed interests of national industry, is to encroach upon their liberty—it is to prohibit an act; namely, the act of exchange, that has in it nothing contrary to good morals; in a word, it is to do them an act of injustice.

And yet this is necessary, we are told, unless we wish to see national labor at a standstill, and public prosperity sustain a fatal shock.

Writers of the protectionist school, then, have arrived at the melancholy conclusion that there is a radical incompatibility between Justice and Utility.

---

[1]The French word employed is *meture*, probably a Spanish word Gallicised—*mestura*, meslin, mixed corn, as wheat and rye.—Translator.

On the other hand, if it be the interest of each nation to sell, and not to buy, the natural state of their relations must consist in a violent action and reaction, for each will seek to impose its products on all, and all will endeavor to repel the products of each.

A sale, in fact, implies a purchase, and since, according to this doctrine, to sell is beneficial, and to buy is the reverse, every international transaction would imply the amelioration of one people and the deterioration of another.

But if men are, on the one hand, irresistibly impelled toward what is for their profit, and if, on the other, they resist instinctively what is hurtful, we are forced to conclude that each nation carries in its bosom a natural force of expansion, and a not less natural force of resistance, which forces are equally injurious to all other nations; or, in other words, that antagonism and war are the natural state of human society.

Thus the theory we are discussing may be summed up in these two axioms:

Utility is incompatible with Justice at home.

Utility is incompatible with Peace abroad.

Now, what astonishes and confounds me is that a publicist, a statesman, who sincerely holds an economical doctrine that runs so violently counter to other principles that are incontestable, should be able to enjoy one moment of calm or peace of mind.

For my own part, it seems to me that if I had entered the precincts of the science by the same gate, if I had failed to perceive clearly that Liberty, Utility, Justice, Peace, are things not only compatible, but strictly allied with each other, and, so to speak, identical, I should have endeavored to forget what I had learned, and I should have asked:

"How God could have willed that men should attain prosperity only through Injustice and War? How He could have willed that they should be unable to avoid Injustice and War except by renouncing the possibility of attaining prosperity?

"Dare I adopt, as the basis of the legislation of a great nation, a science that thus misleads me by false lights, that has conducted me to this horrible blasphemy, and landed me in so dreadful an alternative? And when a long train of illustrious philosophers have been conducted by this science, to which they have devoted their lives, to more consoling results—when they affirm that Liberty and Utility are perfectly reconcilable with Justice and Peace—that all these great principles run in infinitely extended parallels, and will do so to all eternity, without running counter to each other—I would ask, Have they not in their favor that presumption which results from all that we know of the goodness and wisdom of God, as manifested in the sublime harmony of the material creation? In the face of such a presumption, and of so many reliable authorities, ought I to believe lightly that God has been pleased to implant antagonism and dissonance in the laws of the moral world? No; before I should venture to conclude that the principles of social order run counter to and neutralize each other, and are in eternal and irreconcilable opposition—before I should venture to impose on my fellow-citizens a system so impious as that to which my reasonings would appear to lead—I should set myself to re-examine the whole chain of these reasonings, and assure myself that at this stage of the journey I had not missed my way."

But if, after a candid and searching examination, twenty times repeated, I arrived always at this frightful conclusion, that we must choose between the Right and the Good, discouraged, I should reject the science, and bury myself in voluntary ignorance; above all, I should decline all participation in public affairs, leaving to men of another temper and constitution the burden and responsibility of a choice so painful.

15

RECIPROCITY AGAIN

Mr. De Saint-Cricq inquires: "Whether it is certain that the foreigner will buy from us as much as he sells?"

Mr. de Dombasle asks: "What reason we have to believe that English producers will take from us, rather than from some other country of the world, the commodities they have need of, and an amount of commodities equivalent in value to that of their exports to France?"

I wonder how so many men who call themselves practical men should have all reasoned without reference to practice!

In practice, does a single exchange take place, out of a hundred, out of a thousand, out of ten thousand, perhaps, which represents the direct barter of commodity for commodity? Never since the introduction of money has any agriculturist said: I want to buy shoes, hats, advice, lessons; but only from the shoemaker, the hat-maker, the lawyer, the professor, who will purchase from me corn to an exactly equivalent value. And why should nations bring each other under a yoke of this kind?

Practically, how are such matters transacted?

Let us suppose people shut out from external relations. A man, we will suppose, produces wheat. He sends it to the home market, and offers it for the highest price he can obtain. He receives in exchange—what? Coins, which are just so many drafts or orders, varying very much in amount, by means of which he can draw, in his turn, from the national stores, when he judges it proper, and subject to due competition, everything which he may want or desire. Ultimately, and at the end of the operation, he will have drawn from the mass the exact equivalent of what he has contributed to it, and, in value, his consumption will exactly equal his production.

If the exchanges of the supposed nation with foreigners are left free, it is no longer to the national, but to the general, market that each sends his contributions, and, in turn, derives his supplies for consumption. He has no need to care whether what he sends into the market of the world is purchased by a fellow countryman or by a foreigner; whether the drafts or orders he receives come from a Frenchman or an Englishman; whether the commodities for which he afterwards exchanges these drafts or orders are produced on this or on the other side of the Rhine or the Pyrenees. There is always in each individual case an exact balance between what is contributed and what is received, between what is poured into and what is drawn out of the great common reservoir; and if this is true of each individual it is true of the nation at large.

The only difference between the two cases is that in the last each has to face a more extended market both as regards sales and purchases, and has consequently more chances of transacting both advantageously.

This objection may perhaps be urged: If everybody enters into a league not to take from the general mass the commodities of a certain individual, that individual cannot, in his turn, obtain from the mass what he is in want of. It is the same of nations.

The reply to this is, that if a nation cannot obtain what it has need of in the general market, it will no longer contribute anything to that market. It will work for itself. It will be forced in that case to submit to what you want to impose on it beforehand—isolation.

And this will realize the ideal of the prohibitive system.

Is it not amusing to think that you inflict upon the nation, now and beforehand, this very system, from a fear that it might otherwise run the risk of arriving at it independently of your exertions?

16

Obstruction—The Plea
of the Protectionist

Some years ago I happened to be at Madrid, and went to the Cortes. The subject of debate was a proposed treaty with Portugal for improving the navigation of the Douro. One of the deputies rose and said: "If the navigation of the Douro is improved in the way now proposed, the traffic will be carried on at less expense. The grain of Portugal will, in consequence, be sold in the markets of Castile at a lower price, and will become a formidable rival to our national industry. I oppose the project, unless, indeed, our ministers will undertake to raise the tariff of customs to the extent required to re-establish the equilibrium." The Assembly found the argument unanswerable.

Three months afterwards I was at Lisbon. The same question was discussed in the Senate. A noble hidalgo made a speech: "Mr. President," he said, "this project is absurd. You place guards, at great expense, along the banks of the Douro to prevent Portugal being invaded by Castilian grain; and at the same time you propose, also at great expense, to facilitate that invasion. This is a piece of inconsistency to which I cannot assent. Let us leave the Douro to our children as it has come to us from our fathers."

Afterwards, when the subject of improving the navigation of the Garonne was discussed, I remembered the arguments of the Iberian orators, and I said to myself: If the Toulouse deputies were as good economists as the Spanish deputies, and the representatives of Bordeaux as acute logicians at those of Oporto, assuredly they would leave the Garonne.

"*Dormir au bruit flatteur de son onde naissante*," for the canalisation of the Garonne would favor the invasion of Toulouse products, to the prejudice of Bordeaux, and the inundation of Bordeaux products would do the same thing to the detriment of Toulouse.

17

A Negative Railway

I have said that when, unfortunately, one has regard to the interest of the producer, and not to that of the consumer, it is impossible to avoid running counter to the general interest because the demand of the producer, as such, is only for efforts, wants, and obstacles.

I find a remarkable illustration of this in a Bordeaux newspaper.

Mr. Simiot proposes this question:

Should the proposed railway from Paris to Madrid offer a break of continuity at Bordeaux?

He answers the question in the affirmative, and gives a multiplicity of reasons, which I shall not stop to examine except this one:

The railway from Paris to Bayonne should have a break at Bordeaux for if goods and passengers are forced to stop at that town, profits will accrue to bargemen, porters, commissionaires, hotel-keepers, etc.

Here we have clearly the interest of labor put before the interest of consumers.

But if Bordeaux has a right to profit by a gap in the line of railway, and if such profit is consistent with the public interest, then Angouleme, Poitiers, Tours, Orleans, nay, more, all the intermediate places, Ruffec, Chatellerault, etc., should also demand gaps, as being for the general interest, and, of course, for the interest of national industry; for the more these breaks in the line are multiplied, the greater will be the increase of consignments, commissions, trans-shipments, etc., along the whole extent of the railway. In this way, we shall succeed in having a line of railway composed of successive gaps, and which may be denominated a Negative Railway.

Let the protectionists say what they will, it is not the less certain that the principle of restriction is the very same as the principle of gaps; the sacrifice of the consumer's interest to that of the producer—in other words, the sacrifice of the end to the means.

18

There Are No
Absolute Principles

We cannot wonder enough at the facility with which men resign themselves to continue ignorant of what it is most important that they should know; and we may be certain that such ignorance is incorrigible in those who venture to proclaim this axiom: There are no absolute principles.

You enter the legislative precincts. The subject of debate is whether the law should prohibit international exchanges, or proclaim freedom.

A deputy rises, and says:

If you tolerate these exchanges the foreigner will inundate you with his products: England with her textile fabrics, Belgium with coals, Spain with wools, Italy with silks, Switzerland with cattle, Sweden with iron, Prussia with wheat; so that home industry will no longer be possible.

Another replies—

If you prohibit international exchanges, the various bounties which nature has lavished on different climates will be for you as if they did not exist. You cannot participate in the mechanical skill of the English, in the wealth of the Belgian mines, in the fertility of the Polish soil, in the luxuriance of the Swiss pastures, in the cheapness of Spanish labor, in the warmth of the Italian climate; and you must obtain from an unprofitable and misdirected production those commodities which, through exchange, would have been furnished to you by an easy production.

Assuredly, one of these deputies must be wrong. But which? We must take care to make no mistake on the subject, for this is not a matter of abstract opinion merely. You have to choose between two roads, and one of them leads necessarily to poverty.

To get rid of the dilemma we are told that there are no absolute principles.

This axiom, which is so much in fashion nowadays, not only countenances indolence, but ministers to ambition.

If the theory of prohibition comes to prevail, or if the doctrine of Free Trade comes to triumph, one brief enactment will constitute our whole economic code. In the first case, the law will proclaim that all exchanges with foreign countries are prohibited; in the second, that all exchanges with foreign countries are free; and many grand and distinguished personages will thereby lose their importance.

But if exchange does not possess a character that is peculiar to it; if it is not governed by any natural law; if, capriciously, it be sometimes useful and sometimes detrimental; if it does not find its motive force in the good it accomplishes, its limit in the good it ceases to accomplish; if its consequences cannot be estimated by those who effect exchanges—in a word, if there be no absolute principles, then we must proceed to weigh, balance, and regulate transactions, we must equalize the conditions of labor, and try to find out the average rate of profits—a colossal task, well deserving the large emoluments and powerful influence awarded to those who undertake it.

On entering Paris, which I had come to visit, I said to myself—here are a million human beings who would all die in a short time if provisions of every kind ceased to flow toward this great metropolis. Imagination is baffled when it tries to appreciate the vast multiplicity of commodities that must enter tomorrow through the barriers in order to preserve the inhabitants from falling a prey to the convulsions of famine, rebellion and pillage. And yet all sleep at this moment, and their peaceful slumbers are not disturbed for a single instant by the prospect of such a frightful catastrophe. On the other hand, eighty departments have been laboring today, without concert, without any mutual understanding, for the provisioning of Paris. How does each succeeding day bring what is wanted, nothing more, nothing less, to so gigantic a market? What, then, is the ingenious and secret power that governs the astonishing regularity of movements so complicated, a regularity in which everybody has implicit faith, although happiness and life itself are at stake? That power is an absolute principle, the principle of freedom in transactions. We have faith in that inward light that Providence has placed in the heart of all men, and to which He has confided the preservation and indefinite amelioration of our species, namely, a regard to personal interest—since we must give it its right name—a principle so active, so vigilant, so foreseeing, when it is free in its action. In what situation, I would ask, would the inhabitants of Paris be if a minister should take it into his head to substitute for this power the combinations of his own genius, however superior we might suppose them to be—if he thought to subject to his supreme direction this prodigious mechanism, to hold the springs of it in his hands, to decide by whom, or in what manner, or on what conditions, everything needed should be produced, transported, exchanged and consumed? Truly, there may be much suffering within the walls of Paris—poverty, despair, perhaps starvation, causing more tears to flow than ardent charity is able to dry up; but I affirm that it is probable, nay, that it is certain, that the arbitrary intervention of government would multiply infinitely those sufferings, and spread over all our fellow-citizens those evils which at present affect only a small number of them.

This faith, then, which we repose in a principle, when the question relates only to our home transactions, why should we not retain when the same principle is applied to our international transactions, which are undoubtedly less numerous, less delicate, and less complicated? And if it is not necessary that the municipality should regulate our Parisian industries, weigh our chances, balance our profits and losses, see that our circulating medium is not exhausted, and equalize the conditions of our home labor, why should it be necessary that the customhouse, departing from its fiscal duties, should pretend to exercise a protective action over our external commerce?

19

NATIONAL INDEPENDENCE

Among the arguments we hear adduced in favor of the restrictive regime we must not forget that which is founded on national independence.

"What should we do in case of war," it is said, "if we are placed at the mercy of England for iron and coal?"

English monopolists do not fail to cry out in their turn:

"What would become of Great Britain in case of war if she is dependent on France for provisions?"

One thing is overlooked, which is this: That the kind of dependence that results from exchange, from commercial transactions, is a reciprocal dependence. We cannot be dependent on the foreigner without the foreigner being dependent on us. Now, this is the very essence of society. To break up natural relations is not to place ourselves in a state of independence, but in a state of isolation.

Note this: A nation isolates itself looking forward to the possibility of war; but is not this very act of isolating itself the beginning of war? It renders war more easy, less burdensome, and, it may be, less unpopular. Let countries be permanent markets for each other's produce; let their reciprocal relations be such that they cannot be broken without inflicting on each other the double suffering of privation and a glut of commodities; and they will no longer stand in need of naval armaments, which ruin them, and overgrown armies, which crush them; the peace of the world will not then be compromised by the caprice of a Thiers or of a Palmerston; and war will disappear for want of what supports it, for want of resources, inducements, pretexts, and popular sympathy.

I am quite aware that I shall be reproached (it is the fashion of the day) with basing the fraternity of nations on men's personal interest—vile, prosaic self-interest. Better far, it may be thought, that it should have had its basis in charity, in love, even in a little self-abnegation, and that, interfering somewhat with men's material comforts, it should have had the merit of a generous sacrifice.

When shall we be done with these puerile declamations? When will hypocrisy be finally banished from science? When shall we cease to exhibit this nauseous contradiction between our professions and our practice? We hoot at and execrate personal interest; in other words, we denounce what is useful and good (for to say that all men are interested in anything is to say that the thing is good in itself), as if personal interest were not the necessary, eternal and indestructible mainspring to which Providence has confided human perfectibility. Are we not represented as being all angels of disinterestedness? And does the thought never occur to those who say so that the public begins to see with disgust that this affected language disfigures the pages of those very writers who are most successful in filling their own pockets at the public expense? Oh! Affectation! Affectation! Thou are verily the besetting sin of our times!

What! Because material prosperity and peace are things correlative, because it has pleased God to establish this beautiful harmony in the moral world, am I not to admire, am I not to adore His ordinances, am I not to accept with gratitude laws that make justice the condition of happiness? You desire peace only in so far as it runs counter to material prosperity; and liberty is rejected because it does not impose sacrifices. If abnegation has indeed so many charms for you, why do you fail to practice it in private life? Society will be grateful to you, for someone, at least, will reap the fruit; but to desire to impose it upon mankind as a principle is the very height of absurdity, for the abnegation of all is the sacrifice of all, which is evil erected into a theory.

But, thank Heaven, one can write or read many of these declamations without the world ceasing on that account to obey the social motive force, which leads us to shun evil and seek after good, and which, whether they like it or not, we must denominate personal interest.

After all, it is ironic enough to see sentiments of the most sublime self-denial invoked in support of spoliation itself. See to what this boasted disinterestedness tends! These men who are so fantastically delicate as not to desire peace itself, if it is founded on the vile interest of mankind, put their hand into the pockets of others, and especially of the poor.

For what article of the tariff protects the poor? Be pleased, gentlemen, to dispose of what belongs to yourselves as you think proper, but leave us the disposal of the fruit of our own toil, to use it or exchange it as we see best. Declaim on self-sacrifice as much as you choose, it is all very fine and very beautiful, but be at least consistent.

20

Human Labor—
National Labor

Machine-breaking and the prohibition of foreign commodities—are two acts founded on the same doctrine.

We see men who clap their hands when a great invention is introduced, and who nevertheless adhere to the protectionist system. Such men are grossly inconsistent!

With what do they reproach free trade? With encouraging the production by foreigners who are more skilled or more favorably situated than we are, of commodities that, but for free trade, would be produced at home. In a word, they accuse free trade of being injurious to national Labor?

For the same reason, should they not reproach machinery with accomplishing by natural agents what otherwise would have been done by manual Labor, and so of being injurious to human Labor?

The foreign workman, better and more favorably situated than the home workman for the production of certain commodities, is, with reference to the latter, a veritable economic machine, crushing him by competition. In like manner, machinery, which executes a piece of work at a lower price than a certain number of men could do by manual Labor, is, in relation to these manual laborers, a veritable foreign competitor, who paralyzes them by his rivalry.

If, then, it is politic to protect national Labor against the competition of foreign Labor, it is not less so to protect human Labor against the rivalry of mechanical Labor.

Thus, every adherent of the system of protection, if he is logical, should not content himself with prohibiting foreign products; he should proscribe also the products of the shuttle and the plough.

And this is the reason why I like better the logic of those men who, declaiming against the invasion of foreign merchandise, declaim likewise against the excess of production that is due to the inventive power of the human mind.

Such a man is Mr. de Saint-Chamans.

> One of the strongest arguments against free trade," he says, "is the too extensive employment of machinery, for many workmen are deprived of employment, either by foreign competition, which lowers the price of our manufactured goods, or by instruments, which take the place of men in our workshops.[1]

Mr. de Saint-Chamans has seen clearly the analogy, or, we should rather say, the identity, that obtains between imports and machinery. For this reason, he proscribes both; and it is really agreeable to have to do with such intrepid reasoners, who, even when wrong, carry out their argument to its logical conclusion.

But here is the mess in which they land themselves:

If it be true, a priori, that the domain of invention and that of Labor cannot be simultaneously extended but at each other's

---

[1] *Du Systeme d'Impots*, p. 438.

expense, it must be in those countries where machinery most abounds—in Lancashire, for example—that we should expect to find the fewest workmen. And if, on the other hand, we establish the fact that mechanical power and manual Labor coexist, and to a greater extent, among rich nations than among savages, the conclusion is inevitable that these two powers do not exclude each other.

I cannot understand how any thinking being can enjoy a moment's repose in presence of the following dilemma:

Either the inventions of man are not injurious to manual Labor, as general facts attest, since there are more of both in England and France than among the Hurons and Cherokees, and, that being so, I am on a wrong road, though I know neither where nor when I missed my way; at all events, I see I am wrong, and I should commit the crime of treason to humanity were I to introduce my error into the legislation of my country!

Or else, the discoveries of the human mind limit the amount of manual Labor, as special facts appear to indicate; for I see every day some machine or other superseding twenty or a hundred workmen; and then I am forced to acknowledge a flagrant, eternal, and incurable antithesis between the intellectual and physical powers of man—between his progress and his present well-being; and in these circumstances I am forced to say that the Creator of man might have endowed him with reason, or with physical strength, with moral force, or with brute force; but that He mocked him by conferring on him, at the same time, faculties that are destructive of each other.

The difficulty is pressing and puzzling; but you contrive to find your way out of it by adopting the strange mantra:

In political economy there are no absolute principles.

In plain language, this means:

"I know not whether it be true or false; I am ignorant of what constitutes general good or evil. I give myself no trouble about that. The immediate effect of each measure upon my own personal interest is the only law which I can consent to recognize."

There are no principles! You might as well say there are no facts; for principles are merely formulas that classify such facts as are well established.

Machinery, and the importation of foreign commodities, certainly produce effects. These effects may be good or bad; on that there may be difference of opinion. But whatever view we take of them, it is reduced to a formula, by one of these two principles: Machinery is a good; or, machinery is an evil: Importations of foreign produce are beneficial; or, such importations are hurtful. But to assert that there are no principles, certainly exhibits the lowest degree of abasement to which the human mind can descend; and I confess that I blush for my country when I hear such a monstrous heresy proclaimed in the French Chambers, and with their assent; that is to say, in the face and with the assent of the elite of our fellow-citizens; and this in order to justify their imposing laws upon us in total disregard for the real state of the case.

But then I am told to destroy the fallacy by proving that machinery is not hurtful to human Labor, nor the importation of foreign products to national Labor.

A work like the present cannot well include very full or complete demonstrations. My design is rather to state difficulties than to resolve them; to excite reflection rather than to satisfy doubts. No conviction makes so lasting an impression on the mind as that which it works out for itself. But I shall endeavor nevertheless to put the reader on the right road.

What misleads the adversaries of machinery and foreign importations is that they judge of them by their immediate and transitory effects, instead of following them out to their general and definite consequences.

The immediate effect of the invention and employment of an ingenious machine is to render superfluous, for the attainment of a given result, a certain amount of manual Labor. But its action does not stop there. For the very reason that the desired result is obtained with fewer efforts, the product is handed over to the public at a lower price; and the aggregate of savings thus realized by all purchasers enables them to procure other satisfactions; that is to say, to encourage manual Labor in general to exactly the extent of the manual Labor which has been saved in the special branch of industry which has been recently improved. So that the level of Labor has not fallen, while that of enjoyments has risen.

Let us render this evident by an example.

Suppose there are used annually in this country ten million hats at 15 shillings each; this makes the sum which goes to the support of this branch of industry £7,500,000 sterling. A machine is invented that allows these hats to be manufactured and sold at 10 shillings. The sum now wanted for the support of this industry is reduced to £5,000,000, provided the demand is not augmented by the change. But the remaining sum of £2,500,000 is not by this change withdrawn from the support of human Labor. That sum, economized by the purchasers of hats, will enable them to satisfy other wants, and consequently, to that extent will go to remunerate the aggregate industry of the country. With the five shillings saved, John will purchase a pair of shoes, James a book, Jerome a piece of furniture, etc. Human Labor, taken in the aggregate, will continue, then, to be supported and encouraged to the extent of £7,500,000; but this sum will yield the same number of hats, plus all the satisfactions and enjoyments corresponding to £2,500,000 that the employment of the machine has enabled the consumers of hats to save. These additional enjoyments constitute the clear profit that the country will have derived from the invention. This is a free gift, a tribute that human genius will have derived from nature. We do not at all dispute that in the course of the transformation a certain amount of Labor will have been displaced; but we cannot allow that it has been destroyed or diminished.

The same thing holds of the importation of foreign commodities. Let us revert to our former hypothesis.

The country manufactures ten millions of hats, of which the cost price was 15 shillings. The foreigner sends similar hats to our market, and furnishes them at 10 shillings each. I maintain that the national Labor will not be thereby diminished.

For it must produce to the extent of £5,000,000 to enable it to pay for 10 million hats at 10 shillings.

And then there remains to each purchaser five shillings saved on each hat, or in all, £2,500,000, which will be spent on other enjoyments—that is to say, which will go to support Labor in other departments of industry.

Then the aggregate Labor of the country will remain what it was, and the additional enjoyments represented by £2,500,000 saved upon hats will form the clear profit accruing from imports under the system of free trade.

It is of no use to try to frighten us by a picture of the sufferings that, on this hypothesis, the displacement of Labor will entail.

For, if the prohibition had never been imposed, the Labor would have found its natural place under the ordinary law of exchange, and no displacement would have taken place.

If, on the other hand, prohibition has led to an artificial and unproductive employment of Labor, it is prohibition, and not liberty, that is to blame for a displacement that is inevitable in the transition from what is detrimental to what is beneficial.

At all events, let no one claim that because an abuse cannot be done away with, without inconvenience to those who profit by it, what has been suffered to exist for a time should be allowed to exist forever.

21

RAW MATERIALS

It is said that the most advantageous of all branches of trade is that which supplies manufactured commodities in exchange for raw materials. For these raw materials are the aliment and support of national labor.

Hence the conclusion is drawn:

That the best law of customs is that which gives the greatest possible facility to the importation of raw materials, and which throws most obstacles in the way of importing finished goods.

There is no fallacy in political economy more widely disseminated than this. It is cherished not only by the protectionist school, but also, and above all, by the school that dubs itself Liberal; and it is unfortunate that it should be so, for what can be more injurious to a good cause than that it should be at the same time vigorously attacked and feebly defended?

Commercial liberty is likely to have the fate of liberty in general; it will only find a place in the statute book after it has taken possession of men's minds and convictions. But if it be true that a reform, in order to be solidly established, should be generally understood, it follows that nothing can so much retard reform as that which misleads public opinion. And what is more calculated to mislead public opinion than works that, in advocating freedom, invoke aid from the doctrines of monopoly?

Some years ago three of the great towns of France—Lyons, Bordeaux, and Havre—united in a movement against the restrictive regime. All Europe was stirred on seeing raised what they took for the banner of liberty. Alas! it proved to be also the banner of monopoly—of a monopoly a little more niggardly and much more absurd than that of which they seemed to desire the overthrow. By the aid of the fallacy that I have just endeavored to expose, the petitioners did nothing more than reproduce the doctrine of protection to national industry, tacking to it an additional inconsistency.

It was, in fact, nothing else than the system of prohibition. Just listen to Mr. de Saint-Cricq:

"Labor constitutes the wealth of a nation, because labor alone creates those material objects which our wants demand; and universal ease and comfort consist in the abundance of these things." So much for the principle.

"But this abundance must be produced by national labor. If it were the result of foreign labor, national labor would be immediately brought to a stand." Here lies the error. (See the preceding chapter.)

"What course should an agricultural and manufacturing country take under such circumstances? Reserve its markets for the products of its own soil and of its own industry." Such is the end and design.

"And for that purpose restrain by duties, and, if necessary, prohibit importation of the products of the soil and industry of other nations." Such are the means.

Let us compare this system with that which the Bordeaux petition advocates.

Commodities are there divided into three classes:

"The first includes provisions, and raw materials upon which no human labor has been bestowed. In principle, a wise economy would demand that this class should be free of duties." Here we have no labor, no protection.

"The second consists of products that have, to some extent, been prepared. This preparation warrants such products being charged with a certain amount of duty." Here protection begins, because here, according to the petitioners, begins national labor.

"The third comprises goods and products in their finished and perfect state. These contribute nothing to national labor, and we regard this class as the most taxable." Here labor, and protection along with it, reach their maximum.

We thus see that the petitioners profess their belief in the doctrine that foreign labor is injurious to national labor; and this is the error of the prohibitive system.

They demand that the home market should be reserved for home industry. That is the design of the system of prohibition.

They demand that foreign labor should be subjected to restrictions and taxes. These are the means employed by the system of prohibition. What difference, then, can we possibly discover between the Bordeaux petitioners and the Corypheus of restriction? One difference, and one only: the greater or less extension given to the word labor.

Mr. de Saint-Cricq extends it to everything, and so he wishes to protect all.

"Labor constitutes all the wealth of a people," he says; "to protect agricultural industry, and all agricultural industry; to protect manufacturing industry, and all manufacturing industry, is the cry which should never cease to be heard in this Chamber."

The Bordeaux petitioners take no labor into account but that of the manufacturers; and for that reason they would admit them to the benefits of protection.

"Raw materials are commodities upon which no human labor has been bestowed. In principle, we should not tax them. Manufactured products can no longer serve the cause of national industry, and we regard them as the best subjects for taxation."

It is not our business in this place to inquire whether protection to national industry is reasonable. Mr. de Saint-Cricq and the Bordeaux gentlemen are at one upon this point, and, as we have shown in the preceding chapters, we on this subject differ from both.

Our present business is to discover whether it is by Mr. de Saint-Cricq, or by the Bordeaux petitioners, that the word labor is used in a correct sense.

Now, in this view of the question, we think that Mr. de Saint-Cricq has very much the best of it; and to prove this we may suppose them to hold some such dialogue as the following:

Mr. DE SAINT-CRICQ: You grant that national labor should be protected. You grant that the products of no foreign labor can be introduced into our market without superseding a corresponding amount of our national labor. Only you contend that there are a multiplicity of products possessed of value (for they sell), but upon which no human labor has been bestowed (virgin material). And you enumerate, among other things, wheat, flour, meat, cattle, tallow, salt, iron, copper, lead, coal, wool, hides, seeds, etc.

If you will only prove to me that the value of these things is not due to labor, I will grant that it is useless to protect them.

But, on the other hand, if I demonstrate to you that there is as much labor worked up in 100 francs worth of wool as in 100 francs worth of textile fabrics, you will allow that the one is as worthy of protection as the other.

Now, why is this sack of wool worth 100 francs? Is it not because that is its cost price? And what does its cost price represent but the aggregate wages of all the labor and profits of all the capital which have contributed to the production of the commodity?

THE BORDEAUX PETITIONERS: Well, perhaps as regards wool you may be right. But take the case of a sack of corn, a bar of iron, a hundredweight of coal—are these commodities produced by labor? Are they not created by nature?

MR. DE SAINT-CRICQ: Undoubtedly nature creates the elements of all these things, but it is labor that produces the value. I was wrong myself in saying that labor created material objects, and that unfortunate form of expression has led me into other errors. It does not belong to man to create, to make anything out of nothing, be he agriculturist or manufacturer; and if by production is meant creation, all our labor must be marked down as unproductive, and yours, as merchants, more unproductive than all others, excepting perhaps my own.

The agriculturist, then, cannot pretend to have created wheat but he has created value; I mean to say, he has, by his labor and that of his servants, laborers, reapers, etc., transformed into wheat substances which had no resemblance to it whatever. The miller who converts the wheat into flour, the baker who converts the flour into bread, do the same thing.

In order that man may be enabled to clothe himself a multitude of operations are necessary. Prior to all intervention of human labor the true raw materials of cloth are the air, the water, the heat, the gases, the light, the salts, that enter into its composition. These are the raw materials upon which, strictly speaking, no human labor has been employed. They are virgin materials; and since they have no value, I should never dream of protecting them. But the first application of labor converts these substances into grass and fodder, a second into wool, a third into yarn, a fourth into a woven fabric, a fifth into clothing. Who can assert that the whole of these operations, from the first furrow laid open by the plough to the last stitch of the tailor's needle, do not resolve themselves into labor?

And it is because these operations are spread over several branches of industry, in order to accelerate and facilitate the accomplishment of the ultimate object, which is to furnish clothing to those who have need of it, that you desire, by an arbitrary distinction, to rank the importance of such works in the order in which they succeed each other, so that the first of the series shall not merit even the name of labor, and that the last, being labor par excellence, shall be worthy of the favors of protection?

THE PETITIONERS: Yes, we begin to see that wheat, like wool, is not exactly a product of which it can be said that no human labor has been bestowed upon it; but the agriculturist has not, at least, like the manufacturer, done everything himself or by means of his workmen; nature has assisted him, and if there is labor worked up in wheat it is not the simple product of labor.

MR. DE SAINT-CRICQ: But its value resolves itself exclusively into labor. I am happy that nature concurs in the material formation of grain. I could even wish that it were entirely her work; but you must allow that I have constrained this assistance of nature by my labor, and when I sell you my wheat you will remark this: That it is not for the labor of nature that I ask you to pay, but for my own.

But, as you state the case, manufactured commodities are no longer the exclusive products of labor. Is the manufacturer not beholden to nature in his processes? Does he not avail himself of the assistance of the steam-engine, of the pressure of the atmosphere, just as, with the assistance of the plough, I avail myself of its humidity? Has he created the laws of gravitation, of the transmission of forces, of affinity?

THE PETITIONERS: Well, this is the case of the wool over again; but coal is assuredly the work, the exclusive work, of nature. It is indeed a product upon which no human labor has ever been bestowed.

MR. DE SAINT-CRICQ: Yes, nature has undoubtedly created the coal, but labor has imparted value to it. For the millions of years during which it was buried 100 fathoms under ground, unknown to everybody, it was destitute of value. It was necessary to search for it—that is labor; it was necessary to send it to market—that is additional labor. Then the price you pay for it in the market is nothing else than the remuneration of the labor of mining and transport.[1]

---

[1] I do not particularize the parts of the remuneration falling to the lessee, the capitalist, etc., for several reasons: First, because, on looking at the thing more closely, you will see that the remuneration always resolves itself into the reimbursement of advances or the payment of previous labor. Second, because, under the term labor, I include not only the wages of the workmen, but the legitimate recompense of everything that co-operates in

Thus far we see that Mr. de Saint-Cricq has the best of the argument; that the value of raw materials, like that of manufactured commodities, represents the cost of production, that is to say, the labor worked up in them; that it is not possible to conceive of a product possessing value, that has had no human labor bestowed on it; that the distinction made by the petitioners is futile in theory; that, as the basis of an unequal distribution of favors, it would be iniquitous in practice, since the result would be that one-third of our countrymen, who happened to be engaged in manufactures, would obtain the advantages of monopoly, on the alleged ground that they produce by labor, while the other two-thirds—namely, the agricultural population—would be abandoned to competition under the pretext that they produce without labor.

The rejoinder to this, I am quite sure, will be that a nation derives more advantages from importing what are called raw materials, whether produced by labor or not, and exporting manufactured commodities. This will be repeated and insisted on, and it is an opinion very widely accredited.

"The more abundant raw materials are," says the Bordeaux petition, "the more are manufactures promoted and multiplied."

"Raw materials," says the same document in another place, "open up an unlimited field of work for the inhabitants of the countries into which they are imported."

"Raw materials," says the Havre petition, "constituting as they do the elements of labor, must be submitted to a different treatment, and be gradually admitted at the lowest rate of duty."

The same petition expresses a wish that manufactured products should be admitted, not gradually, but after an indefinite

---

the work of production. Third (and above all), because the production of manufactured products is, like that of raw materials, burdened with auxiliary remunerations other than the mere expense of manual labor; and, moreover, this objection, frivolous in itself, would apply as much to the most delicate processes of manufacture, as to the rudest operations of agriculture.

lapse of time, not at the lowest rate of duty, but at a duty of 20 percent.

"Among other articles, the low price and abundance of which are a necessity," says the Lyons petition, "manufacturers include all raw materials."

All this is founded on an illusion.

We have seen that all value represents labor. Now, it is quite true that manufacturing labor increases tenfold, sometimes a hundredfold, the value of the raw material; that is to say, it yields ten times, a hundred times, more profit to the nation. Hence men are led to reason thus: The production of a hundredweight of iron brings in a gain of only 15 shillings to workmen of all classes. The conversion of this hundredweight of iron into the mainsprings of watches raises their earnings to £500; and will anyone venture to say that a nation has not a greater interest to secure for its labor a gain of £500 than a gain of fifteen shillings? We do not exchange a hundredweight of un-wrought iron for a hundred-weight of watchsprings, nor a hundredweight of unwashed wool for a hundredweight of cashmere shawls; but we exchange a certain value of one of these materials for an equal value of another. Now, to exchange equal value for equal value is to exchange equal labor for equal labor. It is not true, then, that a nation that sells five pounds' worth of wrought fabrics or watch-springs gains more than a nation that sells five pounds' worth of wool or iron.

In a country where no law can be voted, where no tax can be imposed, but with the consent of those whose dealings the law is to regulate, and whose pockets the tax is to affect, the public cannot be robbed without first being imposed on and misled. Our ignorance is the raw material of every extortion from which we suffer, and we may be certain beforehand that every fallacy is the precursor of an act of plunder. My good friends! when you detect a fallacy in a petition, button up your wallet-pocket, for you may be sure that this is the mark aimed at. Let us see, then, what is the real object secretly aimed at by the shipowners of Bordeaux and Havre, and the manufacturers of Lyons, and which is concealed under the distinction they attempt to draw between agricultural and manufactured commodities.

"It is principally this first class (that which comprises raw materials, upon which no human labor has been bestowed) which affords," say the Bordeaux petitioners, "the principal support to our merchant shipping. . . . In principle, a wise economy would not tax this class. . . . The second (commodities partly wrought up) may be taxed to a certain extent. The third (commodities which call for no more exertion of labor) we regard as the fittest subjects of taxation."

The Havre petitioners "consider that it is indispensable to reduce gradually the duty on raw materials to the lowest rate, in order that our manufacturers may gradually find employment for the shipping interest, which furnishes them with the first and indispensable materials of labor."

The manufacturers could not remain behindhand in politeness toward the shipowners. So the Lyons petition asks for the free introduction of raw materials, "in order to prove," as they express it, "that the interests of the manufacturing are not always opposed to those of the maritime towns."

No; but then the interests of both, understood as the petitioners understand them, are in direct opposition to the interests of agriculture and of consumers.

Well, gentlemen, we have come at length to see what you are aiming at, and the object of your subtle economical distinctions. You desire that the law should restrain the transport of finished goods across the ocean, in order that the more costly conveyance of raw and rough materials, bulky, and mixed up with refuse, should afford greater scope for your merchant shipping, and more largely employ your marine resources. This is what you call a wise economy.

On the same principle, why do you not ask that the pines of Russia should be brought to you with their branches, bark, and roots; the silver of Mexico in its mineral state; the hides of Buenos Aires sticking to the bones of the putrefying carcasses from which they have been torn?

I expect that railway shareholders, the moment they are in a majority in the Chambers, will proceed to make a law forbidding the manufacture of the brandy that is consumed in Paris. And why not? Would not a law enforcing the conveyance of ten casks of wine for every cask of brandy afford Parisian industry the indispensable materials of its labor, and give employment to our locomotive resources?

How long will men shut their eyes to this simple truth?

Manufactures, shipping, labor—all have for end the general, the public good; to create useless industries, to favor superfluous conveyances, to support a greater amount of labor than is necessary, not for the good of the public, but at the expense of the public—is to realize a true *petitio principii*. It is not labor that is desirable for its own sake; it is consumption. All labor without a commensurate result is a loss. You may as well pay sailors for skipping pebbles on the surface of the water as pay them for transporting useless refuse. Thus, we arrive at the result to which all economic fallacies, numerous as they are, conduct us, namely, confounding the means with the end, and developing the one at the expense of the other.

22

METAPHORS

A fallacy sometimes expands, and runs through the whole texture of a long and elaborate theory. More frequently, it shrinks and contracts, assumes the guise of a principle, and lurks in a word or a phrase.

"May God protect us from the devil and from metaphors!" was the exclamation of Paul-Louis.[1] And it is difficult to say which of them has done most mischief in this world of ours. The devil, you will say; for he has put the spirit of plunder into all our hearts. True, but he has left free the means of repressing abuses by the resistance of those who suffer from them. It is the fallacy that paralyzes this resistance. The sword that malice puts into the hands of assailants would be powerless, did sophistry not break the buckler that should shield the party assailed. It was with reason, therefore, that Malebranche inscribed on the title-page of his work this sentence: *L'erreur est la cause de la misere des hommes* (Error is the cause of mankind's misery).

---

[1] Paul-Louis Courier.

Let us see in what way this takes place. Ambitious men are often actuated by sinister and wicked intentions; their design, for example, may be to implant in the public mind the germ of international hatred. This fatal germ may develop itself, light up a general conflagration, arrest civilization, cause torrents of blood to be shed, and bring upon the country the most terrible of all scourges, invasion. At any rate, and apart from this, such sentiments of hatred lower us in the estimation of other nations, and force Frenchmen who retain any sense of justice to blush for their country. These are undoubtedly most serious evils; and to guard the public against the underhand practices of those who would expose the country to such hazard, it is only necessary to see clearly into their designs. How do they manage to conceal them? By the use of metaphors. They twist, distort, and pervert the meaning of three or four words, and the thing is done.

The word invasion itself is a good illustration of this. A French ironmaster exclaims: Preserve us from the invasion of English iron. An English landowner exclaims in return: Preserve us from the invasion of French wheat. And then they proceed to interpose barriers between the two countries. These barriers create isolation, isolation gives rise to hatred, hatred to war, war to invasion. What does it signify? cry the two sophists; is it not better to expose ourselves to a possible invasion than accept an invasion that is certain? And the people believe them, and the barriers are kept up.

And yet what analogy is there between an exchange and an invasion? What possible similarity can be imagined between a ship of war that comes to vomit fire and devastation on our towns, and a merchant ship that comes to offer a free voluntary exchange of commodities for commodities?

The same thing holds of the use made of the word inundation. This word is ordinarily used in a bad sense, for we often see our fields injured, and our harvests carried away by floods. If, however, they leave on our soil something of greater value than what they carry away, like the inundations of the Nile, we should be thankful for them, as the Egyptians are. Before we declaim, then, against the inundations of foreign products—before proceeding to restrain them by irksome and costly obstacles—we should inquire to what class they belong, and whether they ravage or fertilize. What should we think of Mehemet Ali, if, instead of raising at great cost, dams across the Nile, to extend wider its inundations, he were to spend his money in digging a deeper channel to prevent Egypt being soiled by the foreign slime that descends upon her from the Mountains of the Moon? We display exactly the same degree of wisdom and sense, when we desire, at the cost of millions, to defend our country—From what? From the benefits that nature has bestowed on other climates.

Among the metaphors that conceal a pernicious theory, there is none more in use than that presented by the words tribute and tributary.

These words have now become so common that they are used as synonymous with purchase and purchaser, and are employed indiscriminately.

And yet a tribute is as different from a purchase as a theft is from an exchange; and I should like quite as well to hear it said, Cartouche has broken into my strong-box and purchased a thousand pounds, as to hear one of our deputies repeat, We have paid Germany tribute for a thousand horses that she has sold us.

For what distinguishes the act of Cartouche from a purchase is that he has not put into my strong-box, and with my consent, a value equivalent to what he has taken out of it.

And what distinguishes our remittance of £20,000 that we have made to Germany from a tribute paid to her is this, that she has not received the money gratuitously, but has given us in exchange a thousand horses, which we have judged to be worth the £20,000.

Is it worthwhile exposing seriously such an abuse of language? Yes; for these terms are used seriously both in newspapers and in books.

Do not let it be supposed that these are instances of a mere *lapsus linguae* on the part of certain ignorant writers! For one writer who abstains from so using them, I will point you out ten who admit them, and among the rest, the D'Argouts, the Dupins, the Villeles—peers, deputies, ministers of state—men, in short, whose words are laws, and whose fallacies, even the most transparent, serve as a basis for the government of the country.

A celebrated modern philosopher has added to the categories of Aristotle the fallacy that consists in employing a phrase that includes a *petitio principii*. He gives many examples of it; and he should have added the word tributary to his list. The business, in fact, is to discover whether purchases made from foreigners are useful or hurtful. They are hurtful, you say. And why? Because they render us tributaries to the foreigner. This is just to use a word that implies the very thing to be proved.

It may be asked how this abuse of words first came to be introduced into the rhetoric of the monopolists?

Money leaves the country to satisfy the rapacity of a victorious enemy. Money also leaves the country to pay for commodities. An analogy is established between the two cases by taking into account only the points in which they resemble each other, and keeping out of view the points in which they differ.

Yet this circumstance—that is to say, the non-reimbursement in the first case, and the reimbursement voluntarily agreed upon in the second—establishes between them such a difference that it is really impossible to class them in the same category. To hand over a hundred pounds by force to a man who has caught you by the throat, or to hand them over voluntarily to a man who furnishes you with what you want, are things as different as light and darkness. You might as well assert that it is a matter of indifference whether you throw your bread into the river or eat it, for in both cases the bread is destroyed. The vice of this reasoning, like that applied to the word tribute, consists in asserting an entire similitude between two cases, looking only at their points of resemblance, and keeping out of sight the points in which they differ.

23

Conclusion

All the Sophisms I have so far combated relate to the restrictive policy; and some of the most notable on this subject I have, in pity to the reader, even passed over: acquired rights; unsuitableness; exhaustion of money, etc., etc.

But Social economy is not confined within this narrow circle. Fourierism, Saint Simonism, Commonism, agrarianism, anti-rentism, mysticism, sentimentalism, false philanthropy, affected aspirations for a chimerical equality and fraternity; questions relative to luxury, wages, machinery; to the pretended tyranny of capital; to colonies, outlets, population; to emigration, association, imposts, and loans, have encumbered the field of Science with a crowd of parasitical arguments—Sophisms, whose rank growth calls for the spade and the weeding-hoe.

I am perfectly aware of the defect of my plan, or rather absence of plan. By attacking as I do, one by one, so many incoherent Sophisms, which clash and then again often mingle with each other, I am conscious that I condemn myself to a disorderly and capricious struggle, and am exposed to perpetual repetitions.

I should certainly much prefer to state simply how things are, without troubling myself to contemplate the thousand aspects under which ignorance supposes them to be. . . . To lay down all together the laws under which society prospers or perishes, would be virtually to destroy at once all Sophisms. When Laplace described what, up to his time, was known of the movements of celestial bodies, he dissipated, without even naming them, all the astrological reveries of the Egyptians, Greeks, and Hindus, much more certainly than he could have done by attempting to refute them directly, through innumerable volumes. Truth is one, and the work that expounds it is an imposing and durable edifice. Error is multiple, and of ephemeral nature. The work that combats it, cannot bear in itself a principle of greatness or of durability.

But if power, and perhaps opportunity, have eluded me, to enable me to proceed in the manner of Laplace and of Say, I still cannot but believe that the mode adopted by me has also its modest usefulness. It appears to me likewise to be well suited to the wants of the age, and to the broken moments that it is now the habit to snatch for study.

A treatise has without doubt an incontestable superiority. But it requires to be read, meditated, and understood. It addresses itself to the select few. Its mission is first to fix attention, and then to enlarge the circle of acquired knowledge.

A work that undertakes the refutation of vulgar prejudices, cannot have so high an aim. It aspires only to clear the way for the steps of Truth; to prepare the minds of men to receive her; to rectify public opinion, and to snatch from unworthy hands dangerous weapons they misuse.

It is above all in social economy that this hand-to-hand struggle, this ever-reviving combat with popular errors, has a true practical utility.

Sciences might be arranged in two categories. Those of the first class whose application belongs only to particular professions, can be understood only by the learned; but the most ignorant may profit by their fruits. We may enjoy the comforts of a watch; we may be transported by locomotives or steamboats, although knowing nothing of mechanism and astronomy. We walk according to the laws of equilibrium, while entirely ignorant of them.

But there are sciences whose influence upon the public is proportioned only to the information of that public itself, and whose efficacy consists not in the accumulated knowledge of some few learned heads, but in that which has diffused itself into the reason of man in the aggregate. Such are morals, hygiene, social economy, and (in countries where men belong to themselves) political economy. Of these sciences Bentham might above all have said: "It is better to circulate, than to advance them." What does it profit us that a great man, even a God, should promulgate moral laws, if the minds of men, steeped in error, will constantly mistake vice for virtue, and virtue for vice? What does it benefit us that Smith, Say and, according to Mr. de St. Chamans, political economists of every school, should have proclaimed the superiority in all commercial transactions, of liberty above restraint, if those who make laws, and for whom laws are made, are convinced of the contrary? These sciences, which have very properly been named social, are again peculiar in this, that they, being of common application, no one will confess himself ignorant of them. If the object be to determine a question in chemistry or geometry, nobody pretends to have an innate knowledge of the science, or is ashamed to consult Mr. Thenard, or to seek information from the pages of Legendre or Bezout. But in the social sciences authorities are rarely acknowledged. As each individual daily acts upon his own notions whether right or wrong, of morals, hygiene, and economy; of politics, whether reasonable or absurd, each one thinks he has a right to prattle, comment, decide, and dictate in these matters. Are you sick? There is not a good old woman in the country who is not ready to tell you the cause and the remedy of your sufferings. "It is from humors in the blood," says she, "you must be purged." But what are these humors, or are there any humors at all? On this subject she troubles herself but little. This good old woman comes into my mind whenever I hear an attempt made to account for all the maladies of the social body, by some trivial form of words. It is super-abundance of produce, tyranny of capital, industrial surplus, or other such nonsense, of which it would be fortunate if we could say: *Verba et voces proetereaque nihil*, for these are errors from which fatal consequences follow.

From what has just been stated, the two following results may be deduced: First, that the social sciences, more than others, necessarily abound in Sophisms, because in their application, each individual consults only his own judgment and his own instincts. Second, that in these sciences Sophisms are especially injurious, because they mislead opinion on a subject in which opinion is power—is law.

Two kinds of books then are necessary in these sciences, those that teach, and those that circulate; those that expound the truth, and those that combat error.

I believe that the inherent defect of this little work, repetition, is what is likely to be the cause of its principal utility. Among the Sophisms it has discussed, each has undoubtedly its own formula and tendency, but all have a common root; and this is, the forgetfulness of the interests of men considered as consumers. By showing that a thousand mistaken roads all lead to this great seminal Sophism, I may perhaps teach the public to recognize, to know, and to mistrust it, under all circumstances.

After all, I am less at forcing convictions, than at waking doubts.

I have no hope that the reader as he lays down my book will exclaim, I know. My aspirations will be fully satisfied if he can but sincerely say, I doubt.

"I doubt, for I begin to fear that there may be something illusory in the supposed blessings of scarcity." (Sophism 1)

"I am not so certain of the beneficial effect of obstacles." (Sophism 2)

"Effort without result no longer appears to me so desirable as result without effort." (Sophism 3)

"I understand that the more an article has been labored upon, the more is its value. But in trade, do two equal values cease to be equal, because one comes from the plough, and the other from the workshop?" (Sophism 21)

"I confess that I begin to think it doubtful that mankind should be the better of hindrances and obstacles, or should grow rich upon taxes; and truly I would be relieved from some anxiety, would be really happy to see the proof of the fact, as stated by the author of "the Sophisms," that there is no incompatibility between prosperity and justice, between peace and liberty, between the extension of labor and the advance of intelligence." (Sophisms 14 and 20)

"Without, then, giving up entirely to arguments that I am yet in doubt whether to look upon as fairly reasoned, or as self-contradictory, I will at least seek enlightenment from the masters of the science."

I will now terminate this sketch by a last and important recapitulation.

The world is not sufficiently conscious of the influence exercised over it by Sophistry.

When might ceases to be right, and the government of mere strength is dethroned, Sophistry transfers the empire to cunning and subtlety. It would be difficult to determine which of the two tyrannies is most injurious to mankind.

Men have an immoderate love for pleasure, influence, consideration, power—in a word, for riches; and they are, by an almost unconquerable inclination, pushed to procure these at the expense of others.

But these others, who form the public, have a no less strong inclination to keep what they have acquired; and this they will do, if they have the strength and the knowledge to effect it.

Spoliation, which plays so important a part in the affairs of this world, has then two agents; Force and Cunning. She has also two checks; Courage and Knowledge.

Force applied to spoliation furnishes the great material for the annals of men. To retrace its history would be to present almost the entire history of every nation: Assyrians, Babylonians, Medes, Persians, Greeks, Romans, Goths, Franks, Huns, Turks, Arabs,

Tartars, without counting the more recent expeditions of the English in India, the French in Africa, the Russians in Asia, etc., etc.

But among civilized nations surely the producers of riches are now become sufficiently numerous and strong to defend themselves.

Does this mean that they are no longer robbed? They are as much so as ever, and moreover they rob one another.

The only difference is that Spoliation has changed her agent She acts no longer by Force, but by Cunning.

To rob the public, it is necessary to deceive them. To deceive them, it is necessary to persuade them that they are robbed for their own advantage, and to induce them to accept in exchange for their property, imaginary services, and often worse. Hence spring Sophisms in all their varieties. Then, since Force is held in check, Sophistry is no longer only an evil; it is the genius of evil, and requires a check in its turn. This check must be the enlightenment of the public, which must be rendered more subtle than the subtle, as it is already stronger than the strong.

GOOD PUBLIC! I now dedicate to you this first essay; though it must be confessed that the Preface is strangely transposed, and the Dedication a little tardy.

VII.

ECONOMIC SOPHISMS—
SECOND SERIES

1

Natural History of Spoliation

Why do I give myself up to that dry science, political economy?

The question is a proper one. All labor is so repugnant in its nature that one has the right to ask of what use it is.

Let us examine and see.

I do not address myself to those philosophers who, if not in their own names, at least in the name of humanity, profess to adore poverty.

I speak to those who hold wealth in esteem—and understand by this word, not the opulence of the few, but the comfort, the well-being, the security, the independence, the instruction, the dignity of all.

There are only two ways by which the means essential to the preservation, the adornment and the perfection of life may be obtained—production and spoliation. Some persons may say: "Spoliation is an accident, a local and transient abuse, denounced by morality, punished by the law, and unworthy of the attention of political economy."

Still, however benevolent or optimistic one may be, he is compelled to admit that spoliation is practiced on so vast a scale in this world, and is so generally connected with all great human events, that no social science, and least of all political economy, can refuse to consider it.

I go farther. That which prevents the perfection of the social system (at least in so far as it is capable of perfection) is the constant effort of its members to live and prosper at the expense of each other. So that, if spoliation did not exist, society being perfect, the social sciences would be without an object.

I go still farther. When spoliation becomes a means of subsistence for a body of men united by social ties, in course of time they make a law that sanctions it, a morality that glorifies it.

It is enough to name some of the best defined forms of spoliation to indicate the position it occupies in human affairs.

First comes war. Among savages the conqueror kills the conquered to obtain an uncontested, if not incontestable, right to game.

Next slavery. When man learns that he can make the earth fruitful by labor, he makes this division with his brother: "You work and I eat."

Then comes superstition. "According as you give or refuse me that which is yours, I will open to you the gates of heaven or of hell."

Finally, monopoly appears. Its distinguishing characteristic is to allow the existence of the grand social law—service for service—while it brings the element of force into the discussion, and thus alters the just proportion between service received and service rendered.

Spoliation always bears within itself the germ of its own destruction. Very rarely the many despoil the few. In such a case the latter soon become so reduced that they can no longer satisfy the cupidity of the former, and spoliation ceases for want of sustenance.

Almost always the few oppress the many, and in that case spoliation is none the less undermined, for, if it has force as an agent, as in war and slavery, it is natural that force in the end should be on the side of the greater number. And if deception is the agent, as with superstition and monopoly, it is natural that the many should ultimately become enlightened.

Another law of Providence wars against spoliation. It is this:

Spoliation not only displaces wealth, but always destroys a portion.

War annihilates values.

Slavery paralyzes the faculties.

Monopoly transfers wealth from one pocket to another, but it always occasions the loss of a portion in the transfer.

This is an admirable law. Without it, provided the strength of oppressors and oppressed were equal, spoliation would have no end.

A moment comes when the destruction of wealth is such that the despoiler is poorer than he would have been if he had remained honest.

So it is with a people when a war costs more than the booty is worth; with a master who pays more for slave labor than for free labor; with a priesthood which has so stupefied the people and destroyed its energy that nothing more can be gotten out of it; with a monopoly which increases its attempts at absorption as there is less to absorb, just as the difficulty of milking increases with the emptiness of the udder.

Monopoly is a species of the genus spoliation. It has many varieties, among them sinecure, privilege, and restriction upon trade.

Some of the forms it assumes are simple and naive, like feudal rights. Under this regime the masses are despoiled, and know it.

Other forms are more complicated. Often the masses are plundered, and do not know it. It may even happen that they believe that they owe every thing to spoliation, not only what is left them but what is taken from them, and what is lost in the operation. I also assert that, in the course of time, thanks to the ingenious machinery of habit, many people become spoilers without knowing it or wishing it. Monopolies of this kind are begotten by fraud and nurtured by error. They vanish only before the light.

I have said enough to indicate that political economy has a manifest practical use. It is the torch that, unveiling deceit and dissipating error, destroys that social disorder called spoliation. Someone, a woman I believe, has correctly defined it as "the safety-lock upon the property of the people."

COMMENTARY

If this little book were destined to live three or four thousand years, to be read and re-read, pondered and studied, phrase by phrase, word by word, and letter by letter, from generation to generation, like a new Koran; if it were to fill the libraries of the world with avalanches of annotations, explanations and paraphrases, I might leave to their fate, in their rather obscure conciseness, the thoughts that precede. But since they need a commentary, it seems wise to me to furnish it myself.

The true and equitable law of humanity is the free exchange of service for service. Spoliation consists in destroying by force or by trickery the freedom of exchange, in order to receive a service without rendering one.

Forcible spoliation is exercised thus: Wait till a man has produced something; then take it away from him by violence.

It is solemnly condemned in the Ten Commandments: Thou shalt not steal.

When practiced by one individual on another, it is called robbery, and leads to the prison; when practiced among nations, it takes the name of conquest, and leads to glory.

Why this difference? It is worth while to search for the cause. It will reveal to us an irresistible power, public opinion, which, like the atmosphere, envelopes us so completely that we do not notice it. Rousseau never said a truer thing than this: "A great deal of philosophy is needed to understand the facts that are very near to us."

The robber, for the reason that he acts alone, has public opinion against him. He terrifies all who are about him. Yet, if he has companions, he boasts to them on his exploits, and here we may begin to notice the power of public opinion, for the approbation of his band serves to obliterate all consciousness of his turpitude, and even to make him proud of it. The warrior lives in a different atmosphere. The public opinion that would rebuke him is among the vanquished. He does not feel its influence. But the opinion of those by whom he is surrounded approves his acts and sustains him. He and his comrades are vividly conscious of the common interest that unites them. The country, which has created enemies and dangers, needs to stimulate the courage of its children. To the most daring, to those who have enlarged the frontiers, and gathered the spoils of war, are given honors, reputation, glory. Poets sing their exploits. Fair women weave garlands for them. And such is the power of public opinion that it separates the idea of injustice from spoliation, and even rids the despoiler of the consciousness of his wrong-doing.

The public opinion that reacts against military spoliation, (as it exists among the conquered and not among the conquering people) has very little influence. But it is not entirely powerless. It gains in strength as nations come together and understand one another better. Thus, it can be seen that the study of languages and the free communication of peoples tend to bring about the supremacy of an opinion opposed to this sort of spoliation.

Unfortunately, it often happens that the nations adjacent to a plundering people are themselves spoilers when opportunity offers, and hence are imbued with the same prejudices.

Then there is only one remedy—time. It is necessary that nations learn by harsh experience the enormous disadvantage of despoiling each other.

You say there is another restraint—moral influences. But moral influences have for their object the increase of virtuous actions. How can they restrain these acts of spoliation when these very acts are raised by public opinion to the level of the highest virtues? Is there a more potent moral influence than religion? Has there ever been a religion more favorable to peace or more universally received than Christianity? And yet what has been witnessed during eighteen centuries? Men have gone out to battle, not merely in spite of religion, but in the very name of religion.

A conquering nation does not always wage offensive war. Its soldiers are obliged to protect the hearthstones, the property, the families, the independence and liberty of their native land. At such a time war assumes a character of sanctity and grandeur. The flag, blessed by the ministers of the God of Peace, represents all that is sacred on earth; the people rally to it as the living image of their country and their honor; the warlike virtues are exalted above all others. When the danger is over, the opinion remains, and by a natural reaction of that spirit of vengeance that confounds itself with patriotism, they love to bear the cherished flag from capital to capital. It seems that nature has thus prepared the punishment of the aggressor.

It is the fear of this punishment, and not the progress of philosophy, that keeps arms in the arsenals, for it cannot be denied that those people who are most advanced in civilization make war, and bother themselves very little with justice when they have no reprisals to fear. Witness the Himalayas, the Atlas, and the Caucasus.

If religion has been impotent, if philosophy is powerless, how is war to cease?

Political economy demonstrates that even if the victors alone are considered, war is always begun in the interest of the few, and at the expense of the many. All that is needed, then, is that the masses should clearly perceive this truth. The weight of public opinion, which is yet divided, would then be cast entirely on the side of peace.

Forcible spoliation also takes another form. Without waiting for a man to produce something in order to rob him, they take possession of the man himself, deprive him of his freedom, and force him to work. They do not say to him, "If you will do this for me, I will do that for you," but they say to him, "You take all the troubles; we, all the enjoyments." This is slavery.

Now it is important to inquire whether it is not in the nature of uncontrolled power always to abuse itself.

For my part I have no doubt of it, and should as soon expect to see the power that could arrest a stone in falling proceed from the stone itself, as to trust force within any defined limits.

I should like to be shown a country where slavery has been abolished by the voluntary action of the masters.

Slavery furnishes a second striking example of the impotence of philosophical and religious sentiments in a conflict with the energetic activity of self interest.

This may seem sad to some modern schools which seek the reformation of society in self-denial. Let them begin by reforming the nature of man.

In the West Indies the masters, from father to son, have, since slavery was established, professed the Christian religion. Many times a day they repeat these words: "All men are brothers. Love thy neighbor as thyself; in this are the law and the prophets fulfilled." Yet they hold slaves, and nothing seems to them more legitimate or natural. Do modern reformers hope that their moral creed will ever be as universally accepted, as popular, as authoritative, or as often on all lips as the Gospel? If that has not passed from the lips to the heart, over or through the great barrier of self-interest, how can they hope that their system will work this miracle?

Well, then, is slavery invulnerable? No; self-interest, which founded it, will one day destroy it, provided the special interests that have created it do not stifle those general interests that tend to overthrow it.

Another truth demonstrated by political economy is that free labor is progressive, and slave labor stationary. Hence the triumph of the first over the second is inevitable. What has become of the cultivation of indigo by the blacks?

Free labor, applied to the production of sugar, is constantly causing a reduction in the price. Slave property is becoming proportionately less valuable to the master. Slavery will soon die out in the West Indies unless the price of sugar is artificially raised by legislation. Accordingly we see today the masters, their creditors and representatives, making vigorous efforts to maintain these laws, which are the pillars of the edifice.

Unfortunately they still have the sympathy of people among whom slavery has disappeared, from which circumstances the sovereignty of public opinion may again be observed. If public opinion is sovereign in the domain of force, it is much more so in the domain of fraud. Fraud is its proper sphere. Stratagem is the abuse of intelligence. Imposture on the part of the despoiler implies credulity on the part of the despoiled, and the natural antidote of credulity is truth. It follows that to enlighten the mind is to deprive this species of spoliation of its support.

I will briefly pass in review a few of the different kinds of spoliation that are practiced on an exceedingly large scale. The first which presents itself is spoliation through the avenue of superstition. In what does it consist? In the exchange of food, clothing, luxury, distinction, influence, power—substantial services for fictitious services. If I tell a man: "I will render you an immediate service," I am obliged to keep my word, or he would soon know what to depend upon, and my trickery would be unmasked.

But if I should tell him, "In exchange for your services I will do you immense service, not in this world but in another; after this life you may be eternally happy or miserable, and that happiness or misery depends upon me; I am a vicar between God and man, and can open to you the gates of heaven or of hell," if that man believes me he is at my mercy.

This method of imposture has been very extensively practiced since the beginning of the world, and it is well known what omnipotence the Egyptian priests attained by such means.

It is easy to see how impostors proceed. It is enough to ask one's self what he would do in their place.

If I, entertaining views of this kind, had arrived in the midst of an ignorant population, and were to succeed by some extraordinary act or marvelous appearance in passing myself off as a supernatural being, I would claim to be a messenger from God, having an absolute control over the future destinies of men.

Then I would forbid all examination of my claims. I would go still farther, and, as reason would be my most dangerous enemy, I would interdict the use of reason—at least as applied to this dangerous subject. I would taboo, as the savages say, this question, and all those connected with it. To question them, discuss them, or even think of them, should be an unpardonable crime.

Certainly it would be the acme of arts thus to put the barrier of the taboo upon all intellectual avenues which might lead to the discovery of my imposture. What better guarantee of its perpetuity than to make even doubt sacrilege?

However, I would add accessory guarantees to this fundamental one. For instance, in order that knowledge might never be disseminated among the masses, I would appropriate to myself and my accomplices the monopoly of the sciences. I would hide them under the veil of a dead language and hieroglyphic writing; and, in order that no danger might take me unawares, I would be careful to invent some ceremony which day by day would give me access to the privacy of all consciences.

It would not be amiss for me to supply some of the real wants of my people, especially if by doing so I could add to my influence and authority. For instance, men need education and moral teaching, and I would be the source of both. Thus I would guide as I pleased the minds and hearts of my people. I would join morality to my authority by an indissoluble chain, and I would proclaim that one could not exist without the other, so that if any audacious individual attempted to meddle with a tabooed question, society, which cannot exist without morality, would feel the very earth tremble under its feet, and would turn its wrath upon the rash innovator.

When things have come to this pass, it is plain that these people are more mine than if they were my slaves. The slave curses his chain, but my people will bless theirs, and I shall succeed in stamping, not on their foreheads, but in the very center of their consciences, the seal of slavery.

Public opinion alone can overturn such a structure of iniquity; but where can it begin, if each stone is tabooed? It is the work of time and the printing press.

God forbid that I should seek to disturb those consoling beliefs that link this life of sorrows to a life of felicity. But, that the irresistible longing that attracts us toward religion has been abused, no one, not even the Head of Christianity, can deny. There is, it seems to me, one sign by which you can know whether the people are or are not dupes. Examine religion and the priest, and see whether the priest is the instrument of religion, or religion the instrument of the priest.

If the priest is the instrument of religion, if his only thought is to disseminate its morality and its benefits on the earth, he will be gentle, tolerant, humble, charitable, and full of zeal; his life will reflect that of his divine model; he will preach liberty and equality among men, and peace and fraternity among nations; he will repel the allurements of temporal power, and will not ally himself with that which, of all things in this world, has the most need of restraint; he will be the man of the people, the man of good advice and tender consolations, the man of public opinion, the man of the Evangelist.

If, on the contrary, religion is the instrument of the priest, he will treat it as one does an instrument which is changed, bent and twisted in all ways so as to get out of it the greatest possible advantage for one's self. He will multiply tabooed questions; his morality will be as flexible as seasons, men, and circumstances. He will seek to impose on humanity by gesticulations and studied attitudes; a hundred times a day he will mumble over words whose sense has evaporated and which have become empty conventionalities. He will traffic in holy things, but just enough not to shake faith in their sanctity, and he will take care that the more intelligent the people are, the less open shall the traffic be. He will take part in the intrigues of the world, and he will always side with the powerful, on the simple condition that they side with him. In a word, it will be easy to see in all his actions that he does not desire to advance religion by the clergy, but the clergy by religion, and as so many efforts indicate an object, and as this object according to the hypothesis, can be only power and wealth, the decisive proof that the people are dupes is when the priest is rich and powerful.

It is very plain that a true religion can be abused as well as a false one. The higher its authority the greater the fear that it may be severely tested. But there is much difference in the results. Abuse always stirs up to revolt the sound, enlightened, intelligent portion of a people. This inevitably weakens faith, and the weakening of a true religion is far more lamentable than of a false one. This kind of spoliation, and popular enlightenment, are always in an inverse ratio to one another, for it is in the nature of abuses to go as far as possible. Not that pure and devoted priests cannot be found in the midst of the most ignorant population, but how can the knave be prevented from donning the cassock and nursing the ambitious hope of wearing the mitre? Despoilers obey the Malthusian law; they multiply with the means of existence, and the means of existence of knaves is the credulity of their dupes. Turn whichever way you please, you always find need of an enlightened public opinion. There is no other antidote.

Another species of spoliation is commercial fraud, a term that seems to me too limited because the tradesman who changes his weights and measures is not alone culpable, but also the physician who receives a fee for evil counsel, the lawyer who provokes litigation, etc. In the exchange of two services one may be of less value than the other, but when the service received is that which has been agreed upon, it is evident that spoliation of that nature will diminish with the increase of public intelligence.

The next in order is the abuse in the public service—an immense field of spoliation, so immense that we can give it but partial consideration.

If God had made man a solitary animal, everyone would labor for himself. Individual wealth would be in proportion to the services each one rendered to himself. But since man is a social animal, one service is exchanged for another. A proposition you can transpose if it suits you.

In society there are certain requirements so general, so universal in their nature, that provision has been made for them in the organizing of the public service. Among these is the necessity of security. Society agrees to compensate in services of a different nature those who render it the service of guarding the public safety. In this there is nothing contrary to the principles of political economy. Do this for me, I will do that for you. The principle of the transaction is the same, although the process is different, but the circumstance has great significance.

In private transactions each individual remains the judge both of the service he renders and of that which he receives. He can always decline an exchange, or negotiate elsewhere. There is no necessity of an interchange of services, except by previous voluntary agreement. Such is not the case with the State, especially before the establishment of representative government. Whether or not we require its services, whether they are good or bad, we are obliged to accept such as are offered and to pay the price.

It is the tendency of all men to magnify their own services and to disparage services rendered them, and private matters would be poorly regulated if there was not some standard of value. This guarantee we have not (or we hardly have it), in public affairs. But still society, composed of men, however strongly the contrary may be insinuated, obeys the universal tendency. The government wishes to serve us a great deal, much more than we desire, and forces us to acknowledge as a real service that which sometimes is widely different, and this is done for the purpose of demanding contributions from us in return.

The State is also subject to the law of Malthus. It is continually living beyond its means, it increases in proportion to its means, and draws its support solely from the substance of the people. Woe to the people who are incapable of limiting the sphere of action of the State. Liberty, private activity, riches, well-being, independence, dignity, depend upon this.

There is one circumstance that must be noticed: Chief among the services we ask of the State is security. That it may guarantee this to us it must control a force capable of overcoming all individual or collective domestic or foreign forces that might endanger it. Combined with that fatal disposition among men to live at the expense of each other, which we have before noticed, this fact suggests a danger patent to all.

You will accordingly observe on what an immense scale spoliation, by the abuses and excesses of the government, has been practiced.

If one should ask what service has been rendered the public, and what return has been made therefor, by such governments as Assyria, Babylon, Egypt, Rome, Persia, Turkey, China, Russia, England, Spain and France, he would be astonished at the enormous disparity.

At last representative government was invented, and, a priori, one might have believed that the disorder would have ceased as if by enchantment.

The principle of these governments is this:

"The people themselves, by their representatives, shall decide as to the nature and extent of the public service and the remuneration for those services."

The tendency to appropriate the property of another, and the desire to defend one's own, are thus brought in contact. One might suppose that the latter would overcome the former. Assuredly I am convinced that the latter will finally prevail, but we must concede that thus far it has not.

Why? For a very simple reason. Governments have had too much sagacity; people too little.

Governments are skillful. They act methodically, consecutively, on a well concerted plan, which is constantly improved by tradition and experience. They study men and their passions. If they perceive, for instance, that they have warlike instincts, they incite and inflame this fatal propensity. They surround the nation with dangers through the conduct of diplomats, and then naturally ask for soldiers, sailors, arsenals and fortifications. Often they have but the trouble of accepting them. Then they have pensions, places, and promotions to offer. All this calls for money. Hence loans and taxes.

If the nation is generous, the government proposes to cure all the ills of humanity. It promises to increase commerce, to make agriculture prosperous, to develop manufactures, to encourage letters and arts, to banish misery, etc. All that is necessary is to create offices and to pay public functionaries.

In other words, their tactics consist in presenting as actual services things that are but hindrances; then the nation pays, not for being served, but for being subservient. Governments assuming gigantic proportions end by absorbing half of all the revenues. The people are astonished that while marvelous labor-saving inventions, destined to infinitely multiply productions, are ever increasing in number, they are obliged to toil on as painfully as ever, and remain as poor as before.

This happens because, while the government manifests so much ability, the people show so little. Thus, when they are called upon to choose their agents, those who are to determine the sphere of, and compensation for, governmental action whom do they choose? The agents of the government. They entrust the executive power with the determination of the limit of its activity and its requirements. They are like the Bourgeois Gentilhomme, who referred the selection and number of his suits of clothes to his tailor.

However, things go from bad to worse, and at last the people open their eyes, not to the remedy, for there is none as yet, but to the evil.

Governing is so pleasant a trade that everybody desires to engage in it. Thus the advisers of the people do not cease to say: "We see your sufferings, and we weep over them. It would be otherwise if we governed you."

This period, which usually lasts for some time, is one of rebellions and insurrections. When the people are conquered, the expenses of the war are added to their burdens. When they conquer, there is a change of those who govern, and the abuses remain.

This lasts until the people learn to know and defend their true interests. Thus we always come back to this: there is no remedy but in the progress of public intelligence.

Certain nations seem remarkably inclined to become the prey of governmental spoliation. They are those where men, not considering their own dignity and energy, would believe themselves lost if they were not governed and administered upon in all things. Without having traveled much, I have seen countries where they think agriculture can make no progress unless the State keeps up experimental farms; that there will presently be no horses if the State has no stables; and that fathers will not have their children educated, or will teach them only immoralities, if the State does not decide what it is proper to learn. In such a country revolutions may rapidly succeed one another, and one set of rulers after another be overturned. But the governed are none the less governed at the caprice and mercy of their rulers, until the people see that it is better to leave the greatest possible number of services in the category of those which the parties interested exchange after a fair discussion of the price.

We have seen that society is an exchange of services, and should be but an exchange of good and honest ones. But we have also proven that men have a great interest in exaggerating the relative value of the services they render one another. I cannot indeed, see any other limit to these claims than the free acceptance or free refusal of those to whom these services are offered.

Hence it comes that certain men resort to the law to curtail the natural prerogatives of this liberty. This kind of spoliation is called privilege or monopoly. We will carefully indicate its origin and character.

Everyone knows that the services he offers in the general market are the more valued and better paid for, the scarcer they are. Each one, then, will ask for the enactment of a law to keep out of the market all who offer services similar to his.

When the monopoly is an isolated fact, it never fails to enrich the person to whom the law has granted it. It may then happen that each class of workmen, instead of seeking the overthrow of this monopoly, claim a similar one for themselves. This kind of spoliation, thus reduced to a system, becomes then the most ridiculous of illusions for everyone, and the definite result is that each one believes that he gains more from a general market impoverished by all.

It is not necessary to add that this singular regime also brings about an universal antagonism between all classes, all professions, and all peoples; that it requires the constant but always uncertain interference of government; that it swarms with the abuses that have been the subject of the preceding paragraph; that it places all industrial pursuits in hopeless insecurity; and that it accustoms men to place upon the law, and not upon themselves, the responsibility for their very existence. It would be difficult to imagine a more active cause of social disturbance.

JUSTIFICATION

It may be asked, "Why this ugly word—spoliation? It is not only coarse, but it wounds and irritates; it turns calm and moderate men against you, and embitters the controversy."

I earnestly declare that I respect individuals; I believe in the sincerity of almost all the friends of Protection, and I do not claim that I have any right to suspect the personal honesty, delicacy of feeling, or philanthropy of any one. I also repeat that Protection is the work, the fatal work, of a common error, of which all, or nearly all, are at once victims and accomplices. But I cannot prevent things being what they are.

Just imagine some Diogenes putting his head out of his tub and saying, "Athenians, you are served by slaves. Have you never thought that you practice on your brothers the most iniquitous spoliation?" Or a tribune speaking in the forum, "Romans! you have laid the foundations of all your greatness on the pillage of other nations."

They would state only undeniable truths. But must we conclude from this that Athens and Rome were inhabited only by dishonest persons? That Socrates and Plato, Cato and Cincinnatus were despicable characters?

Who could harbor such a thought? But these great men lived amidst surroundings that relieved their consciences of the sense of this injustice. Even Aristotle could not conceive the idea of a society existing without slavery. In modern times slavery has continued to our own day without causing many scruples among the planters. Armies have served as the instruments of grand conquests—that is to say, of grand spoliations. Is this saying that they are not composed of officers and men as sensitive of their honor, even more so, perhaps, than men in ordinary industrial pursuits—men who would blush at the very thought of theft, and who would face a thousand deaths rather than stoop to a base action?

It is not individuals who are to blame, but the general movement of opinion that deludes and deceives them—a movement for which society in general is culpable.

Thus is it with monopoly. I accuse the system, and not individuals; society as a mass, and not this or that one of its members. If the greatest philosophers have been able to deceive themselves as to the iniquity of slavery, how much easier is it for farmers and manufacturers to deceive themselves as to the nature and effects of the protective system.

2

TWO SYSTEMS OF MORALS

Arrived at the end of the preceding chapter, if he gets so far, I imagine I hear the reader say:

"Well, now, was I wrong in accusing political economists of being dry and cold? What a picture of humanity! Spoliation is a fatal power, almost normal, assuming every form, practiced under every pretext, against law and according to law, abusing the most sacred things, alternately playing upon the feebleness and the credulity of the masses, and ever growing by what it feeds on. Could a more mournful picture of the world be imagined than this?"

The problem is, not to find whether the picture is mournful, but whether it is true. And for that we have the testimony of history.

It is singular that those who decry political economy, because it investigates men and the world as it finds them, are more gloomy than political economy itself, at least as regards the past and the present. Look into their books and their journals. What do you find? Bitterness and hatred of society. They have even come to curse liberty, so little confidence have they in the development of the human race, the result of its natural organization. Liberty, according to them, is something that will bring humanity nearer and nearer to destruction.

It is true that they are optimists as regards the future. For although humanity, in itself incapable, for six thousand years has gone astray, a revelation has come, which has pointed out to men the way of safety and, if the flock is docile and obedient to the shepherd's call, will lead them to the promised land, where well-being may be attained without effort, where order, security and prosperity are the easy reward of improvidence.

To this end humanity, as Rousseau said, has only to allow these reformers to change the physical and moral constitution of man.

Political economy has not taken upon itself the mission of finding out the probable condition of society had it pleased God to make men different from what they are. It may be unfortunate that Providence, at the beginning, neglected to call to his counsels a few of our modern reformers. And, as the celestial mechanism would have been entirely different had the Creator consulted Alphonso the Wise, society, also, had He not neglected the advice of Fourier, would have been very different from that in which we are compelled to live, and move, and breathe. But, since we are here, our duty is to study and to understand His laws, especially if the amelioration of our condition essentially depends upon such knowledge.

We cannot prevent the existence of unsatisfied desires in the hearts of men.

We cannot satisfy these desires except by labor.

We cannot deny the fact that man has as much repugnance for labor as he has satisfaction with its results.

Since man has such characteristics, we cannot prevent the existence of a constant tendency among men to obtain their part of the enjoyments of life while throwing upon others, by force or by trickery, the burdens of labor. It is not for us to belie universal history, to silence the voice of the past, which attests that this has been the condition of things since the beginning of the world. We cannot deny that war, slavery, superstition, the abuses of government, privileges, frauds of every nature, and monopolies, have been incontestable and terrible manifestations of these two sentiments united in the heart of man: desire for enjoyment; repugnance to labor.

"In the sweat of thy brow shalt thou eat bread!" But everyone wants as much bread and as little sweat as possible. This is the conclusion of history.

Thank heaven, history also teaches that the division of blessings and burdens tends to a more exact equality among men. Unless one is prepared to deny the light of the sun, it must be admitted that, in this respect at least, society has made some progress.

If this be true, there exists in society a natural and providential force, a law that causes iniquity gradually to cease, and makes justice more and more a reality.

We say that this force exists in society, and that God has placed it there. If it did not exist we should be compelled, with the socialists, to search for it in those artificial means, in those arrangements which require a fundamental change in the physical and moral constitution of man, or rather we should consider that search idle and vain, for the reason that we could not comprehend the action of a lever without a place of support.

Let us, then, endeavor to indicate that beneficent force that tends progressively to overcome the maleficent force to which we have given the name spoliation, and the existence of which is only too well explained by reason and proved by experience.

Every maleficent act necessarily has two terms— the point of beginning and the point of ending; the man who performs the act and the man upon whom it is performed; or, in the language of the schools, the active and the passive agent. There are, then, two means by which the maleficent act can be prevented: by the voluntary absence of the active, or by the resistance of the passive agent. Whence two systems of morals arise, not antagonistic but concurrent; religious or philosophical morality, and the morality to which I permit myself to apply the name economical (utilitarian).

Religious morality, to abolish and extirpate the maleficent act, appeals to its author, to man in his capacity of active agent. It says to him: "Reform yourself; purify yourself; cease to do evil; learn to do well; conquer your passions; sacrifice your interests; do not oppress your neighbor, to succor and relieve whom is your duty; be first just, then generous." This morality will always be the most beautiful, the most touching, that which will exhibit the human race in all its majesty; which will the best lend itself to the offices of eloquence, and will most excite the sympathy and admiration of mankind.

Utilitarian morality works to the same end, but especially addresses itself to man in his capacity of passive agent. It points out to him the consequences of human actions, and, by this simple exhibition, stimulates him to struggle against those who injure, and to honor those who are useful to him. It aims to extend among the oppressed masses enough good sense, enlightenment and just defiance, to render oppression both difficult and dangerous.

It may also be remarked that utilitarian morality is not without its influence upon the oppressor. An act of spoliation causes good and evil—evil for him who suffers it, good for him in whose favor it is exercised—else the act would not have been performed. But the good by no means compensates the evil. The evil always, and necessarily, predominates over the good, because the very fact of oppression occasions a loss of force, creates dangers, provokes reprisals, and requires costly precautions. The simple exhibition of these effects is not then limited to retaliation of the oppressed; it places all whose hearts are not perverted, on the side of justice, and alarms the security of the oppressors themselves.

But it is easy to understand that this morality, which is simply a scientific demonstration, and would even lose its efficiency if it changed its character; which addresses itself not to the heart but to the intelligence; which seeks not to persuade but to convince;

which gives proofs not counsels; whose mission is not to move but to enlighten, and which obtains over vice no other victory than to deprive it of its spoils—it is easy to understand, I say, how this morality has been accused of being dry and prosaic. The reproach is true without being just. It is equivalent to saying that political economy is not everything, does not comprehend everything, is not the universal solvent. But who has ever made such an exorbitant pretension in its name? The accusation would not be well founded unless political economy presented its processes as final, and denied to philosophy and religion the use of their direct and proper means of elevating humanity. Look at the concurrent action of morality, properly so called, and of political economy—the one inveighing against spoliation by an exposure of its moral ugliness, the other bringing it into discredit in our judgment, by showing its evil consequences. Concede that the triumph of the religious moralist, when realized, is more beautiful, more consoling and more radical; at the same time it is not easy to deny that the triumph of economical science is more facile and more certain.

In a few lines more valuable than many volumes, J.B. Say has already remarked that there are two ways of removing the disorder introduced by hypocrisy into an honorable family; to reform Tartuffe, or sharpen the wits of Orgon. Moliere, that great painter of human life, seems constantly to have had in view the second process as the more efficient.

Such is the case on the world's stage. Tell me what Caesar did, and I will tell you what were the Romans of his day.

Tell me what modern diplomacy has accomplished, and I will describe the moral condition of the nations.

We should not pay such staggering sums of taxes if we did not appoint those who consume them to vote them.

We should not have so much trouble, difficulty and expense with the African question if we were as well convinced that two and two make four in political economy as in arithmetic.

Mr. Guizot would never have had occasion to say: "France is rich enough to pay for her glory," if France had never conceived a false idea of glory.

The same statesman never would have said: "Liberty is too precious for France to traffic in it," if France had well understood that liberty and a large budget are incompatible.

Let religious morality then, if it can, touch the heart of the Tartuffes, the Caesars, the conquerors of Algeria, the sinecurists, the monopolists, etc. The mission of political economy is to enlighten their dupes. Of these two processes, which is the more efficient aid to social progress? I believe it is the second. I believe that humanity cannot escape the necessity of first learning a defensive morality. I have read, observed, and made diligent inquiry, and have been unable to find any abuse, practiced to any considerable extent, that has perished by voluntary renunciation on the part of those who profited by it. On the other hand, I have seen many that have yielded to the manly resistance of those who suffered by them.

To describe the consequences of abuses, is the most efficient way of destroying the abuses themselves. And this is true particularly in regard to abuses that, like the protective system, while inflicting real evil upon the masses, are to those who seem to profit by them only an illusion and a deception.

Well, then, does this species of morality realize all the social perfection that the sympathetic nature of the human heart and its noblest faculties cause us to hope for? This I by no means pretend. Admit the general diffusion of this defensive morality—which, after all, is only a knowledge that the best-understood interests are in accord with general utility and justice. A society, although very well regulated, might not be very attractive, where there were no knaves, only because there were no fools; where vice, always latent, and, so to speak, overcome by famine, would only need available plunder in order to be restored to vigor; where the prudence of the individual would be guarded by the vigilance of the mass and, finally, where reforms, regulating external acts, would not have penetrated to the consciences of men.

Such a state of society we sometimes see typified in one of those exact, rigorous and just men who is ever ready to resent the slightest infringement of his rights, and shrewd in avoiding impositions. You esteem him—possibly you admire him. You may make him your deputy, but you would not necessarily choose him for a friend.

Let, then, the two moral systems, instead of blaming each other, act in concert, and attack vice at its opposite poles. While the economists perform their task in uprooting prejudice, stimulating just and necessary opposition, studying and exposing the real nature of actions and things, let the religious moralist, on his part, perform his more attractive, but more difficult, labor; let him attack the very body of iniquity, follow it to its most vital parts, paint the charms of beneficence, self-denial and devotion, open the fountains of virtue where we can only choke the sources of vice—this is his duty. It is noble and beautiful. But why does he dispute the utility of that which belongs to us?

In a society that, though not superlatively virtuous, should nevertheless be regulated by the influences of economical morality (which is the knowledge of the economy of society), would there not be a field for the progress of religious morality?

Habit, it has been said, is a second nature. A country where the individual had become unaccustomed to injustice simply by the force of an enlightened public opinion might, indeed, be pitiable; but it seems to me it would be well prepared to receive an education more elevated and more pure. To be disaccustomed to evil is a great step toward becoming good. Men cannot remain stationary. Turned aside from the paths of vice that would lead only to infamy, they appreciate better the attractions of virtue. Possibly it may be necessary for society to pass through this prosaic state, where men practice virtue by calculation, to be thence elevated to that more poetic region where they will no longer have need of such an exercise.

3

THE TWO HATCHETS

PETITION OF JACQUES BONHOMME, CARPENTER, TO
MR. CUNINGRIDAINE, MINISTER OF COMMERCE

Mr. Manufacturer Minister,

I am a carpenter by trade, as was St. Joseph of old, and I handle the hatchet and adze for your benefit.

Now, while engaged in hewing and chopping from morning to night upon the lands of our Lord the King,[1] the idea has struck me that my labor may be regarded as national, as well as yours.

And, in these circumstances, I cannot see why protection should not visit my woodyard as well as your workshop.

For, sooth to say, if you make cloths I make roofs; and both, in their own way, shelter our customers from cold and from rain.

And yet I run after customers, and customers run after you. You have found out the way of securing them by hindering them

---

[1]Published in January 1848.

from supplying themselves elsewhere, while mine apply to whomsoever they think proper.

What is astonishing in all this? Mr. Cunin, the Minister of State, has not forgotten Mr. Cunin, the manufacturer—all quite natural. But alas! My humble trade has not given a Minister to France, although practiced in Biblical times by far more august personages.

And in the immortal code which I find embodied in Scripture I cannot discover the slightest expression that could be quoted by carpenters as authorizing them to enrich themselves at the expense of other people.

You see, then, how I am situated. I earn fifteen pence a day, when it is not Sunday or holiday. I offer you my services at the same time as a Flemish carpenter offers you his, and, because he abates a halfpenny, you give him the preference.

But I desire to clothe myself; and if a Belgian weaver presents his cloth alongside of yours, you drive him and his cloth out of the country. So that, being forced to frequent your shop, although the dearest, my poor fifteen pence go no further in reality than fourteen.

Nay, they are not worth more than thirteen! For in place of expelling the Belgian weaver, at your own cost (which was the least you could do), you, for your own ends, make me pay for the people you set at his heels.

And as a great number of your co-legislators, with whom you are on a marvelously good footing, take each a halfpenny or a penny, under pretext of protecting iron, or coal, or oil, or corn, I find, when everything is taken into account, that of my fifteen pence I have only been able to save sevenpence or eightpence from pillage.

You will no doubt tell me that these small halfpence, which pass in this way from my pocket to yours, maintain workpeople who reside around your castle, and enable you to live in a style of magnificence. To which I will only reply that, if the pence had been left with me, the person who earned them, they would have maintained workpeople in my neighborhood.

Be this as it may, Mr. Minister Manufacturer, knowing that I should be but ill received by you, I have not come to require you, as I had good right to do, to withdraw the restriction which you impose on your customers. I prefer following the ordinary course, and I approach you to solicit a little bit of protection for myself.

Here, of course, you will interpose a difficulty. "My good friend," you will say, "I would protect you and your fellow workmen with all my heart; but how can I confer custom-house favors on carpenter work? What use would it be to prohibit the importation of houses by sea or by land?

That would be a good joke, to be sure; but, by dint of thinking, I have discovered another mode of favoring the children of St. Joseph, which you will welcome the more willingly, I hope, as it differs in nothing from that which constitutes the privilege you vote year after year in your own favor.

The means of favoring us that I have thus marvelously discovered is to prohibit the use of sharp axes in this country.

I maintain that such a restriction would not be in the least more illogical or more arbitrary than the one to which you subject us in the case of your cloth.

Why do you drive away the Belgians? Because they sell cheaper than you. And why do they sell cheaper than you? Because they have a certain degree of superiority over you as manufacturers.

Between you and a Belgian, therefore, there is exactly the same difference as in my trade there would be between a blunt and a sharp axe.

And you force me, as a tradesman, to purchase from you the product of the blunt hatchet!

Regard the country at large as a workman who desires, by his labor, to procure all things he has want of, and, among others, cloth.

There are two means of effecting this.

The first is to spin and weave the wool.

The second is to produce other articles, as, for example, French clocks, paper-hangings, or wines, and exchange them with the Belgians for the cloth wanted.

Of these two processes the one that gives the best result may be represented by the sharp axe, and the other by the blunt one.

You do not deny that at present, in France, we obtain a piece of cloth by the work of our own looms (that is the blunt axe) with more labor than by producing and exchanging wines (that is the sharp axe). So far are you from denying this that it is precisely because of this excess of labor (in which you say wealth consists) that you recommend, nay, that you compel the employment of the worse of the two hatchets.

Now, only be consistent, be impartial, and if you mean to be just, treat the poor carpenters as you treat yourselves.

Pass a law to this effect:

"No one shall henceforth be permitted to employ any beams or rafters but such as are produced and fashioned by blunt hatchets,"

And see what will immediately happen.

Whereas at present we give a hundred blows of the axe we shall then give three hundred. The work we now do in an hour will then require three hours. What a powerful encouragement will thus be given to labor! Masters, journeymen, apprentices, our sufferings are now at an end! We shall be in demand; and, therefore, well paid. Whoever shall henceforth desire to have a roof to cover him must comply with our exactions, just as at present whoever desires clothes to his back must comply with yours.

And should the theoretical advocates of Free Trade ever dare to call in question the utility of the measure we know well where to seek for reasons to confute them. Your inquiry of 1834 is still to be had. With that weapon we shall conquer; for you have there admirably pleaded the cause of restriction and of blunt axes, which are in reality the same thing.

4

LOWER COUNCIL OF LABOR

"What! You have the nerve to demand for all citizens a right to sell, buy, barter, and exchange; to render and receive service for service, and to judge for themselves, on the single condition that they do all honestly, and comply with the demands of the public treasury? Then you simply desire to deprive our workmen of employment, of wages, and of bread?"

That is what is said to us. I know very well what to think of it; but what I wish to know is, what the workmen themselves think of it.

I have at hand an excellent instrument of inquiry. Not those Upper Councils of Industry, where extensive proprietors who call themselves laborers, rich shipowners who call themselves sailors, and wealthy shareholders who pass themselves off for workmen, turn their philanthropy to advantage in a way that we all know.

No; it is with workmen who are workmen in reality that we have to do—joiners, carpenters, masons, tailors, shoemakers, dyers, blacksmiths, innkeepers, grocers, etc. etc.—and who in my village have founded a friendly society.

I have transformed this friendly society, by my own hand, into a Lower Council of Labor, and instituted an inquiry that will be found of great importance, although it is not crammed with figures, or inflated to the bulk of a quarto volume printed at the expense of the State.

My object was to interrogate these plain, simple people as to the manner in which they are, or believe themselves to be, affected by the policy of protection. The president pointed out that this would be infringing to some extent on the fundamental conditions of the Association. For in France, this land of liberty, people who associate give up their right to talk politics—in other words, their right to discuss their common interests. However, after some hesitation, he agreed to include the question in the order of the day.

They divided the assembly into as many committees as there were groups of distinct trades, and delivered to each committee a schedule to be filled up after fifteen days' deliberation.

On the day fixed, the worthy president (we adopt the official style) took the chair, and there were laid upon the table (still the official style) fifteen reports, which he read in succession.

The first that was taken into consideration was that of the tailors. Here is an exact and literal copy of it.

EFFECTS OF PROTECTION.
REPORT OF THE TAILORS

ADVANTAGES

None.
Note: After all our inquiries, deliberations, and discussions, we have been quite unable to discover that in any respect whatever the policy of protection has been of advantage to our trade.

INCONVENIENCES

1st. In consequence of the policy of protection, we pay dearer for bread, meat, sugar, firewood, thread, needles, etc., which is equivalent in our case to a considerable reduction of wages.

2nd. In consequence of the policy of protection, our customers also pay dearer for everything, and this leaves them less to spend upon clothing: whence it follows that we have less employment, and, consequently, smaller returns.

3rd. In consequence of the policy of protection, the materials we sew are dear, and people on that account wear their clothes longer, or dispense with part of them. This, again, is equivalent to a diminution of employment, and forces us to offer our services at a lower rate of remuneration.

Here is another report:

EFFECTS OF PROTECTION.
REPORT OF THE BLACKSMITHS

ADVANTAGES	INCONVENIENCES
None.	1st. The policy of protection imposes a tax upon us every time we eat, drink, or warm or clothe ourselves, and this tax does not go to the treasury.
	2nd. It imposes a like tax upon all our fellow-citizens who are not of our trade, and they, being so much the poorer, have recourse to cheap substitutes for our work, which deprives us of the employment we should otherwise have had.
	3rd. It keeps up iron at so high a price that it is not employed in the country for ploughs, grates, gates, balconies, etc.; and our trade, which might furnish employment to so many other people who are in want of it, no longer furnishes employment to ourselves.
	4th. The revenue that the treasury fails to obtain from commodities that are not imported, is levied upon the salt we use, postages, etc.

All the other reports (with which it is unnecessary to trouble the reader) are to the same tune. Gardeners, carpenters, shoemakers, clogmakers, boatmen, millers, all give vent to the same complaints.

I regret that there are no agricultural laborers in our association. Their report would assuredly have been very instructive.

But alas! In our country of the Landes, the poor laborers, protected though they be, have not the means of joining an association and, having insured their cattle, they find they cannot themselves become members of a friendly society. The boon of protection does not hinder them from being the pariahs of our social order. What shall I say of the grape pickers?

What I notice, especially, is the good sense displayed by our villagers in perceiving not only the direct injury the policy of protection does them, but the indirect injury, which, although in the first instance affecting their customers, rebounds upon themselves.

This is what the economists of the *Moniteur Industriel* do not appear to understand.

And perhaps those men whose eyes a dash of protection has fascinated, especially our agriculturists, would be willing to give it up if they were enabled to see this side of the question.

In that case they might perhaps say to themselves, "Better far to be self-supported in the midst of a set of customers in easy circumstances than to be protected in the midst of an impoverished clientele.

For to desire to enrich by turns each separate branch of industry by creating a moat around each in succession, is as vain an attempt as it would be for a man to try to leap over his own shadow.

5

DEARNESS—CHEAPNESS

I think it necessary to submit to the reader some theoretical remarks on the illusions to which the words dearness and cheapness give rise. At first sight, these remarks may, I feel, be regarded as subtle, but the question is not whether they are subtle or the reverse, but whether they are true. Now, I not only believe them to be perfectly true, but to be well fitted to suggest matter for reflection to men (of whom there are not a few) who have sincere faith in the efficacy of a protectionist policy.

The advocates of Liberty and the defenders of Restriction are both obliged to employ the expressions, dearness and cheapness. The former declare themselves in favor of cheapness with a view to the interest of the consumer; the latter pronounce in favor of dearness, having regard especially to the interest of the producer. Others content themselves with saying: The producer and consumer are one and the same person; which leaves undecided the question whether the law should promote cheapness or dearness.

In the midst of this conflict it would seem that the law has only one course to follow, and that is to allow prices to settle and adjust themselves naturally. But then we are attacked by the bitter enemies of *laissez faire*. Regardless of risks they want the law to interfere, without knowing or caring in what direction. And yet it lies with those who desire to create by legal intervention an artificial dearness or an unnatural cheapness to explain the grounds of their preference. The burden of proof rests upon them exclusively. Liberty is always esteemed good till the contrary is proved; and to allow prices to settle and adjust themselves naturally is liberty.

But the parties to this dispute have changed positions. The advocates of dearness have secured the triumph of their system, and it lies with the defenders of natural prices to prove the goodness of their cause. On both sides the argument turns on two words; and it is therefore very essential to ascertain what these two words really mean.

But we must first of all notice a series of facts which are fitted to disconcert the champions of both camps. To engender dearness the restrictionists have obtained protective duties, and a cheapness, which is to them inexplicable, has come to deceive their hopes.

To create cheapness, the free traders have occasionally succeeded in securing liberty, and, to their astonishment, an elevation of prices has been the consequence.

For example, in France, in order to favor agriculture, a duty of 22 percent has been imposed on foreign wool, and it has turned out that French wool has been sold at a lower price after the measure than before it.

In England, to satisfy the consumer, they lowered, and ultimately removed, the duty on foreign wool; and it has come to pass that in that country the price of wool is higher than ever.

And these are not isolated facts; for the price of wool is governed by precisely the same laws that govern the price of everything else. The same result is produced in all analogous cases. Contrary to expectation, protection has, to some extent, brought about a fall, and competition, to some extent, a rise of prices.

When the confusion of ideas thence arising had reached its height, the protectionists began saying to their adversaries: "It is our system that brings about the cheapness of which you boast so much." To which the reply was: "It is liberty that has induced the dearness which you find so useful."[1]

Evidently there is in all this a misconception, an illusion, that it is necessary to clear up; and this is what I shall now endeavor to do.

Put the case of two isolated nations, each composed of a million inhabitants. Grant that, other things being equal, the one possesses double the quantity of everything—wheat, meat, iron, furniture, fuel, books, clothing, etc.—that the other possesses.

It will be granted that the one is twice as rich as the other.

And yet there is no reason to affirm that a difference in actual money prices[2] exists in the two countries. Nominal prices may perhaps be higher in the richer country. It may be that in the United States everything is nominally dearer than in Poland, and that the population of the former country should, nevertheless, be better provided with all that they need; whence we infer that it is not the nominal price of products but their comparative abundance, that constitutes wealth. When, then, we desire to pronounce an opinion on the comparative merits of restriction and free trade, we should not inquire which of the two systems engenders dearness or cheapness, but which of the two brings abundance or scarcity.

For observe this, that products being exchanged for each other, a relative scarcity of all, and a relative abundance of all, leave the nominal prices of commodities in general at the same

---

[1] Recently, Mr. Duchatel, who had formerly advocated free trade, with a view to low prices, said to the Chamber: "It would not be difficult for me to prove that protection leads to cheapness."

[2] The expression, *prix absolus* (absolute prices), which the author employs here and in chapter 9 of the first series (ante), is not, I think, used by English economists, and from the context in both instances I take it to mean actual money prices; or what Adam Smith terms nominal prices.— Translator.

point; but this cannot be affirmed of the relative condition of the inhabitants of the two countries.

Let us dip a little deeper still into this subject.

When we see an increase and a reduction of duties produce effects so different from what we had expected, depreciation often following taxation, and enhancement following free trade, it becomes the imperative duty of political economy to seek an explanation of phenomena so much opposed to received ideas; for it is needless to say that a science, if it is worthy of the name, is nothing else than a faithful statement and a sound explanation of facts.

Now the phenomenon we are here examining is explained very satisfactorily by a circumstance of which we must never lose sight.

Dearness is due to two causes, and not to one only.

The same thing holds good of cheapness.

It is one of the least disputed points in political economy that price is determined by the relative state of supply and demand.

There are then two terms that affect price—supply and demand. These terms are essentially variable. They may be combined in the same direction, in contrary directions, and in infinitely varied proportions. Hence the combinations of which price is the result are inexhaustible. High price may be the result either of diminished supply or of increased demand.

Low price may be the result of increased supply or of diminished demand.

Hence there are two kinds of dearness, and two kinds of cheapness.

There is a dearness of an injurious kind, that which proceeds from a diminution of supply, for that implies scarcity, privation (such as has been felt this year from the scarcity of wheat); and there is a dearness of a beneficial kind, that which results from an increase of demand, for the latter presupposes the development of general wealth.

In the same way, there is a cheapness that is desirable, that which has its source in abundance; and an injurious cheapness, that has for its cause the failure of demand, and the impoverishment of consumers.

Now, please note this: that restriction tends to induce, at the same time, both the injurious cause of dearness, and the injurious cause of cheapness—injurious dearness, by diminishing the supply, for this is the avowed object of restriction; and injurious cheapness, by diminishing also the demand; seeing that it gives a false direction to labor and capital, and fetters consumers with taxes and trammels.

So that, as regards price, these two tendencies neutralize each other; and this is the reason why the restrictive system, restraining as it does, demand and supply at one and the same time, does not in the long run realize even that dearness which is its object.

But, as regards the condition of the population, these causes do not at all neutralize each other; on the contrary, they concur in making it worse.

The effect of freedom of trade is exactly the opposite. In its general result, it may be that it does not realize the cheapness it promises; for it has two tendencies, one toward desirable cheapness through the extension of supply, or abundance; the other toward appreciable dearness by the development of demand, or general wealth. These two tendencies neutralize each other in what concerns nominal price, but they concur in what regards the material prosperity of the population.

In short, under the restrictive system, in so far as it is operative, men recede toward a state of things in which both demand and supply are enfeebled. Under a system of freedom, they progress toward a state of things in which both are developed simultaneously, and without necessarily affecting nominal prices. Such prices form no good criterion of wealth. They may remain the same while society is falling into a state of the most abject poverty or while it is advancing toward a state of the greatest prosperity.

We shall now, in a few words, show the practical application of this doctrine.

A cultivator of the south of France believes himself to be very rich, because he is protected by duties from external competition.

He may be as poor as Job; but he nevertheless imagines that sooner or later he will get rich by protection. In these circumstances, if we ask him the question that was put by the Odier Committee in these words:

"Do you desire—yes or no—to be subject to foreign competition?" His first impulse is to answer "No," and the Odier Committee proudly welcomes his response.

However, we must go a little deeper into the matter. Unquestionably, foreign competition—nay, competition in general—is always troublesome; and if one branch of trade alone could eliminate it, that branch of trade would for some time profit largely.

But protection is not an isolated favor; it is a system. If, to the profit of the agriculturist, protection tends to create a scarcity of wheat and of meat, it tends likewise to create, to the profit of other industries, a scarcity of iron, of cloth, of fuel, tools, etc.—a scarcity, in short, of everything.

Now, if a scarcity of wheat tends to enhance its price through a diminution of supply, the scarcity of all other commodities for which wheat is exchanged tends to reduce the price of wheat by a diminution of demand, so that it is not at all certain that ultimately wheat will be a penny dearer than it would have been under a system of free trade. There is nothing certain in the whole process but this—that as there is upon the whole less of every commodity in the country, each man will be less plentifully provided with everything he has occasion to buy.

The agriculturist should ask himself whether it would not be more to his interest that a certain quantity of wheat and cattle should be imported from abroad, and that he should at the same time find himself surrounded by a population in easy circumstances, able and willing to consume and pay for all sorts of agricultural produce.

Imagine a place in which the people are clothed in rags, fed upon chestnuts, and lodged in hovels. How can agriculture flourish in such a locality? What can the soil be made to produce with a well-founded expectation of fair remuneration? Meat? The people do not eat it. Milk? They must content themselves with water. Butter? It is regarded as a luxury. Wool? The use of it is dispensed with as much as possible. Does anyone imagine that all the ordinary objects of consumption can thus be put beyond the reach of the masses, without tending to lower prices as much as protection is tending to raise them?

What has been said of the agriculturist holds equally true of the manufacturer. Our manufacturers of cloth assure us that external competition will lower prices by increasing the supply. Granted; but will not these prices be again raised by an increased demand? Is the consumption of cloth a fixed and invariable quantity? Has every man as much of it as he would wish to have? And if general wealth is advanced and developed by the abolition of all these taxes and restrictions, will the first use to which this emancipation is turned by the population not be to dress better?

The question—the constantly-recurring question—then, is not to find out whether protection is favorable to any one special branch of industry, but whether, when everything is weighed, balanced, and taken into account, restriction is in its own nature, more productive than liberty.

Now, no one will venture to maintain this. On the contrary, we are perpetually met with the admission, "You are right in principle."

If it be so, if restriction confers no benefit on individual branches of industry without doing a greater amount of injury to general wealth, we are forced to conclude that actual money prices, considered by themselves, only express a relation between each special branch of industry and industry in general, between supply and demand; and that, on this account, a remunerative price, which is the professed object of protection, is rather injured than favored by the system.

Supplement

The article we have published under the title of Dearness, Cheapness, has brought us several letters. We give them, along with our replies:

MR. EDITOR—You upset all our ideas. I endeavored to aid the cause of free trade, and found it necessary to urge the consideration of cheapness. I went about everywhere, saying, "When freedom of trade is accorded, bread, meat, cloth, linen, iron, fuel, will go on falling in price." This displeased those who sell, but gave great pleasure to those who buy these commodities. And now you throw out doubts as to whether free trade will bring us cheapness or not. What, then, is to be gained by it? What gain will it be to the people if foreign competition, which may damage their sales, does not benefit them in their purchases?

MR. FREE-TRADER—Allow us to tell you that you must have read only half the article that has called forth your letter. We said that free trade acts exactly in the same way as roads, canals, railways, and everything else that facilitates communication by removing obstacles. Its first tendency is to increase the supply of the commodity freed from duty, and consequently to lower its price. But by augmenting at the same time the supply of all other commodities for which this article is exchanged, it increases the demand, and the price by this means rises again. You ask what gain this would be to the people? Suppose a balance with several scales, in each of which is deposited a certain quantity of the articles you have enumerated. If you add to the wheat in one scale it will tend to fall; but if you add a little cloth, a little iron, a little fuel, to what the other scales contained, you will redress the equilibrium. If you look only at the beam, you will find nothing changed. But if you look at the people for whose use these articles are produced, you will find them better fed, clothed, and warmed.

MR. EDITOR—I am a manufacturer of cloth, and a protectionist. I confess that your article on dearness and cheapness has made me reflect. It contains something specious that would require to be well established before we declare ourselves converted.

MR. PROTECTIONIST—We say that your restrictive measures have an iniquitous object in view, namely, artificial dearness. But we do not affirm that they always realize the hopes of those who promote them. It is certain that they inflict on the consumer all the injurious consequences of scarcity. It is not certain that they always confer a corresponding advantage on the producer. Why? Because if they diminish the supply, they diminish also the demand.

This proves that there is in the economic arrangement of this world a moral force, a *vis medicatrix*, which causes unjust ambition in the long run to fall prey to self-deception.

Would you have the goodness, sir, to remark that one of the elements of the prosperity of each individual branch of industry is the general wealth of the community. The value of a house is not always in proportion to what it has cost, but likewise in proportion to the number and fortune of the tenants. Are two houses exactly similar necessarily of the same value? By no means, if the one is situated in Paris and the other in Lower Brittany. Never speak of price without taking into account collateral circumstances, and let it be remembered that no attempt is so vain as to endeavor to found the prosperity of parts on the ruin of the whole. And yet this is what the policy of restriction pretends to do.

Consider what would have happened at Paris, for example, if this strife of interests had been attended with success.

Suppose that the first shoemaker who established himself in that city had succeeded in ejecting all others; that the first tailor, the first mason, the first printer, the first watchmaker, the first physician, the first baker, had been equally successful. Paris would at this moment have been still a village of 1,200 or 1,500 inhabitants. It has turned out very differently. The market of Paris has been open to all (excepting those whom you still keep out), and it is this freedom that has enlarged and aggrandized it. The struggles of competition have been bitter and long continued, and this is what has made Paris a city of a million inhabitants. The general wealth has increased, no doubt; but has the individual wealth of the shoemakers and tailors been diminished? This is the question you have to ask. You may say that according as the number of competitors increased, the price of their products would go on falling. Has it done so? No; for if the supply has been augmented, the demand has been enlarged.

The same thing will hold good of your commodity, cloth; let it enter freely. You will have more competitors in the trade, it is true; but you will have more customers, and, above all, richer customers. Is it possible you can never have thought of this, when you see nine-tenths of your fellow citizens underclothed in winter, for want of the commodity you manufacture?

If you wish to prosper, allow your customers to thrive. This is a lesson you have been very long in learning. When it is thoroughly learned, each man will seek his own interest in the general good; and then jealousies between man and man, town and town, province and province, nation and nation, will no longer trouble the world.

6

TO ARTISANS AND WORKMEN

M any journals have attacked me in your presence and hearing.[1] Perhaps you will not object to read my defense.

I am not suspicious. When a man writes or speaks, I take it for granted that he believes what he says.

And yet, after reading and re-reading the journals to which I now reply, I seem unable to discover any other than melancholy tendencies.

Our present business is to inquire which is more favorable to your interests—liberty or restriction.

I believe that it is liberty; they believe that it is restriction. It is for each party to prove his own thesis.

Was it necessary to insinuate that we free traders are the agents of England, of the south of France, of the Government?

On this point you see how easy recrimination would be.

---

[1]This article appeared in the *Courier Francaise* of September, 1846, in reply to articles that had appeared in *L'Atelier*.

We are the agents of England, they say, because some of us employ the words "meeting" and "free trader"!

And do they not make use of the words "drawback" and "budget"?

We, it would seem, imitate Cobden and the English democracy!

And do they not parody Lord George Bentinck and the British aristocracy?

We borrow from perfidious Albion the doctrine of liberty!

And do they not borrow from the same source the quibbles of protection?

We follow the lead of Bordeaux and the south!

And do they not avail themselves of the cupidity of Lille and the north?

We favor the secret designs of the ministry, whose object is to divert public attention from their real policy!

And do they not act in the interest of the civil list, which profits most of all from the policy of protection?

You see, then, very clearly, that if we did not despise this war of disparagement, arms would not be wanting to carry it on.

But this is beside the question.

The question, and we must never lose sight of it, is this:

Whether it is better for the working classes to be free, or not to be free to purchase foreign commodities?

Workmen! They tell you that: "If you are free to purchase from the foreigner those things that you now produce yourselves, you will cease to produce them; you will be without employment, without wages, and without bread. It is therefore for your own good to restrain your liberty."

This objection recurs in every form: They say, for example, "If we clothe ourselves with English cloth; if we make our ploughs of English iron; if we cut our bread with English knives; if we wipe our hands with English towels—what will become of French workmen, what will become of national labor?"

Tell me, workmen! If a man should stand on the quay at Boulogne and say to every Englishman who landed, "If you will give me those English boots, I will give you this French hat"; or, "If you will give me that English horse I will give you this French tilbury"; or ask him, "Will you exchange that machine made at Birmingham for this clock made at Paris?"; or, again, "Can you arrange to barter this Newcastle coal against this champagne wine?" Tell me whether, assuming this man to make his proposals with discernment, anyone would be justified in saying that our national labor, taken in the aggregate, would suffer in consequence?

Would it make the slightest difference in this respect were twenty such offers to be made in place of one, or a million such barters to be effected in place of four, or were merchants and money to intervene, whereby such transactions would be greatly facilitated and multiplied?

Now, when one country buys from another wholesale to sell again in retail, or buys in retail to sell again in bulk, if we trace the transaction to its ultimate results we shall always find that commerce resolves itself into barter, products for products, services for services. If, then, barter does no injury to national labor, since it implies as much national labor given as foreign labor received, it follows that a hundred thousand millions of such acts of barter would do as little injury as one. But where would be the profit? you will ask. The profit consists in turning to most account the resources of each country, so that the same amount of labor shall yield everywhere more satisfaction and well-being.

There are some who in your case have recourse to a singular system of tactics. They begin by admitting the superiority of the free to the prohibitive system, in order, doubtless, not to have the battle to fight on this ground.

Then they remark that the transition from one system to another is always attended with some displacement of labor.

Last, they enlarge on the sufferings, which, in their opinion, such displacements must always entail. They exaggerate these sufferings, they multiply them, they make them the principal subject of discussion, they present them as the exclusive and definite result of reform, and in this way they endeavor to enlist you under the banners of monopoly.

This is just the system of tactics that has been employed to defend every system of abuse; and one thing I must plainly avow that it is this system of tactics that constantly embarrasses those who advocate reforms, even those most useful to the people. You will soon see the reason of this.

When an abuse has once taken root everything is arranged on the assumption of its continuance. Some men depend upon it for subsistence, others depend upon them, and so on, till a formidable edifice is erected.

Would you venture to pull it down? All cry out, and—remark this well—the men who bawl out appear always at first sight to be in the right, because it is far easier to show the derangements that must accompany a reform than the arrangements that must follow it.

The supporters of abuses cite particular instances of sufferings; they point out particular employers who, with their workmen and the people who supply them with materials, are about to be injured; and the poor reformer can only refer to the general good that must gradually diffuse itself over the masses. That by no means produces the same effect.

Thus, when the question turns on the abolition of slavery, "Poor men!" they say to the negroes, "who is henceforth to support you? The manager handles the lash, but he likewise distributes the cassava."

And the slave regrets his chain, for he asks, "Whence will come the cassava?"

He fails to see that it is not the manager who feeds him, but his own labor that feeds both him and the manager.

When they set about reforming the convents in Spain, they asked the beggars: "Where will you now find food and clothing? The prior is your best friend. Is it not very convenient to be in a situation to address yourself to him?"

And the mendicants replied: "True; if the prior goes away we see very clearly that we shall be losers, and we do not see at all so clearly who is to come in his place."

They did not take into account that, if the convents bestowed alms, they lived upon them; so that the nation had more to give away than to receive.

In the same way, workmen! monopoly, quite imperceptibly, saddles you with taxes, and then, with the produce of these taxes, finds you employment.

And your sham friends exclaim: "But for monopolies where would you find employment?"

And you, like the Spanish beggars, reply: "True, true; the employment the monopolists find us is certain. The promises of liberty are of uncertain fulfillment."

For you do not see that they take from you in the first instance the money with part of which they afterwards afford you employment.

You ask: Who is to find you employment? and the answer is that you will give employment to one another! With the money of which he is no longer deprived by taxation the shoemaker will dress better, and give employment to the tailor. The tailor will more frequently renew his foot-gear, and afford employment to the shoemaker; and the same thing will take place in all other departments of trade.

It has been said that under a system of free trade we should have fewer workmen in our mines and spinning mills.

I do not think so. But if this happened, we should necessarily have a greater number of people working freely and independently, either in their own houses or at outdoor employment. For if our mines and spinning mills are not capable of supporting themselves, as is asserted, without the aid of taxes levied from the public at large, the moment these taxes are repealed everybody will be by so much in better circumstances; and it is this improvement in the general circumstances of the community that lends support to individual branches of industry.

Pardon my dwelling a little longer on this view of the subject; for my great anxiety is to see you all ranged on the side of liberty.

Suppose that the capital employed in manufactures yields 5 percent profit. But Mondor has an establishment in which he employs £100,000, at a loss, instead of a profit, of 5 percent. Between the loss and the gain supposed, there is a difference of £10,000. What takes place? A small tax of £10,000 is coolly levied from the public, and handed over to Mondor. You don't see it, for the thing is skillfully disguised. It is not the taxgatherer who waits upon you to demand your share of this burden; but you pay it to Mondor, the ironmaster, every time that you purchase your trowels, hatchets, and planes. Then they tell you that unless you pay this tax, Mondor will not be able to give employment; and his workmen, James and John, must go without work. And yet, if they gave up the tax, it would enable you to find employment for one another, independently of Mondor.

And then, you may be sure, after this smooth pillow of protection has been taken away, Mondor will set his wits to work to convert his loss into a profit, and James and John will not be sent away, in which case there will be profit for everybody.

You may still rejoin, "We allow that, after the reform, there will be more employment upon the whole than before; in the meantime, James and John are starving."

To which I reply:

First—That when labor is only displaced, to be augmented, a man who has a head and hands is seldom left long in a state of destitution.

Second—There is nothing to hinder the State's reserving a fund to meet, during the transition, any temporary want of employment, in which, however, for my own part, I do not believe.

Third—If I do not misunderstand the workmen, they are quite prepared to encounter any temporary suffering necessarily attendant on a transfer of labor from one department to another, by which the community are more likely to be benefited and have justice done them. I only wish I could say the same thing of their employers!

What! Will it be said that because you are workmen you are for that reason unintelligent and immoral? Your pretended friends seem to think so. Is it not surprising that in your hearing they should discuss such a question, talking exclusively of wages and profits without ever once allowing the word justice to pass their lips? And yet they know that restriction is unjust. Why have they not the courage to admit it, and say to you, "Workmen! An iniquity prevails in this country, but it is profitable to you, and we must maintain it." Why? Because they know you would answer, No.

But it is not true that this injustice is profitable to you. Give me your attention for a few moments longer, and then judge for yourselves.

What is it that we protect in France? Things that are produced on a great scale by rich capitalists and in large establishments, as iron, coal, cloth, and textile fabrics; and they tell you that this is done not in the interest of employers, but in yours, and in order to secure you employment.

And yet whenever foreign labor presents itself in our markets, in such a shape that it may be injurious to you but advantageous for your employers, it is allowed to enter without any restriction being imposed.

Are there not in Paris 30,000 Germans who make clothes and shoes? Why are they permitted to establish themselves alongside you while the importation of cloth is restricted? Because cloth is manufactured in grand establishments that belong to manufacturing legislators. But clothes are made by workmen in their own houses. In converting wool into cloth, these gentlemen desire to have no competition, because that is their trade; but in converting cloth into coats, they allow it, because that is your trade.

In making our railways, an embargo was laid on English rails, but English workmen were brought over. Why was this? Simply because English rails came into competition with the iron produced in our great establishments, while the English laborers were only your rivals.

We have no wish that German tailors and English navies should be kept out of France. What we ask is, that the entry of cloth and rails should be left free. We simply demand justice and equality before the law, for all.

It is a mockery to tell us that customs restrictions are imposed for your benefit. Tailors, shoemakers, carpenters, masons, blacksmiths, shopkeepers, grocers, watchmakers, butchers, bakers, dressmakers! I defy you all to point out a single way in which restriction is profitable to you, and I shall point out, whenever you desire it, four ways in which it is hurtful to you.

And, after all, see how little foundation your journalists have for attributing self-abnegation to the monopolists.

I may venture to denominate the rate of wages that settles and establishes itself naturally under a system of freedom, the natural rate of wages. When you affirm, therefore, that restriction is profitable to you, it is tantamount to affirming that it adds a premium to your natural wages. Now, a surplus of wages beyond the natural rate must come from some quarter or other; it does not fall from the skies, but comes from those who pay it.

You are landed, then, in this conclusion by your pretended friends, that the policy of protection has been introduced in order that the interests of capitalists should be sacrificed to those of the workmen.

Do you think this probable?

Where is your place, then, in the Chamber of Peers? When did you take your seat in the Palais Bourbon? Who has consulted you? Whence did this idea of establishing a policy of protection come to you?

I think I hear you answer, "It is not we who have established it. Alas! We are neither Peers, nor Deputies, nor Councillors of State. The capitalists have done it all."

Verily, they must have been in a good humour that day! What! these capitalists have made the law; they have established a policy of prohibition for the express purpose of enabling you to profit at their expense!

But here is something stranger still.

How does it come to pass that your pretended friends, who hold forth to you on the goodness, the generosity, and the self-abnegation of capitalists, never cease sympathizing with you on your being deprived of your political rights? From their point of view, I would ask what you could make of such rights if you had them? The capitalists have a monopoly of legislation—granted. By means of this monopoly, they have adjudged themselves a monopoly of iron, of cloth, of textile fabrics, of coal, of wood, of meat—granted likewise. But here are your pretended friends, who tell you that in acting thus, capitalists have impoverished themselves, without being under any obligation to do so, in order to enrich you who have no right to be enriched! Assuredly, if you were electors and deputies tomorrow, you could not manage your affairs better than they are managed for you; you could not even manage them so well.

If the industrial legislation under which you live is intended for your profit, it is an act of perfidy to demand for your political rights; for these new-fashioned democrats never can escape this dilemma—the law made by the middle classes either gives you more, or it gives you less, than your natural wages. If that law gives you less, they deceive you, in soliciting you to maintain it. If it gives you more, they still deceive you, by inviting you to demand political rights at the very time when they are making sacrifices for you, which, in common honesty, you could not by your votes exact, even if you had the power.

Workmen! I should be sorry indeed if this address should excite in your minds feelings of irritation against the rich. If self-interest, badly understood, or too apt to be alarmed, still maintains monopoly, let us not forget that monopoly has its root in errors that are common to both capitalists and workmen; instead of exciting the one class against the other, let us try to bring them together. And for that end what ought we to do? If it be true that the natural social tendencies concur in levelling inequalities among men, we have only to allow these tendencies to act, remove artificial obstructions that retard their operation, and allow the relations of the various classes of society to be established on the principle of JUSTICE, which, in my mind at least, is identical with the principle of LIBERTY.

7

A CHINESE STORY

There is nothing that is not pretended by the writers in favor of Protection to be established as an aid to the working classes—there is positively no exception, not even the custom house. You fancy, perhaps, that the custom house is merely an instrument of taxation like property taxes or the toll-bar! Nothing of the kind. It is essentially an institution for promoting the march of civilization, fraternity, and equality. What would you be at? It is the fashion to introduce, or affect to introduce, sentiment and sentimentalism everywhere, even into the toll-gatherer's booth.

The custom house, we must allow, has a very singular machinery for realizing philanthropical aspirations.

It includes an army of directors, subdirectors, inspectors, subinspectors, comptrollers, examiners, heads of departments, clerks, supernumeraries, aspirant-supernumeraries, not to speak of the officers of the active service; and the object of all this complicated machinery is to exercise over the industry of the people a negative action, which is summed up in the word "obstruct."

Observe, I do not say that the object is to tax, but to obstruct. To prevent, not acts that are repugnant to good morals or public order, but transactions that are in themselves not only harmless but fitted to maintain peace and union among nations.

And yet the human race is so flexible and elastic that it always surmounts these obstructions. And then we hear of the labor market being glutted.

If you hinder a people from obtaining its subsistence from abroad it will produce it at home. The labor is greater and more painful, but subsistence must be had. If you hinder a man from traversing the valley he must cross the hills. The road is longer and more difficult, but he must get to his journey's end.

This is lamentable, but we come now to what is ludicrous. When the law has thus created obstacles, and when in order to overcome them society has diverted a corresponding amount of labor from other employments, you are no longer permitted to demand a reform. If you point to the obstacle you are told of the amount of labor to which it has given employment. And if you rejoin that this labor is not created, but displaced, you are answered in the words of the Esprit Public, "The impoverishment alone is certain and immediate; as to our enrichment, it is more than problematical."

This reminds me of a Chinese story, which I will relate to you.

There were in China two large towns, called Tchin and Tchan. A magnificent canal united them. The Emperor thought fit to order enormous blocks of stone to be thrown into it for the purpose of rendering it useless.

On seeing this, Kouang, his first mandarin, said to him,

"Son of Heaven! This is a mistake."

To which the Emperor replied,

"Kouang, you talk nonsense."

I give you only the substance of their conversation.

At the end of three months the Celestial Emperor sent again for the mandarin, and said to him,

"Kouang, behold!"

And Kouang opened his eyes, and looked.

And he saw at some distance from the canal a multitude of men at work. Some were excavating, others were filling up hollows, levelling and paving. And the mandarin, who was very cultivated, said to himself: They are making a highway.

When other three months had elapsed the Emperor again sent for Kouang, and said to him,

"Look!"

And Kouang looked.

And he saw the road completed, and from one end of it to the other he saw here and there inns for travellers erected. Crowds of pedestrians, carts, litters, came and went, and innumerable Chinese, overcome with fatigue, carried back and forth heavy burdens from Tchin to Tchan, and from Tchan to Tchin. And Kouang said to himself: It is the destruction of the canal that gives employment to these poor people. But the idea never struck him that their labor was simply diverted from other employments.

Three months more passed, and the Emperor said to Kouang, "Look!"

And Kouang looked. And he saw that the hostelries were full of travellers, and that to supply their wants there were grouped around them butchers' and bakers' stalls, shops for the sale of edible birds' nests. He also saw that, the artisans having need of clothing, there had settled among them tailors, shoemakers, and those who sold parasols and fans; and as they could not sleep in the open air, even in the Celestial Empire, there were also masons, carpenters, and slaters. Then there were officers of police, judges, fakirs; in a word, a town with its suburbs had risen round each hostelry.

And the Emperor asked Kouang what he thought of all this.

And Kouang said that he never could have imagined that the destruction of a canal could have provided employment for so many people; for the thought never struck him that this was not employment created but labor diverted from other employments, and that men would have eaten and drunk in passing along the canal as well as in passing along the highroad.

However, to the astonishment of the Chinese, the Son of Heaven at length died and was buried.

His successor sent for Kouang, and ordered him to have the canal cleared out and restored.

And Kouang said to the new Emperor,

"Son of Heaven! You commit a blunder."

And the Emperor replied,

"Kouang, you talk nonsense."

But Kouang persisted, and said: "Sire, what is your object?"

"My object is to facilitate the transit of goods and passengers between Tchin and Tchan, to render carriage less expensive, in order that the people may have tea and clothing cheaper."

But Kouang was ready with his answer. He had received the night before several numbers of the *Moniteur Industriel,* a Chinese newspaper. Knowing his lesson well, he asked and obtained permission to reply, and after having prostrated himself nine times, he said,

"Sire, your object is, by increased facility of transit, to reduce the price of articles of consumption, and bring them within reach of the people; and to effect that you begin by taking away from them all the employment to which the destruction of the canal had given rise. Sire, in political economy, nominal cheapness. . . ."

The Emperor: "I believe you are repeating by rote."

Kouang: "True, Sire; and it will be better to read what I have to say." So, producing the Esprit Public, he read as follows: "In political economy, the nominal cheapness of articles of consumption is only a secondary question. The problem is to establish an equilibrium between the price of labor and that of the means of subsistence. The abundance of labor constitutes the wealth of nations; and the best economic system is that which supplies the people with the greatest amount of employment. The question is not whether it is better to pay four or eight cash for a cup of tea, or five or ten taels (Chinese money) for a shirt. These are puerilities unworthy of a thinking mind. Nobody disputes your proposition. The question is whether it is better to pay dearer for a commodity you want to buy, and have, through the abundance of employment and the higher price of labor, the means of acquiring it; or whether it is better to limit the sources of employment, and with them the mass of the national population, in order to transport, by improved means of transit, the objects of consumption, cheaper, it is true, but taking away at the same time from many of our people the means of purchasing these objects even at their reduced price.

Seeing the Emperor still unconvinced, Kouang added: "Sire, deign to give me your attention. I have still the *Moniteur Industriel* to bring under your notice."

But the Emperor said,

"I don't require your Chinese journals to enable me to find out that to create obstacles is to divert and misapply labor. But that is not my mission. Go and clear out the canal; and we shall reform the custom house afterwards."

And Kouang went away tearing his beard, and appealing to his God, "O Fo! Take pity on thy people; for we have now got an Emperor of the English school, and I see clearly that in a short time we shall be in want of everything, for we shall no longer require to do anything."

8

POST HOC, ERGO PROPTER HOC

This is the greatest and most common fallacy in reasoning.

Real sufferings, for example have manifested themselves in England.[1]

These sufferings come in the train of two other phenomena:

First, The reformed tariff;

Second, Two bad harvests in succession.

To which of these two last circumstances are we to attribute the first?

The protectionists exclaim:

It is this accursed free trade that does all the harm. It promised us wonderful things; we accepted it; and here are our manufacturers at a standstill, and the people suffering: *Cum hoc, ergo propter hoc*.

Free trade distributes in the most uniform and equitable manner the fruits that Providence accords to human labor. If we are

---

[1]This was written in December 1846.—French editor.

deprived of part of these fruits by natural causes, such as a succession of bad seasons, free trade does not fail to distribute in the same manner what remains. Men are, no doubt, not so well provided with what they want; but are we to impute this to free trade, or on the bad harvests?

Liberty acts on the same principle as insurance. When an accident, like a fire, happens, insurance spreads over a great number of men and a great number of years, losses that, in the absence of insurance, would have fallen all at once upon one individual. But will anyone undertake to affirm that fire has become a greater evil since the introduction of insurance?

In 1842, 1843, and 1844, the reduction of taxes began in England. At the same time the harvests were very abundant; and we are led to conclude that these two circumstances concurred in producing the unparalleled prosperity which England enjoyed during that period.

In 1845 the harvest was bad, and in 1846 worse still.

Provisions rose in price; and the people were forced to expend their resources on necessaries, and to limit their consumption of other commodities. Clothing was less in demand, manufactories had less work, and wages tended to fall.

Fortunately, in that same year, the barriers of restriction were still more effectually removed, and an enormous quantity of provisions reached the English market. Had this not been so, it is nearly certain that a formidable revolution would have taken place.

And yet free trade is blamed for disasters that it tended to prevent, and in part, at least, to repair!

A poor leper lived in solitude. Whatever he happened to touch, no one else would touch. Obliged to pine in solitude, he led a miserable existence. An eminent physician cured him, and now our poor hermit was admitted to all the benefits of free trade, and had full liberty to effect exchanges. What brilliant prospects were opened to him! He delighted in calculating the advantages that, through his restored intercourse with his fellow-men, he was able to derive from his own vigorous exertions. He happened to break both his arms, and was landed in poverty and misery. The journalists who were witnesses of that misery said, "See to what this liberty of making exchanges has reduced him! Verily, he was less to be pitied when he lived alone." "What!" said the physician, "do you make no allowance for his broken arms? Has that accident nothing to do with his present unhappy state? His misfortune arises from his having lost the use of his hands, and not from his having been cured of his leprosy. He would have been a fitter subject for your compassion had he been lame and leprous into the bargain."

Post hoc, ergo propter hoc. Beware of that fallacy.

9

THE PREMIUM THEFT—
ROBBERY BY SUBSIDY

This little book of FALLACIES is found to be too theoretical, scientific, and metaphysical. Be it so. Let us try the effect of a more trivial and hackneyed, and, if necessary, a ruder style. Convinced that the public is duped in this matter of protection, I have endeavored to prove it. But if outcry is preferred to argument, let us vociferate,

"King Midas has a snout, and asses' ears."[1]

A burst of plain speaking has more effect frequently than the most polished circumlocution. You remember Oronte, and the difficulty that the Misanthrope had in convincing him of his folly.[2]

Alceste. *On s'expose a jouer un mauvais personnage.*
Oronte. *Est-ce que vous voulez me declarer par la*
         Que j'ai tort de vouloir. . . .

---

[1]"Auriculas asini Mida rex habet."—Persius, sat. i. The line as given in the text is from Dryden's translation.—Translator.

[2]See Moliere's play of *The Misanthrope*.

Alceste.	*Je ne dis pas cela. Mais. . . .*
Oronte.	*Est-ce que j'ecris mal?*
Alceste.	*Je ne dis pas cela. Mais enfin. . . .*
Oronte.	*Mais ne puis-je savoir ce que dans mon sonnet?*
Alceste.	*Franchement, il est bon a mettre au Cabinet.*

To speak plainly, Good Public! you are robbed. This is speaking bluntly, but the thing is very evident. It is crude, but clear.

The words theft, to steal, robbery, thief, may appear ugly words to many people. I ask such people, as Harpagon asks Elise,[3] "Is it the word or the thing that frightens you?"

"Whoever has possessed himself fraudulently of a thing that does not belong to him is guilty of theft."[4]

To steal: To take by stealth or by force.[5]

Thief: He who exacts more than is due to him.[6]

Now, does not the monopolist, who, by a law of his own making, obliges me to pay him 20 francs for what I could get elsewhere for 15, take from me fraudulently 5 francs that belonged to me?

Does he not take them by stealth or by force?

Does he not exact more than is due to him?

He takes, purloins, exacts, it may be said; but not by stealth or by force, which are the characteristics of theft.

When our bulletins de contributions have included in them 5 francs for the premium that the monopolist takes, exacts, or abstracts, what can be more stealthy for the unsuspecting? And for those who are not dupes, and who do suspect, what savors more of force, seeing that on the first refusal the taxgatherer's bailiff is at the door?

---

[3]See Moliere's play of *L'Avare*.

[4]*C. Pen.*, art. 379.

[5]*Dictionnaire de l'Aca-demie*.

[6]Ibid.

But let monopolists take courage. Premium thefts, tariff thefts, if they violate equity as much as theft *a l'Americaine*, do not violate the law; on the contrary, they are perpetrated according to law and if they are worse than common thefts, they do not come under the cognizance of the magistrate.

Besides, willingly or unwillingly, we are all robbed or robbers in this business. The author of this volume might very well cry "Stop, thief!" when he buys; and with equal reason he might have that cry addressed to him when he sells;[7] and if he is in a situation different from that of many of his countrymen, the difference consists in this, that he knows that he loses more than he gains by the game, and they don't know it. If they knew it, the game would soon be given up.

Nor do I boast of being the first to give the thing its right name. Adam Smith said, sixty years ago, that "when manufacturers hold meetings, we may be sure a plot is hatching against the pockets of the public." Can we be surprised at this, when the public says nothing?

Well, then, suppose a meeting of manufacturers deliberating formally, under the title of general councils. What takes place, and what is resolved upon?

Here is a very abridged report of one of their meetings:

"SHIPOWNER: Our shipping is at the lowest ebb. That is not to be wondered at. I cannot construct ships without iron. I can buy it in the market of the world at 10 francs; but by law the French ironmaster forces me to pay him 15 francs, which takes 5 francs out of my pocket. I demand liberty to purchase iron wherever I see proper.

"IRONMASTER: In the market of the world I find freights at 20 francs. By law I am obliged to pay the French shipowner 30;

---

[7]Possessing some landed property, on which he lives, he belongs to the protected class. This circumstance should disarm criticism. It shows that if he uses hard words, they are directed against the thing itself, and not against men's intentions or motives.

he takes 10 francs out of my pocket. He robs me, and I rob him; all quite right.

"STATESMAN: The shipowner has arrived at an unwise conclusion. Let us cultivate the union that constitutes our strength. If we give up a single point of the theory of protection, the whole theory falls to the ground.

"SHIPOWNER: For us shipowners protection has been a failure. I repeat that shipping is at its lowest ebb.

"SHIPMASTER: Well, let us raise the surtax, and let the shipowner who now exacts 30 francs from the public for his freight charge 40.

"A MINISTER: The government will make all the use they can of the beautiful mechanism of the surtax; but I fear that will not be sufficient.

"A GOVERNMENT FUNCTIONARY: You are all very easily frightened. Does the tariff alone protect you? and do you lay taxation out of account? If the consumer is kind and benevolent, the taxpayer is not less so. Let us heap taxes upon him, and let the shipowner be satisfied. I propose a premium of 5 francs to be levied from the public taxpayers, to be handed over to the shipbuilder for each cwt. of iron he shall employ.

"Confused voices: Agreed! Agreed! An agriculturist: Three francs premium upon each hectolitre of wheat for me! A manufacturer: Two francs premium on each yard of cloth for me! etc., etc.

"THE PRESIDENT: This then is what we have agreed upon. Our session has instituted a system of premiums, and it will be its eternal honor. What branch of industry can possibly henceforth be a loser, since we have two means, and both so very simple, of converting our losses into gains—the tariff and the premium? The sitting is adjourned."

I really think some supernatural vision must have foreshadowed to me in a dream the near approach of the premium (who knows but I may have first suggested the idea to Mr. Dupin?) when six months ago I wrote these words:

"It appears evident to me that protection, without changing its nature or the effects it produces, might take the form of a direct tax, levied by the state, and distributed in premiums of indemnification among privileged branches of industry."

And after comparing a protective duty to a premium, I added:

"I confess candidly my preference for the last system. It seems to me juster, more economical, and more fair. Juster, because if society desires to make presents to some of its members, all ought to bear the expense; more economical, because it would save a great deal in the cost of collection, and do away with many of the trammels with which trade is hampered; more fair, because the public would see clearly the nature of the operation, and act accordingly."

Since the occasion presents itself to us so opportunely, let us study this system of plunder by premium; for all we say of it applies equally to the system of plunder by tariff; and as the latter is a little better concealed, the direct may help us to detect and expose the indirect system of cheating. The mind will thus be led from what is simple to what is more complicated.

But it may be asked: Is there not a species of theft which is more simple still? Undoubtedly; there is highway robbery, which lacks only to be legalized, and made a monopoly of, or, in the language of the present day, organized.

I have been reading what follows in a book of travels:

"When we reached the kingdom of A., all branches of industry declared themselves in a state of suffering. Agriculture groaned, manufactures complained, trade murmured, the shipping interest grumbled, and the government was at a loss what to do. First of all, the idea was to lay a pretty smart tax on all the malcontents, and afterwards to divide the proceeds among them after retaining its own quota; this would have been on the principle of the Spanish lottery. There are a thousand of you, and the State takes a piastre from each; then by sleight of hand it conveys away 250 piastres, and divides the remaining 750 in larger and smaller proportions among the ticketholders. The gallant Hidalgo who gets three-fourths of a piastre, forgetting that he had contributed a whole piastre, cannot conceal his delight, and rushes off to spend his fifteen reals at the alehouse. This is very much the same thing as we see taking place in France. But the government had overrated the stupidity of the population when it endeavored to make them accept such a species of protection, and at length it lighted upon the following expedient.

"The country was covered with a network of highways. The government had these roads accurately measured; and then it announced to the agriculturist: 'All that you can steal from travellers between these two points is yours; let that serve as a premium for your protection and encouragement.' Afterward it assigned to each manufacturer, to each shipowner, a certain portion of road, to be made available for their profit, according to this formula:

> *Dono tibi et concedo*
> *Virtutem et puissantiam*
> *Volandi,*
> *Pillandi,*
> *Derobandi,*
> *Filoutandi,*
> *Et escroquandi,*
> *Impune per totam istam*
> *Viam."*

Now it has come to pass that the natives of the kingdom of A. have become so habituated to this system, that they take into account only what they are enabled to steal, not what is stolen from them, being so determined to regard pillage only from the standpoint of the thief that they look upon the sum total of individual thefts as a national gain, and refuse to abandon a system of protection, without which they say no branch of industry could support itself.

You demur to this. It is not possible, you exclaim, that a whole people should be led to ascribe an increase of wealth to mutual robbery.

And why not? We see that this conviction pervades France, and that we are constantly organizing and improving the system of reciprocal robbery under the respectable names of premiums and protective tariffs.

We must not, however, be guilty of exaggeration. As regards the mode of levying, and other collateral circumstances, the system adopted in the kingdom of A. may be worse than ours; but we must at the same time admit that, as regards the principle and its necessary consequences, there is not an atom of difference between all these species of theft, which are organized by law for the purpose of supplementing the profits of particular branches of industry.

Note also, that if highway robbery presents some inconveniences in its actual perpetration, it has likewise some advantages which we do not find in robbery by tariff.

For example, it is possible to make an equitable division among all the producers. It is not so in the case of customs duties. The latter are incapable of protecting certain classes of society, such as artisans, shopkeepers, men of letters, lawyers, soldiers, laborers, etc.

It is true that the robbery by premium assumes an infinite number of shapes, and in this respect is not inferior to highway robbery; but, on the other hand, it leads frequently to results so arbitrary and awkward that the natives of the kingdom of A. may well laugh at us.

What the victim of a highway robbery loses the thief gains, and the articles stolen remain in the country. But under the system of robbery by premium, what the tax exacts from the Frenchman is conferred frequently on the Chinese, on the Hottentots, on the Caffres, etc., and here is the way in which this takes place:

A piece of cloth, we will suppose, is worth 100 francs at Bordeaux. It cannot be sold below that price without a loss. It is impossible to sell it above that price because the competition of merchants prevents the price rising. In these circumstances, if a Frenchman desires to have the cloth, he must pay 100 francs, or do without it. But if it is an Englishman who wants the cloth, the government steps in, and says to the merchant, "Sell your cloth, and we will get you 20 francs from the taxpayers." The merchant who could not get more than 100 francs for his cloth, sells it to the Englishman for 80. This sum, added to the 20 francs produced by the premium theft, makes all square. This is exactly the same case as if the taxpayers had given 20 francs to the Englishman, upon condition of his buying French cloth at 20 francs discount, at 20 francs below the cost of production, at 20 francs below what it has cost ourselves. The robbery by premium, then, has this peculiarity, that the people robbed are resident in the country that tolerates it, while the people who profit by the robbery are scattered over the world.

Verily, it is marvellous that people should persist in maintaining that all that an individual steals from the masses is a general gain. Perpetual motion, the philosopher's stone, the quadrature of the circle, are obsolete myths long abandoned; but the theory of progress by plunder is still held in honor. A priori, we should have thought that, of all imaginable puerilities, it was the least likely to survive.

Some people will say, You are partisans, then, of the *laissez-faire* economists of the school of Smith and Say? You do not desire the organization of labor. Yes, gentlemen, organize labor as much as you choose, but have the goodness not to organize theft.

Another, and a more numerous, set keep repeating, premiums, tariffs, all that has been exaggerated. We should use them without abusing them. A judicious liberty, combined with a moderate protection, that is what discreet and practical men desire. Let us steer clear of fixed principles.

This is precisely what the traveller tells us takes place in the kingdom of A. "Highway robbery," say the sages, "is neither good nor bad in itself; that depends upon circumstances. All we are concerned with is to weigh things, and see our functionaries well paid for the work of weighing. It may be that we have given too great latitude to pillage; perhaps we have not given enough. Let us examine and balance the accounts of each man employed in the work of pillage. To those who do not earn enough, let us assign a larger portion of the road. To those who gain too much, we must limit the hours, days or months of pillage."

Those who talk in this way gain a great reputation for moderation, prudence, and good sense. They never fail to attain to the highest offices in the state.

Those who say: Repress all injustice, whether on a greater or a smaller scale, suffer no dishonesty, to however small an extent, are marked down for ideologues, idle dreamers, who keep repeating over and over again the same thing. The people, moreover, find their arguments too clear, and why should they be expected to believe what is so easily understood?

10

THE TAX GATHERER

JACQUES BONHOMME, a Vintner.

Mr. LASOUCHE, Tax gatherer.

L.: You have secured twenty tuns of wine?

J.: Yes, by dint of my own skill and labor.

L.: Have the goodness to deliver up to me six of the best.

J.: Six tuns out of twenty! Good Heaven! you are going to ruin me. And please, Sir, for what purpose do you intend them?

L.: The first will be handed over to the creditors of the State. When people have debts, the least thing they can do is to pay interest upon them.

J.: And what has become of the capital?

L.: That is too long a story to tell you at present. One part was converted into cartridges, which emitted the most beautiful smoke in the world. Another went to pay the men who had got crippled in foreign countries after having laid them waste. Then, when this expenditure brought invasion upon us, our gracious enemy was unwilling to take leave of us without carrying away some money, and this money had to be borrowed.

J.: And what benefit do I derive from this now?

L.: The satisfaction of saying—

> *Que je suis fier d'etre Francois*
> *Quand je regarde la colonne!*

J.: And the humiliation of leaving to my heirs an estate burdened with a perpetual rent-charge. Still, it is necessary to pay one's debts, whatever foolish use is made of the proceeds. So much for the disposal of one tun; but what about the five others?

L.: One goes to support the public service, the civil list, the judges who protect your property when your neighbor wishes wrongfully to appropriate it, the policemen who protect you from robbers when you are asleep, the roadmen who maintain the highways, the curé who baptizes your children, the schoolmaster who educates them, and, lastly, your humble servant, who cannot be expected to work exactly for nothing.

J.: All right; service for service is quite fair, and I have nothing to say against it. I should like quite as well, no doubt, to deal directly with the rector and the schoolmaster on my own account; but I don't stand upon that. This accounts for the second tun— but we have still other four to account for.

L.: Would you consider two tuns as more than your fair contribution to the expense of the army and navy?

J.: Alas! that is a small affair, compared with what the two services have cost me already, for they have deprived me of two sons whom I dearly loved.

L.: It is necessary to maintain the balance of power.

J.: And would that balance not be quite as well maintained if the European powers were to reduce their forces by one-half or three-fourths? We should preserve our children and our money. All that is requisite is to come to a common understanding.

L.: Yes; but they don't understand one another.

J.: It is that which fills me with astonishment, for they suffer from it in common.

L.: It is partly your own doing, Jacques Bonhomme.

J.: You are joking, Mr. Taxgatherer. Have I any voice in the matter?

L.: Whom did you vote for as deputy?

J.: A brave general officer, who will soon be a marshal, if God spares him.

L.: And upon what does the gallant general live?

J.: Upon my six tuns, I should think.

L.: What would happen to him if he voted a reduction of the army, and of your contingent?

J.: Instead of being made a marshal he would be forced to retire.

L.: Do you understand now that you have yourself?

J.: Let us pass on to the fifth tun, if you please.

L.: That goes to Algeria.

L.: To Algeria! And yet they tell us that all the Muslims are wine-haters, barbarians as they are! I have often inquired whether it is their ignorance of claret which has made them infidels, or their infidelity which has made them ignorant of claret. And then, what service do they render me in return for this nectar that has cost me so much toil?

L.: None at all; nor is the wine destined for the Muslim, but for good Christians who spend their lives in Barbary.

J.: And what service do they render me?

L.: They make raids, and suffer from them in their turn; they kill and are killed; they are seized with dysentery and sent to the hospital; they make harbors and roads, build villages, and people them with Maltese, Italians, Spaniards, and Swiss, who live upon your wine; for another supply of which, I can tell you, I shall soon come back to you.

J.: Good gracious! that is too much. I give you a flat refusal. A vintner who could be guilty of such folly would be sent to Bedlam. To make roads through Mount Atlas—good Heavens! when I can scarcely leave my house for want of roads! To create harbors in Barbary, when the Garonne is silted up! To carry off my children whom I love, and send them to torment the Kabyles! To make me pay for houses, seed, and horses, to be handed over to Greeks and Maltese, when we have so many poor people to provide for at home!

L.: The poor! Just so; they rid the country of the redundant population.

J.: And we are to send after them to Algeria the capital on which they could live at home!

L.: But then you are laying the foundations of a great empire, you carry civilization into Africa, thus crowning your country with immortal glory.

J.: You are a poet, Mr. Taxgatherer. I am a plain vintner, and I refuse your demand.

L.: But think that in the course of some thousands of years your present advances will be recouped and repaid a hundredfold. The men who direct the enterprise assure us that it will be so.

J.: In the meantime, in order to defray the expense, they asked me first of all for one cask of wine, then for two, then for three, and now I am taxed by the tun! I persist in my refusal.

L.: Your refusal comes too late. Your representative has stipulated for the whole quantity I demand.

J.: Too true. Cursed weakness on my part! Surely, in making him my representative I was guilty of a piece of folly; for what is there in common between a general officer and a poor vintner?

L.: Oh, yes; there is something in common—namely, your wine which he has voted to himself in your name.

J.: You may well laugh at me, Mr. Taxgatherer, for I richly deserve it. But be reasonable. Leave me at least the sixth tun. You have already secured payment of the interest of the debt, and provided for the civil list and the public service, besides perpetuating the war in Africa. What more would you have?

L.: It is needless to higgle with me. Communicate your views to the General, your representative. For the present he has voted away your vintage.

J.: Confound the fellow! But tell me what you intend to make of this last cask, the best of my whole stock? Stay, taste this wine. How ripe, mellow and full-bodied it is!

L.: Excellent! delicious! It will suit Mr. D., the cloth manufacturer, admirably.

J.: Mr. D., the cloth manufacturer? What do you mean?

L.: That he will reap the benefit.

J.: How? What? I'll be hanged if I understand you!

L.: Don't you know that Mr. D. has set in motion a grand undertaking that will prove most useful to the country, but which, when everything is taken into account, causes each year a considerable pecuniary loss?

J.: I am sorry to hear it, but what can I do?

L.: The Chamber has come to the conclusion that, if this state of things continues, Mr. D. will be under the necessity of either working more profitably, or of shutting up his manufacturing establishment altogether.

J.: But what have these losing speculations of Mr. D. to do with my wine?

L.: The Chamber has found out that, by making over to Mr. D. some wine taken from your cellar, some wheat taken from your neighbor's granaries, some money taken from the workmen's wages, the losses of D. may be converted into profits.

J.: The recipe is as infallible as it is ingenious. But, zounds! it is awfully iniquitous. Mr. D., forsooth, is to make up his losses by laying hold of my wine!

L.: Not exactly of the wine, but of its price. This is what we denominate premiums of encouragement, or bounties. Don't you see the great service you are rendering to the country?

J.: You mean to Mr. D.?

L.: To the country. Mr. D. assures us that his manufacture prospers in consequence of this arrangement, and in this way he says the country is enriched. He said so the other day in the Chamber, of which he is a member.

J.: This is a wretched quibble! A speculator enters into a losing trade, and dissipates his capital; and if he extorts from me and from my neighbors wine and wheat of sufficient value, not only to repair his losses, but afford him a profit, this is represented as a gain to the country at large.

L.: Your representative having come to this conclusion you have nothing more to do but to deliver up to me the six tuns of wine that I demand, and sell the remaining fourteen tuns to the best advantage.

J.: That is my business.

L.: It will be unfortunate if you do not realize a large price.

J.: I will think of it.

L.: For this price will enable you to meet many more things.

J.: I am aware of that, Sir.

L.: In the first place, if you purchase iron to renew your ploughs and your spades, the law decrees that you must pay the ironmaster double what the commodity is worth.

J.: Yes, this is very consolatory.

L.: Then you have need of coal, of butchers' meat, of cloth, of oil, of wood, of sugar, and for each of these commodities the law makes you pay double.

J.: It is horrible, frightful, abominable!

L.: Why should you indulge in complaints? You yourself, through your representative:

J.: Say nothing more of my representative. I am amazingly represented, it is true. But they will not impose upon me a second time. I shall be represented by a good and honest peasant.

L.: Bah! you will re-elect the gallant General.

J.: Shall I re-elect him to divide my wine among Africans and manufacturers?

L.: I tell you, you will re-elect him.

J.: This is too much. I am free to re-elect him or not, as I choose.

L.: But you will so choose.

J.: Let him come forward again, and he will find whom he has to deal with.

L.: Well, we shall see. Farewell. I carry away your six tuns of wine, to be distributed as your friend, the General, has determined.

11

PROTECTION; OR, THE THREE CITY ALDERMEN

DEMONSTRATION IN FOUR TABLEAUX

SCENE I—House of Master Peter

Window looking out on a fine park.—Three gentlemen seated near a good fire.

PETER: Bravo! Nothing like a good fire after a good dinner. It does feel so comfortable. But alas! how many honest folks, like the Rio d'Yvetot,

> *Soufflent, faute de bois*
> *Dans leurs doigts.*

Miserable creatures! A charitable thought has just come into my head. You see these fine trees; I am about to fell them, and distribute the timber among the poor.

PAUL and JOHN: What! gratis?

PETER: Not exactly. My good works would soon have an end were I to dissipate my fortune. I estimate my park as worth £1,000. By cutting down the trees I shall pocket much more.

PAUL: Wrong. Your wood as it stands is worth more than that of the neighboring forests, for it renders services that they cannot render. When cut down it will be only good for firewood, like any other, and will not bring a penny more the load.

PETER: Oh! oh! Mr. Theorist, you forget that I am a practical man. My reputation as a speculator is sufficiently well established, I believe, to prevent me from being taken for an idiot. Do you imagine I am going to amuse myself by selling my timber at the price of float-wood?

PAUL: It would seem so.

PETER: Simpleton! And what if I can hinder floatwood from being brought into Paris?

PAUL: That alters the case. But how can you manage it?

PETER: Here is the whole secret. You know that float-wood on entering the city pays 5d. the load. Tomorrow I induce the commune to raise the duty to £4, £8, £12—in short, sufficiently high to prevent the entry of a single log. Now, do you follow me? If the good people are not to die of cold they have no alternative but to come to my woodyard. They will bid against each other for my wood, and I will sell it for a high price; and this act of charity, successfully carried out, will put me in a situation to do other acts of charity.

PAUL: A fine invention, truly! It suggests to me another of the same kind.

JOHN: And what is that? Is philanthropy to be again brought into play?

PAUL: How do you like this Normandy butter?

JOHN: Excellent.

PAUL: Hitherto I have thought it passable. But do you not think it is a little strong? I could make better butter in Paris. I shall have four or five hundred cows, and distribute milk, butter and cheese among the poor.

PETER and JOHN: What! in charity?

PAUL: Bah! let us put charity always in the foreground. It is so fine a figure that its very mask is a good passport. I shall give my butter to the people, and they will give me their money. Is that what is called selling?

JOHN: No; not according to the Bourgeois Gentilhomme. But call it what you please, you will ruin yourself. How can Paris ever compete with Normandy in dairy produce?

PAUL: I shall be able to save the cost of carriage.

JOHN: Be it so. Still, while paying that cost, the Normans can beat the Parisians.

PAUL: To give a man something at a lower price—is that what you call beating him?

JOHN: It is the usual phrase; and you will always find yourself beaten.

PAUL.: Yes, as Don Quixote was beaten. The blows will fall upon Sancho. John, my friend, you forget the town dues.

JOHN: The town dues! What have they to do with your butter?

PAUL: To-morrow I shall demand protection, and induce the commune to prohibit butter being brought into Paris from Normandy and Brittany. The people must then either dispense with it, or purchase mine, and at my own price, too.

JOHN: Upon my honor, gentlemen, your philanthropy has quite made a convert of me.

"*On apprend a hurler, dit l'autre, avec les loups.*"

My mind is made up. It shall not be said that I am an unworthy alderman. Peter, this sparkling fire has inflamed your soul. Paul, this butter has lubricated the springs of your intelligence. I, too, feel stimulated by this piece of salted pork; and tomorrow I shall vote, and cause to be voted, the exclusion of swine, dead or alive. That done, I shall construct superb sheds in the heart of Paris.

"*Pour l'animal immonde aux Hebreux defendu.*"

I shall become a pig-driver and pork-butcher. Let us see how the good people of Paris can avoid coming to provide themselves at my shop.

PETER: Softly, my good friends; if you enhance the price of butter and salt meat to such an extent you cut down beforehand the profit I expect from my wood.

PAUL: And my speculation will be no longer so wondrously profitable if I am overcharged for my firewood and bacon.

JOHN: And I, what shall I gain by overcharging you for my sausages if you overcharge me for my faggots and bread and butter?

PETER: Very well, don't let us quarrel. Let us rather put our heads together and make reciprocal concessions. Moreover, it is not good to consult one's self-interest exclusively—we must exercise humanity, and see that the people do not lack fuel.

PAUL: Very right; and it is proper that the people should have butter to their bread.

JOHN: Undoubtedly; and a bit of bacon for the pot.

ALL: Three cheers for charity; three cheers for philanthropy; and tomorrow we take the town dues by assault.

PETER: Ah! I forgot. One word more; it is essential. My good friends, in this age of selfishness the world is distrustful, and the purest intentions are often misunderstood. Paul, you take the part of pleading for the wood; John will do the same for the butter; and I shall devote myself to the home-bred pig. It is necessary to prevent malignant suspicions.

PAUL and JOHN (leaving): Upon my word, that is a clever fellow.

SCENE II—Council Chamber

PAUL: My dear colleagues, every day there are brought to Paris great masses of firewood, which drain away large sums of money. At this rate, we shall all be ruined in three years, and what will become of the poorer classes? (Cheers.) We must prohibit foreign timber. I don't speak for myself, for all the wood I possess would not make a toothpick. In what I mean to say, then, I am entirely free from any personal interest or bias. (Hear, hear.) But here is my friend Peter, who possesses a park, and he will guarantee an adequate supply of fuel to our fellow citizens, who will no longer be dependent on the charcoal-burners of the Yonne. Have you ever turned your attention to the risk we run of dying of cold if the proprietors of forests abroad should take it into their heads to send no more firewood to Paris? Let us put a prohibition, then, on the bringing in of wood. By this means we shall put a stop to the draining away of our money, create an independent interest charged with supplying the city with firewood, and open up to workmen a new source of employment and remuneration. (Cheers.)

JOHN: I support the proposal of my honorable friend, the preceding speaker, which is at once so philanthropic, and, as he himself has explained, so entirely disinterested. It is indeed high time that we should put an end to this insolent *laissez passer*, which has brought immoderate competition into our markets, and to such an extent that there is no province that possesses any special facility for providing us with a product, be it what it may, that does not immediately inundate us, undersell us, and bring ruin on the Parisian workman. It is the duty of Government to equalize the conditions of production by duties wisely adapted to each case, so as not to allow to enter from without anything that is not dearer than in Paris, and so relieve us from an unequal struggle. How, for example, can we possibly produce milk and butter in Paris, with Brittany and Normandy at our door? Remember, gentlemen, that the agriculturists of Brittany have cheaper land, a more abundant supply of hay, and manual labor on more advantageous terms. Does not common sense tell us that we must equalize the conditions by a protective town tariff? I demand that the duty on milk and butter should be raised by 1,000 percent, and still higher if necessary. The workman's break-fast will cost a little more, but see to what extent his wages will be raised! We shall see rising around us cow-barns, dairies, and barrel churns, and the foundations laid of new sources of industry. Not that I have any interest in this proposition. I am not a rancher, nor have I any wish to be so. The sole motive that actuates me is a wish to be useful to the working classes. (Applause.)

PETER: I am delighted to see in this assembly statesmen so pure, so enlightened, and so devoted to the best interests of the people. (Cheers.) I admire their disinterestedness, and I cannot do better than imitate the noble example which has been set me. I give their motions my support, and I shall only add another, for prohibiting the entry into Paris of the pigs of Poitou. I have no desire, I assure you, to become a pig-driver or a pork-butcher. In that case I should have made it a matter of conscience to be silent. But is it not shameful, gentlemen, that we should be the tributaries of the peasants of Poitou, who have the audacity to come into our own market and take possession of a branch of industry that we ourselves have the means of carrying on? And who, after having inundated us with their hams and sausages, take perhaps nothing from us in return? At all events, who will tell us that the balance of trade is not in their favor, and that we are not obliged to pay them a tribute in hard cash? Is it not evident that if the industry of Poitou were transplanted to Paris it would open up a steady demand for Parisian labor? And then gentlemen, is it not very possible, as M. Lestiboudois has so well remarked that we may be buying the salt pork of Poitou, not with our incomes, but with our capital? Where will that land us? Let us not suffer, then, that rivals who are at once avaricious, greedy, and perfidious, should come here to undersell us, and put it out of our power to provide ourselves with the same commodities. Gentlemen, Paris has reposed in you her confidence; it is for you to justify that confidence. The people are without employment; it is for you to create employment for them; and if salt pork shall cost them a somewhat higher price, we have, at least, the consciousness of having sacrificed our own interests to those of the masses, as every good magistrate ought to do. (Loud and long-continued cheers.)

A VOICE: I have heard much talk of the poor; but under pretext of affording them employment you begin by depriving them of what is worth more than employment itself—namely, butter, firewood, and meat.

PETER, PAUL and JOHN: Vote, vote! Down with Utopian dreamers, theorists, generalizers! Vote, vote! (The three motions are carried.)

SCENE III—Twenty Years Afterwards

SON: Father, make up your mind; we must leave Paris. Nobody can any longer live here—no work, and everything dear.

FATHER: You don't know, my son, how much it costs one to leave the place where he was born.

SON: The worst thing of all is to perish from want.

FATHER: Go you, then, and search for a more hospitable country. For myself, I will not leave the place where are the graves of your mother, and of your brothers and sisters. I long to obtain with them that repose which has been denied me in this city of desolation.

SON: Courage, father; we shall find employment somewhere else—in Poitou, or Normandy, or Brittany. It is said that all the manufactures of Paris are being removed by degrees to these distant provinces.

FATHER: And naturally so. Not being able to sell firewood and provisions, the people of these provinces have ceased to produce them beyond what their own wants call for. The time and capital at their disposal are devoted to making for themselves those articles with which we were accustomed formerly to furnish them.

SON: Just as at Paris they have given up making pretty dresses and furniture, and betaken themselves to the planting of trees and the rearing of pigs and cows. Although still young, I have lived to see vast warehouses, sumptuous parts of the city, and quays once teeming with life and animation on the banks of the Seine turned into meadows and copses.

FATHER: While towns are spread over the provinces, Paris is turned into country. What a deplorable revolution! And this terrible calamity has been brought upon us by three magistrates, backed by public ignorance.

SON: Pray tell me the history of this change.

FATHER: It is short and simple. Under pretext of planting in Paris three new branches of industry, and by this means giving employment to the working classes, these men got the commune to prohibit the entry into Paris of firewood, butter and meat. They claimed for themselves the right of providing for their fellow-citizens. These commodities rose at first to exorbitant prices. No one earned enough to procure them, and the limited number of those who could procure them spent all their income on them, and had no longer the means of buying anything else. A check was thus given at once to all other industries, and all the more quickly that the provinces no longer afforded a market. Poverty, death, and emigration then began to depopulate Paris.

SON: And when is this to stop?

FATHER: When Paris has become a forest and a prairie.

SON: The three magistrates must have made a large fortune.

FATHER: At first they realized enormous profits, but at length they fell into the common poverty.

SON: How did that happen?

FATHER: Look at that ruin. That was a magnificent mansion-house surrounded with a beautiful park. If Paris had continued to progress, Master Peter would have realized more rent than his entire capital now amounts to.

SON: How can that be, seeing he has got rid of competition?

FATHER: Competition in selling has disappeared, but competition in buying is also disappearing, and will continue every day to disappear more and more until Paris becomes a bare field, and until the copses of Master Peter have no more value than the copses of an equal extent of land in the Forest of Bondy. It is thus that monopoly, like every other system of injustice, carries in itself its own punishment.

SON: That appears to me not very clear, but the decadence of Paris is an incontestable fact. Is there no means, then, of counteracting this iniquitous measure that Peter and his colleagues got adopted twenty years ago?

FATHER: I am going to tell you a secret. I remain in Paris on purpose. I shall call in the people to my assistance. It rests with them to replace the town dues on their ancient basis, and repeal that fatal principle that was engrafted on them, and that still vegetates there like a parasitical fungus.

SON: You will succeed in this at once.

FATHER: On the contrary, the work will be difficult and laborious. Peter, Paul and John understand one another marvelously. They will do anything rather than allow firewood, butter, and butchers' meat to enter Paris. They have on their side the people, who see clearly the employment that these three protected branches of industry afford, who know well to how many ranchers and wood-merchants they give employment, but who have by no means the same exact idea of the labor that would be developed in the grand air of liberty.

SON: If that is all, you will soon enlighten them.

FATHER: At your age, my son, one doubts of nothing. If I write, the people will not read; for, to support their miserable existence, they have no spare time at their disposal. If I speak, the aldermen will shut my mouth. The people, therefore, will long remain under their fatal mistake. Political parties, whose hopes are founded on popular passions, will set themselves, not to dissipate their prejudices, but to make use of them. I shall have to combat at one and the same time the powerful men of the day, the people, and the political parties. In truth, I see a frightful storm ready to burst over the head of the bold man who shall venture to protest against an iniquity so deeply rooted in this country.

SON: You will have truth and justice on your side.

FATHER: And they will have force and calumny on theirs. Were I but young again; but age and suffering have exhausted my strength!

SON: Very well, father; what strength remains to you, devote it to the service of the country. Begin this work of enfranchisement, and leave to me the task of finishing it.

SCENE IV—The Agitation

JACQUES BONHOMME: Parisians, let us insist upon a reform of the town duties; let us demand that they be instantly put back to what they were. Let every citizen be FREE to buy his firewood, butter, and butchers' meat where he sees fit.

THE PEOPLE: Hurrah for Liberty!

PETER: Parisians, don't allow yourselves to be seduced by that word, liberty. What good can result from liberty to purchase if you want the means, and how can you have the means if you are out of employment? Can Paris produce firewood as cheaply as the Forest of Bondy? Meat as cheaply as Poitou? Butter as cheaply as Normandy? If you open your gates freely to these rival products, what will become of the ranchers, woodcutters, and pork-butchers? They cannot dispense with protection.

THE PEOPLE: Hurrah for Protection!

JACQUES BONHOMME: Protection! But who protects you workmen? Do you not compete with one another? Let the wood-merchants, then, be subject to competition in their turn. They ought not to have right by law to raise the price of firewood, unless the rate of wages is also raised by law. Are you no longer in love with equality?

THE PEOPLE: Hurrah for Equality!

PETER: Don't listen to these agitators. We have, it is true, raised the price of firewood, butchers' meat, and butter; but we have done so for the express purpose of being enabled to give good wages to the workmen. We are actuated by motives of charity.

THE PEOPLE: Hurrah for Charity!

JACQUES BONHOMME: Cause the rate of wages to be raised by the town dues, if you can, or cease to use them to raise the prices of commodities. We Parisians ask for no charity—we demand justice.

THE PEOPLE: Hurrah for Justice!

PETER: It is precisely the high price of commodities that will lead, indirectly, to a rise of wages.

THE PEOPLE: Hurrah for Dearness!

JACQUES BONHOMME: If butter is dear, it is not because you pay high wages to the workmen, it is not even because you make exorbitant profits; it is solely because Paris is ill-adapted for that branch of industry; it is because you have wished to make in the town what should be made in the country, and in the country what should be made in the town. The people have not more employment—only they have employment of a different kind. They have no higher wages; while they can no longer buy commodities as cheaply as formerly.

THE PEOPLE: Hurrah for Cheapness!

PETER: This man seduces you with fine words. Let us place the question before you in all its simplicity. Is it, or is it not true, that if we admit firewood, meat, and butter freely or at a lower duty, our markets will be inundated? Believe me there is no other means of preserving ourselves from this new species of invasion but to keep the door shut, and to maintain the prices of commodities by rendering them artificially scarce.

A VERY FEW VOICES IN THE CROWD: Hurrah for Scarcity!

JACQUES BONHOMME: Let us bring the question to the simple test of truth. You cannot divide among the people of Paris commodities that are not in Paris. If there be less meat, less firewood, less butter, the share falling to each will be smaller. Now there must be less if we prohibit what should be allowed to enter the city. Parisians, abundance for each of you can be secured only by general abundance.

THE PEOPLE: Hurrah for Abundance!

PETER: It is in vain that this man tries to persuade you that it is your interest to be subjected to unbridled competition.

THE PEOPLE: Down with Competition!

JACQUES BONHOMME: It is in vain that this man tries to make you fall in love with restriction.

THE PEOPLE: Down with Restriction!

PETER: I declare, for my own part, if you deprive the poor ranchers and pig-drivers of their daily bread, if you sacrifice them to theories, I can no longer be answerable for public order.

Workmen, distrust that man. He is the agent of perfidious Normandy, and is prompted by the foreigner. He is a traitor, and ought to be hanged!

(The people preserve silence.)

JACQUES BONHOMME: Parisians, what I have told you today, I told you twenty years ago, when Peter set himself to work the town dues for his own profit and to your detriment. I am not, then, an agent of Normandy. Hang me, if you will, but that will not make oppression anything else than oppression. Friends, it is neither Jacques nor Peter that you must kill, but liberty if you fear it, or restriction if it does you harm.

THE PEOPLE: Hang nobody, and set everybody free.

12

SOMETHING ELSE

"What is restriction?"

"It is partial prohibition." "What is prohibition?" "Absolute restriction."

"So that what holds true of the one, holds true of the other?"

"Yes; the difference is only one of degree. There is between them the same relation as there is between a circle and the arc of a circle."

"Then, if prohibition is bad, restriction cannot be good?"

"No more than the arc can be correct if the circle is irregular."

"What is the name which is common to restriction and prohibition?"

"Protection."

"What is the definitive effect of protection?"

"To exact from men a greater amount of labor for the same result."

"Why are men attached to the system of protection?"

"Because as liberty enables us to obtain the same result with less labor, this apparent diminution of employment frightens them."

"Why do you say apparent?"

"Because all labor saved can be applied to something else."

"To what?"

"That I cannot specify, nor is there any need to specify it."

"Why?"

"Because if the amount of satisfactions the country at present enjoys could be obtained with one-tenth less labor, no one can enumerate the new enjoyments that men would desire to obtain from the labor left disposable. One man would desire to be better clothed, another better fed, another better educated, another better amused."

"Explain to me the mechanism and the effects of protection."

"That is not an easy matter. Before entering on consideration of the more complicated cases, we must study it in a very simple one."

"Take as simple a case as you choose."

"You remember how Robinson Crusoe managed to make a plank when he had no saw."

"Yes; he felled a tree, and then, cutting the trunk right and left with his hatchet, he reduced it to the thickness of a board."

"And that cost him much labor?"

"Fifteen whole days' work."

"And what did he live on during that time?"

"He had provisions."

"What happened to the hatchet?"

"It was blunted by the work."

"Yes; but you perhaps do not know this: that at the moment when Robinson was beginning the work he perceived a plank thrown by the tide upon the seashore."

"Happy accident! He of course ran to appropriate it?"

"That was his first impulse; but he stopped short, and began to reason thus with himself: If I get this plank, it will cost me only the trouble of carrying it, and the time needed to descend and remount the cliff."

"But if I form a plank with my hatchet, first of all, it will procure me fifteen days' employment; then my hatchet will get blunt, which will furnish me with the additional employment of sharpening it; then I shall consume my stock of provisions, which will be a third source of employment in replacing them. Now, labor is wealth. It is clear that I should ruin myself by getting the plank. I must protect my personal labor; and, now that I think of it, I can even increase that labor by throwing back the plank into the sea."

"But this reasoning was absurd."

"No doubt. It is nevertheless the reasoning of every nation that protects itself by prohibition. It throws back the plank that is offered in exchange for a small amount of labor in order to exert a greater amount of labor. Even in the labor of the Customhouse officials it discovers a gain. That gain is represented by the pains Robinson takes to render back to the waves the gift they had offered him. Consider the nation as a collective being, and you will not find between its reasoning and that of Robinson an atom of difference."

"Did Robinson not see that he could devote the time saved to something else?"

"What else?"

"As long as a man has wants to satisfy and time at his disposal, there is always something to be done. I am not bound to specify the kind of labor he would in such a case undertake."

"I see clearly what labor he could have escaped."

"And I maintain that Robinson, with incredible blindness, confounded the labor with its result, the end with the means, and I am going to prove to you. . . ."

"There is no need. Here we have the system of restriction or prohibition in its simplest form. If it appears to you absurd when so put, it is because the two capacities of producer and consumer are in this case mixed up in the same individual."

"Let us pass on, therefore, to a more complicated example."

"With all my heart. Some time afterwards, Robinson having met with Friday, they united their labor in a common work. In the morning they hunted for six hours, and brought home four baskets of game. In the evening they worked in the garden for six hours, and obtained four baskets of vegetables.

"One day a canoe touched at the island. A good-looking foreigner landed, and was admitted to the table of our two recluses. He tasted and commended very much the produce of the garden, and before taking leave of his entertainers, spoke as follows:

" 'Generous islanders, I inhabit a country where game is much more plentiful than here, but where horticulture is quite unknown. It would be an easy matter to bring you every evening four baskets of game, if you will give me in exchange two baskets of vegetables.' "

"At these words Robinson and Friday retired to consult, and the debate that took place is too interesting not to be reported *in extenso*.

"FRIDAY: What do you think of it?

"ROBINSON: If we accept the proposal, we are ruined.

"F.: Are you sure of that? Let us consider.

"R.: The case is clear. Crushed by competition, our hunting as a branch of industry is annihilated.

"F.: What matters it, if we have the game?

"R.: Theory! It will no longer be the product of our labor.

"F.: I beg your pardon, sir; for in order to have game we must part with vegetables.

"R.: Then, what shall we gain?

"F.: The four baskets of game cost us six hours' work. The foreigner gives us them in exchange for two baskets of vegetables, which cost us only three hours' work. This places three hours at our disposal.

"R.: Say, rather, which are subtracted from our exertions. There is our loss. Labor is wealth, and if we lose a fourth part of our time we shall be less rich by a fourth.

"F.: You are greatly mistaken, my good friend. We shall have as much game, and the same quantity of vegetables, and three hours at our disposal into the bargain. This is progress, or there is no such thing in the world.

"R.: You lose yourself in generalities! What should we make of these three hours?

"F.: We would do something else.

"R.: Ah! I understand you. You cannot come to particulars. Something else, something else—that is easily said.

"F.: We can fish, we can ornament our cottage, we can read the Bible.

"R.: Utopia! Is there any certainty that we should do either the one or the other?

"F.: Very well, if we have no wants to satisfy we can rest. Is repose nothing?

"R.: But while we repose we may die of hunger.

"F.: My dear friend, you have got into a vicious circle. I speak of a repose which will subtract nothing from our supply of game and vegetables. You always forget that by means of our foreign trade nine hours' labor will give us the same quantity of provisions that we obtain at present with twelve.

"R.: It is very evident, Friday, that you have not been educated in Europe, and that you have never read the *Moniteur Industriel*. If you had, it would have taught you this: that all time saved is sheer loss. The important thing is not to eat or consume, but to work. All that we consume, if it is not the direct produce of our labor, goes for nothing. Do you want to know whether you are rich? Never consider the enjoyments you obtain, but the labor you undergo. This is what the *Moniteur Industriel* would teach you. For myself, who have no pretensions to be a theorist, the only thing I look at is the loss of our hunting.

"F.: What a strange turning upside down of ideas! But . . .

"R.: No buts. Moreover, there are political reasons for rejecting the interested offers of the perfidious foreigner.

"F.: Political reasons!

"R.: Yes, he only makes us these offers because they are advantageous to him.

"F.: So much the better, since they are for our advantage likewise.

"R.: Then by this traffic we should place ourselves in a situation of dependence upon him.

"F.: And he would place himself in dependence on us. We should have need of his game, and he of our vegetables, and we should live on terms of friendship.

"R.: System! Do you want me to shut your mouth?

"F.: We shall see about that. I have as yet heard no good reason.

"R.: Suppose the foreigner learns to cultivate a garden, and that his island should prove more fertile than ours. Do you see the consequence?

"F.: Yes; our relations with the foreigner would cease. He would take from us no more vegetables, since he could have them at home with less labor. He would bring us no more game, since we should have nothing to give him in exchange, and we should then be in precisely the situation that you wish us in now.

"R.: Improvident savage! You don't see that after having annihilated our hunting by inundating us with game, he would annihilate our gardening by inundating us with vegetables.

"F.: But this would only last so long as we were in a situation to give him something else; that is to say, so long as we found something else that we could produce with economy of labor for ourselves.

"R.: Something else, something else! You always come back to that. You are at sea, my good friend Friday; there is nothing practical in your views.

"The debate was long prolonged, and, as often happens, each remained wedded to his own opinion. But Robinson possessing a great influence over Friday, his opinion prevailed, and when the foreigner arrived to demand a reply, Robinson said to him:

" 'Stranger, in order to induce us to accept your proposal, we must be assured of two things:

" 'The first is, that your island is no better stocked with game than ours, for we want to fight only with equal weapons.

"'The second is that you will lose by the bargain. For, as in every exchange there is necessarily a gaining and a losing party, we should be dupes, if you were not the loser. What have you got to say?'"

" 'Nothing,' replied the foreigner; and, bursting out laughing, he got back into his canoe."

"The story would not be amiss if Robinson were not made to argue so very absurdly."

"He does not argue more absurdly than the committee of the Rue Hauteville."

"Oh! the case is very different. Sometimes you suppose one man, and sometimes (which comes to the same thing) two men living in company. That does not tally with the actual state of things. The division of labor and the intervention of merchants and money change the state of the question very much."

"That may complicate transactions, but does not change their nature."

"What! you want to compare modern commerce with a system of barter."

"Trade is nothing but a multiplicity of barters. Barter is in its own nature identical with commerce, just as labor on a small scale is identical with labor on a great scale, or as the law of gravitation that moves an atom is identical with the same law of gravitation that moves a world."

"So, according to you, these arguments, which are so untenable in the mouth of Robinson, are equally untenable when urged by our protectionists."

"Yes; only the error is better concealed under a complication of circumstances."

"Then, pray, let us have an example taken from the present order of things."

"With pleasure. In France, owing to the exigencies of climate and habits, cloth is a useful thing. Is the essential thing to make it, or to get it?"

"A very sensible question, truly! In order to have it, you must make it."

"Not necessarily. To have it, someone must make it, that is certain; but it is not at all necessary that the same person or the same country that consumes it should also produce it. You have not made that stuff which clothes you so well. France does not produce the coffee on which our citizens breakfast."

"But I buy my cloth, and France her coffee.

"Exactly so; and with what?"

"With money."

"But neither you nor France produce the material of money."

"We buy it."

"With what?"

"With our products, which are sent to Peru."

"It is then, in fact, your labor that you exchange for cloth, and French labor that is exchanged for coffee."

"Undoubtedly."

"It is not absolutely necessary, therefore, to manufacture what you consume?"

"No; if we manufacture something else that we give in exchange."

"In other words, France has two means of procuring a given quantity of cloth. The first is to make it; the second is to make something else, and to exchange this something else with the foreigner for cloth. Of these two means, which is the best?"

"I don't very well know."

"Is it not that which, for a determinate amount of labor, obtains the greater quantity of cloth?"

"It seems so."

"And which is best for a nation, to have the choice between these two means, or that the law should prohibit one of them, on the chance of stumbling on the better of the two?"

"It appears to me that it is better for the nation to have the choice, inasmuch as in such matters it invariably chooses right."

"The law, which prohibits the importation of foreign cloth, decides, then, that if France wishes to have cloth, she must make it, and she is prohibited from making the something else with which she could purchase foreign cloth."

"True."

"And as the law obliges us to make the cloth, and forbids our making the something else, precisely because that something else would exact less labor (but for which reason the law would not interfere with it) the law virtually decrees that for a determinate amount of labor, France shall only have one yard of cloth, when for the same amount of labor she might have two yards, by applying that labor to something else."

"But the question recurs, 'What else?'"

"And my question recurs, 'What does it signify?' Having the choice, she will only make the something else to such an extent as there may be a demand for it."

"That is possible; but I cannot divest myself of the idea that the foreigner will send us his cloth, and not take from us the something else, in which case we would be entrapped. At all events, this is the objection even from your own point of view. You allow that France could make this something else to exchange for cloth, with a less expenditure of labor than if she had made the cloth itself?"

"Undoubtedly."

"There would, then, be a certain amount of her labor rendered inert?"

"Yes; but without her being less well provided with clothes, a little circumstance which makes all the difference. Robinson lost sight of this, and our protectionists either do not see it, or pretend not to see it. The shipwrecked plank rendered fifteen days of Robinson's labor inert, in so far as that labor was applied to making a plank, but it did not deprive him of it. Discriminate, then, between these two kinds of diminished labor—the diminution that has for effect privation, and that which has for its cause satisfaction. These two things are very different, and if you mix them up, you reason as Robinson did. In the most complicated, as in the most simple cases, the fallacy consists in this: Judging of the utility of labor by its duration and intensity, and not by its results; which gives rise to this economic policy: To reduce the results of labor for the purpose of augmenting its duration and intensity."[1]

---

[1]See chapters 2 and 3, first series; and *Economic Harmonies*, chap. 6.

13

THE LITTLE ARSENAL
OF THE FREE-TRADER

If anyone tells you that there are no absolute principles, no inflexible rules; that prohibition may be bad and yet that restriction may be good,

Reply: "Restriction prohibits all that it hinders from being imported."

If anyone says that agriculture is the mother's milk of the country,

Reply: "What nourishes the country is not exactly agriculture, but wheat."

If anyone tells you that the basis of the food of the people is agriculture,

Reply: "The basis of the people's food is wheat. This is the reason why a law that gives us, by agricultural labor, two quarters of wheat, when we could have obtained four quarters without such labor, and by means of labor applied to manufactures, is a law not for feeding, but for starving the people."

If anyone remarks that restriction upon the importation of foreign wheat gives rise to a more extensive culture, and consequently to increased home production,

Reply: "It induces men to sow grain on comparatively barren and ungrateful soils. To milk a cow and go on milking her, puts a little more into the pail, for it is difficult to say when you will come to the last drop. But that drop costs dear."

If anyone tells you that when bread is dear, the agriculturist, having become rich, enriches the manufacturer,

Reply: "Bread is dear when it is scarce, and then men are poor, or, if you like it better, they become rich starvelings."

If you are further told that when bread gets dearer, wages rise,

Reply by pointing out that in April 1847, five-sixths of our workmen were receiving charity.

If you are told that the wages of labor should rise with the increased price of provisions,

Reply: "This is as much as to say that in a ship without provisions, everybody will have as much biscuit as if the vessel were fully victualled."

If you are told that it is necessary to secure a good price to the man who sells wheat,

Reply: "That in that case it is also necessary to secure good wages to the man who buys it."

If it is said that the proprietors, who make the laws, have raised the price of bread without taking thought about wages, because they know that when bread rises wages naturally rise,

Reply: "Upon the same principle, when the workmen come to make the laws, don't blame them if they fix a high rate of wages without busying themselves about protecting wheat, because they know that when wages rise, provisions naturally rise also."

If you are asked what, then, is to be done?

Reply: "Be just to everybody."

If you are told that it is essential that every great country should produce iron,

Reply: "What is essential is, that every great country should have iron."

If you are told that it is indispensable that every great country should produce cloth,

Reply: "The indispensable thing is that the citizens of every great country should have cloth."

If it be said that labor is wealth,

Reply: "This is not true."

And, by way of development, add: "Letting blood is not health, and the proof of it is that it is resorted to for the purpose of restoring health."

If it is said: "To force men to mine rocks, and extract an ounce of iron from a hundredweight of ore, is to increase their labor and consequently their wealth."

Reply: "To force men to dig wells by prohibiting them from taking water from the brook is to increase their useless labor, but not their wealth."

If you are told that the sun gives you his heat and light without remuneration,

Reply: "So much the better for me, for it costs me nothing to see clearly."

And if you are answered that industry in general loses what would have been paid for artificial light,

Rejoin: "No; for having paid nothing to the sun, what he saves me enables me to buy clothes, furniture, and candles."

In the same way, if you are told that these rascally English possess capital that is dormant,

Reply: "So much the better for us; they will not make us pay interest for it."

If it is said: "These perfidious English find coal and iron in the same pit,"

Reply: "So much the better for us; they will charge us nothing for bringing them together." `

If you are told that the Swiss have rich pasturages, which cost little:

Reply: "The advantage is ours, for they will demand a smaller amount of our labor in return for giving an impetus to our agriculture, and supplying us with provisions."

If they tell you that the lands of the Crimea have no value, and pay no taxes,

Reply: "The profit is ours, who buy corn free from such charges."

If they tell you that the serfs of Poland work without wages,

Reply: "The misfortune is theirs and the profit is ours, since their labor does not enter into the price of the wheat their masters sell us."

Finally, if they tell you that other nations have many advantages over us,

Reply: "By means of exchange, they are forced to allow us to participate in these advantages."

If they tell you that under free-trade we are about to be inundated with bread, beef *a la mode*, coal, and winter clothing,

Reply: "In that case we shall be neither hungry nor thirsty."

If they ask how we are to pay for these things?

Reply: "Don't let that disquiet you. If we are inundated, it is a sign we have the means of paying for the inundation; and if we have not the means of paying, we shall not be inundated."

If anyone says: I should approve of free trade, if the foreigner, in sending us his products, would take our products in exchange; but he carries off our money,

Reply: "Neither money nor coffee grows in the fields of Beauce, nor are they turned out by the workshops of Elbeuf. So far as we are concerned, to pay the foreigner with money is the same thing as paying him with coffee."

If they bid you eat butcher's meat,

Reply: "Allow it to be imported."

If they say to you, in the words of *La Presse*, "When one has not the means to buy bread, he is forced to buy beef,"

Reply: "This is advice quite as judicious as that given by M. Vautour to his tenant:

" '*Quand on n'a pas de quoi payer son terme,
Il faut avoir une maison a soi.*'"

If, again, they say to you, in the words of *La Presse*, "The government should teach the people how and why they must eat beef,"

Reply: "The government has only to allow the beef to be imported, and the most civilized people in the world will know how to use it without being taught by a master."

If they tell you that the government should know everything, and foresee everything, in order to direct the people, and that the people have simply to allow themselves to be led,

Reply by asking: "Is there a state apart from the people? Is there a human foresight apart from humanity? Archimedes might repeat every day of his life, 'With a fulcrum and lever I can move the world;' but he never did move it, for want of a fulcrum and lever. The lever of the state is the nation, and nothing can be more foolish than to found so many hopes upon the state, which is simply to take for granted the existence of collective science and foresight, after having set out with the assumption of individual imbecility and improvidence."

If anyone says, "I ask no favor, but only such a duty on bread and meat as shall compensate the heavy taxes to which I am subjected; only a small duty equal to what the taxes add to the cost price of my wheat,"

Reply: "A thousand pardons; but I also pay taxes. If, then, the protection you vote in your own favor has the effect of burdening me as a purchaser of corn with exactly your share of the taxes, your modest demand amounts to nothing less than establishing this arrangement as formulated by you: 'Seeing that the public charges are heavy, I, as a seller of wheat, am to pay nothing, and you my neighbor, as a buyer of wheat, are to pay double, viz., your own share and mine into the bargain.' Mr. Grain-merchant, my good friend, you may have force at your command, but assuredly you have not reason on your side."

If anyone says to you, "It is, however, exceedingly hard upon me, who pays taxes, to have to compete in my own market with the foreigner, who pays none,"

Reply: "In the first place, it is not your market, but our market. I who live upon wheat and pay for it, should surely be taken into account.

"Second, Few foreigners at the present day are exempt from taxes.

"Third, If the taxes you vote yield you in roads, canals, security, etc., more than they cost you, you are not justified in repelling, at my expense, the competition of foreigners, who, if they do not pay taxes, have not the advantages you enjoy in roads, canals, and security. You might as well say, 'I demand a compensating duty because I have finer clothes, stronger horses, and better ploughs than the hard-working peasant of Russia.'"

"Fourth, If the tax does not repay you for what it costs, don't vote it."

"Fifth, In short, after having voted the tax, do you wish to get free from it? Try to frame a law that will throw it on the foreigner. But your tariff makes your share of it fall upon me, who have already my own burden to bear."

If anyone says, "For the Russians free trade is necessary to enable them to exchange their products with advantage" (Opinion of M. Thiers in the Bureaux, April, 1847),

Reply: "Liberty is necessary everywhere, and for the same reason."

If you are told, "Each country has its wants, and we must be guided by that in what we do" (M. Thiers),

Reply: "Each country acts thus of its own accord, if you don't throw obstacles in the way."

If they tell you, "We have no sheet-iron, and we must allow it to be imported" (M. Thiers),

Reply: "Many thanks."

If you are told, "We have no freights for our merchant shipping. The want of return cargoes prevents our shipping from competing with foreigners" (M. Thiers),

Reply: "When a country wishes to have everything produced at home, there can be no freights either for exports or imports. It is just as absurd to desire to have a mercantile marine under a system of prohibition as it would be to have carts when there is nothing to carry."

If you are told that, assuming protection to be unjust, everything has been arranged on that footing; capital has been embarked; rights have been acquired; and the system cannot be changed without suffering to individuals and classes,

Reply: "All injustice is profitable to somebody (except, perhaps, restriction, which in the long run benefits no one). To argue from the derangement that the cessation of injustice may occasion to the man who profits by it is as much as to say that a system of injustice, for no other reason than that it has had a temporary existence, ought to exist for ever."

14

THE RIGHT HAND AND THE LEFT

REPORT ADDRESSED TO THE KING[1]

S IRE—When we observe these free trade advocates boldly disseminating their doctrines, and maintaining that the right of buying and selling is implied in the right of property (as has been urged by Mr. Billauit in the true style of a special pleader), we may be permitted to feel serious alarm as to the fate of our national labor; for what would Frenchmen make of their heads and their hands were they free?

The administration that you have honored with your confidence has turned its attention to this grave state of things, and has sought in its wisdom to discover a species of protection that may be substituted for that which appears to be getting out of repute. They propose a law TO PROHIBIT YOUR FAITHFUL SUBJECTS FROM USING THEIR RIGHT HANDS.

Sire, we beseech you not to do us the injustice of supposing that we have adopted lightly and without due deliberation a

---

[1]Written in 1847.

measure that at first sight may appear somewhat whimsical. A profound study of the system of protection has taught us this syllogism, upon which the whole doctrine reposes:

The more men work, the richer they become;

The more difficulties there are to be overcome, the more work:

Ergo, the more difficulties there are to be overcome, the richer they become.

In fact, what is protection, if it is not an ingenious application of this reasoning—reasoning so close and conclusive as to balk the subtlety of Mr. Billauit himself?

Let us personify the country, and regard it as a collective being with thirty million mouths, and, as a natural consequence, with sixty million hands. Here is a man who makes a French clock, which he can exchange in Belgium for ten hundredweights of iron. But we tell him to make the iron himself. He replies, "I cannot, it would occupy too much of my time; I should produce only five hundredweights of iron during the time I am occupied in making a clock." Utopian dreamer, we reply, that is the very reason why we forbid you to make the clock, and order you to make the iron. Don't you see we are providing employment for you?

Sire, it cannot have escaped your sagacity that this is exactly the same thing in effect as if we were to say to the country, "Work with your left hand, and not with the right."

To create obstacles in order to furnish labor with an opportunity of developing itself, was the principle of the old system of restriction, and it is the principle likewise of the new system that is now being inaugurated. Sire, to regulate industry in this way is not to innovate, but to persevere.

As regards the efficiency of the measure, it is incontestable. It is difficult, much more difficult than one would suppose, to do with the left hand what we have been accustomed to do with the right. You will be convinced of this, Sire, if you will condescend to make trial of our system in a process which must be familiar to you; as, for example, in shuffling a deck of cards. For this reason we flatter ourselves that we are opening to labor an unlimited career.

When workmen in all departments of industry are thus confined to the use of the left hand, we may figure to ourselves, Sire, the immense number of people that will be wanted to supply the present consumption, assuming it to continue invariable, as we always do when we compare two different systems of production with one another. So prodigious a demand for manual labor cannot fail to induce a great rise of wages, and poverty will disappear as if by magic.

Sire, your paternal heart will rejoice to think that this new law of ours will extend its benefits to that interesting part of the community whose destinies engage all your solicitude. What is the present destiny of women in France? The bolder and more hardy sex drives them insensibly out of every department of industry.

Formerly, they had the resource of the lottery offices. These offices have been shut up by a pitiless philanthropy, and on what pretext? "To save the money of the poor." Alas! the poor man never obtained for a piece of money enjoyments as sweet and innocent as those afforded by the mysterious turn of fortune. Deprived of all the comforts of life, when he, fortnight after fortnight, risked a day's wages, how many delicious hours did he afford his family! Hope was always present at his fireside. The garret was peopled with illusions. The wife hoped to rival her neighbors in her style of living; the son saw himself the drum-major of a regiment; and the daughter fancied herself led to the altar by her betrothed.

"C'est quelque chose encor que de faire un beau reve!"

The lottery was the poetry of the poor, and we have lost it.

The lottery gone, what means have we of providing for our wards? Tobacco-shops and the post-office.

Tobacco, all right; its use progresses, thanks to distinguished examples.

But the post-office! . . . We shall say nothing of it, it will be the subject of a special report.

Except, then, the sale of tobacco, what employment remains for your female subjects? Embroidery, lace making, and sewing—melancholy resources, which the barbarous science of mechanics goes on limiting more and more.

But the moment your new law comes into operation, the moment right hands are amputated or tied up, the face of everything will be changed. Twenty times, thirty times, more embroiderers, polishers, laundresses, seamstresses, milliners, shirtmakers, will not be sufficient to supply the wants of the kingdom, always assuming, as before, the consumption to be the same.

This assumption may very likely be disputed by some cold theorists, for dress and everything else will then be dearer. The same thing may be said of the iron we extract from our own mines, compared with the iron we could obtain in exchange for our wines. This argument, therefore, does not tell more against left-handed men than against protection, for this very dearness is the effect and the sign of an excess of work and exertion, which is precisely the basis upon which, in both cases, we contend that the prosperity of the working classes is founded.

Yes, we can make a touching picture of the prosperity of the millinery business. What movement! What activity! What life! Every dress will occupy a hundred fingers, instead of ten. No young woman will be idle, and we have no need, Sire, to indicate to your perspicacity the moral consequences of this great revolution. Not only will there be more young women employed, but each of them will earn more, for they will be unable to supply the demand; and if competition shall again show itself, it will not be among the seamstresses who make the dresses, but among the fine ladies who wear them.

You must see then, Sire, that our proposal is not only in strict conformity with the economic traditions of the government, but is in itself essentially moral and popular.

To appreciate its effects, let us suppose the law passed and in operation—let us transport ourselves in imagination into the future—and assume the new system to have been in operation for twenty years. Idleness is banished from the country; ease and concord, contentment and morality, have, with employment, been introduced into every family—no more poverty, no more vice. The left hand being very awkward at all work, employment will be abundant, and the remuneration adequate. Everything is arranged on this footing, and the workshops in consequence are full. If, in such circumstances, Sire, Utopian dreamers were all at once to agitate for the right hand being again set free, would they not throw the whole country into alarm? Would such a pretended reform not overturn the whole existing state of things? Then our system must be good, since it could not be put an end to without universal suffering.

And yet we confess we have the melancholy presentiment (so great is human perversity) that some day there will be formed an association for right-hand freedom.

We think that already we hear the free right-handers, assembled in the Salle Montesquieu, holding this discourse:

"Good people, you think yourselves richer because the use of one of your hands has been denied you; you take account only of the additional employment that that brings you. But consider also the high prices that result from it, and the forced diminution of consumption. That measure has not made capital more abundant, and capital is the fund from which wages are paid. The streams that flow from that great reservoir are directed toward other channels; but their volume is not enlarged; and the ultimate effect, as far as the nation at large is concerned, is the loss of all that wealth which that of right hands could produce, compared with what is now produced by an equal number of left hands. At the risk of some inevitable derangements, then, let us form an association, and enforce our right to work with both hands."

Fortunately, Sire, an association has been formed in defense of left-hand labor, and the Left-handers will have no difficulty in demolishing all these generalities, suppositions, abstractions, reveries, and Utopias. They have only to exhume the *Moniteur Industriel* for 1846, and they will find ready-made arguments against freedom of trade, which refute so admirably all that has been urged in favor of right-hand liberty that it is only necessary to substitute one word for the other.

"The Parisian free-trade league has no doubt of securing the concurrence of the workmen. But the workmen are no longer men who can be led by the nose. They have their eyes open, and they know political economy better than our professors. Free trade, they say, will deprive us of employment, and labor is our wealth. With employment, with abundant employment, the price of commodities never places them beyond our reach. Without employment, were bread at a halfpenny a pound, the workman would die of hunger. Now your doctrines instead of increasing the present amount of employment, would diminish it, that is to say, would reduce us to poverty."

"When there are too many commodities in the market, their price falls, no doubt. But as wages always fall when commodities are cheap, the result is that, instead of being in a situation to purchase more, we are no longer able to buy anything. It is when commodities are cheap that the workman is worst off."

It will not be amiss for the Left-handers to intermingle some menaces with their theories. Here is a model for them:

"What! you desire to substitute right-hand for left-hand labor, and thus force down, or perhaps annihilate, wages, the sole resource of the great bulk of the nation!"

"And, at a time when a deficient harvest is imposing painful privations on the workman, you wish to disquiet him as to his future, and render him more accessible to bad advice, and more ready to abandon that wise line of conduct which has hitherto distinguished him."

After such conclusive reasoning as this, we entertain a confident hope, Sire, that if the battle is once begun, the left hand will come off victorious.

Perhaps an association may be formed for the purpose of inquiring whether the right hand and the left are not both wrong, and whether a third hand cannot be found to conciliate everybody.

After having depicted the Right-handers as seduced by the apparent liberality of a principle, the soundness of which experience has not verified, and the Left-handers as maintaining the position they have gained, they go on to say:

"It is denied that there is any third position that it is possible to take up in the midst of the battle! Is it not evident that the workmen have to defend themselves at one and the same time against those who desire to change nothing in the present situation, because they are heavily invested in it, and against those who dream of an economic revolution of which they have calculated neither the direction nor the extent?"

We cannot, however, conceal from your Majesty that our project has a vulnerable side; for it may be said that twenty years hence left hands will be as skilful as right hands are at present, and that then you could no longer trust to left-handedness for an increase of national employment.

To that we reply, that according to the most learned physicians the left side of the body has a natural feebleness, which is quite reassuring as regards the labor of the future.

Should your Majesty consent to pass the measure now proposed, a great principle will be established: All wealth proceeds from the intensity of labor. It will be easy for us to extend and vary the applications of this principle. We may decree, for example, that it shall no longer be permissible to work but with the foot; for this is no more impossible (as we have seen) than to extract iron from the mud of the Seine. You see then, Sire, that the means of increasing national labor can never fail. And after all has been tried, we have still the practically exhaustless resource of amputation.

To conclude, Sire, if this report were not intended for publicity, we should take the liberty of soliciting your attention to the great influence that measures of this kind are calculated to confer on men in power. But that is a matter that we must reserve for a private audience.

15

DOMINATION BY LABOR

"In the same way that in time of war we attain the mastery by superiority in arms, can we not, in time of peace, arrive at domination by superiority in Labor?"

This is a question of the highest interest at a time when no doubt seems to be entertained that in the field of industry, as on the field of battle, the stronger crushes the weaker.

To arrive at this conclusion, we must have discovered between the Labor that is applied to commodities and the violence exercised upon men, a melancholy and discouraging analogy; for why should these two kinds of operations be identical in their effects, if they are essentially different in their own nature?

And if it be true that in industry, as in war, domination is the necessary result of superiority, what have we to do with progress or with social economy, seeing that we inhabit a world where everything has been so arranged by Providence that one and the same effect—namely, oppression—proceeds necessarily from two opposite principles?

With reference to the new policy toward which commercial freedom is drawing England, many persons make this objection, which, I admit, preoccupies the most candid minds among us: "Is England doing anything else than pursuing the same end by different means? Does she not always aspire at universal supremacy? Assured of her superiority in capital and Labor, does she not invite free competition in order to stifle Continental industry, and so put herself in a situation to reign as a sovereign, and conquer the privilege of feeding and clothing the populations she has ruined?"

It would be easy to show that these alarms are chimerical; that our alleged inferiority is much exaggerated; that our great branches of industry not only maintain their ground, but are actually developed under the action of external competition, and that the infallible effect of such competition is to bring about an increase of general consumption, capable of absorbing both home and foreign products.

At present, I desire to make a direct answer to the objection, leaving it all the strength and the advantage of the ground it has chosen. Keeping out of view for the present the special case of England and France, I shall inquire in a general way whether, when, by its superiority in one branch of industry, a nation comes to wipe out a similar branch of industry existing among another people, the former has advanced one step toward domination, or the latter toward independence; in other words, whether both nations do not gain by the operation, and whether it is not the nation that is outrivalled that gains the most.

If we saw in a product nothing more than an opportunity of working, the alarms of the protectionists would undoubtedly be well founded. Were we to consider iron for example, only in its relations with ironmasters, we might be led to fear that the competition of a country where it is the gratuitous gift of nature would extinguish the furnaces of another country where both ore and fuel are scarce.

But is this a complete view of the subject? Has iron relations only with those who make it? Has it no relations with those who use it? Is its sole and ultimate destination to be produced? And if it is useful, not on account of the Labor to which it gives employment, but on account of the qualities it possesses, of the numerous purposes to which its durability and malleability adapt it, does it not follow that the foreigner cannot reduce its price, even so far as to render its production here at home unprofitable, without doing us more good in this last respect than harm in the other?

Pray consider that there are many things that foreigners, by reason of the natural advantages by which they are surrounded, prevent our producing directly, and with reference to which we are placed in reality in the hypothetical position we have been examining with reference to iron. We produce at home neither tea nor coffee, gold nor silver. Is our industry as a whole diminished in consequence? No; only in order to create the counter-value of these imported commodities, in order to acquire them by means of exchange, we detach from our national Labor a portion less great than would be required to produce these things ourselves. More Labor thus remains to be devoted to the procuring of other enjoyments. We are so much the richer and so much the stronger. All that external competition can do, even in cases where it puts an end absolutely to a particular branch of industry, is to economize Labor, and increase our productive power. Is this, for the foreigner, the road to domination? If we should find in France a gold mine, it does not follow that it would be for our interest to work it. Nay, it is certain that the enterprise should be neglected if each ounce of gold absorbed more of our Labor than an ounce of gold purchased abroad with cloth. In this case we should do better to find our mines in our workshops. And what is true of gold is true of iron.

The illusion proceeds from our failure to see one thing, which is, that foreign superiority never puts a stop to national industry, except in a particular sector, and in that sector only renders it superfluous by placing at our disposal the result of the very Labor thus superseded. If men lived in diving-bells under water, and had to provide themselves with air by means of a pump, this would be a great source of employment. To throw obstacles in the way of such employment, as long as men were left in this condition, would be to inflict upon them a frightful injury. But if the Labor ceases because the necessity for its exertion no longer exists, because men are placed in a medium where air is introduced into their lungs without effort, then the loss of that Labor is not to be regretted, except in the eyes of men who obstinately persist in appreciating in Labor nothing but Labor in the abstract.

It is exactly this kind of Labor that machinery, commercial freedom, progress of every kind, gradually supersedes; not useful Labor, but Labor becomes superfluous, without object, and without result. On the contrary, protection sets that sort of useless Labor to work; it places us again under water, to bring the air-pump into play; it forces us to apply for gold to the inaccessible national mine, rather than to the national workshops. All the effect is expressed by the words, loss of power.

It will be understood that I am speaking here of general effects, not of the temporary inconvenience that is always caused by the transition from a bad system to a good one. A momentary derangement accompanies necessarily all progress. This may be a reason for making the transition gently and gradually. It is no reason for putting a stop systematically to all progress, still less for misunderstanding it.

Industry is often represented as a struggle. That is not a true representation of it, or only true when we confine ourselves to the consideration of each branch of industry in its effects upon a similar branch, regarding them both apart from the interests of the rest of mankind. But there is always something else to be considered, namely, the effect upon consumption and upon general prosperity.

It is an error to apply to trade, as is but too often done, phrases that are applicable to war.

In war the stronger overcomes the weaker.

In industry the stronger imparts vigor to the weaker. This entirely does away with the analogy.

Let the English be as powerful and skillful as they are represented, let them be possessed of as large an amount of capital, and have as great a command of the two great agents of production, iron and fuel, as they are supposed to have; all this simply means cheapness. And who gains by the cheapness of products? The man who buys them.

It is not in their power to annihilate any part whatever of our national Labor. All they can do is to render it superfluous in the production of what has been already acquired, to furnish us with air without the aid of the pump, to enlarge in this way our disposable forces, and so render their alleged domination so much the more impossible as their superiority becomes the more incontestable.

Thus, by a rigorous and heartening demonstration, we arrive at this conclusion; Labor and violence, which are so opposite in their nature, are not less so in their effects.

All we are called upon to do is to distinguish between Labor annihilated and Labor economized.

To have less iron because we work less, and to have less iron although we work less, are things not only different, but opposed to each other. The protectionists confound them; we do not. That is all.

We may be very certain of one thing, that if the English employ a large amount of activity, Labor, capital, intelligence, and natural forces, it is not done for show. It is done in order to procure a multitude of enjoyments in exchange for their products. They most certainly expect to receive at least as much as they give. What they produce at home is destined to pay for what they purchase abroad. If they inundate us with their products, it is because they expect to be inundated with ours in return. That being so, the best means of having much for ourselves is to be free to choose between these two modes of acquisition, direct production and indirect production. British Machiavellianism cannot force us to make a wrong choice.

Let us give up, then, the puerility of applying to industrial competition phrases applicable to war—a false way of speaking that is only specious when applied to competition between two rival trades. The moment we come to take into account the effect produced on the general prosperity, the analogy disappears.

In a battle everyone who is killed diminishes by so much the strength of the army. In industry, a workshop is shut up only when what it produced is obtained by the public from another source and in greater abundance. Picture a state of things where for one man killed on the spot two should rise up full of life and vigor. Were such a state of things possible, war would no longer merit its name.

This, however, is the distinctive character of what is so absurdly called industrial war.

Let the Belgians and the English lower the price of their iron ever so much; let them, if they will, send it to us for nothing; this might extinguish some of our blast-furnaces; but immediately, and as a necessary consequence of this very cheapness, there would rise up a thousand other branches of industry more profitable than the one that had been superseded.

We arrive, then, at the conclusion that domination by Labor is impossible, and a contradiction in terms, seeing that all superiority that manifests itself among a people means cheapness, and tends only to impart power to all other nations. Let us banish, then, from political economy all terms borrowed from the military vocabulary: to fight with equal weapons, to conquer, to crush, to stifle, to be beaten, invasion, tribute, etc. What do such phrases mean? Squeeze them, and you obtain nothing. . . . Yes, you do obtain something; for from such words proceed absurd errors, and fatal and infectious prejudices. Such phrases tend to arrest the fusion of nations, are inimical to their peaceful, universal, and indissoluble alliance, and retard the progress of the human race.

VIII.

HARMONIES OF POLITICAL ECONOMY

BOOK ONE

To the Youth of France

Love of study, and lack of fixed opinions—a mind free from prejudice, a heart devoid of hate, zeal for the propagation of truth—ardent sympathies, disinterestedness, devotion, candor—enthusiasm for all that is good and fair, simple and great, honest and religious—such are the precious attributes of youth. It is for this reason that I dedicate my work to you. And the seed must have in it no kernel of life if it fail to take root in a soil so generous.

I had thought to offer you a picture, and all I have given you is a sketch; but you will pardon me; for who, in times like the present,[1] can sit down to finish a grave and important work? My hope is that some one among you, on seeing it, will be led to exclaim, with the great artist, *Anch' io son pittore!* and seizing the pencil, impart to my rude canvas color and flesh, light and shade, sentiment and life.

You may think the title of the work somewhat ambitious; and assuredly I make no pretension to reveal the designs of Providence in the social order, and to explain the mechanisms of all the forces with which God has endowed man for the realization of

---

[1]The first edition of the *Harmonies Economiques* appeared in 1850.

progress. All that I have aimed at is to put you on the right track, and make you acquainted with the truth that *all legitimate interests are in harmony*. That is the predominant idea of my work, and it is impossible not to recognize its importance.

For some time it has been the fashion to laugh at what has been called the social problem; and no doubt some of the solutions that have been proposed afford but too much ground for raillery. But in the problem itself there is nothing laughable. It is the ghost of Banquo at the feast of Macbeth—and no dumb ghost either; for in formidable tones it calls out to terror-stricken society—a solution or death!

Now this solution, you will at once see, must be different according as men's interests are held to be naturally harmonious or naturally antagonistic.

In the one case, we must seek for the solution in Liberty—in the other, in Constraint. In the one case, we have only to be passive—in the other, we must necessarily offer opposition.

But Liberty assumes only one shape. Once convinced that each of the molecules that compose a fluid possesses in itself the force by which the general level is produced, we conclude that there is no surer or simpler way of seeing that level realized than not to interfere with it. All, then, who set out with this fundamental principle, that men's interests are harmonious, will agree as to the practical solution of the social problem—to abstain from displacing or thwarting these interests.

Constraint, on the other hand, may assume a thousand shapes, according to the views we take of it, and which are infinitely varied. Those schools that set out with the principle that men's interests are antagonistic, have done nothing yet toward the solution of the problem, unless it be that they have thrust aside Liberty. Among the infinite forms of Constraint, they have still to choose the one they consider good, if indeed any of them be so. And then, as a crowning difficulty, they have to obtain universal acceptance, among men who are free agents, for the particular form of Constraint to which they have awarded the preference.

But, on this hypothesis, if human interests are, by their very nature urged into fatal collision, and if this shock can be avoided only by the accidental invention of an artificial social order, the destiny of the human race becomes very hazardous, and we ask in terror:

First, if any man is to be found who has discovered a satisfactory form of Constraint?

Second, can this man bring to his way of thinking the innumerable schools who give the preference to other forms?

Third, will mankind give in to that particular form which, by hypothesis, runs counter to all individual interests?

Fourth, assuming that men will allow themselves to be rigged out in this new attire, what will happen if another inventor presents himself, with a coat of a different and improved cut? Are we to persevere in a vicious organization, knowing it to be vicious; or must we resolve to change that organization every morning according as the caprices of fashion and the fertility of inventors' brains may dictate?

Fifth, would not all the inventors whose plans have been rejected unite together against the particular organization that had been selected, and would not their success in disturbing society be in exact proportion to the degree in which that particular form of organization ran counter to all existing interests?

Sixth, and last of all, may be asked, Does there exist any human force capable of overcoming an antagonism that we presuppose to be itself the very essence of human force?

I might multiply such questions ad infinitum, and propose, for example, this difficulty:

If individual interest is opposed to the general interest, where are we to place the active principle of Constraint? Where is the fulcrum of the lever to be placed? Beyond the limits of human society? It must be so if we are to escape the consequences of your law. If we are to entrust some men with arbitrary power, prove first of all that these men are formed of a different clay from other mortals; that they in their turn will not be acted upon by the fatal principle of self-interest; and that, placed in a situation that excludes the idea of any curb, any effective opposition, their judgments will be exempt from error, their hands from rapacity, and their hearts from covetousness.

The radical difference between various Socialist schools (I mean here, those which seek the solution of the social problem in an artificial organization) and the Economist school, does not consist in certain views of detail or of governmental combination. We encounter that difference at the starting point, in the preliminary and pressing question: Are human interests, when left to themselves, antagonistic or harmonious?

It is evident that the Socialists have set out in quest of an artificial organization only because they judge the natural organization of society bad or insufficient; and they have judged the latter bad and insufficient only because they think they see in men's interests a radical antagonism, for otherwise they would not have had recourse to Constraint. It is not necessary to constrain into harmony what is in itself harmonious.

Thus they have discovered antagonism everywhere:

> Between the proprietor and the proletarian
> Between capital and labor
> Between the masses and the bourgeoisie
> Between agriculture and manufactures
> Between the rustic and the burgess
> Between the native and the foreigner
> Between the producer and the consumer
> Between civilization and organization
> In a word, Between Liberty and Harmony.

And this explains why it happens that, although a certain kind of sentimental philanthropy finds a place in their hearts, gall and bitterness flow continually from their lips. Each reserves all his love for the new state of society he has dreamt of; but as regards the society in which we actually live and move, it cannot, in their opinion, be too soon crushed and overthrown, to make room for the New Jerusalem they are to rear upon its ruins.

I have said that the Economist school, setting out with the natural harmony of interests, is the advocate of Liberty.

And yet I must allow that if Economists in general stand up for liberty, it is unfortunately not equally true that their principles establish solidly the foundation on which they build—the harmony of interests.

Before proceeding further, and to forewarn you against the conclusions that will no doubt be drawn from this avowal, I must say a word on the situations that Socialism and Political Economy respectively occupy.

It would be folly in me to assert that Socialism has never lighted upon a truth, and that Political Economy has never fallen into an error.

What separates, radically and profoundly, the two schools is their difference of methods. The one school, like the astrologer and the alchemist, proceeds on hypothesis; the other, like the astronomer and the chemist, proceeds on observation.

Two astronomers, observing the same fact, may not be able to arrive at the same result.

In spite of this transient disagreement, they feel themselves united by the common process that sooner or later will cause that disagreement to disappear. They recognize each other as of the same communion. But between the astronomer, who observes, and the astrologer, who imagines, the gulf is impassable, although accidentally they may sometimes approximate.

The same thing holds of Political Economy and Socialism.

The Economists observe man, the laws of his organization, and the social relations that result from those laws. The Socialists conjure up an imaginary society, and then create a human heart to suit that society.

Now, if philosophy never errs, philosophers often do. I deny not that Economists may make false observations; I will add that they must necessarily begin by doing so.

But then what happens? If men's interests are harmonious, it follows that every incorrect observation will lead logically to antagonism. What, then, are the Socialist tactics? They gather from the works of Economists certain incorrect observations, follow them out to their consequences, and show those consequences to be disastrous. Thus far they are right. Then they set to work upon the observer, whom we may assume to be Malthus or Ricardo. Still they have right on their side. But they do not stop there. They turn against the science of Political Economy itself, accusing it of being heartless, and leading to evil. Here they do violence to reason and justice, inasmuch as science is not responsible for incorrect observation. At length they proceed another step. They lay the blame on society itself—they threaten to overthrow it for the purpose of reconstructing the edifice—and why? Because, say they, it is proved by science that society as now constituted is urged onwards to destruction. In this they outrage good sense—for either science is not mistaken, and then why attack it? Or it is mistaken, and in that case they should leave society in repose, since society is not menaced.

But these tactics, illogical as they are, have not been the less fatal to economic science, especially when the cultivators of that science have had the misfortune, from a chivalrous and not unnatural feeling, to render themselves liable, *singuli in solidum*, for their predecessors and for one another. Science is a queen whose gait should be frank and free—the atmosphere of the clique stifles her.

I have already said that in Political Economy every erroneous proposition must lead ultimately to antagonism. On the other hand, it is impossible that the voluminous works of even the most eminent economists should not include some erroneous propositions. It is ours to mark and to rectify them in the interest of science and of society. If we persist in maintaining them for the honor of the fraternity, we shall not only expose ourselves, which is of little consequence, but we shall expose truth itself, which is a serious affair, to the attacks of Socialism.

To return: the conclusion of the Economists is for Liberty. But in order that this conclusion should take hold of men's minds and hearts, it must be solidly based on this fundamental principle, that interests, left to themselves, tend to harmonious combinations, and to the progressive preponderance of the general good.

Now many Economists, some of them writers of authority, have advanced propositions, which, step by step, lead logically to absolute evil, necessary injustice, fatal and progressive inequality, and inevitable pauperism, etc.

Thus, there are very few of them who, so far as I know, have not attributed value to natural agents, to the gifts that God has vouchsafed gratuitously to his creatures. The word value implies that we do not give away the portion of it we possess except for an equivalent consideration. Here, then, we have men, especially proprietors of land, bartering for effective labor the gifts of God, and receiving recompense for utilities in the creation of which their labor has had no share—an evident, but a necessary, injustice, say these writers.

Then comes the famous theory of Ricardo, which may be summed up in a few words: The price of the necessaries of life depends on the labor required to produce them on the least productive land in cultivation. Then the increase of population obliges us to have recourse to soils of lower and lower fertility.

Consequently mankind at large (all except the landowners) are forced to give a larger and larger amount of labor for the same amount of subsistence; or, what comes to the same thing, to receive a less and less amount of subsistence for the same amount of labor—while the landowners see their rental swelling by every new descent to soils of an inferior quality. Conclusion: Progressive opulence of men of leisure—progressive poverty of men of labor; in other words, fatal inequality.

Finally, we have the still more celebrated theory of Malthus, that population has a tendency to increase more rapidly than the means of subsistence, and has done so every moment throughout time. Now, men cannot be happy, or live in peace, if they have not the means of support; and there are but two obstacles to this increase of population that is always threatening us, namely, a diminished number of births, or an increase of mortality in all its dreadful forms. Moral restraint, to be efficacious, must be universal, and no one expects that. There remains, then, only the

440 The Bastiat Collection

repressive obstacles—vice, poverty, war, pestilence, famine—in other words, pauperism and death.

I forbear to mention other systems of a less general scope, which tend in the same way to bring us to a dead-stand. Monsieur de Tocqueville, for example, and many others, tell us, if we admit the right of primogeniture, we arrive at the most concentrated aristocracy—if we do not admit it, we arrive at ruin and sterility.

And it is worthy of note that these four melancholy theories do not in the least degree run foul of each other. If they did, we might console ourselves with the reflection that they are alike false, since they refute each other. But no—they are in unison, and make part of one and the same general theory, which, supported by numerous and specious facts, would seem to explain the spasmodic state of modern society and, fortified by the assent of many masters in the science, presents itself with frightful authority to the mind of the confused and discouraged inquirer.

We have still to discover how the authors of this melancholy theory have been able to lay down as their principle the harmony of interests and as their conclusion, Liberty.

For if mankind is indeed urged on by the laws of Value toward Injustice; by the laws of Rent toward Inequality; by the laws of Population toward Poverty; by the laws of Inheritance toward Sterility—we can no longer affirm that God has made the moral as he has made the natural world—a harmonious work; we must bow the head, and confess that it has pleased Him to base it on revolting and irremediable dissonance.

You must not suppose, young men, that the socialists have refuted and repudiated what, in order to wound no one's susceptibilities, I shall call the theory of dissonances. No; let them say as they will, they have assumed the truth of that theory, and it is just because they have assumed its truth that they propose to substitute Constraint for Liberty, artificial for natural organization, their own inventions for the work of God. They say to their opponents (and in this, perhaps, they are more consistent than the latter)—if, as you have told us, human interests when left to themselves tend to harmonious combination, we cannot do better than welcome and magnify Liberty as you do. But you have demonstrated unanswerably that those interests, if allowed to develop themselves freely, urge mankind toward injustice, inequality, pauperism, and sterility. Your theory, then, provokes reaction precisely because it is true. We desire to break up the existing fabric of society just because it is subject to the fatal laws you have described; we wish to make trial of our own powers, seeing that the power of God has miscarried.

Thus they are agreed as regards the premises, and differ only on the conclusion.

The Economists to whom I have alluded say that the great providential laws urge on society to evil; but that we must take care not to disturb the action of those laws, because such action is happily impeded by the secondary laws that retard the final catastrophe; and arbitrary intervention can only weaken the embankment, without stopping the fatal rising of the flood.

The Socialists say that the great providential laws urge on society to evil; we must therefore abolish them, and select others from our inexhaustible storehouse.

The Catholics say that the great providential laws urge on society to evil; we must therefore escape from them by renouncing worldly interests, and taking refuge in abnegation, sacrifice, asceticism, and resignation.

It is in the midst of this tumult, of these cries of anguish and distress, of these exhortations to subversion, or to resignation and despair, that I endeavor to obtain a hearing for this assertion, in presence of which, if it be correct, all difference of opinion must disappear—it is not true that the great providential laws urge on society to evil.

It is with reference to the conclusions to be deduced from their common premises that the various schools are divided and combat each other. I deny those premises, and I ask, Is not that the best way of putting an end to these disputes?

The leading idea of this work, the harmony of interests, is simple. Is simplicity not the touchstone of truth? The laws of light, of sound, of motion, appear to us to be all the truer for being simple—Why should it be otherwise with the law of interests?

This idea is conciliatory. What is more fitted to reconcile parties than to demonstrate the harmony of the various branches of industry: the harmony of classes, of nations, even of doctrines?

It is consoling, seeing that it points out what is false in those systems that adopt, as their conclusion, progressive evil.

It is religious, for it assures us that it is not only the celestial but the social mechanism that reveals the wisdom of God, and declares His glory.

It is practical, for one can scarcely conceive anything more easily reduced to practice than this—to allow men to labor, to exchange, to learn, to associate, to act and react on each other—for, according to the laws of Providence, nothing can result from their intelligent spontaneity but order, harmony, progress, good, and better still; better ad infinitum.

Bravo, you will say; here we have the optimism of the Economists with a vengeance! These Economists are so much the slaves of their own systems that they shut their eyes to facts for fear of seeing them. In the face of all the poverty, all the injustice, all the oppressions that desolate humanity, they coolly deny the existence of evil. The smell of revolutionary gunpowder does not reach their blunted senses—the pavement of the barricades has no voice for them; and were society to crumble to pieces before their eyes, they would still keep repeating, "All is for the best in the best of worlds."

No indeed—we do not think that all is for the best; but I have faith in the wisdom of the laws of Providence, and for the same reason I have faith in Liberty.

The question is, Have we Liberty?

The question is, Do these laws act in their plenitude, or is their action not profoundly troubled by the countervailing action of human institutions?

Deny evil! deny suffering! Who can? We must forget that our subject is man. We must forget that we are ourselves men. The laws of Providence may be regarded as harmonious without their necessarily excluding evil. Enough that evil has its explanation and its mission, that it checks and limits itself, that it destroys itself by its own action, and that each suffering prevents a greater suffering by repressing the cause of suffering.

Society has for its element man, who is a free agent; and since man is free, he may choose—since he may choose, he may be mistaken—since he may be mistaken, he may suffer.

I go further. I say he must be mistaken and suffer—for he begins his journey in ignorance, and for ignorance there are endless and unknown roads, all of which, except one, lead to error.

Now, every Error engenders suffering; but either suffering reacts upon the man who errs, and then it brings Responsibility into play—or, if it affects others who are free from error, it sets in motion the marvellous reactionary machinery of Solidarity.

The action of these laws, combined with the faculty that has been vouchsafed to us of connecting effects with their causes, must bring us back, by means of this very suffering, into the way of what is good and true.

Thus, not only do we not deny the existence of evil, but we acknowledge that it has a mission in the social, as it has in the material world.

But in order that it should fulfill this mission, we must not stretch Solidarity artificially, so as to destroy Responsibility—in other words, we must respect Liberty.

Should human institutions step in to oppose in this respect the divine laws, evil would not the less flow from error, only it would shift its position. It would strike those whom it ought not to strike. It would be no longer a warning and a monitor. It would no longer have the tendency to diminish and die away by its own proper action. Its action would be continued, and increase, as would happen in the physiological world if the imprudences and excesses of the men of one hemisphere were felt in their unhappy effects only by the inhabitants of the opposite hemisphere.

Now this is precisely the tendency not only of most of our governmental institutions, but likewise, and above all, of those we seek to establish as remedies for the evils we suffer. Under the philanthropical pretext of developing among men a factitious Solidarity, we render Responsibility more and more inert and inefficacious. By an improper application of the public force, we alter the relation of labor to its remuneration, we disturb the laws of industry and of exchange, we offer violence to the natural development of education, we give a wrong direction to capital and labor, we twist and invert men's ideas, we inflame absurd pretensions, we dazzle with chimerical hopes, we occasion a strange loss of human energy, we change the centers of population, we render experience itself useless—in a word, we give to all interests artificial foundations, we turn them upside-down, and then we exclaim that—Interests are antagonistic: Liberty has done all the evil—let us denounce and stifle Liberty.

And yet, as this sacred word has still power to stir men's hearts and make them palpitate, we despoil Liberty of its prestige by depriving it of its name; and it is under the brand of Competition that it is led to the sacrificial altar, amid the applause of a mob stretching forth their hands to receive the shackles of servitude.

It is not enough, then, to exhibit, in their majestic harmony, the natural laws of the social order; we must also explain the disturbing causes that paralyze their action; and this is what I have endeavored to do in the second part of this work.

I have striven to avoid controversy; and, in doing so, I have no doubt lost an opportunity of giving to the principles I desire to disseminate the stability that results from a thorough and searching discussion. And yet, might not the attention of the reader, seduced by digressions, have been diverted from the argument taken as a whole? If I exhibit the edifice as it stands, what matters it in what light it has been regarded by others, even by those who first taught me to look at it?

And now I would appeal with confidence to men of all schools who prefer truth, justice, and the pubic good to their own systems.

Economists! Like you, I am the advocate of LIBERTY; and if I succeed in shaking some of those premises that sadden your generous hearts, perhaps you will see in this an additional incentive to love and to serve our sacred cause.

Socialists! You have faith in ASSOCIATION. I entreat you, after having read this book, to say whether society as it is now constituted, apart from its abuses and shackles, that is to say, under the condition of Liberty, is not the most beautiful, the most complete, the most durable, the most universal, the most equitable, of all Associations.

Egalitarians! You admit but one principle, the MUTUALITY OF SERVICES. Let human transactions be free, and I assert that they are not and cannot be anything else than a reciprocal exchange of services—services always diminishing in price, always increasing in utility.

Communists! You desire that men, having become brothers, should enjoy in common the goods that Providence has lavished on them. My aim is to demonstrate that society as it exists has only to acquire freedom in order to realize and surpass your wishes and your hopes. For all things are common to all, on the single condition that each man takes the trouble to gather what God has given, which is very natural; or remunerate freely those who take that trouble for him, which is very just.

Christians of all communions! Unless you stand alone in casting doubt on the divine wisdom, manifested in the most magnificent of all God's works that have come within the range of our knowledge, you will find in this book no expression that can shock even the severest morals, or the most sacred dogmas of your faith.

Proprietors! Whatever be the extent of your possessions, if I establish that your rights, now so much contested, are limited, like those of the most ordinary workman, to the receiving of services in exchange for real and substantial services that have been actually rendered by you, or by your forefathers, those rights will henceforth repose on a basis that cannot be shaken.

Proletaires! Men who live by wages! I undertake to demonstrate that you obtain the fruits of the land of which you are not the owners with less pain and effort than if you were obliged to raise those fruits by your own direct labor—with less than if that land had been given to you in its primitive state, and before being prepared for cultivation by labor.

Capitalists and laborers! I believe myself in a position to establish the law that, in proportion as capital is accumulated, the absolute share of the total product falling to the capitalist increases, and his proportional share is diminished; while both the absolute and relative share of the product falling to the laborer is augmented—the reverse effects being produced when capital is lessened or dissipated.[2] If this law be established, the obvious deduction is, a harmony of interests between laborers and those who employ them.

Disciples of Malthus! Sincere and calumniated philanthropists, whose only fault has been in warning mankind against the effects of a law you believe to be fatal, I shall have to submit to you another law more reassuring: "Ceteris paribus, increasing density of population is equivalent to increasing facility of production." And if it be so, I am certain it will not be you who will grieve to see a stumbling block removed from the threshold of our favorite science.

Men of spoliation! You who, by force or fraud, by law or in spite of law, batten on the people's substance; you who live by the errors you propagate, by the ignorance you cherish, by the wars you light up, by the trammels with which you hamper trade; you who tax labor after having rendered it unproductive, making it

---

[2]I shall explain this law by figures: Suppose three periods during which capital increases, labor remaining the same. Let the total production at these three periods be as 80—100—120. It will be thus divided:

	Capitalist's share	Laborer Share	Total
First Period	45	35	80
Second Period	50	50	100
Third Period	55	65	120

Of course these proportions are merely given for the sake of illustration.

lose an armload for every handful you yourselves pluck from it; you who cause yourselves to be paid for creating obstacles, in order to get afterwards paid for partially removing those obstacles; incarnations of selfishness in its worst sense; parasitical excrescences of a vicious policy, prepare for the sharpest and most unsparing criticism. To you, alone, I make no appeal, for the design of this book is to sacrifice you, or rather to sacrifice your unjust pretensions. In vain we cherish conciliation. There are two principles that can never be reconciled—Liberty and Constraint.

If the laws of Providence are harmonious, it is when they act with freedom, without which there is no harmony. Whenever, then, we remark an absence of harmony, we may be sure that it proceeds from an absence of liberty, an absence of justice. Oppressors, spoliators, contempters of justice, you can have no part in the universal harmony, for it is you who disturb it.

Do I mean to say that the effect of this work may be to enfeeble power, to shake its stability, to diminish its authority? My design is just the opposite. But let me not be misunderstood.

It is the business of political science to distinguish between what ought and what ought not to fall under State control; and in making this important distinction we must not forget that the State always acts through the intervention of Force. The services it renders us, and the services it exacts from us in return, are alike imposed upon us under the name of contributions.

The question then comes back to this: What are the things that men have a right to impose upon each other by force? Now I know but one thing in this situation, and that is Justice. I have no right to force any one whatever to be religious, charitable, well educated, or industrious; but I have a right to force him to be just—this is a case of legitimate defense.

Now, individuals in the aggregate can possess no right that did not pre-exist in individuals as such. If, then, the employment of individual force is justified only by legitimate defense, the fact that the action of government is always manifested by Force should lead us to conclude that it is essentially limited to the maintenance of order, security, and justice.

All action of governments beyond this limit is a usurpation upon conscience, upon intelligence, upon industry; in a word, upon human Liberty.

This being granted, we ought to set ourselves unceasingly and without compunction to emancipate the entire domain of private enterprise from the encroachments of power. Without this we shall not have gained Freedom, or the free play of those laws of harmony God has provided for the development and progress of the human race.

Will Power by this means be enfeebled? Will it have lost in stability because it has lost in extent? Will it have less authority because it has fewer functions to discharge? Will it attract to itself less respect because it calls forth fewer complaints? Will it be more the sport of factions when it has reduced those enormous budgets and that coveted influence which are the baits and allurements of faction? Will it encounter greater danger when it has less responsibility?

To me it seems evident that to confine public force to its one, essential, undisputed, beneficent mission—a mission desired and accepted by all—would be the surest way of securing to it respect and universal support. In that case, I see not whence could proceed systematic opposition, parliamentary struggles, street insurrections, revolutions, sudden changes of fortune, factions, illusions, the pretensions of all to govern under all forms, those dangerous and absurd systems that teach the people to look to government for everything, that compromising diplomacy, those wars that are always in perspective, or armed truces that are nearly as fatal, those crushing taxes that it is impossible to levy on any equitable principle, that absorbing and unnatural mixing up of politics with everything, those great artificial displacements of capital and labor, which are the source of fruitless heartburnings, fluctuations, stoppages, and commercial crises. All those causes of trouble, of irritation, of disaffection, of covetousness, and of disorder, and a thousand others, would no longer have any foundation, and the depositaries of power, instead of disturbing, would contribute to the universal harmony—a harmony that does not indeed exclude evil, but that leaves less and less room for those ills that are inseparable from the ignorance and perversity of our feeble nature, and whose mission it is to prevent or chastise that ignorance and perversity.

Young men! In these days in which a grievous skepticism would seem to be at once the effect and the punishment of the anarchy of ideas that prevails, I shall esteem myself happy if this work, as you proceed in its perusal, should bring to your lips the consoling words, I BELIEVE—words of a sweet-smelling savor, which are at once a refuge and a force, which are said to move mountains, and stand at the head of the Christian's creed—I believe. "I believe, not with a blind and submissive faith, for we are not concerned here with the mysteries of revelation, but with a rational and scientific faith, befitting things that are left to man's investigation. I believe that He who has arranged the material universe has not withheld His regards from the arrangements of the social world. I believe that He has combined, and caused to move in harmony, free agents as well as inert molecules. I believe that His over-ruling Providence shines forth as strikingly, if not more so, in the laws to which He has subjected men's interests and men's wills, as in the laws He has imposed on weight and velocity. I believe that everything in human society, even what is apparently injurious, is the cause of improvement and of progress. I believe that Evil tends to Good, and calls it forth, whilst Good cannot tend to Evil; whence it follows that Good must in the end predominate. I believe that the invincible social tendency is a constant approximation of men toward a common moral, intellectual, and physical level, with, at the same time, a progressive and indefinite elevation of that level. I believe that all that is necessary to the gradual and peaceful development of humanity is that its tendencies should not be disturbed, but have the liberty of their movements restored. I believe these things, not because I desire them, not because they satisfy my heart, but because my judgment accords to them a deliberate assent."

Ah! Whenever you come to pronounce these words, I BELIEVE, you will be anxious to propagate your creed, and the social problem will soon be resolved, for let them say what they will, it is not of difficult solution. Men's interests are harmonious—the solution then lies entirely in this one word—LIBERTY.

1

NATURAL AND ARTIFICIAL ORGANIZATION[1]

Is it quite certain that the mechanism of society, like the mechanism of the heavenly bodies, or that of the human frame, is subject to general laws? Does it form a harmoniously organized whole? Or rather, do we not note in it the absence of all organization? Is not an organization the very thing which all men of heart and of the future, all advanced publicists, all the pioneers of thought are in search of at the present day? Is society anything else than a multitude of individuals placed in juxtaposition, acting without concert, and given up to the movements of an anarchical liberty? Are our countless masses, after having with difficulty recovered their liberties one after the other, not now awaiting the advent of some great genius to arrange them into a harmonious whole? Having pulled down all, must we not now set about laying the foundation of a new edifice?

---

[1]This chapter was first published in the *Journal des Economistes*, January 1848.

And yet, it may be asked, have these questions any other meaning than this: Can society dispense with written laws, rules, and repressive measures? Is every man to make an unlimited use of his faculties, even when in so doing he strikes at the liberties of another, or inflicts injury on society at large? In a word, must we recognize in the maxim, *laissez faire, laissez passer*, the absolute formula of political economy? If that were the question, no one could hesitate about the solution. The economists do not say that a man may kill, sack, burn, and that society has only to be quiescent—*laissez faire*. They say that even in the absence of all law, society would resist such acts; and that consequently such resistance is a general law of humanity. They say that civil and penal laws must regulate, and not counteract, those general laws the existence of which they presuppose. There is a wide difference between a social organization founded on the general laws of human nature, and an artificial organization, invented, imagined—that takes no account of these laws, or repudiates and despises them—such an organization, in short, as many modern schools would impose upon us.

For, if there be general laws that act independently of written laws, and of which the latter can only regulate the action, we must study these general laws. They can be made the object of a science, and Political Economy exists. If, on the other hand, society is a human invention, if men are regarded only as inert matter, to which a great genius, like Rousseau, must impart sentiment and will, movement and life, then there is no such science as Political Economy. There are only an indefinite number of possible and contingent arrangements, and the fate of nations must depend upon the Founder to whom chance shall have committed their destinies.

In order to prove that society is subject to general laws, no elaborate dissertation is necessary. All I shall do is to notice certain facts that, although trite, are not the less important.

Rousseau has said, "*Il faut beaucoup de philosophie pour observer les faits qui sont trop pres de nous*"—"Much philosophy is needed for the correct observation of things which are before our eyes," And such are the social phenomena in the midst of which we live and move. Habit has so familiarized us with these phenomena that we cease to observe them, unless something striking and exceptional forces them on our attention.

Let us take, by way of illustration, a man in the humble walks of life—a village carpenter, for instance—and observe the various services he renders to society, and receives from it; we shall not fail to be struck with the enormous disproportion that is apparent.

This man employs his day's labor in planing boards, and making tables and chests of drawers. He complains of his condition; yet in truth what does he receive from society in exchange for his work?

First of all, on getting up in the morning, he dresses himself; and he has himself personally made none of the numerous articles of which his clothing consists. Now, in order to put at his disposal this clothing, simple as it is, an enormous amount of labor, industry, and locomotion, and many ingenious inventions, must have been employed. Americans must have produced cotton, Indians indigo, Frenchmen wool and flax, Brazilians hides; and all these materials must have been transported to various towns where they have been worked up, spun, woven, dyed, etc.

Then he breakfasts. In order to procure him the bread he eats every morning, land must have been cleared, enclosed, labored, manured, sown; the fruits of the soil must have been preserved with care from pillage, and security must have reigned among an innumerable multitude of people; the wheat must have been cut down, ground into flour, kneaded, and prepared; iron, steel, wood, stone, must have been converted by industry into instruments of labor; some men must have employed animal force, others water power, etc.; all matters of which each, taken singly, presupposes a mass of labor, whether we have regard to space or time, of incalculable amount.

In the course of the day this man will have occasion to use sugar, oil, and various other materials and utensils.

He sends his son to school, there to receive an education, which, although limited, nevertheless implies anterior study and research, and an extent of knowledge that startles the imagination.

He goes out. He finds the street paved and lighted.

A neighbor sues him. He finds advocates to plead his cause, judges to maintain his rights, officers of justice to put the sentence in execution; all which implies acquired knowledge, and, consequently, intelligence and means of subsistence.

He goes to church. It is a stupendous monument, and the book he carries thither is a monument, perhaps still more Stupendous, of human intelligence. He is taught morals, he has his mind enlightened, his soul elevated; and in order to do this we must suppose that another man had previously frequented schools and libraries, consulted all the sources of human learning, and while so employed had been able to live without occupying himself directly with the wants of the body.

If our artisan undertakes a journey, he finds that, in order to save him time and exertion, other men have removed and levelled the soil, filled up valleys, hewed down mountains, united the banks of rivers, diminished friction, placed wheeled carriages on blocks of sandstone or bands of iron, and brought the force of animals and the power of steam into subjection to human wants.

It is impossible not to be struck with the measureless disproportion between the enjoyments which this man derives from society and what he could obtain by his own unassisted exertions. I venture to say that in a single day he consumes more than he could himself produce in ten centuries.

What renders the phenomenon still more strange is that all other men are in the same situation. Every individual member of society has absorbed millions of times more than he could himself produce; yet there is no mutual robbery. And, if we regard things more nearly, we perceive that the carpenter has paid, in services, for all the services others have rendered to him. If we bring the matter to a strict reckoning, we shall be convinced that he has received nothing he has not paid for by means of his modest industry; and that everyone who, at whatever interval of time or space, has been employed in his service, has received, or will receive, his remuneration.

The social mechanism, then, must be very ingenious and very powerful, since it leads to this singular result, that each man, even he whose lot is cast in the humblest condition, has more enjoyment in one day than he could himself produce in many ages.

Nor is this all. The mechanism of society will appear still more ingenious if the reader will be pleased to turn his regards upon himself.

I suppose him a plain student. What is his business in Paris? How does he live? It cannot be disputed that society places at his disposal food, clothing, lodging, amusements, books, means of instruction, a multitude of things, in short, that would take a long time not only to produce, but even to explain how they were produced. And what services has this student rendered to society in return for all these things that have exacted so much labor, toil, fatigue, physical and intellectual effort, so many inventions, transactions, and conveyances hither and thither? None at all. He is only preparing to render services. Why, then, have so many millions of men abandoned to him the fruits of their positive, effective, and productive labor? Here is the explanation: The father of this student, who was a lawyer, perhaps, or a physician, or a merchant, had formerly rendered services—it may be to society in China—and had been remunerated, not by immediate services, but by a title to demand services, at the time, in the place and under the form that might be most suitable and convenient to him. It is of these past and distant services that society is now acquitting itself, and (astonishing as it seems) if we follow in thought the infinite range of transactions that must have taken place in order for this result to be effected, we shall see that every one has been remunerated for his labor and services; and that these titles have passed from hand to hand, sometimes divided into parts, sometimes grouped together, until, in the consumption of this student, the entire account has been squared and balanced. Is not this a very remarkable phenomenon?

We should shut our eyes to the light of day, did we fail to perceive that society could not present combinations so complicated, and in which civil and penal laws have so little part, unless it obeyed the laws of a mechanism wonderfully ingenious. The study of that mechanism is the business of Political Economy.

Another thing worthy of observation is, that of the incalculable number of transactions to which the student owed his daily subsistence, there was not perhaps a millionth part that contributed to it directly. The things of which he has now the enjoyment, and which are innumerable, were produced by men the greater part of whom have long since disappeared from the earth. And yet they were remunerated as they expected to be, although he who now profits by the fruit of their labors had done nothing for them. They knew him not; they will never know him. He who reads this page, at the very moment he is reading it, has the power, although perhaps he has no consciousness of it, to put in motion men of every country, of all races, I had almost said of all time—white, black, red, tawny—to make bygone generations, and generations still unborn, contribute to his present enjoyments; and he owes this extraordinary power to the services his father had formerly rendered to other men, who apparently had nothing in common with those whose labor is now put in requisition. Yet despite all differences of time and space, so just and equitable a balance has been struck that every one has been remunerated, and has received exactly what he calculated he ought to receive.

But, in truth, could all this have happened, and such phenomena been witnessed, unless society had had a natural and wise organization, which acts, as it were, unknown to us?

Much has been said in our day of inventing a new organization. Is it quite certain that any thinker, whatever genius we may attribute to him, whatever power we may suppose him to possess, could imagine and introduce an organization superior to that of which I have just sketched some of the results?

But what would be thought of it if I described its machinery, its springs, and its motive powers?

The machinery consists of men, that is to say, of beings capable of learning, reflecting, reasoning, of being deceived and undeceived, and consequently of contributing to the amelioration or deterioration of the mechanism itself. They are capable of pleasure and pain; and it is that which makes them not only the wheels but the springs of the mechanism. They are also the motive power; for it is in them that the active principle resides. More than that, they are themselves the very end and object of the mechanism, since it is into individual pains and enjoyments that the whole definitely resolves itself.

Now it has been remarked, and it is unhappily obvious enough, that in the action, the development, and even the progress (by those who acknowledge progress) of this powerful mechanism, many of the wheels have been inevitably, fatally injured; and that, as regards a great number of human beings, the sum of unmerited suffering surpasses by much the sum of enjoyment.

This view of the subject has led many candid minds, many generous hearts, to suspect the mechanism itself. They have repudiated it, they have refused to study it, they have attacked, often with passion, those who have investigated and explained its laws. They have risen against the nature of things, and at length they have proposed to organize society upon a new plan, in which injustice and suffering and error shall have no place.

God forbid that I should set myself against intentions manifestly pure and philanthropical! But I should desert my principles, and do violence to the dictates of my own conscience, did I not declare that these men are in my opinion upon a wrong path.

In the first place, they are reduced, by the very nature of their postulates, to the melancholy necessity of disowning the good that society develops, of denying its progress, of imputing to it all sufferings, of hunting after these with avidity, and exaggerating them beyond measure.

When a man believes that he has discovered a social organization different from that which results from the ordinary tendencies of human nature, it is quite necessary, in order to obtain acceptance for his invention, to paint the organization he wishes to abolish in the most somber color. Thus the publicists to whom I am alluding, after having proclaimed enthusiastically, and perhaps with exaggeration, the perfectibility of man, fall into the strange contradiction of maintaining that society is becoming more and more deteriorated. According to them, men are a thousand times more unhappy than they were in ancient times under the feudal regime, and the yoke of slavery. The world is become a hell. Were it possible to conjure up the Paris of the tenth century, I venture to think that such a thesis would be found untenable.

Then they are led to condemn the very mainspring of human action—I mean a regard to personal interest, because it has brought about such a state of things. Let us note that man is so organized as to seek enjoyment and avoid suffering. From this source I allow that all social evils take their rise—war, slavery, monopoly, privilege; but from the same source springs all that is good, since the satisfaction of wants and repugnance to suffering are the motives of human action. The business then is to discover whether this incitement to action, by its universality—from individual becoming social—is not in itself a principle of progress.

At all events, do the inventors of new organizations not perceive that this principle, inherent in the very nature of man, will follow them into their systems, and that there it will make greater havoc than in our natural organization, in which the interest and unjust pretensions of one are at least restrained by the resistance of all? These writers always make two inadmissible suppositions—the first is, that society, such as they conceive it, will be directed by infallible men denuded of their motive of self-interest; and, second, that the masses will allow themselves to be directed by these men.

Finally, these system-makers appear to give themselves no trouble about the means of execution. How are they to establish their system? How are they to induce all mankind at once to give up the principle upon which they now act—the attraction of enjoyment, and the repugnance to pain? It would be necessary, as

Rousseau has said, to change the moral and physical constitution of man.

In order to induce men at once to throw aside, as a worn-out garment, the existing social order in which the human race has lived and been developed from the beginning to our day, to adopt an organization of human invention and become docile parts of another mechanism, there are, it seems to me, only two means which can be employed—Force, or Universal Consent.

The founder of the new system must have at his disposal a force capable of overcoming all resistance, so that humanity shall be in his hands only as so much melting wax to be molded and fashioned at his pleasure—or he must obtain by persuasion an assent so complete, so exclusive, so blind even, as to render unnecessary the employment of force.

I defy anyone to point out to me a third means of establishing or introducing into human practice a Phalanstere,[2] or any other artificial social organization.

Now, if there be only two assumed means, and if we have demonstrated that the one is as impracticable as the other, we have proved that these system-makers are losing both their time and their trouble.

As regards the command of a material force that should subject to them all the kings and peoples of the earth, this is what these dotards, senile as they are, have never dreamt of. King Alphonsus had presumption and folly enough to exclaim, that "If he had been taken into God's counsels, the planetary system should have been better arranged." But although he set his wisdom above that of the Creator, he was not mad enough to wish to struggle with the power of Omnipotence, and history does not tell us that he ever actually tried to make the stars turn according to the laws of his invention. Descartes likewise contented himself

---

[2] Allusion to a socialist work of the day—"La Reforme industrielle, ou la Phalanstere, by Ch. Fourier."—Translator.

with constructing a tiny world with dice and strings, knowing well that he was not strong enough to move the universe. We know no one but Xerxes who, in the intoxication of his power, dared to say to the waves, "Thus far shall ye come, and no farther." The billows did not recede before Xerxes but Xerxes retreated before the billows; and without this humiliating but wise precaution he would certainly have been drowned.

Force, then, is what the organizers need who would subject humanity to their experiments. When they shall have gained over to their cause the Russian autocrat, the shah of Persia, the khan of Tartary, and all the other tyrants of the world, they will find that they still lack the power to distribute mankind into groups and classes, and to annihilate the general laws of property, exchange, inheritance, and family; for even in Russia, in Persia, and in Tartary, it is necessary to a certain extent to consult the feelings, habits, and prejudices of the people. Were the emperor of Russia to take it into his head to set about altering the moral and physical constitution of his subjects, it is probable that he would soon have a successor, and that his successor would be better advised than to continue the experiment.

But since force is a means quite beyond the reach of our numerous system-makers, no other resource remains to them but to obtain universal consent.

There are two modes of obtaining this—namely, Persuasion and Imposture.

Persuasion! But have we ever found two minds in perfect accord upon all the points of a single science? How then are we to expect men of various tongues, races, and manners, spread over the surface of the globe, most of them unable to read, and destined to die without having even heard the name of the reformer, to accept with unanimity the universal science? What is it that you aim at? At changing the whole system of labor, exchanges, and social relations, domestic, civil, and religious; in a word, at altering the whole physical and moral constitution of man; and you hope to rally mankind, and bring them all under this new order of things, by conviction!

Verily you undertake no light or easy duty.

When a man has the task of saying to his fellows:

"For the last five thousand years there has been a misunderstanding between God and man;

"From the days of Adam to our time, the human race has been upon a wrong course—and, if only a little confidence is placed in me, I shall soon bring them back to the right way;

"God desired mankind to pursue a different road altogether, but they have taken their own way, and hence evil has been introduced into the world. Let them turn round at my call, and take an opposite direction, and universal happiness will then prevail."

When a man sets out in this style it is much if he is believed by five or six adepts; but between that and being believed by one thousand millions of men the distance is great indeed.

And then, remember that the number of social inventions is as vast as the domain of the imagination itself; that there is not a publicist or writer on social economy who, after shutting himself up for a few hours in his library, does not come forth with a ready-made plan of artificial organization in his hand; that the inventions of Fourier, Saint Simon, Owen, Cabet, Blanc, etc., have no resemblance whatever to each other; that every day brings to light a new scheme; and that people are entitled to have some little time given them for reflection before they are called upon to reject the social organization God has vouchsafed them, and to make a definite and irrevocable choice among so many newly invented systems. For what would happen if, after having selected one of these plans, a better one should present itself! Can the institutions of property, family, labor, exchange, be placed every day upon a new basis? Are we to be forced to change the organization of society every morning?

"Thus, then," says Rousseau, "the legislator being able to employ effectively neither force nor persuasion, he is under the necessity of having recourse to an authority of another kind, which carries us along without violence, and persuades without convincing us."

What is that authority? Imposture. Rousseau dares not give utterance to the word, but, according to his invariable practice in such a case, he places it behind the transparent veil of an eloquent tirade.

"This is the reason," says he, "which in all ages has forced the Fathers of nations to have recourse to the intervention of heaven, and to give the credit of their own wisdom to the gods, in order that the people, submitting to the laws of the state as to those of nature, and acknowledging the same power in the formation of man and of the commonwealth, should obey freely and bear willingly the yoke of the public felicity. This sublime reason, which is above the reach of vulgar souls, is that whose decisions the legislator puts into the mouth of the immortals, in order to carry along by divine authority those who cannot be moved by considerations of human prudence. But it is not for every man to make the gods speak," etc.

And in order that there may be no mistake, he cites Machiavelli, and allows him to complete the idea: "*Mai non fu alcuno ordinatore de leggi STRAORDINARIE in un popolo che non ricorresse a Dio.*"

But why does Machiavelli counsel us to have recourse to God, and Rousseau to the gods, to the immortals? The reader can answer that question for himself.

I do not indeed accuse the modern Fathers of nations of making use of these unworthy deceptions. But when we place ourselves in their point of view, we see that they readily allow themselves to be hurried along by the desire of success. When an earnest and philanthropical man is deeply convinced that he possesses a social secret by means of which all his fellow men may enjoy in this world unlimited happiness—when he sees clearly that he can practically establish that idea neither by force nor by reasoning, and that deception is his only resource, he is laid under a very strong temptation. We know that the ministers of religion themselves, who profess the greatest horror of untruth, have not rejected pious frauds; and we see by the example of Rousseau (that austere writer who has inscribed at the head of all his works the motto, *Vitam impendere vero*), that even a proud philosophy can allow itself to be seduced by the attraction of a very different maxim, namely, The end justifies the means. Why then should we be so surprised that modern organisateurs should think also "to place their own wisdom to the credit of the gods, to put their decisions in the mouths of the immortals, hurrying us along without violence, and persuading without convincing us!"

We know that, after the example of Moses, Fourier has preceded his Deuteronomy by a Genesis. Saint Simon and his disciples had gone still farther in their apostolic dotages. Others, more discreet, attached themselves to a latitudinarian faith, modified to suit their views, under the name of New Christianity; and every one must be struck with the tone of mystic affectation that nearly all our modern reformers have introduced into their sermons.

Efforts of this kind have served only to prove one thing, and it is not unimportant—namely, that in our days the man is not always a prophet who wishes to be one. In vain he proclaims himself a god; he is believed by no one; neither by the public, nor by his fellows, nor by himself.

Since I have spoken of Rousseau, I may be permitted to make here some observations on that manufacturer of systems, inasmuch as they will serve to point out the distinctions between artificial and natural organization. This digression, besides, is not out of place, as the Contrat Social has again for some time been held forth as the oracle of the future.

Rousseau was convinced that isolation was man's natural state, and, consequently, that society was a human invention. "The social order," he says in the outset, "comes not from nature, and is therefore founded on convention."

This philosopher, although a passionate lover of liberty, had a very low opinion of men. He believed them to be quite incapable of forming for themselves good institutions. The intervention of a founder, a legislator, a father of nations, was therefore indispensable.

"A people subjected to laws," says he, "should be the authors of them. It belongs alone to those who associate to adjust the conditions of their association; but how are they to regulate them? By common consent, or by sudden inspiration? How should a blind multitude, who frequently know not what they want, because they rarely know what is good for them, accomplish of themselves an enterprise so great and so difficult as the formation of a system of laws? . . . Individuals perceive what is good, and reject it—the public wishes for what is good, but cannot discover it—all are equally in want of guides. . . . Hence the necessity of a legislator."

That legislator, as we have already seen, "not being able to employ force or reason, is under the necessity of having recourse to an authority of another kind;" that is to say, in plain terms, to deception.

It is impossible to give an idea of the immense height at which Rousseau places his legislator above other men:

"Gods would be necessary in order to give laws to men. . . . He who dares to found a nation must feel himself in a condition to change human nature, so to speak . . . to alter the constitution of man in order to strengthen it. . . . He must take from man his own force, in order to give him that which is foreign to him. . . . The lawgiver is in all respects an extraordinary man in the estate . . . his employment is a peculiar and superior function that has nothing in common with ordinary government. . . . If it be true that a great prince is a rare character, what must a great lawgiver be? The first has only to follow the model the other is to propose to him. The one is the mechanician who invents the machine—the other merely puts it together and sets it in motion."

And what is the part assigned to human nature in all this? It is but the base material of which the machine is composed.

In sober reality, is this anything else than pride elevated to madness? Men are the materials of a machine, which the prince, the ruling power, sets in motion. The lawgiver proposes the model. The philosopher governs the lawgiver, placing himself thus at an immeasurable distance above the vulgar herd, above the ruler, above the lawgiver himself. He soars far above the human race, actuates it, transforms it, moulds it, or rather he teaches the Fathers of nations how they are to do all this.

But the founder of a nation must propose to himself a design. He has his human material to set in motion, and he must direct its movements to a definite result. As the people are deprived of the initiative, and all depends upon the legislator, he must decide whether the nation is to be commercial or agricultural, or a barbarous race of hunters and fishers; but it is desirable at the same time that the legislator should not himself be mistaken, and so do too much violence to the nature of things.

Men in agreeing to enter into an association, or rather in associating under the fiat of a lawgiver, have a precise and definite design. "Thus," says Rousseau, "the Hebrews, and, more recently, the Arabs, had for their principal object religion; the Athenians, letters; Carthage and Tyre, commerce; Rhodes, navigation; Sparta, war; and Rome, virtue."

What object is to determine us Frenchmen to leave the state of isolation and of nature, in order to form a society? Or rather—as we are only so much inert matter; the materials of a machine—toward what object shall our great founder direct us?

Following the ideas of Rousseau, there could be but little room for learning, commerce, or navigation. War is a nobler object, and virtue still more so. But there is another, the noblest of all: "The end of every system of legislation is liberty and equality."

But we must first of all discover what Rousseau understands by liberty. To enjoy liberty, according to him, is not to be free, but to exercise the suffrage, when we are "borne along without violence, and persuaded without being convinced;" for then "we obey with freedom, and bear willingly the yoke of the public felicity."

"Among the Greeks," he says, "all that the people had to do they did for themselves; they were constantly assembled in the market-place; they inhabited a genial climate; they were not avaricious; slaves did all their work; their grand concern was their liberty."

"The English people," he remarks in another place, "believe themselves free—they are much mistaken. They are so only during the election of their members of parliament; the moment the election is over, they are slaves—they are nothing."

The people, if they will be free, must, then, themselves perform all duties in connection with the public service, for it is in that that liberty consists. They must be always voting and electing, always in the market-place. Woe to him who takes it into his head to work for his living! The moment a citizen begins to mind his own affairs, that instant (to use Rousseau's favorite phrase) *tout est perdu*—all is over with him.

And yet the difficulty is by no means trifling. How are we to manage? for, after all, before we can either practice virtue or exercise liberty, we must have the means of living.

We have already noted the rhetorical veil under which Rousseau conceals the word Imposture. We shall now see how, by another dash of eloquence, he evades the conclusion of his whole work, which is Slavery.

"Your ungenial climate imposes upon you additional wants. For six months of the year you cannot frequent the marketplace, your hoarse voices cannot make themselves audible in the open air, and you fear poverty more than slavery."

"You see clearly that you cannot be free."

"What! Liberty maintain itself only by the aid of servitude? Very likely!"

Had Rousseau stopped short at this dreadful word, the reader would have been shocked. It was necessary therefore to have recourse to imposing declamation, and Rousseau never fails in that.

"All things that are unnatural (it is society he is speaking of) are inconvenient, and civil society more so than all the rest. There are unfortunate situations in which one man cannot maintain his liberty but at the expense of another, and where the citizen cannot be entirely free unless the rigors of slavery are extreme. As for you, modern people, you have no slavery, but you are yourselves slaves. You purchase other men's liberties with your own. In vain you boast of this choice—I see in it rather cowardice than humanity."

I ask, does not this mean: Modern people, you would do infinitely better not to be slaves, but to possess slaves?

I trust the reader will have the goodness to pardon this long digression, which is by no means useless or inopportune. Rousseau and his disciples of the Convention have been held up to us of late as the apostles of human fraternity. Men for materials, a ruler for mechanician, a father of nations for inventor, a philosopher above them all—imposture for means, slavery for result—is this the fraternity that is promised us?

This work of Rousseau to which I have referred—the "Contrat Social"—appears to me well fitted to exhibit the characteristics of these artificial social organizations. The inventors of such systems set out with the idea that society is a state contrary to nature, and they seek to subject humanity to different combinations. They forget that its motive power, its spring of action, is in itself. They regard men as base materials, and aspire to impart to them movement and will, sentiment and life; placing themselves at an immeasurable height above the whole human race. These are features common to all the inventors of social organizations. The inventions are different—the inventors are alike.

Among the new arrangements that feeble mortals are invited to make trial of, there is one that is presented to us in terms worthy of attention. Its formula is: Association voluntary and progressive.

But Political Economy is founded exactly on the datum that society is nothing else than association (such as the above three words describe it)—association, very imperfect at first, because man is imperfect; but improving as man improves, that is to say, progressive.

Is your object to effect a more intimate association between labor, capital, and talent, insuring thereby to the members of the human family a greater amount of material enjoyment—enjoyment more equally distributed? If such associations are voluntary; if force and constraint do not intervene; if the cost is defrayed by those who enter these associations, without drawing upon those who refuse to enter them, in what respect are they repugnant to Political Economy? Is it not the business of Political Economy, as a science, to examine the various forms in which men may unite their powers, and divide their employments, with a view to greater and more widely diffused prosperity? Does trade not frequently afford us examples of two, three, or four persons uniting to form such associations? Is Metayage[3] not a sort of informal association of capital and labor? Have we not in recent times seen joint stock companies formed that afford to the smallest capitals the opportunity of taking part in the most extensive enterprises? Have we not certain manufactures in which it is sought to give the laborers an interest in the profits? Does Political Economy condemn those efforts of men to make their industry more productive and profitable? Does she affirm anywhere that human nature has reached perfection? Quite the contrary. I believe that there is no science that demonstrates more clearly that society is still in its infancy.

But whatever hopes we may entertain as to the future, whatever ideas we may conceive as to the measures that men may adopt for the improvement of their mutual relations, and the diffusion of happiness, knowledge, and morality, we must never forget that society is an organization that has for its element a moral and intelligent agent, endowed with free will and susceptible of improvement. If you take away Liberty from man, he becomes nothing else than a rude and wretched machine.

Liberty would seem not to be lacking in our days. In France, the privileged land of fads, freedom appears to be no longer in repute. For myself, I say that he who rejects liberty has no faith in human nature. Of late the distressing discovery seems to have

---

[3]Metayage is a mode of sharecropping farms in the south of Europe where the landlord furnishes a proportion of the means of cultivation, and shares the produce with the cultivator, or metayer.—Translator.

been made that liberty leads inevitably to monopoly. This monstrous union, this unnatural conjunction, does not exist; it is the imaginary fruit of an error that the light of Political Economy speedily dissipates. Freedom engender monopoly! Oppression the offspring of liberty! To affirm this is to affirm that the tendencies of human nature are radically bad—bad in themselves, in their nature, in their essence. It is to affirm that the natural bent of man is to deterioration; that the human mind is irresistibly attracted toward error. To what end, then, our schools, our studies, our inquiries, our discussions, unless to accelerate our progress toward that fatal descent; since to teach men to judge, to distinguish, to select, is only to teach them to commit suicide. And if the tendencies of human nature are essentially perverse, where are the organizers of new social systems to place the fulcrum of that lever by which they hope to effect their changes? It must be somewhere beyond the limits of the present domain of humanity. Do they search for it in themselves—in their own minds and hearts? They are not gods yet; they are men, and tending, consequently, along with the whole human race, toward the fatal abyss. Shall they invoke the intervention of the state? The state also is composed of men. They must therefore prove that they form a distinct class, for whom the general laws of society are not intended, since it is their province to make these laws. Unless this be proved, the difficulty is not removed, it is not even diminished.

Let us not thus condemn human nature before studying its laws, its forces, its energies, its tendencies. Newton, after he discovered attraction, never pronounced the name of God without uncovering his head. Yet the celestial mechanism is subject to laws of which it has no consciousness; and the social world is as much superior to that which called forth the admiration of Newton as mind is superior to matter. How much more reason, then, have we to bow before Omniscience when we behold the social mechanism, which universal intelligence no less pervades (*mens agitat molem*); and which presents, moreover, this extraordinary phenomenon, that every atom of which it is composed is an animated thinking being, endowed with marvelous energy, and with that principle of all morality, all dignity, all progress, the exclusive attribute of man—LIBERTY.[4]

---

[4]"It is averred that the regime of free competition demanded by an ignorant Political Economy, and intended to do away with monopolies, tends only to the general organization of monster monopolies in all departments."—*Principes du Socialisme*, by Mr. Considerant, p. 15.

2

WANTS, EFFORTS, SATISFACTIONS[1]

What a profoundly afflicting spectacle France presents to us!

It would be difficult to say if anarchy has passed from ideas to facts, or from facts to ideas, but it is certain that it pervades all, and abounds everywhere.

The poor rise up against the rich, men without fortune or profession against property; the populace against the bourgeoisie; labor against capital; agriculture against manufactures; the country against the town; the provinces against the metropolis; the denizen against the stranger.

And theorists step in and form a system of this antagonism. "It is the inevitable result," they say, "of the nature of things, that is to say, of Liberty. Man is endowed with self-love, and hence comes all the evil; for since he is endowed with self-love, he seeks

---

[1]This and the following chapter were published in the *Journal des Economistes*, September and December 1848.

to better his own condition, and he can only do so by imposing misery on his brethren. Let us hinder him, then, from following his inclinations; let us stifle his liberty, change the human heart, substitute other motives for those God has placed there; let us invent and constitute an artificial society!"

When they have reached this point, an unlimited career opens itself to their reason or imagination. If they are possessed of a disputatious turn and a peevish temper, they enter with eagerness into an analysis of Evil. They dissect it, they put it in the crucible, they interrogate it, they remount to its causes, they pursue it to its consequences; and, as by reason of our native imperfection there is nothing in which Evil is not present, they asperse and disparage everything. They exhibit to us Property, Family, Capital, Labor, Competition, Liberty, Personal Interest, only in one of their aspects, and always on the dark side, the side that injures or destroys. Their lectures on the natural history of man are, if I may use the expression, clinical lectures—the subject is always on his deathbed. They impiously defy God to reconcile what is said of his infinite goodness with the existence of evil. They stain and sully everything; they disgust us with everything; they dispute everything; and yet they obtain only a melancholy and dangerous success with those classes whom suffering disposes but too much to despair.

If, on the other hand, such theorists have a heart open to benevolence, a mind that is pleased with illusions, they rush to the region of chimeras. They dream of an Oceana, an Atlantis, a Salente, a Spensonie, an Icarie, a Utopia, a Phalanstere,[2] and they people these imaginary regions with a docile, loving, devoted race who always avoid setting themselves up against the fancies of the dreamer. He installs himself complacently in the seat of Providence. He arranges, he disposes, he molds men after his own fancy. Nothing stops him. He never encounters deceit. He resembles the

---

[2]Icarie, Phalanstere, etc.—allusion to Socialist works of the day.—Translator.

Roman preacher, who, after having transformed his square cap into Rousseau, refuted warmly the "Contrat Social," and triumphantly reduced his adversary to silence. It is thus that our Reformers dazzle those who suffer by means of seductive pictures of ideal felicity, well fitted to disgust them with the hard necessities of real life.

The theorist, however, rarely confines himself to such innocent chimeras. The moment he aims at leading mankind, he finds the people impatient of attempted transformations. Men resist—they get angry. In order to win them over, he harangues them not only on the happiness they reject, but more especially on the evils from which he professes to deliver them. He finds it impossible to make too striking a picture. He is continually refilling his palette and deepening his colors. He hunts out the evils of existing society with as much zeal as another employs in discovering the good. He sees nothing but sufferings, rags, leanness, starvation, pain, oppression. He is enraged that society has not a deeper sense of its misery. He neglects no means of making it throw off its insensibility, and, having begun with benevolence, he ends with misanthropy.[3]

God forbid that I should call into question the sincerity of anyone. But, in truth, I cannot explain to myself how these writers, who see a radical antagonism in the natural order of things, can ever taste a moment's calm or repose. Discouragement and despair would seem to be their unhappy portion. For, to sum up all, if nature is mistaken in making personal interest the mainspring of human society (and the mistake is manifest if it be claimed that the interests of society are fatally antagonistic), how do they not perceive that the evil is without remedy? Being men ourselves, and being able to have recourse only to men, where can be our point d'appui for changing the tendencies of human

---

[3]"Our industrial regime, founded on competition without guarantee and without organization, is then only a social hell, a vast realization of all the torments and all the punishments of the ancient Taenarus. There is one difference, however—namely, the victims."—(Vide Considerant.)

nature? Shall we invoke the Police, the Magistracy, the State, the Legislature? That would only be to invoke men, that is to say, beings subject to the common infirmity. Shall we address ourselves to Universal Suffrage? That would be to give the freest course to the universal tendency.

Only one expedient remains to these gentlemen. It is to hold themselves out as discoverers, as prophets, made of different clay from their fellow-men, and deriving their inspiration from a different source. This is the reason, no doubt, why we find them so frequently enveloping their systems and their counsels in a mystic phraseology. But if they are ambassadors of God, let them exhibit their credentials. In effect, what they demand is sovereign power, despotism the most absolute that ever existed. They not only wish to govern our acts, but to revolutionize our thoughts. Do they hope that mankind will believe them on their word, when they are not able to agree among themselves?

But before even examining their projects of artificial societies, is there not one point upon which it is necessary to assure ourselves, namely, whether they are not mistaken in the very foundation of their argument? Is it quite certain that MEN'S INTERESTS ARE NATURALLY ANTAGONISTIC; that an irremediable cause of inequality is fatally developed in the natural order of human society under the influence of personal interest, and that Providence is manifestly in error in ordaining that the progress of man should be toward ease and competency?

This is what I propose to inquire into.

Taking man as it has pleased God to constitute him, capable of foresight and experience, perfectible, endowed with self-love, it is true—but self-love qualified by the sympathetic principle, and at all events restrained and balanced by encountering an analogous sentiment universally prevailing in the medium in which it acts—I proceed to inquire what social order must necessarily result from the combination and free play of such elements.

If we find that this result is nothing else than a progressive march toward prosperity, improvement, and equality—a sustained approximation of all classes toward the same physical, intellectual, and moral level, accompanied by a constant elevation of that level, the ways of God to man will be vindicated. We shall learn with delight that there is no gap, no blank, in creation, and that the social order, like everything else, attests the existence of those harmonious laws before which Newton bowed his head, and which elicited from the Psalmist the exclamation, "the heavens declare the glory of God."

Rousseau has said, "If I were a prince or a legislator, I should not lose my time in pointing out what was necessary to be done—I should do it, or hold my tongue."

I am not a prince, but the confidence of my fellow citizens has made me a legislator. Perhaps they will tell me that this is the time for me to act and not to write.

Let them pardon me. Whether it be truth itself that urges me on, or that I am the dupe of an illusion, I have never ceased to feel the want of concentrating those ideas that have hitherto failed to find acceptance when presented in detached portions. I think I discover in the play of the natural laws of society sublime and consoling harmonies. What I see, or think I see, ought I not to try to exhibit to others, in order to rally round a sentiment of concord and fraternity many unsettled minds, many embittered hearts? If, when the much-loved vessel of the state is beat by the tempest, I sometimes appear to absent myself from my post in order to collect my scattered thoughts, it is because I feel my feeble hands unfitted for the work. Is it, besides, to betray my mission to reflect upon the causes of the tempest itself, and endeavor to act upon these causes? And then, what I find I cannot do today, who knows but it may be given me to accomplish tomorrow?

I shall begin by establishing some Economical ideas. Availing myself of the works of my predecessors, I shall endeavor to sum up the science in one principle—true, simple, and prolific—of which we have had a glimpse from the beginning, to which we are constantly drawing nearer and nearer, and of which, perhaps, the time is now come to fix the formula. By the light thus afforded, I shall afterwards essay the solution of some yet disputed problems—Competition, Machinery, Foreign trade, Luxury, Capital,

Rent, etc. I shall note some of the relations, or, I should rather say, the harmonies, of Political Economy, with the other moral and social sciences, glancing at the important subjects indicated by the terms—Personal Interest, Property, Community, Liberty, Equality, Responsibility, Solidarity, Fraternity, Unity. Last of all, I shall invite attention to the artificial obstacles that the pacific, regular, and progressive development of human society encounters. From these two ideas—Natural harmonious Laws—Artificial disturbing Causes—will be deduced the solution of the Social Problem.

It is easy to see that there are two rocks ahead upon which this undertaking may founder. In the middle of the vortex in which we are carried along, if this work is abstruse, it will not be read; if it obtains readers, the questions of which it treats will be but lightly dealt with. How are we to reconcile the exactions of the reader with the requirements of science? To satisfy all conditions both in form and substance, each word would require to be weighed, and have its proper place assigned to it. It is thus that the crystal is formed drop by drop in silence and obscurity. Retirement, quiet, time, freedom from care—all are lacking to me—and I am forced to trust to the sagacity of the public, and throw myself on its indulgence.

The subject of Political Economy is Man.

But it does not embrace the whole range of human affairs. The science of morals has appropriated all that comes within the attractive regions of Sympathy—the religious sentiment, paternal and maternal tenderness, filial piety, love, friendship, patriotism, charity, politeness. To Political Economy is left only the cold domain of Personal interest. This is unjustly forgotten when economic science is reproached with lacking the charm and unction of morals. How can it be otherwise? Dispute its right to existence as a science, but don't force it to counterfeit what it is not, and cannot be. If human transactions that have wealth for their object are vast enough, complicated enough, to afford materials for a special science, leave to it its own attractions, such as they are, and don't force it to speak of men's Interests in the language of Sentiment. For my own part, I believe that little good has been effected of late in exacting from Writers on Political Economy a tone of enthusiastic sentimentality which in their mouth can only be feigned. Of what do they treat? Of transactions that take place between people who know nothing of each other, who owe each other nothing but common Justice, who seek to defend or advance certain interests. It has to do with claims and pretensions that limit and restrain each other, and with which disinterestedness and devotion have nothing to do. Take a lyre, and chant such themes! As well might Lamartine sing his odes with the aid of the logarithm tables.

Not that Political Economy is without its poetry. There is poetry wherever order and harmony exist. But it is in the results, not in the demonstrations. It is brought out, not created. Kepler did not hold himself out as a poet, and yet the laws he discovered are the true poetry of mind.

Thus, Political Economy regards man only in one aspect, and our first care must be to study man in that point of view. This is the reason why we cannot avoid going back to the primary phenomena of human Sensibility and Activity. Don't worry, gentle reader! We shall not detain you long in those cloudy regions of metaphysics, and we shall borrow from that science only such notions as are clear, simple, and, if possible, incontestable.

The soul, or (to get rid of the spiritual question) man, is endowed with Sensibility. Whether this sensibility be either in the soul or in the body, man, as a passive being, always experiences sensations either painful or agreeable. As an active being, he makes an effort to drive away the one set of sensations and to multiply the other. The result, which affects him again as a passive being, may be called Satisfaction.

The general idea of Sensibility springs from other ideas that are more precise: pain, want, desire, taste, appetite, on one side; and, on the other, pleasure, enjoyment, competence.

Between these two extremes a middle term is interposed, and from the general idea of Activity spring the more precise ideas of pain, effort, fatigue, labor, production.

In analyzing Sensibility and Activity we encounter a word common to both; the word Pain. To experience certain sensations is a pain, and we cannot put an end to it but by an effort that is also a pain. We feel pains; we take pains. This advertises to us that here below we have only a choice of evils.

In the aggregate of these phenomena all is personal, as well the Sensation that precedes the effort, as the Satisfaction that follows it.

We cannot doubt, then, that Personal interest is the great mainspring of human nature. It must be perfectly understood, however, that this term is here employed as the expression of a universal fact, incontestable, and resulting from the organization of man—and not of a critical judgment on his conduct and actions, as if, instead of it, we should employ the word selfishness. Moral science would be rendered impossible if we were to pervert beforehand the terms of which it is compelled to make use.

Human effort does not always come necessarily to place itself between the sensation and the satisfaction. Sometimes the satisfaction comes of its own accord. More frequently the effort is exercised upon materials by the intervention of forces that nature has placed gratuitously at our disposal.

If we give the name of Utility to all that effects the satisfaction of wants, there are, then, utilities of two kinds—one, vouchsafed to us gratuitously by Providence; the other (if I may use the expression), requiring to be purchased by an Effort.

Thus the complete evolution embraces, or may embrace, these four ideas:

Wants (Gratuitous Utility) Satisfaction.
(Onerous Utility)

Man is endowed with progressive faculties. He compares, he foresees, he learns, he reforms himself, by experience. If want is a pain, effort is a pain also, and there is therefore no reason why he should not seek to diminish the latter, when he can do so without diminishing the satisfaction, which is his ultimate object. This is the reason of his success when he comes to replace onerous by gratuitous Utility, which is the perpetual object of his search.

It follows from the interested nature of the human heart, that we constantly seek to increase the proportion that our Satisfactions bear to our Efforts; and it results from the intelligent nature of our mind that we manage at each step to augment the proportion that gratuitous bears to onerous Utility.

Every time a success of this nature is achieved, a part of our efforts is, so to speak, rendered disposable, and we have the option of either indulging ourselves with longer repose or of working for the satisfaction of new desires, if these are strong enough to stimulate our activity.

Such is the principle of all economic progress; and it is easy to see that it is the principle also of all deception; for progress and error have both their root in that marvelous gift of God to man— Free will.

We are endowed with the faculty of comparing, of judging, of choosing, and of acting in consequence; which implies that we may form a right or a wrong judgment, and make a good or a bad choice. It is never useless to remind men of this when they talk of Liberty.

We never deceive ourselves, it is true, regarding the particular nature of our sensations, and we discern with an infallible instinct whether they are painful or agreeable. But how many various forms may our errors take! We may be laboring under a mistake as to the cause, and pursue with ardor as likely to afford us enjoyment what can only inflict pain upon us; or we may be mistaken as to the chain of consequences, and be ignorant that an immediate satisfaction will be followed by greater ulterior pain; or, again, we may mistake the relative importance of our wants and our desires.

Not only may we thus give a false direction to our efforts through ignorance, but also through a perverse will. "Man," says Mr. Bonald, "is an intelligence served by organs." What! Is there nothing else in us? Have we no passions?

When we speak of harmony, then, we must not be understood to mean that the natural arrangement of the social world is such that error and vice have been excluded from it. To maintain that thesis in the face of plain facts would be to carry the love of system to madness. To have harmony without dissonance man must either be devoid of free will or he must be infallible. All we say is this, that the great social tendencies are harmonious, inasmuch as—all error leading to deception and all vice to chastisement—the dissonances have a continual tendency to disappear.

A first and vague notion of property may be deduced from these premises. Since it is the individual who experiences the sensation, the desire, the want—since it is he who makes the Effort—the satisfaction must necessarily redound to him, for otherwise the effort would be without cause or reason.

The same may be said of Inheritance. No theory, no declamation, is required in order to make fathers love their children. People who sit down to manufacture imaginary societies may think it strange, but it is so—a father makes as many Efforts for the satisfaction of his children as for his own. Perhaps he makes more. If, then, an unnatural law should interdict the transmission of property, not only would that law violate property by the very act, but it would hinder its formation by abandoning to inaction one-half at least of our Efforts.

We shall have occasion to return to the subjects of Personal interest, Property, and Inheritance. Let us, in the first instance, mark out the limits of the science with which we have more immediately to do.

I am not one of those who think that a science, as such, has natural and unalterable boundaries. In the domain of ideas, as in that of facts, all things are bound up and linked together; truths run into one another; and there is no science that, in order to be complete, might not be made to include all. It has been said with reason that to an infinite intelligence there is but a single verity. It is, then, our weakness that obliges us to study separately a certain order of phenomena, and the classifications that result from it cannot escape a certain degree of arbitrariness.

The true merit is to explain accurately the facts, their causes, and their consequences. It is also a merit, although a much less and a purely relative one, to determine, not rigorously—for that is impossible—but rationally, the order of the facts we propose to study.

I say this in order that it may not be supposed that I intend to criticize my predecessors in giving to Political Economy limits somewhat different from those they have assigned to that science.

Economists have of late been reproached with addicting themselves too much to the study of Wealth. It has been wished that they had found a place in their science for all that, directly or indirectly, contributes to the happiness or sufferings of humanity. They have even been supposed to deny everything which they did not profess to teach—for example, the phenomena of sympathy, which is as natural to the heart of man as the principle of self-interest. It is as if they accused the mineralogist of denying the existence of the animal kingdom. What?

Wealth, the laws of its production, of its distribution, of its consumption—is not this a subject vast enough, and important enough, to be made the object of a special science? If the conclusions of the Economist were at variance with those of morals and politics, I could conceive ground for the accusation. One might say to him, "In limiting your science you are mistaken, for it is not possible for two verities to run counter to each other." Perhaps one result of the work I now submit to the public may be that the Science of Wealth will be found to be in perfect harmony with all the other sciences.

Of the three terms comprehended in the human destinies—Sensation, Effort, Satisfaction—the first and the last are always and necessarily confounded in the same individuality. It is impossible to imagine them separated. We can conceive a sensation unsatisfied, a want unappeased, but it is quite impossible to suppose the want to be in one man and the satisfaction to be in another.

If the same observation applied to the middle term, Effort, man would be a being completely solitary. The Economic phenomena would then manifest themselves in an isolated individual. There might be a juxtaposition of persons, but there could be no society; there might be a Personal, but not a Political, Economy.

But it is not so. It is very possible, and very often happens, that the wants of one owe their satisfaction to the efforts of another. This is a fact. If any one of us were to pass in review all the satisfactions he enjoys, he would acknowledge that he owes them chiefly to efforts which he has not himself made; and in the same way, the labor which we undergo, each in his own profession, goes almost always to satisfy the desires of others.

This tells us that it is neither in the wants nor in the satisfactions (phenomena essentially personal and intransmissible), but in the nature of the intermediate term, human Efforts, that we must search for the social principle—the origin of Political Economy.

It is in fact to this faculty, given to men, and to men alone, among all creatures, to work the one for the other; it is this transmission of efforts, this exchange of services, with all the infinite and involved combinations to which it gives rise, through time and through space, it is this precisely that constitutes Economic Science, points out its origin, and determines its limits.

I say, then:

Every effort capable of satisfying, on condition of a return, the wants of a person other than the man who makes the effort, and consequently the wants and satisfactions relative to this species of effort, constitute the domain of Political Economy.

Thus, to give an example: the act of breathing, although it includes the three terms that constitute the Economic phenomenon, does not pertain to that science, and we see the reason. What we have here to do with is a series of facts, of which not only the two extremes—want and satisfaction—are incapable of transmission (they are always so); but the intermediate term, Effort, is also incapable of transmission. To enable us to respire we invoke the assistance of no one; in that there is neither a service to be received nor a service to render. The fact is in its nature individual, not social, and consequently cannot enter into a science that is essentially one of relation, as its very name indicates.

But if, in peculiar circumstances, people were to render each other assistance to enable them to breathe, as when a workman descends in a diving-bell, when a physician treats a patient for pulmonary complaints, or when the police take measures for purifying the air, in such cases there is a want satisfied by a person other than the person who experiences the want; there is a service rendered; and respiration itself, as far at least as concerns assistance and remuneration, is brought within the sphere of Political Economy.

It is not necessary that the transaction should be completed, it is sufficient that it is possible, in order to impart to the labor employed an economic character. The laborer who raises corn for his own use accomplishes an economic fact in this respect that the corn is capable of being exchanged.

To make an effort in order to satisfy another's wants is to render him a service. If a service is stipulated in return, there is an exchange of services; and as this is the most ordinary case, Political Economy may be defined the Theory of Exchange.

Whatever may be for one of the contracting parties the urgency of the want, or for the other the intensity of the effort, if the exchange is free, the two services exchanged are worth each other. Value, then, consists in the comparative appreciation of reciprocal services, and Political Economy again may be defined the Theory of Value.

I have just defined Political Economy, and marked out its domain, without mentioning an essential element, gratuitous Utility.

All authors have remarked that we derive a multitude of satisfactions from this source. They denominate these utilities, such as air, water, the light of the sun, etc., natural wealth, in contradistinction to social wealth, and having done so, they take no more notice of them; and in fact it would seem that, as they give rise to no effort, to no exchange, to no service, as (being devoid of value) they figure in no inventory of goods, they should not be admitted into the domain of Political Economy.

This exclusion would be rational if gratuitous utility were a fixed invariable quantity, always separated from onerous utility; but they are constantly mixed up, and in inverse proportions. Man's constant endeavor is to substitute the one for the other, that is to say, to arrive, by means of natural and gratuitous agents, at the same results as by efforts. He accomplishes by the wind, by gravitation, by heat, by the elasticity of the air, what he accomplished at first only by muscular exertion.

Now what happens? Although the effect is equally useful, the effort is less. Less effort implies less service, and less service implies less value. Each step of progress, then, annihilates value; but how? Not by suppressing the useful effect, but by substituting gratuitous for onerous utility, natural for social wealth. In one sense the portion of value thus annihilated is excluded from the domain of Political Economy, just as it is excluded from our inventories. It is no longer exchanged, bought, or sold, and mankind enjoys it without effort and almost without consciousness. It is no longer accounted relative wealth, but is ranked among the gifts of God.

But on the other hand, if science takes it no longer into account, the error is assuredly committed of losing sight of what under all circumstances is the main, the essential thing—the result, the useful effect. In that case we overlook the strongest tendencies toward community and equality, and discover much less of harmony in the social order. If this book is destined to advance Political Economy a single step, it will be by keeping constantly before the eyes of the reader that portion of value which is successively annihilated, and recovered, under the form of gratuitous utility, by mankind at large.

I shall here make an observation that will prove how frequently the sciences unite and nearly flow into each other.

I have just defined service. It is the effort in one man, while the want and the satisfaction are in another. Sometimes the service is rendered gratuitously, without remuneration, without any service being exacted in return. It proceeds, then, from the principle of sympathy rather than from the principle of self-interest. It constitutes gift, not exchange. Consequently it would seem to appertain not to Political Economy (which is the theory of exchange), but to morals. In fact, acts of that nature, by reason of their motive, are rather moral than economical. We shall see, however, that, by reason of their effects, they concern the science that now engages us. On the other hand, services rendered for an onerous consideration, on condition of a return, and, by reason of that motive (essentially economic), do not on that account remain excluded from the domain of morals, in so far as their effects are concerned.

Thus these two branches of knowledge have an infinite number of points of contact; and as two truths cannot be antagonistic, when the economist ascribes to a phenomenon injurious consequences, and the moralist ascribes to it beneficial effects, we may affirm that one or other of them is mistaken. It is thus that the sciences verify and fortify one another.

3

WANTS OF MAN

It is perhaps impossible, and, at any rate, it would not be of much use, to present a complete and methodical catalogue of human wants. Nearly all those of real importance are comprised in the following enumeration:

Respiration (I retain here that want, as marking the boundary where the transmission of labor or exchange of services begins): Food—Clothing—Lodging—Preservation or Re-establishment of Health—Locomotion—Security—Instruction—Diversion—Sense of the Beautiful.

Wants exist. This is a fact. It would be puerile to inquire whether we should have been better without wants, and why God has made us subject to them.

It is certain that man suffers, and even dies, when he cannot satisfy the wants that belong to his constitution. It is certain that he suffers, and may even die, when in satisfying certain of his wants he indulges to excess.

We cannot satisfy the greater part of our wants without pain or trouble, which may be considered as suffering. The same may be said of the act by which, exercising a noble control over our appetites, we impose on ourselves a privation.

Thus, suffering is inevitable, and there remains to us only a choice of evils. Nothing comes more home to us than suffering, and hence personal interest—the sentiment that is branded now-a-days with the names of selfishness and individualism—is indestructible. Nature has placed sensibility at the extremity of our nerves, and at all the avenues to the heart and mind, as an advance guard, to give us notice when our satisfactions are either deficient or in excess. Pain has, then, a purpose, a mission. We are asked frequently, whether the existence of evil can be reconciled with the infinite goodness of the Creator—a formidable problem that philosophy will always discuss, and never probably be able to solve. As far as Political Economy is concerned, we must take man as he is inasmuch as it is not given to imagination to figure to itself—far less can the reason conceive—a sentient and mortal being exempt from pain. We should try in vain to comprehend sensibility without pain, or man without sensibility.

In our days, certain sentimentalist schools reject as false all social science that does not go the length of establishing a system by means of which suffering may be banished from the world. They pass a severe judgment on Political Economy because it admits what it is impossible to deny, the existence of suffering. They go farther—they make Political Economy responsible for it. It is as if they were to attribute the frailty of our organs to the physician who makes them the object of his study.

Undoubtedly we may acquire a temporary popularity, attract the regards of suffering classes, and irritate them against the natural order of society, by telling them that we have in our head a plan of artificial social arrangement that excludes pain in every form; we may even pretend to appropriate God's secret, and to interpret his presumed will, by banishing evil from the world. And there will not be lacking those who will treat as impious a science that exposes such pretensions, and who will accuse it of overlooking or denying the foresight of the Author of things.

These schools at the same time give us a frightful picture of the actual state of society, not perceiving that if it be impious to foresee suffering in the future, it is equally so to expose its existence in the past or in the present. For the infinite admits of no limits; and if a single human being has since the creation experienced suffering, that fact would entitle us to state, without impiety, that suffering has entered into the plan of Providence.

Surely it is more philosophical and more manly to acknowledge at once great natural facts that not only exist, but apart from which we can form no just or adequate conception of human nature.

Man, then, is subject to suffering, and consequently society is also subject to it.

Suffering discharges a function in the individual, and consequently in society.

An accurate investigation of the social laws discloses to us that the mission of suffering is gradually to destroy its own causes, to circumscribe suffering itself within narrower limits, and finally to assure the preponderance of the Good and the Fair, by enabling us to purchase or merit that preponderance. The nomenclature we have proposed places material wants in the foreground.

The times in which we live force me to put the reader on his guard against a species of sentimental affectation that is now much in vogue.

There are people who hold very cheap what they disdainfully term material wants, material satisfactions: they will say, as Belise says to Chrysale,

"*Le corps, cette guenille, est-il d'une importance, D'un prix a meriter seulement qu'on y pense?*"

And although, in general pretty well off themselves, they will blame me for having indicated as one of our most pressing wants, that of food, for example.

I acknowledge undoubtedly that moral advancement is a higher thing than physical sustenance. But are we so beset with declamatory affectation that we can no longer venture to say that before we can set about moral culture, we must have the means of living. Let us guard ourselves against these puerilities, which obstruct science. In wishing to pass for philanthropical we cease to be truthful; for it is contrary both to reason and to fact to represent moral development, self-respect, the cultivation of refined sentiments as preceding the requirements of simple preservation. This sort of prudery is quite modern. Rousseau, that enthusiastic panegyrist of the State of Nature, steered clear of it; and a man endowed with exquisite delicacy, of a tenderness of heart full of unction, a spiritualist even to quietism, and, toward himself, a stoic—I mean Fenelon—has said that, "After all, solidity of mind consists in the desire to be exactly instructed as to how those things are managed that lie at the foundation of human life—all great affairs turn upon that."

Without pretending, then, to classify our wants in a rigorously exact order, we may say that man cannot direct his efforts to the satisfaction of moral wants of the highest and most elevated kind until after he has provided for those that concern his preservation and sustenance. Whence, without going farther, we may conclude that every legislative measure that tells against the material well-being of communities injures the moral life of nations—a harmony I commend, in passing, to the attention of the reader.

And since the occasion presents itself, I will here mark another.

Since the inexorable necessities of material life are an obstacle to moral and intellectual culture, it follows that we ought to find more virtue among wealthy than among poor nations and classes. Good Heaven! what have I just said, and with what objections shall I be assailed! But the truth is, it is a perfect mania of our times to attribute all disinterestedness, all self-sacrifice, all that constitutes the greatness and moral beauty of man, to the poorer classes, and this mania has of late been still more developed by a revolution, that, bringing these classes to the surface of society, has not failed to surround them with a crowd of flatterers.

I don't deny that wealth, opulence, especially where it is very unequally spread, tends to develop certain special vices.

But is it possible to state as a general proposition that virtue is the privilege of poverty, and vice the unhappy and unfailing companion of ease? This would be to affirm that moral and intellectual improvement, which is only compatible with a certain amount of leisure and comfort, is detrimental to intelligence and morality.

I appeal to the candor of the suffering classes themselves. To what horrible dissonances would such a paradox conduct us!

We must then conclude that human nature has the frightful alternative presented to it either to remain eternally wretched, or advance gradually on the road to vice and immorality. Then all the forces that conduct us to wealth—such as activity, economy, skill, honesty—are the seeds of vice; while those that tie us to poverty—improvidence, idleness, dissipation, carelessness—are the precious germs of virtue. Could we conceive in the moral world a dissonance more discouraging? Or, were it really so, who would dare to address or counsel the people? You complain of your sufferings (we must say to them), and you are impatient to see an end of these sufferings. You groan at finding yourselves under the yoke of the most imperious material wants, and you sigh for the hour of your deliverance, for you desire leisure to make your voice heard in the political world and to protect your interests. You know not what you desire, or how fatal success would prove to you. Ease, competence, riches, develop only vice. Guard, then, religiously your poverty and your virtue.

The flatterers of the people, then, fall into a manifest contradiction when they point to the region of opulence as an impure sink of greed and vice, and, at the same time, urge them on—and frequently in their eagerness by the most illegitimate means—to a region which they deem so unfortunate.

Such discordances are never encountered in the natural order of society. It is impossible to suppose that all men should aspire to competence, that the natural way to attain it should be by the exercise of the strictest virtue, and that they should reach it nevertheless only to be caught in the snares of vice. Such declamations are calculated only to light up and keep alive the hatred of classes. If true, they place human nature in a dilemma between poverty and immorality. If untrue, they make falsehood the minister of disorder, and set to loggerheads classes who should mutually love and assist each other.

Factitious inequality—inequality generated by law, by disturbing the natural order of development of the different classes of society—is, for all, a prolific source of irritation, jealousy, and crime. This is the reason why it is necessary to satisfy ourselves whether this natural order leads to the progressive amelioration and progressive equalization of all classes; and we should be arrested in this inquiry by what lawyers term a *fin de non-recevoir*, a peremptory exception, if this double material progress implied necessarily a double moral degradation.

Upon the subject of human wants, I have to make an important observation—and one that, in Political Economy, may even be regarded as fundamental—it is, that wants are not a fixed immutable quantity. They are not in their nature stationary, but progressive.

We observe this characteristic even in our strictly physical wants; but it becomes more apparent as we rise to those desires and intellectual tastes that distinguish man from the inferior animals.

It would seem that if there be anything in which men should resemble each other, it is in the want of food, for, unless in exceptional cases, men's stomachs are very much alike.

And yet aliments that are rare at one period become common at another, and the regimen that suits a Lazzarone would subject a Dutchman to torture. Thus the want that is the most immediate, the grossest of all, and consequently the most uniform of all, still varies according to age, sex, temperament, climate, custom.

The same may be said of all our other wants. Scarcely has a man found shelter than he desires to be lodged, scarcely is he clothed than he wishes to be decorated, scarcely has he satisfied his bodily cravings than study, science, art, open to his desires an unlimited field.

It is a phenomenon well worthy of remark, how quickly, by continuous satisfaction, what was at first only a vague desire becomes a taste, and what was only a taste is transformed into a want, and even a want of the most imperious kind.

Look at that rude artisan. Accustomed to poor fare, plain clothing, indifferent lodging, he imagines he would be the happiest of men, and would have no further desires, if he could but reach the step of the ladder immediately above him. He is astonished that those who have already reached it should still torment themselves as they do. At length comes the modest fortune he has dreamt of, and then he is happy, very happy—for a few days.

For soon he becomes familiar with his new situation, and by degrees he ceases to feel his fancied happiness. With indifference he puts on the fine clothing for which he once yearned. He has got into a new circle, he associates with other companions, he drinks of another cup, he aspires to mount another step, and if he ever turns his reflections at all upon himself, he feels that if his fortune has changed, his soul remains the same, and is still an inexhaustible spring of new desires.

It would seem that nature has attached this singular power to habit, in order that it should be in us what a ratchet-wheel is in mechanics, and that humanity, urged on continually to higher and higher regions, should not be able to rest content, whatever degree of civilization it attains.

The sense of dignity, the feeling of self-respect, acts with perhaps still more force in the same direction. The stoic philosophy has frequently blamed men for desiring rather to appear than to be. But, taking a broader view of things, is it certain that to appear is not for man one of the modes of being?

When by exertion, order, and economy a family rises by degrees toward those social regions where tastes become nicer and more delicate, relations more polished, sentiments more refined, intelligence more cultivated, who can describe the acute suffering that accompanies a forced return to their former low estate? The body does not alone suffer. The sad reverse interferes with habits that have become as it were a second nature; it clashes with the sense of dignity, and all the feelings of the soul. It is by no means uncommon in such a case to see the victim sink all at once into degrading besottedness, or perish in despair. It is with the social medium as with the atmosphere. The mountaineer, accustomed to the pure air of his native hills, pines and moulders away in the narrow streets of our cities.

But I hear someone exclaim, Economist, you stumble already. You have just told us that your science is in accord with morals, and here you are justifying luxury and effeminacy. Philosopher, I say in my turn, lay aside these fine clothes, which were not those of primitive man, break your furniture, burn your books, dine on raw flesh, and I shall then reply to your objection. It is too much to quarrel with this power of habit, of which you are yourself the living example.

We may find fault with this disposition nature has given to our organs; but our censure will not make it the less universal. We find it existing among all nations, ancient and modern, savage and civilized, at the antipodes as at home. We cannot explain civilization without it; and when a disposition of the human heart is thus proved to be universal and indestructible, social science cannot put it aside, or refuse to take it into account.

This objection will be made by publicists who pride themselves on being the disciples of Rousseau; but Rousseau has never denied the existence of the phenomenon. He establishes undeniably the indefinite elasticity of human wants, and the power of habit, and admits even the part I assign to them in preventing the human race from retrograding; only that which I admire is what he deplores, and he does so consistently. Rousseau fancied there was a time when men had neither rights, nor duties, nor relations, nor affections, nor language; and it was then, according to him, that they were happy and perfect. He was bound, therefore, to abhor the social machinery that is constantly removing mankind from ideal perfection. Those, on the contrary, who are of opinion that perfection is not at the beginning, but at the end, of the human evolution, will admire the spring and motive of action that

I place in the foreground. But as to the existence and play of the spring itself we are at one.

"Men of leisure," he says, "employed themselves in procuring all sorts of conveniences and accommodations unknown to their forefathers, and that was the first yoke that, without intending it, they imposed upon themselves, and the prime source of the inconveniences they prepared for their descendants. For not only did they thus continue to emasculate both mind and body, but these luxuries having by habit lost all their relish, and degenerated into true wants, their being deprived of them caused more pain than the possession of them had given pleasure: they were unhappy at losing what they had no enjoyment in possessing."

Rousseau was convinced that God, nature, and humanity were wrong. That is still the opinion of many; but it is not mine.

After all, God forbid that I should desire to set myself against the noblest attribute, the most beautiful virtue of man, self-control, command over his passions, moderation in his desires, contempt of show. I don't say that he is to make himself a slave to this or that factitious want. I say that wants (taking a broad and general view of them as resulting from man's mental and bodily constitution) combined with the power of habit, and the sense of dignity, are indefinitely expansible, because they spring from an inexhaustible source—namely, desire. Who should blame a rich man for being sober, for despising finery, for avoiding pomp and effeminacy? But are there not more elevated desires to which he may yield? Has the desire for instruction, for instance, any limits? To render service to his country, to encourage the arts, to disseminate useful ideas, to succor the distressed—is there anything in these incompatible with the right use of riches?

For the rest, whatever philosophers may think of it, human wants do not constitute a fixed immutable quantity. That is a certain, a universal fact, liable to no exception. The wants of the fourteenth century, whether with reference to food, or lodging, or instruction, were not at all the wants of ours, and we may safely predict that ours will not be the wants of our descendants.

The same observation applies to all the elements of Political Economy—Wealth, labor, Value, Services, etc.—all participate in the extreme versatility of the principal subject, Man. Political Economy has not, like geometry or physics, the advantage of dealing with objects that can be weighed or measured. This is one of its difficulties to begin with, and it is a perpetual source of errors throughout; for when the human mind applies itself to a certain order of phenomena, it is naturally on the outlook for a criterion, a common measure, to which everything can be referred, in order to give to that particular branch of knowledge the character of an exact science. Thus we observe some authors seeking for fixity in value, others in money, others in wheat, others in labor, that is to say, in things that are themselves all liable to fluctuation.

Many errors in Political Economy proceed from authors thus regarding human wants as a fixed determinate quantity; and it is for this reason that I have deemed it my duty to enlarge on this subject. At the risk of anticipating, it is worth while to notice briefly this mode of reasoning. Economists take generally the enjoyments that satisfy men of the present day, and they assume that human nature admits of no other. Hence, if the bounty of nature, or the power of machinery, or habits of temperance and moderation, succeed in rendering disposable for a time a portion of human labor, this progress disquiets them, they consider it as a disaster, and they retreat behind absurd but specious formulas, such as these: Production is superabundant—we suffer from plethora—the power of producing outruns the power of consuming, etc.

It is not possible to discover a solution of the question of machinery, or that of external competition, or that of luxury, if we persist in considering our wants as a fixed invariable quantity, and do not take into account their indefinite expansibility.

But if human wants are indefinite, progressive, capable of increase like desire, which is their never failing source, we must admit, under pain of introducing discordance and contradiction into the economical laws of society, that nature has placed in man and around him indefinite and progressive means of satisfaction—equilibrium between the means and the end being the primary condition of all harmony. This is what we shall now examine.

I said at the outset of this work that the object of Political Economy is man, considered with reference to his wants, and his means of satisfying these wants.

We must then begin with the study of man and his makeup.

But we have also seen that he is not a solitary being. If his wants and his satisfactions are, from the very nature of sensibility, inseparable from his being, the same thing cannot be said of his efforts, which spring from the active principle. The latter are susceptible of transmission. In a word, men work for one another.

Now a very strange thing takes place.

If we take a general or, if I may be allowed the expression, abstract view, of man, his wants, his efforts, his satisfactions, his constitution, his inclinations, his tendencies, we fall into a train of observation that appears free from doubt and self-evident—so much so that the writer finds a difficulty in submitting to the public judgment truths so commonplace and so palpable. He is afraid of provoking ridicule; and thinks, not without reason, that the impatient reader will throw away his book, exclaiming, "I shall not waste time on such trivialities."

And yet these truths that, when presented to us in an abstract shape we regard as so incontrovertible that we can scarce summon patience to listen to them are considered only as ridiculous errors and absurd theories the moment they are applied to man in his social state. Regarding man as an isolated being, who ever took it into his head to say, "Production is superabundant—the power of consumption cannot keep pace with the power of production—luxury and factitious tastes are the source of wealth—the invention of machinery annihilates labor," and other sayings of the same sort—which, nevertheless, when applied to mankind in the aggregate, we receive as axioms so well established that they are actually made the basis of our commercial and industrial legislation? Exchange produces in this respect an illusion of which even men of penetration and solid judgment find it impossible to disabuse themselves, and I affirm that Political Economy will have attained its design and fulfilled its mission when it shall have conclusively demonstrated this—that what is true of an individual man is true of society at large. Man in an isolated state is at once producer and consumer, inventor and entrepreneur, capitalist and workman. All the economic phenomena are accomplished in his person—he is, as it were, society in miniature. In like manner, humanity viewed in the aggregate, may be regarded as a great, collective, complex individual, to whom you may apply exactly the same truths as to man in a state of isolation.

I have felt it necessary to make this remark, which I hope will be justified in the sequel, before continuing what I had to say upon man. I should have been afraid otherwise, that the reader might reject as superfluous the following developments, which in fact are nothing else than veritable truisms.

I have just spoken of the wants of man, and after presenting an approximate enumeration of them, I observed that they were not of a stationary, but of a progressive nature; and this holds true whether we consider these wants each singly, or all together, in their physical, intellectual, and moral order. How could it be otherwise? There are wants the satisfaction of which is required by our makeup under pain of death, and up to a certain point we may represent these as fixed quantities, although that is not rigorously exact, for however little we may desire to neglect an essential element—namely, the force of habit—however little we may condescend to subject ourselves to honest self-examination, we shall be forced to allow that wants, even of the plainest and most homely kind (the desire for food for example), undergo, under the influence of habit, undoubted transformations. The man who declaims against this observation as materialist and epicurean would think himself very unfortunate, if, taking him at his word, we should reduce him to the black broth of the Spartans, or the scanty pittance of a hermit. At all events, when wants of this kind have been satisfied in an assured and permanent way, there are others that arise in the most expansible of our faculties, desire.

Can we conceive a time when man can no longer form even reasonable desires? Let us not forget that a desire that might be unreasonable in a former state of civilization—at a time when all the human faculties were absorbed in providing for low material wants—ceases to be so when improvement opens to these faculties a more extended field. A desire to travel at the rate of thirty miles an hour would have been unreasonable two centuries ago—it is not so at the present day. To pretend that the wants and desires of man are fixed and stationary quantities, is to mistake the nature of the human soul, to deny facts, and to render civilization inexplicable.

It would still be inexplicable if, side by side with the indefinite development of wants, there had not been placed, as possible, the indefinite development of the means of providing for these wants. How could the expansible nature of our wants have contributed to the realization of progress if, at a certain point, our faculties could advance no farther, and should encounter an impassable barrier?

Our wants being indefinite, the presumption is that the means of satisfying these wants should be indefinite also, unless we are to suppose Nature, Providence, or the Power that presides over our destinies, to have fallen into a cruel and shocking contradiction.

I say indefinite, not infinite, for nothing connected with man is infinite. It is precisely because our faculties go on developing themselves ad infinitum that they have no assignable limits, although they may have absolute limits. There are many points above the present range of humanity, which we may never succeed in attaining, and yet for all that, the time may never come when we shall cease to approach nearer them.[1]

I don't at all mean to say that desire, and the means of satisfying desire, march in parallel lines and with equal rapidity. The former runs—the latter limps after it.

---

[1]A mathematical law of frequent occurrence, but very little understood in Political Economy.

The prompt and adventurous nature of desire, compared with the slowness of our faculties, shows us very clearly that in every stage of civilization, at every step of our progress, suffering to a certain extent is, and ever must be, the lot of man. But it shows us likewise that this suffering has a mission, for desire could no longer be an incentive to our faculties if it followed, instead of preceding, their exercise. Let us not, however, accuse nature of cruelty in the construction of this mechanism, for we cannot fail to remark that desire is never transformed into want, strictly so called, that is, into painful desire, until it has been made such by habit; in other words, until the means of satisfying the desire have been found and placed irrevocably within our reach.[2]

We have now to examine the question—What means have we of providing for our wants?

It seems evident to me there are two—namely, Nature and labor, the gifts of God, and the fruits of our efforts—or, if you will, the application of our faculties to the things nature has placed at our service.

No school that I know of has attributed the satisfaction of our wants to nature alone. Such an assertion is clearly contradicted by experience, and we need not learn Political Economy to perceive that the intervention of our faculties is necessary. But there are schools who have attributed this privilege to labor alone. Their axiom is, "All wealth comes from labor—labor is wealth."

I cannot help anticipating, so far as to remark, that these formulas, taken literally, have led to monstrous errors of doctrine, and, consequently, to deplorable legislative blunders. I shall return to this subject. I confine myself here to establishing as a

---

[2]One of the indirect objects of this work is to combat modern sentimental schools, who, in spite of facts, refuse to admit that suffering to any extent enters into the designs of Providence. As these schools are said to proceed from Rousseau, I must here cite to them a passage from their master: "The evil we see is not absolute evil; and far from being directly antagonistic to the good, it concurs with it in the universal harmony."

fact that Nature and labor cooperate for the satisfaction of our wants and desires.

Let us examine the facts.

The first want we have placed at the head of our list is that of breathing. As regards respiration, we have already shown that nature in general is at the whole cost, and that human labor intervenes only in certain exceptional cases, as where it becomes necessary to purify the atmosphere.

Another want is that of quenching our thirst, and it is more or less satisfied by Nature, in so far as she furnishes us with water, more or less pure, abundant, and within reach; and labor concurs in so far as it becomes necessary to bring water from a greater distance, to filter it, or to obviate its scarcity by constructing wells and cisterns.

The liberality of nature toward us in regard to food is by no means uniform; for who will maintain that the labor to be furnished is the same when the land is fertile, or when it is sterile, when the forest abounds with game, the river with fish, or in the opposite cases?

As regards lighting, human labor has certainly less to do when the night is short than when it is long.

I dare not lay it down as an absolute rule, but it appears to me that in proportion as we rise in the scale of wants, the cooperation of nature is lessened, and leaves us more room for the exercise of our faculties. The painter, the sculptor, and the author even, are forced to avail themselves of materials and instruments that nature alone furnishes, but from their own genius is derived all that makes the charm, the merit, the utility, and the value of their works. To learn is a want which the well-directed exercise of our faculties almost alone can satisfy. Yet here nature assists, by presenting objects of observation and comparison to us in every direction. With an equal amount of application, may not botany, geology, or natural history, make everywhere equal progress?

It would be superfluous to cite other examples. We have already shown undeniably that Nature gives us the means of satisfaction, in placing at our disposal things possessed of higher or lower degrees of utility (I use the word in its etymological sense, as indicating the property of serving, of being useful). In many cases, in almost every case, labor must contribute, to a certain extent, in rendering this utility complete; and we can easily comprehend that the part labor has to perform is greater or less in proportion as nature had previously advanced the operation in a less or greater degree.

We may then lay down these two formulas:

Utility is communicated sometimes by Nature alone, sometimes by labor alone, but almost always by the cooperation of both.

To bring anything to its highest degree of UTILITY, the action of Labor is in an inverse ratio to the action of Nature.

From these two propositions, combined with what I have said of the indefinite expansibility of our wants, I may be permitted to deduce a conclusion, the importance of which will be demonstrated in the sequel. Suppose two men, having no connection with each other, to be unequally situated in this respect, that nature has been liberal to the one, and niggardly to the other; the first would evidently obtain a given amount of satisfaction at a less expense of labor. Would it follow that the part of his forces thus left disposable, if I may use the expression, would be abandoned to inaction? and that this man, on account of the liberality of nature, would be reduced to compulsory idleness? Not at all. It would follow that he could, if he wished it, dispose of these forces to enlarge the circle of his enjoyments; that with an equal amount of labor he could procure two satisfactions in place of one; in a word, that his progress would become more easy.

I may be mistaken, but it appears to me that no science, not even geometry, is founded on truths more unassailable. Were any one to prove to me that all these truths were so many errors, I should not only lose confidence in them, but all faith in evidence itself; for what reasoning could one employ that should better deserve the acquiescence of our judgment than the evidence thus overturned? The moment an axiom is discovered that shall contradict this other axiom—that a straight line is the shortest road from one point to another—that instant the human mind has no other refuge, if it be a refuge, than absolute skepticism.

I positively feel ashamed thus to insist upon first principles that are so plain as to seem puerile. And yet we must confess that, amid the complications of human transactions, such simple truths have been overlooked; and in order to justify myself for detaining the reader so long upon what the English call truisms, I shall notice here a singular error by which excellent minds have allowed themselves to be misled. Setting aside, neglecting entirely, the cooperation of nature in relation to the satisfaction of our wants, they have laid down the absolute principle that all wealth comes from labor. On this foundation they have reared the following erroneous syllogism:

"All wealth comes from labor:

"Wealth, then, is in proportion to labor.

"But labor is in an inverse ratio to the liberality of nature:

"Ergo, wealth is inversely as the liberality of nature."

Right or wrong, many economical laws owe their origin to this singular reasoning. Such laws cannot be otherwise than subversive of every sound principle in relation to the development and distribution of wealth; and this it is that justifies me in preparing beforehand, by the explanation of truths very trivial in appearance, for the refutation of the deplorable errors and prejudices under which society is now laboring.

Let us analyze the cooperation of Nature of which I have spoken. Nature places two things at our disposal—materials and forces.

Most of the material objects that contribute to the satisfaction of our wants and desires are brought into the state of utility that renders them fit for our use only by the intervention of labor, by the application of the human faculties. But the elements, the atoms, if you will, of which these objects are composed, are the gifts, I will add the gratuitous gifts, of nature. This observation is of the very highest importance, and will, I believe, throw a new light upon the theory of wealth.

The reader will have the goodness to bear in mind that I am inquiring at present in a general way into the moral and physical constitution of man, his wants, his faculties, his relations with nature—apart from the consideration of Exchange, which I shall enter upon in the next chapter. We shall then see in what respect, and in what manner, social transactions modify the phenomena.

It is very evident that if man in an isolated state must, so to speak, purchase the greater part of his satisfaction by an exertion, by an effort, it is rigorously exact to say that prior to the intervention of any such exertion, any such effort, the materials he finds at his disposal are the gratuitous gifts of nature. After the first effort on his part, however slight it may be, they cease to be gratuitous; and if the language of Political Economy had been always exact, it would have been to material objects in this state, and before human labor had been bestowed upon them, that the term raw materials (*matieres premieres*) would have been exclusively applied.

I regret that this gratuitous quality of the gifts of nature, anterior to the intervention of labor, is of the very highest importance. I said in my second chapter that Political Economy was the theory of value; I add now, and by anticipation, that things begin to possess value only when it is given to them by labor. I intend to demonstrate afterwards that everything that is gratuitous for man in an isolated state is gratuitous for man in his social condition, and that the gratuitous gifts of nature, whatever be their UTILITY, have no value. I say that a man who receives a benefit from nature, directly and without any effort on his part, cannot be considered as rendering himself an onerous service, and, consequently, that he cannot render to another any service with reference to things that are common to all. Now, where there are no services rendered and received there is no value.

All that I have said of materials is equally applicable to the forces nature places at our disposal. Gravitation, the elasticity of air, the power of the winds, the laws of equilibrium, vegetable life, animal life, are so many forces we learn to turn to account. The pains and intelligence we bestow in this way always admit of remuneration, for we are not bound to devote our efforts to the advantage of others gratuitously. But these natural forces in themselves, and apart from all intellectual or bodily exertion are gratuitous gifts of Providence, and in this respect they remain devoid of value through all the complications of human transactions. This is the leading idea of the present work.

This observation would be of little importance, I allow, if the cooperation of nature were constantly uniform, if each man, at all times, in all places, in all circumstances, received from nature equal and invariable assistance. In that case, science would be justified in not taking into account an element that, remaining always and everywhere the same, would affect the services exchanged in equal proportions on both sides. As in geometry we eliminate portions of lines common to two figures we compare with each other, we might neglect a cooperation that is invariably present, and content ourselves with saying, as we have done hitherto, "There is such a thing as natural wealth—Political Economy acknowledges it, and has no more concern with it."

But this is not the true state of the matter. The irresistible tendency of the human mind, stimulated by self-interest and assisted by a series of discoveries, is to substitute natural and gratuitous cooperation for human and onerous concurrence; so that a given utility, although remaining the same as far as the result and the satisfactions it procures us are concerned, represents a smaller and smaller amount of labor. In fact, it is impossible not to perceive the immense influence of this marvelous phenomenon on our notion of value. For what is the result of it? This, that in every product the gratuitous element tends to take the place of the onerous; that utility, being the result of two collaborations, of which one is remunerated and the other is not, Value, which has relation only to the first of these united forces, is diminished, and makes room for a utility that is identically the same, and this in proportion as we succeed in constraining nature to a more efficacious cooperation. So that we may say that men have as many more satisfactions, as much more wealth, as they have less value. Now the majority of authors having employed these three terms, utility, wealth, value, as synonymous, the result has been a theory that is not only not true, but the reverse of true. I believe sincerely that a more exact description of this combination of natural forces and human forces in the business of production, in other words, a juster definition of Value, would put an end to inextricable theoretical confusion, and would reconcile schools that are now divergent; and if I am now anticipating somewhat in entering on this subject here, my justification with the reader is the necessity of explaining in the outset certain ideas of which otherwise he would have difficulty in perceiving the importance.

Returning from this digression, I resume what I had to say upon man considered exclusively in an economical point of view.

Another observation, which we owe to J.B. Say, and which is almost self-evident, although too much neglected by many authors, is that man creates neither the materials nor the forces of nature, if we take the word create in its exact signification. These materials, these forces, have an independent existence. Man can only combine them or displace them for his own benefit or that of others. If for his own, he renders a service to himself—if for the benefit of others, he renders service to his fellows and has the right to exact an equivalent service. Whence it also follows that value is proportional to the service rendered, and not at all to the absolute utility of the thing. For this utility may be in great part the result of the gratuitous action of nature, in which case the human service, the onerous service, the service to be remunerated, is of little value. This results from the axiom above established—namely, that to bring a thing to the highest degree of utility, the action of man is inversely as the action of nature.

This observation overturns the doctrine that places value in the materiality of things. The contrary is the truth. The materiality is a quality given by nature, and consequently gratuitous, and devoid of value, although of incontestable utility. Human action, which can never succeed in creating matter, constitutes alone the service that man in a state of isolation renders to himself, or that men in society render to each other; and it is the free appreciation of these services that is the foundation of value. Far, then, from concluding with Adam Smith that it is impossible to conceive of value otherwise than as residing in material substance, we conclude that between Matter and Value there is no possible relation.

This erroneous doctrine Smith deduced logically from his principle that those classes alone are productive who operate on material substances. He thus prepared the way for the modern error of the socialists, who have never ceased representing as unproductive parasites those whom they term intermediaries between the producer and consumer—the merchant, the retail dealer, etc. Do they render services? Do they save us trouble by taking trouble for us? In that case they create value, although they do not create matter; and as no one can create matter, and we all confine our exertions to rendering reciprocal services, we pronounce with justice that all, including agriculturists and manufacturers, are intermediaries in relation one to another.

This is what I had to say at present upon the cooperation of nature. Nature places at our disposal, in various degrees depending on climate, seasons, and the advance of knowledge, but always gratuitously, materials and forces. Then these materials and forces are devoid of value; it would be strange if they had any. According to what rule should we estimate them? In what way could nature be paid, remunerated, compensated? We shall see afterwards that exchange is necessary in order to determine value. We don't purchase the goods of nature—we gather them; and if, in order to appropriate them, a certain amount of effort is necessary, it is in this effort, and not in the gifts of nature, that the principle of value resides.

Let us now consider that action of man which we designate, in a general way, by the term labor.

The word labor, like almost all the terms of Political Economy, is very vague. Different authors use it in a sense more or less extended. Political Economy has not had, like most other sciences, Chemistry for example, the advantage of constructing her own vocabulary. Treating of subjects that have been familiar to men's thoughts since the beginning of the world, and the constant subject of their daily talk, she has found a nomenclature ready made, and has been forced to adopt it.

The meaning of the word labor is often limited exclusively to the muscular action of man upon materials. Hence those who execute the mechanical part of production are called the working classes.

The reader will comprehend that I give to this word a more extended sense. I understand by labor the application of our faculties to the satisfaction of our wants. Wants, efforts, satisfactions, this is the circle of Political Economy. Effort may be physical, intellectual, or even moral, as we shall immediately see.

It is not necessary to demonstrate in this place that all our organs, all or nearly all our faculties, may concur and in point of fact do concur, in production. Attention, sagacity, intelligence, imagination, have assuredly their part in it.

Mr. Dunoyer, in his excellent work, *Sur la Liberté du Travail*, has included, and with scientific exactness, our moral faculties among the elements to which we are indebted for our wealth—an idea as original and suggestive as it is just. It is destined to enlarge and ennoble the field of Political Economy.

I shall not dwell here upon that idea farther than as it may enable me to throw a faint light upon the origin of a powerful agent of production of which I shall have occasion to speak hereafter—I mean Capital.

If we examine in succession the material objects that contribute to the satisfaction of our wants, we shall discover without difficulty that all or nearly all require, in order to bring them to perfection, more time, a larger portion of our life, than a man can expend without recruiting his strength, that is to say, without satisfying his wants. This supposes that those who had made these things had previously reserved, set aside, accumulated, provisions, to enable them to subsist during the operation.

The same observation applies to satisfactions that have nothing material belonging to them.

A clergyman cannot devote himself to preaching, a professor to teaching, a magistrate to the maintenance of order, unless by themselves or by others, they are put in possession of means of subsistence previously created.

Let us go a little higher. Suppose a man isolated and forced to live by hunting. It is easy to comprehend that if every night he consumed the whole game that his day's hunting had furnished, he could never set himself to any other work, to build a cottage for example, or repair his arms or implements. All progress would be interdicted in his case.

This not the proper place to define the nature and functions of Capital. My sole object at present is to show that certain moral virtues cooperate very directly in the amelioration of our condition, even when viewed exclusively with reference to wealth—among other virtues, order, foresight, self-control, economy.

To foresee is one of our noblest privileges, and it is scarcely necessary to say that, in all situations of life, the man who most clearly foresees the probable consequences of his acts and decisions has the best chance of success.

To control his appetites, to govern his passions, to sacrifice the present to the future, to submit to privations for the sake of greater but more distant advantages—such are the conditions essential to the formation of capital; and capital, as we have already partially seen, is itself the essential condition of all labor that is in any degree complicated or prolonged. It is quite evident that if we suppose two men placed in identically the same position, and possessed of the same amount of intelligence and activity, that man would make the most progress who, having accumulated provisions, had placed himself in a situation to undertake protracted works, to improve his implements, and thus to make the forces of nature cooperate in the realization of his designs.

I shall not dwell longer on this. We have only to look around us to be convinced that all our forces, all our faculties, all our virtues, concur in furthering the advancement of man and of society.

For the same reason, there are none of our vices that are not directly or indirectly the causes of poverty. Idleness paralyzes efforts, which are the sinews of production. Ignorance and error give our efforts a false direction. Improvidence lays us open to deceptions. Indulgence in the appetites of the hour prevents the accumulation of capital. Vanity leads us to devote our efforts to factitious enjoyments, in place of such as are real. Violence and fraud provoke reprisals, oblige us to surround ourselves with troublesome precautions, and entail a great waste and destruction of power.

I shall wind up these preliminary observations on man with a remark I have already made in relation to his wants. It is this, that the elements discussed and explained in this chapter, and that enter into and constitute economic science, are in their nature flexible and changeable. Wants, desires, materials and powers furnished by nature, our muscular force, our organs, our intellectual faculties, our moral qualities, all vary with the individual, and change with time and place. No two men, perhaps, are entirely alike in any one of these respects, certainly not in all—nay more, no man entirely resembles himself for two hours together. What one knows, another is ignorant of—what one values, another despises—here nature is prodigal, there niggardly—a virtue that it is difficult to practice in one climate or latitude becomes easy in another. Economic science has not, then, like the exact sciences, the advantages of possessing a fixed measure, and absolute unconditional truths—a graduated scale, a standard, which can be employed in measuring the intensity of desires, of efforts, and of satisfactions. Were we even to devote ourselves to solitary labor, like certain animals, we should still find ourselves placed in circumstances in some degree different; and were our external circumstances alike, were the medium in which we act the same for all, we should still differ from each other in our desires, our wants, our ideas, our sagacity, our energy, our manner of estimating and appreciating things, our foresight, our initiative—so that a great and inevitable inequality would manifest itself. In truth, absolute isolation, the absence of all relations among men, is only an idle fancy coined in the brain of Rousseau. But supposing that this antisocial state, called the state of nature, had ever existed, I cannot help inquiring by what chain of reasoning Rousseau and his adepts have succeeded in planting Equality there? We shall afterwards see that Equality, like Wealth, like Liberty, like Fraternity, like Unity, is the end; it is not the starting point. It rises out of the natural and regular development of societies. The tendency of human nature is not away from, but toward, Equality. This is most consoling and most true.

Having spoken of our wants, and our means of providing for them, it remains to say a word respecting our satisfactions. They are the result of the entire mechanism we have described.

It is by the greater or less amount of physical, intellectual, and moral satisfactions that mankind enjoys, that we discover whether the machine works well or ill. This is the reason why the word consumption (consumption[3]), adopted by our Economists would have an apposite meaning if we used it in its etymological signification as synonymous with end, or completion. Unfortunately, in common, and even in scientific, language, it presents to the mind a gross and material idea, exact without doubt when applied to our physical wants, but not at all so when used with reference to those of a more elevated order. The cultivation of wheat, the manufacture of woolen cloth, terminate in consumption (consummation). But can this be said with equal propriety of the works of the artist, the songs of the poet, the studies of the lawyer, the prelections of the professor, the sermons of the clergyman? It is here that we again experience the inconvenience of that fundamental error that caused Adam Smith to circumscribe Political Economy within the limits of a material circle; and the reader will pardon me for frequently making use of the term satisfaction, as applicable to all our wants and all our desires, and as more in accordance with the larger scope I hope to be able to give to the science.

Political Economists have been frequently reproached with confining their attention exclusively to the interests of the consumer. "You forget the producer," we are told. But satisfaction

---

[3]The term consumption employed by English Economists, the French Economists translate by consummation.—Translator.

being the end and design of all our efforts—the grand consummation or termination of the economic phenomena—is it not evident that it is there that the touchstone of progress is to be found? A man's happiness and well-being are not measured by his efforts but by his satisfactions, and this holds equally true of society in the aggregate. This is one of those truths that are never disputed when applied to an individual, but that are constantly disputed when applied to society at large. The phrase to which exception has been taken only means this, that Political Economy estimates the worth of what we do not by the labor it costs us to do it, but by the ultimate result, which resolves itself definitively into an increase or diminution of the general prosperity.

We have said, in reference to our wants and desires, that there are no two men exactly alike. The same thing may be said of our satisfactions: they are not held in equal estimation by all, which verifies the common saying that tastes differ. Now it is by the intensity of our desires, and the variety of our tastes, that the direction of our efforts is determined. It is here that the influence of morals upon industry becomes apparent. Man, as an individual, may be the slave of tastes which are factitious, puerile, and immoral. In this case it is self-evident that, his powers being limited, he can only satisfy his depraved desires at the expense of those that are laudable and legitimate. But when society comes into play, this evident axiom is marked down as an error. We are led to believe that artificial tastes, illusory satisfactions, which we acknowledge as the source of individual poverty, are nevertheless the cause of national wealth, as providing an outlet to manufactures. If it were so, we should arrive at the miserable conclusion that the social state places man between poverty and vice. Once more, Political Economy reconciles, in the most rigorous and satisfactory manner, these apparent contradictions.

4

EXCHANGE

Exchange is Political Economy—it is Society itself—for it is impossible to conceive Society as existing without Exchange, or Exchange without Society. I shall not pretend in this chapter to exhaust so vast a subject. To present even an outline of it would require the entire volume.

If men, like snails, lived in complete isolation, if they did not exchange their ideas and exertions, and had no bargain or transactions with each other, we might have multitudes indeed—human units—individuals living in juxtaposition—but we could not have Society.

Nay, we should not even have individuals. To man isolation is death. But then, if he cannot live out of society, the legitimate conclusion is that the social state is his natural state.

All the sciences tend to establish this truth, which was so little understood by the men of the eighteenth century that they founded morals and politics on the contrary assertion. They were not content with placing the state of nature in opposition to the social state—they gave the first a decided preference. "Men were blessed," said Montaigne, "when they lived without bonds, without laws, without language, without religion." And we know that the system of Rousseau, which exercised, and still exercises, so powerful an influence over opinions and facts, rests altogether on this hypothesis—that men, unhappily, agreed one fine morning to abandon the innocent state of nature for the stormy state of society.

It is not the design of this chapter to bring together all possible refutations of this fundamental error, the most fatal that has ever infested the political sciences; for if society is the fruit of invention and convention, it follows that everyone may propose a new model, and this, since Rousseau's time, has in fact been the direction in which men's minds have tended. I could easily demonstrate, I believe, that isolation excludes language, as the absence of language excludes thought; and man, deprived of thought, instead of being a child of nature, ceases to be man at all. But a peremptory refutation of the idea upon which Rousseau's doctrine reposes flows naturally from some considerations on Exchange.

Want, Effort, Satisfaction—such is man in an economical point of view.

We have seen that the two extreme terms are essentially intransmissible, for they terminate in sensation, they are sensation, which is the most personal thing in the world, as well the sensation that precedes the effort and determines it, as the sensation that follows the effort and rewards it.

It is then the Effort that is exchanged; indeed it cannot be otherwise, since exchange implies action, and Effort alone manifests the principle of activity. We cannot suffer or enjoy for one another, unless we could experience personally the pains and pleasures of others. But we can assist each other, work for one another, render reciprocal services, and place our faculties, or the results of their exercise, at the disposal of others, in consideration of a return. This is society. The causes, the effects, the laws, of these exchanges constitute the subject of political and social economy.

We not only can exchange efforts and render reciprocal services, but we do so necessarily. What I affirm is this, that our makeup is such that we are obliged to work for one another under pain of death, of instant death. If it be so, society is our state of nature, since it is the only state in which we can live at all.

There is one observation that I have to make upon the equilibrium between our wants and our faculties, an observation that has always led me to admire the providential plan that regulates our destinies:

In the state of isolation our wants exceed our powers;

In the social state our powers exceed our wants. Hence it follows that man in an isolated state cannot subsist, while in the social state his most imperious wants give place to desires of a higher order, and continue to do so in an ascending career of progress and improvement to which it is impossible to set limits.

This is not declamation, but an assertion capable of being rigorously demonstrated by reasoning and analogy, if not by experience. And why can it not be demonstrated by experience, by direct observation? Precisely because it is true—precisely because man not being able to exist in a state of isolation, it becomes impossible to exhibit in actual nature the effects of absolute solitude. You cannot lay hold of a nonentity. You can prove to me that a triangle never has four sides, but you cannot, in support of your demonstration, place before my eyes a tetragonal triangle. If you could, the exhibition of such a triangle would disprove your assertion. In the same way to ask me for experimental proof, to ask me to study the effects of isolation in actual nature, is to palm a contradiction upon me; for life and isolation being incompatible, we have never seen, and never shall see, men without social relations.

If there are animals (of which I am ignorant) destined by their constitution to make the round of their existence in absolute isolation, it is very clear that nature must exactly proportion their wants and their powers. It is possible to conceive that their powers have the superiority, in which case these animals would be progressive and capable of improvement. An equilibrium of wants and powers would render them stationary beings; but the superiority of their wants to their powers it is impossible to conceive. From their birth, from their first appearance in life, their faculties must be complete—relatively to the wants for which they have to provide, or at least both must be developed in just proportion. Otherwise the species would die the moment they came into existence, and, consequently, could not be the subject of our observation.

Of all the species of living beings that surround us, undoubtedly none have so many wants as man. In none is infancy so long, so feeble, and so helpless—in none is maturity loaded with so much responsibility—in none is old age so frail and so liable to suffering. And, as if we had not enough of wants, man has tastes also, satisfaction of which exercises his faculties quite as much as his wants. Scarcely has he appeased his hunger than he begins to pamper himself with dainties—no sooner has he clothed himself than he sighs for finery—no sooner has he obtained shelter than he proceeds to embellish and decorate his residence. His mind is as restless as his body is exacting. He seeks to fathom the secrets of nature, to tame animals, to control the elements, to dive into the bowels of the earth, to traverse broad seas, to soar above the clouds, to annihilate time and space. He desires to know the motions, the springs, the laws, of his mind and heart—to control his passions—to conquer immortality—to become a god—to bring all things into subjection: nature, his fellow-men, himself. In a word, his desires and aspirations expand continually, and tend towards the infinite.

Thus, in no other species are the faculties so susceptible of vast development as in man. It is his alone to compare and to judge, to reason and to speak, to foresee, to sacrifice the present to the future. He alone can transmit, from generation to generation, his works, his thoughts, the treasures of his experience. He alone is capable of a perfectibility that is indefinite, that forms a chain the countless links of which would seem to stretch beyond the limits of the present world.

Let me here set down an observation that belongs properly to Political Economy. However extended may be the domain of our faculties, they do not reach the length of creating anything. Man cannot, in truth, augment or diminish the number of existing particles of matter. His action is limited to subjecting the substances that he finds around him to modifications and combinations that fit them for his use.[1]

To modify substances, so as to increase their utility in relation to us, is to produce, or rather it is one mode of producing. From this I conclude that value (as we shall afterwards more fully explain) does not reside in these substances themselves, but in the effort that intervenes in order to modify them, and that exchange brings into comparison with other analogous efforts. This is the reason why value is simply the appreciation of services exchanged, whether a material commodity does or does not intervene. As regards the notion of value, it is a matter of perfect indifference whether I render to another a direct service, as, for example, in performing for him a surgical operation, or an indirect service in preparing for him a curative substance. In this last case the utility is in the substance, but the value is in the service, in the effort, intellectual and muscular, made by one man for the benefit of another. It is by a pure metonymy that we attribute value to the material substance itself, and here, as on many other occasions, metaphor leads science astray.

I return to the subject of man's makeup. If we adhere to the preceding notions, he differs from other animals only in the greater extent of his wants, and the superiority of his powers. All, in fact, are subject to the one and provided with the other. A bird undertakes long journeys in search of the temperature that suits it best—the beaver crosses the river on a bridge of his own construction—the hawk pursues his prey openly—the cat watches for it with patience—the spider prepares a snare—all labor in order to live and multiply.

---

[1] J.B. Say.

But while nature has established an exact proportion between the wants of animals and their faculties, if she has treated man with greater bounty and munificence, if, in order to force him to be sociable, she has decreed that in a state of isolation his wants should surpass his faculties, while, on the contrary, in the social state, his powers, superior to his wants, open to him an unlimited field for nobler enjoyments, we ought to acknowledge that, as in his relation with the Creator man is elevated above the beasts by the religious sentiment, in his relations with his fellow-creatures by his sense of justice, in his relations with himself by the moral principle—in like manner, in relation to the means of living and multiplying, he is distinguished by a remarkable phenomenon, namely, EXCHANGE.

Shall I essay to paint the state of poverty, of destitution, and of ignorance, into which, but for the power of exchanging, the human species would have been sunk, had it not, indeed, as is more likely, disappeared altogether?

One of the most popular philosophers, in a romance that has been the charm of the young from generation to generation, has shown us man surmounting by his energy, his activity, his intelligence, the difficulties of absolute solitude. For the purpose of setting clearly before us what are the resources of that noble creature, the author has exhibited him as accidentally cut off from civilization. It was part of Defoe's plan to throw Robinson Crusoe into the Island of Juan Fernandez alone, naked, deprived of all that the union of efforts, the division of employments, exchange, society, add to the human powers.

And yet, although the fancied obstacles are but imaginary, Defoe would have taken away from his tale even the shadow of probability if, too faithful to the thought he wished to develop, he had not made forced concessions to the social state, by admitting that his hero had saved from shipwreck some indispensable things, such as provisions, gunpowder, a gun, a hatchet, a knife, cords, planks, iron, etc.; a decisive proof that society is the necessary medium in which man lives, and out of which not even a romance writer could figure him as existing.

And observe that Robinson Crusoe carried with him into solitude another social treasure, a thousand times more precious than all these, and which the waves could not engulf, I mean his ideas, his recollections, his experience, above all, his language, without which he would not have been able to hold conversation with himself, that is to say, to think.

We have the unfortunate and unreasonable habit of attributing to the social state the sufferings which we see around us. We are right so far, if our object be to compare society with itself in different degrees of advancement and improvement; but we are wrong if our object be to compare the social state, however imperfect, with a state of isolation. To authorize us to assert that society impairs the condition, I do not say of man in general, but of some men, and these the poorest and most wretched of the species, we must begin by proving that the worst provided of our fellow-creatures have to support in the social state a heavier load of privations and sufferings than the man whose lot has been cast in solitude. Now, examine the life of the humblest day-laborer. Pass in review, in all their details, the articles of his daily consumption. He is covered with some coarse clothing, he eats a little common bread, he sleeps under shelter, and on boards, at least if he has no better couch. Now, let us ask if man in a state of isolation, deprived of the resources of Exchange, could by any possibility procure for himself that coarse clothing, that common bread, that rude bed, that humble shelter? Rousseau himself, the passionate enthusiast of the state of nature, proves the utter impossibility of it. Men dispensed with everything he says; they went naked, they slept in the open air. Thus Rousseau, to exalt the state of nature, was led to make happiness consist in privation. And yet I affirm that this negative happiness is a chimera, and that man in a state of isolation would infallibly perish in a very few hours. Perhaps Rousseau would have gone to the length of saying that that would have been the perfection of his system; and he would have been consistent, for if privation be happiness, death is perfection.

I trust the reader will not conclude from what precedes that we are insensible to the social sufferings of our fellow-men. Because these sufferings are less even in an imperfect state of society than in a state of isolation, it does not follow that we should not encourage, with all earnestness, that progress that constantly diminishes them. But if isolation is something worse than all that is bad in the social state, then I am justified in saying that it places our wants, even the most imperious, far above our faculties and our means of providing for wants.

In what way does Exchange advantageously reverse all this, and place our faculties above our wants?

And first this is proved by the very fact of civilization. If our wants surpassed our faculties, we should be beings invincibly retrograde; if there were an equilibrium between them, we should be invincibly stationary. But we advance; which shows that at every stage of social life, as compared with the period that preceded it, a certain portion of our powers, relatively to a given amount of satisfactions, is left disposable. We shall endeavor to explain this marvelous phenomenon.

The explanation Condillac has given appears to me to be quite unsatisfactory and empirical—in fact it explains nothing. "From the very fact," he says, "that an exchange is made, it follows that there must be profit for the two contracting parties, for otherwise it would not take place. Then each exchange includes two gains for humanity."

Holding this proposition as true, we see in it only the statement of a result. It is in this way that the *Malade Imaginaire* explains the narcotic virtue of opium:

> *Quia est in eo*
> *Virtus dormitiva*
> *Quae facit dormire.*

Exchange includes two gains, you say. How? Why? It results from the fact that it takes place. But why does it take place? What motive has induced the contracting parties to effect the exchange? Has Exchange in itself a mysterious virtue, necessarily beneficial, and incapable of explanation?

Others make the advantage consist in this, that the one gives away a commodity of which he has too much in order to receive another of which he has too little. Exchange, they say, is a barter of the superfluous for the necessary. This is contradicted by facts that pass under our own eyes; for who can say that the peasant, in giving away the wheat that he has raised, but which he is never to eat, gives away a superfluity? I see in this axiom very clearly how two men may make an accidental arrangement, but I see no explanation of progress.

Observation gives us a more satisfactory explanation of the power of Exchange.

Exchange has two manifestations—namely, union of forces, and separation of occupations.

It is very clear that in many cases the united force of several men is superior, all things considered, to the sum of their individual forces. Suppose that what is wanted is to remove a heavy load. Where a thousand men in succession may fail, it is possible that four men may succeed by uniting their efforts. Just let us reflect how few things were ever accomplished in this world without union!

And yet this is only the concurrence of muscular forces in a common design. Nature has endowed us with very varied physical, intellectual, and moral faculties. There are in the co-operation of these faculties endless combinations. Is it wished to accomplish a useful work, like the construction of a road, or the defense of a country? One gives the community the benefit of his strength, another of his agility, another of his courage, another of his experience, foresight, imagination, even of his reputation. It is easy to comprehend that the same men acting singly could not have attained, or ever conceived, the same results.

Now, union of forces implies Exchange. To induce men to co-operate, they have the prospect of participating in the benefit to be obtained. Each makes the other profit by his Efforts, and he profits by the other's Efforts in return, which is Exchange.

We see how Exchange in this way augments our Satisfactions. The benefit consists in this, that efforts of equal intensity tend, by the mere fact of their union, to superior results. There is here no trace of the pretended barter of the superfluous for the necessary, any more than of the double and empirical profit alleged by Condillac.

The same remark applies to division of labor. Indeed, if we regard the matter more closely, we shall be convinced that the separation of employments is only another and more permanent manner of uniting our forces—of cooperating, of associating; and it is quite correct to say, as we shall afterwards demonstrate, that the present social organization, provided Exchange is left free and unfettered, is itself a vast and beautiful association—a marvelous association, very different indeed from that dreamed of by the Socialists, since, by an admirable mechanism, it is in perfect accordance with individual independence. Every one can enter and leave it at any moment that suits his convenience. He contributes to it voluntarily, and reaps a satisfaction superior to his contribution, and always increasing—a satisfaction determined by the laws of justice and the nature of things, not by the arbitrary will of a chief. But this is anticipating. All we have to do at present is to explain how the division of labor increases our power.

Without dwelling much on this subject, as it is one of the few that do not give rise to controversy, a remark or two may not be out of place. Its importance has perhaps been somewhat disparaged. In order to demonstrate the powerful effects of the Division of labor, it has been usual to describe its marvelous results in certain manufactures—in the making of pins, for example. But the subject admits of being viewed in a more general and philosophical light. The force of habit has the singular effect of concealing from us, and rendering us unconscious of, the phenomena in the midst of which we live and move. No saying is more profoundly true than that of Rousseau, "Much philosophy is needed for the observation of what we see every day." It may not then be without use to recall what we owe to Exchange, without perceiving it.

In what way has the power of exchanging elevated mankind to the height of civilization we have now attained? I answer, by the influence it exerts on labor, upon the cooperation of natural agents, upon the powers and faculties of man, and upon Capital.

Adam Smith has clearly demonstrated its influence on labor.

"The great increase in the quantity of work, which, in consequence of the division of labor, the same number of people are capable of performing, is owing to three circumstances," says that celebrated Economist; "First, to the increase of dexterity in every particular workman; second, to the saving of time, which is commonly lost in passing from one species of work to another; third, to this, that men are much more likely to discover easier and readier methods of attaining an object when the whole attention of their minds is directed to that single object, than when it is dissipated among a great variety of things."

Those who, like Adam Smith, see in labor the exclusive source of wealth, confine themselves to inquiring in what way the division of labor increases its efficiency. But we have seen in the preceding chapter that labor is not the sole agent in procuring us satisfaction. Natural forces cooperate. That is beyond doubt.

Thus in agriculture, the action of the sun and of the rain, the moisture of the earth, and the gases diffused in the atmosphere, are undoubtedly agents that cooperate with human labor in the production of vegetable substances.

Manufacturing industry owes analogous services to the chemical qualities of certain substances, to water power, to the elasticity of steam, to gravitation, to electricity.

Commerce has turned to the profit of man the vigor and instincts of certain races of animals, the force of the winds that fill the sails of his ships, the laws of magnetism, that, acting on the compass, direct the course of these ships through the pathless ocean.

There are two verities that are beyond all dispute. The first is that the more man avails himself of the forces of nature, the better he is provided with everything he requires.

It is sufficiently evident that, with equal exertion, we obtain more wheat from a rich loamy soil than from sterile rocks or arid sands.

The second is that natural agents are unequally diffused over the various countries of the world.

Who would venture to maintain that all soils are equally well fitted for all kinds of culture, or all countries for the same description of manufactures?

Now, if it be true on the one hand that natural forces are unequally diffused in the different countries of the world, and on the other that men are richer in proportion as they avail themselves of them, it follows that the faculty of Exchange immeasurably augments the useful cooperation of these forces.

And here we recur once more to gratuitous and onerous utility, the former being substituted for the latter by virtue of Exchange. Is it not very clear that if men were deprived of the power of Exchange, and were obliged to produce ice under the equator, and sugar at the poles, they must spend much pains in doing what heat and cold do gratuitously, and that for them an immense proportion of the Forces of nature would remain inoperative? Thanks to Exchange, these forces are rendered useful to us wherever we encounter them. Wheat land is sown with wheat—in wine-growing countries the land is planted with vines—there are fishermen on the coasts, and wood-cutters among the mountains. In one place a wheel that does the work of ten men is set in motion by water—in another, by wind. Nature becomes a slave, whom we have neither to feed, nor to clothe, nor to pay—who costs nothing either to our purse or our conscience.[2] The same amount of human efforts, that is to say, the same services, the same value, realizes a constantly increasing amount of utility. For each given result a certain portion only of human exertion is absorbed; the remainder, by means of the intervention of natural Forces, is rendered disposable, and it sets to work to overcome new obstacles, to minister to new desires, to realize new utilities.

_____

[2]Moreover, this slave, by reason of his superiority, ends in the long-run by depreciating and emancipating all others. This is a harmony I leave to the sagacity of the reader to follow to its consequences.

The effects of Exchange upon our intellectual Faculties are so great that we can scarcely even imagine their extent.

"Knowledge," says Mr. de Tracy, "is the most precious of all our acquisitions, since it directs and governs the employment of our forces, and renders them more prolific in proportion as it is sounder and more extensive. No man can himself observe everything, and it is much easier to learn than to invent. But when several men communicate with each other, what is observed by one is soon known to the rest; and if there be among them but one person of superior ingenuity, precious discoveries speedily become the property of all. In such circumstances, knowledge is much more rapidly increased than it could be in a state of isolation, without taking into account the power of preserving it, and consequently of accumulating it from one generation to another."

If the resources nature has accumulated around man and placed at his disposal are varied, the human faculties themselves are not less so. We are not all equally endowed with strength, courage, intelligence, patience, or with artistic, literary, and industrial aptitudes. Without exchange, this diversity, far from contributing to our well-being, would contribute to our misery, each feeling less the advantage of those Faculties he possessed than the deprivation of those he lacked. Thanks to exchange, a man possessed of bodily strength may, up to a certain point, dispense with genius, and a man of intelligence with bodily strength; for by the admirable community that the power of exchange establishes among men, each individual participates in the distinctive qualities of his neighbors.

In order to obtain the satisfactions he desires, it is not enough, in most cases, to work—to exercise his faculties upon, or by means of, natural agents. He requires also to have tools, instruments, machines, provisions—in a word, Capital. Imagine a small tribe, composed of ten families, each, in working exclusively for itself, being obliged to engage in ten different employments. In that case each family must have ten sets of industrial apparatus. The tribe would require to possess ten ploughs, ten teams of oxen, ten forges, ten joiner's and carpenter's workshops, ten looms, etc.; while, with the power of exchange, a single plough, a single team, a single forge, a single loom, would be sufficient. It is impossible to conceive the economy of Capital which we owe to exchange.

The reader now sees clearly what constitutes the true power of exchange. It is not, as Condillac says, that it implies two gains, because of each of the contracting parties valuing more highly what he receives than what he gives. Neither is it that each gives away what is superfluous for what is necessary. It lies simply in this, that when one man says to another—"Do you only this, and I shall do only that, and we shall divide," there is a better and more advantageous employment of labor, of faculties, of natural agents, of capital, and consequently there is more to divide. And these results take place to a still greater extent when three, ten, a hundred, a thousand, or several million men enter into the association.

The two propositions I have laid down, then, are rigorously true, viz.:

In isolation our wants exceed our powers;

In society our powers exceed our wants.

The first is true, seeing that the whole surface of our country would not maintain one man in a state of absolute isolation.

The second is true, seeing that, in fact, the population that is spread over that same surface multiplies and grows richer.

Progress of Exchange: The primitive form of exchange is Barter. Two persons, one of whom desires an object, and is possessed of an object that the other desires, agree to cede these objects reciprocally, or they agree to work separately, each at one thing, but for the purpose of dividing the total product of their labor in arranged proportions. This is Barter, which is, as the Socialists would say, Exchange, traffic, commerce in embryo. We observe here two Desires as motives—two Efforts as means—two Satisfactions as results, or as the termination and completion of the entire cycle; and this evolution is not essentially different from the same evolution accomplished in a state of isolation, except that the desires and satisfactions have, as their nature requires, remained intransmissible, and that Efforts alone have been exchanged. In other words, the two persons have worked for each other, and have rendered each other reciprocal services.

It is at this point that Political Economy truly begins, for it is here that value first makes its appearance. Barter takes place only after an arrangement, a discussion. Each of the contracting parties is governed by considerations of self-interest. Each of them makes a calculation, which in effect comes to this, "I shall barter if the barter procures me the satisfaction I desire with a less Effort." It is certainly a marvelous phenomenon that diminished efforts can yet keep pace with undiminished desires and satisfactions; and this is explained by the considerations I have presented in the first part of this chapter. When two commodities or two services are bartered, we may conclude that they are of equal value. We shall have to analyze afterwards the notion of value, but this vague definition is sufficient for the present.

We may suppose a round-about barter, including three contracting parties. Paul renders a service to Peter, who renders an equivalent service to James, who in turn renders an equivalent service to Paul, by means of which all is balanced. I need not say that this round-about transaction only takes place because it suits all the parties, without changing either the nature or the consequences of barter.

The essence of Barter is discovered in all its purity even when the number of contracting parties is greater. In my commune the vintner pays with wine for the services of the blacksmith, the barber, the tailor, the constable, the curate, the grocer; while the blacksmith, the barber, the tailor, in turn deliver to the grocer, for the commodities consumed during the year, the wine they have received from the vintner.

This round-about Barter, I cannot too often repeat, does not change in the least degree the primary notions explained in the preceding chapters. When the evolution is complete, each of those who have had part in it presents still the triple phenomenon, want, effort, satisfaction. We have but to add the exchange of efforts, the transmission of services, the separation of employments, with all their resulting advantages—advantages to which every one of the parties has contributed, seeing that isolated individual labor is a last resort—always reserved an option—and which is only renounced in consideration of a certain advantage.

It is easy to comprehend that Barter in kind, especially the indirect and round-about barter I have described, cannot be much extended, and it is unnecessary to dwell upon the obstacles that set limits to it. How could he manage, for example, who wished to exchange his house against the thousand articles that enter into his annual consumption? In any case, Barter could never take place but among the few persons who happen to be acquainted with each other. Progress and the Division of labor would soon reach their limits if mankind had not discovered the means of facilitating exchanges.

This is the reason why men, from the earliest ages of society, have employed an intermediate commodity to effect their trans-actions—wheat, wine, animals, and almost always, the precious metals. Such commodities perform this function of facilitating exchanges more or less conveniently; still any one of them can perform it, provided that, in the transaction, Effort is represented by value, the transmission of which is the thing to be effected.

When recourse is had to an intermediate commodity, two eco-nomic phenomena make their appearance, which we denominate Sale and Purchase. It is evident that the idea of sale and purchase is not included in direct Barter, or even in roundabout Barter. When a man gives another something to drink in consideration of receiving from him something to eat, we have a simple fact that we cannot analyze farther. Now, what we must note in the very outset of the science is, that exchanges that are effected by means of an intermediate commodity do not lose the nature, the essence, the quality of barter—only the barter is no longer sim-ple, but compound. To borrow the very judicious and profound observation of J.B. Say, it is a barter of two factors (*troc a deux facteurs*), of which the one is called sale and other purchase—fac-tors whose union is indispensable in order to constitute a com-plete barter.

In truth, this discovery of a convenient means of effecting exchanges makes no alteration in the nature either of men or of things. We have still in every case the want that motivates the effort, and the satisfaction that rewards it. The Exchange is complete only when the man who has made an effort in favor of another has obtained from him an equivalent service, that is to say satisfaction. To effect this, he sells his service for the intermediate commodity, and then with that intermediate commodity he purchases equivalent services, when the two factors bring back the transaction to simple barter.

Take the case of a physician for instance. For many years he has devoted his time and his faculties to the study of diseases and their remedies. He has visited patients, he has prescribed for them, in a word, he has rendered services. Instead of receiving compensation from his patients in direct services, which would have constituted simple barter, he receives from them an intermediate commodity, the precious metals, wherewith he purchases the satisfactions that were the ultimate object he had in view. His patients have not furnished him with bread, wine, or other goods, but they have furnished him with the value of these. They could not have given him money unless they had themselves rendered services. As far as they are concerned, therefore, there is a balance of services, and there is also a balance as regards the physician; and could we in thought follow this circulation of services out and out, we should see that Exchange carried on by the intervention of money resolves itself into a multitude of acts of simple barter.

In the case of simple barter, value is the appreciation of two services exchanged and directly compared with each other. In the case of Compound Exchange the two services measure each other's value, not directly, but by comparison with this mean term, this intermediate commodity, which is called Money. We shall see, by and by, what difficulties, what errors, have sprung from this complication. At present it is sufficient to remark that the intervention of this intermediate commodity makes no change whatever in the notion of value.

Only admit that exchange is at once the cause and the effect of the division of labor and the separation of employments; only admit that the separation of occupations multiplies satisfactions in proportion to efforts, for the reasons explained at the beginning of this chapter, and you will comprehend at once the services that Money has rendered to mankind, by the simple fact that it facilitates Exchanges. By means of Money, Exchange is indefinitely extended and developed. Each man casts his services into the common fund, without knowing who is to enjoy the satisfactions they are calculated to procure. In the same way he obtains from society not immediate services, but money with which he can afterwards purchase services, where, when, and how it may best suit him. In this way the ultimate transactions occur at various times and places, between people totally unacquainted with each other, and in the greater number of cases no one knows by whose efforts his wants will be satisfied, or to the satisfaction of whose desires his own efforts will contribute. Exchange, by the intervention of Money, resolves itself into innumerable acts of barter, of which the contracting parties themselves are ignorant.

Exchange, however, confers so great a benefit on society (is it not society itself?) that it facilitates and extends it by other means besides the introduction of money. In logical order, after Want and Satisfaction united in the same individual with isolated Effort—after simple barter—after barter *a deux facteurs*, or Exchange composed of sale and purchase—come other transactions, extended farther over time and space by means of credit, mortgages, bills of exchange, bank notes, etc. By means of this wondrous machinery, the result of civilization, the improver of civilization, and itself becoming more perfect at the same time, an exertion made at the present hour in Paris may contribute to the satisfaction and enjoyment of an unknown stranger, separated from us by oceans and centuries; and he who makes the exertion will not the less receive for it a present recompense, through the intervention of persons who advance the remuneration, and wait to be reimbursed in a distant country or at a future day. Marvelous and astonishing complication which, when subjected to analysis, shows us finally the accomplishment of the entire economic cycle—want, effort, satisfaction, taking place in each individual, according to a just law.

Limits of Exchange: The general character of Exchange is to diminish the proportion that the Effort bears to the Satisfaction. Between our wants and our satisfactions obstacles are interposed, which we succeed in diminishing by the union of forces or the division of occupations, that is to say, by Exchange. But Exchange itself encounters obstacles and demands efforts. The proof of this is the immense amount of human labor it sets in motion. The precious metals, roads, canals, railways, wheeled carriages, ships—all these things absorb a considerable portion of human activity. Observe, besides, how many men are exclusively occupied in facilitating exchanges—how many bankers, merchants, shopkeepers, brokers, draymen, sailors! This vast and costly apparatus shows us, better than any reasoning, how much efficacy there is in the power of Exchange, for why otherwise should society be encumbered with it?

Since it is the nature of Exchange to save efforts and to consume them, it is easy to understand what are its natural limits. In virtue of that motive which urges man to choose always the least of two evils, Exchange will go on extending itself indefinitely as long as the effort it exacts is less than the effort it saves. And its extension will stop naturally when, upon the whole, the aggregate of satisfactions obtained by the division of labor becomes less, by reason of the increasing difficulties attending Exchange, than if we procured them by direct production.

Suppose the case of a small tribe. If they desire to procure themselves satisfactions they must make an effort. They may address themselves to another tribe, and say to them, "Make this effort for us, and we shall make another for you." The stipulation may suit all parties, if, for example, the second tribe is in a situation to obtain greater assistance than the other from natural and gratuitous forces. In that case it may be able to realize the result with an effort equal to eight, while the first could only accomplish it by an effort equal to twelve. There is thus an economy equal to

four for the first. But then come the cost of transport, the remuneration of intermediate agents, in a word, the effort exacted by
the machinery of Exchange. This cost must then clearly be added
to the figure eight. Exchange will continue to take place as long
as the Exchange itself does not cost four. The moment it reaches
that figure it will stop. It is quite unnecessary to make laws on this
subject; for either the law intervenes before this level is attained,
and then it is injurious—it prevents an economy of efforts—or it
comes after it, and then it is useless, like an ordinance forbidding
people to light their lamps at noonday.

When Exchange is thus arrested, from ceasing to be advantageous, the slightest improvement in the commercial apparatus gives it a new activity. Between Orleans and Angouleme a
certain number of transactions take place. These towns effect an
Exchange as often as they can obtain a greater amount of enjoyments by that means than by direct production. They stop
short the moment the cost of obtaining commodities by means of
exchange, aggravated by the cost of effecting the exchange itself,
surpasses, or reaches, that of obtaining them by means of direct
production. In these circumstances, if we improve the conditions
under which Exchanges are effected—if the merchants' profits are
diminished, or the means of transport facilitated—if roads and
railways are made, mountains levelled, and bridges thrown over
rivers—in a word, if obstacles are removed, the number of
Exchanges will be increased; for men are always desirous to avail
themselves of the great advantages we have ascribed to Exchange,
and to substitute gratuitous for onerous utility. The improvement
of the commercial apparatus, then, is equivalent to bringing two
cities locally nearer to each other. Whence it follows that bringing
men physically, locally, nearer each other is equivalent to improving the conditions of exchange. This is very important. It is, in fact,
the solution of the problem of population; and this is precisely
the element in that great problem that Malthus has neglected.
Where Malthus saw Discordance, attention to this element
enables us to discover Harmony.

When men effect an exchange, it is because they succeed by that means in obtaining an equal amount of satisfaction at a less expense of effort; and the reason of this is that on both sides services are rendered that are the means of procuring a greater proportion of what we have termed gratuitous utility.

Now you have always a greater number of exchanges in proportion as you remove the obstacles which impede exchanges, and diminish the efforts these exchanges require.

And Exchange encounters fewer obstacles, and requires fewer efforts, just in proportion as you bring men nearer each other, and mass them more together. A greater density of population, then, is accompanied by a greater proportion of gratuitous utility. That density imparts greater power to the machinery of exchange; it sets free and renders disposable a portion of human efforts; it is a cause of progress.

Now, if you please, let us leave generalities and look at facts.

Does not a street of equal length render more service in Paris than in a remote village? Is not a mile of railway of more use in the Department of the Seine than in the Department of the Landes? Is not a London merchant content with smaller markups on account of the greater amount of business he transacts? In everything we shall discover two sets of exchange agencies at work, which although identical in kind, act very differently, according as they operate in a densely or a thinly peopled locality.

The density of population not only enables us to reap more advantage from the machinery of exchange, it permits us to improve that machinery, and increase its power. Where the population is condensed, these improvements are advantageous, because they save us more efforts than they cost; but where the population is scattered and thin-spread, they cost more efforts than they save.

On leaving the metropolis for a time, and going to reside in a small provincial town, one is astonished to find that in many instances the most ordinary services can only be obtained at great expense, and with time and difficulty.

It is not the material part of the commercial mechanism only that is turned to account and improved by the single circumstance of the density of population, but the moral part also. When men are massed together, they have more facility in dividing their employments, in uniting their powers, and in combining to found churches and schools, to provide for their common security, to establish banks and insurance companies, in a word, to procure themselves all the common enjoyments with a much smaller proportion of efforts.

We shall revert to these considerations when we come to enter on the subject of Population. At present we shall make only this remark:

Exchange enables men to turn their faculties to better account, to economize capital, to obtain more assistance from the gratuitous agencies of nature, to increase the proportion of gratuitous to onerous utility, to diminish, consequently, the ratio of efforts to results, and to leave at their disposal a part of their forces, so that they may withdraw a greater and greater portion of them from the business of providing for their primary and more urgent wants, and devote them to procuring enjoyments of a higher and higher order.

If Exchange saves efforts, it also exacts them. It extends, and spreads and increases, up to the point at which the effort it costs becomes equal to the effort it saves, and it stops there until, by the improvement of the commercial apparatus, or by the circumstance exclusively of the concentration of population, and bringing men together in masses, it again returns to the conditions that are essential to its onward and ascending march. Whence it follows that laws that limit or hamper Exchanges are always either hurtful or superfluous.

Governments that persuade themselves that nothing good can be done but through their instrumentality, refuse to acknowledge this harmonic law.

Exchange develops itself naturally until it becomes more onerous than useful, and at that point it naturally stops.

In consequence, we find governments everywhere busying themselves in favoring or restraining trade.

In order to carry it beyond its natural limits, they set to conquering colonies and opening new markets. In order to confine it below its natural bounds, they invent all sorts of restrictions and fetters.

This intervention of Force in human transactions is the source of innumerable evils.

The Increase of this force itself is an evil to begin with; for it is very evident that the State cannot make conquests, retain distant countries under its rule, or divert the natural course of trade by the action of tariffs, without greatly increasing the number of its agents.

The Diversion of the public power from its legitimate functions is an evil still greater than its Increase. Its rational mission was to protect Liberty and Property; and here you have it violating Liberty and Property. All just notions and principles are thus effaced from men's minds. The moment you admit that Oppression and Spoliation are legitimate, provided they are legal—provided they interfere only by means of the Law or public power, you find by degrees each class of citizens demanding that the interest of every other class should be sacrificed to it.

This intervention of power in the business of Exchanges, whether it succeeds in promoting or in restraining them, cannot fail to occasion both the Loss and Displacement of labor and capital, and, in consequence, a disturbance of the natural distribution of the population. On one side, natural interests disappear, on the other, artificial interests are created, and men are forced to follow the course of these interests. It is thus we see important branches of industry established where they ought not to be. France makes sugar; England spins cotton, brought from the plains of India. Centuries of war, torrents of blood, the dissipation of vast treasures, have brought about these results, and the effect has been to substitute in Europe sickly and precarious for sound and healthy enterprises, and to open the door to commercial crises, to stoppages, to instability, and finally to Pauperism.

But I find I am anticipating. What we ought first to do is to acquaint ourselves with the free and natural development of human societies, and then investigate the Disturbances.

Moral Force of Exchange: We must repeat, at the risk of wounding modern sentimentalism, that Political Economy belongs to the region of business, and business is transacted under the influence of personal interest. In vain the puritans of socialism cry out, "This is frightful; we shall change all this." Such declamations involve a flat contradiction. Do we make purchases in the marketplace in the name of Fraternity?

It would be to fall into another kind of cant to attribute morality to acts determined and governed by self-interest. But a good and wise Providence may so have arranged the social order that these very acts, devoid of morality in their motives, may nevertheless tend to moral results. Is it not so in the case of labor? Now, I maintain that Exchange, whether in the incipient state of simple barter, or expanded into a vast and complicated commerce, develops in society tendencies more noble than the motive that gives rise to it.

I have certainly no wish to attribute to only one of our powers all that constitutes the grandeur, the glory, and the charm of our existence. As there are two forces in the material world—one that goes from the circumference to the center, the other from the center to the circumference—there are also two principles in the social world, self-interest and sympathy. It would be a misfortune indeed if we failed to recognize the benefits and joys of the sympathetic principle, as manifested in friendship, love, filial piety, parental tenderness, charity, patriotism, religion, enthusiasm for the good and the beautiful. Some have maintained that the sympathetic principle is only a magnificent form of self-love, that to love others is at bottom only an intelligent way of loving ourselves. This is not the place to enter on the solution of that problem. Whether these two native energies are distinct or confounded, it is enough for us to know that far from being antagonistic, as is constantly said, they act in combination, and concur in the realization of one and the same result, the general good.

I have established these two propositions:

In a state of isolation, our wants exceed our powers;

In consequence of Exchange, our powers exceed our wants.

These propositions show the end and purpose of society. There are two others that guarantee its indefinite improvement:

In a state of isolation, the gain of one may be the loss of another;

In consequence of Exchange, the gain of each is the gain of all.

Is it necessary to prove that, if nature had destined man to a solitary life, the prosperity of one would have been incompatible with that of another, and the more numerous men had been, the less chance would they have had of attaining prosperity? At all events, we see clearly in what way numbers might have been injurious, and we do not see how they could have been beneficial. And then, I would ask, under what form could the principle of sympathy have manifested itself? How, or on what occasion, could it have been called forth? Could we have even comprehended it?

But men exchange, and Exchange, as we have seen, implies the separation of employments. It gives birth to professions and trades. Each man sets himself to overcome a certain class of obstacles, for the benefit of the Community. Each makes it his business to render a certain description of services. Now, a complete analysis of value demonstrates that each service has value in the first instance in proportion to its intrinsic utility, and afterwards in proportion to the wealth of those to whom it is furnished— that is to say, in proportion as the community to whom the service is rendered has a greater demand for it, and is in a better situation to pay for it. Experience shows us that the artisan, the physician, the lawyer, the merchant, the carrier, the professor, the savant, derive greater returns from their services in Paris, in London, or at New York, than in the lands of Gascony, or the mountains of Wales, or the prairies of the Far West. And does not this confirm the truth, that each man is more likely to prosper in proportion to the general prosperity of the community in which he lives?

Of all the harmonies that have come under my observation, this is beyond doubt the most important, the finest, the most decisive, the most suggestive. It sums up and includes all the others. This is why I can give only a very incomplete demonstration of it in this place. The whole scope and spirit of this work will establish it; and I shall deem it a fortunate thing if its probability at least is made so apparent as to induce the reader to convince himself of its truth by further inquiry and reflection.

For it is beyond question that on this turns our decision between natural and artificial Organizations—that on this, and this alone, hangs the solution of the Social Problem. If the prosperity of all be the condition of the prosperity of each, then we can repose with confidence not only on the economic power of free trade, but on its moral force. If men only understood their true interests, restrictions, mercantile jealousies, commercial wars, monopolies, would go down under the influence of public opinion; and before soliciting the interposition of government in any case, the question would be, not "How am I to be benefited by it?" but "What advantage is likely to result from it to the community?" This last question, I grant, is sometimes elicited by the principle of sympathy; but let men be once enlightened, and it will be called forth by Self-interest. Then we shall be enabled to say with truth that the two motive principles of our nature tend toward the same result—the General Good; and it will be impossible to deny Moral Power to self-interest, and the transactions that spring from it, as far at least as their effects are concerned.

Consider the relations of man to man, family to family, province to province, nation to nation, hemisphere to hemisphere, capitalist to laborer, the man of property to the man of no property—it seems evident to me that it is impossible to resolve the social problem from any one of these points of view, or even to enter upon its solution, before choosing between these two maxims:

The profit of one is the loss of another;

The profit of one is the gain of another.

For if nature has arranged matters so that antagonism is the law of free transactions, our only resource is to vanquish nature and stifle Freedom. If, on the other hand, these free transactions are harmonious, that is to say, if they tend to ameliorate and equalize the conditions of men, our efforts must be confined to allowing nature to act, and maintaining the rights of human Liberty.

This is the reason why I conjure the young people to whom this work is dedicated to scrutinize with care the formulas which it lays down, and to analyze the peculiar nature and effects of Exchange. I hope yet to find at least one among them who will be able to demonstrate rigorously this proposition: "The good of each tends to the good of all, as the good of all tends to the good of each;" and who will, moreover, be able to impress this truth upon men's minds by rendering the proof of it simple, lucid, and irrefutable. The man who does this will have resolved the social problem, and be the benefactor of the human race.

Depend upon it, that according as this axiom is true or false, the natural laws of society are harmonious or antagonistic; and that according as they are harmonious or antagonistic, it is our interest to conform to them or to deviate from them. Were it once thoroughly demonstrated, then, that under the empire of freedom men's interests harmonize and favor each other, all the efforts we now see governments making to disturb the action of these natural social laws we should see directed to giving them force, or rather, no efforts whatever would then be necessary, and all they would have to do would be to abstain from interfering. In what does the restraining action of governments consist? We may infer it from the design they have in view. What is that design? To remedy the Inequality that is supposed to spring from Liberty. Now, there is only one way of re-establishing the equilibrium, namely, to take from one in order to give to another. Such, in fact, is the mission that governments have arrogated to themselves, or have received; and it is a rigorous consequence of the formula that the gain of one is the loss of another. If that axiom be true, Force must repair the evils of Liberty. Thus governments, instituted for the protection of liberty and property, have undertaken the task of violating liberty and property in every shape; and they have done so consistently, if it be in liberty and property that the germ and principle of evil reside. Hence we see them everywhere engaged in the artificial displacement and redistribution of labor, capital, and responsibility.

On the other hand, an incalculable amount of intellectual force is thrown away in the pursuit of artificial social organizations. To take from one in order to give to another, to violate both liberty and property, is a very simple design, but the means of carrying out that design may be varied to infinity. Hence arise multitudes of systems, which strike the producing classes with terror, since from the very nature of the object they have in view, they menace all existing interests.

Thus arbitrary and complex systems of government, the negation of liberty and property, the antagonism of classes and nations, all these are logically included in the axiom that the gain of one is the loss of another. And, for the same reason, simplicity in government, respect for individual dignity, freedom of labor and exchange, peace among nations, security for person and property, are all contained and shut up in this truth—Interests are harmonious. They are so, however, only on one condition, which is, that this truth should be generally admitted.

But it is very far from being so. On reading what I have said on this subject many people will be led to say, You break through an open door. Who ever thought of contesting seriously the superiority of Exchange to Isolation? In what book, unless indeed in the works of Rousseau, have you encountered this strange paradox?

Those who stop me with this reflection forget only two things, two symptoms, or rather two aspects of modern society, the doctrines with which theorists inundate us, and the practice that governments impose on us. It is quite impossible that the harmony of interests can be universally recognized, since on the one hand, public force is constantly engaged in interfering to disturb natural combinations, while on the other, the great complaint against the ruling power is that it does not interfere enough.

The question is this, Are the evils (I do not speak here of evils that arise from our native infirmity)—are the evils to which society is subject imputable to the action of natural social laws, or to our disturbance of that action?

Now, here we have two co-existent facts, Evil—and Public Force, engaged to counteract the natural social laws. Is the first of these facts the consequence of the second? For my own part, I believe so; I should even say, I am certain of it. But at the same time I can attest to this, that in proportion as evil is developed, governments invariably seek for a remedy in new disturbances of the natural laws, and theorists reproach them with not going far enough. Am I not thence entitled to conclude that they have but little confidence in these laws?

Undoubtedly, if the question is between Isolation and Exchange we are at one. But if the question be between free and compulsory exchange, does the same thing hold? Is there nothing forced, factitious, restrained, constrained, in France, in the manner in which services related to trade, to credit, to conveyances, to the arts, to education, to religion, are exchanged? Are labor and capital distributed naturally between agriculture and manufactures? When existing interests are disturbed, are they allowed of their own accord to return to their natural channels? Do we not encounter trammels and obstacles on all sides? Are there not a hundred professions that are interdicted to the majority of the people? Is the Roman-Catholic not forced to pay for the services of the Jewish rabbi, and the Jew for the services of the Catholic priest? Is there a single man in France who has received the education that his parents would have given him had they been free? Are not our minds, our manners, our ideas, our employments, fashioned under the regime of the arbitrary, or at least of the artificial? Now, I ask whether thus to disturb the free exchange of services is not to abjure and deny the harmony of interests? On what ground am I robbed of my liberty, unless it be that it is judged hurtful to others? Is it pretended that it is injurious to myself? This would be but to add one antagonism the more. And only think! in what a situation should we find ourselves if nature had placed in each man's heart a permanent irrepressible spring of action, urging him to injure those around him, and at the same time to injure himself?

Alas! we have tried everything—when shall we make trial of the simplest thing of all—Liberty? Liberty in all that does not offend against justice—liberty to live, advance, improve—the free exercise of our faculties—the free interchange of services. A beautiful and rare spectacle it would have been, had the Power that sprang from the revolution of February thus addressed our citizens:

"You have invested me with the public Force. I shall apply it exclusively to those things in which the intervention of Force is permissible, and there is but one—Justice. I shall force everyone to conform himself within the bounds of right. You may work freely and as you please during the day, and sleep in peace at night. I have taken under my charge the security of person and property—that is my mission, and I will fulfill it—but I accept no other. Let there then be no longer any misunderstanding between us. Henceforth you shall pay me only the light tribute that is necessary for the maintenance of order and the administration of justice. Keep in mind that henceforth every man must depend upon himself for his subsistence and advancement. Turn no longer your longing eyes to me. Ask me no longer for wealth, for employment, for credit, for education, for religion, for morality. Never forget that the mainspring of your development is in yourselves. As for me, I never act but through the intervention of force. I have nothing, absolutely nothing, but what I derive from you, and for this reason I cannot confer even the smallest advantage on one except at the expense of another. Cultivate your fields, then, manufacture and export your products, carry on trade, afford each other credit, render and receive services freely, educate your children, set them out in life, cultivate the arts, improve your minds, refine and purify your tastes and sentiments, unite, form industrial and charitable associations, join your efforts for your individual good and that of the public, follow your inclinations, fulfill your destinies by the free exercise of your powers, your ideas, and your foresight. Expect from me only two things—Liberty and Security—and depend upon it you cannot ask me for a third without losing the other two."

I am thoroughly persuaded that if the revolution of February had proclaimed these principles we never should have had another revolution. Is it possible to conceive that citizens, left perfectly free in all other respects, would conspire to overturn a power whose action was limited to the satisfaction of the most pressing, the most deeply felt of all our social requirements, the requirement of Justice?

But it was unfortunately impossible for the National Assembly to adopt this course, or make these sentiments heard. They were not in accordance either with the ideas of the Assembly or the expectations of the public. They would have terrified society as much as the proclamation of Communism. To be responsible to ourselves, of all things! To trust to the State only for the maintenance of order and peace! To expect from it neither wealth nor knowledge! To be able no longer to make it responsible for our faults, our folly, our imprudence! To trust only to ourselves for the means of subsistence and physical amelioration, or moral and intellectual improvement! What on earth is to become of us? Is not society on the eve of being invaded by poverty, ignorance, error, irreligion, and perversity?

We allow that such undoubtedly would have been the fears that would have manifested themselves on all sides had the revolution of February proclaimed Liberty, that is to say, the reign of the natural laws of society. Then we were either unacquainted with these laws, or we wanted confidence in them. We could not get rid of the idea that the motives and springs of action that God has implanted in the mind of man are essentially perverse; that rectitude resides nowhere but in the views and intentions of the governing power; that the tendencies of human nature lead to disorganization, to anarchy—in a word, we believed in the inevitable antagonism of interests.

So far was the revolution of February from displaying any tendency toward a natural organization that never were the hopes and ideas of French society so decidedly turned to artificial combinations as at that epoch. Which of these combinations was in most favor? I really cannot very well tell. The business, in the language of the day, was to make experiments—*Faciamus experimentum in corpore vili*. Such was their contempt for individuality, so thoroughly did they equate human nature to inert matter, that they talked of making social experiments with men, just as we make chemical experiments with acids and alkalies. The first tentative was begun at the Luxembourg, we know with what success. Before long, the Constituent Assembly instituted a Committee of labor, in which a thousand social schemes were engulfed and swallowed up. A Fourierist representative seriously demanded lands and money (he would soon have asked for men also) to enable him to manipulate his model society. Another Egalitaire representative offered his recipe, which was rejected. The manufacturers were more lucky, and succeeded in maintaining theirs. In the meantime, the Legislative Assembly named a commission to organize "assistance."

Now, what strikes us with surprise in all this is that the Ruling Power, for the sake of its own stability, did not from time to time thus enter its protest: "You are habituating thirty-six million men to regard the State as responsible for all the good or evil that may befall them in this world. At this rate, Government is impossible."

At any rate, if these various social inventions, dignified with the high sounding title of organization, differ from each other in their manner of proceeding, they are all founded on the same principle: Take from one to give to another. Now such a principle clearly could not meet with such universal sympathy from the people, unless they were thoroughly convinced that men's interests are naturally antagonistic, and that the tendencies of human nature are essentially perverse.

To take from one to give to another! I know well that things have gone on in this way for a long time. But before you set yourselves to imagine various means of realizing this whimsical principle for the remedy of existing distress, would it not be well to inquire whether that distress has not proceeded from the very fact that this principle in a certain form has been realized already? Before seeking a remedy in new disturbances of the natural social laws, should you not make sure that such perturbations do not themselves constitute the very evil from which society suffers, and which it is your object to cure?

To take from one in order to give to another! Just allow me to mark here the danger and the absurdity, from an economical point of view, of this so-called social aspiration, which, fermenting among the masses of our population, broke forth with so terrific a force in the revolution of February.

Where society consists of several grades, we are apt to think that people of the highest rank enjoy Privileges or Monopolies at the expense of all the other members of the community. This is odious, but it is not absurd.

The second grade, the class immediately below the first, will not fail to attack and batter down monopolies; and, with the assistance of the masses, they will succeed sooner or later in bringing about a Revolution. In that case, power passes into their hands, and they still think that power implies Monopoly. This is still odious, but it is not absurd, at least it is not impracticable; for Monopolies are impossible as long as there is, below the grade that enjoys them, a lower stratum—namely, the public at large, that supports and feeds them. If the third and fourth grade succeed, in their turn, in effecting a revolution, they will, if they can, so arrange as to make the most of the masses, by means of privileges or monopolies skillfully combined. But then the masses, emaciated, ground down, trampled upon, must also have their revolution. Why? What are they going to do? You think, perhaps, that they are going to abolish all monopolies and privileges, and to inaugurate the reign of universal justice; that they are about to exclaim—away with restrictions—away with shackles and trammels—away with monopolies—away with Government interferences for the profit of certain classes; begone taxes and grinding impositions; down with political and diplomatic intrigues? Not at all. They have quite another aim. They become their own solicitors, and in their turn demand to be privileged! The public at large, imitating their superiors, ask for monopolies! They urge their right to employment, their right to credit, their right to education, their right to assistance! But at whose expense? They are easy on that score. They feel only that, if they are ensured employment, credit, education for their children, repose for their old days, and all gratis, they will be exceedingly happy; and, truly, no one disputes it. But is it possible? Alas! no; and this is the reason why I say that here the odious disappears, and the absurd has reached its climax.

Monopolies to the masses! Good people, reflect a little on the vicious circle in which you are placing yourselves. Monopoly implies someone to enjoy it, and someone to pay for it. We can understand a privileged man, or a privileged class, but not a privileged people. Is there below you a still lower stratum of society upon which you can throw back the burden? Will you never comprehend the whimsical mystification of which you are the dupes? Will you never understand that the State can give you nothing with the one hand but what it has taken from you with the other? that, far from there being for you in this combination any possible increase of prosperity, the final result of the operation must be an arbitrary Government, more vexatious, more exacting, more uncertain, more expensive; heavier taxes—more injustice, more offensive favoritism—liberty more restrained—power thrown away—occupations, labor and capital displaced—covetousness excited—discontent provoked—and individual energy extinguished?

The upper classes have gotten alarmed, and not without reason, at this unhappy disposition of the masses. They see in it the germ of incessant revolutions; for what Government can hold together that has ventured to say—"I am in possession of force, and I will employ it to support everybody at the expense of everybody? I undertake to become responsible for the general happiness." But is not the alarm that has seized these classes a just and merited punishment? Have they not themselves set the people the fatal example of that grasping disposition of which they now complain? Have they not had their own eyes perpetually turned to the treasury? Have they ever failed to secure some monopoly, some privilege, great or small, to manufactures, to banks, to mines, to landed property, to the arts, even to the means of diversion, to the ballet, to the opera, to everything and everybody in short; except to the industry of the people—to manual labor? Have they not multiplied beyond bounds public employments, in order to increase, at the expense of the people, their own resources? and is there at this day a single head of a family in France who is not on the lookout for a place for his son? Have they ever endeavored to get rid of any one of the acknowledged inequalities of taxation? Have they not for a long time turned to account everything, even the electoral franchise? And yet they are astonished and horrified that the people should adopt the same course. When the spirit of mendicity has so long infected the wealthy orders, how can we suppose that it will not penetrate to the heart of the suffering masses?

However, a great Revolution has taken place. Political power, the power of making laws, the disposal of the public force, has passed virtually, if not yet in fact, into the hands of the people along with universal suffrage. Thus the people, who have proposed the problem for solution, will be called upon to solve it themselves; and woe to the country, if, following the example that has been set them, they seek its solution in Privilege, which is always an invasion of another's rights. They will find themselves mistaken, and the mistake will bring with it a great lesson; for if it be possible to violate the rights of the many for the benefit of the few, how can we violate the rights of all for the benefit of all? But at what cost will this lesson be taught us? And, in order to obviate so frightful a danger, what ought the upper classes to do? Two things—renounce all privileges and monopolies themselves, and enlighten the masses, for there are only two things that can save society—Justice and Knowledge. They ought to inquire with earnestness whether they do not enjoy some monopoly or other, in order that they may renounce it—whether they do not profit by some artificial inequalities, in order that they may efface them—whether Pauperism is not in some measure attributable to a disturbance of the natural social laws, in order that they may put an end to it. They should be able to hold out their hands to the people, and say to them, These hands are full, but they are clean. Is this what they actually do? If I am not very much mistaken, they do just the reverse. They begin by guarding their monopolies, and we have seen them even turning the revolution to profit by attempting to extend these monopolies. After having deprived themselves of even the possibility of speaking the truth and appealing to principles, they endeavor to vindicate their consistency by engaging to treat the people as they have treated themselves, and dazzle them with the bait of Privilege. Only, they think themselves very knowing in conceding at present only a small privilege, the right to "assistance," in the hope of diverting them from demanding a greater one—the right to employment. They do not perceive that to extend and systematize more and more the maxim, "Take from one to give to another," is only to strengthen the illusion that creates difficulties for the present and dangers for the future.

We must not exaggerate, however. When the superior classes seek in privilege a remedy for the evils privilege has caused, they are sincere, and act, I am convinced, rather from ignorance than from any desire to commit injustice. It is an irreparable misfortune that the governments that have succeeded each other in France have invariably discouraged the teaching of Political Economy. And it is a still greater misfortune that University Education fills all our heads with Roman prejudices; in other words, with all that is repugnant to social truth. This is what leads the upper classes astray. It is the fashion at present to declaim against these classes. For my own part, I believe that at no period have their intentions been more benevolent. I believe that they ardently desire to solve the social Problem. I believe that they would do more than renounce their privileges—that they would sacrifice willingly, in works of charity, a part of the property they have acquired, if by that means they were satisfied that an end could be put to the sufferings of the working classes. It may be said, no doubt, that they are actuated by interest or fear, and that it is no great generosity to abandon a part of their fortune to save the remainder—that it is, in fact, but the vulgar prudence of a man who insures his property against fire. But let us not thus calumniate human nature. Why should we refuse to recognize a motive less selfish? Is it not very natural that the democratic sentiments that prevail in our country should render men alive to the sufferings of their brethren? But whatever may be the dominant sentiment, it cannot be denied that everything by which public opinion is influenced—philosophy, literature, poetry, the drama, the pulpit, the tribune, the daily press—all these organs of opinion reveal not only a desire, but an ardent longing on the part of the wealthier classes to resolve the great problem. Why, then, is there no movement on the part of our Legislative Assemblies? Because they are ignorant. Political Economy proposes to them this solution—PUBLIC JUSTICE—PRIVATE CHARITY. But they got off upon the wrong scent, and, obeying socialist influences, without being aware of the fact, they give charity a place in the statute book, thereby banishing justice from it, and destroying by the same act private charity, which is ever prompt to recede before a compulsory poor-rate.

Why, then, do our legislators thus run counter to all sound notions? Why do they not leave things in their proper place—Sympathy in its natural domain, which is Liberty—Justice in its own, which is Law? Why do they not leave law to do its own exclusive work in furthering justice? Is it that they have no love of justice? No; it is that they have no confidence in it. Justice is Liberty and Property. But they are Socialists without knowing it; and, for the progressive diminution of poverty, and the indefinite expansion of wealth, let them say what they will, they have no faith either in liberty or property, nor, consequently, in justice. This is why we see them, in the sincerity of their hearts, seeking the realization of what is Good by the perpetual violation of what is Right.

Natural social laws are the phenomena, taken in the aggregate, and considered in reference both to their motives and their results, that govern the transactions of men in a state of freedom.

That being granted, the question is, Are we to allow these laws to act, or are we to hinder them from acting?

The question, in fact, comes to this:

Are we to leave every man master of his liberty and property, his right to produce, and exchange his produce, as he chooses, whether to his benefit or detriment; or are we to interfere by means of law, which is Force, for the protection of these rights? Or, can we hope to secure a greater amount of social happiness by violating liberty and property, by interfering with and regulating labor, by disturbing exchanges, and shifting responsibility?

In other words:

Is Law to enforce rigorous Justice, or to be the instrument of Spoliation, organized with more or less adroitness?

It is very evident that the solution of these questions depends upon our knowledge and study of the natural laws of society. We cannot pronounce conclusively upon them until we have discovered whether property, liberty, the combination of services freely and voluntarily exchanged, lead to improvement and material prosperity, as the economists believe, or to ruin and degradation, as the socialists affirm.

In the first case, social evils must be attributed to disturbances of the natural laws, to legal violations of liberty and property, and these disturbances and violations must be put an end to. In that case Political Economy is right.

In the second case, it may be said, we have not yet had enough of Government interference. Forced and factitious combinations have not yet sufficiently superseded free and natural combinations. These three fatal principles, Justice, Liberty, and Property, have still too powerful a sway. Our legislators have not yet attacked them boldly enough. We have not yet acted sufficiently on the maxim of taking from one in order to give to another. Hitherto we have taken from the many to give to the few. Now, we must take from all and give to all. In a word, we must organize Spoliation, and from Socialism must come our salvation.

5

OF VALUE

All dissertations are wearisome—a dissertation on Value the most wearisome of all.

What unpracticed writer, who has had to face an Economic problem, has not tried to resolve it without reference to any definition of value?

Yet he soon finds he has engaged in a vain attempt. The theory of Value is to Political Economy what numbers are to arithmetic. In what inextricable confusion would not Bezout have landed himself if, to save labor to his pupils, he had undertaken to teach them the four rules and proportion, without having previously explained the value the figures derive from their form and position?

The truth is, if the reader could only foresee the beautiful consequences deducible from the theory of Value, he would undertake the labor of mastering the first principles of Economical Science with the same cheerfulness that one submits to the drudgery of Geometry, in prospect of the magnificent field it opens to our intelligence.

But this intuitive foresight is not to be expected; and the more pains I should take to establish the distinction between Value and Utility, or between Value and labor, in order to show how natural it is that this should form a stumbling-block at the very threshold of the science, the more wearisome I should become. The reader would see in such a discussion only barren and idle subtleties, calculated at best to satisfy the curiosity of professional Economists.

You are inquiring laboriously, it may be said, whether wealth consists in the Utility of things, or in their Value, or in their rarity. Is not this like the question of the schoolmen, Does form reside in the substance or in the accident? Are you not afraid that some street Moliere will hold you up to public ridicule at the *Theatre des Varietes*?

Yet truth obliges me to say that, from an economical point of view, Society is Exchange. The primary element of Exchange is the notion of Value, so that every truth and every error this word introduces into men's minds is a social truth or error. I undertake in this work to demonstrate the Harmony of those laws of Providence that govern human society. What makes these laws harmonious and not discordant is, that all principles, all motives, all springs of action, all interests, co-operate toward a grand final result, which humanity will never reach by reason of its native imperfection, but to which it will always approximate more and more by reason of its unlimited capability of improvement. And that result is, the indefinite approximation of all classes toward a level, which is always rising; in other words, the equalization of individuals in the general amelioration.

But to attain my object, I must explain two things, namely,

First, that Utility has a tendency to become more and more gratuitous, more and more common, as it gradually recedes from the domain of individual appropriation.

Second, that Value, on the other hand, which alone is capable of appropriation, which alone legitimately constitutes property and in fact, has a tendency to diminish more and more in relation to the utility to which it is attached.

Such a demonstration—founded on Property, but only on the property of which Value is the subject, and on Community, but only on the community of utility—such a demonstration, I say, must satisfy and reconcile all schools, by conceding to them that all have had a glimpse of the truth, but only of partial truth, regarded from different points of view.

Economists! you defend property. There is in the social order no other property than that of which Value is the subject, and that is immutable and unassailable.

Communists! you dream of Community. You have got it. The social order renders all utilities common, provided the exchange of those values that have been appropriated is unhindered.

You are like architects who dispute about a monument of which each has seen only one side. They don't see ill, but they don't see all. To make them agree, it is only necessary to ask them to walk round the edifice.

But how am I to reconstruct the social edifice so as to exhibit to mankind all its beautiful harmony if I reject its two corner stones, Utility and Value? How can I bring about the desired reconciliation of various schools upon the platform of truth if I shun the analysis of these two ideas, although the dissidence has arisen from the unhappy confusion they have caused?

I have felt this kind of introduction necessary, in order, if possible, to secure from the reader a moment's attention and relieve him from fatigue and ennui. I am much mistaken if the consoling beauty of the consequences will not amply make up for the dryness of the premises. Had Newton allowed himself to be repulsed at the outset by a distaste for elementary mathematics, never would his heart have beat with rapture on beholding the harmonies of the celestial mechanism; and I maintain that it is only necessary to make our way manfully to an acquaintance with certain first principles in order to be convinced that God has displayed in the social mechanism goodness no less touching, simplicity no less admirable, splendor no less magnificent.

In the first chapter we viewed man as both active and passive, and we saw that Want and Satisfaction, acting on sensibility alone, were in their own nature personal, peculiar, and intransmissible; that Effort, on the contrary, the connecting link between Want and Satisfaction, the mean term between the motive principle of action and the end we have in view, proceeding from our activity, our spontaneity, our will, was susceptible of conventions and of transmission. I know that, metaphysically, no one can contest this assertion, and maintain that Effort also is personal. I have no desire to enter the territory of ideology, and I hope that my view of the subject will be admitted without controversy when put in this fundamental form: We cannot feel the wants of others—we cannot feel the satisfactions of others; but we can render service one to another.

It is this transmission of efforts, this exchange of services, that forms the subject of Political Economy; and since, on the other hand, economic science is condensed and summed up in the word Value, of which it is only a lengthened explanation, it follows that the notion of value would be imperfectly, erroneously conceived if we were to found it upon the extreme phenomena of our sensibility—namely, our Wants and Satisfactions—phenomena that are personal, intransmissible, and incommensurable as between two individuals, in place of founding it on the manifestations of our activity, upon efforts, upon reciprocal services, which are interchanged because they are susceptible of being compared, evaluated, estimated, and which are capable of being estimated precisely because they are capable of being interchanged.

In the same chapter we arrived at the following formulas:

"Utility (the property that certain things and certain acts have of serving us, of being useful to us) is complex—one part we owe to the action of nature, another to the action of man."—"With reference to a given result, the more nature has done the less remains for human action to do."—"The co-operation of nature is essentially gratuitous—the co-operation of man, whether intellectual or muscular, exchanged or not, collective or solitary, is essentially onerous, as indeed the word Effort implies."

And as what is gratuitous cannot possess value, since the idea of value implies onerous acquisition, it follows that the notion of Value would be still erroneously conceived if we were to extend it in whole or in part to the gifts or to the cooperation of nature, instead of restricting it exclusively to human cooperation.

Thus, from both sides, by two different roads, we arrive at this conclusion, that value must have reference to the efforts men make in order to obtain the satisfaction of their wants.

In the third chapter we have established that man cannot exist in a state of isolation. But if, by an effort of imagination, we fancy him placed in that chimerical situation, that state contrary to nature, which the writers of the eighteenth century extolled as the state of nature, we shall not fail to see that it does not disclose to us the idea of Value, although it presents the manifestation of the active principle we have termed effort. The reason is obvious. Value implies comparison, evaluation, estimation, measure. In order that two things should measure each other, it is necessary that they be commensurable, and, in order to be that, they must be of the same kind. In a state of isolation, with what could we compare effort? With want? With satisfaction? In that case, we could go no farther than to pronounce that the effort was more or less appropriate, more or less opportune. In the social state, what we compare (and it is this comparison that gives rise to the idea of Value) is the effort of one man with the effort of another man—two phenomena of the same nature, and, consequently, commensurable.

Thus, the definition of the word Value, in order to be exact, must have reference not only to human efforts, but likewise to those efforts that are exchanged or exchangeable. Exchange does more than exhibit and measure values—it gives them existence. I do not mean to say that it gives existence to the acts and the things that are exchanged, but it imparts to their existence the notion of value.

Now, when two men transfer to each other their present efforts, or make over mutually the results of their previous efforts, they serve each other; they render each other reciprocal service.

I say, then, VALUE IS THE RELATION OF TWO SERVICES EXCHANGED.

The idea of value entered into the world the first time that a man having said to his brother, Do this for me, and I shall do that for you—they have come to an agreement; for then, for the first time, we could say—The two services exchanged are worth each other.

It is singular enough that the true theory of value, which we search for in vain in many a ponderous volume, is to be found in Florian's beautiful fable of *l'Aveugle et le Paralytique*—

> *Aidons—nous mutuellement,*
> *La charge des malheurs en sera plus legere.*
> *. . . . . A nous deux*
> *Nous possedons le bien a chacun necessaire.*
> *J'ai des jambes, et vous des yeux.*
> *Moi, je vais vous porter; vous, vous serez mon guide:*
> *Ainsi, sans que jamais notre amitie decide*
> *Qui de nous deux remplit le plus utile emploi,*
> *Je marcherai pour vous, vous y verrez pour moi.*

Here you have value discovered and defined. Here you have it in its rigorous economic exactitude, excepting the touching trait relative to friendship, which carries us into another sphere, that of sympathy. We may conceive two unfortunates rendering each other reciprocal service, without inquiring too curiously which of the two discharged the most useful employment. The exceptional situation imagined by the fabulist explains sufficiently that the principle of sympathy, acting with great force, comes to absorb, so to speak, the minute appreciation of the services exchanged—an appreciation, however, that is indispensable in order to disengage completely the idea of Value. That idea would be complete if all men, or the majority of them, were struck with paralysis or blindness; for the inexorable law of supply and demand would then predominate and, causing the permanent sacrifices accepted by him who fulfills the more useful employment to disappear, would restore the transaction to the domain of justice.

We are all blind or impotent in some respects, and we soon come to understand that by assisting each other, the burden of misfortune is lightened. Hence EXCHANGE. We labor in order to feed, clothe, shelter, enlighten, cure, defend, instruct one another. Hence reciprocal SERVICES. We compare, we discuss, we estimate or evalute these services. Hence VALUE.

A multitude of circumstances may augment the relative importance of a Service. We find it greater or less according as it is more or less useful to us—according as a greater or less number of people are disposed to render it to us—according as it exacts from them more or less labor, trouble, skill, time, previous study—and according as it saves more or less of these to ourselves. Value depends not only on these circumstances, but on the judgment we form of them; for it may happen, and it happens frequently, that we esteem a service very highly because we judge it very useful, while in reality it is hurtful. This is the reason why vanity, ignorance, error exert a certain influence on the essentially elastic and flexible relation that we denominate value; and we may affirm that the evaluation of services tends to approximate more to absolute truth and justice in proportion as men become more enlightened, more moral, and more refined.

Hitherto the principle of Value has been sought for in one of those circumstances that augment or which diminish it, materiality, durableness, utility, scarcity, labor, difficulty of acquisition, judgment, etc., and hence a false direction has been given to the science from the beginning; for the accident that modifies the phenomenon is not the phenomenon itself. Moreover, each author has constituted himself the sponsor, so to speak, of some special circumstance he thinks preponderates—the constant result of generalizing; for all is in all, and there is nothing we cannot subsume under a term by means of extending its sense. Thus the principle of value, according to Adam Smith, resides in materiality and durability; according to Jean Baptiste Say, in utility; according to Ricardo, in labor; according to Senior, in rarity; according to Storch, in the judgment we form, etc.

The consequence has been what might have been expected. These authors have unwittingly injured the authority and dignity of the science by appearing to contradict each other; while in reality each is right, as from his own point of view. Besides, they have involved the first principles of Political Economy in a labyrinth of inextricable difficulties; for the same words, as used by these authors, no longer represent the same ideas; and, moreover, although a circumstance may be proclaimed fundamental, other circumstances stand out too prominently to be neglected, and definitions are thus constantly enlarged.

The object of the present work is not controversy, but exposition. I explain what I myself see, not what others have seen. I cannot avoid, however, calling the attention of the reader to the circumstances in which the foundation of Value has hitherto been sought for. But first of all, I must bring Value itself before him in a series of examples, for it is by diverse applications that the mind lays hold of a theory.

I shall demonstrate how all is definitely resolved into a barter of services; but it is necessary to keep in mind what has been said on the subject of barter in the preceding chapter. It is rarely simple—sometimes it forms a circular or round-about transaction among several parties—most frequently, by the intervention of money, it resolves itself into two factors, sale and purchase; but as this complication does not change its nature, I may be permitted, for the sake of perspicuity, to assume the barter to be direct and immediate. This will lead to no mistake as to the nature of Value.

We are all born with an urgent material want, which must be satisfied under pain of death, I mean that of breathing. On the other hand, we all exist in a medium that, in general, supplies that want without the intervention of any effort on our part. Atmospheric air, then, has utility, without having value. It has no Value, because, requiring no Effort, it gives rise to no service. To render a service to anyone is to save him trouble; and where it is not necessary to take pains in order to realize a satisfaction, no trouble can be saved.

But if a man descend to the bottom of a river in a diving bell, a foreign substance is interposed between the air and his lungs, and, in order to re-establish the communication, a pump must be employed. Here there is an effort to make, pains to take, and the man below desires the exertion, for it is a matter of life or death, and he cannot possibly secure to himself a greater service.

Instead of making this effort himself, he calls on me to make it for him, and, in order to induce me to do so, he undertakes in turn to make an exertion from which I may reap satisfaction. We discuss the matter, and come to an agreement. Now, what do we discover here? Two wants, two satisfactions, which are not inconsistent with each other; two efforts, which are the subject of a voluntary transaction; two services, which are exchanged—and value makes its appearance.

Now, we are told that utility is the foundation of value; and as utility is inherent in the air, we are led to think that it is the same in regard to value. There is here an evident confusion of ideas. The air, from its nature, has physical properties in harmony with one of our physical organs, the lungs. The portion I draw from the atmosphere in order to fill the diving bell does not change its nature—it is still oxygen and nitrogen. No new physical quality is combined with it, no reacting power brings out of it a new element called value. That springs exclusively from the service rendered.

If, in laying down the general principle that Utility is the foundation of Value, you mean that the Service has value because it is useful to him who receives it and pays for it, I allow the truth of what you say. It is a truism implied in the very word service.

But we must not confound the utility of the air with the utility of the service. They are two utilities distinct from each other, different in nature, different in kind, that bear no proportion to one another, and have no necessary relation. There are circumstances in which with very slight exertion, by rendering a very small service, or saving very little trouble, I may bring within the reach of another an article of very great intrinsic utility.

Take the case of the diving bell, and consider how the parties to the supposed bargain manage to estimate the value of the service rendered by the one to the other in supplying him with atmospheric air. We must have a point of comparison, and that point of comparison can only be in the service the diver renders in return. Their reciprocal demands will depend on their relative situation, on the intensity of their desires, on the greater or less need they have of each other, and on a multitude of circumstances that demonstrate that the value is in the Service, since it increases with the service.

The reader may easily vary the hypothesis, so as to convince himself that the Value is not necessarily proportionate to the intensity of the efforts—a remark which I set down here as a connecting link in the chain of reasoning, and of which I shall afterwards have occasion to make use; for my object is to prove that Value no more resides in labor than it does in utility.

Nature has so constituted me that I must die if I am deprived of an opportunity from time to time of quenching my thirst, and the well is miles from the village. For this reason, I take the trouble every morning to go there to fetch the water of which I have need, for in water I have recognized those useful qualities that are calculated to assuage the suffering called thirst. Want, Effort, Satisfaction—we have them all here. I have found Utility—I have not yet found Value.

But, as my neighbor goes also to the fountain, I say to him— "Save me the pains of this journey—render me the service of bringing me water. During the time you are so occupied, I shall do something for you, I shall teach your child to spell." This arrangement suits us both. Here is an exchange of two services, and we are enabled to pronounce that the one is worth the other. The things compared here are two efforts, not two wants and two satisfactions; for by what common standard should we compare the benefit of drinking water and that of learning to spell?

By and by, I say to my neighbor, "Your child troubles me—I should like better to do something else for you. You shall continue to bring me water, and I shall give you twopence." If the proposal is agreed to, the Economist may, without fear of mistake, pronounce that the SERVICE IS WORTH twopence.

Afterwards, my neighbor no longer waits to be requested. He knows by experience that every day I want water. He anticipates my wishes. At the same time, he provides water for the other villagers. In short, he becomes a water merchant. It is then that we begin to say, the WATER IS WORTH twopence.

Has the water, then, changed its nature? Has the Value, which was previously in the service, become materialized and incorporated in the water, as if it were a new chemical element? Has a slight modification in the form of the arrangement between my neighbor and me had the power to displace the principle of value and change its nature? I am not purist enough to find fault with your saying that the water is worth twopence, just as you say the sun sets. But we must remember that metaphors and metonymies do not affect the truth of facts; and that, in strict scientific language, value can no more be said to reside in the water, than the sun can be said to go to rest in the sea.

Let us attribute, then, to things the peculiar qualities that belong to them—to air, to water, utility—to services, value. We may say with propriety that water is useful, because it has the property of allaying thirst; and it is the service that has value, because it is the subject of a convention previously debated and discussed. So true is this that if the well is brought nearer, or removed to a greater distance, the Utility of the water remains the same, but its Value is diminished or increased. Why? because the service is less or greater. The value, then, is in the service, seeing that it is increased or diminished according as the service is increased or diminished.

The diamond makes a great figure in works of Political Economy. It is adduced as an illustration of the laws of Value, or of the supposed disturbance of those laws. It is a brilliant weapon with which all the schools do battle. The English school asserts that "Value resides in labor." The French school exhibits a diamond, and says, "Here is a commodity that exacts no labor and yet is of immense value." The French school affirms that the foundation of value is utility, and the English school immediately brings forward the diamond in opposition to the illustrations drawn from air, light, and water. "The air is very useful," says the English Economist, "but it possesses no value; the utility of the diamond is almost inappreciable, and yet it possesses more value than the whole atmosphere;" and the reader is inclined to say with Henri Quatre—"In sooth, they are both right." They end by landing themselves in an error more fatal than both the others, and are forced to avow that value resides in the works of nature, and that that value is material.

My definition, as it seems to me, gets rid of these anomalies, and is confirmed rather than invalidated by the illustration just mentioned.

I take a walk along the sea-beach, and I find by chance a magnificent diamond. I am thus put in possession of a great value. Why? Am I about to confer a great benefit on the human race? Have I devoted myself to a long and laborious work? Neither the one nor the other. Why, then, does this diamond possess so much value? Undoubtedly because the person to whom I transfer it considers that I have rendered him a great service—all the greater that many rich people desire it, and that I alone can render it. The grounds of his judgment may be controverted—be it so. It may be founded on pride, on vanity—granted again. But this judgment has, nevertheless, been formed by a man who is disposed to act upon it, and that is sufficient for my argument.

Far from the judgment being based on a reasonable appreciation of utility, we may allow that the very reverse is the case. Ostentation makes great sacrifices for what is utterly useless.

In this case, the value, far from bearing a necessary proportion to the labor performed by the person who renders the service, may be said rather to bear proportion to the labor saved to the person who receives it. This general law of value, which has not, so far as I know, been observed by theoretical writers, nevertheless prevails universally in practice. We shall explain afterwards the admirable mechanism by which value tends to proportion itself to labor when it is unfettered; but it is not the less true that it has its principle and foundation less in the effort of the person who serves than in the effort saved to him who is served.

The transaction relative to the diamond may be supposed to give rise to the following dialogue:

"Give me your diamond, Sir."

"With all my heart; give me in exchange your labor for an entire year."

"Your acquisition has not cost you a minute's work."

"Very well, Sir, try to find a similar lucky minute."

"Yes, but, in strict equity, the exchange ought to be one of equal labor."

"No, in strict equity, you put a value on your own services, and I upon mine; I don't force you; why should you lay a constraint upon me? Give me a whole year's labor, or seek out a diamond for yourself."

"But that might entail upon me ten years' work, and would probably end in nothing. It would be wiser and more profitable to devote these ten years to another employment."

"It is precisely on that account that I imagined I was rendering you a service in asking for only one year's work. I thus save you nine, and that is the reason why I attach great value to the service. If I appear to you exacting, it is because you regard only the labor that I have performed; but consider also the labor that I save you, and you will find me reasonable in my demand."

"It is not the less true that you profit by a work of nature."

"And if I were to give away what I have found for little or nothing, it is you who would profit by it. Besides, if this diamond possesses great value, it is not because nature has been elaborating it since the beginning of time: she does as much for a drop of dew."

"Yes, but if diamonds were as common as dew-drops, you could no longer lay down the law to me, and make your own conditions."

"Very true; because, in that case, you would not address yourself to me, or would not be disposed to recompense me highly for a service you could easily perform for yourself."

The result of this dialogue is that Value no more resides in the diamond than in the air or in the water. It resides exclusively in the services we suppose to be rendered and received with reference to these things, and is determined by the free bargaining of the parties who make the exchange.

Take up the *Collection des Economistes*, and read and compare all the definitions you will find there. If there be one of them that meets the cases of the air and the diamond, two cases in appearance so opposite, throw this book into the fire. But if the definition I propose, simple as it is, solves, or rather obviates, the difficulty, you are bound in conscience, gentle reader, to go on to the end of the work, or it is in vain that we have placed an inviting sign-board over the vestibule of the science.

Allow me to give some more examples, in order to elucidate clearly my thoughts and familiarize the reader with a new definition. By exhibiting this fundamental principle in different aspects, we shall clear the way for a thorough comprehension of the consequences, which I venture to predict will be found no less important than unexpected.

Among the wants to which our physical constitution subjects us is that of food; and one of the articles best fitted to satisfy that want is Bread.

As the need of food is personal to me, I should, naturally, myself perform all the operations necessary to provide the needful supply of bread. I can the less expect my fellow-men to render me gratuitously this service that they are themselves subject to the same want, and condemned to the same exertion.

Were I to make my own bread, I must devote myself to a labor infinitely more complicated, but strictly analogous to that which the necessity of fetching water from the spring would have imposed upon me. The elements of bread exist everywhere in nature. As J.B. Say has judiciously remarked, it is neither possible nor necessary for man to create anything. Gases, salts, electricity, vegetable life, all exist; my business is to unite them, assist them, combine them, transport them, availing myself of that great laboratory called the earth, in which mysteries are accomplished from which human science has scarcely raised the veil. If the operations to which I must devote myself in the pursuit of my design are in the aggregate very complicated, each of them, taken singly, is as simple as the act of drawing water from the fountain. Every effort I make is simply a service I render to myself; and if, in consequence of a bargain freely entered into, it happens that other persons save me some of these efforts, or the whole of them, these are so many services which I receive. The aggregate of these services, compared with those I render in return, constitute the value of the Bread and determine its amount.

A convenient intermediate commodity intervenes to facilitate this exchange of services, and even to serve as a measure of their relative importance—Money. But this makes no substantial difference—the principle remains exactly the same, just as in mechanics the transmission of forces is subject to the same law, whether there be one or several intermediate wheels.

This is so true that, when the loaf is worth fourpence, for example, if a good bookkeeper wishes to analyze its value, he will succeed in discovering, amid the multiplicity of transactions that go to the accomplishment of the final result, all those whose services have contributed to form that value—all those who have saved labor to the man who finally pays for it as the consumer. He discovers, first of all, the baker, who retains his five percent, and from that percentage remunerates the mason who has built his oven, the wood-cutter who prepares his billets, etc. Then comes the miller, who receives not only the recompense of his own labor, but the means of remunerating the quarryman who has furnished his millstones, the laborer who has formed his dam, etc. Other portions of the total value go to the thresher, the reaper, the laborer, the sower, until you account for the last farthing. No part of it assuredly goes to remunerate God and nature. The very idea is absurd, and yet this is rigorously implied in the theory of the Economists, who attribute a certain portion of the value of a product to matter or natural forces. No; we still find that what has value is not the Loaf, but the series of services that have put me in possession of it.

It is true that among the elementary parts of the value of the loaf, our bookkeeper will find one that he will have difficulty in connecting with a service, at least a service implying effort. He will find of the fourpence of which the price is made up, a part goes to the proprietor of the soil, to the man who has the keeping of the laboratory. That small portion of the value of the loaf constitutes what is called the rent of land; and, misled by the form of expression, by the metonymy that again makes its appearance here, our calculator may be tempted to think that this portion is allotted to natural agents—to the soil itself.

I maintain that, if he exercises sufficient skill, he will find that this is still the price of real services—services of the same kind as all the others. This will be demonstrated with the clearest evidence when we come to treat of landed property. At present, I shall only remark that I am not concerned here with property, but with value. I don't inquire whether all services are real and legitimate, or whether men do not sometimes succeed in getting paid for services they do not render. The world, alas! is full of such injustices, but rent must not be included among them.

All that I have to demonstrate here is that the value attributed to commodities is only the value of services, real or imaginary, received and rendered in connection with them—that value does not reside in the commodities themselves, and is no more to be found in the loaf than in the diamond, the water, or the air—that no part of the remuneration goes to nature—that it proceeds from the final consumer of the article, and is distributed exclusively among men—and that it would not be accorded to them by him for any other reason than that they have rendered him services, except, indeed, in the case of violence or fraud.

Two men agree that ice is a good thing in summer, and coal a still better thing in winter. They supply two of our wants—the one cools, the other warms us. We do not fail to note that the Utility of these commodities consists in certain material properties suitably adapted to our material organs. We note, moreover that among those properties, that physics and chemistry might enumerate, we do not find value, or anything like it. How, then, have we come to regard value as inherent in matter and material?

If the two men we have supposed wished to obtain the satisfaction of their wants without acting in concert, each would labor to provide for himself both the articles wanted. If they came to an understanding, the one would provide coal for two from the coal mine, the other ice for two from the mountain. This presupposes a bargain. They must then adjust the relation of the two services exchanged. They would take all circumstances into account—the difficulties to be overcome, the dangers to be braved, the time to be spent, the pains to be taken, the skill to be displayed, the risks to be run, the possibility of providing for their wants in some other way, etc., etc. When they came to an understanding, the Economist would say, The two services exchanged are worth each other. In common language, it would be said by metonymy: Such a quantity of coal is worth such a quantity of ice, as if the value had passed physically into these bodies. But it is easy to see that if the common form of expression enables us to state the results, the scientific expression alone reveals to us the true causes.

In place of two services and two persons, the agreement may embrace a greater number, substituting a complex Exchange for simple Barter. In that case, money would intervene to facilitate the exchange. Need I say that the principle of value would be neither changed nor displaced?

But I must add here a single observation apropos of coal. It may be that there is only one coal mine in a country, and that an individual has got possession of it. If so, this man will make conditions: that is to say, he will put a high price upon his services, or ostensible services.

We have not yet come to the question of right and justice, to the distinction between true and loyal services, and those that are fraudulent and pretended. What concerns us at this moment is, to consolidate the true theory of value, and to disabuse it of one error with which Economic science is infected. When we say that what nature has done or given, she has done or given gratuitously, and that the notion of value is excluded, we are answered by an analysis of the price of coal, or some other natural product. It is acknowledged, indeed, that the greater part of this price is the remuneration of the services of man. One man has excavated the ground, another has drained away the water, another has raised the fuel to the surface, another has transported it to its destination; and it is the aggregate of these works, it is allowed, that constitutes nearly the entire value. Still there remains one portion of the value that does not correspond with any labor or service. This is the value of the coal as it lies under the soil, still virgin, and untouched by human labor. It forms the share of the proprietor; and, since this portion of Value is not of human creation, it follows necessarily that it is the creation of nature.

I reject that conclusion, and I premonish the reader that if he admits it to a greater or lesser extent, he cannot proceed a single step farther in the science. No; the action of nature does not create Value, any more than the action of man creates matter. Of two things one: either the proprietor has usefully co-operated toward the final result, and has rendered real services, and then the portion of value he has conferred on the coal enters into my definition; or else he obtrudes himself as a parasite, and, in that case, he has had the effrontery to get paid for services that he had not rendered, and the price of the coal is unduly augmented. That circumstance may prove, indeed, that injustice has entered into the transaction; but it cannot overturn the theory so as to authorize us to say that this portion of value is material—that it is combined as a physical element with the gratuitous gifts of Providence. Here is the proof of it. Cause the injustice to cease, if injustice there be, and the corresponding value will disappear, which it assuredly would not have done had the value been inherent in matter and of natural creation.

Let us now pass to one of our most urgent wants, that of security.

A certain number of men land upon an inhospitable coast. They begin to work. But each of them finds himself constantly drawn away from his employment by the necessity of defending himself against wild beasts, or men still more savage. Besides the time and the exertion he devotes directly to the work of defense, he has to provide himself with arms and munitions. At length it is discovered that, on the whole, infinitely less power and effort would be wasted if some of them, abandoning other work, were to devote themselves exclusively to this service. This duty is assigned to those who are most distinguished for boldness, courage, and vigor—and they improve in an art that they make their exclusive business. While they watch over the public safety, the community reaps from its labors, now no longer interrupted, more satisfactions for all than it loses by the diversion of ten men from other avocations. This arrangement is in consequence made. What do we see in it but a new progress in the division of occupations, inducing and requiring an exchange of services?

Are the services of these soldiers, guards, militiamen, or whatever you may call them, productive? Undoubtedly they are, seeing that the sole object of the arrangement is to increase the proportion that the aggregate Satisfactions of the community bear to the general efforts.

Have they Value? They must have it, since we esteem them, appreciate them, estimate their worth, and, in the end, pay for them with other services with which they are compared.

The form in which this remuneration is stipulated for, the mode of levying it, the process we adopt in adjusting and concluding the arrangement, make no alteration on the principle. Are there efforts saved to some men by others? Are there satisfactions procured for some by others? In that case there are services exchanged, compared, estimated—there is Value.

The kind of services we are now discussing, when social complications occur, lead sometimes to frightful consequences.

The very nature of the services we demand from this class of functionaries requires us to put into their hands Power—power sufficient to subdue all resistance—and it sometimes happens that they abuse it, and turn it against the very community that employs them. Deriving from the community services proportioned to the want we have of security, they themselves may cause insecurity, in order to display their own importance, and, by a too skillful diplomacy, involve their fellow-citizens in perpetual wars.

All this has happened, and still happens. Great disturbances of the just equilibrium of reciprocal services are the result of it. But it makes no change in the fundamental principle and scientific theory of Value.

I must still give another example or two; but I pray the reader to believe that I feel quite as much as he how tiresome and fatiguing this series of hypotheses must be—throwing us Back, as they all do, on the same kind of proof, tending to the same conclusion, expressed in the same terms. He must understand, however, that this process, if not the most interesting, is at least the surest way of establishing the true theory of Value, and of thus clearing the road we have to traverse.

We suppose ourselves in Paris. In that great metropolis there is a vast fermentation of desires, and abundant means also of satisfying them. Multitudes of rich men, or men in easy circumstances, devote themselves to industry, to the arts, to politics—and in the evening they are all eager to obtain an hour's recreation. Among the amusements they relish most is the pleasure of hearing the music of Rossini sung by Malibran, or the admirable poetry of Racine interpreted by Rachel. There are in the world only two women who can furnish these noble and delicate kinds of entertainment, and unless we could subject them to torture, which would probably not succeed, we have no other way of procuring their services but by addressing ourselves to their good will. Thus the services which we expect from Malibran and Rachel are possessed of great Value. This explanation is prosaic enough, but it is true.

If an opulent banker should desire to gratify his vanity by having the performance of one of these great artists in his salons, he will soon find by experience the full truth of my theory. He desires a rich treat, a lively satisfaction—he desires it eagerly—and only one person in the world can furnish it. He cannot procure it otherwise than by offering a large remuneration.

Between what extreme limits will the transaction oscillate? The banker will go on till he reaches the point at which he prefers rather to lose the satisfaction than to pay what he deems an extravagant price for it; the singer to that point at which she prefers to accept the remuneration offered, rather than not be remunerated at all. This point of equilibrium determines the value of this particular service, as it does of all others. It may be that in many cases custom fixes this delicate point. There is too much taste in the beau monde to higgle about certain services. The remuneration may even be gracefully disguised, so as to veil the vulgarity of the economic law. That law, however, presides over this transaction, just as it does over the most ordinary bargain; and Value does not change its nature because experience or urbanity dispenses with discussing it formally on every occasion.

This explains how artists above the usual standard of excellence succeed in realizing great fortunes. Another circumstance favors them. Their services are of such a nature that they can render them, at one and the same time, and by one and the same effort, to a multitude of individuals. However large the theatre, provided the voice of Rachel can fill it, each spectator enjoys the full pleasure of her inimitable declamation. This is the foundation of a new arrangement. Three or four thousand people, all experiencing the same desire, may come to an understanding, and raise the requisite sum; and the contribution of each to the remuneration of the great tragedienne constitutes the equivalent of the unique service rendered by her to all at once. Such is Value.

As a great number of spectators may combine in order to witness an entertainment of this description, so a number of actors may combine in order to perform in an opera or play. Managers may intervene, to save them the trouble of a multiplicity of trifling accessory arrangements. Value is thus multiplied, ramified, distributed, and rendered complex—but it does not change its nature.

We shall finish with some exceptional cases. Such cases form the best test of a sound theory. When the rule is correct, exceptions do not invalidate, but confirm it.

An aged priest moves slowly along, pensive, with staff in hand, and breviary under his arm. His air is serene, his countenance expressive—he looks inspired! Where is he going? Do you see that church in the distance? The youthful village parson, distrustful as yet of his own powers, has called to his assistance the old missionary. But first of all he has some arrangements to make. The preacher will find indeed food and shelter at the parsonage—but he must live from one year's end to another. Mr. le Cure, then, has promoted a subscription among the rich people of the village, moderate in amount, but sufficient; for the aged pastor is not exacting, and answered the person who wrote to him—"*Du pain pour moi, voila mon necessaire; une obole pour le pauvre, voila mon superflu.*"

Thus are the economic preliminaries complied with; for this meddling Political Economy creeps into everything, and is to be found everywhere—*Nil humani a me alienum puto.*

Let us enlarge a little on this example, which is very apposite to what we are now discussing.

Here you have an exchange of services. On the one hand you have an old man who devotes his time, his strength, his talents, his health, to enlighten the minds of a few villagers, and raise them to a higher moral level. One the other hand, bread for a few days, and a hat and cassock, are assured to the man of eloquence.

But there is something more here. There is a rivalry of sacrifices. The old priest refuses everything that is not absolutely indispensable. Of that poor pittance the cure takes one half on his own shoulders; the village Croesuses exempt their brethren from the other half, who nevertheless profit by the sermons.

Do these sacrifices invalidate our definition of value? Not at all. Each is free to render his services only on such terms as are agreeable to himself. If these conditions are made easy, or if none are stipulated for, what is the consequence? The service, preserving its utility, loses its value. The old priest is persuaded that his services will find their reward in another world, and he cares not for their being recompensed here below. He feels, no doubt, that he is rendering a service to his listeners in addressing them, but he also feels that they do him a service in listening to him. Hence it follows that the transaction is based upon advantage to one of the contracting parties, with the full consent of the other. That is all. In general, exchanges are determined and estimated by reference to self-interest; but, thank God, that is not always the case: they are sometimes based on the principle of sympathy, and in that case we either transfer to another a satisfaction we might have reserved for ourselves, or we make an effort for him which we might have devoted to our own profit and advantage. Generosity, devotion, self-sacrifice, are impulses of our nature that, like many other circumstances, influence the actual value of a particular service, but they make no change on the general law of values.

In contrast to this consoling example, I might adduce another of a very opposite character. In order that a service should possess value, in the economical sense of the word, it is not at all indispensable that it should be a real, conscientious, and useful service; it is sufficient that it is accepted, and paid for by another service. The world is full of people who palm upon the public services of a quality more than doubtful, and make the public pay for them. All depends on the judgment we form in each case; and this is the reason why morals will be always the best auxiliary of Political Economy.

Impostors succeed in propagating a false belief. They represent themselves as the ambassadors of Heaven. They open at pleasure the gates of heaven or of hell. When this belief has once taken firm root, "Here," say they, "are some little images to which we have communicated the virtue of securing eternal happiness to those who carry them about their persons. In bestowing upon you one of these images, we render you an immense service. You must render us, then, certain services in return." Here you have a Value created. It is founded on a false appreciation, you say, and that is true. We might say as much of many material things that possess a certain value, for they would find purchasers if set up to auction. Economic science would become impossible if we admitted as values only values correctly and judiciously appreciated. At every step we must begin a new course of the moral and physical sciences. In a state of isolation, depraved desires and a warped intelligence may cause a man to pursue with great effort and exertion a chimerical satisfaction—a delusion. In like manner, in the social state, it sometimes happens, as the philosopher says, that we buy regret too dear. But if truth is naturally more in keeping with the human mind than error, all these frauds are destined to disappear—all these delusive services to be spurned and lose their value. Civilization will, in the long run, put everybody and everything in the right place.

But we must conclude this analysis, which has already extended to too great a length. Among the various wants of our nature, respiration, hunger, thirst—and the wants and desires that take their rise in our vanity, in our heads, hearts, and opinions, in our hopes for the future, whether well or ill grounded—everywhere we have sought for Value—and we have found it wherever an exchange of service takes place. We have found it everywhere of the same nature, based upon a principle clear, simple, absolute, although influenced by a multitude of varying circumstances. We might have passed in review all our other wants; we might have cited the carpenter, the mason, the manufacturer, the tailor, the physician, the officer of justice, the lawyer, the merchant, the painter, the judge, the president of the republic, and we should have found exactly the same thing. Frequently a material substance; sometimes forces furnished gratuitously by nature; always human services interchanged, measuring each other, estimating, appreciating, valuing one another, and exhibiting simply the result of that Valuation—or Value.

There is, however, one of our wants, very special in its nature, the cement of society, at once the cause and the effect of all our transactions, and the everlasting problem of Political Economy, of which it is necessary to say something in this place—I allude to the need to exchange.

In the preceding chapter we have described the marvelous effects of Exchange. They are such that men must naturally feel a desire to facilitate it, even at the expense of considerable sacrifices. It is for this end that we have roads, canals, railways, carriages, ships, merchants, tradesmen, bankers; and it is impossible to believe that society would submit to such enormous draughts upon its forces for the purpose of facilitating exchange if it did not find in exchange itself an ample compensation.

We have also seen that direct barter could give rise only to transactions at once inconvenient and restrained.

It is on that account that men have thought of resolving barter into two factors, sale and purchase, by means of an intermediate commodity, readily divisible, and, above all, possessed of value, in order to secure public confidence. This intermediate commodity is Money.

And it is worthy of remark that what, by an ellipsis or metonymy, we designate the value of gold and silver rests on exactly the same foundation as that of the air, the water, the diamond, the sermons of our old missionary, or the roulades of Malibran—that is to say, upon services rendered and received.

The gold, indeed, which we find spread on the favored banks of the Sacramento, derives from nature many precious qualities—ductility, weight, beauty, brilliancy, utility even, if you will. But there is one quality that nature has not given it, because nature has nothing to do with that—Value. A man knows that gold supplies a want that is sensibly felt, and that it is much coveted. He goes to California to seek for gold, just as my neighbor went to the spring to fetch water. He devotes himself to hard work—he digs, he excavates, he washes, he melts down—and then he comes to me and says: I will render you the service of transferring to you this gold; what service will you render me in return? We discuss the matter, we weigh all the circumstances that should influence our determination; at last we conclude a bargain, and Value is manifested and fixed. Misled by this curt form of expression, "Gold is valuable," we might suppose that the value resides in the gold, just as the qualities of ductility and specific gravity reside in it, and that nature has put it there. I hope the reader is already satisfied that this is a mistake. By and by he will be convinced that it is a deplorable fallacy.

Another misconception exists on the subject of gold, or rather of money. As it is the constant medium that enters into all transactions, the mean term between the two factors of compound barter, it is always with its value that we compare the value of the two services to be exchanged; and hence we are led to regard gold or money as a measure of value. In practice it cannot be otherwise. But science ought never to forget that money, so far as its value is concerned, is subject to the same fluctuations as any other product or service. Science does forget this sometimes; nor is it surprising. Everything tends to make us consider money as the measure of value, in the same way as the litre (or quart) is the measure of capacity. It plays an analogous part in actual business. One is not aware of its own fluctuations, because the franc, like its multiples and sub-multiples, always retains the same denomination. And arithmetic itself tends to propagate the confusion by ranking the franc as a measure, along with the measures of quantity in daily use.

I have given a definition of Value, at least of value according to my idea of it. I have subjected that definition to the test of diverse facts. None of them, so far as I can see, contradict it; and the scientific meaning I have given to the word agrees with its commonly accepted one, which is no small advantage, no slight guarantee—for what is science but experience classified? What is theory but the methodical exposition of universal practice?

I may now be permitted to glance rapidly at the systems that have hitherto prevailed. It is not in a spirit of controversy, much less of criticism, that I enter upon this examination, and I should willingly avoid it were I not convinced that it will throw new light upon the fundamental principles I am advocating.

We have seen that writers on Political Economy have sought for the principle of Value in one or more of the accidents that exercise a notable influence over it, such as materiality, conservability, utility, rarity, labor, etc.; just like a physiologist who should seek the principle of life in one or more of the external phenomena that are necessary to its development, as air, water, light, electricity, etc.

Materiality: "Man," says Mr. de Bonald, "is mind served by organs." If the economists of the materialist school had simply meant that men can render reciprocal services to each other only through the medium of their bodily organs, and had thence concluded that there is always something material in these services, and, consequently, in Value, I should not have proceeded a step farther, as I have a horror at word-catching and subtleties, which wit revels in.

But they have not thus understood it. What they believe is that Value has been communicated to matter, either by the labor of man or by the action of nature. In a word, deceived by the elliptical form of expression, gold is worth so much, corn is worth so much, they think they see in matter a quality called Value, just as the natural philosopher sees in it resistance and weight—and yet these attributes have been disputed.

Be that as it may, I dispute formally the existence of Value as an attribute of matter.

And first of all, it cannot be denied that Matter and Value are often found separated. When we say to a man—Carry that letter to its destination—fetch me some water—teach me this science or that manufacturing process—give me advice as to my sickness, or my law-suit—watch over my security, while I give myself up to labor or to sleep—what we demand is a Service, and in that service we acknowledge in the face of the world that there resides a Value, seeing that we pay for it voluntarily by an equivalent service. It would be strange that we should refuse to admit in theory what universal consent admits in practice.

True, our transactions have reference frequently to material objects; but what does that prove? Why, that men, by exercising foresight, prepare to render services they know to be in demand. I purchase a coat ready made, or I have a tailor come to my house to work by the day; but does that change the principle of Value, so as to make it reside at one time in the coat and at another time in the service?

One might ask here this puzzling question: Must we not see the principle of Value first of all in the material object, and then attribute it by analogy to the services? I say that it is just the reverse. We must recognize it first of all in the services, and attribute it afterwards, if we choose, by a figure of speech, by metonymy, to the material objects.

The numerous examples I have adduced render it unnecessary for me to pursue this discussion further. But I cannot refrain from justifying myself for having entered on it, by showing to what fatal consequences an error, or, if you will, an incomplete truth, may lead, when placed at the threshold of a science.

The least inconvenience of the definition that I am combating has been to curtail and mutilate Political Economy. If Value resides in matter, then where there is no matter there can be no Value. The Physiocrats designated three-fourths of the entire population as sterile, and Adam Smith, softening the expression, as unproductive classes.

But as facts in the long run are stronger than definitions, it became necessary in some way to bring back these classes, and make them re-enter the circle of economic studies. They were introduced by way of analogy; but the language of the science, formed beforehand on other definitions, had been so materialized as to render this extension repulsive. What mean such phrases as these: "To consume an immaterial product? Man is accumulated capital? Security is a commodity?" etc., etc.

Not only was the language of the science materialized beyond measure, but writers were forced to surcharge it with subtle distinctions, in order to reconcile ideas that had been erroneously separated. Hence Adam Smith's expression of Value in use, in contradistinction to Value in exchange, etc.

A greater evil still has been that, in consequence of this confusion of two great social phenomena, property and community, the one has seemed incapable of justification, and the other has been lost sight of.

In fact, if Value resides in matter, it becomes mixed up with the physical qualities of bodies that render them useful to man. Now, these qualities are frequently placed there by nature. Then nature co-operates in creating Value, and we find ourselves attributing value to what is essentially common and gratuitous. On what basis, then, do you place property? When the remuneration I give in order to obtain a material product, wheat for example, is distributed among all the laborers, near or at a distance, who have rendered me a service in the production of that commodity—who is to receive that portion of the value which corresponds to the action of nature, and with which man has nothing to do? Is it Providence who is to receive it? No one will say so, for we never heard of Nature demanding wages. Is man to receive it? What title has he to it, seeing that, by the hypothesis, he has done nothing?

Do not suppose that I am exaggerating, and that, for the sake of my own definition, I am torturing the definition of the economists, and deducing from it too rigorous conclusions. No, these consequences they have themselves very explicitly deduced, under the pressure of logic.

Thus, Senior has said that "those who have appropriated natural agents receive, in the form of rent, a recompense without having made any sacrifice. They merely hold out their hands to receive the offerings of the rest of the community." Scrope tells us that "landed property is an artificial restriction imposed upon the enjoyment of those gifts which the Creator has intended for the satisfaction of the wants of all." J.B. Say has these words: "Arable lands would seem to form a portion of natural wealth, seeing that they are not of human creation, and that nature has given them to man gratuitously. But as this description of wealth is not fugitive, like air and water—as a field is a space fixed and marked out which certain men have succeeded in appropriating, to the exclusion of all others who have given their consent to this appropriation, land, which was natural and gratuitous property, has now become social wealth, the use of which must be paid for."

Truly, if it be so, Proudhon is justified in proposing this terrible question, followed by an affirmation still more terrible:

"To whom belongs the rent of land? To the producer of land without doubt. Who made the land? God. Then, proprietor, begone!"

Yes, by a vicious definition, Political Economy has handed over logic to the Communists. I will break this terrible weapon in their hands, or rather they shall surrender it to me cheerfully. The consequences will disappear when I have annihilated the principle. And I undertake to demonstrate that if, in the production of wealth, the action of nature is combined with the action of man, the first—gratuitous and common in its own nature—remains gratuitous and common in all our transactions; that the second alone represents services, value; that the action of man alone is remunerated; and that it alone is the foundation, explanation, and justification of Property. In a word, I maintain that, relative to each other, men are proprietors only of the value of things, and that in transferring products from hand to hand, what they stipulate for exclusively is value, that is to say, reciprocal services;—all the qualities, properties, and utilities these products derive from nature being obtained by them into the bargain.

If Political Economy hitherto, in disregarding this fundamental consideration, has shaken the guardian principle of property by representing it as an artificial institution, necessary indeed, but unjust, she has by the same act left in the shade, and completely unperceived, another admirable phenomenon, the most touching dispensation of Providence to the creature—the phenomenon of progressive community.

Wealth, taking the word in its general acceptation, results from the combination of two agencies: the action of nature, and the action of man. The first is gratuitous and common by the destination of Providence, and never loses that character. The second alone is provided with value, and, consequently, appropriated: But with the development of intelligence, and the progress of civilization, the one takes a greater and greater part, the other a less and less part, in the realization of each given utility; whence it follows that the domain of the Gratuitous and the Common is continually expanding among men relatively to the domain of Value and Property; a consoling and suggestive view of the subject, entirely hidden from the eye of science, so long as we continue to attribute Value to the co-operation of nature.

Men of all religions thank God for his benefits. The father of a family blesses the bread that he breaks and distributes to his children—a touching custom, that reason would not justify were the liberality of Providence other than gratuitous.

Durableness, conservability—that pretended sine qua non of Value, is connected with the subject which I have just been discussing. It is necessary to the very existence of value, as Adam Smith thinks, that it should be fixed and realized in something that can be exchanged, accumulated, preserved, consequently in something material.

"There is one sort of labor that adds[1] to the value of the subject upon which it is bestowed. There is another which has no such effect."

"The labor of the manufacturer," he adds, "fixes and realizes itself in some particular subject or vendible commodity, which lasts for some time at least after the labor is past. The labor of the menial servant, on the contrary" (to which the author compares in this respect that of soldiers, magistrates, musicians, professors, etc.), "does not fix or realize itself in any particular subject or vendible commodity. His services perish in the very instant of their performance, and leave no trace of value behind them."

Here we find Value connected rather with the modifications of matter than with the satisfactions of men—a profound error; for the sole good to be obtained from the modification of material things is the attainment of that satisfaction which is the design, the end, the consummation of every Effort. If, then, we realize that satisfaction by a direct and immediate effort, the result is the same; and if that effort can be made the subject of transactions, exchanges, estimation, it includes the principle of Value.

---

[1] Adds! The subject had then intrinsic value anterior to the bestowal of labor upon it. That could only come from nature. The action of nature is not then gratuitous, according to this showing; but in that case, who can have the audacity to exact payment for this portion of superhuman value?

As regards the interval that may elapse between the effort and the satisfaction, surely Adam Smith attributes far too much importance to it when he says that the existence or non-existence of Value depends upon it. "The value of a vendible commodity," he says, "lasts for some time at least." Undoubtedly it lasts until the commodity has answered its purpose, which is to satisfy a want; and exactly the same thing may be said of a service. As long as that plate of strawberries remains on the sideboard it preserves its value. Why? Because it is the result of a service I have designed to render to myself, or that another has rendered to me by way of compensation, and of which I have not yet made use. The moment I have made use of it, by eating the strawberries, the value will disappear. The service will vanish and leave no trace of value behind. The very same thing holds of personal services. The consumer makes the value disappear, for it has been created only for that purpose. It is of little consequence as regards the principle of value, whether the service is undertaken to satisfy a want today, tomorrow, or a year hence.

Take another case. I am afflicted with a cataract. I call in an oculist. The instrument he makes use of has value, because it has durability; the operation he performs, it is said, has none, and yet I pay for it, and I have made choice of one among many rival operators, and arranged his remuneration beforehand. To maintain that this service has no value is to run counter to well-known facts and notions universally received. And of what use, I would ask, is a theory that, far from taking universal practice into account, ignores it altogether?

I would not have the reader suppose that I am carried away by an inordinate love of controversy. If I dwell upon these elementary notions, it is to prepare his mind for consequences of the highest importance, which will be afterwards developed. I know not whether it be to violate the laws of method to indicate these consequences by anticipation, but I venture to depart slightly from the regular course in order to obviate the danger of becoming tedious. This is the reason why I have spoken prematurely of Property and Community; and for the same reason I shall here say a word respecting Capital.

As Adam Smith made value to reside in matter, he could not conceive Capital as existing otherwise than in an accumulation of material objects. How, then, can we attribute Value to Services not susceptible of being accumulated or converted into capital?

Among the different descriptions of Capital, we give the first place to tools, machines, instruments of labor. They serve to make natural forces co-operate in the work of production and, attributing to these forces the faculty of creating value, people were led to imagine that instruments of labor, as such, were endowed with the same faculty, independently of any human services. Thus the spade, the plough, the steam engine, were supposed to co-operate simultaneously with natural agents and human forces in creating not only Utility, but Value also. But all value is remunerated by exchange. Who, then, is to receive that portion of value which is independent of all human service?

It is thus that the school of Proudhon, after having brought the rent of land into question, has contested also the interest of capital—a larger thesis, because it includes the other. I maintain that the Proudhon error, viewed scientifically, has its root in the prior error of Adam Smith. I shall demonstrate that capital, like natural agents, considered in itself, and with reference to its own proper action, creates utility, but never creates value. The latter is essentially the fruit of a legitimate service. I shall demonstrate also that in the social order, capital is not an accumulation of material objects, depending on material durability, but an accumulation of Values, that is to say, of services. This will put an end (virtually at least, by removing its foundation) to the recent attack upon the productiveness of Capital, and in a way satisfactory to the objectors themselves; for if I prove that there is nothing in the business of exchange but a mutuality of services, Mr. Proudhon must admit himself vanquished by my victory over his principle.

Labor. Adam Smith and his disciples have assigned the principle of Value to labor under the condition of Materiality. This is contrary to the other opinion that natural forces play a certain part in the production of Value. I have not here to combat the contradictions that become apparent in all their fatal consequences when these authors come to discuss the rent of land and the interest of capital.

Be that as it may, when they refer the principle of Value to labor, they would be very near the truth if they did not allude to manual labor. I have said, in fact, at the beginning of this chapter, that Value must have reference to Effort—an expression I prefer to the word labor, as more general, and embracing the whole sphere of human activity. But I hasten to add that it can spring only from efforts exchanged—from reciprocal Services; because value is not a thing having independent existence, but a relation.

There are then, strictly speaking, two flaws in Adam Smith's definition. The first is that it does not take exchange into account, without which value can be neither produced nor conceived. The second is that it makes use of too restricted a term—labor; unless we give to that term an unusual extension, and include in it the ideas not only of intensity and duration, but of skill, sagacity, and even of good or bad fortune.

The word service, which I substitute in my definition, removes these defects. It implies, necessarily, the idea of transmission, for no service can be rendered that is not received; and it implies also the idea of Effort, without taking for granted that the value is proportionate.

It is in this, above all, that the definition of the English Economists is lacking. To say that Value resides in labor induces us to suppose that Value and labor are proportional, and serve as reciprocal measures of each other. This is contrary to fact, and a definition that is contrary to fact must be defective.

It often happens that an exertion, considered insignificant in itself, passes with the world as of enormous value. (Take, for example, the diamond, the performance of the prima donna, a dash of a banker's pen, a fortunate privateering adventure, a touch of Raphael's pencil, a bull of plenary indulgence, the easy duty of an English queen, etc.) It still more frequently happens that laborious and overwhelming labor tends to what is absolutely valueless; and if it be so, how can we establish correlation and proportion between Value and labor?

My definition removes the difficulty. It is clear that in certain circumstances one can render a great service at the expense of a very small exertion, and that in others, after great exertion, we render no service at all. And this is another reason why, in this respect, it is correct to say that the Value is in the Service rendered, rather than in the labor bestowed, seeing that it bears proportion to the one and not to the other.

I go further. I affirm that value is estimated as much by the labor saved to the recipient as by the labor performed by the cedant (the man who cedes or makes it over). Let the reader recall the dialogue we supposed to take place between the two parties who bargained for the diamond. In substance, it has reference to no accidental circumstances, but enters, tacitly, into the essence and foundation of all transactions. Keep in mind that we here take for granted that the two parties are at entire liberty to exercise their own will and judgment. Each of them, in making the exchange, is influenced by various considerations among which we must certainly rank, as of the greatest importance, the difficulty experienced by the recipient in procuring for himself, by a direct exertion, the satisfaction that is offered to him. Both parties have their eyes on the difficulty, the one with the view of being more yielding, the other with the view of being more exacting. The labor undergone by the cedant also exerts an influence on the bargain. It is one of the elements of it, but it is not the only one. It is not, then, exact to say that value is determined by labor. It is determined by a multitude of considerations, all comprised in the word service.

What may be affirmed with great truth is this; that, in consequence of competition, Value tends to become more proportioned to Effort—recompense to merit. It is one of the beautiful Harmonies of the social state. But as regards Value, this equalizing pressure exercised by competition is quite external, and it is not allowable in strict logic to confound the influence a phenomenon undergoes from an external cause, with the phenomenon itself.

Utility. J.B. Say, if I am not mistaken, was the first who threw off the yoke of materiality. He made out value very expressly to be a moral quality—an expression that perhaps goes too far, for value can scarcely be said to be either a physical or a moral quality—it is simply a relation.

But the great French Economist has himself said, that "It is not given to anyone to reach the limits of science, and Philosophers mount on each other's shoulders to explore a more and more extended horizon." Perhaps the glory of Mr. Say (in what regards the special question with which we are now occupied, for his titles to glory in other respects are as numerous as they are imperishable) is to have bequeathed to his successors a view of the subject that is prolific and suggestive.

Mr. Say's principle was this: "Value is founded on Utility." If we had here to do with utility as connected with human services, I should not contest this principle. At most, I could only observe that it is superfluous, as being self-evident. It is very clear, as a matter of fact that no one consents to remunerate a service unless, right or wrong, he judges it to be useful. The word service includes the idea of utility—so much so that it is nothing else than a literal reproduction of the Latin word *uti*; in French, *servir*.

But, unfortunately, it is not in this sense that Say understands it. He discovers the principle of value not only in human services rendered by means of material things, but in the useful qualities put by nature into the things themselves. In this way he places himself once more under the yoke of materiality, and is very far, we are obliged to confess, from clearing away the mist in which the English Economists had enveloped the question of Property.

Before discussing Say's principle on its own merits, I must explain its logical import, in order to avoid the reproach of landing myself and the reader in an idle discussion.

We cannot doubt that the Utility of which Say speaks is that which resides in material objects. If wheat, timber, coal, broad cloth, have value, it is because these products possess qualities which render them proper for our use, fit to satisfy the want we experience for food, fuel, and clothing.

Hence, as nature has created Utility, it is inferred that she has created also Value—a fatal confusion of ideas, out of which the enemies of property have forged a terrible weapon.

Take a commodity, wheat for example. I purchase it at the Halle au Ble for sixteen francs. A great portion of these sixteen francs is distributed—in infinite ramifications, and an inextricable complication of advances and reimbursements—among all the men here or abroad who have cooperated in furnishing this wheat. Part goes to the laborer, the sower, the reaper, the thresher, the carter—part to the blacksmith and plough-wright who have prepared the agricultural implements. Thus far all are agreed, whether Economists or Communists.

But I perceive that four out of the sixteen francs go to the pro-prietor of the soil, and I have a good right to ask if that man, like the others, has rendered me a Service to entitle him incontestably, like them, to remuneration.

According to the doctrine that the present work aspires to establish, the answer is categorical. It consists of a peremptory yes. The proprietor has rendered me a service. What is it? This, that he has by himself, or his ancestor, cleared and enclosed the field—he has cleared it of weeds and stagnant water—he has enriched and thickened the vegetable mould—he has built a house and a homestead. All this presupposes much labor executed by him in person; or, what comes to the same thing, by others whom he has paid. These are services, certainly, that, according to the just law of reciprocity, must be reimbursed to him. Now, this proprietor has never been remunerated, at least to the full extent. He cannot be so by the first man who comes to buy from him a bag of wheat. What is the arrangement, then, that takes place? Assuredly the most ingenious, the most legitimate, the most equi-table arrangement it is possible to imagine. It consists in this—That whoever wishes to purchase a sack of wheat shall pay, besides the services of the various laborers whom we have enumerated, a small portion of the services rendered by the proprietor. In other words, the Value of the proprietor's services is spread over all the sacks of wheat that are produced by this field.

Now, it may be asked if the supposed remuneration of four francs be too great or too small. I answer that Political Economy has nothing to do with that. That science establishes that the value of the services rendered by the landed proprietor are regulated by exactly the same laws as the value of other services, and that is enough.

It may be a subject of surprise, too, that this bit-by-bit reimbursement should not at length amount to a complete liquidation and, consequently, to an extinction of the proprietor's claim. They who make this objection do not reflect that it is of the nature of Capital to produce a perpetual return, as we shall see in the sequel.

I shall not dwell longer on that question in this place; and shall simply remark, that there is not in the entire price of the wheat a single farthing that does not go to remunerate human services—not one that corresponds to the value that nature is supposed to have given to the wheat by imparting to it utility.

But if, adhering to the principle of Say and the English Economists, you assert that, of the sixteen francs, there are twelve that go to the laborers, sowers, reapers, carters, etc.—two that recompense the personal services of the proprietor; and, finally, that there are two others that represent a value that has for its foundation the utility created by God, by natural agents, and without any co-operation of man, do you not perceive that you immediately lay yourself open to be asked, Who is to profit by this portion of value? Who has a title to this remuneration? Nature does not demand it, and who dare take nature's place?

The more Say tries to explain Property on this hypothesis, the more he exposes himself to attack. He sets out by justly comparing nature to a laboratory, in which various chemical operations take place, the result of which is useful to man. "The soil, then," he adds, "is the producer of utility, and when IT (the soil) receives payment in the form of a profit or a rent to its proprietor, it is not without giving something to the consumer in exchange for what he pays IT (the soil). IT (still the soil) gives him the utility it has produced, and it is in producing this utility that the earth is productive as well as labor."

This assertion is unmistakable. Here we have two pretenders, who present themselves to share the remuneration due by the consumer of wheat—namely, the earth and labor. They urge the same title, for the soil, Mr. Say affirms, is productive as well as labor. Labor asks to be remunerated for a service; the soil demands to be remunerated for a utility, and this remuneration it demands not for itself (for in what form should we give it?) but for its proprietor.

Whereupon Proudhon summons the proprietor, who represents himself as having the powers of the soil at his disposal, to exhibit his title.

You wish me to pay; in other words, to render a service, in order that I may receive the utility produced by natural agents, independently of the assistance of man, already paid for separately. But, I ask again, Who is to profit by my service?

Is it the producer of utility—that is to say, the soil? That is absurd—the fear of any demand from that quarter need give no great uneasiness.

Is it man? but by what title does he demand it? If for having rendered me a service, well and good. In that case, we are at one. It is the human service that has value, not the natural service; and that is just the conclusion to which I desire to bring you.

That, however, is contrary to your hypothesis. You say that all the human services are remunerated with fourteen francs, and that the two francs that make up the price of the wheat correspond to the value created by nature. In that case, I repeat my question—By what title does anyone present himself to receive them? Is it not, unfortunately, too clear that if you give specially the name of proprietor to the man who claims right to these two francs, you justify the too famous saying that Property is theft?

And don't imagine that this confusion between utility and value shakes only the foundation of landed property. After having led you to contest the rent of land, it leads you to contest also the interest of capital.

In fact, machines, the instruments of labor, are, like the soil, producers of utility. If that utility has value, it is paid for, for the word value implies right to payment. But to whom is the payment made? To the proprietor of the machine without doubt. Is it for a personal service? Then say at once that the value is in the service. But if you say that it is necessary to make a payment first for the service, and a second payment for the utility produced by the machine independently of the human action, which has been already recompensed, then I ask you to whom does this second payment go, and how has the man who has been already remunerated for all his services a right to demand anything more?

The truth is, that the utility that is produced by nature is gratuitous, and therefore common, like that produced by the instruments of labor. It is gratuitous and common on one condition, that we take the trouble, that we render ourselves the service of appropriating it; or if we give that trouble to or demand that service from another, that we cede to him in return an equivalent service. It is in these services, thus compared, that value resides, and not at all in natural utility. The exertion may be more or less great—that makes a difference in the value, not in the utility. When we stand near a spring, water is gratuitous for us all on condition that we stoop to lift it. If we ask our neighbor to take that trouble for us, then a convention, a bargain, a value makes its appearance, but that does not make the water otherwise than gratuitous, If we are an hour's walk from the spring, the basis of the transaction will be different; but the difference is one of degree, not of principle. The value has not, on that account, passed into the water or into its utility. The water continues still gratuitous on condition of fetching it, or of remunerating those who, by a bargain freely made and discussed, agree to spare us that exertion by making it themselves.

It is the same thing in every case. We are surrounded by utilities, but we must stoop to appropriate them. That exertion is sometimes very simple, and often very complicated. Nothing is more easy, in the general case, than to draw water, the utility of which has been prepared by nature beforehand. It is not so easy to obtain wheat, the utility of which nature has equally prepared. This is why these two efforts differ in degree, though not in principle. The service is more or less onerous; therefore more or less valuable—the utility is, and remains always, gratuitous.

Suppose an instrument of labor to intervene, what would be the result? That the utility would be more easily obtained. The service has thus less value. We certainly pay less for our books since the invention of printing. Admirable phenomenon, too little understood! You say that the instruments of labor produce Value—you are mistaken—it is Utility, and gratuitous Utility, you should say. As to Value, instead of producing it, they tend more and more to annihilate it.

It is quite true that the person who made the machine has rendered a service. He receives a remuneration by which the value of the product is augmented. This is the reason why we fancy we recompense the utility the machine produces. It is an illusion. What we remunerate is the services all those who have co-operated in making and working the machine have rendered to us. So little does the value reside in the utility produced that even after having recompensed these new services, we acquire the utility on easier and cheaper terms than before.

Let us accustom ourselves to distinguish Utility from Value. Without this there can be no Economic science. I give utterance to no paradox when I affirm that Utility and Value, so far from being identical, or even similar, are ideas opposed to one another. Want, Effort, Satisfaction: here we have man regarded in an Economic point of view. The relation of Utility is with Want and Satisfaction. The relation of Value is with Effort. Utility is the Good, which puts an end to the want by the satisfaction. Value is the Evil, for it springs from the obstacle that is interposed between the want and the satisfaction. But for these obstacles, there would have been no Effort either to make or to exchange; Utility would be infinite, gratuitous, and common, without condition, and the notion of Value would never have entered into the world. In consequence of these obstacles, Utility is gratuitous only on condition of Efforts exchanged, which, when compared with each other, give rise to Value. The more these obstacles give way to the liberality of nature and the progress of science, the more does utility approximate to the state of being absolutely common and gratuitous, for the onerous condition, and consequently the value, diminish as the obstacles diminish. I shall esteem myself fortunate if, by these dissertations, which may appear subtle, and of which I am condemned to fear at the same time both the length and the conciseness, I succeed in establishing this encouraging truth—the legitimate property of value and this other truth, equally consoling—the progressive community of utility.

One observation more. All that serves us is useful (uti, ser-vir), and in this respect it is extremely doubtful whether there be anything in the universe (whether in the shape of forces or materials) that is not useful to man.

We may affirm at least, without fear of mistake, that a multitude of things possess a utility that is unknown to us. Were the moon placed either higher or lower than she is, it is very possible that the inorganic kingdom, consequently the vegetable kingdom, consequently also the animal kingdom, might be profoundly modified. But for that star which shines in the firmament while I write, it may be that the human race had not existed. Nature has surrounded us with utilities. The quality of being useful we recognize in many substances and phenomena;—in others, science and experience reveal it to us every day—in others, again, it may exist in perfection, and yet we may remain for ever ignorant of it.

When these substances and phenomena exert upon us, but independently of us, their useful action, we have no interest in comparing the degree of their utility to mankind; and, what is more, we have scarcely the means of making the comparison. We know that oxygen and nitrogen are useful to us, but we don't try, and probably we should try in vain, to determine in what proportion. We have not here the elements of appreciation—the elements of value. I should say as much of the salts, the gases, the forces that abound in nature. When all these agents are moved and combined so as to produce for us, but without our co-operation, utility, that utility we enjoy without estimating its value. It is when our co-operation comes into play, and above all, when it comes to be exchanged—it is then, and then only, that Estimation and Value make their appearance, in connection not with the utility of the substances or phenomena, of which we are often ignorant, but with the co-operation itself.

This is my reason for saying that "Value is the appreciation of services exchanged." These services may be very complicated; they may have exacted a multitude of operations recent or remote; they may be transmitted from one generation or one hemisphere to another generation or another hemisphere, embracing countless contracting parties, necessitating credits, advances, various arrangements, until a general balance is effected. But the principle of value is always in the services, and not in the utility of which these services are the vehicle—utility that is gratuitous in its nature and essence, and that passes from hand to hand, if I may be allowed the expression, into the bargain.

After all, if you persist in seeing in Utility the foundation of Value, I am very willing, but it must be distinctly understood that it is not that utility that is in things and phenomena by the dispensation of Providence or the power of art, but the utility of human services compared and exchanged.

Rarity. According to Senior, of all the circumstances that determine value, rarity is the most decisive. I have no objection to make to that remark, if it is not that the form in which it is made presupposes that value is inherent in things themselves—a hypothesis the very appearance of which I shall always combat. At bottom, the word rarity, as applied to the subject we are now discussing, expresses in a concise manner this idea that, *ceteris paribus*, a service has more value in proportion as we have more difficulty in rendering it to ourselves; and that, consequently, a larger equivalent is exacted from us when we demand it from another. Rarity is one of these difficulties. It is one obstacle more to be surmounted. The greater it is, the greater remuneration do we award to those who surmount it for us. Rarity gives rise frequently to large remunerations, and this is my reason for refusing to admit with the English Economists that Value is proportional to labor. We must take into account the parsimony with which nature treats us in certain respects. The word service embraces all these ideas and shades of ideas.

Judgment. Storch sees value in the judgment by which we recognize it. Undoubtedly, whenever we have to do with relation, it is necessary to compare and to judge. Nevertheless, the relation is one thing and the judgment is another. When we compare the height of two trees, their magnitude, and the difference of their magnitude, are independent of our appreciation.

But in the determination of value, what is the relation of which we have to form a judgment? It is the relation of two services exchanged. The business is to discover what the services rendered are worth in relation to those received, in connection with acts or things exchanged, and taking all circumstances into account—not what intrinsic utility resides in these acts or things, for this utility may, to some extent, be altogether independent of human exertion, and consequently devoid of value.

Storch falls into the error I am now combating when he says,

"Our judgment enables us to discover the relation which exists between our wants and the utility of things. The determination which our judgment forms upon the utility of things constitutes their value."

And, farther on, he says,

"In order to create a value, we must have the conjunction of these three circumstances—first, that man experiences or conceives a want; second, that there exists something calculated to satisfy that want; and third, that a judgment is pronounced in favor of the utility of the thing. Then the value of things is their relative utility."

During the day I experience the want of seeing clearly. There exists one thing calculated to satisfy that want—namely, the light of the sun. My judgment pronounces in favor of the utility of that thing, and . . . it has no value. Why? Because I enjoy it without calling for the services of anyone.

At night I experience the same want. There exists one thing capable of satisfying it very imperfectly, a wax candle. My judgment pronounces in favor of the utility, but far inferior utility, of that thing—and it has value. Why? Because the man who has taken the trouble to make the candle will not give it to me except upon condition of my rendering him an equivalent service.

What we have, then, to compare and to judge of, in order to determine Value, is not the relative utility of things, but the relation of two services.

On these terms, I do not reject Storch's definition.

Permit me to recapitulate a little, in order to show clearly that my definition contains all that is true in the definitions of my predecessors, and eliminates everything in them that is erroneous either through excess or defect.

The principle of Value, we have seen, resides in a human service, and results from the appreciation of two services compared.

Value must have relation to Effort. Service implies a certain Effort.

Value supposes a comparison of Efforts exchanged, or at least exchangeable. Service implies the terms to give and to receive.

Value is not, however, in fact proportional to the intensity of the Efforts. Service does not necessarily imply that proportion.

A multitude of external circumstances influence value without constituting value itself. The word service takes all these circumstances in due measure into account.

Materiality. When the service consists in transferring a material thing, nothing hinders us from saying, by metonymy, that it is the thing that has value. But we must not forget that this is a figure of speech, by which we attribute to things themselves the value of the services that produced them.

Conservability. Without reference to the consideration of materiality, value endures until the satisfaction is obtained, and no longer. Whether the satisfaction follows the effort more or less nearly—whether the service is personal or real, makes no change in the nature of value.

Capability of Accumulation. In a social point of view, what is accumulated by saving is not matter, but value or services.

Utility. I admit, with Mr. Say, that Utility is the foundation of Value, provided it is granted me that we have no concern with the utility that resides in commodities, but with the relative utility of services.

Labor. I admit, with Ricardo, that labor is the foundation of Value, provided, first of all, the word labor is taken in the most general sense, and that you do not afterwards assert a proportionality that is contrary to fact; in other words, provided you substitute for the word labor the word service.

Rarity. I admit, with Senior, that rarity influences value. But why? Because it renders the service so much more precious.

Judgment. I admit, with Storch, that value results from a judgment formed, provided it be granted me that the judgment so formed is not upon the utility of things, but on the utility of services.

Thus I hope to satisfy Economists of all shades of opinion. I admit them all to be right, because all have had a glimpse of the truth in one of its aspects. Error is no doubt on the reverse of the medal; and it is for the reader to decide whether my definition includes all that is true, and rejects all that is false.

I cannot conclude without saying a word on that quadrature of Political Economy—the measure of value; and here I shall repeat, and with still more force, the observation with which I terminated the preceding chapters.

I said our wants, our desires, our tastes, have neither limit nor exact measure.

I said also that our means of providing for our wants—the gifts of nature, our faculties, activity, discernment, foresight—had no precise measure. Each of these elements is variable in itself—it differs in different men and it varies from hour to hour in the same individual—so that the whole forms an aggregate that is mobility itself.

If, again, we consider what the circumstances are that influence value—utility, labor, rarity, judgment—and reflect that there is not one of these circumstances that does not vary *ad infinitum*, we may well ask why men should set themselves so pertinaciously to try to discover a fixed measure of Value?

It would be singular, indeed, if we were to find fixity in a mean term composed of variable elements, and which is nothing else than a Relation between two extreme terms more variable still!

The Economists, then, who go in pursuit of an absolute measure of value are pursuing a chimera; and, what is more, a thing that, if found, would be positively useless. Universal practice has adopted gold and silver as standards, although practical men are not ignorant how variable is the value of these metals. But of what importance is the variability of the measure, if, affecting equally and in the same manner the two objects that are exchanged, it does not interfere with the fairness and equity of the exchange? It is a mean proportional, which may rise or fall, without, on that account, failing to perform its office, which is to show the Relation of two extremes.

The design of the science is not, like that of exchange, to discover the present Relation of two services, for in that case, money would answer the purpose in view. What the science aims at discovering is the Relation between Effort and Satisfaction; and for this purpose, a measure of value, did it exist, would teach us nothing, for the effort brings always to the satisfaction a varying proportion of gratuitous utility that has no value. It is because this element of our well-being has been lost sight of that the majority of writers have deplored the absence of a measure of Value. They have not reflected that it would not enable them to answer the question proposed—What is the comparative Wealth or prosperity of two classes, of two countries, of two generations?

In order to resolve that question, the science would require a measure that should reveal to it not only the relation of two services, which might be the vehicle of very different amounts of gratuitous utility, but the relation of the Effort to the Satisfaction, and that measure could be no other than the effort itself, or labor.

But how can labor serve as a measure? Is it not itself a most variable element? Is it not more or less skillful, laborious, precarious, dangerous, repugnant? Does it not require, more or less, the intervention of certain intellectual faculties, of certain moral virtues? And according as it is influenced by these circumstances, is it not rewarded by a remuneration that is in the highest degree variable?

There is one species of labor that, at all times, and in all places, is identically the same, and it is that which must serve as a type. I mean labor the most simple, rude, primitive, muscular—that which is freest from all natural co-operation—that which every man can execute—that which renders services of a kind that one can render to himself—that which exacts no exceptional force or skill, and requires no apprenticeship—industry such as is found in the very earliest stages of society: the work, in short, of the simple day-laborer. That kind of labor is everywhere the most abundantly supplied, the least special, the most homogeneous, and the worst remunerated. Wages in all other departments are proportioned and graduated on this basis, and increase with every circumstance that adds to its importance.

If, then, we wish to compare two social states with each other, we cannot have recourse to a standard of value, and for two reasons, the one as logical as the other—first, because there is none; and, second, because, if there were, it would give a wrong answer to our question, neglecting, as it must, a considerable and progressive element in human prosperity—gratuitous utility.

What we must do, on the contrary, is to put Value altogether out of sight, particularly the consideration of money; and ask the question, What, in such and such a country, and at such and such an epoch, is the amount of each kind of special utility, and the sum total of all utilities, that correspond to a given amount of unskilled labor? In other words, what amount of material comfort and prosperity can an unskilled workman earn as the reward of his daily toil?

We may affirm that the natural social order is harmonious, and goes on improving, if, on the one hand, the number of unskilled laborers receiving the smallest possible remuneration continues to diminish; and if, on the other, that remuneration, measured not in value or in money, but in real satisfactions, continues constantly on the increase.

The ancients have well described all the combinations of Exchange—Do ut des (commodity against commodity), *Do ut facias* (commodity against service), *Facio ut des* (service against commodity), *Facio ut facias* (service against service).[2]

Seeing that products and services are thus exchanged for one another, it is quite necessary that they should have something in common, something by which they can be compared and estimated—namely, Value.

But value is always identically the same. Whether it be in the product or in the service, it has always the same origin and foundation.

This being so, we may ask, is Value originally and essentially in the commodity, and is it only by analogy that we extend the notion to the service?

Or, on the contrary, does Value reside in the service, and is it not mixed up and amalgamated with the product, simply and exclusively because the service is so?

Some people seem to think that this is a question of pure subtlety. We shall see by and by. At present I shall only observe, that it would be strange if, in Political Economy a good or a bad definition of Value were a matter of indifference.

I cannot doubt that at the outset, Political Economists thought they discovered value rather in the product as such, than in the matter of the product. The Physiocrats (the Economists of Quesnay's School) attributed value exclusively to land, and stigmatized as sterile such classes as added nothing to matter—so strictly in their eyes were value and matter bound up together.

---

[2]These are the words by which the Roman lawyers designated what they termed innominate contracts, as distinguished from contracts with known names, as purchase and sale, letting, hiring, borrowing, lending, etc.—Translator.

Adam Smith ought to have discarded this idea, since he makes value flow from labor. Do not pure services, services *per se*, exact labor and consequently, do they not imply value? Near to the truth as Smith had come, he did not make himself master of it; for, besides pronouncing formally that labor, in order to possess value, must be applied to matter, to something physically tangible and capable of accumulation, we know that, like the Physiocrats, he ranked those who simply render services among the unproductive classes.

These classes, in fact, occupy a prominent position in the Wealth of Nations. But this only shows us that the author, after having given a definition, found himself straitened by it, and consequently, that that definition is erroneous. Adam Smith would not have gained his great and just renown had he not written his magnificent chapters on Education, on the Clergy, and on Public Services, and if he had, in treating of Wealth, confined himself within the limits of his own definition. Happily, by this inconsistency, he freed himself from the fetters that his premises imposed upon him. This always happens. A man of genius who sets out with a false principle never escapes inconsistency, without which he would get deeper and deeper into error, and, far from appearing a man of genius, would show himself no longer a man of sense.

As Adam Smith advanced a step beyond the Physiocrats, Jean Baptiste Say advanced a step beyond Smith. By degrees Say was led to refer value to services, but only by way of analogy. It is in the product that he discovers true value, and nothing shows this better than his whimsical denomination of services as "immaterial products"—two words that absolutely shriek out on finding themselves side by side. Say, in the outset, agrees with Smith; for the entire theory of the master is to be found in the first ten lines of the work of the disciple.[3] But he thought and meditated on the

---

[3]*Traite d'Economie Politique*, p. 1.

subject for thirty years, and he made progress. He approximated more and more to the truth, without ever fully attaining it.

Moreover, we may imagine that Say might have done his duty as an Economist as well by referring the value of the service to the product as by referring the value of the product to the service if the Socialist propaganda, founding on his own deductions, had not come to reveal to us the insufficiency and the danger of his principle.

The question I propose, then, is this—Seeing that certain products are possessed of value, seeing that certain services are possessed of value, and seeing that value is one and identical, and can have but one origin, one foundation, one explanation—is this origin, this explanation, to be found in the product or in the service?

The reply to that question is obvious, and for this unanswerable reason, that every product that has value implies service, but every service does not necessarily imply a product.

This appears to me mathematically certain—conclusive. A service, as such, has value, whether it assume a material form or not.

A material object has value if in transferring it to another, we render him a service—if not, it has no value.

Then value does not proceed from the material object to the service, but from the service to the material object.

Nor is this all. Nothing is more easily explained than this pre-eminence, this priority, given to the service over the product, so far as value is concerned. We shall immediately see that this is owing to a circumstance that might have been easily perceived, but that has not been observed, just because it is under our eyes. It is nothing else than that foresight which is natural to man, and in virtue of which, in place of limiting himself to the services that are demanded of him, he prepares himself beforehand to render those services that he foresees are likely to be demanded. It is thus that the *facio ut facias* transforms itself into the *do ut des,* without its ceasing to be the dominant fact that explains the whole transaction.

John says to Peter, I want a cup. I could make it myself, but if you will make it for me, you will render me a service, for which I will pay you by an equivalent service.

Peter accepts the offer, and, in consequence, sets out in quest of suitable materials, mixes them, manipulates them, and, in the end, makes the article John wants.

It is very evident that here it is the service that determines the value. The dominant word in the transaction is *facio*. And if, afterwards, the value is incorporated with the product, it is only because it flows from the service, which combines the labor executed by Peter with the labor saved to John.

Now, it may happen that John may make frequently the same proposal to Peter, and that other people may also make it; so that Peter can foresee with certainty the kind of services that will be demanded of him, and prepare himself for rendering them. He may say, I have acquired a certain degree of skill in making cups. Experience tells me that cups supply a want that must be satisfied, and I am therefore enabled to manufacture them beforehand.

Henceforth John says no longer to Peter *facio ut facias*, but *facio ut des*. If he in turn has foreseen the wants of Peter, and labored beforehand to provide for them, he can then say *do ut des*.

But in what respect, I ask, does this progress, which flows from human foresight, change the nature and origin of value? Does service cease to be its foundation and measure? As regards the true idea of value, what difference does it make whether Peter, before he makes the cup, waits till there is a demand for it, or, foreseeing a future demand, manufactures the article beforehand?

There is another remark that I would like to make here. In human life, inexperience and thoughtlessness precede experience and foresight. It is only in the course of time that men are enabled to foresee each other's wants, and to make preparations for satisfying them. Logically, the facio ut facias must precede the *do ut des*. The latter is at once the fruit and the evidence of a certain amount of knowledge diffused, of experience acquired, of political security obtained, of a certain confidence in the future—in a word, of a certain degree of civilization. This social prescience, this faith in a future demand, which causes us to provide a present supply; this sort of intuitive acquaintance with statistics that each possesses in a greater or less degree, and that establishes a surprising equilibrium between our wants and the means of supplying them, is one of the most powerful and efficacious promoters of human improvement. To it we owe the division of labor, or at least the separation of trades and professions. To it we owe one of the advantages men seek for with the greatest ardor, the fixity of remuneration, under the form of wages as regards labor, and interest as regards capital. To it we are indebted for the institution of credit, transactions having reference to the future, those which are designed to equalize risk, etc. It is surprising, in an Economical point of view, that this noble attribute of man, Foresight, has not been made more the subject of remark. This arises, as Rousseau has said, from the difficulty we experience in observing the medium in which we live and move, and which forms our natural atmosphere. We notice only exceptional appearances and abnormal facts, while we allow to pass unperceived those that act permanently around us, upon us, and within us, and that modify profoundly both individual men and society at large.

To return to the subject that at present engages us. It may be that human foresight, in its infinite diffusion, tends more and more to substitute the *do ut des* for the *facio ut facias*; but we must never forget that it is in the primitive and necessary form of exchange that the notion of value first makes its appearance, that this primitive form is that of reciprocal service; and that, after all, as regards exchange, the product is only a service foreseen and provided for.

But although I have shown that value is not inherent in matter, and cannot be classed among its attributes, I am far from maintaining that it does not pass from the service to the product, so as (if I may be allowed the expression) to become incorporated with it. I hope my opponents will not believe I am pedant enough to wish to exclude from common language such phrases as these—gold has value, wheat has value, land has value. But I have a right to demand of science why this is so; and if I am answered, because gold, wheat, and land possess in themselves intrinsic value, then I think I have a right to say—"You are mistaken, and your error is dangerous. You are mistaken, for there are gold and land that are devoid of value, gold and land that have not yet had any human labor bestowed upon them. Your error is dangerous, for it leads men to regard what is simply a right to a reciprocity of services as a usurpation of the gratuitous gifts of God."

I am quite willing, then, to acknowledge that products are possessed of value, provided you grant me that it is not essential to them, and that it attaches itself to services, and proceeds from them.

This is so true, that a very important consequence, and one that is fundamental in Political Economy, flows from it—a consequence that has not been, and indeed could not be, remarked. It is this:

Where value has passed from the service to the product, it undergoes in the product all the risks and chances to which it is subject in the service itself.

It is not fixed in the product, as it would have been had it been one of its own intrinsic qualities. It is essentially variable; it may rise indefinitely, or it may fall until it disappears altogether, just as the species of service to which it owes its origin would have done.

The man who makes a cup today for the purpose of selling it a year hence confers value on it, and that value is determined by that of the service—not the value the service possesses at the present moment, but that which it will possess at the end of the year. If at the time when the cup comes to be sold such services are more in demand, the cup will be worth more, or it will be depreciated in the opposite case.

This is the reason why man is constantly stimulated to exercise foresight, in order to turn it to account. He has always in perspective a possible rise or fall of value—a recompense for just and sagacious forecasts, and chastisement when they are erroneous. And, observe, his success or failure coincides with the public good or the public detriment. If his foresight has been well directed, if he has made preparations beforehand to give society the benefit of services that are more in request, more appreciated, more efficacious, that supply more adequately wants that are deeply felt, he has contributed to diminish the scarcity, to augment the abundance, of that description of service, and to bring it within the reach of a greater number of persons at less expense. If, on the other hand, he is mistaken in his calculations for the future, he contributes by his competition to depress still farther those services for which there is little demand. He only effects, and at his own expense, a negative good—he advertises the public that a certain description of wants no longer call for the exertion of much social activity, which activity must now take another direction, or go without recompense.

This remarkable fact—that value incorporated in a product, depends on the value of the kind of service to which it owes its origin—is of the very highest importance, not only because it demonstrates more and more clearly the theory that the principle of value resides in the service, but because it explains, easily and satisfactorily, phenomena that other systems regard as abnormal and exceptional.

When once the product has been thrown upon the market of the world, do the general tendencies of society operate toward elevating or toward depressing its value? This is to ask whether the particular kind of services that have engendered this value are liable to become more or less appreciated, and better or worse remunerated. The one is as possible as the other, and it is this which opens an unlimited field to human foresight.

This we may remark at least, that the general law of beings, capable of making experiments, of acquiring information, and of rectifying mistakes, is progress. The probability, then, is, that at any given period a certain amount of time and pains will effect greater results than were effected by the same agency at an anterior period; whence we may conclude that the prevailing tendency of value incorporated with a commodity is to fall. If, for example, we suppose the cup I took by way of illustration, and as a symbol of other products, to have been made many years ago, the probability is that it has undergone depreciation, inasmuch as we have at the present day more resources for the manufacture of such articles, more skill, better tools, capital obtained on easier terms, and a more extended division of labor. In this way the person who wishes to obtain the cup does not say to its possessor, Tell me the exact amount of labor (quantity and quality both taken into account) that cup has cost you, in order that I may remunerate you accordingly. No, he says, Nowadays, in consequence of the progress of art, I can make for myself, or procure by exchange, a similar cup at the expense of so much labor of such a quality; and that is the limit of the remuneration I can consent to give you.

Hence it follows that all labor incorporated with commodities, in other words, all accumulated labor, all capital, has a tendency to become depreciated in presence of services naturally improvable and increasingly and progressively productive; and that, in exchanging present labor against anterior labor, the advantage is generally on the side of present labor, as it ought to be, seeing that it renders a greater amount of service.

This shows us how empty are the declamations we hear continually directed against the value of landed property. That value differs from other values in nothing—neither in its origin, nor in its nature, nor in the general law of its slow depreciation, as compared with the labor it originally cost.

It represents anterior services—the clearing away of trees and stones, draining, enclosing, levelling, manuring, building: it demands the recompense of these services. But that recompense is not regulated with reference to the labor that has been actually performed. The landed proprietor does not say, "Give me in exchange for this land as much labor as it has received from me." (But he would so express himself if, according to Adam Smith's theory, value came from labor, and were proportional to it.) Much less does he say, as Ricardo and a number of economists suppose, "Give me first of all as much labor as this land has had bestowed upon it, and a certain amount of labor over and above, as an equivalent for the natural and inherent power of the soil." No, the proprietor, who represents all the possessors of the land who have preceded him, up to those who made the first clearance, is obliged, in their name, to hold this humble language:

"We have prepared services, and what we ask is to exchange these for equivalent services. We worked hard formerly, for in our days we were not acquainted with your powerful means of execution—there were no roads—we were forced to do everything by muscular exertion. Much sweat and toil, many human lives, are buried under these furrows. But we do not expect from you labor for labor—we have no means of effecting an exchange on these terms. We are quite aware that the labor bestowed on land now-a-days, whether in this country or abroad, is much more perfect and much more productive than formerly. All that we ask, and what you clearly cannot refuse us, is that our anterior labor and the new labor shall be exchanged, not in proportion to their comparative duration and intensity, but proportionally to their results, so that we may both receive the same remuneration for the same service. By this arrangement we are losers as regards labor, seeing that three or four times more of ours than of yours is required to accomplish the same service; but we have no choice, and can no longer effect the exchange on any other terms."

And, in point of fact, this represents the actual state of things. If we could form an exact estimate of the amount of efforts, of incessant labor, and toil, expended in bringing each acre of our land to its present state of productiveness, we should be thoroughly convinced that the man who purchases that land does not give labor for labor—at least in ninety-nine cases out of the hundred.

I add this qualification, because we must not forget that an incorporated service may gain value as well as lose it. And although the general tendency be toward depreciation, nevertheless the opposite phenomenon manifests itself sometimes, in exceptional circumstances, as well in the case of land as of anything else, and this without violating the law of justice, or affording adequate cause for the cry of monopoly.

Services always intervene to bring out the principle of value. In most cases the anterior labor probably renders a lesser amount of service than the new labor, but this is not an absolute law that admits of no exception. If the anterior labor renders a lesser amount of service than the new, as is nearly always the case, a greater quantity of the first than of the second must be thrown into the scale to establish the equiponderance, seeing that the equiponderance is regulated by services. But if it happen, as it sometimes may, that the anterior labor renders greater service than the new, the latter must make up for this by the sacrifice of quantity.

6

WEALTH

We have seen that in every commodity that is adapted to satisfy our wants and desires, there are two things to be considered and distinguished: what nature does, and what man does—what is gratuitous, and what is onerous—the gift of God and the service of man—utility and value. In the same commodity the one may be immense, and the other imperceptible. The former remaining invariable, the latter may be indefinitely diminished; and is diminished, in fact, as often as an ingenious process or invention enables us to obtain the same result with less effort.

One of the greatest difficulties, one of the most fertile sources of misunderstanding, controversy, and error, here presents itself to us at the very threshold of the science.

What is wealth?

Are we rich in proportion to the utilities we have at our disposal—that is, in proportion to the wants and desires we have the means of satisfying? "A man is rich or poor," says Adam Smith, "according as he possesses a greater or smaller amount of useful commodities which minister to his enjoyments."

Are we rich in proportion to the values we possess—that is to say, the services we can command? "Wealth," says J.B. Say, "is in proportion to Value. It is great if the sum of the value of which it is composed is great—it is small if the value be small."

The casual employ the word Wealth in two senses. Sometimes we hear them say—"The abundance of water is Wealth to such a country." In this case, they are thinking only of Utility. But when one wishes to reckon up his own wealth, he makes what is called an Inventory, in which only commercial Value is taken into account.

With deference to the savants, I believe that the casual are right for once. Wealth is either actual or relative. In the first point of view, we judge of it by our satisfactions. Mankind becomes richer in proportion as men acquire a greater amount of ease or material prosperity, whatever be the commodities by which it is procured. But do you wish to know what proportional share each man has in the general prosperity; in other words, his relative wealth? This is simply a relation, which value alone reveals, because value is itself a relation.

Our science has to do with the general welfare and prosperity of men, with the proportion that exists between their Efforts and their Satisfactions—a proportion the progressive participation of gratuitous utility in the business of production modifies advantageously. You cannot, then, exclude this element from the idea of Wealth. In a scientific point of view, actual or effective wealth is not the sum of values, but the aggregate of the utilities, gratuitous and onerous, that are attached to these values. As regards satisfactions—that is to say, as regards actual results of wealth, we are as much enriched by the value annihilated by progress as by that which still subsists.

In the ordinary transactions of life, we cease to take utility into account, in proportion as that utility becomes gratuitous by the lowering of value. Why? because what is gratuitous is common, and what is common alters in no respect each man's share or proportion of actual or effective wealth. We do not exchange what is common to all; and as in our everyday transactions we only require to be made acquainted with the proportion that value establishes, we take no account of anything else.

This subject gave rise to a controversy between Ricardo and J.B. Say. Ricardo gave to the word Wealth the sense of Utility—Say, that of Value. The exclusive triumph of one of these champions was impossible, since the word admits of both senses, according as we regard wealth as actual or relative.

But it is necessary to remark, and the more so on account of the great authority of Say in these matters, that if we confound wealth (in the sense of actual or effective prosperity) with value; above all, if we affirm that the one is proportional to the other, we shall be apt to give the science a wrong direction. The works of second-rate Economists, and those of the Socialists, show this but too clearly. To set out by concealing from view precisely that which forms the fairest patrimony of the human race, is an unfortunate beginning. It leads us to consider as annihilated that portion of wealth which progress renders common to all, and exposes us to the danger of falling into petitio principii, and studying Political Economy backwards—the end, the design, which it is our object to attain, being perpetually confounded with the obstacle that impedes our efforts.

In truth, but for the existence of obstacles, there could be no such thing as Value, which is the sign, the symptom, the witness, the proof of our native weakness. It reminds us incessantly of the decree that went forth in the beginning—"In the sweat of thy face shalt thou eat bread." With reference to Omnipotence, the words Effort, Service, and consequently Value, have no meaning. As regards ourselves, we live in an atmosphere of utilities, of which utilities the greater part are gratuitous, but there are others that we can acquire only by an onerous title. Obstacles are interposed between these utilities and the wants to which they minister. We are condemned either to forgo the Utility, or vanquish these obstacles by Efforts. Sweat must drop from the brow before bread can be eaten, whether the toil be undergone by ourselves or by others for our benefit.

The greater the amount of value we find existing in a country, the greater evidence we have that obstacles have been surmounted, but the greater evidence we also have that there are obstacles to surmount. Are we to go so far as to say that these obstacles constitute Wealth because, apart from them, Value would have no existence?

We may suppose two countries. One of them possesses the means of enjoyment to a greater extent than the other with a less amount of Value, because it is favored by nature, and it has fewer obstacles to overcome. Which is the richer?

Or, to put a stronger case, let us suppose the same people at different periods of their history. The obstacles to be overcome are the same at both periods. But, nowadays, they surmount these obstacles with so much greater facility; they execute, for instance, the work of transport, of tillage, of manufactures, at so much less an expense of effort that values are considerably reduced. There are two courses, then, that a people in such a situation may take— they may content themselves with the same amount of enjoyments as formerly—progress in that case, resolving itself simply into the attainment of additional leisure; and, in such circumstances, should we be authorized to say that the Wealth of the society had retrograded because it is possessed of a smaller amount of value? Or, they may devote the efforts that progress and improvement have rendered disposable to the increase and extension of their enjoyments; but should we be warranted to conclude that, because the amount of values had remained stationary, the wealth of the society had remained stationary also? It is to this result, however, that we tend if we confound the two things, Riches and Value.

Political Economists may here find themselves in a dilemma. Are we to measure wealth by Satisfactions realized, or by Values created?

Were no obstacles interposed between utilities and desires, there would be neither efforts, nor services, nor Values in our case, any more than in that of God and nature. In such circumstances, were wealth estimated by the satisfactions realized, mankind, like nature, would be in possession of infinite riches; but, if estimated by the values created, they would be deprived of wealth altogether. An economist who adopted the first view might pronounce us infinitely rich—another, who adopted the second view, might pronounce us infinitely poor.

The infinite, it is true, is in no respect an attribute of humanity. But mankind direct their exertions to certain ends; they make efforts, they have tendencies, they gravitate toward progressive Wealth or progressive Poverty. Now, how could Economists make themselves mutually intelligible if this successive diminution of effort in relation to result, of labor to be undergone or to be remunerated; in a word, of value, were considered by some of them as a progress toward Wealth, and by others as a descent toward Poverty?

If the difficulty, indeed, concerned only Economists, we might say, let them settle the matter among themselves. But legislators and governments have every day to introduce measures that exercise a serious influence on human affairs; and in what condition should we be if these measures were taken in the absence of that light that enables us to distinguish Riches from Poverty?

I affirm that the theory that defines Wealth as Value is only the glorification of Obstacles. Its syllogism is this: "Wealth is in proportion to Value, value to efforts, efforts to obstacles; ergo, wealth is in proportion to obstacles." I affirm also that, by reason of the division of labor, which includes the case of every one who exercises a trade or profession, the illusion thus created is very difficult to be got rid of. We all of us see that the Services we render are called forth by some obstacle, some want, some suffering—those of the physician by disease, those of the agricultural laborer by hunger, those of the manufacturer of clothing by cold, those of the carrier by distance, those of the advocate by injustice, those of the soldier by danger to his country. There is not, in fact, a single obstacle, the disappearance of which does not prove very inopportune and very troublesome to somebody, or which does not even appear fatal in a public point of view, because it seems to dry up a source of employment, of services, of values, of wealth. Very few Economists have been able to preserve themselves entirely from this illusion; and if the science shall ever succeed in dispelling it, its practical mission will have been fulfilled. For I venture to make a third affirmation—namely, that our official practice is saturated with this theory, and that when governments believe it to be their duty to favor certain classes, certain professions, or certain manufactures, they have no other mode of accomplishing their objective than by setting up Obstacles, in order to give to particular branches of industry additional development, in order to enlarge artificially the circle of services to which the community is forced to have recourse—and thus to increase Value, falsely assumed as synonymous with Wealth.

And, in fact, it is quite true that such legislation is useful to the classes that are favored by it—they exult in it—congratulate each other upon it—and what is the consequence? Why this, that the same favors are successively accorded to all other classes.

What more natural than to confound Utility with Value, and Value with Riches! The Science has never encountered a snare she has less suspected. For what has happened? At every step of progress the reasoning has been this: "The obstacle is diminished, then effort is lessened, then value is lessened, then utility is lessened, then wealth is lessened—then we are the most unfortunate people in the world to have taken it into our heads to invent and exchange, to have five fingers in place of three, and two hands in place of one; and then it is necessary to engage government, which is in possession of force, to take order with this abuse."

This Political Economy *a rebours*—this Political Economy read backwards—is the staple of many of our journals, and the life of legislative assemblies. It has misled the candid and philanthropic Sismondi, and we find it very logically set forth in the work of Mr. de Saint-Chamans.

"There are two kinds of national wealth," he tells us. "If we have regard only to useful products with reference to their quantity, their abundance, we have to do with a species of wealth that procures enjoyments to society, and that I shall denominate the Wealth of enjoyment.

"If we regard products with reference to their exchangeable value, or simply with reference to their value, we have to do with a species of Wealth that procures values to society, and that I call the Wealth of value.

"It is this last species of Wealth that forms the special subject of Political Economy, and it is with it, above all, that governments have to do."

This being so, how are Economists and Statesmen to proceed? The first are to point out the means of increasing this species of riches, this wealth of value; the second to set about adopting these means.

But this kind of wealth bears proportion to efforts, and efforts bear proportion to obstacles. Political Economy, then, is to teach, and Government to contrive, how to multiply obstacles. Mr. de Saint-Chamans does not flinch in the least from this consequence.

Does exchange facilitate our acquiring more of the wealth of enjoyment with less of the wealth of value? We must, then, counteract this tendency of exchange.[1]

Is there any portion of gratuitous Utility we can replace by onerous Utility; for example, by prohibiting the use of a tool or a machine? We must not fail to do so; for it is very evident, he says, that if machinery augments the wealth of enjoyment, it diminishes the wealth of value. "Let us bless the obstacles that the dearness and scarcity of fuel in this country has opposed to the multiplication of steam-engines."[2]

Has nature favored us in any particular respect? It is our misfortune; for, by that means, we are deprived of the opportunity of exerting ourselves. "I avow that I could desire to see manufactured by manual labor, forced exertion, and the sweat of the brow, things that are now produced without trouble and spontaneously."[3]

---

[1]*Nouvel essai sur la Richesse des Nations*, p. 438.

[2]Ibid., p. 263.

[3]*Nouvel essai sur la Richesse des Nations*, p. 456.

What a misfortune, then, is it for us that we are not obliged to manufacture the water we drink! It would have been a fine opportunity of producing the wealth of value. Happily we take our revenge upon wine. "Discover the secret of drawing wine from springs in the earth as abundantly as you draw water, and you will soon see that this fine order of things will ruin a fourth part of France."[4]

According to the ideas this Economist sets forth with such naivete, there are many methods, and very simple methods too, of obliging men to create what he terms the wealth of value.

The first is to deprive them of what they have. "If taxation lays hold of money where it is plentiful, to distribute it where it is scarce, it is useful, and far from being a loss, it is a gain, to the state."[5]

The second is to dissipate what you take. "Luxury and prodigality, which are so hurtful to individual fortunes, benefit public wealth. You teach me a fine moral lesson, it may be said—I have no such pretension—my business is with Political Economy, and not with morals. You seek the means of rendering nations richer, and I preach up luxury."[6]

A more prompt method still is to destroy the wealth you take from the taxpayer by good sweeping wars. "If you grant me that the expenditure of prodigals is as productive as any other, and that the expenditure of governments is equally productive, . . . you will no longer be astonished at the wealth of England after so expensive a war."[7]

But, as tending to promote the creation of this Wealth of value, all these means—taxes, luxury, wars—must hide their

---

[4]Ibid., p. 456.

[5]Ibid., p. 161.

[6]Ibid., p. 168.

[7]Ibid.

diminished heads before an expedient infinitely more efficacious—namely, conflagration.

"To build is a great source of wealth, because it supplies revenues to proprietors, who furnish the materials, to workmen, and
to various classes of artisans and artists. Melon cites Sir William
Petty, who regards as a national profit the labor employed in
rebuilding the streets of London after the great fire that consumed two-thirds of the city, and he estimates it (the profit!) at a
million sterling per annum (in money of 1666) during four years,
and this without the least injury having been done to other
branches of trade. Without regarding this pecuniary estimate of
profit as quite accurate," adds Mr. de Saint-Chamans, "it is certain at least that this event had no detrimental effect upon the
wealth of England at that period. . . . The result stated by Sir W.
Petty is not impossible, seeing that the necessity of rebuilding
London must have created a large amount of new revenues."[8]

All Economists, who set out by confounding wealth with
value, must infallibly arrive at the same conclusions, if they are
logical; but they are not logical; for on the road of absurdity men
of any common sense always sooner or later stop short. Mr. de
Saint-Chamans seems himself to recede a little before the consequences of his principle when it lands him in a eulogium on conflagration. We see that he hesitates, and contents himself with a
negative panegyric. He should have carried out his principle to its
logical conclusions, and told us outright what he so clearly indicates.

Of all our Economists, Mr. de Sismondi has succumbed to the
difficulty now under consideration in the manner most to be
regretted. Like Mr. de Saint-Chamans, he set out with the idea
that value forms an element of wealth; and like him, he has built
upon this datum a Political Economy a rebours, denouncing
everything that tends to diminish value. Sismondi, like Saint-
Chamans, exalts obstacles, proscribes machinery, anathematizes

---

[8]*Nouvel essai sur la Richesse des Nations,* p. 63.

exchange, competition, and liberty, extols luxury and taxation, and arrives at length at this conclusion, that the more we possess the poorer we become.

From beginning to end of his work, however, Mr. de Sismondi seems to have a lurking consciousness that he is mistaken, and that a dark veil may have interposed itself between his mind and the truth. He does not venture, like Mr. de Saint-Chamans, to announce roughly and bluntly the consequences of his principle—he hesitates, and is troubled. He asks himself sometimes if it is possible that all men from the beginning of the world have been in error, and on the road to self-destruction, in seeking to diminish the proportion that Effort bears to Satisfaction—that is to say, value. At once the friend and the enemy of liberty, he fears it, since the abundance that depreciates value leads to universal poverty, and yet he knows not how to set about the destruction of this fatal liberty. He thus arrives at the confines of socialism and artificial organization, and insinuates that government and science should regulate and control everything. Then he sees the danger of the advice he is giving, retracts it, and ends by falling into despair, exclaiming—"Liberty leads to the abyss of poverty—Constraint is as impossible as it is useless—there is no escape." In truth and reality, there is none, if Value be Riches; in other words, if the obstacle to prosperity be prosperity itself—that is to say, if Evil be Good.

The latest writer, as far as I know, who has stirred this question is Mr. Proudhon. It made the fortune of his book, *Des Contradictions Economiques.* Never was there a finer opportunity of seizing a paradox by the forelock, and snapping his fingers at science. Never was there a fairer occasion of asking—"Do you see in the increase of value a good or an evil? *Quidquid dixeris argumentabor.*" Just think what a treat![9]

"I call upon any earnest Economist to explain to me, otherwise than by varying and repeating the question, why value diminishes

---

[9]"Do you take the side of Competition, you are wrong—do you argue against Competition, you are still wrong; which means that you are always right."—P.J. Proudhon, *Contradictions Economiques*, p. 182.

in proportion as production increases, and vice versa. . . . In technical phrase, value in use and value in exchange, although necessary to each other, are in inverse ratio to each other. . . . Value in use and value in exchange remain, then, fatally enchained, although in their own nature they tend to exclude each other."

"For this contradiction, which is inherent in the notion of value, no cause can be assigned, nor is any explanation of it possible. . . . From the data, that man has need of a great variety of commodities, and that he must provide them by his labor, the necessary conclusion is that there exists an antagonism between value in use and value in exchange, and from this antagonism a contradiction arises at the very threshold of Political Economy. No amount of intelligence, no agency divine or human can make it otherwise. In place, then, of beating about for a useless explanation, let us content ourselves with pointing out clearly the necessity of the contradiction."

We know that the grand discovery of Mr. Proudhon is, that everything is at once true and false, good and bad, legitimate and illegitimate, that there exists no principle that is not self-contradictory, and that contradiction lurks not only in erroneous theories, but in the very essence of things—"it is the pure expression of necessity, the peculiar law of existence," etc.; so that it is inevitable, and would be incurable, rationally, but for progression, and, practically, but for the Banque du Peuple. Nature is a contradiction, liberty a contradiction, competition a contradiction, property a contradiction—value, credit, monopoly, community, all contradictions. When Mr. Proudhon achieved this wonderful discovery his heart must have leaped for joy; for since contradiction is everywhere and in everything, he can never want something to gainsay, which for him is the supreme good. He said to me one day, "I should rather like to go to heaven, but I fear that everybody there will be of one mind, and I should find nobody to argue with."

We must confess that the subject of Value gave him an excellent opportunity of indulging his taste. But, with great deference to him, the contradictions and paradoxes to which the word

Value has given rise are to be found in the false theories that have been constructed, and not at all, as he would have us believe, in the nature of things.

Theorists have set out, in the first instance, by confounding Value with Utility—that is to say, evil with good; for utility is the desired result, and value springs from the obstacle that is interposed between the desire and the result. This was their first error, and when they perceived the consequences of it, they thought to obviate the difficulty by imagining a distinction between value in use and value in exchange—an unwieldy tautology, that had the great fault of attaching the same word—Value—to two opposite phenomena.

But if, putting aside these subtleties, we adhere strictly to facts, what do we perceive? Nothing, assuredly, but what is quite natural and consistent.

A man, we shall suppose, works exclusively for himself. If he acquires skill, if his force and intelligence are developed, if nature becomes more liberal, or if he learns how to make nature co-operate better in his work, he obtains more wealth with less trouble. Where is the contradiction, and what is there in this to excite so much wonder?

Well, then, in place of remaining an isolated being, suppose this man to have relations with his fellow-men. They exchange; and I repeat my observation—in proportion as they acquire skill, experience, power, and intelligence—in proportion as nature (become more liberal or brought more into subjection) lends them more efficacious co-operation, they obtain more wealth with less trouble; they have at their disposal a greater amount of gratuitous utility; in their transactions they transfer to one another a greater sum of useful results in proportion to a given amount of labor. Where, then, is the contradiction?

If, indeed, following the example of Adam Smith and his successors, you commit the error of applying the same denomination—value—both to the results obtained and to the exertion made; in that case, an antinomy or contradiction will show itself. But be assured that that contradiction is not at all in the facts, but in your own erroneous explanation of those facts.

Mr. Proudhon ought, then, to have shaped his proposition thus: It being granted that man has need of a great variety of products, that he can only obtain them by his labor, and that he has the precious gift of educating and improving himself, nothing in the world is more natural than the sustained increase of results in relation to efforts; and there is nothing at all contradictory in a given value serving as the vehicle of a greater amount of realized utility.

Let me repeat, once more, that for man Utility is the fair side of the medal and Value the reverse. Utility has relation only to our Satisfactions, Value only with our Pains. Utility realizes our enjoyments, and is proportioned to them; Value attests our native weakness, springs from obstacles, and is proportioned to those Obstacles.

In virtue of the law of human perfectibility, gratuitous utility tends more and more to take the place of onerous utility, expressed by the word value. Such is the phenomenon, and it presents assuredly nothing contradictory.

But the question recurs—Should the word Wealth comprehend these two kinds of utility united, or only the last? If we could form, once and for all, two classes of utilities, putting on the one side all those that are gratuitous, and on the other all those that are onerous, we should form, at the same time, two classes of Wealth, which we should denominate, with Mr. Say, Natural Wealth and Social Wealth; or else, with Mr. de Saint-Chamans, the Wealth of Enjoyment and the Wealth of Value; after which, as these authors propose, we should have nothing more to do with the first of these classes.

"Things which are accessible to all," says Mr. Say, "and which every one may enjoy at pleasure, without being forced to acquire them, and without the fear of exhausting them, such as air, water, the light of the sun, etc., are the gratuitous gifts of nature, and may be denominated Natural Wealth. As these can be neither produced nor distributed, nor consumed by us, they come not within the domain of Political Economy."

"The things which this science has to do with are things which we possess, and which have a recognized value. These we denominate Social Wealth, because they exist only among men united in society."

"It is the Wealth of Value," says Mr. de Saint-Chamans, "which forms the special subject of Political Economy, and whenever in this work I mention Wealth without being more specific, I mean that description of it."

Nearly all Economists have taken the same view.

"The most striking distinction," says Storch, "which presents itself in the outset, is, that there are certain kinds of value which are capable of appropriation, and other kinds which are not so.[10] The first alone are the subject of Political Economy, for the analysis of the others would furnish no result worthy of the attention of the statesman."

For my own part, I think that that portion of utility which, in the progress of society, ceases to be onerous and to possess value, but which does not on that account cease to be utility, and is about to fall into the domain of the common and gratuitous, is precisely that which should constantly attract the attention of the statesman and of the Economist. If it do not, in place of penetrating and comprehending the great results that affect and elevate the human race, the science will be left to deal with what is quite contingent and flexible—with what has a tendency to diminish, if not to disappear—with a relation merely; in a word, with Value. Without being aware of it, Economists are thus led to consider only labor, obstacles, and the interest of the producer; and, what is worse, they are led to confound the interest of the producer with the interest of the public—that is to say, to mistake evil for

---

[10]Always this perpetual and lamentable confusion between Value and Utility! I can show you many utilities that are not appropriated, but I defy you to show me in the whole world a single value that has not a proprietor.

good, and, under the guidance of the Sismondis and Saint-Chamans, to land at length in the Utopia of the socialists, or the *Systeme des Contradictions* of Proudhon.

And then, is not this line of demarcation you attempt to draw between the two descriptions of utility chimerical, arbitrary, and impossible? How can you thus disjoin the cooperation of nature and that of man when they combine and get mixed up everywhere, much more when the one tends constantly to replace the other, which is precisely what constitutes progress? If economic science, so dry in some respects, in other aspects elevates and fascinates the mind, it is just because it describes the laws of this association between man and nature—it is because it shows gratuitous utility substituting itself more and more for onerous utility, enjoyments bearing a greater and greater proportion to labor and fatigue, obstacles constantly lessening, and, along with them, value; the perpetual mistakes and miscalculations of producers more than compensated by the increasing prosperity of consumers; natural wealth, gratuitous and common, coming more and more to take the place of wealth that is personal and appropriated. What! are we to exclude from Political Economy what constitutes its religious Harmony?

Air, light, water, are gratuitous, you say. True, and if we enjoyed them under their primitive form, without making them co-operate in any of our works, we might exclude them from Political Economy just as we exclude from it the possible and probable utility of comets. But observe the progress of man. At first he is able to make air, light, water, and other natural agents co-operate very imperfectly. His satisfactions were purchased by laborious personal efforts, they exacted a large amount of labor, and they were transferred to others as important services; in a word, they were possessed of great value. By degrees, this water, this air, this light, gravitation, elasticity, heat, electricity, vegetable life, have abandoned this state of relative inactivity. They mingle more and more with our industry. They are substituted for human labor. They do for us gratuitously what labor does only for an onerous consideration.

They annihilate value without diminishing our enjoyments. To speak in common language, what cost us a hundred francs, costs us only ten—what required ten days' labor now demands only one. The whole value thus annihilated has passed from the domain of Property to that of Community. A considerable proportion of human efforts has been set free, and placed at our disposal for other enterprises; so that with equal labor, equal services, equal value, mankind has enlarged prodigiously the circle of enjoyments; and yet you tell me that I must eliminate and banish from the science this utility, which is gratuitous and common, which alone explains progress, as well upward as forward, if I may so speak, as well in wealth and prosperity as in freedom and equality!

We may, then, legitimately attach to the word Wealth two meanings.

Effective Wealth, real, and realizing satisfactions, or the aggregate of utilities that human labor, aided by the co-operation of natural agents, places within the reach of Society.

Relative Wealth—that is to say, the proportional share of each in the general Riches, a share that is determined by Value.

This Economic Harmony, then, may be thus stated:

By labor the action of man is combined with the action of nature.

Utility results from that co-operation.

Each man receives a share of the general utility proportioned to the value he has created—that is to say, to the services he has rendered; in other words, to the utility he has himself produced.

ADDENDUM

Morality of Wealth. We have just been engaged in studying wealth from an Economical point of view; it may not perhaps be useless to say something here of its Moral effects.

In all ages, wealth, from a moral point of view, has been the subject of controversy. Certain philosophers and certain religionists have commanded us to despise it; others have greatly prided themselves on the golden mean, *aurea mediocritas*. Few, if any, have admitted as moral an ardent longing after the goods of fortune.

Which are right? Which are wrong? It does not belong to Political Economy to treat of individual morality. I shall make only one remark: I am always inclined to think that in matters that lie within the domain of everyday practice, theorists, savants, philosophers, are much less likely to be right than this universal practice itself when we include in the meaning of the word practice not only the actions of the generality of men, but their sentiments and ideas.

Now, what does universal practice demonstrate in this case? It shows us all men endeavoring to emerge from their original state of poverty—all preferring the sensation of satisfaction to the sensation of want, riches to poverty; all, I should say, or almost all, without excepting even those who declaim against wealth.

The desire for wealth is ardent, incessant, universal, irrepressible. In almost every part of the globe, it has triumphed over our natural aversion to toil. Whatever may be said to the contrary, it displays a character of avidity still baser among savage than among civilized nations. All our navigators who left Europe in the eighteenth century imbued with the fashionable ideas of Rousseau and expecting to find the men of nature at the antipodes disinterested, generous, hospitable, were struck with the devouring rapacity of these primitive barbarians. Our military men can tell us, in our own day, what we are to think of the boasted disinterestedness of the Arab tribes.

On the other hand, the opinions of all men, even of those who do not act up to their opinions, concur in honoring disinterestedness, generosity, self-control, and in branding that ill-regulated, inordinate love of wealth that causes men not to shrink from any means of obtaining it. The same public opinion surrounds with esteem the man who, in whatever rank of life, devotes his honest and persevering labor to ameliorating the lot and elevating the condition of his family. It is from this combination of facts, ideas, and sentiments, it would seem to me, that we must form our judgment on wealth in connection with individual morality.

First of all, we must acknowledge that the motive that urges us to the acquisition of riches is of providential creation—natural, and consequently moral. It has its source in that original and general destitution that would be our lot in everything if it did not create in us the desire to free ourselves from it. We must acknowledge, in the second place, that the efforts men make to emerge from the primitive destitution, provided they keep within the limits of justice, are estimable and respectable, seeing that they are universally esteemed and respected. No one, moreover, will deny that labor is in itself of a moral nature. This is expressed in the common proverb we find in all countries: Idleness is the parent of vice. And we should fall into a glaring contradiction were we to say, on the one hand, that labor is indispensable to the morality of men, and on the other, that men are immoral when they seek to realize wealth by their labor.

We must acknowledge, in the third place, that the desire for wealth becomes immoral when it goes the length of inducing us to depart from the rules of justice, and that avarice becomes more unpopular in proportion to the wealth of those who addict themselves to that passion.

Such is the judgment pronounced, not by certain philosophers or sects, but by the generality of men; and I adopt it.

I must guard myself, however, by adding that this judgment may be different at the present day from what it was in ancient times, without involving a contradiction.

The Essenians and Stoics lived in a state of society where wealth was always the reward of oppression, of pillage, and of violence. Not only was it deemed immoral in itself, but, in consequence of the immoral means employed in its acquisition, it revealed the immorality of those who possessed it. A reaction, even an exaggerated reaction, against riches and rich men was to be expected. Modern philosophers who declaim against wealth without taking into account this difference in the means of acquiring wealth, believe themselves Senecas, while they are only parrots, repeating what they do not understand.

But the question Political Economy proposes is this: Is wealth for mankind a moral good or a moral evil? Does the progressive development of wealth imply, in a moral point of view, improvement or decadence?

The reader anticipates my answer, and will understand that I must say a few words on the subject of individual morality in order to avoid the contradiction, or rather of the impossibility, that would be implied in asserting that what is individual immorality is general morality.

Without having recourse to statistics, or the records of our prisons, we must handle a problem that may be enunciated in these terms:

Is man degraded by exercising more power over nature—by constraining nature to serve him—by obtaining additional leisure—by freeing himself from the more urging and pressing wants of his makeup—by being enabled to rouse from sleep and inactivity his intellectual and moral faculties—faculties that assuredly have not been given him to remain in eternal lethargy?

Is man degraded by being removed from a state the most inorganic, so to speak, and raised to a state of the highest spiritualism it is possible for him to reach?

To enunciate the problem in this form is to resolve it.

I willingly grant that when wealth is acquired by means that are immoral, it has an immoral influence, as among the Romans.

I also allow that when it is developed in a very unequal manner, creating a great gulf between classes, it has an immoral influence, and gives rise to revolutionary passions.

But does the same thing hold when wealth is the fruit of honest industry and free transactions, and is uniformly distributed over all classes? That would be a doctrine impossible to maintain.

Socialist works, nevertheless, are crammed with declamations against the rich.

I really cannot comprehend how these schools, so opposite in other respects, but so unanimous in this, should not perceive the contradiction into which they fall.

On the one hand, wealth, according to the leaders of these schools, has a deleterious and demoralizing action, which debases the soul, hardens the heart, and leaves behind only a taste for depraved enjoyments. The rich have all manner of vices. The poor have all manner of virtues—they are just, sensible, disinterested, generous—such is the favorite theme of these authors.

On the other hand, all the efforts of the Socialists' imagination, all the systems they invent, all the laws they wish to impose upon us, tend, if we are to believe them, to convert poverty into riches. Morality of wealth proved by this maxim; the profit of one is the profit of another.

7

CAPITAL

The economic laws will be found to act on the same principle whether we take the case of a numerous agglomeration of men or of only two individuals, or even of a single individual condemned by circumstances to live in a state of isolation.

Such an individual, if he could exist for some time in an isolated state, would be at once capitalist, employer, workman, producer, and consumer. The whole economic evolution would be accomplished in him. Observing each of the elements of which that evolution is made up—want, effort, satisfaction, gratuitous utility, and onerous utility—he would be enabled to form an idea of the entire mechanism, even when thus reduced to its greatest simplicity.

One thing is obvious enough, that he could never confound what was gratuitous with what exacted efforts; for that would imply a contradiction in terms. He would know at once when a material or a force was furnished to him by nature without the co-operation of his labor, even when his own labor was assisted by natural agents, and thus rendered more productive.

An isolated individual would never think of applying his own labor to the production of a commodity as long as he could procure it directly from nature. He would not travel a league to fetch water if he had a well at his door. For the same reason, whenever his own labor was called into requisition, he would endeavor to substitute for it, as much as he possibly could, the co-operation of natural agents.

If he constructed a canoe, he would make it of the lightest materials, in order to take advantage of the specific gravity of water. He would furnish it with a sail, that the wind might save him the trouble of rowing, etc.

In order to obtain in this way the co-operation of natural agents, tools and instruments would be wanted.

And here the isolated individual would begin to calculate. He would ask himself this question: At present I obtain a satisfaction at the expense of a given effort: when I am in possession of the proper tool or instrument, shall I obtain the same satisfaction with less effort, taking into account the labor required for the construction of the instrument itself?

No one will throw away his labor for the mere pleasure of throwing it away. Our supposed Robinson Crusoe, then, will be induced to set about constructing the instrument only if he sees clearly that, when completed, he will obtain an equal satisfaction at a smaller expense of effort, or a greater amount of satisfaction with the same effort.

One circumstance will form a great element in his calculation—the number of commodities in the production of which this instrument will assist while it lasts. He has a primary standard of comparison—the present labors to which he is subjected every time he wishes to procure the satisfaction directly and without assistance. He estimates how much labor the tool or instrument will save him on each occasion; but labor is required to make the tool, and this labor he will in his own mind spread over all the occasions on which such an instrument can be made available. The greater the number of these occasions, the stronger will be his motive for seeking the co-operation of natural agents. It is here—in this spreading of an advance over an aggregate of products—that we discover the principle and foundation of Interest.

When Robinson Crusoe has once made up his mind to construct the instrument, he perceives that his willingness to make it, and the advantage it is to bring him, are not enough. Tools are necessary to the manufacture of tools—iron must be hammered with iron—and so you go on, mounting from difficulty to difficulty, till you reach the first difficulty of all, which appears to be insuperable. This shows us the extreme slowness with which Capital must have been formed at the beginning, and what an enormous amount of human labor each satisfaction must originally have cost.

Again, in order to construct the instruments of labor, not only tools, but materials are wanted. If these materials, as for instance stones, are furnished gratuitously by nature, we must still combine them, which costs labor. But the possession of these materials supposes, in almost every case, anterior labor both long and complicated, as in the manufacture of wool, flax, iron, lead, etc.

Nor is this all. While a man is thus working for the exclusive purpose of facilitating his ulterior labor, he can do nothing to supply his present wants. Now, here we encounter an order of phenomena in which there can be no interruption. Each day the laborer must be fed, clothed, and sheltered. Robinson will perceive, then, that he can undertake nothing for the purpose of procuring the co-operation of natural forces until he has previously accumulated a stock of provisions. He must every day redouble his activity in the chase, and store up a portion of the game he kills, and subject himself to present privations, in order that he may have at his disposal the time requisite for the construction of the instrument he has projected. In such circumstances, it is most probable that all he will accomplish will be the construction of an instrument that is rude and imperfect, and not very well fitted for the purpose he has in view.

Afterwards, he will obtain greater facilities. Reflection and experience will teach him to work better; and the first tool he makes will furnish him with the means of fabricating others, and of accumulating provisions with greater promptitude.

Tools, materials, provisions—these, doubtless, Robinson will denominate his Capital; and he will readily discover that the more considerable his capital becomes, the greater command will he obtain over natural agents—that the more he makes such agents co-operate in his labor, the more will he augment his satisfactions in proportion to his efforts.

Let us now vary the hypothesis, and place ourselves in the midst of the social order. Capital is still composed of instruments of labor, materials, and provisions, without which no enterprise of any magnitude can be undertaken, either in a state of isolation or in the social state. Those who are possessed of capital have been put in possession of it only by their labor, or by their privations; and they would not have undergone that labor (which has no connection with present wants), they would not have imposed on themselves those privations, but with the view of obtaining ulterior advantages—with the view, for example, of procuring in larger measure the future co-operation of natural agents. On their part, to give away this capital would be to deprive themselves of the special advantage they have in view; it would be to transfer this advantage to others; it would be to render others a service. We cannot, then, without abandoning the most simple principles of reason and justice, fail to see that the owners of capital have a perfect right to refuse to make this transfer unless in exchange for another service, freely bargained for and voluntarily agreed to. No man in the world, I believe, will dispute the equity of the mutuality of services, for mutuality of services is, in other words, equity. Will it be said that the transaction cannot be free and voluntary, because the man who is in possession of capital is in a position to lay down the law to the man who has none? But how is a bargain to be made? In what way are we to discover the equivalence of services if it be not in the case of an exchange voluntarily effected on both sides? Do you not perceive, moreover, that the man who borrows capital, being free either to borrow it or not, will refuse to do so unless he sees it to be for his advantage, and that the loan cannot make his situation worse? The question he asks himself is evidently this: Will the employment of this capital afford me advantages that are more than sufficient to make up for the conditions that are demanded of me? Or this: Is the effort I am now obliged to make, in order to obtain a given satisfaction greater or less than the sum of the efforts the loan will entail upon me—first of all in rendering the services that are demanded of me by the lender, and afterwards in procuring the special satisfaction I have in view with the aid of the capital borrowed? If, taking all things into account, there be no advantage to be got, he will not borrow, he will remain as he is, and what injury is done him? He may be mistaken, you will say. Undoubtedly he may. One may be mistaken in all imaginable transactions. Are we then to abandon our liberty? If you go that length, tell us what we are to substitute for free will and free consent. Constraint? for if we give up liberty, what remains but constraint? No, you say—the judgment of a third party. Granted, on these conditions: First, that the decision of this third party, whatever name you give him, shall not be put in force by constraint. Second, that he be infallible, for to substitute one fallible man for another would be to no purpose; and the parties whose judgment I should least distrust in such a matter are the parties who are interested in the result. The third and last condition is that this arbitrator shall not be paid for his services; for it would be a singular way of manifesting his sympathy for the borrower, first of all to take away from him his liberty, and then to lay on his shoulders an additional burden as the recompense of this philanthropical service. But let us leave the question of right, and return to Political Economy.

A Capital which is composed of materials, provisions, and instruments presents two aspects—Utility and Value. I must have failed in my exposition of the theory of value if the reader does not understand that the man who transfers capital is paid only for its value, that is to say, for the service rendered in creating that capital; in other words, for the pains taken by the cedant combined with the pains saved to the recipient. Capital consists of commodities or products. It assumes the name of capital only by reason of its ulterior destination. It is a great mistake to suppose that capital, as such, is a thing having an independent existence. A sack of wheat is still a sack of wheat, although one man sells it for revenue, and another buys it for capital. Exchange takes place on the invariable principle of value for value, service for service; and the portion of gratuitous utility that enters into the commodity is so much into the bargain. At the same time, the portion that is gratuitous has no value, and value is the only thing regarded in bargains. In this respect, transactions that have reference to capital are in no respect different from others.

This consideration opens up some admirable views with reference to the social order, but which I cannot do more than indicate here. Man, in a state of isolation, is possessed of capital only when he has brought together materials, provisions, and tools. The same thing does not hold true of man in the social state. It is enough for the latter to have rendered services, and to have thus the power of drawing upon society, by means of the mechanism of exchange for equivalent services. I mean by the mechanism of exchange money, bills, bank notes, and even bankers themselves. Whoever has rendered a service, and has not yet received the corresponding satisfaction is the bearer of a warrant, either possessed of value, as money, or fiduciary, like bank notes, which warrant gives him the power of receiving back from society, when he will, where he will, and in what form he will, an equivalent service. This impairs neither in principle nor in effect, nor in an equitable point of view, the great law I seek to elucidate, that services are exchanged for services. It is still the embryo barter, which has been developed, enlarged, and rendered more complex, but without losing its identity.

The bearer of such a warrant as I have just described may then demand back from society, at pleasure, either an immediate satisfaction, or an object that, in another aspect, may be regarded as capital. The person who lends or transfers has nothing to do with that. He satisfies himself as to the equivalence of the services—that is all.

Again, he may transfer this warrant to another, to use it as he pleases, under the double condition of restitution, and of a service, at a fixed date. If we go to the bottom of the matter, we shall find that in this case the person who lends or transfers capital deprives himself, in favor of the cessionary or recipient, either of an immediate satisfaction, which he defers for some years, or of an instrument of labor which would have increased his power of production, procured him the cooperation of natural agents, and augmented, to his profit, the proportion of satisfactions to efforts. He strips himself of these advantages in order to invest another with them. This is undoubtedly to render a service, and in equity this service is entitled to a return. Mere restitution at the year's end cannot be considered as the remuneration of this special service. Observe that the transaction here is not a sale, where the delivery of the thing sold is immediate, and the return or remuneration is immediate also. What we have to do with here is delay. And this delay is in itself a special service, seeing that it imposes a sacrifice on the person who accords it, and confers an advantage on the person who asks for it. There must, then, be remuneration, or we must give up that supreme law of society, service for service. This remuneration is variously denominated, according to circumstances—hire, rent, yearly income—but its generic name is Interest.[1]

Every service then is, or may become, a Capital, an admirable phenomenon due to the mechanism of exchange. If workmen are to commence the construction of a railway ten years hence, we could not at the present moment store up in kind the wheat that is to feed them, the cloth that is to clothe them, and the barrows and implements they will need during that protracted operation. But we can save up and transmit to them the value of these things. For this purpose it is enough that we render present services to society, and obtain for these services the warrants, in money or credits of which I have spoken, which can be converted into

---

[1] See my brochure, entitled *Capital et Rente*.

636   The Bastiat Collection

wheat or cloth ten years hence. It is not even necessary that we should leave these warrants dormant and unproductive in the interval. There are merchants, bankers, and others in society who, for the use of our services or their results, render us the service of imposing upon themselves these privations in our place.

And it is still more remarkable that we can effect an inverse operation, however impossible at first sight this may appear. We can convert into instruments of labor, into railways, into houses, a capital that as yet has no existence—thus making available at once services that will not be actually rendered till the twentieth century. There are bankers who are ready to make present advances on the faith that workmen and railway travellers of the third and fourth generation will provide for their payment, and these drafts upon the future are transmitted from hand to hand, without remaining for a moment unproductive. I confess I do not believe that the numerous inventors of artificial societies ever imagined anything at once so simple and so complex, so ingenious and so equitable, as this. They would at once abandon their insipid and stupid Utopias if they but knew the fine harmonies of the social mechanism that has been instituted by God. It was a king of Aragon who bethought him what advice he should have given to Providence on the construction of the celestial mechanism, had he been called to the counsels of Omniscience. Newton never conceived so impious a thought.

We thus see that all transmissions of services from one point of time or of space to another repose upon this datum, that to accord delay is to render service; in other words, they repose on the legitimacy of Interest. The man who, in our days, has wished to suppress interest, does not see that he would bring back exchange to its embryo form—barter, present barter—without reference either to the future or the past. He does not see that, imagining himself the most advanced, he is in reality the most retrograde of men, since he would reconstruct society on its most primitive model. He desires, he says, mutuality of services. But he begins by taking away the character of services exactly from that kind of services which unite, tie together, and solidarize all places and all times. In spite of the practical audacity of his socialist aphorisms, he has paid an involuntary homage to the present order of things. He has but one reform, which is negative. It consists in suppressing in society the most powerful and marvelous part of its machinery.

I have explained in another place the legitimacy and perpetuity of Interest. I shall content myself at present with reminding the reader:

First, That the legitimacy of interest rests upon the fact, that he who accords delay renders service. Interest, then, is legitimate in virtue of the principle of service for service.

Second, That the perpetuity of interest reposes on this other fact, that he who borrows must pay back all that he has borrowed at a fixed date. When the thing lent, or its value, is restored to its owner, he can lend it anew. When returned to him a second time, he can lend it a third time, and so on to perpetuity. Which of the successive and voluntary borrowers can find fault with this?

But since the legitimacy of interest has been contested so seriously in our day as to put capital to flight, or force it to conceal itself, I may be permitted to show how utterly foolish and insensate this controversy is.

And first of all, let me ask, would it not be absurd and unjust, either that no remuneration should be given for the use of capital, or that that remuneration should be the same, whether the loan were granted and obtained at one year's, or two years', or ten years' date? If, unhappily, under this doctrine of pretended equality, such a law should find a place in our code, an entire category of human transactions would be suppressed on the instant. We should still have barter, and sales for ready money, but we could no longer have sales on credit, nor loans. The advocates of equality would relieve borrowers from the burden of paying interest; but they would, at the same time, deprive them of their loans. At the same rate, we might relieve men from the inconvenient necessity of paying for what they buy. We should only have to prohibit them from purchasing; or, what would come to the same thing, declare prices illegal.

There is levelling enough in all conscience in this pretended principle of equality. First of all, it would put a stop to the creation of capital; for who would desire to save, when he could reap no advantage from saving? Then it would reduce wages to zero, for where there is no capital (instruments, materials, and provisions), there can be neither future work nor wages. We should very soon arrive at the most perfect of all equalities, the equality of nothingness.

But is there any man so blind as not to see that delay is in itself a circumstance that is onerous, and, consequently, entitled to remuneration? Apart even from the consideration of loans, would not everyone endeavor to abridge delays? It is the object of our perpetual solicitude. Every employer of workmen lays great stress on the time that must elapse before his returns come in. He sells dearer or cheaper according as his returns are more or less distant. Were he indifferent on that subject, he must forget that capital is power; for if he is alive to that consideration, he must naturally desire that it should perform its work in the shortest possible time, so as to enable him the oftener to engage it in a new operation.

They are but short-sighted Economists who think that we pay interest for capital only when we borrow it. The general rule is that he who reaps the satisfaction should bear all the charges of production, delay included, whether he renders the service to himself or has it rendered to him by another. A man in a state of isolation, who has no bargains or transactions with anyone, would consider it an onerous circumstance to be deprived of the use of his weapons for a year. Why, then, should an analogous circumstance not be considered as onerous in society? But if a man submits to it voluntarily for the sake of another who agrees voluntarily to remunerate it, what should render that remuneration illegitimate?

Nothing would be transacted in the world; no enterprise requiring advances would be undertaken; we should neither plant, nor sow, nor labor, were not delay considered as in itself an onerous circumstance, and treated and paid for as such. Universal consent is so unanimous on this point that no exchange takes place but on this principle. Delays, hindrances, enter into the evaluation of services, and, consequently, into the constitution of value.

Thus, in their crusade against interest, the advocates of equality not only trample under foot the most obvious notions of equity—they ignore not only their own principle of service for service, but also the authority of mankind and universal practice. How can they, in the light of day, exhibit the overweening pride such a pretension supposes? Is it not, indeed, a very strange and a very sad thing that these radicals should adopt, not only tacitly, but often in so many words, the motto that since the beginning of the world, all men have been mistaken except themselves? *Omnes, ego non.*

Pardon me for thus insisting on the legitimacy of interest, which is founded on this principle that, since delay is costly, it must be paid for—to cost and to pay being correlative terms. The fault lies in the spirit of our age. It is quite necessary to defend vital truths, admitted generally by mankind, but attacked and brought into question by a few fanatical innovators. For a writer who aspires to demonstrate the harmony of phenomena in the aggregate, it is a painful thing, you may believe, to be constantly stopped by the necessity of elucidating the most elementary notions. Would Laplace have been able to explain the planetary system in all its simplicity, if, among his readers, there had not existed certain common and received ideas—if it had been necessary for him, in order to prove that the earth turns upon its axis, to begin by teaching arithmetic? Such is the hard fate of the Economist of our day. If he neglects the rudiments, he is not understood—if he explains them, the beauty and simplicity of his system is lost sight of in the multiplicity of details.

It is a happy thing for mankind that Interest can be shown to be legitimate. We should otherwise be placed in a miserable dilemma—we must either perish by remaining just, or make progress by means of injustice.

Every branch of industry is an aggregate of Efforts. But, as regards efforts, there is an important distinction to be made. Some efforts are connected with services that we are presently engaged in rendering; others with an indefinite series of analogous services. Let me explain myself.

The day's work of the water carrier must be paid for by those who profit by his labor. But his anterior labor in making his barrow and his water cask must, as regards remuneration, be spread over an indeterminate number of consumers.

In the same way, ploughing, sowing, harrowing, weeding, cutting down, thrashing, apply only to the present harvest; but clearing, enclosing, draining, building, improving, apply to and facilitate an indefinite number of future harvests.

According to the general law of service for service, those who receive the ultimate satisfaction must recompense the efforts that have been made for them. As regards the first class of efforts, there is no difficulty. They are bargained for and estimated by the man who makes them, and the man who profits by them. But how are those of the second class to be estimated? How is a just proportion of the permanent advances, the general costs, and what the Economists term fixed capital, to be spread over the whole series of satisfactions they are destined to realize? By what process can we distribute the burden among those to whom the water is furnished down to the time when the barrow shall be worn out, and among all the consumers of wheat until the period when the field will produce no more?

I know not how they resolve this problem in Icarie, or at the Phalanstere.[2] But I am inclined to think that the gentlemen who manufacture artificial societies, and who are so fertile in arrangements and expedients, and so prompt to compel their adoption by

---

[2]Allusion to Socialist works—*La Reforme industrielle, ou le Phalanstere, Recueil periodique, redige* by Ch. Fourier, 1832, *Visite au Phalanstere,* by Mr. Briancourt, 1848, and *Voyage en Icarie*, by Cabet, 1848, etc.—Translator.

Law (or constraint), could imagine no solution more ingenious than the very natural process men have adopted since the beginning of the world, and it is now sought to prohibit them from following. Here is the process—it flows from the law of Interest.

Suppose a thousand francs to be laid out on agricultural improvements, the rate of interest to be five percent, and the average return fifty hectolitres of wheat. In these circumstances, each hectolitre would be burdened with one franc.

This franc is obviously the legitimate recompense of an actual service, rendered by the proprietor (whom we might term a laborer), as well to the person who shall acquire a hectolitre of corn ten years hence as to the man who buys it today. The law of strict justice, then, is observed here.

But if the agricultural improvement, or the barrow and the water barrel, have only a limited duration, which we can reckon approximately, a sinking fund must be added to the interest, in order that, when these portions of capital are worn out, the proprietor may be enabled to renew them. Still it is the law of justice that governs the transaction.

We must not suppose, however, that the franc with which each hectolitre is burdened as interest is an invariable quantity. It represents a value, and is subject to the law of values. It rises or falls with the variation of supply and demand—that is to say, according to the exigencies of the times and the interests of society.

It is generally thought that this species of remuneration has a tendency to rise, if not in the case of manufacturing, at least in the case of agricultural improvements. Supposing this rent to have been equitable at the beginning, it has a tendency, it is said, to degenerate into abuse; because the proprietor, sitting with his hands folded, sees it increase year after year, solely in consequence of the increase of population and the enlarged demand for wheat.

I allow that this tendency exists, but it is not peculiar to the rent of land—it is common to all departments of industry, in all, value increases with the density of population, and even the common day-laborer earns more in Paris than he could in Brittany.

And then, as regards the rent of land, the tendency to which we have referred is powerfully counterbalanced by another tendency—that of progress. An amelioration, realized at the present day by improved processes, effected with less manual labor, and at a time when the rate of interest has fallen, saves our paying too dearly for improvements effected in former times. The fixed capital of the landed proprietor, like that of the manufacturer, is deteriorated in the long run by the invention of instruments of equal value and greater efficiency. This is a magnificent Law, which overturns the melancholy theory of Ricardo; and it will be explained more in detail when we come to the subject of landed property.

Observe that the problem of the distribution of the services that form the remuneration of permanent improvements can be resolved only by a reference to the law of interest. The capital itself cannot be spread over a succession of purchasers, for this is rendered impossible by their indeterminate number. The first would pay for the last, which would be unjust. Besides, a time would arrive when the proprietor would become possessed both of the capital laid out in the improvement and of the improvement itself, which would be equally unfair. Let us acknowledge, then, that the natural mechanism of society is too ingenious to require the substitution of artificial contrivances.

I have presented the phenomenon in its simplest form in order to render it intelligible; but in practice, things do not take place quite as I have described them.

The proprietor does not regulate the distribution himself, or determine that each hectolitre shall be charged with one franc, more or less, as in the hypothetical case I have put. He finds an established order of things, as well with reference to the average price of wheat as to the rate of interest. Upon these data he decides how he shall invest his capital. He will devote it to agricultural improvements if he finds that the average price of corn will return him the ordinary rate of interest. If not, he will devote his capital to a more lucrative branch of industry—a branch of industry that, just because it is more lucrative, presents, happily for society, greater attractions for capital. This movement of capital from one department to another, which is what actually takes place, tends to the same result, and presents us with another Harmony.

The reader will understand that I confine myself to a special instance only for the sake of elucidating a general law, which applies to all trades and professions.

A lawyer, for example, cannot expect, from the first suit of which he happens to have charge, to be reimbursed the expense of his education, of his course of probation, of his establishment in business, which we may suppose to amount to 20,000 francs. Not only would this be unjust—it would be impracticable; for were he to make such a stipulation, his first brief would never make its appearance, and our Cujacius would be obliged to imitate the gentleman who, on taking up house, could get nobody to come to his first ball, and declared that next year he would begin with his second.

The same thing holds with the merchant, the physician, the shipowner, the artist. In every career we encounter these two classes of efforts—the second imperatively requires to be spread over an indeterminate number of consumers, employers, or customers, and it is impossible to imagine such a distribution without reference to the mechanism of interest.

Great efforts have been made of late to remove the hatred that exists in the popular mind against capital—infamous, infernal capital, as it is called. It has been exhibited to the masses as a voracious and insatiable monster, more destructive than cholera, more frightful than revolution, exercising on the body politic the action of a vampire, whose power of suction goes on increasing indefinitely. *Vires acquirit eundo.* The tongue of this blood-sucker is called usury, revenue, hire, rent, interest. A writer, who might have acquired reputation by his great powers, and who has preferred to gain notoriety by his paradoxes, has been pleased to scatter these paradoxes among a people already in the delirium of a revolutionary fever. I, too, have an apparent paradox to submit to the reader; and I beg him to examine it, and see whether it be not in reality a great and consoling truth.

But first, I must say a word as to the manner in which Mr. Proudhon and his school explain what they term the illegitimacy of interest.

Capital is an instrument of labor. The use of instruments of labor is to procure us the co-operation of the gratuitous forces of nature. By the steam engine we avail ourselves of the elasticity of air; by the watch spring, of the elasticity of steel; by weights or waterfalls, of gravitation; by the voltaic pile, of the rapidity of the electric spark; by the sun's rays, of the chemical and physical combinations we call vegetation, etc., etc. Now, by confounding Utility with Value, we suppose that these natural agents possess a value that is inherent in them; and that, consequently, those who appropriate them, are paid for their use, inasmuch as value implies payment. We imagine that products are burdened with one item for the services of man, which we admit to be just; and with another item for the services of nature, which we reject as iniquitous. Why, it is asked, should we pay for gravitation, electricity, vegetable life, elasticity, and so forth?

The answer to this question is to be found in the theory of value. Those Socialists who take the name of Egalitarians confound the legitimate value of the instrument, which is the offspring of human labor, with its useful result, which, under deduction of that legitimate value, or of the interest that represents it, is always gratuitous. When I remunerate an agricultural laborer, a miller, a railway company, I give nothing, absolutely nothing, for the phenomena of vegetation, gravitation, or the elasticity of steam. I pay for the human labor required for making the instruments by means of which these forces are constrained to act; or, what suits my purpose better, I pay interest for that labor. I render service for service, by means of which the useful action of these forces is turned gratuitously to my profit. It is the same thing as in the case of Exchange, or simple barter. The presence of capital does not at all modify this law, for capital is nothing else than an accumulation of values, of services, to which is committed the special duty of procuring the co-operation of nature.

And now for my paradox.

Of all the elements of which the total value of any product is made up, the part we should pay for most cheerfully is that element we term the interest of the advances, or capital.

And why? Because that element enables us, by paying for one, to save two. Because, by its very presence, it shows clearly that natural forces have concurred in the final result without our having had to pay for their co-operation; and the consequence is, that the same general utility is placed at our disposal, while at the same time a certain portion of gratuitous utility has, happily for us, been substituted for onerous utility; and in short, the price of the product has been reduced. We acquire it with a less proportion of our own labor, and what happens to society at large is just what would happen to an isolated individual who should succeed in realizing an ingenious invention.

Suppose the case of a common artisan who earns four francs a day. With two francs—that is to say, with half-a-day's labor, he purchases a pair of cotton stockings. Were he to try to produce these stockings by his own direct labor, I sincerely believe that his whole life would not suffice for the work. How, then, does it happen that his half-day's work pays for all the human services that have been rendered to him on this occasion? According to the law of service for service, why is he not forced to give several years' labor?

For this reason, that the stockings are the result of human services of which natural agents, by the intervention of Capital, have enormously diminished the proportion. Our artisan, however, pays not only for the actual labor of all those who have concurred in the work, but also the interest of the capital by means of which the co-operation of nature was procured; and it is worthy of note, that, without this last remuneration, or were it held to be illegitimate, capital would not have been employed to secure the assistance of the natural agents. There would have been in the product only onerous utility; for in that case the commodity would have been the exclusive result of human labor; and our artisan would have been brought back to the point whence he started—that is to say, he would have been placed in the dilemma of either dispensing with the stockings, or of paying for them the price of several years' labor.

If our artisan had learned to analyze phenomena, he would soon get reconciled to Capital, on seeing how much he is indebted to it. He would be convinced above all that the gratuitous nature of the gifts of God has been completely preserved, and that these gifts have been lavished on him with a liberality that he owes not to his own merit, but to the beautiful mechanism of the natural social order. Capital does not consist in the vegetative force that has made cotton germinate and flower, but in the pains taken by the planter. Capital is not the wind that fills the sails of the ship, or the magnetism that acts upon the needle, but the pains taken by the sailmaker and the optician. Capital is not the elasticity of steam that turns the spindles of the mill, but the pains taken by the machine-maker. Vegetation, the power of the winds, magnetism, elasticity—all these are plenty gratuitous; and hence the stockings have so little value. As regards the pains taken by the planter, the sailmaker, the optician, the shipbuilder, the sailor, the manufacturer, the merchant, they are spread—or, rather, so far as capital is concerned, the interest of that capital is spread—over innumerable purchasers of stockings; and this is the reason why the portion of labor given by each of these purchasers is so small.

Modern reformers! when I see you desiring to replace this admirable natural order by an arrangement of your own invention, there are two things (although they are in reality one and the same) that confound me—namely, your want of faith in Providence, and your faith in yourselves—your ignorance, and your presumption.

It follows from what I have said that the progress of mankind coincides with the rapid creation of Capital; for to say that new capital is formed is just to say, in other words that obstacles, formerly onerously combated by labor are now gratuitously combated by nature; and that, be it observed, not for the profit of the capitalist, but for the profit of the community.

This being so, the paramount interest of all (in an economical point of view, and rightly understood) is to favor the rapid creation of capital. But capital, if I may say so, increases of its own accord under the triple influence of activity, frugality, and security. We can scarcely exercise any direct influence on the activity and frugality of our neighbors, except through the medium of public opinion, by an intelligent communication of our antipathies and our sympathies. But as regards security we can do much, for without security, capital, far from being formed and accumulated, conceals itself, takes flight, and perishes; and this shows us how suicidal that popular ardor is that displays itself in disturbing the public tranquillity. Let the working classes be well assured that the mission of Capital from the beginning has been to set men free from the yoke of ignorance, of want, and of despotism; and that to frighten away Capital is to rivet a triple chain on the energies of the human race.

The *vires acquirit eundo* may be applied with rigorous exactitude to capital, and its beneficent influence. Capital, when formed, necessarily leaves disposable both labor and the remuneration of that labor. It carries in itself, then, a power of progression. There is in it something that resembles the law of velocities. This progression economical science has omitted hitherto to oppose to the other progression that Malthus has noted. It is a Harmony that we cannot explain in this place, but must reserve for the chapter on Population.

But I must here put the reader on his guard against a specious objection. If the mission of capital, it may be said, is to cause nature to execute work that has been hitherto executed by human labor, whatever good it may confer upon mankind, it must do injury to the working classes, especially to those classes who live by wages; for everything that throws hands out of employment and renders them disposable, renders competition more intense; and this, undoubtedly, is the secret reason of the antipathy of the working classes to men of capital. If this objection were well founded, we should have a discordant note in the social harmony.

The illusion arises from losing sight of this, that capital, in proportion as its action is extended, sets free and renders disposable a certain amount of human efforts, only by setting free and rendering disposable a corresponding fund of remuneration, so that these two elements meet and compensate one another. The labor is not paralyzed. Replaced in a special department of industry by gratuitous forces, it sets to work upon other obstacles in the general march of progress, and with more certainty, inasmuch as it finds its recompense prepared beforehand.

Recurring to our former illustration, it is easy to see that the price of stockings (like that of books, and all things else) is lowered by the action of capital only by leaving in the hands of the purchaser the former price. This is too clear for illustration. The workman who now pays two francs for what he paid six francs for formerly, has four francs left at his disposal. Now, it is exactly in that proportion that human labor has been replaced by natural forces. These forces, then, are a pure and simple acquisition, which alters in no respect the relation of labor to available remuneration. It will be remembered that the answer to this objection was given formerly, when, observing upon man in a state of isolation, or reduced once more to the primitive law of barter, I put the reader on his guard against the illusion which it is my object here to dispel.

We may leave capital, then, to take care of itself, to be created and accumulated according to its own proper tendencies, and the wants and desires of men. Do not imagine that, when the common laborer economizes for his old days, when the father of a family sets his son up in business, or provides a dowry for his daughter, they are exercising to the detriment of the public that noble attribute of man, Foresight; but it would be so, and private virtues would be in direct antagonism with the general good, were there an incompatibility between Capital and labor.

Far from mankind being subjected to this contradiction, or, I might rather say, this impossibility (for how can we conceive progressive evil in the aggregate to result from progressive good in individual cases?) we must acknowledge that Providence, in justice and mercy, has assigned a nobler part to labor than to Capital in the work of progress, and has afforded a stimulant more efficacious, a recompense more liberal, to the man who lives by the sweat of his brow, than to the man who subsists upon the exertions of this forefathers.

In fact, having established that every increase of capital is followed by a necessary increase in general prosperity, I venture to lay down the following principle with reference to the distribution of wealth—a principle I believe will be found unassailable:

"In proportion to the increase of Capital, the absolute share of the total product falling to the capitalist is augmented, and his relative share is diminished; while, on the contrary, the laborer's share is increased both absolutely and relatively."

I shall explain this more clearly by figures:

Suppose the total products of society, at successive epochs, to be represented by the figures 1,000, 2,000, 3,000, 4,000, etc.

I maintain that the share falling to the capitalists will descend, successively, from 50 percent, to 40, 35, 30 percent, and that the share of the laborers will rise, consequently, from 50 percent, to 60, 65, 70 percent—so that the absolute share of the capitalist will be always greater at each period, although his relative share will be smaller.

The division will take place in this way:

	Total Product	Share of Capitalist	Share of Laborer
First period.......	1,000	500	500
Second period.....	2,000	800	1,200
Third period......	3,000	1,050	1,950
Fourth period.....	4,000	1,200	2,800

Such is the great, admirable, reassuring, necessary, and inflexible law of Capital. To demonstrate it, appears to me to be the true way to strike with discredit the declamations that have so long been dinned into our ears against the avidity, the tyranny, of the most powerful instrument of civilization and of equality that has ever proceeded from the human faculties.

The demonstration is twofold. First of all, we must prove that the relative share of the product falling to the capitalist goes on continually diminishing. This is not difficult; for it only amounts to saying that the more abundant capital becomes, the more interest falls. Now, this is a matter of fact, incontestable and uncontested. Not only does science explain it—it is self-evident. Schools the most eccentric admit it. It forms the basis of their theory, for it is from this very fall of interest that they infer the necessary, the inevitable annihilation of what they choose to brand as infernal Capital. Now, say they, inasmuch as this annihilation is necessary, is inevitable, and must take place in a given time; and, moreover, implies the realization of a positive good, it is incumbent on us to hasten it and insure it. I am not concerned to refute these principles, or the deductions drawn from them. It is enough that Economists of all schools, as well as socialists, egalitarians, and others all admit, in point of fact, that interest falls in proportion as capital becomes more abundant. Whether they admit it or not, indeed, the fact is not less certain. It rests upon the authority of universal experience, and on the acquiescence, involuntary it may be, of all the capitalists in the world. It is a fact that the interest of capital is lower in Spain than in Mexico, in France than in Spain, in England than in France, in Holland than in England. Now, when interest falls from 20 to 15 percent, and then to 10, to 8, to 6, to 5, to 4½, to 4, to 3½, to 3 percent, what does that mean in relation to the question that now engages us? It means that capital, as the recompense of its co-operation in the work of production, in the realization of wealth, is content or, if you will, is forced to be content, with a smaller and smaller share of the product in proportion as capital increases. Does it constitute one-third of the value of corn, of cloth, of houses, of ships, of canals? in other words, when these things are sold, does one-third of the price fall to the capitalist, and two-thirds to the laborer? By degrees, the capitalist receives no more than a fourth, a fifth, a sixth. His relative share goes on diminishing, while that of the laborer goes on increasing in the same proportion; and the first part of my demonstration is complete.

It remains for me to prove that the absolute share falling to the capitalist goes on constantly increasing. It is very true that the tendency of interest is to fall. But when, and why? When, and because, the capital becomes more abundant. It is then quite possible that the total product should be increased while the percentage is diminished. A man has a larger income with 200,000 francs at four percent, than with 100,000 francs at five percent, although, in the first case, he charges less to the manufacturer for the use of his capital. The same thing holds of a nation, and of the world at large. Now, I maintain that the percentage, in its tendency to fall, neither does nor can follow a progression so rapid that the sum total of interest should be smaller when capital is abundant than when it is scarce. I admit, indeed, that if the capital of mankind be represented by 100 and interest by 5—this interest will amount to no more than 4 when the capital shall have mounted to 200. Here we see the simultaneousness of the two effects. The less the relative part, the greater the absolute part. But my hypothesis does not admit that the increase of capital from 100 to 200 is sufficient to make interest fall from 5 to 2 percent, for example; because, if it were so, the capitalist who had an income of 5,000 francs with 100,000 francs of capital, would have no greater income than 4,000 francs with 200,000 francs of capital. A result so contradictory and impossible, an anomaly so strange, would be met with the simplest and most agreeable of remedies; for then, in order to increase your income, it would only be necessary to consume half your capital. A happy and whimsical age it would be when men could enrich by impoverishing themselves!

We must take care, then, not to lose sight of the combination of these two correlative facts. The increase of capital, and the fall of interest, take place necessarily in such a way that the total product is continually augmented.

And let us remark in passing that this completely exposes the fallacy of those who imagine that because interest falls, it tends to annihilation. The effect of that would be that a time would arrive when capital would be so much increased as to yield nothing to its possessors. Keep your mind easy on that score—before that time comes, capitalists will dissipate the stock in order to ensure the reappearance of interest.

Such is the great law of Capital and labor in what concerns the distribution of the product of their joint agency. Each of them has a greater and greater absolute share, but the proportional share of the capitalist is continually diminished as compared with that of the laborers.

Cease, then, capitalists and workmen, to regard each other with an eye of envy and distrust. Shut your ears against those absurd declamations that proceed from ignorance and presumption, which, under pretense of insuring future prosperity, fan the flame of present discord. Be assured that your interests are one and identical; that they are indisputably knit together; that they tend together toward the realization of the public good; that the toils of the present generation mingle with the labors of generations past; that all who co-operate in the work of production receive their share of the produce; and that the most ingenious and most equitable distribution is effected among you by the wise laws of Providence, and under the empire of freedom, independently altogether of a parasite sentimentalism, which would impose upon you its decrees at the expense of your well-being, your liberty, your security, and your self-respect.

Capital has its root in these attributes of man—Foresight, Intelligence, and Frugality. To set about the creation of capital we must look forward to the future, and sacrifice the present to it—we must exercise a noble empire over ourselves and over our appetites; we must resist the seduction of present enjoyments, the impulses of vanity and the caprices of fashion and of public opinion, always so indulgent to the thoughtless and the prodigal. We must study cause and effect in order to discover by what processes, by what instruments, nature can be made to co-operate in the work of production. We must be animated by love for our families, and not grudge present sacrifices for the sake of those who are dear to us, and who will reap the fruits after we ourselves have disappeared from the scene. To create capital is to prepare food, clothing, shelter, leisure, instruction, independence, dignity, for future generations. Nothing of all this can be effected without bringing into play motives that are eminently social and, what is more, converting these virtues into habits.

And yet it is very usual to attribute to capital a sort of fatal efficacy, the effect of which is to introduce greed, miserliness, Machiavelism, into the hearts of those who aspire to possess it. But let us not be misunderstood. There are countries where labor is of little value, and the little that is earned is shared by the government. In order to snatch from you the fruit of your toil, what is called the State surrounds you with a multitude of trammels. It interferes with all your actions, and mixes itself up in all your concerns. It domineers over your mind and your faith. It disarranges all interests, and places them in an artificial and precarious position. It enervates individual energy and activity, by usurping the direction of all affairs. It makes the responsibility of actions fall upon people with whom it amounts to nothing, so that by degrees all notions of what is just or unjust are effaced. By its diplomacy it embroils the nation in quarrels with all the world, and then the army and navy are brought into play. It warps the popular mind as much as it can upon all economic questions; for it is necessary to make the masses believe that its foolish expenditure, its unjust aggressions, its conquests, its colonies, are for them a source of riches. In such countries it is difficult to create capital by natural means. The great object is to purloin it by force or by fraud from those who have created it. We there see man enriching themselves by war, by places at court, by gambling, by purveying, by stockjobbing, by commercial frauds, by hazardous enterprises, by public contracts, etc. The qualities requisite for thus snatching capital from the hands of those who create it are precisely the opposite of those necessary for its formation. It cannot surprise us, then, that in countries so situated an association is established between these two ideas—capital and greed; and this association becomes ineradicable when all the moral ideas of the country exhaust themselves on ancient and medieval history.

But when we turn our regards, not to this embezzlement and abuse of capital, but to its creation by intelligence and activity, foresight and frugality, it is impossible not to perceive that a moral and social virtue is attached to its acquisition.

Nor is there less moral and social virtue in the action of capital than in its formation. Its peculiar effect is to procure us the co-operation of nature, to set us free from all that is most material, muscular, brutal, in the work of production; to render the intelligent principle more and more predominant; to enlarge the domain, I do not say of idleness, but of leisure; to render less urgent the physical wants of our nature by rendering their satisfactions more easy, and to substitute for them wants and enjoyments of a nature more elevated, more delicate, more refined, more artistic, more spiritual.

Thus, in whatever point of view we place ourselves, whether we regard Capital in connection with our wants, which it ennobles; with our efforts, which it facilitates; with our enjoyments, which it purifies with nature, which it enlists in our service; with morality, which it converts into habit; with sociability, which it develops; with equality, which it promotes; with freedom, in which it lives; with equity, which it realizes by methods the most ingenious—everywhere, always, provided that it is created and acts in the regular order of things, and is not diverted from its natural uses, we recognize in Capital what forms the indubitable note and stamp of all great providential laws—Harmony.

8

PROPERTY—COMMUNITY

Recognizing in the soil, in natural agents, and in instruments of labor, what they incontestably possess, the gift of engendering Utility, I have endeavored to denude them of what has been erroneously attributed to them, namely, the faculty of creating Value—a faculty that pertains exclusively to the Services men exchange with each other.

This simple rectification, while it strengthens and confirms Property by restoring to it its true character, brings to light a most important fact hitherto, if I am not mistaken, overlooked by Economic science—the fact that there exists a real, essential, and progressive Community—the natural result of every social system in which liberty prevails, and the evident design of which is to conduct all men, as brethren, from primitive Equality, which is the equality of ignorance and destitution, toward an ultimate Equality in the possession of truth and material prosperity.

If this radical distinction between the Utility of things and the value of services be true in itself, and in the consequences that have been deduced from it, it is impossible to misunderstand its implications; for it leads to nothing less than the absorption of

Utopian theories in science, and the reconcilement of antagonistic schools in a common faith, which satisfies all minds and all aspirations.

Men of property and leisure!—whatever be your rank in the social scale, whatever step of the social ladder you may have reached by dint of activity, probity, order, and economy—whence come the fears that have seized upon you? The perfumed but poisoned breath of Utopia menaces your existence. You are loudly told that the fortune you have amassed for the purpose of securing a little repose in your old age, and food, instruction, and an outset in life for your children, has been acquired by you at the expense of your brethren; that you have placed yourselves between the gifts of God and the poor; that, like greedy tax-gatherers, you have levied a tribute on those gifts, under the name of Property, of Interest, and of Rent; that you have intercepted the benefits that the common Father has bestowed on his children, in order to make merchandise of them. You are called upon for restitution; and what augments your terror is that your advocates, in conducting your defense, feel themselves too often obliged to avow that the usurpation is flagrant, but that it is necessary. Such accusations I meet with a direct and emphatic negative. You have not intercepted the gifts of God. You have received them gratuitously, it is true, at the hands of nature; but you have also gratuitously transferred them to your brethren without receiving anything. They have acted the same way toward you; and the only things that have been reciprocally compensated are physical or intellectual efforts, toils undergone, dangers braved, skill exercised, privations submitted to, pains taken, services rendered and received. You may perhaps have thought only of yourselves and your own selfish interest, but that very selfish interest has been an instrument in the hand of an infinitely prescient and wise Providence to enlarge unceasingly among men the domain of Community; for without your efforts all those useful effects you have obtained from nature, in order to distribute them without remuneration among your brethren, would have remained forever inert. I say without remuneration, because what you have received is simply the recompense of your efforts, and not at all the price of the gifts of God. Live, then, in peace, without fear and without misgiving. You have no other property in the world but your right to services, in exchange for other services by you faithfully rendered, and by your brethren voluntarily accepted. Such property is legitimate, unassailable; no Utopia can prevail against it, for it enters into the very constitution of our being. No theory can ever succeed in blighting or in shaking it.

Men of toil and privations! you cannot shut your eyes to this truth, that the primitive condition of the human race is that of an entire Community—a perfect Equality—of poverty, of destitution, and of ignorance. Man redeems himself from this estate by the sweat of his brow, and directs his course toward another Community, that of the gifts of God, successively obtained with less effort—toward another Equality, that of material prosperity, knowledge, and moral dignity. The progress of men on the road of improvement is unequal indeed; and you could not complain were the more hurried and precipitate march of the vanguard of progress to retard in some measure your own advance. But in truth it is quite the reverse. No ray of light penetrates a single mind without in some degree enlightening yours. No step of progress, prompted by the conscious possession of property, but is a step of progress for you. No wealth is created that does not tend to your enfranchisement; no capital, that does not increase your enjoyments in proportion to your labor; no acquisition, that does not increase your facilities of acquisition; no Property, that does not tend to enlarge, for your benefit, the domain of Community. The natural social order has been so skillfully arranged by the Divine Architect that those who are more advanced on the road of civilization hold out to you voluntarily or unconsciously, a helping hand; for the order of things has been so disposed that no man can work honestly for himself without at the same time working for all. And it is rigorously true to affirm that every attack upon this marvelous order would on your part be not only a homicide, but a suicide. Human nature is an admirable chain, that exhibits this standing miracle, that the first links communicate to all the others a progressive movement more and more rapid, onwards to the last.

Men of philanthropy! lovers of equality! blind defenders, dangerous friends, of the suffering classes, who are yet far behind on the road of civilization, you who expect the reign of Community in this world, why do you begin by unsettling all interests and shaking all received opinions? Why, in your pride, should you seek to subjugate men's wills, and bring them under the yoke of your social inventions? Do you not see that this Community after which you sigh, and which is to inaugurate the kingdom of God upon earth, has been already thought of and provided for by God himself? Does He need your aid to provide a patrimony for His children? Has He need either of your conceptions or of your violence? Do you not see that this Community is realized more and more every day, in virtue of His admirable decrees; that for the execution of these decrees He has not trusted to your chance services and puerile arrangements, nor even to the growing expression of the sympathetic principle manifested by charity; but that He has confided the realization of His providential designs to the most active, the most personal, the most permanent of all our energies: Self-interest—a principle imbedded in our inmost nature, and that never flags, never takes rest? Study, then, the social mechanism as it comes from the hand of the Great Mechanician, and you will find that it testifies to a universal solicitude that far outstrips your dreams and chimeras. You will then, I hope, in place of presumptuously pretending to reconstruct the divine workmanship, be content to admire and to bless it.

I say not that there is no room in this world of ours for reforms and reformers. I say not that mankind is not to call to its service, and encourage with its gratitude, men of investigation, of science, and of earnestness—hearts faithful to the people. Such are still but too much wanted—not to overturn the social laws—but to combat the artificial obstacles that disturb and reverse the action of these laws. In truth, it is difficult to understand why people should keep repeating such commonplaces as this: "Political Economy is an optimist, as far as existing facts are concerned;

and affirms that whatever is, is right. At the sight of what is evil, as at the sight of what is good, Economists are content to exclaim, *Laissez faire*." Optimists with reference to existing facts! Then we must be ignorant that the primitive condition of man is poverty, ignorance, the reign of brute force! We must be ignorant that the moving spring of human nature is aversion to all suffering, to all fatigue; and that labor being fatigue, the earliest manifestation of selfishness among men is shown in their effort to throw this painful burden on the shoulders of each other! The words cannibalism, war, slavery, privilege, monopoly, fraud, spoliation, imposture, must either have never reached our ears, or else we must see in these abominations the necessary machinery of progress! But is there not in all this a certain amount of willful misrepresentation, a confounding of all things for the purpose of accusing us of confounding them? When we admire the providential laws that govern human transactions—when we assert that men's interests are harmonious—when we thence conclude that they naturally tend and gravitate toward the realization of relative equality and general progress—it is surely from the play and action of these laws, not from their perturbations and disturbances, that we educe harmony. When we say *laissez faire*, we surely mean allow these laws to act, not allow these laws to be disturbed. According as we conform to these laws or violate them, good or evil is produced; in other words, men's interests are in harmony, provided right prevail, and services are freely and voluntarily exchanged against services. But does this imply that we are ignorant of the perpetual struggle of Wrong against Right? Does this imply that we lose sight of, or approve, the efforts that have been made in all ages, and that are still being made, to alter, by force or fraud, the natural equivalence of services? This is exactly what we repudiate as a violation of the natural social laws as an attack upon property—for in our view, the terms free exchange of services, justice, property, liberty, security, all express the same idea under different aspects. It is not the principle of Property we contest, but the antagonistic principle of Spoliation.

Proprietors of all ranks! reformers of all schools! this is the mission that should reconcile and unite us.

It is time, high time, that this crusade should begin. A mere theoretical war against Property is by no means the most virulent or the most dangerous. Since the beginning of the world there has existed a practical conspiracy against it that is not likely soon to cease. War, slavery, imposture, oppressive imposts, monopolies, privileges, commercial frauds, colonies, right to employment, right to credit, right to assistance, right to instruction, progressive taxation imposed in direct or inverse proportion to our power of bearing it, are so many battering-rams directed against the tottering edifice; and if the truth must come out, would you tell me whether there are many men in France, even among those who think themselves conservative, who do not, in one form or another, lend a hand to this work of destruction?

There are people in whose views property never appears in any other form than that of a field or a bag of crown-pieces. If you do not overstep sacred landmarks, or sensibly empty their pockets, they feel quite comfortable. But is there no other kind of Property? Is there not the Property of muscular force and intellectual power, of faculties, of ideas—in a word, the Property of Services? When I throw a service into the social scale, is it not my right that it should be held there, if I may use the expression, suspended, according to the laws of its natural equivalence; that it may there form a counterpoise to any other service my neighbor may consent to throw into the opposite scale and tender me in exchange? The law of common consent agreed to establish a public force for the protection of property thus understood. But in what situation are we placed if this very force assumes to itself the mission of disturbing the equilibrium, under the socialist pretext that liberty gives birth to monopoly, and that the doctrine of *laissez faire* is odious and heartless? When things go on in this way, individual theft may be rare, and may be severely punished, but spoliation is organized, legalized, and erected into a system. Comfort yourselves, Reformers! your work is not yet done—only try to understand what that work really is.

But before proceeding to analyze spoliation, whether public or private, legal or illegal, and to consider its bearing as an element in the social problem, and the part it plays in the business of the world, it is necessary to form just ideas, if possible, of Community and Property; for as we shall by and by see, spoliation forms a limit to property, just as property forms a limit to community.

From the preceding chapters, especially that which treats of Utility and Value, we may deduce this formula:

Every man enjoys GRATUITOUSLY all the utilities furnished or created by nature, on condition of taking the trouble to appropriate them, or of returning an equivalent service to those who render him the service of taking that trouble for him.

Here we have two facts combined and mixed up together, although in their own nature distinct.

We have the gifts of nature—gratuitous materials, gratuitous forces. This is the domain of Community.

We have also human efforts devoted to the appropriation of these materials, to the direction of these forces—efforts that are exchanged, estimated, and compensated. This is the domain of Property.

In other words, as regards both, we are not owners of the Utility of things, but of their Value, and value is simply the appreciation of reciprocal services.

Property and Community are two ideas correlative to the ideas of onerousness and gratuitousness, on which they are founded.

That which is gratuitous is common, for everyone enjoys a portion of it, and enjoys it unconditionally.

That which is onerous is appropriated, because trouble taken, effort made, is the condition of its enjoyment, as the enjoyment is the reason for taking the trouble, or making the effort.

Does an exchange intervene? It is effected by a comparative estimate of the two efforts or the two services.

This reference to trouble, to pains, implies the existence of an Obstacle. We may then conclude that the object sought for approximates more nearly to the gratuitous and the common, in proportion as the obstacle is less; as, by hypothesis, the complete absence of obstacle would render it perfectly gratuitous and common.

Now, with reference to human nature, which is progressive and perfectible, the obstacle can never be regarded as an absolute and invariable quantity. It diminishes. Then the pains taken diminish along with it—and the service with the pains—and value with the service—and property with value.

And the Utility remains the same. Then the gratuitous and the common have gained all that onerousness and property have lost.

For a man to decide to labor he must have a motive, and that motive is the satisfaction he has in view, or utility. His undoubted and irrepressible tendency is to realize the greatest possible satisfaction with the least possible labor, to cause the greatest amount of utility to correspond with the greatest amount of property. Whence it follows that the mission of Property, or rather of the spirit of property, is to realize, in a greater and greater degree, Community.

The starting point of the human race being the maximum of poverty, or the maximum of obstacles to be overcome, it is clear that for all that is gained from one age to another we are indebted to the spirit of property.

This being so, is there to be found in the world a single theoretical adversary of the institution of property? Is it possible to imagine a social force at once so just and so popular? The fundamental dogma of Proudhon himself is the mutuality of services. On this point we are agreed. What we differ upon is that I give this the name of Property, because, on going to the root of the matter, I am convinced that men, if they are free, neither have, nor can have, any other property than that of value, or of services. On the contrary, Proudhon, like most Economists, thinks that certain natural agents have a value that is inherent in them, and that in consequence of that they are appropriated. But as regards property in services, far from contesting it, he adopts it as his creed. Do you wish to go still farther? To go to the length of asserting that a man should not have a right of property in his own exertions? Will it be said that by exchange it is not enough to transfer gratuitously the co-operation of natural agents, but also to cede gratuitously one's own efforts? This is indeed a dangerous doctrine; it is to glorify slavery; for to assert that certain men must render, is to assert that other men must receive, services that are not remunerated, and that is slavery. But if you say that this gratuitous interchange must be reciprocal, you get into a conundrum; for either there is some equity in exchange, and then the services will, in one way or another, be estimated and compensated; or they will not be estimated and compensated—in which case the one party will render a great amount of service, and the other a small amount, and you will fall back again into slavery.

But it is impossible to contest the legitimate nature of Property in services that are exchanged on the principle of equivalence. To explain their legitimacy we have no need to have recourse to philosophy, or jurisprudence, or metaphysics. Socialists, Economists, Advocates of Equality and Fraternity—I defy the whole body, numerous as it is, to raise even the shadow of an objection against the legitimate mutuality of voluntary services, and consequently against Property, such as I have defined it, such as it actually exists in the natural social order.

I know very well that in practice the reign of Property is far from being always pure, and that we have always to deal with tainted cases. There are services that are not voluntary; there is remuneration that is not freely stipulated; there are services whose equivalence is impaired by force or by fraud; in a word, there is Spoliation. The legitimate principle of Property, however, is not thereby invalidated but confirmed. The very fact of its being violated proves its existence. If we put faith in anything in this world—in facts, in justice, in universal assent, in human language—we must admit that these two words, Property and Spoliation, express ideas that are as opposite, as irreconcilable, as far from being identical as yes and no, light and darkness, good and evil, harmony and discord. Taken literally, the celebrated formula that property is theft is absurd in the very highest degree. It would not be more monstrous to say that theft is property, that what is legitimate is illegitimate, that what is, is not, etc. The author of this whimsical aphorism probably wished to show how ingeniously he could support a paradox, and meant no more than this, that certain men are paid not only for work they do but for work they don't do, thus appropriating to themselves exclusively, gratuitous utility—the gifts vouchsafed by God for the good of all. In this case all that we have to do is to prove the assertion, and substitute the truism that theft is theft.

To steal means, in ordinary language, to appropriate by force or fraud, a value, to the prejudice and without the consent of the person who has created that value. It is easy to see how a false Political Economy has succeeded in enlarging the sense of that ugly word steal. You begin by confounding utility with value. Then, as nature co-operates in the creation of utility, you conclude that nature also concurs in the creation of value, and you say that this portion of value, being the fruit of no one's labor, belongs to all. At length, finding that value is never transferred without remuneration, you add, that the man who exacts a recompense for a value that is the creation of nature, that is independent of all human labor, that is inherent in things, and is by the destination of Providence one of their intrinsic qualities, like weight or porosity, form or color, commits a robbery.

An exact analysis of value overturns this scaffolding of subtleties intended to prop up a monstrous identification of Property with Spoliation.

God has placed certain Materials and certain Forces at the disposal of man. In order to obtain possession of these materials and forces, labor is necessary, or it is not. If it be not necessary, no one will voluntarily consent to purchase from another, by means of an effort, what, without any effort, he can obtain from the hands of Nature. In this case, services, exchange, value, Property, are out of the question. If on the other hand, labor be necessary, in equity it falls upon the person who is to receive the satisfaction; whence it follows that the satisfaction is the recompense of the pains taken, the effort made, the labor undergone. Here you have the principle of Property. This being so, a man takes pains, or submits to labor, for his own benefit, and becomes possessed of the whole utility realized by this labor co-operating with nature. He takes pains, or submits to labor, for another, and in that case he bargains to receive in return an equivalent service, which is likewise the vehicle of utility, and the result exhibits two Efforts, two Utilities that have changed hands, and two Satisfactions. But we must not lose sight of this, that the transaction is effected by the comparison, by the evaluation, not of the two utilities (they cannot be brought to this test), but of the two services exchanged. It is then exact to say that, in a personal point of view, man, by means of labor, becomes proprietor of natural utility (that is the object of his labor), whatever be the relation (which may vary *ad infinitum*) of labor to utility. But in a social point of view, or in reference to each other, men are never proprietors except of value, the foundation of which is not the liberality of nature, but human service, pains taken, danger encountered, skill displayed, in securing that liberality. In a word, in what concerns natural and gratuitous utility, the last acquirer, the person who is the recipient of the satisfaction, is placed, by exchange, in the shoes of the first laborer. The latter has found himself in presence of a gratuitous utility that he has taken the pains to appropriate; the former returns him an equivalent service, and thus substitutes himself in the other's right and place; utility is acquired by him by the same title, that is to say, by a gratuitous title, on condition of pains taken. There is here, neither in fact nor in appearance, any improper interception of the gifts of God.

I venture, then, to lay down this proposition as unassailable:

In relation to one another, men are proprietors only of values, and values represent only services compared, and voluntarily received and rendered.

That, on the one hand, the true meaning of the word value is what I have already demonstrated it to be (chapter 5); and that, on the other, men are never, and never can be, as regards each other, proprietors of anything but value, is evident as well from reasoning as from experience. From reasoning—for why should I go to purchase from a man, by means of an effort what without any effort I can obtain from nature? From universal experience, which is too weighty to be dismissed in this question—nothing being more fitted to give us confidence in a theory than the rational and practical acquiescence of men of all ages and all countries. Now I say that universal consent ratifies the sense I give here to the word Property. When a public officer makes an inventory after a death, or by authority of justice, or when a merchant, manufacturer, or farmer does the same thing for his own satisfaction, or when it is done by officials under a bankruptcy—what do they inscribe on the stamped rolls as each object presents itself? Is it its utility, its intrinsic merit? No, it is its value, that is to say, the equivalent of the trouble that any purchaser taken at random would have in procuring himself a similar commodity. Does a jury named by a judge to report upon a work or a commodity inquire whether it be more useful than another work or commodity? Do they take into consideration the enjoyments that may be thereby procured? Do they esteem a hammer more than a china jar, because the hammer is admirably adapted to make the law of gravitation available to its possessor? or a glass of water more than a diamond, because the former is capable of rendering more substantial service? or the work of Say more than the work of Fourier, because from the former we can draw more rational enjoyment and more solid instruction? No, they value, they set down the value, in rigorous conformity, observe, with my definition, or, to say better, it is my definition that is in conformity with their practice. They take into account not the natural advantages, or the gratuitous utility, attached to each commodity, but the exertion each acquirer should have to make for himself, or to require another to make for him, in order to procure it. They never think of the exertion nature has made, I may hazard the expression, but upon the exertion the purchaser would have had to make. And when the operation is terminated, when the public is told the sum total of Value that is carried to the balance sheet, they exclaim with one voice, Here is the wealth that is available to the Proprietor.

As property includes nothing but value, and as value expresses only a relation, it follows that property itself is only a relation.

When the public, on the inspection of two inventories, pronounces one man to be richer than another, it is not meant to say that the relative amount of the two properties is indicative of the relative absolute wealth of the two men, or the amount of enjoyments they can command. There enters into positive satisfactions and enjoyments a certain amount of common and gratuitous utility that alters this proportion very much. As regards the light of day, the air we breathe, the heat of the sun, all men are equal; and Inequality—as indicative of a difference in property or value—has reference only to onerous utility. Now I have often said, and I shall probably have occasion frequently to repeat the remark (for it is the finest and most striking, although perhaps the least understood, of the social harmonies, and includes all the others), that it is of the essence of progress—and indeed in this alone progress consists—to transform onerous into gratuitous utility—to diminish value without diminishing utility—to permit each individual to procure the same things with less effort, either to make or to remunerate; to increase continually the mass of things that are common, and the enjoyment of which, being distributed in a uniform manner among all, effaces by degrees the Inequality that results from difference of fortune.

We must not omit to analyze very carefully the result of this mechanism.

In contemplating the phenomena of the social world, how often have I had occasion to feel the profound justice of Rousseau's saying: "*Il faut beaucoup de philosophie pour observer ce qu'on voit tous les jours!*" It is difficult to observe accurately what we see every day; Custom, that veil that blinds the eyes of the common, and which the attentive observer cannot always throw off, prevents our discerning the most marvelous of all the Economic phenomena: real wealth falling incessantly from the domain of Property into that of Community.

Let us endeavor to demonstrate and explain this democratic evolution, and, if possible, test its range and its effects.

I have remarked elsewhere that if we desire to compare two epochs as regards real wealth and prosperity, we must refer all to a common standard, which is unskilled labor measured by time, and ask ourselves this question—What difference in the amount of satisfaction, according to the degree of advancement society has reached, is a determinate quantity of unskilled labor—for example, a day's work of a common laborer—capable of yielding us?

This question implies two others:

What was the relation of the satisfaction to unskilled labor at the beginning of the period? What is it now?

The difference will be the measure of the advance gratuitous utility has made relatively to onerous utility—the domain of community relatively to that of property.

I believe that for the politician no problem can be proposed more interesting and instructive than this; and the reader must pardon me if, in order to arrive at a satisfactory solution of it, I fatigue him with too many examples.

I made, at the outset, a sort of catalogue of the most common human wants: respiration, food, clothing, lodging, locomotion, instruction, amusement, etc.

Let us resume the same order, and inquire what amount of satisfactions a common day-laborer could at the beginning, and can now, procure himself, by a determinate number of days' labor.

Respiration. Here all is completely gratuitous and common from the beginning. Nature does all, and leaves us nothing to do. Efforts, services, value, property, progress are all out of the question. As regards utility, Diogenes is as rich as Alexander—as regards value, Alexander is as rich as Diogenes.

Food. At present, the value of a hectoliter of wheat in France is the equivalent of from 15 to 20 days' work of a common unskilled laborer. This is a fact which we may regard as unimportant, but it is not the less worthy of remark. It is a fact that in our day, viewing humanity in its least advanced aspect, and as represented by a penniless workman, enjoyment measured by a hectoliter of wheat can be obtained by an expenditure of 15 days' unskilled labor. The ordinary calculation is that three hectoliters of wheat annually are required for the subsistence of one man. The common laborer, then, produces, if not his subsistence, what comes to the same thing, the value of his subsistence by an expenditure of from 45 to 60 days' labor in the year. If we represent the type of value by one (in this case one day's unskilled labor), the value of a hectoliter of wheat will be expressed by 15, 18, or 20, according to the year. The relation of these two values is, say, one to fifteen.

To discover if progress has been made, and to measure it, we must inquire what this relation was in the early days of the human race. In truth, I dare not hazard a figure, but there is one way of clearing up the difficulty. When you hear a man declaiming against the social order, against the appropriation of the soil, against rent, against machinery, lead him into the middle of a primitive forest and in sight of a pestilential morass. Say to him, I wish to free you from the yoke of which you complain—I wish to withdraw you from the atrocious struggles of anarchical competition, from the antagonism of interests, from the selfishness of wealth, from the oppression of property, from the crushing rivalry of machinery, from the stifling atmosphere of society. Here is land exactly like what the first clearers had to encounter. Take as much of it as you please—take it by tens, by hundreds of acres. Cultivate it yourself. All that you can make it produce is yours. I make but one condition, that you will not have recourse to that society of which you represent yourself as the victim.

As regards the soil, observe, this man would be placed in exactly the same situation that mankind at large occupied at the beginning. Now I fear not to be contradicted when I assert that this man would not produce a hectoliter of wheat in two years: Ratio 15 to 600.

And now we can measure the progress that has been made. As regards wheat—and despite his being obliged to pay rent for his land, interest for his capital, and hire for his tools—or rather because he pays them—a laborer now obtains with 15 days' work what he would formerly have had difficulty in procuring with 600 days' work. The value of wheat, then, measured by unskilled labor, has fallen from 600 to 15, or from 40 to 1. A hectoliter of wheat has for man the same utility it had the day after the deluge—it contains the same quantity of alimentary substance—it satisfies the same want, and in the same degree. It constitutes an equal amount of real wealth—it does not constitute an equal amount of relative wealth. Its production has been transferred in a great measure to the charge of nature. It is obtained with less human effort. It renders less service in passing from hand to hand, it has less value. In a word, it has become gratuitous, not absolutely, but in the proportion of 40 to 1.

And not only has it become gratuitous—it has become common to the same extent. For it is not to the profit of the person who produces the wheat that 39/40ths of the effort has been annihilated, but to the advantage of the consumer, whatever be the kind of labor to which he devotes himself.

Clothing. We have here again the same phenomenon. A common day laborer enters one of the warehouses at the Marais,[1] and there obtains clothing corresponding to twenty days of his labor, which we suppose to be unskilled. Were he to attempt to make this clothing himself, his whole life would be insufficient. Had he desired to obtain the same clothing in the time of Henry IV, it would have cost him three or four hundred days' work. What then has become of this difference in the value of these materials in relation to the quantity of unskilled labor? It has been annihilated, because the gratuitous forces of nature now perform a great portion of the work, and it has been annihilated to the advantage of mankind at large.

For we must not fail to note here that every man owes his neighbor a service equivalent to what he has received from him.

---

[1] Public warehouses where goods were deposited, and negotiable receipts issued in exchange for them.—Translator.

If, then, the art of the weaver had made no progress, if weaving were not executed in part by gratuitous forces, the weaver would still be occupied two or three hundred days in fabricating these materials, and our workmen would be required to give him two or three hundred days' work in order to obtain the clothing they want. And since the weaver cannot succeed, with all his wish to do so, in obtaining two or three hundred days' labor in recompense for the intervention of gratuitous forces, and for the progress achieved, we are warranted in saying that this progress has been effected to the advantage of the purchaser or consumer, and that it is a gain to society at large.

Conveyance. Prior to all progress, when the human race, like our day laborer, was obliged to make use of primitive and unskilled labor, if a man had desired to have a load of a hundred-weight transported from Paris to Bayonne, he would have had only this alternative, either to take the load on his own shoulders, and perform the work himself, travelling over hill and dale, which would have required a year's labor, or else to ask someone to perform this rough piece of work for him; and as, by hypothesis, the person who undertook this work would have to employ the same means and the same time, he would undoubtedly demand a remuneration equal to a year's labor. At that period, then, the value of unskilled labor being one, that of transport was 300 for the weight of a cwt. and a distance of 200 leagues.

But things are changed now. In fact there is no workman in Paris who cannot obtain the same result by the sacrifice of two days' labor. The alternative indeed is still the same. He must either do the work himself or get others to do it for him by remunerating them. If our day laborer perform it himself, it will still cost him a year of fatigue; but if he applies to men who make it their business, he will find twenty carriers to do what he wants for three or four francs, that is to say, for the equivalent of two days' unskilled labor. Thus the value of such labor being represented by one, that of transport, which was represented by 300, is now reduced to two.

In what way has this astonishing revolution been brought about? Ages have been required to accomplish it. Animals have been trained, mountains have been pierced, valleys have been filled up, bridges have been thrown across rivers, sledges and afterwards wheeled carriages have been invented, obstacles, which give rise to labor, services, value, have been removed, in short, we have succeeded in accomplishing, with labor equal to two, what our remote ancestors would have effected only by labor equal to 300. This progress has been realized by men who had no thought but for their own interests. And yet, who profits by it now? Our poor day laborer, and with him society at large.

Let no one say that this is not Community. I say that it is Community in the strictest sense of the word. At the outset the satisfaction in question was, in the estimation of all, the equivalent of 300 days' unskilled labor, or a proportionally smaller amount of skilled labor. Now 298 parts of this labor out of 300 are performed by nature, and mankind is exonerated to a corresponding extent. Now, evidently all men are in exactly the same situation as regards the obstacles that have been removed, the distance that has been wiped out, the fatigue that has been obviated, the value that has been annihilated, since all obtain the result without having to pay for it. What they pay for is the human effort that remains still to be made, as compared with and measured by two days' work of an unskilled laborer. In other words, the man who has not himself effected this improvement, and who has only muscular force to offer in exchange, has still to give two days' labor to secure the satisfaction he wishes to obtain. All other men can obtain it with a smaller sacrifice of labor. The Paris lawyer, earning 30,000 francs a year, can obtain it for a twenty-fifth part of a day's labor, etc.—by which we see that all men are equal as regards the value annihilated, and that the inequality is restrained within the limits of the portion of value which survives the change, that is, within the domain of Property.

Economic science labors under a disadvantage in being obliged to have recourse to hypothetical cases. The reader is taught to believe that the phenomena we wish to describe are to be discovered only in special cases, adduced for the sake of illustration. But it is evident that what we have said of wheat, clothing, and means of transport is true of everything else. When an author generalizes, it is for the reader to particularize; and when the former devotes himself to cold and forbidding analysis, the latter may at least indulge in the pleasures of synthesis.

The synthetic law may be reduced to this formula:

Value, which is social property, springs from Effort and Obstacle.

In proportion as the obstacle is lessened, effort, value, or the domain of property, is diminished along with it.

With reference to each given satisfaction, Property always recedes and Community always advances.

Must we then conclude with Mr. Proudhon that the days of Property are numbered? Because, as regards each useful result to be realized, each satisfaction to be obtained, Property recedes before Community, are we thence to conclude that the former is about to be absorbed and annihilated altogether?

To adopt this conclusion would be to mistake completely the nature of man. We encounter here a sophism analogous to the one we have already refuted on the subject of the interest of capital. Interest has a tendency to fall, it is said; then it is destined ultimately to disappear altogether. Value and property go on diminishing; then they are destined, it is now said, to be annihilated.

The whole sophism consists in omitting the words, for each determinate result. It is quite true that men obtain determinate results with a less amount of effort—it is in this respect that they are progressive and perfectible—it is on this account that we are able to affirm that the relative domain of property becomes narrower, looking at it as regards each given satisfaction.

But it is not true that all the results that it is possible to obtain are ever exhausted, and hence it is absurd to suppose that it is in the nature of progress to lessen or limit the absolute domain of property.

We have repeated often, and in every shape, that each given effort may, in course of time, serve as the vehicle of a greater amount of gratuitous utility, without our being warranted thence to conclude that men should ever cease to make efforts. All that we can conclude from it is that their forces, thus rendered disposable, will be employed in combating other obstacles, and will realize, with equal labor, satisfactions hitherto unknown.

I must enlarge still further on this idea. These are not times to leave anything to possible misconstruction when we venture to pronounce the fearful words, Property and Community.

Man in a state of isolation can, at any given moment of his existence, exert only a certain amount of effort; and the same thing holds of society.

When man in a state of isolation realizes a step of progress by making natural agents co-operate with his own labor, the sum of his efforts is reduced by so much in relation to the useful result sought for. It would be reduced not relatively only, but absolutely, if this man, content with his original condition, should convert his progress into leisure, and should abstain from devoting to the acquisition of new enjoyments that portion of effort that is now rendered disposable. That would take for granted that ambition, desire, aspiration, were limited forces, and that the human heart was not indefinitely expansible; but it is quite otherwise. Robinson Crusoe has no sooner handed over part of his work to natural agents than he devotes his efforts to new enterprises. The sum total of his efforts remains the same—but one portion of these efforts, aided by a greater amount of natural and gratuitous co-operation, has become more productive, more prolific. This is exactly the phenomenon we see realized in society.

Because the plough, the harrow, the hammer, the saw, oxen and horses, the sail, water power, steam, have successively relieved mankind from an enormous amount of labor, in proportion to each result obtained, it does not necessarily follow that this labor, thus set free and rendered disposable, should lie dormant. Remember what has been already said as to the indefinite expansibility of our wants and desires—and note what is passing around you—and you will not fail to see that as often as man succeeds in vanquishing an obstacle by the aid of natural agents, he sets his own forces to grapple with other obstacles. We have more facility in the art of printing than we had formerly, but we print more. Each book corresponds to a less amount of human effort, to less value, less property; but we have more books and, on the whole, the same amount of effort, value, property. The same thing might be said of clothing, of houses, of railways, of all human productions. It is not the aggregate of values that has diminished; it is the aggregate of utilities that has increased. It is not the absolute domain of Property that has been narrowed; it is the absolute domain of Community that has been enlarged. Progress has not paralyzed labor; it has augmented wealth.

Things that are gratuitous and common to all are within the domain of natural forces; and it is true in theory as in fact that this domain is constantly extending.

Value and Property are within the domain of human efforts, of reciprocal services, and this domain becomes narrower and narrower as regards each given result, but not as regards the aggregate of results; as regards each determinate satisfaction, but not as regards the aggregate of satisfactions, because the amount of possible enjoyments is without limit.

It is as true, then, that relative Property gives place to Community, as it is false that absolute Property tends to disappear altogether. Property is a pioneer that accomplishes its work in one circle, and then passes into another. Before property could disappear altogether we must suppose every obstacle to have been removed, labor to have been superseded, human efforts to have become useless; we must suppose men to have no longer need to effect exchanges, or render services to each other; we must suppose all production to be spontaneous, and enjoyment to spring directly from desire; in a word, we must suppose men to have become equal to gods. Then, indeed, all would be gratuitous, and we should have all things in common. Effort, service, value, property, everything indicative of our native weakness and infirmity, would cease to exist.

In vain man raises himself in the social scale, and advances on the road of civilization—he is as far as ever from Omnipotence. It is one of the attributes of the Divinity, as far as we can understand what is so much above human reason, that between volition and result no obstacle is interposed. God said, Let there be light, and there was light. And it is the powerlessness of man to express that to which there is so little analogous in his own nature that reduced Moses to the necessity of supposing between the divine will and the creation of light the intervention of an obstacle, in the shape even of a word to be pronounced. But whatever advance man, in virtue of his progressive nature, may be destined yet to make, we may safely affirm that he will never succeed in freeing himself entirely from the obstacles that encumber his path, or in rendering himself independent of the labor of his head and of his hands. The reason is obvious. In proportion as certain obstacles are overcome, his desires dilate and expand, and new obstacles oppose themselves to new efforts. We shall always, then, have labor to perform, to exchange, to estimate, and to value. Property will exist until the consummation of all things, increasing in mass in proportion as men become more active and more numerous; while at the same time each effort, each service, each value, each portion of property, considered relatively, will, in passing from hand to hand, serve as the vehicle of an increasing proportion of common and gratuitous utility.

The reader will observe that we use the word Property in a very extended sense, but a sense that on that account is not the less exact. Property is the right a man possesses of applying to his own use his own efforts, or of not giving them away except in consideration of equivalent efforts. The distinction between Proprietors and Proletaires, then, is radically false, unless it is pretended that there is a class of men who do no work, who have no control over their own exertions, or over the services they render and those they receive in exchange.

It is wrong to restrict the term Property to one of its special forms, to capital, to land, to what yields interest or rent; and it is in consequence of this erroneous definition that we proceed afterwards to separate men into two antagonist classes. Analysis demonstrates that interest and rent are the fruit of services rendered, and have the same origin, the same nature, the same rights as manual labor.

The world may be regarded as a vast workshop that Providence has supplied abundantly with materials and forces of which human labor makes use. Anterior efforts, present efforts, even future efforts, or promises of efforts, are exchanged for each other. Their relative merit, as established by exchange, and independently of gratuitous forces and materials, brings out the element of value; and it is of the value created by each individual that each is owner or proprietor.

But what does it signify, it may be said, that a man is proprietor only of the value, or of the acknowledged merit of his service? The possession of the value carries along with it that of the utility that is mingled with it. John has two sacks of wheat. Peter has only one. John, you say, is twice as rich in value. Surely, then, he is also twice as rich in utility, even natural utility. He has twice as much to eat.

Unquestionably it is so; but has he not performed double the labor?

Let us come, nevertheless, to the root of the objection.

Essential, absolute wealth resides, as we have said, in utility. The very word implies this. It is utility alone that renders service (uti—in French, *servir*). It alone has relation to our wants, and it is it alone that man has in view when he devotes himself to labor. Utility at all events is the ultimate object of pursuit; for things do not satisfy our hunger or quench our thirst because they include value, but because they possess utility.

We must take into account, however, the phenomenon that society exhibits in this respect.

Man in a state of isolation seeks to realize utility without thinking about value, of which, in that state, he can have no idea.

In the social state, on the contrary, man seeks to realize value irrespective of utility. The commodity he produces is not intended to satisfy his own wants, and he has little interest in its being useful or not. It is for the person who desires to acquire it to judge of that. What concerns the producer is, that it should bear as high a value as possible in the market, as he is certain that the utilities he has to receive in return will be in proportion to the value of what he carries to it.

The division of labor and of occupations leads to this result, that each produces what he does not himself consume, and consumes what he does not himself produce. As producers, what we are in quest of is value; as consumers, what we seek is utility. Universal experience testifies to this. The man who polishes a diamond, or embroiders lace, or distills brandy, or cultivates the poppy, never inquires whether the consumption of these commodities is good or bad in itself. He gives his work, and if his work realizes value, that is enough for him.

And let me here remark in passing, that the moral or immoral has nothing to do with labor, but with desire; and that society is improved, not by rendering the producer, but the consumer, more moral. What an outcry was raised against the English on account of their cultivating opium in India for the deliberate purpose, it was said, of poisoning the Chinese! This was to misunderstand and misapply the principle of morality. No one will ever be effectually prevented from producing a commodity that, being in demand, is possessed of value. It is for the man who demands a particular species of enjoyment to calculate the effects of it; and it is in vain that we attempt to divorce foresight from responsibility. Our vine-growers produce wine, and will produce it as long at it possesses value, without troubling themselves to inquire whether this wine leads to drunkenness in Europe or to suicide in America. It is the judgment men form as to their wants and satisfactions that determines the direction of labor. This is true even of man in an isolated state; and if a foolish vanity had spoken more loudly to Robinson Crusoe than hunger, he would, in place of devoting his time to hunting, have employed it in arranging feathers for his hat. It is the same with nations as with individuals—serious people have serious pursuits, and frivolous people devote themselves to frivolous occupations.

But to return:

The man who works for himself has in view utility.

The man who works for others has in view value.

Now Property, as I have defined it, is founded on Value, and value being simply a relation, it follows that property is also a relation.

Were there only one man upon the earth, the idea of Property would never enter his mind. Monarch of all he surveyed, surrounded with utilities he had only to adapt to his use, never encountering any analogous right to serve as a limit to his own, how should it ever come into his head to say This is mine? That would imply the correlative assertion, This is not mine, or This belongs to another. Meum and tuum are inconsistent with isolation, and the word Property necessarily implies relation; but it gives us emphatically to understand that a thing is proper to one person, only by giving us to understand that it is not proper to anybody else.

"The first man," says Rousseau, "who having enclosed a field, took it into his head to say This is mine, was the true founder of civil society."

What does the enclosure mean if it be not indicative of exclusion, and consequently of relation? If its object were only to defend the field against the intrusion of animals, it was a precaution, not a sign of property. A boundary, on the contrary, is a mark of property, not of precaution.

Thus men are truly proprietors only in relation to one another; and this being so, of what are they proprietors? Of value, as we discover very clearly in the exchanges they make with each other.

Let us, according to our usual practice, take a very simple case by way of illustration.

Nature labors, and has done so probably from all eternity, to invest spring water with those qualities that fit it for quenching our thirst, and which qualities, so far as we are concerned, constitute its utility. It is assuredly not my work, for it has been elaborated without my assistance, and quite unknown to me. In this respect, I can truly say that water is to me the gratuitous gift of God. What is my own proper work is the effort I have made in going to fetch my supply of water for the day.

Of what do I become proprietor by that act?

As regards myself, I am proprietor, if I may use the expression, of all the utility with which nature has invested this water. I can turn it to my own use in any way I think proper. It is for that purpose that I have taken the trouble to fetch it. To dispute my right would be to say that, although men cannot live without drinking, they have no right to drink the water which they have procured by their own exertions. I do not believe that the Communists, although they go very far, will go the length of asserting this, and even under the regime of Cabet, the lambs of Icaria would be allowed to quench their thirst in the limpid stream.

But in relation to other men, who are free to do as I do, I am not, and cannot be, proprietor except of what is called, by metonymy, the value of the water, that is to say, the value of the service I render in procuring it.

My right to drink this water being granted, it is impossible to contest my right to give it away. And the right of the other contracting party to go to the spring, as I did, and draw water for himself, being admitted, it is equally impossible to contest his right to accept the water I have fetched. If the one has a right to give, and the other, in consideration of a payment voluntarily bargained for, to accept, this water, the first is then the proprietor in relation to the second. It is sad to write upon Political Economy at a time when we cannot advance a step without having recourse to demonstrations so puerile.

But on what basis is the arrangement we have supposed come to? It is essential to know this, in order to appreciate the whole social bearing of the word Property—a word that sounds so ill in the ears of democratic sentimentalism.

It is clear that, both parties being free, we must take into consideration the trouble I have had, and the trouble I have saved to the other party, as the circumstances that constitute value. We discuss the conditions of the bargain, and, if we come to terms, there is neither exaggeration nor subtlety in saying that my neighbor has acquired gratuitously, or, if you will, as gratuitously as I did, all the natural utility of the water. Do you desire proof that the conditions, more or less onerous, of the transaction are determined by the human efforts and not by the intrinsic utility? It will be granted that the utility remains the same whether the spring is distant or near at hand. It is the amount of exertion made, or to be made, which depends upon the distance; and since the remuneration varies with the exertion, it is in the latter, and not in the utility, that the principle of relative value and Property resides.

It is certain, then, that, in relation to others, I am, and can be, proprietor only of my efforts, of my services, that have nothing in common with the recondite and mysterious processes by which nature communicates utility to the things which are the subject of those services. It would be in vain for me to carry my pretensions farther—at this point we must always in fact encounter the limit of Property—for if I demand more than the value of my services, my neighbor will do the work for himself. This limit is absolute and unchangeable. It fully explains and vindicates Property, thus reduced to the natural and simple right of demanding one service for another.

It shows that the enjoyment of natural utility is appropriated only nominally and in appearance; that the expression Property in an acre of land, in a hundredweight of iron, in a quarter of wheat, in a yard of cloth, is truly a metonymy, like the expression, Value of water, of iron, and so forth; and that so far as nature has given these things to men, they enjoy them gratuitously and in common; in a word, that Community is in perfect harmony with Property, the gifts of God remaining in the domain of the one, and human services forming alone the very legitimate domain of the other.

But from my having chosen a very simple example in order to point out the line of demarcation that separates the domain of what is common from the domain of what has been appropriated, you are not to conclude that this line loses itself and disappears, even in the most complicated transactions. It continues always to show itself in every free transaction. The labor of going to fetch water from the spring is very simple no doubt; but when you examine the thing more narrowly, you will be convinced that the labor of raising wheat is only more complicated because it embraces a series of efforts quite as simple, in each of which the work of nature co-operates with that of man, so that in fact the example I have shown may be regarded as the type of every economical fact. Take the case of water, of wheat, of cloth, of books, of transport, of pictures, of the ballet, of the opera—in all, certain circumstances, I allow, may impart such value to certain services, but no one is ever paid for anything else than services—never certainly for the co-operation of nature—and the reason is obvious, because one of the contracting parties has it always in his power to say, If you demand from me more than your service is worth, I shall apply to another quarter, or do the work for myself.

But I am not content to vindicate Property: I should wish to make it an object of cherished affection even to the most determined Communists. And to accomplish this, all that is necessary is to describe the popular, progressive, and equalizing part it plays; and to demonstrate clearly, not only that it does not monopolize and concentrate in a few hands the gifts of God, but that its special mission is to enlarge continually the sphere of Community. In this respect the natural laws of society are much more ingenious than the artificial systems of Plato, Sir Thomas More, Fenelon, or Mr. Cabet.

That there are satisfactions that men enjoy, gratuitously and in common, upon a footing of the most perfect equality—that there is in the social order underlying Property, a real Community—no one will dispute. To see this it is not necessary that you should be either an Economist or a Socialist, but that you should have eyes in your head. In certain respects all the children of God are treated in precisely the same way. All are equal as regards the law of gravitation that attaches them to the earth, as regards the air we breathe, the light of day, the water of the brook. This vast and measureless common fund, which has nothing whatever to do with Value or Property, J.B. Say denominates natural wealth, in opposition to social wealth; Proudhon, natural property, in opposition to acquired property; Considerant, natural capital, in opposition to capital that is created; Saint-Chamans, the wealth of enjoyment, in opposition to the wealth of value. We have denominated it gratuitous utility, in contradistinction to onerous utility. Call it what you will, it exists, and that entitles us to say that there is among men a common fund of gratuitous and equal satisfactions.

And if wealth, social, acquired, created, of value, onerous, in a word, Property, is unequally distributed, we cannot affirm that it is unjustly so, seeing that it is in each man's case proportional to the services that give rise to it, and of which it is simply the measure and estimate. Besides, it is clear that this Inequality is lessened by the existence of the common fund, in virtue of the mathematical rule: the relative inequality of two unequal numbers is lessened by adding equal numbers to each of them. When our inventories, then, show that one man is twice as rich as another man, that proportion ceases to be exact when we take into consideration their equal share in the gratuitous utility furnished by nature, and the inequality would be gradually effaced and wiped away if the common fund were itself progressive.

The problem, then, is to find out whether this common fund is a fixed invariable quantity, given to mankind by Providence in the beginning, and once for all, above which the appropriated fund is superimposed, apart from the existence of any relation or action between these two orders of phenomena.

Economists have concluded that the social order had no influence upon this natural and common fund of wealth; and this is their reason for excluding it from the domain of Political Economy.

The Socialists go farther. They believe that the constitution of society tends to make this common fund pass into the region of Property, that it consecrates, to the profit of a few, the usurpation of what belongs to all; and this is the reason why they rise up against Political Economy, which denies this fatal tendency, and against modern society, which submits to it.

The truth is that Socialism, in this particular, accuses Political Economy of inconsistency, and with some justice too; for after having declared that there are no relations between common and appropriated wealth, Economists have invalidated their own assertion, and prepared the way for the socialist grievance. They did so the moment that, confounding value with utility, they asserted that the materials and forces of nature, that is to say, the gifts of God, had an intrinsic value, a value inherent in them—for value implies, always and necessarily, appropriation. From that moment they lost the right and the means of logically vindicating Property.

What I maintain—and maintain with a conviction amounting to absolute certainty—is this: that the appropriated fund exerts a constant action upon the fund that is common and unappropriated, and in this respect the first assertion of the Economists is erroneous. But the second assertion, as developed and explained by socialism, is still more fatal; for the action in question does not take place in a way to make the common fund pass into the appropriated fund but, on the contrary, to make the appropriated fund pass incessantly into the common domain. Property, just and legitimate in itself, because always representing services, tends to transform onerous, into gratuitous utility. It is the spur that urges on human intelligence to make latent natural forces operative. It struggles, and undoubtedly for our benefit, against the obstacles that render utility onerous. And when the obstacle has been to a certain extent removed, it is found that, to that extent, it has been removed to the profit and advantage of all. Then indefatigable Property challenges and encounters other obstacles, and goes on, raising, always and without intermission, the level of humanity, realizing more and more Community, and with Community, Equality, among the great family of mankind.

In this consists the truly marvelous Harmony of the natural social order. This harmony I am unable to describe without combating objections that are perpetually recurring, and without falling into wearisome repetitions. No matter, I submit—let the reader also exercise a little patience on his side.

Make yourself master, first of all, of this fundamental idea, that when, in any case, there is no obstacle between desire and satisfaction (there is none, for instance, between our eyes and the light of day)—there is no effort to make, no service to render, either to ourselves or to other people, and value and Property have no existence. When an obstacle exists, the whole series comes into play. First, we have Effort—then a voluntary exchange of efforts or Services—then a comparative evaluation of those services, or Value; lastly, the right of each to enjoy the utilities attached to these values, or Property.

If in this struggle against obstacles, which are always uniform, the co-operation of nature and that of labor were also always in equal proportion, Property and Community would advance in parallel lines, without changing their relative proportions.

But it is not so. The universal aim of men in all their enterprises is to diminish the proportion between effort and result, and for that purpose to enlist more and more in their work the assistance of natural agents. There is no agriculturist, manufacturer, merchant, artisan, shipowner, artist, but makes this his constant study. In that direction all their faculties are bent. For that purpose they invent tools and machines and avail themselves of the chemical and mechanical forces of the elements, divide their occupations, and unite their efforts. To accomplish more with less, such is the eternal problem they propose to themselves at all times, in all places, in all situations, in everything. Who doubts that in all this they are prompted by self-interest? What other stimulant could excite them to the same energy? Every man moreover is charged with the care of his own existence and advancement. What, then, should constitute the mainspring of his movements but self-interest? You express your astonishment, but wait till I am done, and you will find that if each cares for himself, God cares for us all.

Our constant study, then, is to diminish the proportion the effort bears to the useful effect sought to be produced. But when the effort is lessened, whether by the removal of obstacles or the intervention of machinery, by the division of labor, the union of forces, or the assistance of natural agents, etc., this diminished effort is less highly appreciated in relation to others—we render less service in making the effort for another. There is less value, and we are justified in saying that the domain of Property has receded. Is the useful effect on that account lost? By hypothesis it is not. Where then has it gone to? It has passed into the domain of Community. As regards that portion of human effort that the useful effect no longer absorbs, it is not on that account sterile—it is turned to other acquisitions. Obstacles present themselves, and will always present themselves, to the indefinite expansibility of our physical, moral, and intellectual wants, to an extent sufficient to ensure that the labor set free in one department will find employment in another. And it is in this way that the appropriated fund remaining always the same, the common fund dilates and expands, like a circle the radius of which is always enlarging.

Apart from this consideration, how could we explain progress or civilization, however imperfect? Let us turn our regards upon ourselves, and consider our feebleness. Let us compare our own individual vigor and knowledge with the vigor and knowledge necessary to produce the innumerable satisfactions we derive from society. We shall soon be convinced that were we reduced to our proper efforts, we could not obtain a hundred thousandth part of them, even if millions of acres of uncultivated land were placed at the disposal of each one of us. It is positively certain that a given amount of human effort will realize an immeasurably greater result at the present day than it could in the days of the Druids. If that were true only of an individual, the natural conclusion would be that he lives and prospers at the expense of his fellows. But since this phenomenon is manifested in all the members of the human family, we are led to the comfortable conclusion that things not our own have come to our aid; that the gratuitous cooperation of nature is in larger and larger measure added to our own efforts, and that it remains gratuitous through all our transactions; for were it not gratuitous, it would explain nothing.

From what we have said, we may deduce these formulas:

Property is Value, and Value is Property; That which has no Value is gratuitous, and what is gratuitous is common;

A fall of Value is an approximation toward the gratuitous;

Such approximation is a partial realization of Community.

There are times when one cannot give utterance to certain words without being exposed to false interpretations. There are always people ready to cry out in a critical or in a laudatory spirit according to the sect they belong to: "The author talks of Community—he must be a Communist." I expect this, and resign myself to it. And yet I must endeavor to guard myself against such hasty inferences.

The reader must have been very inattentive (and the most formidable class of readers are those who turn over books without attending to what they read) if he has not observed the great gulf that interposes itself between Community and Communism. The two ideas are separated by the entire domain not only of property, but of liberty, right, justice, and even of human personality.

Community applies to those things we enjoy in common by the destination of Providence; because, exacting no effort in order to adapt them to our use, they give rise to no service, no transaction, no Property. The foundation of property is the right we possess to render services to ourselves, or to others on condition of a return.

What Communism wishes to render common is, not the gratuitous gift of God, but human effort—service.

It desires that each man should carry the fruit of his labor to the common stock, and that afterwards an equitable distribution of that stock should be made by authority.

Now, of two things, one. Either the distribution is proportional to the stake each has contributed, or it is made upon another principle.

In the first case, Communism aims at realizing, as regards result, the present order of things—only substituting the arbitrary will of one for the liberty of all.

In the second case, what must be the basis of the division? Communism answers, Equality. What! Equality, without regard to the difference of pains taken, of labor undergone! You are to have an equal share whether you have worked six hours or twelve— mechanically, or with intelligence! Of all inequalities surely that would be the most shocking; besides it would be the destruction of all liberty, all activity, all dignity, all sagacity. You pretend to put an end to competition, but in truth you only transform it. The competition at present is, who shall work most and best. Under your regime it would be, who should work worst and least.

Communism misunderstands or disowns the very nature of man. Effort is painful in itself. What urges us to make it? It can only be a feeling more painful still, a want to satisfy, a suffering to remove, a good to be realized. Our moving principle, then, is self-interest. When you ask the Communists what they would substitute for this, they answer, by the mouth of Louis Blanc, The point of honor, and by that of Mr. Cabet, Fraternity. Enable me, then, to experience the sensations of others, in order that I may know what direction to impress upon my industry.

I should like to have it explained what this point of honor, this fraternity, which are to be set to work in society at the instigation and under the direction of Misters Louis Blanc and Cabet, really mean.

But it is not my business in this place to refute Communism, which is opposed in everything to the system that it is my object to establish.

We recognize the right of every man to serve himself, or to serve others on conditions freely stipulated. Communism denies this right, since it masses together and centralizes all services in the hands of an arbitrary authority.

Our doctrine is based upon Property. Communism is founded on systematic spoliation. It consists in handing over to one, without compensation, the labor of another. In fact if, it distributed to each according to his labor, it would recognize property, and would be no longer Communism.

Our doctrine is founded on liberty. In truth, property and liberty are in our eyes one and the same thing, for that which constitutes a man the proprietor of his service is his right and power of disposing of it. Communism annihilates liberty, since it leaves to no one the free disposal of his labor.

Our doctrine is founded on justice—Communism on injustice. That follows clearly from what has been already said.

There is only one point of contact, then, between the communists and us—it is similarity of two syllables, in the words communism and community.

But this similarity of sounds should not mislead the reader. While communism is the negation of Property, we find in our doctrine of Community the most explicit affirmation and the most positive demonstration of property.

If the legitimacy of property has appeared doubtful and inexplicable, even to men who are not communists, the reason is that they believe it concentrates in the hands of some, to the exclusion of others, those gifts of God that were originally common. We believe we have entirely dissipated that doubt by demonstrating that what is common by providential destination remains common in all human transactions—the domain of property never extending beyond that of value—of right onerously acquired by services rendered.

Thus explained, property is vindicated; for who but a fool could pretend that men have no right to their own labor—no right to receive the voluntary services of those to whom they have rendered voluntary services?

There is another word upon which I must offer some explanation, for of late it has been strangely misapplied—I mean the word gratuitous. I need not say that I denominate gratuitous, not what costs a man nothing because he has deprived another of it, but what has cost nothing to anyone.

When Diogenes warmed himself in the sun, he might be said to warm himself gratuitously, for he obtained from the divine liberality a satisfaction that exacted no labor either from himself or his contemporaries. Nor does the heat of the sun's rays cease to be gratuitous when the proprietor avails himself of it to ripen his wheat and his grapes, seeing that in selling his grapes or his wheat he is paid for his own services and not for those of the sun. This may be an erroneous view (in which case we have no alternative but to become communists); but at any rate this is the sense in which I use the word gratuitous, and this is what it evidently means.

Much has been said since the establishment of the Republic of gratuitous credit and gratuitous instruction. But it is evident that there is a serious fallacy in this word. Can the State shed abroad instruction like the light of day without its costing anything to anybody? Can it cover the country with institutions and professors without their being paid in one shape or another? Instead of leaving each individual to demand and to remunerate voluntarily this description of service, the State may lay hold of the remuneration, taken by taxation from the pockets of the citizens, and distribute among them instruction of its own selection, without exacting from them a second remuneration. This is all that can be effected by government interference—and in this case, those who do not learn pay for those who do, those who learn little for those who learn much, those who are destined to manual labor for those who embrace learned professions. This is Communism applied to one branch of human activity. Under this regime, of which I am not called upon here to give an opinion, it might very well be said that instruction is common, but it would be ridiculous to say that instruction is gratuitous. Gratuitous! Yes, for some of those who receive it, but not for those who have to pay for it, if not to the teacher, at least to the tax-gatherer.

For that matter, there is nothing the State can give gratuitously; and if the word were not a mystification, it is not only gratuitous education we should demand from the State, but gratuitous food, gratuitous clothing, gratuitous lodging, etc. Let us take care. The people are not far from going this length, and there are already among us those who demand gratuitous credit, gratuitous tools, and instruments of labor, etc. Dupes of a word, we have made one step toward Communism; why should we not make a second, and a third, until all liberty, all justice, and all property have passed away? Will it be urged that instruction is so universally necessary that we may depart somewhat from right and principle in this instance? But then, are not food and sustenance still more necessary than education? *Primo vivere, deinde philosophari*, the people may say; and I know not in truth what answer we can make to them.

Who knows? Those who charge me with Communism for having demonstrated the natural community of the gifts of God are perhaps the very people who seek to violate justice in the matter of education, that is to say, to attack property in its essence. Such inconsistencies are more surprising than uncommon.

9

LANDED PROPERTY

If the leading idea of this work is well founded, the relations of mankind with the external world must be viewed in this way:

God created the earth. On it, and within it, he has placed a multitude of things that are useful to man, inasmuch as they are adapted to satisfy his wants.

God has, besides, endowed matter with forces—gravitation, elasticity, porosity, compressibility, heat, light, electricity, crystallization, vegetable life.

He has placed man in the midst of these materials and forces, which he has delivered over to him gratuitously.

Men set themselves to exercise their activity upon these materials and forces; and in this way they render service to themselves. They also work for one another, and in this way render reciprocal services. These services, compared by the act of exchange, give rise to the idea of Value, and Value to that of Property.

Each man, then, becomes an owner or proprietor in proportion to the services he has rendered. But the materials and forces given by God to man gratuitously, at the beginning, have continued gratuitous, and are and must continue to be so through all our transactions; for in the estimates and appreciations to which exchange gives rise, the equivalents are human services, not the gifts of God.

Hence it follows that no human being, so long as transactions are free, can ever cease to be the beneficiary of these gifts. A single condition is laid down, which is that we shall execute the labor necessary to make them available to us, or, if any one makes this exertion for us, that we make for him an equivalent exertion.

If this account of the matter be true, Property is indeed unassailable.

The universal instinct of mankind, more infallible than the ponderings of any individual, had adopted this view of the subject without refining upon it, when theory began to scrutinize the foundations of Property.

Theory unhappily began in confusion, mistaking Utility for Value, and attributing an inherent value, independent of all human service, to the materials or forces of nature. From that moment property became unintelligible, and incapable of justification.

For utility is the relation between commodities and our preferences. It necessarily implies neither efforts nor transactions nor comparisons. We can conceive of it *per se*, and in relation to man in a state of isolation. Value, on the contrary, is a relation of man to man. To exist at all, it must exist in duplicate. Nothing isolated can be compared. Value implies that the person in possession of it does not transfer it except for an equivalent value. The theory, then, that confounds these two ideas, takes for granted that a person, in effecting an exchange, gives pretended value of natural creation for true value of human creation, utility that exacts no labor for utility that does exact it; in other words, that he can profit by the labor of another without working himself. Property, thus understood is called first of all a necessary monopoly, then simply a monopoly—then it is branded as illegitimate, and last of all as robbery.

Landed Property receives the first blow, and so it should. Not that natural agents do not bear their part in all manufactures, but these agents manifest themselves more strikingly to the eyes of the masses in the phenomena of vegetable and animal life, in the production of food, and of what are improperly called *matieres premieres* (raw materials), which are the special products of agriculture.

Besides, if there be any one monopoly more revolting than another, it is undoubtedly a monopoly that applies to the first necessities of life.

The confusion that I am exposing, and that is specious in a scientific view, since no theorist I am acquainted with has got rid of it, becomes still more specious when we look at what is passing around us.

We see the landed Proprietor frequently living without labor, and we draw the conclusion, which is plausible enough, that "he must surely be remunerated for something else than his work." And what can this something else be, if not the fecundity, the productiveness, the co-operation of the soil as an instrument? It is, then, the rent of land that we must brand, in the language of the times, with names of necessary monopoly, privilege, illegitimacy, theft.

We must admit that the authors of this theory have encountered a fact that must have powerfully tended to mislead them. Few land estates in Europe have escaped from conquest and all its attendant abuses; and science has confounded the violent methods by which landed property has been acquired with the methods by which it is naturally formed.

But we must not imagine that the false definition of the word value tends only to unsettle landed property. Logic is a terrible and indefatigable power, whether it sets out with a good or a bad principle! As the earth, it is said, makes light, heat, electricity, vegetable life, etc., co-operate in the production of value, does not capital in the same way make gravitation, elasticity, the wind, etc., concur in producing value? There are other men, then, besides agriculturists who are paid for the intervention of natural agents.

This remuneration comes to capitalists in the shape of Interest, just as it comes to proprietors in the shape of Rent. War, then, must be declared against Interest as it has been against Rent!

Property has had a succession of blows aimed at it in the name of this principle, which I think false, but true according to the Economists and Egalitaires, namely, that natural agents possess or create value. This is a postulate upon which all schools are agreed. They differ only in the boldness or timidity of their deductions.

The Economists say that property (in land) is a monopoly, but a monopoly that is necessary, and which must be maintained.

The Socialists say that property (in land) is a monopoly, but a monopoly that is necessary, and that must be maintained—and they demand compensation for it in the shape of right to employment (*le droit au travail*).

The Communists and Egalitaires say that property (in general) is a monopoly, and must be destroyed.

For myself, I say most emphatically that PROPERTY IS NOT A MONOPOLY. Your premises are false, and your three conclusions, although they differ, are false also. PROPERTY IS NOT A MONOPOLY, and consequently it is not incumbent on us either to tolerate it by way of favor, or to demand compensation for it, or to destroy it.

Let us pass briefly in review the opinions of writers of various schools on this important subject.

The English Economists lay down this principle, upon which they appear to be unanimous, that value comes from labor. Were they consistent in their use of terms, it might be so; but are they consistent? The reader will judge. He will see whether they do not always and everywhere confound gratuitous Utility, which is incapable of remuneration, and devoid of value, with onerous Utility, which we owe exclusively to labor, and which according to them is alone possessed of value.

ADAM SMITH. "In agriculture nature labors with man; and although her labor costs no expense, its produce has its value, as well as that of the most expensive workmen."

Here we have nature producing value. The purchaser of corn must pay for it, although it has cost nothing to anybody, not even labor. Who then dares come forward to demand this pretended value? Substitute for that word the word utility, and all becomes clear, Property is vindicated, and justice satisfied.

"This rent," proceeds Smith, "may be considered as the produce of those powers of nature, the use of which the landlord lends to the farmer. . . . It (rent!) is the work of nature, which remains after deducting or compensating everything that can be regarded as the work of man. It is seldom less than a fourth, and frequently more than a third of the whole produce. No equal quantity of productive labor employed in manufactures can ever occasion so great a reproduction. In them nature does nothing; man does all."[1]

Is it possible in as few words to include a greater number of dangerous errors? At this rate a fourth or a third part of the value of human subsistence is due exclusively to the power of nature. And yet the proprietor is paid by the farmer, and the farmer by the wheat consumer, for this pretended value that remains after the work of man has been remunerated. And this is the basis on which it is desired to place Property! And, then, what becomes of the axiom that all value comes from labor?

Next, we have nature doing nothing in manufactures! Do gravitation, the elasticity of the air, and animal force, not aid the manufacturer? These forces act in our manufactures just as they act in our fields; they produce gratuitously not value, but utility. Were it otherwise, property in capital would be as much exposed to the attacks of Communism as property in land.

BUCHANAN. This commentator, adopting the theory of his master on Rent, is pressed by logic to blame him for having represented it as advantageous:

---

[1]*Wealth of Nations* (Buchanan's 2nd edition), vol. 2, pp. 53 and 54.

"In dwelling on the reproduction of rent as so great an advantage to society, Smith does not reflect that rent is the effect of high price, and that what the landlord gains in this way, he gains at the expense of the community at large. There is no absolute gain to society by the reproduction of rent. It is only one class profiting at the expense of another class."[2]

Here the logical deduction makes its appearance—rent is an injustice.

RICARDO. "Rent is that portion of the produce of the earth which is paid to the landlord for the use of the original and indestructible powers of the soil."

And, in order that there may be no mistake, the author adds:

"It is often confounded with the interest and profit of capital. . . . It is evident that a portion only of the money annually to be paid for the improved farm would be given for the original and indestructible powers of the soil, the other portion would be paid for the use of the capital which had been employed in ameliorating the quality of the land, and in erecting such buildings as were necessary to secure and preserve the produce. . . . In the future pages of this work, then, whenever I speak of the rent of the land, I wish to be understood as speaking of that compensation which is paid to the owner of land for the use of its original and indestructible powers."[3]

M'CULLOCH. What is properly termed Rent is the sum paid for the use of the natural and inherent powers of the soil. It is entirely distinct from the sum paid for the use of buildings, enclosures, roads, or other ameliorations. Rent is then always a monopoly."

SCROPE. "The value of land, and its power of yielding Rent, are due to two circumstances—first, the appropriation of its natural powers; second, the labor applied to its amelioration."

We are not kept long waiting for the consequences:

---

[2]Ibid., p. 55, note.
[3]Ricardo's *Political Works* (M'Culloch's edition), pp. 34, 35.

"Under the first of these relations rent is a monopoly. It restricts our usufruct and enjoyment of the gifts which God has given to men for the satisfaction of their wants. This restriction is just, only in as far as it is necessary for the common good."

In what perplexity must those good souls be landed who refuse to admit anything to be necessary which is not just?

Scrope ends with these words:

"When it goes beyond this point, it must be modified on the same principle which caused it to be established."

It is impossible for the reader not to perceive that these authors lead us to a negation of Property, and lead us to it very logically, in setting out with the proposition that the proprietor is paid for the gifts of God. Here we have rent held up as an injustice established by Law under the pressure of necessity, and that laws may modify or destroy under the pressure of another necessity. The Communists have never gone farther than this.

SENIOR. "The instruments of production are labor and natural agents. Natural agents having been appropriated, proprietors charge for their use under the form of Rent, which is the recompense of no sacrifice whatever, and is received by those who have neither labored nor put by, but who merely hold out their hands to accept the offerings of the rest of the community."

After giving this heavy blow to property, Mr. Senior explains that one portion of Rent resolves itself into the Interest of Capital, and then adds:

"The surplus is taken by the proprietor of the natural agent, and is his reward, not for having labored or abstained, but simply for not having withheld what he was able to withhold; for having permitted the gifts of nature to be accepted."

You will observe that this is still the same theory. The proprietor is supposed to interpose himself between the hungry mouth and the food that God has vouchsafed under the condition of labor. The proprietor who has co-operated in the work of production, charges first of all for his co-operation, which is just, and then he makes a second charge for the work of nature, for the use of natural agents, for the indestructible powers of the soil, which is iniquitous.

This theory of the English Economists, which has been farther developed by Mill, Malthus, and others, we are sorry to find making its way also on the Continent.

"When a franc's worth of seed," says SCIALOJA, "produces a hundred francs' worth of wheat, this augmentation of value is mainly due to the soil."

This is to confound Utility with value. He might just as well have said, when water that costs only one sou at ten yards distance from the spring, costs ten sous at 100 yards, this augmentation of value is due in part to the intervention of nature.

FLOREZ ESTRADA. "Rent is that portion of the agricultural product which remains after all the costs of production have been defrayed."

Then the proprietor receives something for nothing.

The English Economists all set out by announcing the principle that value comes from labor, and they are guilty of inconsistency when they afterwards attribute value to the inherent powers of the soil.

The French Economists in general make value to consist in utility; but, confounding gratuitous with onerous utility, they have not the less assisted in shaking the foundation of Property.

J.B. SAY. "Land is not the only natural agent which is productive, but it is the only one, or almost the only one, that man has been able to appropriate. The waters of the sea and of our rivers, by their aptitude to impart motion to machines, to afford nourishment to fishes, to float our ships, are likewise possessed of productive power. The wind and the sun's rays work for us; but happily no one has been able to say, The wind and the sun are mine, and I must be paid for their services."

Mr. Say appears from this to lament that anyone should be able to say, The land belongs to me, and I must be paid for the service it renders. Happily, say I, it is no more in the power of the proprietor to charge for the services of the soil than for the services of the sun and the wind.

"The earth," continues Mr. Say, "is an admirable chemical workshop, in which are combined and elaborated a multitude of materials and elements which are produced in the shape of grain, fruit, flax, etc. Nature has presented to man, gratuitously, this vast workshop divided into a great number of compartments fitted for various kinds of production. But certain individual members of society have appropriated them, and proclaimed—This compartment is mine—that other is mine, and all that is produced in it is my exclusive property. And the astonishing thing is, that this usurped privilege, far from having been fatal to the community, has been found productive of advantage to it."

Undoubtedly this arrangement has been advantageous; but why? Just because it is neither a privilege nor usurped, and that the man who exclaims, "This domain is mine," has not had it in his power to add, "What has been produced on it is my exclusive property." On the contrary, he says, "What has been produced is the exclusive property of whoever desires to purchase it, by giving me back simply the same amount of labor which I have undergone, and which in this instance I have saved his undergoing." The co-operation of nature in the work of production, which is gratuitous for me, is gratuitous for him also.

Mr. Say indeed distinguishes in the value of wheat, the parts contributed by Property, by Capital, and by labor. He has with the best intention been at great pains to justify this first part of the remuneration that accrues to the proprietor, and that is the recompense of no labor, either anterior or present; but he fails; for, like Scrope, he is obliged to fall back on the last and least satisfactory of all grounds of vindication, necessity.

"If it be impossible," he remarks, "for production to be effected, not only without land and without capital, but without these means of production previously becoming property, may it not be said that proprietors of land and capital exercise a productive function, since, without the employment of these means, production would not take place?—a convenient function no doubt, but which, in the present state of society, presupposes accumulation, which is the result of production or saving," etc.

The confusion here is palpable. The accumulation has been effected by the proprietor in his character of Capitalist—a character with which at present we have no concern. But what Mr. Say represents as convenient is the part played by the proprietor, in his proper character of proprietor, exacting a price for the gifts of God. It is this part that it is necessary to vindicate, and it has no connection with either accumulation or saving.

"If, then, property in land and in capital" (why equate the two?) "be the fruit of production, I am warranted in representing such property as a working and productive machine, for which its author, although sitting with his hands folded, is entitled to exact a recompense."

Still the same confusion. The man who constructs a machine is proprietor of a capital, from which he legitimately derives an income, because he is paid, not for the labor of the machine, but for his own labor in constructing it. But land, or territorial property, is not the result of human production. What right, then, have we to be paid for its co-operation? The author has here mixed up two different kinds of property in the same category, in order that the same reasons that justify the one may serve for the vindication of the other.

BLANQUI. "The agriculturist who tills, manures, sows, and reaps his field, furnishes labor, without which nothing would be produced. But the action of the soil in making the seed germinate, and of the sun in bringing the plant to maturity, are independent of that labor, and co-operate in the formation of the value represented by the harvest . . . Smith and other Economists pretend that the labor of man is the exclusive source of value. Assuredly the industry of the laborer is not the exclusive source of the value of a sack of wheat or a bushel of potatoes. His skill can no more succeed in producing the phenomenon of germination than the patience of the alchemist could succeed in discovering the philosopher's stone. This is evident."

It is impossible to imagine a more complete confusion than we have here, first between utility and value, and then between onerous and gratuitous utility.

JOSEPH GARNIER. "The rent of the proprietor differs essentially from the wages of the laborer and the profits of the capitalist, inasmuch as these two kinds of remuneration are the recompense, the one of trouble or pains taken, the other of a privation submitted to, and a risk encountered, whilst Rent is received by the proprietor gratuitously, and in virtue alone of a legal convention which recognizes and maintains in certain individuals the right to landed property."[4] In other words, the laborer and capitalist are paid, in the name of equity, for the services they render; and the proprietor is paid, in the name of law, for services that he does not render.

"The boldest innovators do not go farther than to propose the substitution of collective for individual property. It seems to us that they have reason on their side as regards human right; but they are wrong practically, inasmuch as they are unable to exhibit the advantages of a better Economical system."[5]

"But at the same time, in avowing that property is a privilege, a monopoly, we must add, that it is a natural and a useful monopoly. . . .

"In short, it seems to be admitted by Political Economy" (it is so, alas! and here lies the evil) "that property does not flow from divine right, demesnial right, or any other speculative right, but simply from its utility. It is only a monopoly tolerated in the interest of all," etc.

This is precisely the judgment pronounced by Scrope, and repeated in modified terms by Say.

I think I have now satisfactorily shown that Political Economy, setting out with the false datum, that "natural agents possess or create value," has arrived at this conclusion, "that property (in as far as it appropriates and is remunerated for this value, which is independent of all human service) is a privilege, a monopoly, a usurpation; but that it is a necessary monopoly, and must be maintained."

---

[4]*Elements de l'Economie Politique*, 2nd edition, p. 293.

[5]Ibid, pp. 377, 378.

It remains for me to show that the Socialists set out with the same postulate, only they modify the conclusion in this way: "Property is a necessary monopoly; it must be maintained, but we must demand, from those who have property, compensation to those who have none, in the shape of Right to Employment."

I shall, then, dispose of the doctrine of the Communists who, arguing from the same premises, conclude that "Property is a monopoly, and ought to be abolished."

Finally, and at the risk of repetition, I shall, if I can, expose the fallacy of the premises on which all the three conclusions are based, namely, that natural agents possess or create value. If I succeed in this, if I demonstrate that natural agents, even when appropriated, produce, not Value, but Utility, which, passing from the hands of the proprietor without leaving anything behind it, reaches the consumer gratuitously—in that case, all—Economists, Socialists, Communists—must at length come to a common understanding to leave the world, in this respect, just as it is.

Mr. CONSIDERANT. "In order to discover how and under what conditions private property may Legitimately manifest and develop itself we must get possession of the fundamental principle of the Right of Property; and here it is;

"Every man POSSESSES LEGITIMATELY THE THINGS which have been CREATED by his labor, his intelligence, or, to speak more generally, BY HIS ACTIVITY.[6]

"This Principle is incontestable, and it is right to remark that it contains implicitly the acknowledgment of the Right of all to the Soil. The earth not having been created by man, it follows in fact, from the fundamental principle of Property, that the Soil, which is a common fund given over to the species, can in no shape legitimately become the absolute and exclusive property of this or that individual who has not created this value. Let us establish, then, the true Theory of Property, by basing it exclusively on the unexceptionable principle which makes the legitimacy of

---

[6]The words in CAPITALS are thus printed in the original text.

Property hinge upon the fact of the CREATION of the thing, or of the value possessed. To accomplish this we must direct our reasoning to the origin of industry, that is to say, to the origin and development of agriculture, manufactures, the arts, etc., in human society.

"Suppose that on a solitary island, on the territory of a nation, or on the entire surface of the earth (for the extent of the field of action makes no difference in our estimate of facts), a generation of mankind devotes itself for the first time to industry—for the first time engages in agriculture, manufactures, etc. Each generation, by its labor, by its intelligence, by the exertion of its own proper activity, creates products, develops value, which did not exist on the earth in its rude and primitive state. Is it not perfectly evident that, among the first generation of laborers, Property would conform to Right, PROVIDED the value or wealth produced by the activity of all were distributed among the producers in PROPORTION TO THE COOPERATION of each in the creation of the general riches? That is beyond dispute.

"Now, the results of the labor of this generation may be divided into two categories, which it is important to distinguish.

"The first category includes the products of the soil, which belong to this first generation in its character of usufructuary, as having been increased, refined, or manufactured by its labor, by its industry. These products, whether raw or manufactured, consist either of objects of consumption or of instruments of labor. It is clear that these products belong, in entire and legitimate property, to those who have created them by their activity. Each of them, then, has RIGHT, either to consume these products immediately, to store them up to be disposed of afterwards at pleasure, or to employ them, exchange them, give them away, or transmit them to any one he chooses, without receiving authority from anyone. On this hypothesis, this Property is evidently Legitimate, respectable, sacred. We cannot assail it without assailing Justice, Right, individual liberty—without, in short, being guilty of Spoliation.

"Second category. But the creations attributable to the industrious activity of this first generation are not all included in the preceding category. This generation has created not only the products which we have just described (objects of consumption and instruments of labor)—it has also added an additional value to the primitive value of the soil, by cultivation, by erections, by the permanent improvements which it has executed.

"This additional value constitutes evidently a product, a value, due to the activity of the first generation. Now, if by any means (we are not concerned at present with the question of means)—if by any means whatever the property of this additional value is equitably distributed among the different members of society, that is to say, is distributed among them proportionally to the co-operation of each in its creation, each will possess legitimately the portion which has fallen to him. He may, then, dispose of this individual Property, legitimate as he sees it to be, exchange it, give it away, or transmit it without control, society having over these values no right or power whatsoever.

"We may, therefore, easily conceive that when the second generation makes its appearance, it will find upon the land two sorts of Capital: first, The primitive or natural capital, which has not been created by the men of the first generation—that is, the value of the land in its rough, uncultivated state.

"Second, The capital created by the first generation; including (1.) the products, commodities, and instruments, which shall not have been consumed or used by the first generation; (2.) the additional value which the labor of the first generation has added to the value of the rough, uncultivated land.

"It is evident, then, and results clearly and necessarily from the fundamental principle of the Right of Property, which I have just explained, that each individual of the second generation has an equal right to the primitive or natural capital, whilst he has no right to the other species of capital which has been created by the labor of the first generation. Each individual of the first generation may, then, dispose of his share of this created capital in favor of whatever individual of the second generation he may please to select, children, friends, etc.; and no one, not even the State itself, as we have just seen, has the slightest right (on pretense of Property) to control the disposal which, as donor or testator, he may have made of such capital.

"Observe that on this hypothesis the man of the second generation is already in a better situation than the man of the first, seeing that, besides his right to the primitive capital, which is preserved to him, he has his chance of receiving a portion of the created capital, that is to say, of a value which he has not produced, and which represents anterior labor.

If, then, we suppose things to be arranged in society in such a way that,

"First, The right to the primitive capital, that is, the usufruct of the soil in its natural state, is preserved, or that an EQUIV-ALENT RIGHT is conferred on every individual born within the territory;

"Second, That the created capital is continually distributed among men, as it is produced, in proportion to the co-operation of each in the production of that capital;

"If, we say, the mechanism of the social organization shall satisfy these two conditions, PROPERTY, under such a regime, would be established IN ITS ABSOLUTE LEGITIMACY, and Fact would be in unison with Right."[7]

We see here that the socialist author distinguishes between two kinds of value, created value that is the subject of legitimate property, and uncreated value that he denominates the value of land in its natural state, primitive capital, natural capital, which cannot become individual property but by usurpation. Now, according to the theory I am anxious to establish, the ideas expressed by the words uncreated, primitive, natural, exclude radically these other ideas, value, capital. This is the error in Mr. Considerant's premises, by which he is landed in this melancholy conclusion:

"That, under the regime of Property, in all civilized nations, the common fund, over which the entire species has a full right of usufruct, has been invaded—has been confiscated—by the few, to

---

[7]*Theorie du droit de propriete et du droit au travail,* 3rd Edition, p. 17.)

the exclusion of the many. Why, were even a single human being excluded from his Right to the Usufruct of this common fund, that very exclusion would of itself constitute an attack upon Right by the institution of Property, and that institution, by sanctioning such invasion of right, would be unjust and illegitimate."

Mr. Considerant, however, acknowledges that the earth could not be cultivated but for the institution of individual property. Here, then, is a necessary monopoly. What can we do, then, to reconcile all, and preserve the rights that the proletaires, or men of no property, have to the primitive, natural, uncreated capital, and to the value of the land in its rough and uncultivated state?

"Why, let Society, which has taken possession of the land, and taken away from man the power of exercising, freely and at will, his four natural rights on the surface of the soil—let this industrious society cede to the individual, in compensation for the rights of which it has deprived him, the Right to Employment."

Now, nothing in the world is clearer than that this theory, except the conclusion it seeks to establish, is exactly the theory of the Economists. The man who purchases an agricultural product remunerates three things: first, the actual labor—nothing more legitimate; second, the additional value imparted to the soil by anterior labor—still nothing more legitimate; third, and lastly, the primitive, or natural, or uncreated capital—that gratuitous gift of God, which Mr. Considerant denominates the value of the land in its rough and natural state; Adam Smith, the indestructible powers of the soil; Ricardo, the productive and indestructible powers of the land; Say, natural agents. This is the part that has been usurped, according to Mr. Considerant; this is what has been usurped, according to J.B. Say. It is this that constitutes legitimacy and spoliation in the eyes of the Socialists; that constitutes monopoly and privilege in the eyes of the Economists. They are at one as to the necessity and the utility of this arrangement. Without it the earth would produce nothing, say the disciples of Smith; without it we should return to the savage state, re-echo the disciples of Fourier.

---

[8]Ibid.

We find that in theory, and as regards right (at least with reference to this important question) the understanding between the two schools is much more cordial than we should have imagined. They differ only as to the legislative consequences to be deduced from the fact on which they agree. "Seeing that property is tainted with illegitimacy, inasmuch as it assigns to the proprietor a part of the remuneration to which he has no right; and seeing, at the same time, that it is necessary, let us respect it, but demand indemnities." "No," say the Economists, "although it is a monopoly, yet seeing that it is a necessary monopoly, let us respect it, and let it alone." And yet they urge this weak defense but feebly; for one of their latest organs, Mr. J. Garnier, adds, "You have reason on your side, as regards human right, but you are wrong practically, inasmuch as you have failed to point out the effects of a better system." To which the Socialists immediately reply, "We have found it; it is the Right to Employment—try it."

In the meantime, Mr. Proudhon steps in. You imagine, perhaps, that this redoubtable objector is about to question the premises on which the Economists and Socialists ground their agreement. Not at all. He can demolish Property without that. He appropriates the premises, grasps them, closes with them, and most logically deduces his conclusion. "You grant," he says, "that the gifts of God are possessed not only of utility but of value, and that these gifts the proprietor usurps and sells. Then Property is theft; and it is not necessary to maintain it; it is not necessary to demand compensation for it; what is necessary is to abolish it."

Mr. Proudhon has brought forward many arguments against landed Property. The most formidable one—indeed the only formidable one—is that with which these authors have furnished him, by confounding utility with value.

"Who has the right," he asks, "to charge for the use of the soil—for that wealth which does not proceed from man's act? Who is entitled to the rent of land? The producer of the land, without doubt. Who made it? God. Then, proprietor, begone.

"But the Creator of the earth does not sell it—he gives it; and in giving it he shows no respect of persons. Why, then, among all his children, are some treated as eldest sons, and some as bastards? If equality of inheritance be our original right, why should our posthumous right be inequality of conditions?"

Replying to J.B. Say, who had compared land to an instrument, he says:

"I grant it, that land is an instrument; but who is the workman? Is it the proprietor? Is it he who, by the efficacious virtue of the right of property, communicates to it vigor and fertility? It is precisely here that we discover in what consists the monopoly of the proprietor—he did not make the instrument, and he charges for its use. Were the Creator to present Himself and demand the rent of land, we must account for it to Him; but the proprietor, who represents himself as invested with the same power, ought to exhibit his procuration."

That is evident. The three systems in reality make only one. Economists, Socialists, Egalitaires, all direct against landed proprietors the same reproach, that of charging for what they have no right to charge for. This wrong some call monopoly, some illegitimacy, others theft—these are but different phases of the same complaint.

Now I would appeal to every intelligent reader whether this complaint is or is not well founded? Have I not demonstrated that there is but one thing that comes between the gifts of God and the hungry mouth, namely, human service?

Economists say, that "Rent is what we pay to the proprietor for the use of the productive and indestructible powers of the soil." I say, No—Rent is like what we pay to the water carrier for the pains he has taken to construct his barrow, and the water would cost us more if he had carried it on his back. In the same way, wheat, flax, wool, timber, meat, fruits, would have cost us more if the proprietor had not previously improved the instrument that furnishes them.

Socialists assert that "originally the masses enjoyed their right to the land on condition of labor, but that now they are excluded and robbed of their natural patrimony." I answer, No—they are neither excluded nor robbed—they enjoy, gratuitously, the utility contributed by the soil on condition of labor, that is to say, by repaying that labor to those who have saved it to them.

Egalitarians allege that "the monopoly of the proprietor consists in this, that not having made the instrument, he yet charges for its use." I answer, No—the land-instrument, so far as it is the work of God, produces utility, and that utility is gratuitous; it is beyond the power of the proprietor to charge for it. The land-instrument, so far as it is prepared by the proprietor—so far as he has worked it, enclosed it, drained it, improved it, and furnished it with other necessary instruments, produces value, and that value represents actual human services, and for these alone is the proprietor paid. You must either admit the legitimacy of this demand, or reject your own principle—the mutuality of services.

In order to satisfy ourselves as to the true elements of the value of land, let us attend to the way in which landed property is formed—not by conquest and violence, but according to the laws of labor and exchange. Let us see what takes place in the United States.

Brother Jonathan, a hard-working water carrier of New York, set out for the Far west, carrying in his purse a thousand dollars, the fruit of his labor and frugality.

He journeyed across many fertile provinces where the soil, the sun, and the rain worked wonders, but which nevertheless were entirely devoid of value in the economical and practical sense of the word.

Being a little of a philosopher, he said to himself, "Let Adam Smith and Ricardo say what they will, value must be something else than the natural and indestructible productive power of the soil."

At length, having reached the State of Arkansas, he found a beautiful property of about 100 acres, which the government had advertised for sale at the price of a dollar an acre.

A dollar an acre! he said—that is very little, almost nothing. I shall purchase this land, clear it, and sell the produce, and the drawer of water shall become a lord of the soil!

Brother Jonathan, being a merciless logician, liked to have a reason for everything. He said to himself, But why is this land worth even a dollar an acre? No one has yet put a spade in it, or has bestowed on it the least labor. Can Smith and Ricardo, and the whole string of theorists down to Proudhon, be right after all? Can land have a value independent of all labor, all service, all human intervention? Must I admit that the productive and indestructible powers of the soil have value? In that case, why should they have no value in the countries through which I have passed? And besides, since the powers of the soil surpass so enormously the powers of men, which, as Blanqui well remarks, can never go the length of creating the phenomena of germination, why should these marvelous powers be worth no more than a dollar?

But he was not long in perceiving that this value, like all other values, is of human and social creation. The American government demanded a dollar for the concession of each acre; but, on the other hand, it undertook to guarantee to a certain extent the security of the acquirer; it had formed in a rough way a road to the neighborhood, facilitated the transmission of letters and newspapers, etc. Service for service, said Jonathan—the government makes me pay a dollar, but it gives me an adequate equivalent. With deference to Ricardo, I can now account naturally for the value of this land, which value would be still greater if the road were extended and improved, the post more frequent and regular, and the protection more efficacious and secure.

While Jonathan argued, he worked; for we must do him the justice to say that he always made thinking and acting keep pace.

He expended the remainder of his dollars in buildings, enclosures, clearances, trenching, draining, improving, etc.; and after having dug, labored, sowed, harrowed, reaped, at length came the time to dispose of his crop. "Now I shall see," said Jonathan, still occupied with the problem of value, "if in becoming a landed proprietor I have transformed myself into a monopolist, a privileged aristocrat, a plunderer of my neighbor, an engrosser of the bounties of divine Providence."

He carried his grain to market, and began to talk with a Yankee—Friend, said he, how much will you give me for this Indian corn?

The current price, replied the other.

The current price! but will that yield me anything beyond the interest of my capital and the wages of my labor?

I am a merchant, said the Yankee, and I know that I must content myself with the recompense of my present and former labor.

And I was content with it when I was a mere drawer of water, replied the other, but now I am a landed proprietor. The English and French Economists have assured me that in that character I ought, over and above the double remuneration you point at, to derive a profit from the productive and indestructible power of the soil, and levy a tax on the gifts of God.

The gifts of God belong to all, said the merchant. I avail myself of the productive power of the wind for propelling my ships, but I make no one pay for it.

Still, as far as I am concerned, I expect that you will pay me something for these powers in order that Messieurs Senior, Considerant, and Proudhon should not call me a monopolist and usurper for nothing. If I am to have the disgrace, I may at least have the profit of a monopolist.

In that case, friend, I must bid you good-morning. To obtain the maize I am in quest of, I must apply to other proprietors, and if I find them of your mind, I shall cultivate it for myself.

Jonathan then understood the truth that, under the empire of freedom, a man cannot be a monopolist at pleasure. As long as there are lands in the Union to clear, said he, I can never be more than the simple setter in motion of these famous productive and indestructible forces. I shall be paid for my trouble, that is all, just as when I was a drawer of water I was paid for my own labor, and not for that of nature. I see now very clearly that the true usufructuary of the gifts of God is not the man who raises the corn, but the man who consumes it.

Some years afterward, another enterprise having engaged the attention of Jonathan, he set about finding a tenant for his land.

The dialogue that took place between the two contracting parties was curious, and would throw much light on the subject under consideration were I to quote it in full.

Here is part of it:

Proprietor. What! you would give me no greater rent than the interest, at the current rate, of the capital I have actually laid out?

Farmer. Not a cent more.

Proprietor. Why so, pray?

Farmer. Just for this reason, that, with the outlay of an equal capital, I can put as much land in as good condition as yours.

Proprietor. That seems conclusive. But consider that when you become my tenant, it is not my capital that will work for you, but also the productive and indestructible powers of the soil. You will have enlisted in your service the marvelous influences of the sun and the moon, of magnetism and electricity. Am I to give you all these things for nothing?

Farmer. Why not, since they cost you nothing, and since you derive nothing from them, any more than I do?

Proprietor. Derive nothing from them? I derive everything from them. Zounds! without these admirable phenomena, all my industry could not raise a blade of grass.

Farmer. Undoubtedly. But remember the Yankee you met at market. He would not give you a farthing for all this co-operation of nature any more than, when you were a water carrier, the housewives of New York would give you a farthing for the admirable elaboration by means of which nature supplied the spring.

Proprietor. Ricardo and Proudhon, however . . .

Farmer. A fig for Ricardo. We must either treat on the basis which I have laid down, or I shall proceed to clear land alongside yours, where the sun and the moon will work for me gratis.

It was always the same argument, and Jonathan began to see that God had wisely arranged so as to make it difficult for man to intercept His gifts.

Disgusted with the trade of proprietor, Jonathan resolved to employ his energies in some other department, and he determined to put up his land to sale.

It is needless to say that no one would give him more for it than it cost himself. In vain he cited Ricardo, and represented the inherent value of the indestructible powers of the soil—the answer always was, "There are other lands close by;" and these few words put an extinguisher on his demands and on his illusions.

There is, moreover, in this transaction a fact of great Economic importance, and to which little attention has been paid.

It is easy to understand that if a manufacturer desires, after ten or fifteen years, to sell his apparatus and materials, even in their new state, he will probably be forced to submit to a loss. The reason is obvious. Ten or fifteen years can scarcely elapse without considerable improvements in machinery taking place. This is the reason why the man who sends to market machinery fifteen years old cannot expect a return exactly equal to the labor he has expended; for with an equal expenditure of labor the purchaser could, owing to the progress subsequently made, procure himself machinery of improved construction—which, we may remark in passing, proves more and more clearly that value is not in proportion to labor, but to services.

Hence we may conclude that machinery and instruments of labor have a tendency to lose part of their value in consequence of the mere lapse of time, without taking into account their deterioration by use—and we may lay down this formula, that "one of the effects of progress is to diminish the value of all existing instruments."

It is clear in fact that the more rapid that progress is, the greater difficulty will the former instruments have in sustaining the rivalry of new and improved ones.

I shall not stop here to remark the harmony exhibited by the results of this law. What I desire you to observe at present is that landed property no more escapes from the operation of this law than any other kind of property.

Brother Jonathan experiences this. He holds this language to the purchaser: "What I have expended on this property in permanent improvements represents a thousands days' labor. I expect that you will, in the first place, reimburse me for these thousand days' work, and then add something for the value that is inherent in the soil and independent of all human exertion."

The purchaser replies:

"In the first place, I shall give you nothing for the value inherent in the soil, which is simply utility, which the adjoining property possesses as well as yours. Such native superhuman utility I can obtain gratis, which proves that it possesses no value.

In the second place, since your books show that you have expended a thousand days' work in bringing your land to its present state, I shall give you only 800 days' labor; and my reason for it is, that with 800 days' labor I can nowadays accomplish the same improvements on the adjoining land as you have executed with 1000 days' labor on yours. Pray consider that in the course of fifteen years the art of draining, clearing, building, sinking wells, designing farm-offices, transporting materials, has made great progress. Less labor is now required to effect each given result, and I cannot consent to give you ten for what I can get for eight, more especially as the price of grain has fallen in proportion to this progress, which is a profit neither to you nor to me, but to mankind at large."

Thus Jonathan was left no alternative but to sell his land at a loss, or to keep it.

Undoubtedly the value of land is not affected by one circumstance exclusively. Other circumstances—such as the construction of a canal, or the erection of a town—may act in an opposite direction, and raise its value; but the improvements of which I have spoken, which are general and inevitable, always necessarily tend to depress it

The conclusion to be deduced from all I have said is that as long as there exists in a country abundance of land to be cleared and brought under cultivation, the proprietor, whether he cultivates, or lets, or sells it, enjoys no privilege, no monopoly, no exceptional advantage—above all, that he levies no tax upon the gratuitous liberality of nature. How could it be so, if we suppose men to be free? Have not people who are possessed of capital and energy a perfect right to make a choice between agriculture, manufactures, commerce, fisheries, navigation, the arts, or the learned professions? Will not capital and industry always tend to those departments that give extraordinary returns? Will they not desert those that entail loss? Is this inevitable shifting and redistribution of human efforts not sufficient to establish, according to our hypothesis, an equilibrium of profit and remuneration? Do agriculturists in the United States make fortunes more rapidly than merchants, shipowners, bankers, or physicians—as would necessarily happen if they received the wages of their labor like other people, and the recompense of nature's work into the bargain?

Would you like to know how a proprietor even in the United States could establish for himself a monopoly? I shall try to explain it.

Suppose Jonathan to assemble all the proprietors of the United States, and hold this language to them:

"I desired to sell my crops, and I found no one who would give me a high enough price for them. I wished then to let my land, and encountered the same difficulty. I resolved to sell it, but still experienced the same disappointment. My exactions have always been met by their telling me that there is more land in the neighborhood; so that, horrible to say, my services are estimated by the community, like the services of other people, at what they are worth, in spite of the flattering promises of theorists. They will give me nothing, absolutely nothing, for those productive and indestructible powers of the soil, for those natural agents, for the solar and lunar rays, for the rain, the wind, the dew, the frost, which I was led to believe were mine, but of which I turn out to be only the nominal proprietor. Is it not an iniquitous thing that I am remunerated only for my services, and at a rate, too, reduced by competition? You are all suffering under the same oppression, you are all alike the victims of anarchical competition. It would be no longer so, you may easily perceive, if we organized landed property, if we laid our heads together to prevent anyone hence-forward from clearing a yard of American soil. In that case, pop-ulation pressing, by its increase, on a nearly fixed amount of sub-sistence, we should be able to make our own prices and attain immense wealth, which would be a great boon for all other classes; for being rich, we should provide them with work."

If, in consequence of this discourse, the combined proprietors seized the reins of government, and passed an act interdicting all new clearances, the consequences undoubtedly would be a tem-porary increase of their profits. I say temporary, for the natural laws of society would be wanting in harmony if the punishment of such a crime did not spring naturally from the crime itself. Speaking with scientific exactitude, I should not say that the new law we have supposed would impart value to the powers of the soil, or to natural agents (were this the case, the law would do harm to no one)—but I should say, that the equilibrium of serv-ices had been violently upset; that one class robbed all other classes, and that slavery had been introduced into that country.

Take another hypothesis, which indeed represents the actual state of things among the civilized nations of Europe—and sup-pose all the land to have passed into the domain of private prop-erty.

We are to inquire whether in that case the mass of consumers, or the community, would continue to be the gratuitous benefici-ary of the productive powers of the soil, and of natural agents; whether the proprietors of land would be owners of anything else than of its value, that is to say, of their services fairly estimated according to the laws of competition; and whether, when they are recompensed for those services, they are not forced like everyone else to give the gifts of God into the bargain.

Suppose, then, the entire territory of Arkansas alienated by the government, parceled into private domains, and subjected to culture. When Jonathan brings his grain or his land to market, can he not now take advantage of the productive power of the soil, and make it an element of value? He could no longer be met, as in the preceding case, with the overwhelming answer, "There is more uncultivated land adjacent to yours."

This new state of things presupposes an increase of population, which may be divided into two classes: first, that which furnishes to the community agricultural services; second, that which furnishes manufacturing, intellectual, or other services.

Now this appears to me quite evident. Laborers (other than owners of land) who wished to procure supplies of grain, being perfectly free to apply either to Jonathan or to his neighbors, or to the proprietors of adjoining states, being in circumstances even to proceed to clear lands beyond the territory of Arkansas, it would be absolutely impossible for Jonathan to impose an unjust law upon them. The very fact that lands that have no value exist elsewhere would oppose to monopoly an invincible obstacle, and we should be landed again in the preceding hypothesis. Agricultural services are subject to the law of Universal Competition, and it is quite impossible to make them pass for more than they are worth. I add that they are worth no more (*ceteris paribus*) than services of any other description. As the manufacturer, after charging for his time, his anxiety, his trouble, his risk, his advances, his skill (all which things constitute human service, and are represented by value), can demand no recompense for the law of gravitation, the expansibility of steam, the assistance of which he has availed himself of—so in the same way, Jonathan can include in the value of his grain only the sum total of the personal services, anterior or recent, and not the assistance he has derived from the laws of vegetable physiology. The equilibrium of services is not impaired so long as they are freely exchanged, the one for the other, at an agreed price; and the gifts of God, of which these services are the vehicle, given on both sides into the bargain, remain in the domain of community.

It may be said, no doubt, that in point of fact the value of the soil is constantly increasing; and this is true. In proportion as population becomes more dense and the people more wealthy, and the means of communication more easy, the landed proprietor derives more advantage from his services. Is this law peculiar to him? Does the same thing not hold of all other producers? With equal labor, does not a physician, a lawyer, a singer, a painter, a day laborer, procure a greater amount of enjoyments in the nineteenth than he could in the fourth century? in Paris than in Brittany? in France than in Morocco? But is this increased enjoyment obtained at the expense of any other person? That is the point. For the rest, we shall investigate still farther this law of value (using the word metonymically) of the soil, in a subsequent part of the work, when we come to consider the theory of Ricardo.

At present it is sufficient to show that Jonathan, in the case we have put, can exercise no oppression over the industrial classes, provided the exchange of services is free, and that labor can, without any legal impediment, be distributed, either in Arkansas or elsewhere, among different kinds of production. This liberty renders it impossible for the proprietors to intercept, for their own profit, the gratuitous benefits of nature.

It would no longer be the same thing if Jonathan and his brethren, availing themselves of their legislative powers, were to proscribe or shackle the liberty of trade—were they to decree, for example, that not a grain of foreign wheat should be allowed to enter the territory of Arkansas. In that case the value of services exchanged between proprietors and non-proprietors would no longer be regulated by justice. The one party could no longer control the pretensions of the other. Such a legislative measure would be as iniquitous as the one to which we have just alluded. The effect would be quite the same if Jonathan, having carried to market a sack of wheat, which in other circumstances would have sold for fifteen francs, should present a pistol at the purchaser's head, and say, Give me three francs more, or I will blow out your brains.

This (to give the thing its right name) is extortion. Brutal or legal, the character of the transaction is the same. Brutal, as in the case of the pistol, it violates property; legal, as in the case of the prohibition, it still violates property, and repudiates, moreover, the very principle upon which property is founded. The exclusive subject of property, as we have seen, is value, and Value is the appreciation of two services freely and voluntarily exchanged. It is impossible, then, to conceive anything more directly antagonistic to the very principle of property than that which, in the name of right, destroys the equivalence of services.

It may not be out of place to add that laws of this description are iniquitous and injurious, whatever may be the opinions entertained by those who impose them, or by those who are oppressed by their operation. In certain countries we find the working-classes standing up for these restrictions, because they enrich the proprietors. They do not perceive that it is at their expense, and I know from experience that it is not always safe to tell them so.

Strange! that people should listen willingly to partisans who preach Communism, which is slavery; for when a man is no longer master of his own services, he is a slave—and that they should look askance at those who are always and everywhere the defenders of Liberty, which is the Community of the gifts of God.

We now come to the third hypothesis, which assumes that all the land capable of cultivation throughout the world has passed into the domain of individual appropriation.

We have still to do with two classes—those who possess land—and those who do not. Will the first not oppress the second? and will the latter not be always obliged to give more labor in exchange for the same amount of subsistence?

I notice this objection merely for argument's sake, for hundreds of years must elapse before this hypothesis can become a reality.

Everything forewarns us, however, that the time must at last come when the exactions of proprietors can no longer be met by the words, There are other lands to clear.

I pray the reader to note that this hypothesis implies another—it implies that at the same epoch population will have reached the extreme limit of the means of subsistence that the earth can produce.

This is a new and important element in the question. It is very much as if one should put the question, What will happen when there is no longer enough oxygen in the atmosphere to supply the lungs of a redundant population?

Whatever view we take of the principle of population, it is at least certain that population is capable of increase, nay, that it has a tendency to increase, since in point of fact it does increase. All the economic arrangements of society appear to have been organized with the previous knowledge of this tendency, and are in perfect harmony with it. The landed proprietor always endeavors to get paid for the natural agents he has appropriated, but he is as constantly foiled in this foolish and unjust pretension by the abundance of analogous natural agents that have not been appropriated. The liberality of nature, which is comparatively indefinite, constitutes him a simple custodier. But now you drive me into a corner, by supposing a period at which this liberality reaches its limit. Men have then no longer anything to expect from that quarter. The consequence is inevitable, that the tendency of mankind to increase will be paralyzed, that the progress of population will be arrested. No economic regime can obviate this necessity. According to the hypothesis we have laid down, every increase of population would be repressed by mortality. No philanthropy, no optimism, can make us believe that the increase of human beings can continue its progression when the progressive increase of subsistence has conclusively terminated.

Here, then, we have a new order of things; and the harmony of the social laws might be called in question, had they not provided for a state of matters the existence of which is possible, although very different from that which now obtains.

The difficulty we have to deal with, then, comes to this: When a ship in mid-ocean cannot reach land in less than a month, and has only a fortnight's provisions on board, what is to be done? Clearly this, reduce the allowance of each sailor. This is not cruelty—it is prudence and justice.

In the same way, when population shall have reached the extreme limit that all the land in the world can maintain, a law which, by gentle and infallible means prevents the further multiplication of mankind, cannot be considered either harsh or unjust. Now, it is landed property still which affords us a solution of the difficulty. The institution of property, by applying the stimulant of self-interest, causes the land to produce the greatest possible quantity of subsistence, and by the division of inheritances puts each family in a situation to estimate the danger to itself of an imprudent multiplication. It is very clear that any other regime—Communism, for example—would be at once a less effective spur to production, and a less powerful curb to population.

After all, it appears to me that Political Economy has discharged her duty when she has proved that the great and just law of the mutuality of services operates harmoniously, so long as human progress is not conclusively arrested. Is it not consoling to think that up to that point, and under the empire of freedom, it is not in the power of one class to oppress another? Is economic Science bound to solve this further problem: Given the tendency of mankind to multiply, what will take place when there is no longer room in the world for new inhabitants? Does God hold in reserve for that epoch some creative cataclysm, some marvelous manifestation of His almighty power? Or, as Christians, do we believe in the doctrine of the world's destruction? These evidently are not economical problems, and there is no science that does not encounter similar difficulties. Natural philosophers know well that all bodies that move on the surface of the earth have a tendency to descend, not to ascend. After all, a day must come when the mountains shall have filled up the valleys, when the mouths of our rivers will be on the same level as their source, when the waters can no longer flow, etc., etc. What will happen then? Is Natural Science to cease to observe and to admire the harmony of the actual world, because she cannot divine by what other harmony God will provide for a state of things far distant no doubt, but inevitable? It seems to me that at this point the Economist, like the natural philosopher, should substitute for an exercise of curiosity an exercise of faith. He who has so marvelously arranged the medium in which we now live knows best how to prepare another medium suitable to other circumstances.

We judge of the productiveness of the soil and of human skill by the facts of which we are witnesses. Is this a rational mode of proceeding? Then, adopting it, we may say, Since it has required six thousand years to bring a tenth part of the earth to the sorry state of cultivation in which we find it, how many hundreds of ages must elapse before its entire surface shall be converted into a garden?

Yet in this appreciation, comforting as it is, we suppose merely the more general diffusion of our present knowledge, or rather our present ignorance, of agriculture. But is this, I repeat, an admissible rule? Does not analogy tell us that an impenetrable veil conceals from us the power—the indefinite power it may be—of art? The savage who lives by the chase requires a square league of territory. What would be his surprise were he told that the pastoral life enables ten times the number of men to subsist upon the same space? The nomad shepherd would, in like manner, be quite astonished to be told that a system of triennial cultivation (*la culture triennale*) admits easily of a population ten times greater still. Tell the peasant accustomed to this routine that the same progress will again be the result of alternate culture[9] (*la culture alterne*), and he will not believe you. Alternate culture is for us the latest improvement—Is it the latest improvement for the human race? Let us comfort ourselves regarding the future destiny of the species—a long tract of ages is before us. At all events, let us not require Political Economy to resolve problems that are not within her domain—and let us with confidence commit the destinies of future races to the keeping of that great and good and wise Being who shall have called them into existence.

Let us recapitulate the ideas contained in this chapter.

These two phenomena, Utility and Value—the co-operation of nature and the co-operation of man, consequently Community

---

[9]*Altemer un champ*, is to alternate crops of corn and hay in a field—Translator.

and Property—are combined in the work of agriculture, as in every other department of industry.

In the production of wheat that appeases our hunger, we remark something analogous to what takes place in the formation of water that quenches our thirst. The ocean, which is the theme of the poet's inspiration, offers to the Economist also a fine subject of meditation. It is this vast reservoir that gives drink to all human creatures. And yet how can that be, when many of them are situated at a great distance from its shores, and when its water is besides undrinkable? It is here that we have to admire the marvelous industry of nature. We mark how the sun warms the heaving mass, and subjects it to a slow evaporation. The water takes the form of gas, and, disengaged from the salt, which rendered it unfit for use, it rises into the high regions of the atmosphere. Gales of wind, increasing in all directions, drift it toward inhabited continents. There it encounters cold, which condenses it, and attaches it in a solid form to the sides of mountains. By and by, the gentle heat of spring melts it. Carried along by its weight, it is filtered and purified through beds of schist and gravel. It ramifies and distributes itself, and supplies and feeds refreshing springs in all parts of the world. Here we have an immense and ingenious industry carried on by nature for the benefit of the human race. Change of form, change of place, utility, nothing is wanting. But where is value? Value has not yet come into existence; and if what we must call the work of God is to be paid for (it would be paid for if it possessed exchangeable value)—who could tell the value of a single drop of this precious liquid?

All men, however, have not a spring of pure water at their door. In order to quench their thirst, they must take pains, make efforts, exert foresight and skill. It is this supplementary human labor that gives rise to arrangements, transactions, estimates. It is here, then, that we discover the origin and foundation of value.

Man is originally ignorant. Knowledge is acquired. At the beginning, then, he is forced to carry water, to accomplish the supplementary labor that nature has left him to execute with the maximum of trouble. It is at this stage that water has the greatest value in exchange. By degrees the water carrier invents a barrow and wheels, trains horses, constructs pipes, discovers the law of the siphon, etc.; in short, he transfers part of his labor to the gratuitous forces of nature; and, in proportion as he does so, the value of water, but not its utility, is diminished.

There is here, however, a circumstance it is necessary thoroughly to comprehend, if we would not see discordance where there is in reality only harmony. It is this, that the purchaser of water obtains it on easier terms, that is to say, gives a less amount of labor in exchange for a given quantity of it, each time a step of progress of this kind is gained, although in such circumstances he has to give a remuneration for the instrument by means of which nature is constrained to act. Formerly he paid for the labor of carrying the water; now he pays not only for that, but for the labor expended in constructing the barrow, the wheel, and the pipe—and yet, everything included, he pays less; and this shows us how false and futile the reasoning is that would persuade us that that part of the remuneration that is applicable to capital is a burden on the consumer. Will these reasoners never understand that, for each result obtained, capital supersedes more labor than it exacts?

All that I have said is equally applicable to the production of wheat. In that case also, anterior to all human labor, there has been an immense, a measureless, amount of natural industry at work, the secrets of which the most advanced science can yet give no account of. Gases, salts, are diffused through the soil and the atmosphere. Electricity, magnetism, the wind, the rain, light, heat, vegetable life, play successively their parts, often unknown to us, in transporting, transforming, uniting, dividing, combining these elements; and this marvelous industry, the activity and utility of which elude our appreciation and even our imagination, has yet no value. Value makes its appearance at the first intervention of the labor of man, who has, in this, more perhaps than in the other instance we have given, a supplementary labor to perform, in order to complete what nature has begun.

To direct these natural forces, and remove the obstacles which impede their action, man takes possession of an instrument, which is the soil, and he does so without injury to anyone for this instrument had previously no value. This is not a matter of argument, but a matter of fact. Show me, in any part of the world you choose, land that has not been subjected directly or indirectly to human action, and I will show you land devoid of value.

In the meantime, the agriculturist in order to effect, in conjunction with nature, the production of wheat, executes two kinds of labor that are quite distinct. The one kind is applicable directly and immediately to the crop of the year—is applicable only to that, and must be paid for by that—such as sowing, weeding, reaping, etc. The other, as building, clearing, draining, enclosing, is applicable to an indefinite series of crops, and must be charged to and spread over a course of years, and calculated according to the tables of interest and annuities. The crops constitute the remuneration of the agriculturist if he consumes them himself. If he exchanges them, it is for services of another kind, and the appreciation of the services so exchanged constitutes their value.

Now it is easy to see that this class of permanent works executed by the agriculturist upon the land is a value that has not yet received its entire recompense, but that cannot fail to receive it. It cannot be supposed that he is to throw up his land and allow another to step into his shoes without compensation. The value has been incorporated and mixed up with the soil and this is the reason why we can with propriety employ a metonymy and say the land has value. It has value, in fact, because it can be no longer acquired without giving in exchange the equivalent for this labor. But what I contend for is that this land, on which its natural productive power had not originally conferred any value, has no value yet in this respect. This natural power, which was gratuitous then, is gratuitous now, and will be always gratuitous. We may say, indeed, that the land has value, but when we go to the root of the matter we find that what possesses value is the human labor that has improved the land, and the capital that has been expended on it. Hence it is rigorously exact to say that the proprietor of the land is, after all, the proprietor only of a value he has created, of services he has rendered; and what property can be more legitimate? It is property created at no one's expense, and neither intercepts nor taxes the gifts of God.

Nor is this all. The capital that has been advanced, and the interest of which is spread over the crop of successive years, is so far from increasing the price of the produce, and forming a burden on the consumers, that the latter acquire agricultural products cheaper in proportion as this capital is augmented, that is to say, in proportion as the value of the soil is increased. I have no doubt that this assertion will be thought paradoxical and tainted with exaggerated optimism, so much have people been accustomed to regard the value of land as a calamity, if not a piece of injustice. For my own part, I affirm that it is not enough to say that the value of the soil has been created at no one's expense; it is not enough to say that it injures no one; we should rather say that it benefits everybody. It is not only legitimate, but advantageous, even to those who possess no property.

We have here, in fact, the phenomenon of our previous illustration reproduced. We remarked that from the moment the water carrier invented the barrow and the wheel, the purchaser of the water had to pay for two kinds of labor: first, the labor employed in making the barrow and the wheel, or rather the interest of the capital, and an annual contribution to a sinking fund to replace that capital when worn out; second, the direct labor that the water-carrier must still perform. But it is equally true that these two kinds of labor united do not equal in amount the labor that had to be undergone before the invention. Why? because a portion of the work has now been handed over to the gratuitous forces of nature. It is, indeed, in consequence of this diminution of human labor that the invention has been called forth and adopted.

All this takes place in exactly the same way in the case of land and the production of wheat. As often as an agriculturist expends capital in permanent ameliorations, it is certain that the successive crops are burdened with the interest of that capital. But it is equally certain that the other species of labor—rude, unskilled, present, direct labor—is rendered unnecessary in a still greater proportion; so that each crop is obtained by the proprietor, and consequently by the consumer, on easier terms, on less onerous conditions—the proper action of capital consisting precisely in substituting natural and gratuitous cooperation for human labor that must be paid for.

Here is an example of it. In order to obtain a good crop, it is necessary that the field should be freed from superfluous moisture. Suppose this species of labor to be still included in the first category. Suppose that the cultivator goes every morning with a jar to carry off the stagnant water where it is productive of injury. It is clear that at the year's end the land would have acquired no additional value, but the price of the grain would be enormously enhanced. It would be the same in the case of all who followed the same process while the art of draining was in this primitive state. If the proprietor were to make a drain, that moment the land would acquire value, for this labor pertains to the second category—that which is incorporated with the land—and must be reimbursed by the products of consecutive years; and no one could expect to acquire the land without recompensing this work. Is it not true, however, that it would tend to lower the value of the crop? Is it not true that although during the first year it exacted an extraordinary exertion, it saves in the long run more labor than it has occasioned? Is it not true that the draining thenceforth will be executed by the gratuitous law of hydrostatics more economically than it could be by muscular force? Is it not true that the purchasers of wheat will benefit by this operation? Is it not true that they should esteem themselves fortunate in this new value acquired by the soil? And, having reference to more general considerations, is it not true, in fine, that the value of the soil attests a progress realized, not for the advantage of the proprietor only, but for that of society at large? How absurd, then, and suicidal in society to exclaim: The additional price charged for wheat, to meet the interest of the capital expended on this drain, and ultimately to replace that capital, or its equivalent, as represented in the value of the land, is a privilege, a monopoly, a theft! At this rate, to cease to be a monopolist and a thief, the pro-prietor should have only to fill up his drain, and betake himself to his jar. Would the man who has no property, and lives by wages, be any gainer by that?

Review all the permanent ameliorations of which the sum total makes up the value of land, and you will find that to each of them the same remark applies. Having filled up the drain, demol-ish the fence, and so force the agriculturist to mount guard upon his field; destroy the well, pull down the barn, dig up the road, burn the plough, efface the levelling, remove the artificial mould; replace in the field the loose stones, the weeds, the roots of trees; you will then have realized the Utopia of Equality. The land, and the human race along with it, will have reverted to the primitive state, and will have no longer any value. The crops will have no longer any connection with capital. Their price will be freed from that accursed element called interest. Everything, literally every-thing, will be done by actual labor, visible to the naked eye. Polit-ical Economy will be much simplified. Our country will support one man to the square league. The rest of her inhabitants will have died of hunger—but then it can no longer be said that prop-erty is a monopoly, an injustice, and a theft.

Let us not be insensible, then, to those economic harmonies that unfold themselves to our view more and more as we analyze the ideas of exchange, of value, of capital, of interest, of property, of community. Will it indeed be necessary for me to describe the entire circle, and complete the demonstration?—But we have already, perhaps, advanced sufficiently far to be convinced that the social world, not less than the material world, bears the impress of a Divine hand, from which flows wisdom and good-ness, and toward which we should raise our eyes in gratitude and admiration.

I cannot forbear reverting here to the view of this subject taken by Mr. Considerant.

Setting out with the proposition that the soil has a proper value, independent of all human labor, that it constitutes primi-tive and uncreated capital, he concludes, in perfect consistency with his own views, that appropriation is usurpation. This supposed iniquity leads him to indulge in violent tirades against the institutions of modern society. On the other hand, he allows that permanent ameliorations confer an additional value on this primitive capital, an accessory so mixed up with the principal that we cannot separate them. What are we to do, then? for we have here a total value composed of two elements, of which one, the fruit of labor, is legitimate property; and the other, the gift of God, appropriated by man, is an iniquitous usurpation.

This is no trifling difficulty. Mr. Considerant resolves it by reference to the Right to Employment (*Droit au travail*).

> The development of Mankind evidently demands that the Soil shall not be left in its wild and uncultivated state. The destiny of the human race is opposed to property in land retaining its rude and primitive form.
>
> In the midst of forests and savannah, the savage enjoys four natural rights, namely, the rights of Hunting, of Fishing, of Gathering the fruits, of Pasturing. Such is the primitive form of property in land.
>
> In all civilized societies, the working-classes, the Proletaires, who inherit nothing, and possess nothing, are simply despoiled of these rights. We cannot say that the primitive Right has changed its form, for it no longer exists. The form and the substance have alike disappeared.
>
> Now in what Form can such Rights be reconciled with the conditions of an industrial Society? The answer is plain:
>
> In the savage state, in order to avail himself of his Right, man is obliged to act. The labor of Fishing, of Hunting, of Gathering, of Pasturing, are the conditions of the exercise of his Right. The primitive Right, then, is a Right to engage in these employments.
>
> Very well, let an industrial Society, which has appropriated the land, and taken away from man the power of exercising freely and at will his four natural Rights, let this society cede to the individual, in compensation for those Rights of which it has despoiled him, the Right to Employment. On this principle, rightly understood and applied, the individual has no longer any reason to complain.

The condition *sine qua non*, then, of the Legitimacy of Property is, that Society should concede to the Proletaire—the man who has no property—the Right to Employment; and, in exchange for a given exertion of activity, assure-him of means of subsistence, at least as adequate as such exercise could have procured him in the primitive state.

I cannot, without being guilty of tiresome repetition, discuss this question with Mr. Considerant in all its ramifications. If I demonstrate that what he terms uncreated capital is no capital at all; that what he terms the additional value of the soil, is not an additional value, but the total value; he must acknowledge that his argument has fallen to pieces, and, with it, all complaints of the way in which mankind has judged it proper to live since the days of Adam. But this controversy would oblige me to repeat all that I have already said upon the essentially and indelibly gratuitous character of natural agents.

I shall only note that if Mr. Considerant speaks in behalf of the non-proprietary class, he is so very accommodating that they may think themselves betrayed. What! proprietors have usurped the soil, and all the miracles of vegetation it displays! they have usurped the sun, the rain, the dew, oxygen, hydrogen, and nitrogen, so far at least as these co-operate in the production of agricultural products—and you ask them to assure to the man who has no property, as a compensation, at least as much of the means of subsistence, in exchange for a given exertion of activity, as that exertion could have procured him in the primitive and savage state!

But do you not see that landed property has not waited for your injunctions in order to be a million times more generous? for to what is your demand limited?

In the primitive state, your four rights of fishing, hunting, gathering the fruits, and pasturing, maintain in existence, or rather in a state of vegetation, amid all the horrors of destitution, nearly one man to the square league of territory. The usurpation of the land will then be legitimate, according to you, when those who have been guilty of that usurpation support one man for every square league, exacting from him at the same time as much activity as is displayed by a Huron or an Iroquois. Pray remark that France consists of only thirty thousand square leagues; that consequently, if its whole territory supports thirty thousand inhabitants in that condition of existence which the savage state affords, you renounce in behalf of the non-proprietary class all further demands upon property. Now, there are thirty millions of Frenchmen who have not an inch of land, and among the number we meet with many—the president of the republic, ministers, magistrates, bankers, merchants, notaries, advocates, physicians, brokers, soldiers, sailors, professors, journalists, etc.—who would certainly not be disposed to exchange their condition for that of an Ioway. Landed property, then, must do much more for us than you exact from it. You demand from it the Right to Employment, up to a certain point—that is to say, until it yields to the masses—and in exchange for a given amount of labor too—as much subsistence as they could earn in a state of barbarism. Landed property does much more than that—it gives more than the Right to Employment—it gives Employment itself, and even if it only paid off the land tax, it would do a hundred times more than you ask it to do.

I find to my great regret that I am not yet done with landed property and its value. I have still to state, and to refute, in as few words as possible, an objection that is specious and even formidable.

It is said,

"Your theory is contradicted by facts. Undoubtedly, as long as there is in a country an abundance of uncultivated land, the existence of such land will of itself hinder the cultivated land from acquiring an undue value. It is also beyond doubt that even when all the land has passed into the appropriated domain, if neighboring nations have extensive tracts ready for the plough, freedom of trade is sufficient to restrain the value of landed property within just limits. In these two cases it would seem that the Price of land can only represent the capital advanced, and the Rent of land the interest of that capital. Whence we must conclude, as you do, that the proper action of the soil and the intervention of natural agents, going for nothing, and not influencing the value of the crops, remain gratuitous, and therefore common. All this is specious. We may have difficulty in discovering the error, and yet this reasoning is erroneous. In order to be convinced of it, it is sufficient to point to the fact, that there are in France cultivated lands that are worth from 100 francs to 6,000 francs the hectare, an enormous difference, which is much easier explained by the difference of fertility than by the difference of the anterior labor applied to these lands. It is vain to deny, then, that fertility has its own value, for not a sale takes place that does not attest it. Everyone who purchases a land estate examines its quality, and pays for it accordingly. If, of two properties that lie alongside each other, the one consists of a rich alluvium and the other of barren sand, the first is surely of more value than the second, although both may have absorbed the same capital, and to say truth, the purchaser gives himself no trouble on that score. His attention is fixed upon the future, and not upon the past. What he looks at is not what the land has cost, but what it will yield, and he knows that its yield will be in proportion to its fertility. Then this fertility has a proper and intrinsic value that is independent of all human labor. To maintain the contrary is to endeavor to base the legitimacy of individual appropriation on a trifle, or rather on a paradox."

Let us inquire, then, what is the true foundation of the value of land.

I pray the reader not to forget that this question is of grave importance at the present moment. Hitherto it has been neglected or glossed over by Economists as a question of mere curiosity. The legitimacy of individual appropriation was not formerly contested, but this is no longer the case. Theories that have obtained but too much success have created doubts in the minds of our best thinkers on the institution of property. And upon what do the authors of these theories found their complaints? Why, exactly upon the assertion contained in the objection I have just explained—upon the fact, unfortunately admitted by all schools, that the soil, by reason of its fertility, possesses an inherent value communicated to it by nature and not by human means. Now value is not transferred gratuitously. The very word excludes the idea of gratuitousness. We say to the proprietor, then—you demand from me a value that is the fruit of my labor, and you offer me in exchange a value that is not the fruit of your labor, or of any labor, but of the liberality of nature.

Be assured that this would be a fearful complaint were it well founded. It did not originate with Misters Considerant and Proudhon. We find it in the works of Smith, of Ricardo, of Senior, of all the Economists without exception, not as a theory merely, but as a subject of complaint. These authors have not only attributed to the soil an extra-human value, they have boldly deduced the consequence, and branded landed property as a privilege, a monopoly, a usurpation. No doubt, after thus branding it, they have defended it on the plea of necessity. But what does such a defense amount to but an error of reasoning that the Communist logicians have lost no time in rectifying.

It is not, then, to indulge an unhappy love for minutiae that I enter on this delicate subject. I should have wished to save both the reader and myself the ennui that even now I feel hovering over the conclusion of this chapter.

The answer to the objection now under consideration is to be found in the theory of Value, explained in the fifth chapter of this work. I there said that value does not essentially imply labor; still less is it necessarily proportionate to labor. I have shown that the foundation of value is not so much the pains taken by the person who transfers it as the pains saved to the person who receives it; and it is for that reason that I have made it to reside in something that embraces these two elements—in service. I have said that a person may render a great service with very little effort, or that with a great effort one may render a very trifling service. The sole result is that labor does not obtain necessarily a remuneration that is always in proportion to its intensity, in the case either of man in an isolated condition or of man in the social state.

Value is determined by a bargain between two contracting parties. In making that bargain, each has his own views. You offer to sell me wheat. What matters it to me the time and pains it may have cost you to produce it? What I am concerned about is the time and pains it would cost me to procure it from another quarter. The knowledge you have of my situation may render you more or less demanding; the knowledge I have of yours may render me more or less anxious to make the purchase. There is no necessary measure, then, of the recompense you are to derive from your labor. That depends upon the circumstances, and the value these circumstances confer upon the two services we are desirous to exchange. By and by we shall call attention to an external force called Competition, whose mission is to regulate values, and render them more and more proportional to efforts. Still this proportion is not of the essence of value, seeing that the proportion is established under the pressure of a contingent fact.

Keeping this in view, I maintain that the value of land arises, fluctuates, and is determined, like that of gold, iron, water, the lawyer's advice, the physician's consultation, the singer's or dancer's performance, the artist's picture—in short, like all other values; that it is subject to no exceptional laws; that it constitutes a property the same in origin, the same in nature, and as legitimate, as any other property. But it does not at all follow, as you must now see, that, of two exertions of labor applied to the soil, one should not be much better remunerated than the other.

Let us revert again to that industry, the most simple of all, and the best fitted to show us the delicate point that separates the onerous labor of man from the gratuitous cooperation of nature. I allude to the humble industry of the water carrier.

A man procures and brings home a barrel of water. Does he become possessed of a value necessarily proportionate to his labor? In that case, the value would be independent of the service the water may render. Nay more, it would be fixed; for the labor, once over, is no longer susceptible of increase or diminution.

Well, the day after he procures and brings home this barrel of water, it may lose its value if, for example, it has rained during the night. In that case, everyone is provided—the water can render no service, and is no longer wanted. In economic language, it has ceased to be in demand.

On the other hand, it may acquire considerable value if extraordinary wants, unforeseen and pressing, come to manifest themselves.

What is the consequence? that man, working for the future, is not exactly aware beforehand what value the future will attach to his labor. Value incorporated in a material object will be higher or lower according as it renders more or less service, or to express it more clearly, human labor, which is the source of value, receives according to circumstances a higher or lower remuneration. Such eventualities are an exercise for foresight, and foresight also has a right to remuneration.

But what connection is there, I would ask, between these fluctuations of value, between these variations in the recompense of labor, and that marvelous natural industry, those admirable physical laws, that without our participation have brought the water of the ocean to the spring? Because the value of this barrel of water varies according to circumstances, are we to conclude that nature charges sometimes more, sometimes less, sometimes nothing at all, for evaporation, for carrying the clouds from the ocean to the mountains, for freezing, melting, and the whole of that admirable industry that supplies the spring?

It is exactly the same thing in the case of agricultural products.

The value of the soil, or rather of the capital applied to the soil, is made up not of one element but of two. It depends not only on the labor that has been employed, but also on the ability that society possesses to remunerate that labor—on Demand as well as on Supply.

Take the case of a field. Not a year passes, perhaps, in which there is not some labor bestowed upon it, the effects of which are permanent, and of course an increase of value is the result.

Roads of access, besides, are improved and made more direct, the security of person and property becomes more complete, markets are extended, population increases in number and in

wealth—different systems of culture are introduced, and a new
career is opened to intelligence and skill; the effect of this change
of medium, of this general prosperity, being to confer additional
value on both the present and the anterior labor, and consequently on the field.

There is here no injustice, no exception in favor of landed
property. No species of labor, from that of the banker to that of
the day laborer, fails to exhibit the same phenomenon. No one
fails to see his remuneration improved by the improvement of the
society in which his work is carried on. This action and reaction
of the prosperity of each on the prosperity of all, and vice versa,
is the very law of value. So false is the conclusion that imputes to
the soil and its productive powers an imaginary value, that intellectual labor, professions and trades that have no connection with
matter or the co-operation of physical laws, enjoy the same
advantage, which in fact is not exceptional but universal. The
lawyer, the physician, the professor, the artist, the poet, receive a
higher remuneration for an equal amount of labor, in proportion
as the town or country to which they belong increases in wealth
and prosperity, in proportion as the taste or demand for their
services becomes more generally diffused, in proportion as the
public is more able and more willing to remunerate them. The
acquisition of clients and customers is regulated by this principle.
It is still more apparent in the case of the Basque Giant and Tom
Thumb, who live by the simple exhibition of their exceptional
stature, and reap a much better harvest from the curiosity of the
numerous and wealthy crowds of our large towns than from that
of a few poor and straggling villagers. In this case, demand not
only enhances value, it creates it. Why, then, should we think it
exceptional or unjust that demand should also exert an influence
on the value of land and of agricultural products?

Is it alleged that land may thus attain an exaggerated value?
They who say so have never reflected on the immense amount of
labor that arable land has absorbed. I dare affirm, that there is not
a field in this country that is worth what it has cost, that could be
exchanged for as much labor as has been expended in bringing it

to its present state of productiveness. If this observation is well founded, it is conclusive. It frees landed property from the slightest taint of injustice. For this reason, I shall return to the subject when I come to examine Ricardo's theory of Rent, and I shall show that we must apply to agricultural capital the law I have stated in these terms: In proportion as capital increases, products are divided between capitalists or proprietors and laborers in such a way that the relative share of the former goes on continually diminishing, although their absolute share is increased, while the share of the latter is increased both absolutely and relatively.

The illusion that has induced men to believe that the productive powers of the soil have an independent value because they possess Utility has led to many errors and catastrophes. It has driven them frequently to the premature establishment of colonies, the history of which is nothing else than a lamentable martyrology. They have reasoned in this way: In our own country we can obtain value only by labor, and when we have done our work, we have obtained a value that is only proportionate to our labor. If we emigrate to Guiana, to the banks of the Mississippi, to Australia, to Africa, we shall obtain possession of vast territories, uncultivated but fertile; and our reward will be that we shall become possessed not of the value we have created, but also of the inherent and independent value of the land we may reclaim. They set out, and a cruel experience soon confirms the truth of the theory that I am now explaining. They labor, they clear, they exhaust themselves; they are exposed to privations, to sufferings, to diseases; and then if they wish to dispose of the land that they have rendered fit for production, they cannot obtain for it what it has cost them, and they are forced to acknowledge that value is of human creation. I defy you to give me an instance of the establishment of a colony that has not at the beginning been attended with disaster.

> Upwards of a thousand laborers were sent out to the Swan River Colony; but the extreme cheapness of land (eighteen-pence or less than two francs an acre), and the extravagant rate of wages, afforded them such facilities and inducements

to become landowners, that capitalists could no longer get anyone to cultivate their lands. A capital of £200,000 (five million francs) was lost in consequence, and the colony became a scene of desolation. The laborers having left their employers from the delusive desire to become landowners, agricultural implements were allowed to rust—seeds rotted—and sheep, cattle, and horses perished for want of attention. A frightful famine cured the laborers of their infatuation, and they returned to ask employment from the capitalists; but it was too late.

The association, attributing this disaster to the cheapness of land, raised its price to 12 shillings an acre. But, adds Carey, from whom I borrow this quotation, the real cause was that the laborers, being persuaded that land possesses an inherent value, apart from the labor bestowed on it, were anxious to exercise "the power of appropriation," to which the power to demand Rent is attributed.

What follows supplies us with an argument still more conclusive:

> In 1836, the landed estates in the colony of Swan River were to be purchased from the original settlers at one shilling an acre.

Thus the land that was sold by the company at 12 shillings—upon which the settlers had bestowed much labor and money—was disposed of by them at one shilling! What then became of the value of the natural and indestructible productive powers of the soil?[12]

I feel that the vast and important subject of the Value of Land has not been exhausted in this chapter, written by snatches and amid many distractions. I shall return to it hereafter but in the

---

[10]*Proceedings of the South Australian Association.*

[11]*New Monthly Magazine.*

[12]Ricardo.

meantime I cannot resist submitting one observation to my readers, and more especially to Economists.

The illustrious savants who have done so much to advance the science, whose lives and writings breathe benevolence and philanthropy, and who have disclosed to us, at least in a certain aspect and within the limits of their researches, the true solution of the social problem—the Quesnays, the Turgots, the Smiths, the Malthuses, the Says—have not however escaped, I do not say from refutation, for that is always legitimate, but from calumny, disparagement, and insult. To attack their writings, and even their motives, has become fashionable. It may be said, perhaps, that in this chapter I am furnishing arms to their detractors, and truly the moment would be ill chosen for me to turn against those whom I candidly acknowledge as my initiators, my masters, and my guides.

But supreme homage is, after all, due to Truth, or what I regard as Truth. No book was ever written without some admixture of error. Now a single error in Political Economy, if we press it, torture it, deduce from it rigorously its logical consequences, involves all kinds of errors—in fact, lands us in chaos. There never was a book from which we could not extract one proposition, isolated, incomplete, false, including consequently a whole world of errors and confusion. In my conscience, I believe that the definition the Economists have given of the word Value is of this number. We have just seen that this definition has led them to cast a serious doubt on the legitimacy of property in land, and, by consequence, in capital; and they have only been stopped short on this fatal road by an inconsistency. This inconsistency has saved them. They have resumed their march on the road of Truth; and their error, if it be one, is, in their works, an isolated blot. Then the Socialists have come to lay hold of this false definition, not to refute it, but to adopt it, strengthen it, make it the foundation of their propaganda, and deduce from it all its consequences. Hence has arisen in our day an imminent social danger; and it is for that reason that I have thought it my duty to be explicit on this subject, and trace the erroneous theory to its source. If you conclude that I have separated myself from my masters Smith and Say, from my friends Blanqui and Garnier, because, by an oversight in their learned and admirable works, they have made, as I think, an erroneous application of the word value; if you conclude from this that I have no longer faith in Political Economy and Political Economists, I can only protest, and appeal to the very title of the present volume.

10

COMPETITION

There is not in the whole vocabulary of Political Economy a word that has aroused the fury of modern reformers so much as the word Competition, which, in order to render it the more odious, they never fail to couple with the epithet, anarchical.

What is the meaning of anarchical competition? I really don't know. What could we substitute for it? I am equally ignorant.

I hear people, indeed, calling out Organization! Association! What does that mean? Let us come to an understanding, once for all. I desire to know what sort of authority these writers intend to exercise over me, and all other living men; for I acknowledge only one species of authority, that of reason, if indeed they have it on their side. Is it their wish, then, to deprive me of the right of exercising my judgment on what concerns my own subsistence? Is their object to take from me the power of comparing the services I render with those I receive? Do they mean that I should act under the influence of restraint, exerted over me by them and not by my own intelligence? If they leave me my liberty, Competition remains. If they deprive me of freedom, I am their slave.

Association will be free and voluntary, they say. Be it so. But then each group of associates will, as regards all other groups, be just what individuals now are in relation to each other, and we shall still have Competition. The association will be integral. A good joke truly. What! Anarchical Competition is now desolating society, and we must wait for a remedy, until, by dint of your persuasion, all the nations of the earth—Frenchmen, Englishmen, Chinese, Japanese, Caffres, Hottentots, Laplanders, Cossacks, Patagonians—make up their minds to unite in one of the forms of association you have devised? Why, this is just to avow that Competition is indestructible; and will you venture to say that a phenomenon that is indestructible, and consequently providential, can be mischievous?

After all, what is Competition? Is it a thing that exists and is self-acting like the cholera? No, Competition is only the absence of constraint. In what concerns my own interest, I desire to choose for myself, not that another should choose for me, or in spite of me—that is all. And if anyone pretends to substitute his judgment for mine in what concerns me, I should ask to substitute mine for his in what concerns him. What guarantee have we that things would go on better in this way? It is evident that Competition is Liberty. To take away the liberty of acting is to destroy the possibility, and consequently the power, of choosing, of judging, of comparing; it is to annihilate intelligence, to annihilate thought, to annihilate man. From whatever quarter they set out, to this point all modern reformers tend—to ameliorate society they begin by annihilating the individual, under the pretext that all evils come from this source—as if all good did not come from it too.

We have seen that services are exchanged for services. In reality, every man comes into the world charged with the responsibility of providing for his satisfactions by his own efforts. When another man saves us an effort, we ought to save him an effort in return. He imparts to us a satisfaction resulting from his effort; we ought to do the same for him.

But who is to make the comparison? for between these efforts, these pains, these services exchanged, there is necessarily a comparison to be made, in order to arrive at equivalence, at justice—unless indeed injustice, inequality, chance, is to be our rule, which would just be another way of putting human intelligence *hors de cause*. We must, then, have a judge; and who is this judge to be? Is it not quite natural that in every case wants should be judged of by those who experience them, satisfactions by those who seek them, efforts by those who exchange them? And is it seriously proposed to substitute for this universal vigilance of the parties interested, a social authority (suppose that of the reformer himself), charged with determining in all parts of the world the delicate conditions of these countless acts of interchange? Do you not see that this would be to set up the most fallible, the most universal, the most arbitrary, the most inquisitorial, the most insupportable—we are fortunately able to add, the most impossible—of all despotisms ever conceived in the brain of pasha or mufti?

It is sufficient to know that Competition is nothing else than the absence of an arbitrary authority as judge of exchanges, in order to be satisfied that it is indestructible. Illegitimate force may no doubt restrain, counteract, trammel the liberty of exchanging, as it may the liberty of walking; but it can annihilate neither the one nor the other without annihilating man. This being so, it remains for us to inquire whether Competition tends to the happiness or misery of mankind; a question that amounts to this—Is the human race naturally progressive, or are its tendencies fatally retrograde?

I hesitate not to say that Competition, which, indeed, we might denominate Liberty, despite the repulsion it excites, despite the declamations to which it has given rise, is a law that is democratical in its essence. Of all the laws to which Providence has confided the progress of human society, it is the most progressive, levelling, and communautaire. It is this law which brings successively into the common domain the use and enjoyment of commodities that nature has accorded gratuitously only to certain countries. It is this law, again, that brings into the common domain all the conquests that the genius of each age bequeaths to succeeding generations, leaving them only supplementary labors to execute, which last they continue to exchange with one another, without succeeding, as they desire, in obtaining a recompense for the co-operation of natural agents; and if these labors, as happens always in the beginning, possess a value that is not proportionate to their intensity, it is still Competition that, by its incessant but unperceived action, restores an equilibrium that is sanctioned by justice, and that is more exact than any that the fallible sagacity of a human magistracy could by possibility establish. Far from Competition leading to inequality, as has been erroneously alleged, we may assert that all factitious inequality is imputable to its absence; and if the gulf between the Grand Lama and a Paria is more profound than that which separates the President from an artisan of the United States, the reason is this, that Competition (or Liberty), which is curbed and put down in Asia, is not so in America. This is the reason why, while the Socialists see in Competition the source of all that is evil, we trace to the attacks that have been made upon it the disturbance of all that is good. Although this great law has been misunderstood by the Socialists and their adepts; although it is frequently harsh in its operation, no law is more fertile in social harmonies, more beneficent in general results; no law attests more brilliantly the measureless superiority of the designs of God over the vain and powerless combinations of men.

I must here remind the reader of that singular but unquestionable result of the social order to which I have already invited his attention, and which the power of habit hides too frequently from our view. It is this, that the sum total of satisfactions that falls to each member of society is much superior to those that he could procure for himself by his own efforts. In other words, there is an evident disproportion between our consumption and our labor. This phenomenon, which all of us can easily verify, if we turn our regards upon ourselves, ought, it seems to me, to inspire some gratitude to society, to which we owe it.

We come into this world destitute of everything, tormented with numerous wants, and provided with nothing but faculties to enable us to struggle against them. A priori, it would seem that all we could expect would be to obtain satisfactions proportionate to our labor. If we obtain more, infinitely more, to what do we owe the excess? Precisely to that natural organization against which we are constantly declaiming, when we are not engaged in seeking to subvert it.

In itself the phenomenon is truly extraordinary. That certain men consume more than they produce is easily explained, if in one way or other they usurp the rights of other people—if they receive services without rendering them. But how can that be true of all men at the same time? How happens it that, after having exchanged their services without constraint, without spoliation, upon a footing of equivalence, each man can say to himself with truth, I consume in a day more than I could produce in a century?

The reader has seen that the additional element that resolves the problem is the co-operation of natural agents, constantly becoming more and more effective in the work of production; it is gratuitous utility falling continually into the domain of Community; it is the labor of heat and of cold, of light, of gravitation, of magnetism, of elasticity, coming progressively to be added to the labor of man, diminishing the value of services by rendering them more easy.

I must have but feebly explained the theory of value if the reader imagines that value diminishes immediately and of its own accord, by the simple fact of the co-operation of natural forces, and the relief thereby afforded to human labor. It is not so; for then we might say with the English Economists that value is proportional to labor. The man who is aided by a natural and gratuitous force renders his services more easily; but he does not on that account renounce voluntarily any portion whatever of his accustomed remuneration. To induce him to do that, external coercion—pressure from without—severe but not unjust pressure—is necessary. It is Competition that exerts this pressure. As long as Competition does not intervene, as long as the man who has availed himself of a natural agent preserves his secret, that natural agent is gratuitous, but it is not yet common. The victory has been gained, but to the profit only of a single man, or a single class. It is not yet a benefit to mankind at large. No change has yet taken place, except that one description of services, although partly relieved from the pain of muscular exertion, still exacts all its former remuneration. We have, on the one hand, a man who exacts from all his fellows the same amount of labor as formerly, although he offers them a limited amount of his own labor in return. On the other, we have mankind at large, which is still obliged to make the same sacrifice of time and of labor in order to obtain a product now realized in part by nature.

Were things to remain in this state, a principle of indefinite inequality would be introduced into the world with every new invention. Not only could we not say that value is proportional to labor; we could not even say that value tends to become proportional to labor. All that we have said in the preceding chapters about gratuitous utility and progressive community would be chimerical. It would not be true that services are exchanged against services, in such a way that the gifts of God are transferred gratuitously from one man to another, down to the ultimate recipient, who is the consumer. Each would continue to be paid, not only for his labor, but for the natural forces he had once succeeded in setting to work; in a word, society would be constituted on the principle of universal Monopoly, in place of on the principle of progressive Community.

But it is not so. God, who has bestowed on all his creatures heat, light, gravitation, air, water, the soil, the marvel of vegetable life, electricity, and countless other benefits that it is beyond my power to enumerate—God, who has placed in the human breast the feeling of personal interest, which, like a magnet, attracts everything to itself—God, I say, has placed also in the bosom of society another spring of action, which he has charged with the care of preserving to his benefits their original destination, which was, that they should be gratuitous and common. This spring of action is Competition.

Thus, Personal Interest is that irrepressible force belonging to the individual that urges on to progress and discovery, that spurs us on to exertion, but leads also to monopoly. Competition is that force belonging to the species that is not less irrepressible, and that snatches progress, as it is realized, from individual hands, and makes it the common inheritance of the great family of mankind. These two forces, in each of which, considered individually, we might find something to blame, thus constitute social Harmony, by the play of their combinations when regarded in conjunction.

And we may remark in passing that we ought not to be at all surprised that the individual interests of men, considered as producers, should from the beginning have risen up against Competition, should have rebuked it, and sought to destroy it—calling in for this purpose the assistance of force, fraud, privilege, sophistry, monopoly, restriction, legislative protection, etc. The morality of the means shows us clearly enough the morality of the end. But the astonishing and melancholy thing is, that science herself—false science, it is true—propagated with so much zeal by the socialist schools, in the name of philanthropy, equality, and fraternity, should have espoused the cause of Individualism, in its narrowest and most exclusive manifestation, and should have deserted the cause of humanity.

Let us see now how Competition acts:

Man, under the influence of self-interest, is always and necessarily on the lookout for such circumstances as may give the greatest value to his services. He is not long in discovering that, as regards the gifts of God, he may be favored in three ways:

He may appropriate to his own exclusive use these gifts themselves; or,

He may alone know the process by which they can be made useful; or,

He alone may possess the instrument by means of which their co-operation in the work of production can be secured.

In any of these cases, he gives little of his own labor in exchange for much of the labor of other men. His services have a high relative value, and we are led to believe that this excess of value resides in the natural agent. If it were so, this value would not be subject to fall. Now, what proves that the value is in the service is that we find Competition diminishing both value and service simultaneously.

1. Natural agents—the gifts of God—are not distributed uniformly over the different countries of the world. What an infinite variety of vegetable productions are spread over the wide range extending from the region of the pine to the region of the palm tree! Here the soil is more productive, there the heat is more vivifying. In one quarter we meet with stone, in another with lime, in another with iron, copper, or coal. Water power is not to be found everywhere, nor can we everywhere avail ourselves to an equal extent of the power of the winds. Distance from the objects we find essential of itself makes a vast difference in the obstacles our efforts encounter. Even the human faculties vary in some measure with climate and races.

It is easy to see that but for the law of Competition, this inequality in the distribution of the gifts of God would lead to a corresponding inequality in the condition of men.

Whoever happened to have within reach a natural advantage would profit by it, but his fellow-men would not. He would not permit other men to participate in it through his instrumentality, without stipulating an excessive remuneration, the amount of which he would have the power of fixing arbitrarily. He could attach to his services any value he pleased. We have seen that the extreme limits between which it must be determined are the pains taken by the man who renders the service and the pains saved to the man who receives it. Competition alone hinders its being always raised to the maximum. The inhabitant of the tropics, for example, would say to the European, "Thanks to the sun's rays, I can, with labor equal to ten, procure a given quantity of sugar, coffee, cocoa, or cotton, while you, obliged in your cold climate to have recourse to hot-houses, stoves, and shelter, cannot obtain the same quantity but with labor equal to a hundred. You wish to obtain my coffee, sugar, or cotton, and you would not be sorry were I to take into account in the transaction only the pains I have taken, the labor I have expended. But what I regard principally is the pains, the labor, I have saved you; for, aware that that is the limit of your resistance, I make it the limit of my exaction. As what I produce with an amount of labor equal to ten, you could produce only with labor equal to a hundred, were I to demand in exchange for my sugar a commodity that cost you labor equal to 101, you would certainly refuse; but all that I ask is labor equal to 99. You may higgle and look gruff for a little, but you will come to my terms; for at this rate you have still an advantage by the exchange. You think these terms unfair; but, after all, it is not to you but to me that God has vouchsafed the advantage of a higher temperature. I know that I am in a position to take advantage of this gift of Providence by depriving you of it, unless you pay me a tax, for I have no competitors. Here, then, are my sugar, my cocoa, my coffee, my cotton—take them on the conditions I impose—or raise them for yourself—or do without them."

It is true that the European might hold to the inhabitant of the tropics some such language as this: "Turn over your soil, dig pits, search for iron and coal, and felicitate yourself if you find any; for if not, it is my determination to push my exactions to an extreme also. God has vouchsafed to us both precious gifts. We appropriate as much of them as we require, but we will not suffer others to touch them without paying us a tax."

Even if things took place in this way, scientific exactness would not allow us to attribute to natural agents that Value which resides only in services. But the error would be harmless, for the result would be absolutely the same. Services would still be exchanged against services, but they would exhibit no tendency to conform to efforts, or labor, as a measure. The gifts of God would be personal privileges, not common benefits; and we might perhaps have some reason to complain that the Author of things had treated us in a way so incurably unequal. Should we, then, be brethren? Could we regard ourselves as the children of a common Father? The absence of Competition, that is to say of Liberty, would in the first instance be an insuperable bar to Equality. The absence of Equality would exclude all idea of Fraternity—and nothing of the republican motto[2] would then be left.

But let Competition be introduced, and we shall see it instantly present an insuperable barrier to all such leonine bargains, to all such forestalling of the gifts of God, to all such revolting pretensions in the appreciation of services, to all such inequalities with efforts exchanged.

And let us remark, first of all, that Competition acts forcibly, called forth as it is by these very inequalities. Labor betakes itself instinctively to the quarter where it is best remunerated, and never fails to put an end to this exceptional advantage, so that Inequality is only a spur that urges us on in spite of ourselves toward Equality. It is in truth one of the most beautiful final intentions observable in the social mechanism. Infinite Goodness, which manifests beneficence everywhere, would seem to have made choice of the avaricious producer in order to effect an equitable distribution among all; and truly it is a marvelous sight this, of self-interest realizing continually what it ever desires to avoid. Man, as a producer, is necessarily, inevitably, attracted by excessive returns, which he thus reduces to the ordinary rate. He pursues his own interest; and without knowing it, without wishing it, without seeking it, he promotes the general good.

Thus, to recur to our former example, the inhabitant of the tropics, trafficking in the gifts of God, realizes an excessive remuneration, and by that very means brings down upon himself Competition. Human labor exerts itself in proportion to the magnitude of the inequality if I may use the expression, and never rests until that inequality is effaced. Under the action of Competition, we see the tropical labor, which was equal to ten, exchanged successively for European labor equal to 80, 50, 40, 20, and finally to 10. Under the empire of the natural laws of society, there is no reason why this should not take place; that is to say, there is no reason why services exchanged should not be measured by the labor performed, the pains taken—the gifts of God on both sides being gratuitous and into the bargain. We have only to consider, in order to appreciate and bless the revolution that is thus effected. In the first instance, the labor undergone on both sides is equal, and this satisfies the human mind, which always desires justice.

Then what has become of the gift of God? Attend to this, reader. No one has been deprived of it. In this respect we have not allowed ourselves to be imposed upon by the clamors of the tropical producer. The Brazilian, in so far as he is himself a consumer of sugar, or cotton, or coffee, never ceases to profit by the sun's rays—his good fortune does not cease to aid him in the work of production. What he has lost is only the unjust power of levying a tax upon the consumption of the inhabitants of Europe. The beneficence of Providence, because gratuitous, has become, as it ought to become, common; for common and gratuitous are in reality the same thing.

The gift of God has become common—and the reader will observe that I avail myself here of a special fact to elucidate a phenomenon which is universal—this gift, I say, has become common to all. This is not declamation, but the expression of a truth which is demonstrable. Why has this beautiful phenomenon been misunderstood? Because community is realized under the form of value annihilated, and the mind with difficulty lays hold of negations. But I ask, Is it not true that when, in order to obtain a certain quantity of sugar, coffee, or cotton, I give only one-tenth of the labor I should find it necessary to expend in producing the commodity myself, and this because the Brazilian sun performs the other nine-tenths of the work. Is it not true, I say, that in that case I still exchange labor for labor, and really and truly obtain, over and above the Brazilian labor, and into the bargain, the co-operation of the climate of the tropics? Can I not affirm with rigorous exactitude that I have become, that all men have become, in the same way as the Indians and Americans, that is to say gratuitously, participators in the liberality of nature, so far as the commodities in question are concerned?

England possesses productive coal mines. That is no doubt a great local advantage, more especially if we suppose, as I shall do for the sake of argument, that the Continent possesses no coal mines. Apart from the consideration of exchange, the advantage this gives to the people of England is the possession of fuel in greater abundance than other nations—fuel obtained with less labor, and at less expense of useful time. As soon as exchange comes into operation—keeping out of view Competition—the exclusive possession of these mines enables the people of England to demand a considerable remuneration, and to set a high price upon their labor. Not being in a situation to perform this labor ourselves, or procure what we want from another quarter, we have no alternative but to submit. English labor devoted to this description of work will be well remunerated; in other words, coal will be dear, and the bounty of nature may be considered as conferred on the people of one nation, and not on mankind at large.

But this state of things cannot last; for a great natural and social law is opposed to it—Competition, For the very reason that this species of labor is largely remunerated in England, it will be in great demand there, for men are always in quest of high remuneration. The number of miners will increase, both in consequence of the sons of miners devoting themselves to their fathers' trade, and in consequence of men transferring their industry to mining from other departments. They will offer to work for a smaller recompense, and their remuneration will go on diminishing until it reach the normal rate, or the rate generally given in the country for analogous work. This means that the price of English coal will fall in France; that a given amount of French labor will procure a greater and greater quantity of English coal, or rather of English labor incorporated and worked up in coal; and, finally (and this is what I pray you to remark), that the gift that nature would appear to have bestowed upon England has in reality been conferred on the whole human race. The coal of Newcastle is brought within the reach of all men gratuitously, as far as the mere material is concerned. This is neither a paradox nor an exaggeration—it is brought within their reach like the water of the brook, on the single condition of going to fetch it, or remunerating those who undertake that labor for us. When we purchase coal, it is not the coal that we pay for, but the labor necessary to extract it and transport it. All that we do is to give a corresponding amount of labor that we have worked up or incorporated in wine or in silk. So true is it that the liberality of nature has been extended to France, that the labor we refund is not greater than that which it would have been necessary to undergo had the deposit of coal been in France. Competition has established equality between the two nations as far as coal is concerned, except as regards the inevitable and inconsiderable difference resulting from distance and carriage.

I have given two examples, and, to render the phenomenon more striking, I have selected international transactions, which are effected on a great scale. I fear I may thus have diverted the reader's attention from the same phenomena acting incessantly around us in our every-day transactions. Let him take in his hand the most familiar objects, a glass, a nail, a loaf, a piece of cloth, a book. Let him meditate on such ordinary products, and reflect how great an amount of gratuitous utility would never but for Competition have become common for humanity at large, although remaining gratuitous for the producer. He will find that, thanks to Competition, in purchasing his loaf he pays nothing for the action of the sun, nothing for the rain, nothing for the frost, nothing for the laws of vegetable physiology, nothing even for the powers of the soil, despite all that has been said on that subject; nothing for the law of gravitation set to work by the miller; nothing for the law of combustion set to work by the baker; nothing for the horsepower set to work by the carrier—that he pays only for the services rendered, the pains taken, by human agents; and let him reflect that, but for Competition, he must have paid, over and above, a tax for the intervention of all these natural agents; that that tax would have had no other limit than the difficulty that he might himself have experienced in procuring the loaf by his own efforts, and that consequently a whole life would not have been sufficient to supply the remuneration that would have been demanded of him. Let him think farther that he does not make use of a single commodity which might not give rise to the same reflections, and that these reflections apply not to him only, but to all mankind, and he will then comprehend the radical error of those socialist theories that, looking only at the surface of things, the epidermis of society, have been set up with so much levity against Competition, in other words, against human Liberty. He will then regard Competition, which preserves to the gifts of nature, unequally distributed, their common and gratuitous character, as the principle of a just and natural equalization; he will admire it as the force which holds in check the greed of individual interest, with which at the same time it is so artfully combined as to serve both as a curb to avarice and a spur to exertion; and he will bless it as a most striking manifestation of God's impartial solicitude for the good of all his creatures.

From what has been said, we may deduce the solution of one of the problems that have been most keenly controverted, namely, that of free trade as between nation and nation. If it be true, as seems to me incontestable, that Competition leads the various countries of the globe to exchange with one another nothing else than labor, exertion more and more equalized, and to transfer at the same time reciprocally, and into the bargain, the natural advantages that each possesses; how blind and absurd must those men be who exclude foreign products by legislative measures under the pretext that they are cheap, and have little value in proportion to their aggregate utility; that is to say, precisely because they include a large proportion of gratuitous utility!

I have said, and I repeat it, that I have confidence in a theory when I find it in accordance with universal practice. Now it is certain that countries would effect many exchanges with each other were they not interdicted by force. It requires the bayonet to prevent them; and for that reason it is wrong to prevent them.

2. Another circumstance places certain men in a favorable and exceptional situation as regards remuneration—I mean the personal and exclusive knowledge of the processes by means of which natural agents can alone by appropriated. What we term invention is a conquest by human genius; and these beautiful and pacific conquests, which are, in the first instance, a source of

wealth for those who achieve them, become by and by, under the action of Competition, the common and gratuitous patrimony of all.

The forces of nature belong indeed to all. Gravitation, for instance, is common property; it surrounds us, pervades us, commands us. And yet were there but one mode of making gravitation co-operate toward a useful and determinate result, and but one man acquainted with that mode, this man might set a high price upon his work, or refuse to work except in exchange for a very high remuneration. His demands would have no limit until they reached the point at which the consumers must make greater sacrifices than the old processes entailed upon them. He may have contrived, for example, to annihilate nine-tenths of the labor necessary to produce a certain commodity, x. But x has at present a current market price determined by the labor its production by the ordinary methods exacts. The inventor sells x at the market price; in other words, his labor receives a recompense ten times higher than that of his rivals. This is the first phase of the invention.

So far we discover nothing unjust or unfair. It is just and equitable that the man who makes the world acquainted with a useful process should be rewarded for it; *A chacun selon sa capacite*.

Observe, too, that as yet mankind, with the exception of the inventor, has gained nothing unless virtually, and in perspective, so to speak, since in order to procure the commodity x, each acquirer must make a sacrifice equal to the former cost.

Now, however, the invention enters its second phase—that of imitation. Excessive remuneration awakens covetousness. The new process is more generally adopted; the price of the commodity x continues to fall, and the remuneration goes on diminishing in proportion as the imitation becomes more distant in date from the original invention, that is to say, in proportion as it becomes more easy, and for that reason less meritorious. Surely there is nothing in all this that cannot be avowed by a legislation the most advanced and the most impartial.

At length the invention reaches its third phase, its final stage, that of universal diffusion, when it becomes common and gratuitous. The cycle has been completed when Competition has brought back the remuneration of the producers of x to the general and normal rate yielded by all analogous work. Then the nine-tenths of the labor, which by the hypothesis we supposed to be saved by the invention, becomes an acquisition to mankind at large. The utility of the commodity x remains the same; but nine-tenths of that commodity is now the product of gravitation, a force that was formerly common to all in principle, but has now become common to all in this special application. So true is this that all the consumers of that commodity throughout the world may now acquire it with one-tenth of the labor which it formerly cost. The surplus labor has been entirely annihilated by the new process.

If we consider that there is no human invention that has not traveled this circle, that x is here an algebraical sign that represents wheat, clothing, books, ships—in the production of which an incalculable amount of labor or Value has been annihilated, by the plough, the spinning jenny, the printing press, and the sail; that this observation is applicable to the humblest of tools as well as to the most complicated mechanism, to the nail, the wedge, the lever, as well as to the steam engine and the electric telegraph, we shall come, I trust, to understand the solution of this grand problem of human society, that an amount of utility and enjoyment, always greater, and more and more equally distributed, comes to remunerate each determinate quantity of human labor.

3. I have shown how Competition brings into the domain of the common and gratuitous both natural agents and the processes by which they are made operative. It remains to show that Competition executes the same function with reference to the instruments by means of which we set these agents to work. It is not enough that there should exist in nature a force such as heat, light, gravitation, electricity; it is not enough that intelligence conceives the means of making that force available—there must be instruments to realize this conception of the mind, and provisions

to maintain those who devote themselves to it during the operation.

As regards remuneration, there is a third circumstance that favors a man, or a class of men, namely, the possession of Capital. The man who has in his hands the tools necessary for labor, the materials to work upon, and the provisions for his subsistence during the operation, is in a situation to determine his own remuneration. The principle of this is equitable, for capital is only anterior labor that has not yet been remunerated. The capitalist is in a good position to impose terms; but observe that, even when free from Competition, there is a limit that his demands never can exceed—this limit is the point at which his remuneration would absorb all the advantages of the service he renders. In these circumstances, it is unreasonable to talk, as is so often done, of the tyranny of capital, seeing that even in the most extreme cases neither its presence nor its absence can injure the condition of the laborer. Like the inhabitant of the tropics, who has an intensity of heat at his disposal that nature has denied to colder regions—or like the inventor, who possesses the secret of a process unknown to other men—all that the capitalist can say is: "Would you profit by my labor—I set such a price upon it; if you find it too high, do as you have done hitherto—do without it."

But Competition takes place among capitalists. Tools, materials, and provisions contribute to the creation of utilities only when employed. There is an incentive, then, among capitalists to find employment for their capital. All that this incentive forces them to deduct from the extreme demand, of which I have just assigned the limits, resolving itself into a reduction of the price of the commodity, is so much clear profit, so much gratuitous gain, for the consumer, that is to say, for mankind.

This gain, however, can clearly never be absolutely gratuitous; for, since capital represents labor, that capital must always possess in itself the principle of remuneration.

Transactions relative to Capital are subject to the universal law of exchanges; and exchanges take place only because there is an advantage for the two contracting parties in effecting them—

an advantage that has no doubt a tendency to be equalized, but which accidentally may be greater for the one than for the other. There is a limit to the remuneration of capital beyond which limit no one will consent to borrow it. This limit is the minimum of service for the borrower. In the same way, there is a limit beyond which no one will consent to lend, and this limit is the minimum of remuneration for the lender. This is self-evident. If the requirements of one of the contracting parties are pushed so far as to reduce to zero the benefit to be derived by the other from the transaction, the loan becomes impossible. The remuneration of capital oscillates between these two extreme terms, pressed toward the maximum by the Competition of borrowers, brought back toward the minimum by the Competition of lenders; so that, by a necessity that is in harmony with justice, it rises when capital is scarce, and falls when it is abundant.

Many Economists imagine that the number of borrowers increases more rapidly than it is possible to create capital to lend to them, whence it would follow that the natural tendency of interest is to rise. The fact is decidedly the other way, and on all sides accordingly we perceive civilization lowering the return for capital. This return, it is said, is 30 or 40 percent at Rome, 20 percent in Brazil, 10 percent in Algeria, 8 percent in Spain, 6 percent in Italy, 5 percent in Germany, 4 percent in France, 3 percent in England, and still less in Holland. Now all that part of the return for capital which is annihilated by progress, although lost to the capitalist, is not lost to mankind. If interest, originally at 40 percent, is reduced to 2 percent, all commodities will be freed from 38 parts in 40 of this element of cost. They will reach the consumer freed from this charge to the extent of nineteen-twentieths. This is a force that, like natural agents, like expeditive processes, resolves itself into abundance, equalization, and, finally, into an elevation of the general level of the human race.

I have still to say a few words on the Competition of laborer with laborer—a subject that in these days has given rise to so much sentimental declamation. But have we not already exhausted this subject? I have shown that, owing to the action of

Competition, men cannot long receive an exceptional remuneration for the co-operation of natural forces, for their acquaintance with new processes, or for the possession of instruments by means of which they avail themselves of these forces. This proves that efforts have a tendency to be exchanged on a footing of equality, or, in other words, that value tends to become proportionate to labor. Then I do not see what can justly be termed the Competition of laborers; still less do I see how it can injure their condition, since in this point of view workmen are themselves the consumers. The working class means everybody, and it is precisely this vast community that reaps ultimately the benefits of Competition, and all the advantage of values successively annihilated by progress.

The evolution is this: Services are exchanged against services, values against values. When a man (or a class) appropriates a natural agent, or a new process, his demands are regulated, not by the labor he undergoes, but by the labor which he saves to others. He presses his exactions to the extreme limit without ever being able to injure the condition of others. He sets the greatest possible value on his services. But gradually, by the operation of Competition, this value tends to become proportioned to the labor performed; so that the evolution is brought to a conclusion when equal labor is exchanged for equal labor, both serving as the vehicle of an ever increasing amount of gratuitous utility, to the benefit of the community at large. In such circumstances, to assert that Competition can be injurious to the laborer would be to fall into a palpable contradiction.

And yet this is constantly asserted, and constantly believed; and why? Because by the word laborer is understood not the great laboring community, but a particular class. You divide the community into two classes. On one side, you place all those who are possessed of capital, who live wholly or partly on anterior labor, or by intellectual labor, or the proceeds of taxation; on the other, you place those who have nothing but their hands, who live by wages, or—to use the consecrated expression—the proletaires. You look to the relative position of these two classes, and you ask if, in that relative position, the Competition that takes place among those who live by wages is not fatal to them?

The situation of men of this last class, it is said, is essentially precarious. As they receive their wages from day to day, they live from hand to mouth. In the discussion that, under a free regime, precedes every bargain, they cannot wait; they must find work for tomorrow on any terms, under pain of death. If this be not strictly true of them all, it is at least true of many of them, and that is enough to depress the entire class; for those who are the most pressed and the poorest capitulate first, and establish the general rate of wages. The result is that wages tend to fall to the lowest rate that is compatible with bare subsistence—and in this state of things, the occurrence of the least excess of Competition among the laborers is a veritable calamity; for, as regards them, the question is not one of diminished prosperity, but of simple existence.

Undoubtedly there is much that is true, much that is too true, in fact, in this description. To deny the sufferings and wretchedness of that class of men who bear so material a part in the business of production would be to shut our eyes to the light of day. It is, in fact, this deplorable condition of a great number of our brethren that forms the subject of what has been justly called the social problem; for although other classes of society are visited also with disquietudes, sufferings, sudden changes of fortune, commercial crises, and economic convulsions, it may nevertheless be said with truth that liberty would be accepted as a solution of the problem, mere liberty did not appear powerless to cure that rankling sore that we denominate Pauperism.

And although it is here, pre-eminently, that the social problem lies, the reader will not expect that I should enter upon it in this place. Its solution, please God, may be the result of the entire work, but it clearly cannot be the result of a single chapter.

I am at present engaged in the exposition of general laws, which I believe to be harmonious; and I trust the reader will now begin to be convinced that these laws exist, and that their action tends toward community, and consequently towards equality. But I have not denied that the action of these laws is profoundly troubled by disturbing causes. If, then, we now encounter inequality as stubborn fact, how can we be in circumstances to form a judgment regarding it until we have first of all investigated the regular laws of the social order, and the causes that disturb the action of these laws?

On the other hand, I have ignored neither the existence of evil nor its mission. I have ventured to assert that, free will having been vouchsafed to man, it is not necessary to confine the term harmony to an aggregate from which evil should be excluded; for free will implies error, at least possible error, and error is evil. Social harmony, like everything that concerns man, is relative. Evil is a necessary part of the machinery destined to overcome error, ignorance, injustice, by bringing into play two great laws of our nature—responsibility and solidarity.

Now, taking pauperism as an existing fact, are we to impute it to the natural laws that govern the social order—or to human institutions that act in a sense contrary to these laws—or, finally, to the people themselves, who are the victims, and who, by their errors and their faults, have brought down this severe chastisement on their own heads?

In other words, does pauperism exist by providential destination—or, on the contrary, by what remains of the artificial in our political organization—or as a personal retribution? Bad luck, Exploitation, Irresponsibility—to which of these three causes must we attribute this frightful sore?

I hesitate not to assert that it cannot be the result of the natural laws that have hitherto been the subject of our investigation, seeing that these laws all tend to equalization by amelioration; that is to say, to bring all men to one and the same level, which level is continually rising. This, then, is not the place to seek a solution of the problem of pauperism.

At present, if we would consider specially that class of laborers who execute the most material portion of the work of production, and who, in general, having no interest in the profits, live upon a fixed remuneration called wages, the question we have to investigate is this: Apart from the consideration of good or bad economic institutions—apart from the consideration of the evils that the men who live by wages (the proletaires) bring upon themselves by their faults—what is, as regards them, the proper effect of Competition?

For this class, as for all, the operation of Competition is twofold. They feel it both as buyers and as sellers of services. The error of those who write upon these subjects is never to look but at one side of the question, like natural philosophers, who, if they took into account only centrifugal force, would never cease to believe and to prophesy that all was over with us. Grant their false datum, and you will see with what irrefutable logic they conduct you to this sinister conclusion. The same may be said of the lamentations that the Socialists found upon the exclusive consideration of centrifugal Competition, if I may be allowed the expression. They forget to take into account centripetal Competition, and that is sufficient to reduce their doctrines to puerile cant. They forget that the workman, when he presents himself in the market with the wages he has earned, becomes a center toward which innumerable branches of industry tend, and that he profits then by that universal Competition of which all trades complain in their turn.

It is true that the laborer, when he regards himself as a producer, as the person who supplies labor or services, complains also of Competition. Grant, then, that Competition benefits him on one side, while it pinches him on the other, the question comes to be, Is the balance favorable or unfavorable—or is there cancellation?

I must have explained myself very obscurely if the reader does not see that in the play of this marvelous mechanism, the action of Competition, apparently antagonistic, tends to the singular and consoling result that there is a balance that is favorable to all at the same time; caused by gratuitous Utility continually enlarging the circle of production, and falling continually into the domain of Community. Now, that which becomes common is profitable to all without hurting anyone; we may even say—for this is mathematically certain—it is profitable to each in proportion to his previous poverty. It is this portion of gratuitous utility, forced by Competition to become common, that causes the tendency of value to become proportioned to labor, to the evident benefit of the laborer. This, too, renders evident the social solution I have pressed so much on the attention of the reader, and that is only concealed by the illusions of habit—for a determinate amount of labor each receives an amount of satisfactions that tends to be increased and equalized.

Moreover, the condition of the laborer does not depend upon one economic law, but upon all. To become acquainted with that condition, to discover the prospects and the future of the laborer, this is Political Economy; for what other object could that science have in view? . . . But I am wrong—we have still spoliators. What causes the equivalence of services? Liberty. What impairs that equivalence? Oppression. Such is the circle we have still to traverse.

As regards the condition of that class of laborers who execute the more immediate work of production, it cannot be appreciated until we are in a situation to discover in what manner the law of Competition is combined with that of Wages and Population, and also with the distorting effects of unequal taxes and monopolies.

I shall add but a few words on the subject of Competition. It is very clear that it has no natural tendency to diminish the amount of the enjoyments that are distributed over society. Does Competition tend to make this distribution unequal? If there be anything evident in the world, it is that after having, if I may so express myself, attached to each service, to each value, a larger proportion of utility, Competition labors incessantly to level the services themselves, to render them proportional to efforts. Is Competition not the spur that urges men into profitable branches of industry, and urges them out of those that are unprofitable? Its proper action, then, is to realize equality more and more, by elevating the social level.

Let us not misunderstand each other, however, on this word equality. It does not imply that all men are to have the same

remuneration, but that they are to have remuneration proportioned to the quantity, and even to the quality of their efforts.

A multitude of circumstances contribute to render the remuneration of labor unequal (I speak here only of unhampered
labor, subject to Competition); but if we look at it more narrowly,
we shall find that this fancied inequality, almost always just and
necessary, is in reality nothing else than substantial equality.

Ceteris paribus, there are larger profits in those trades which
are attended with danger than in those which are not so; in those
which require a lengthened apprenticeship, and expensive train-
ing long unremunerated—which imply the patient exercise of certain domestic virtues—than in those where mere muscular exertion is sufficient; in professions that demand a cultivated mind
and refined taste, than in trades which require mere brute force.
Is not all this just? Now, Competition establishes necessarily these
distinctions—and society has no need of the assistance of Fourier
or Louis Blanc in the matter.

Of all these circumstances, that which operates in the greatest
number of cases is the inequality of instruction. Now here, as
everywhere else, we find Competition exerting its twofold action,
levelling classes, and elevating society.

If we suppose society to be composed of two layers or strata,
placed one above another, in one of which the intelligent principle prevails, and in the other the principle of brute force; and if
we study the natural relations of these two layers, we shall easily
discover a force of attraction in the one, and a force of aspiration
in the other, which co-operate toward their fusion. The very
inequality of profits breathes into the inferior ranks an inextinguishable ardor to mount to the region of ease and leisure; and
this ardor is seconded by the superior knowledge that distinguishes the higher classes. The methods of teaching are improved;
books fall in price; instruction is acquired in less time, and at a
smaller cost; science, formerly monopolized by a class or a caste,
and veiled in a dead language, or sealed up in hieroglyphics, is
written and printed in the common tongue; it pervades the

atmosphere, if I may use the expression, and is breathed as freely as the air of heaven.

Nor is this all. At the same time that an education more universal and more equal brings the two classes of society into closer approximation, some very important economic phenomena, which are connected with the great law of Competition, come to aid and accelerate their fusion. The progress of the mechanical arts diminishes continually the proportion of manual labor. The division of labor, by simplifying and separating each of the operations that combine in a productive result, brings within the reach of all branches of industry that could formerly be engaged in only by a few. Moreover, a great many employments that required at the outset much knowledge and varied acquirements, fall, by the mere lapse of time, into routine, and come within the sphere of action of classes generally the least instructed, as has happened in the case of agriculture. Agricultural processes, that in ancient times procured to their discoverers the honors of an apotheosis, are now inherited and almost monopolized by the rudest of men; and to such a degree that this important branch of human industry is, so to speak, entirely withdrawn from the well educated classes.

From the preceding observations it is possible that a false conclusion may be drawn. It may be said—"We perceive, indeed, that Competition lowers remuneration in all countries, in all departments of industry, in all ranks; and levels, by reducing, it; but in that case the wages of unskilled labor, of physical exertion, must become the type, the standard, of all remuneration."

I must have been misunderstood if you have not perceived that Competition, which labors to bring down all excessive remuneration toward an average more and more uniform, raises necessarily this average. I grant that it pinches men in their capacity of producers, but in so doing it ameliorates the condition of the human race in the only way in which it can reasonably be elevated, namely, by an increase of material prosperity, ease, leisure, moral and intellectual improvement, in a word, by enlarging consumption.

Will it be said that, in point of fact, mankind has not made the progress that this theory seems to imply?

I answer in the first place that in modern society Competition is far from occupying the sphere of its natural action. Our laws run counter to it, at least in as great a degree as they favor its action; and when it is asked whether the inequality of conditions is owing to its presence or its absence, it is sufficient to look at the men who make the greatest figure among us, and dazzle us by the display of their scandalous wealth in order to assure ourselves that inequality, so far as it is artificial and unjust, has for foundation conquests, monopolies, restrictions, privileged offices, functions, and places, ministerial trafficking, public borrowing—all things with which Competition has nothing to do.

Moreover, I believe we have overlooked the real progress mankind has made since the very recent epoch to which we must assign the partial enfranchisement of labor. It has been justly said that much philosophy is needed in order to discern facts that are continually passing before us. We are not astonished at what an honest and laborious family of the working class daily consumes, because habit has made us familiar with this strange phenomenon. If, however, we compare the comfortable circumstances in which such a family finds itself, with the condition in which it would be placed under a social order that excluded Competition—if statisticians, armed with an instrument of sufficient precision, could measure, as with a dynamometer, the relation of a working man's labor to his enjoyments at two different periods, we should acknowledge that liberty, restrained as it still is, has accomplished in his favor a prodigy that its very permanency hinders us from detecting. The contingent of human efforts which, in relation to a given result, has been annihilated, is truly incalculable. Time was when the artisan's day's labor would not have sufficed to procure him the most perfunctory broadsheet. At the present day, for a halfpenny, or the fiftieth part of his day's wages, he can obtain a gazette containing the matter of a volume. The same might be said of clothing, locomotion, carriage, lighting, and a multitude of other satisfactions. To what is this result owing? To this, that an enormous proportion of human labor, which had formerly to be paid for, has been handed over to be performed by the gratuitous forces of nature. It is a value annihilated, and to be no longer recompensed. Under the action of Competition, it has been replaced by common and gratuitous utility. And it is worthy of note, that when, in consequence of progress, the price of any commodity comes to fall, the labor saved to the poor purchaser in obtaining it is always proportionally greater than the labor saved to the rich purchaser. That is demonstrable.

In fine, this constantly increasing current of utilities that labor pours into all the veins of the body politic, and that Competition distributes, is not all summed up in an accession of wealth. It is absorbed, in great part, by the stream of advancing numbers. It resolves itself into an increase of population, according to laws that have an intimate affinity with the subject that now engages us, and that will be explained in another chapter.

Let us now stop for a moment, and take a rapid glance at the ground over which we have just travelled.

Man has wants that are unlimited—desires that are insatiable. In order to provide for them, he has materials and agents that are furnished to him by nature—faculties, instruments, all things that labor sets in motion. Labor is the resource that has been most equally distributed to all. Each man seeks instinctively and of necessity to avail himself to the utmost of the co-operation of natural forces, of talents natural and acquired, and of capital, in order that the result of this cooperation may be a greater amount of utilities produced or, what comes to the same thing, a greater amount of satisfactions acquired. Thus, the more active co-operation of natural agents, the indefinite development of intelligence, the progressive increase of capital, give rise to this phenomenon (which at first sight seems strange)—that a given quantity of labor furnishes an always increasing amount of utilities, and that each man can, without despoiling anyone, obtain a mass of consumable commodities out of all proportion to what his own efforts could have realized.

But this phenomenon, which is the result of the divine harmony that Providence has established in the mechanism of society, would have been detrimental to society, by introducing the germ of indefinite inequality, had there not been combined with it a harmony no less admirable, namely, Competition, which is one of the branches of the great law of human solidarity.

In fact, were it possible for an individual, a family, a class, a nation possessed of certain natural advantages, of an important discovery in manufactures, or of the instruments of production in the shape of accumulated capital, to be set permanently free from the law of Competition, it is evident that this individual, this family, this nation, would have forever the monopoly of an exceptionally high remuneration, at the expense of mankind at large. In what situation should we be, if the inhabitants of the tropical regions, set free from all rivalry with each other, could exact from us, in exchange for their sugar, their coffee, their cotton, their spices, not the equivalent of labor equal to their own, but an amount of labor equal to what we must ourselves undergo in order to produce these commodities under our inclement skies? What an incalculable distance would separate the various conditions of men, if the race of Cadmus alone could read, if the direct descendants of Triptolemus alone could handle the plough, if printing were confined to the family of Gutenberg, cotton-spinning to the children of Arkwright, and if the posterity of Watt could alone work the steam engine! Providence has not ordered things thus, but, on the contrary, has placed in the social machine a spring whose power is only less surprising than its simplicity— a spring by the operation of which all productive power, all superiority in manufacturing processes, in a word, all exclusive advantages, slip from the hands of the producer, having remained there, in the shape of exceptional remuneration, only long enough to excite his zeal, and come at length to enlarge the common and gratuitous patrimony of mankind, and resolve themselves into individual enjoyments always progressive, and more and more equally distributed—this spring is Competition. We have already seen its economical effects—and it now remains for us to take a rapid survey of its moral and political consequences. I shall confine myself to the more important of these.

Superficial thinkers have accused Competition of introducing antagonism among men. This is true and inevitable, if we consider men only in the capacity of producers, but regarded from another point of view, as consumers, the matter appears in a very different light. You then see this very Competition binding together individuals, families, classes, nations, and races, in the bonds of universal fraternity.

Seeing that the advantages that appear at first to be the property of certain individuals become, by an admirable law of Divine beneficence, the common patrimony of all; seeing that the natural advantages of situation, of fertility, of temperature, of mineral riches, and even of manufacturing aptitude, slip in a short time from the hands of producers, by reason of their competition with each other, and turn exclusively to the profit of consumers, it follows that there is no country that is not interested in the advancement and prosperity of all other countries. Every step of progress made in the East is wealth in perspective for the West. Fuel discovered in the South warms the men of the North. Great Britain makes progress in her spinning mills; but her capitalists do not alone reap the profit, for the interest of money does not rise; nor do her operatives, for the wages of labor remain the same. In the long run, it is the Russian, the Frenchman, the Spaniard; in a word, it is the human race, who obtain equal satisfactions at a less expense of labor or, what comes to the same thing, superior satisfactions with equal labor.

I have spoken only of the advantages—I might say as much of the disadvantages—which affect certain nations and certain regions. The peculiar action of Competition is to render general what was before exclusive. It acts exactly on the principle of Insurance. A scourge visits the fields of the agriculturist, and the consumers of the bread are the sufferers. An unjust tax is laid upon the vines of France, and this means dear wine for all wine-drinkers. Thus, advantages and disadvantages, that have any permanence only glance upon individuals, classes, or nations. Their providential destination in the long run is to affect humanity at large, and elevate or lower the condition of mankind. Hence to envy a certain people the fertility of their soil, or the beauty of their harbors and rivers, or the warmth of their sun, is to overlook the advantages in which we are called to participate. It is to disdain the abundance that is offered to us. It is to regret the labor that is saved to us. Hence national jealousies are not only perverse feelings—they are absurd. To hurt others is to injure ourselves. To place obstacles in the way of others—tariffs, coalitions, or wars—is to obstruct our own progress. Hence bad passions have their chastisement just as generous sentiments have their reward. The inevitable sanction of an exact distributive justice addresses itself to men's interests, enlightens opinion, proclaims and establishes among men these maxims of eternal truth: that the useful is one of the aspects of the just; that Liberty is the fairest of social Harmonies; and that Honesty is the best Policy.

Christianity has introduced into the world the grand principle of human fraternity. It addresses itself to our hearts, our feelings, our noble instincts. Political Economy recommends the same principle to our cool judgment; and, exhibiting the connection of effects with their causes, reconciles in consoling harmony the vigilant calculations of interest with the inspirations of the sublimest morality.

A second consequence that flows from this doctrine is that society is truly a Community. Misters Owen and Cabet may save themselves the trouble of seeking the solution of the great Communist problem—it is found already—it results not from their arbitrary combinations, but from the organization given by God to man, and to society. Natural forces, expeditive processes, instruments of production, everything is common among men, or has a tendency to become so, everything except pains, labor, individual effort. There is, and there can be, but one inequality—an inequality that Communists the most absolute must admit—that which results from the inequality of efforts. These efforts are what are exchanged for one another at a price bargained for. All the utility that nature, and the genius of ages, and human foresight, have implanted in the commodities exchanged, we obtain into the bargain. Reciprocal remunerations have reference only to reciprocal efforts, whether actual under the name of labor, or preparatory under the name of Capital. Here then is Community in the strictest sense of the word, unless we are to pretend that the personal share of enjoyment should be equal, although the quota of labor furnished is not so, which indeed would be the most iniquitous, the most monstrous, of inequalities—I will add, the most fatal; for it would not destroy Competition—it would only give it a retrograde action. We should still compete, but the Competition would be rivalry of idleness, stupidity, and improvidence.

In fine, the doctrine—so simple, and, as we think, so true—that we have just developed, takes the great principle of human perfectibility out of the domain of empty boasting, and transfers it to that of rigorous demonstration. This internal motive, which is never at rest in the bosom of the individual, but stirs him up to improve his condition, gives rise to the progress of art, which is nothing else than the progressive cooperation of forces, which from their nature call for no remuneration. To Competition is owing the concession to the community of advantages at first individually obtained. The intensity of the labor required for the production of each given result goes on continually diminishing, to the advantage of the human race, which thus sees the circle of its enjoyments and its leisure enlarging from one generation to another, while the level of its physical, intellectual, and moral improvement is raised; and by this arrangement, so worthy of our study and of our profound admiration, we behold mankind recovering the position it had lost.

Let me not be misunderstood, however. I do not say that all fraternity, all community, all perfectibility, are comprised and included in Competition. I say only that Competition is allied and combined with these three great social dogmas—that it forms part of them, that it exhibits them, that it is one of the most powerful agents of their realization.

I have endeavored to describe the general effects of Competition, and consequently its benefits, for it would be impious to suppose that any great law of nature should be at once hurtful and permanent; but I am far from denying that the action of Competition is accompanied with many hardships and sufferings. It appears to me that the theory that has just been developed explains at once those sufferings, and the inevitable complaints to which they give rise. Since the work of Competition consists in levelling, it must necessarily run counter to all who proudly attempt to rise above the general level. Each producer, in order to obtain the highest price for his labor, endeavors, as we have seen, to retain as long as possible the exclusive use of an agent, a process, or an instrument, of production. Now the proper mission and result of Competition being to withdraw this exclusive use from the individual in order to make it common property, it is natural that all men, in their capacity of producers, should unite in a concert of maledictions against Competition. They cannot reconcile themselves to Competition otherwise than by taking into account their interests as consumers, and regarding themselves, not as members of a coterie or a corporation, but as men.

Political Economy, we must say, has not yet exerted herself sufficiently to dissipate this fatal illusion, which has been the source of so much heartache, calamity, and irritation, and of so many wars. This science, from a preference that is narrowminded, has exhausted her efforts in analyzing the phenomena of production. The very nomenclature of the science, in fact, convenient as it is, is not in harmony with its object. Agriculture, manufactures, commerce, may be an excellent classification, when the object is to describe the processes of art; but that description, however essential in technology, has little connection with social economy—I should even say that it is positively dangerous. When we have classed men as agriculturists, manufacturers, and merchants, of what can we speak but of their class interests, of those special interests to which Competition is antagonistic, and which are placed in opposition to the general good? It is not for the sake of agriculturists that agriculture exists, of manufacturers that we have manufactures, or of merchants that we have exchanges, but in order that men should have at their disposal the greatest amount of commodities of every kind. Consumption, its laws, what favors it, and renders it equitable and moral—that is the interest that is truly social, and that truly affects the human race. It is the interest of the consumer that constitutes the real object of Political Economy, and upon which the science should concentrate its cleverest lights. This, in truth, forms the bond that unites classes, nations, races—it is the principle and explanation of human fraternity. It is with regret, then, that we see Economists expending their talents and sagacity on the anatomy of production, and throwing into the twisted conclusions of their books, or into supplementary chapters, a few common-places on the phenomena of consumption. Have we not even seen a justly celebrated professor suppressing entirely that branch of the science, confining himself to the means, without ever speaking of the result, and banishing from his course everything in connection with the consumption of wealth, as pertaining, in his opinion, to morals rather than to Political Economy? Can we be surprised that men are more struck with the inconveniences of Competition than with its advantages, since the former affect them specially as producers—in which character they are constantly considered and talked of; while the latter affect them only in their capacity of consumers—a capacity that is altogether disregarded and overlooked?

I repeat that I do not deny or ignore, on the contrary, I deplore as much anyone can, the sufferings attendant on Competition; but is this any reason for shutting our eyes to its advantages? And it is all the more consoling to observe these advantages, inasmuch as I believe Competition, like all the great laws of nature, to be indestructible. Had it been otherwise, it would assuredly have succumbed to the universal resistance that all the men who have ever co-operated in the production of commodities since the beginning of the world have offered to it, and more especially it would have perished under the combined assault of our modern reformers. But if they have been foolish enough to attempt its destruction, they have not been strong enough to effect it.

And what progressive principle, I would ask, is to be found in the world, the beneficent action of which is not mingled, especially in the beginning, with suffering and misery? The massing together of human beings in vast agglomerations is favorable to boldness and independence of thought, but it frequently sets private life free from the wholesome restraint of public opinion, and gives shelter to debauchery and crime. Wealth and leisure united give birth to mental cultivation, but they also give birth to pride and luxury among the rich, and to irritation and covetousness among the poor. The art of printing brings home knowledge and truth to all ranks of society; but it has brought also afflicting doubt and subversive error. Political liberty has unchained tempests and revolutions, and has modified the simple manners of primitive nations, to such a degree as to induce thinking men to ask themselves whether they would not have preferred tranquillity under the cold shade of despotism. Christianity herself has cast the noble seed of love and charity into a soil saturated with the blood of martyrs.

Why has it entered into the designs of Infinite Goodness and Justice that the happiness of one region or of one era should be purchased at the expense of the sufferings of another region or of another era? What is the Divine purpose that is concealed under this great law of solidarity, of which Competition is only one of the mysterious aspects? Human science cannot answer. What we do know is this, that good always goes on increasing, and that evil goes on diminishing. From the beginning of the social state, such as conquest had made it, when there existed only masters and slaves, and the inequality of conditions was extreme, the work of Competition in approximating ranks, fortunes, intelligences, could not be accomplished without inflicting individual hardships, the intensity of which, however, as the work proceeded, has gone on diminishing, like the vibrations of sound and the oscillations of the pendulum. To the sufferings yet in reserve for them, men learn every day to oppose two powerful remedies—namely, foresight, which is the fruit of knowledge and experience; and association, which is organized foresight.

CONCLUDING OBSERVATIONS

In the first part of this work—alas! too hastily written—I have endeavored to keep the reader's attention fixed upon the line of demarcation, always flexible, but always marked, that separates the two regions of the economic world—natural co-operation and human labor—the bounty of God and the work of man—the gratuitous, and the onerous—that which in exchange is remunerated and that which is transferred without remuneration—aggregate utility and the fractional and supplementary utility that constitutes value—absolute wealth and relative wealth—the co-operation of chemical or mechanical forces, constrained to aid production by the instruments that render them available, and the just recompense of the labor that has created these instruments themselves—Community and Property.

It is not enough to mark these two orders of phenomena that are so essentially different, it is necessary also to describe their relations and, if I may so express myself, their harmonious evolutions. I have essayed to explain how the business of Property consists in conquering utility for the human race and, casting it into the domain of Community, to move on to new conquests—so that each given effort, and consequently the aggregate of efforts, should continually be delivering over to mankind satisfactions which are always increasing. Human services exchanged, while preserving their relative value, become the vehicle of an always increasing proportion of utility that is gratuitous, and, therefore common; and in this consists progress. The possessors of value, then, whatever form it assumes, far from usurping and monopolizing the gifts of God, multiply these gifts; without causing them to lose the character that Providence has affixed to them, of being—Gratuitous.

In proportion as the satisfactions that are handed over by progress to the charge of nature fall by that very fact into the domain of Community, they become equal—it being impossible for us even to conceive inequality except in the domain of human services, which are compared, appreciated, and estimated with a view to an exchange; whence it follows that Equality among men is necessarily progressive. It is so, likewise, in another respect, the action of Competition having for its inevitable result to level and equalize the services themselves, and to bring their recompense more and more into proportion with their merit.

Let us now throw a glance back on the ground over which we have passed.

By the light of the theory, the foundation of which has been laid in the present volume, we shall have to investigate:

The relations of man with the Economic phenomena, in his capacity of producer, and in his character of consumer;

The law of Rent;

That of Wages;

That of Credit;

That of Taxation, which, introducing us into the domain of Politics, properly so called, will lead us to compare those services that are private and voluntary with those that are public and compulsory;

The law of Population.

We shall then be in a situation to solve some practical problems that are still disputed—Free trade, Machinery, Luxury, Leisure, Association, Organization of labor, etc.

I hesitate not to say, that the result of this exposition may be expressed beforehand in these terms: The constant approximation of all men toward a level that is always rising—in other terms: Improvement and Equalization; in a single word, Harmony.

Such is the definitive result of the arrangements of Providence—of the great laws of nature—when they act without impediment, when we regard them as they are in themselves, and apart from any disturbance of their action by error and violence. On beholding this Harmony, the Economist may well exclaim, like the astronomer who regards the planetary movements, or the physiologist who contemplates the structure and arrangement of the human organs—*Digitus Dei est hic!*

But man is a free agent, and consequently fallible. He is subject to ignorance and to passion. His will, which is liable to err, enters as an element into the play of the economic laws. He may misunderstand them, forget them, divert them from their purpose. As the physiologist, after admiring the infinite wisdom displayed in the structure and relations of our organs and viscera, studies these organs likewise in their abnormal state when sickly and diseased, we shall have to penetrate into a new world—the world of social Disturbances.

We shall pave the way for this new study by some considerations on man himself. It would be impossible for us to give an account of social evil, of its origin, its effects, its design—of the limits, always more and more contracted, within which it is shut up by its own action (which constitutes what I might almost venture to call a harmonic dissonance), did we not extend our investigation to the necessary consequences of Free Will, to the errors of Self interest, which are constantly corrected, and to the great laws of human Responsibility and Solidarity.

We have seen the germ of all the social Harmonies included in these two principles—Property and Liberty. We shall see that all social Dissonances are only the development of these two antagonistic principles—Spoliation and Oppression.

The words Property and Liberty, in fact, express only two aspects of the same idea. In an economical point of view, Liberty is allied to the act of production—Property to the things produced. And since Value has its foundation in the human act, we may conclude that Liberty implies and includes Property. The same relation exists between Oppression and Spoliation.

Liberty! here at length we have the principle of harmony. Oppression! here we have the principle of dissonance. The struggle of these two powers fills the annals of the human race.

And as the design of Oppression is to effect an unjust appropriation, as it resolves itself into and is summed up in spoliation, it is Spoliation that must form the subject of our inquiry.

Man comes into this world bound to the yoke of Want, which is pain.

He cannot escape from it but by subjecting himself to the yoke of labor, which is pain also.

He has, then, only a choice of pains, and he detests pain.

This is the reason why he looks around him, and if he sees that his fellow-man has accumulated wealth, he conceives the thought of appropriating it. Hence comes false property, or Spoliation.

Spoliation! here we have a new element in the economy of society. From the day when it first made its appearance in the world down to the day when it shall have completely disappeared, if that day ever come, this element has affected and will affect profoundly the whole social mechanism; it will disturb, and to the extent of rendering them no longer recognizable, those laws of social harmony we have endeavored to discover and describe.

Our duty, then, will not have been accomplished until we have completed the monography of Spoliation.

It may be imagined that we have here to do with an accidental and exceptional fact, a transient derangement unworthy of the investigations of science.

But in truth it is not so. On the contrary, Spoliation, in the traditions of families, in the history of nations, in the occupations of individuals, in the physical and intellectual energies of classes, in the schemes and designs of governments, occupies nearly as prominent a place as Property itself.

No; Spoliation is not an ephemeral scourge, affecting accidentally the social mechanism, and which economical science may disregard as exceptional.

The sentence pronounced upon man in the beginning was, In the sweat of thy brow shalt thou eat bread. Whence it appears that effort and satisfaction are indissolubly united, and that the one must be always the recompense of the other. But on all sides we find man revolting against this law, and saying to his brother, Thine be the labor, and mine the fruit of that labor.

Repair to the hut of the savage hunter, or to the tent of the nomad shepherd, and what spectacle meets your eyes? The wife, lank, pale, disfigured, affrighted, prematurely old, bears the whole burden of the household cares, while the man lounges in idleness. What idea can we form of family Harmonies? The idea has disappeared, for Strength here throws upon Feebleness the weight of labor. And how many ages of civilizing effort will be needed to raise the wife from this state of frightful degradation?

Spoliation, in its most brutal form, armed with torch and sword, fills the annals of the world. Of what names is history made up? Cyrus, Sesostris, Alexander, Scipio, Caesar, Attila, Tamerlane, Mahomet, Pizarro, William the Conqueror—pure Spoliation from beginning to end in the shape of Conquest. Hers are the laurels, the monuments, the statues, the triumphal arches, the song of the poet, the intoxicating enthusiasm of the maidens!

The Conqueror soon finds that he can turn his victories to more profitable account than by putting to death the vanquished; and Slavery covers the earth. Down to our own times, all over the world this has been the form in which societies have existed, bringing with it hatreds, resistance, internal struggles, and revolutions. And what is Slavery but organized oppression—organized for the purpose of Spoliation?

But Spoliation not only arms Force against Feebleness—she turns Intelligence against Credulity. What hard-working people in the world has escaped being mulcted by sacerdotal theocracies, Egyptian priests, Greek oracles, Roman auguries, Gallic druids, Indian brahmans, muftis, ulemas, bonzes, monks, ministers, mountebanks, sorcerers, soothsayers—spoliators of all garbs and of all denominations. Assuming this guise, Spoliation places the fulcrum of her lever in heaven, and sacrilegiously prides herself on the complicity of the gods! She enslaves not men's limbs only, but their souls. She knows how to impress the iron of slavery as well upon the conscience of Seide[1] as upon the forehead of Spartacus—realizing what would seem impossible—Mental Slavery.

Mental Slavery! what a frightful association of words! O Liberty! we have seen thee hunted from country to country, crushed by conquest, groaning under slavery, insulted in courts, banished from schools, laughed at in saloons, misunderstood in workshops, denounced in churches. It seems thou shouldst find in thought an inviolable refuge. But if thou art to surrender in this thy last asylum, what becomes of the hopes of ages, and the boasted courage of the human race?

At length, however, the progressive nature of man causes Spoliation to produce, in the society in which it exists, resistance that paralyzes its force, and knowledge that unveils its impostures. But Spoliation does not confess herself conquered for all that; she only becomes more crafty, and, enveloping herself in the forms of government and in a system of checks and balances, she gives birth to Politics, long a prolific resource. We then see her usurping the liberty of citizens, the better to get hold of their wealth, and draining away their wealth to possess herself more surely of their liberty. Private activity passes into the domain of public activity. Everything is transacted through functionaries, and an unintelligent and meddling bureaucracy overspreads the land. The public treasury becomes a vast reservoir into which laborers pour their savings, to be immediately distributed among bureaucrats.

---

[1]See Voltaire's tragedy, *Le Fanatisme.*—Translator.

Transactions are no longer regulated by free bargaining and discussion, and the mutuality of services disappears.

In this state of things the true notion of Property is extinguished, and everyone appeals to the Law to give his services a factitious value.

We enter then upon the era of privileges. Spoliation, ever improving in subtlety, fortifies herself in Monopoly, and takes refuge behind Restrictions. She displaces the natural current of exchanges, and sends capital into artificial channels, and with capital, labor—and with labor, population. She gets painfully produced in the North what is produced with facility in the South; creates precarious classes and branches of industry; substitutes for the gratuitous forces of nature the onerous fatigues of labor; cherishes establishments that can sustain no rivalry, and invokes against competitors the employment of force; provokes international jealousies; flatters patriotic arrogance; and invents ingenious theories, which make accomplices of her own dupes. She constantly renders imminent industrial crises and bankruptcies, shakes to its foundation all confidence in the future, all faith in liberty, all consciousness of what is just. At length, when science exposes her misdeeds, she stirs up against science her own victims, by proclaiming a Utopia! and ignores not only the science that places obstacles in her path, but the very idea of any possible science, by this crowning sentence of skepticism—There are no principles!

Under the pressure of suffering, at length the masses rise, and overturn everything that is above them. Government, taxes, legislation, everything is at their mercy, and you imagine perhaps that there is now an end to the reign of Spoliation;—that the mutuality of services is about to be established on the only possible, or even imaginable basis—Liberty. Undeceive yourself. The fatal idea, alas! has permeated the masses, that Property has no other origin, no other sanction, no other legitimacy, no other foundation, than Law; and then the masses set to work legislatively to rob one another. Suffering from the wounds that have been inflicted upon them, they undertake to cure each of their members by conceding to him the right to oppress his neighbor, and call this Solidarity and Fraternity. "You have produced—I have not produced—we are solidaires—let us divide." "You have something—I have nothing—we are brethren—let us share." It will be our duty then to examine the improper use that has been made in these latter days of the terms association, organization, labor, *gratuite du credit*, etc. We shall have to subject them to this test—Do they imply Liberty or Oppression? In other words, are they in unison with the great Economic laws, or are they distortions of those laws?

Spoliation is a phenomenon too universal, too persistent, to permit us to attribute to it a character purely accidental. In this, as in many other matters, we cannot separate the study of natural laws from the study of their Perturbations.

But, it may be said, if spoliation enters necessarily into the play of the social mechanism as a dissonance, how can you venture to assert the Harmony of the Economic laws?

I must repeat here what I have said in another place, namely, that in all that concerns man, a being who is only perfectible because he is imperfect, Harmony consists not in the absolute absence of evil, but in its gradual diminution. The social body, like the human body, is provided with a curative force, *a vis medicatrix,* the laws and infallible power of which it is impossible to study without again exclaiming, *Digitus Dei est hic.*

IX.

HARMONIES OF POLITICAL ECONOMY

BOOK TWO

11

PRODUCER—CONSUMER

I f the level of the human race is not continually rising, man is not a perfectible being.

If the social tendency is not a constant approximation of all men toward this progressive elevation, the economic laws are not harmonious.

Now, how can the level of humanity be rising, if each given quantity of labor does not yield a constantly increasing amount of enjoyments, a phenomenon that can be explained only by the transformation of onerous into gratuitous utility?

And, on the other hand, how can this utility, having become gratuitous, bring men nearer and nearer to a common level, if the utility has not at the same time itself become common?

Here, then, we discover the essential law of social harmony.

I should have been pleased had the language of Political Economy furnished me with two words other than the terms production and consumption to designate services that are rendered and received. These terms savor too much of materiality. There are evidently services, like those of the clergyman, the professor, the soldier, the artist, that tend to the furtherance of morality, education, security, taste, that have nothing in common with mechanical or manufacturing industry except this, that the end to be attained is satisfaction or enjoyment.

The terms I have referred to are those generally employed, and I have no wish to become a neologist. But let it be understood that by production I mean what confers utility, and by consumption the enjoyment to which that utility gives rise.

Let the protectionist school—which is in reality a phase of Communism—believe that in employing the terms producer and consumer we are not absurd enough to wish to represent the human race as divided into two distinct classes, the one engaged exclusively in the work of producing, the other exclusively in that of consuming. The naturalist divides the human race into whites and blacks, or into men and women, and the economist, forsooth, is not to classify them as producers and consumers, because, as the protectionist gentlemen sagely remark, producer and consumer make but one person!

Why, it is for the very reason that they do make but one that each individual comes to be considered by the science of Political Economy in this double capacity. Our business is not to divide the human race into two classes, but to study man under two very different aspects. If the protectionists were to forbid grammarians to employ the pronouns I and thou, on the pretext that every man is in turn the person speaking and the person spoken to, it would be a sufficient answer to say, that although it be perfectly true that we cannot place all the tongues on one side, and all the ears on the other, since every man has both ears and a tongue, it by no means follows that, with reference to each proposition enunciated, the tongue does not pertain to one man and the ear to another. In the same way, with reference to every service, the man who renders it is quite distinct from the man who receives it. The producer and consumer are always set opposite each other, so much so that they have always a controversy.

The very people who object to our studying mankind under the double aspect of producers and consumers have no difficulty in making this distinction when they address themselves to legislative assemblies. We then find them demanding monopoly or freedom of trade, according as the matter in dispute refers to a commodity they sell, or a commodity they purchase.

Without dwelling longer, then, on this preliminary exception taken by the protectionists, let us acknowledge that in the social order the separation of employments causes each man to occupy two situations, sufficiently distinct to render their action and relations worthy of our study.

In general, we devote ourselves to some special trade, profession, or career, and it is not from the products of that particular line of work that we expect to derive our satisfactions. We render and receive services; we supply and demand values; we make purchases and sales; we work for others, and others work for us: in short, we are producers and consumers.

According as we present ourselves in the market in one or other of these capacities, we carry thither a spirit that is very different, or rather, I should say, very opposite. Suppose, for example, that corn is the subject of the transaction. The same man has very different views when he goes to market as a purchaser from what he has when he goes there as a seller. As a purchaser, he desires abundance; as a seller, scarcity. In either case, these desires may be traced to the same source—personal interest; but as to sell or buy, to give or to receive, to supply or to demand, are acts as opposite as possible, they cannot but give rise, and from the same motive, to opposite desires.

Antagonistic desires cannot at one and the same time coincide with the general good.

In another work,[1] I have endeavored to show that the wishes or desires of men in their capacity of consumers are those which

---

[1] *Economic Sophisms*, chap. 1 (1st series).

are in harmony with the public interest; and it cannot be otherwise. For seeing that enjoyment is the end and design of labor, and that the labor is determined only by the obstacle to be overcome, it is evident that labor is in this sense an evil, and that everything should tend to diminish it; that enjoyment is a good, and that everything should tend to increase it.

And here presents itself the great, the perpetual, the deplorable illusion that springs from the erroneous definition of value, and from confounding value with utility.

Value being simply a relation, is of as much greater importance to each individual as it is of less importance to society at large.

What renders service to the masses is utility alone; and value is not at all the measure of it.

What renders service to the individual is still only utility. But value is the measure of it; for, with each determinate value, he obtains from society the utility of his choice, in the proportion of that value.

If we regard man as an isolated being, it is as clear as day that consumption, and not production, is the essential thing; for consumption to a certain extent implies labor, but labor does not imply consumption.

The separation of employments has led certain economists to measure the general prosperity not by consumption, but by labor. And by following these economists we have come to this strange subversion of principle, to favor labor at the expense of its results.

The reasoning has been this: The more difficulties are overcome the better. Then augment the difficulties to be conquered.

The error of this reasoning is manifest.

No doubt, a certain amount of difficulties being given, it is fortunate that a certain quantity of labor also given should surmount as many of these difficulties as possible. But to diminish the power of the labor or augment that of the difficulties in order to increase value is positively monstrous.

An individual member of society is interested in this, that his services, while preserving even the same degree of utility, should increase in value. Suppose his desires in this respect to be realized, it is easy to perceive what will happen. He is better off, but his brethren are worse off, seeing that the total amount of utility has not been increased.

We cannot then reason from particulars to generals, and say: Pursue such measures as in their result will satisfy the desire that all individuals seek to see the value of their services augmented.

Value being a relation, we should have accomplished nothing if the increase in all departments were proportionate to the anterior value; if it were arbitrary and unequal for different services, we should have done nothing but introduce injustice into the distribution of utilities.

It is of the nature of every bargain or mercantile transaction to give rise to a debate. But by using this word debate, shall I not bring down upon myself all the sentimental schools that are nowadays so numerous? Debate implies antagonism, it will be said. You admit, then, that antagonism is the natural state of society. Here again I have to break another lance; for in this country economic science is so little understood that one cannot make use of a word without raising up an opponent.

I have been justly reproached for using the phrase that "Between the seller and buyer there exists a radical antagonism." The word antagonism, when strengthened by the word radical, implies much more than I meant to express. It would seem to imply a permanent opposition of interests, consequently an indestructible social dissonance; while what I wished to indicate was merely that transient debate or discussion which precedes every commercial transaction, and which is inherent in the very idea of a bargain.

As long as, to the regret of the sentimental utopian, there shall remain a vestige of liberty in the world, buyers and sellers will discuss their interests, and higgle about prices; nor will the social laws cease to be harmonious on that account. Is it possible to conceive that the man who offers and the man who demands a service should meet each other in the market without having for the moment a different idea of its value? Is that to set the world on fire? Must all commercial transactions, all exchanges, all barter, all liberty, be banished from this earth, or are we to allow each of the contracting parties to defend his position, and urge and put forward his motives? It is this very free debate or discussion that gives rise to the equivalence of services and the equity of transactions. By what other means can our system-makers ensure this equity that is so desirable? Would they by legislation trammel the liberty of one of the parties only? Then the one must be in the power of the other. Would they take away from both the liberty of managing their own affairs, under the pretext that they ought henceforth to buy and sell on the principle of fraternity? Let me tell the Socialists that it is here their absurdity becomes apparent, for, in the long run, these interests will automatically be regulated and adjusted. Is the discussion to be inverted, the purchaser taking the part of the seller, and vice versa? Such transactions would be very diverting, we must allow. "Please, sir, give me only 10 francs for this cloth." "What say you? I will give you 20 for it." "But, my good sir, it is worth nothing—it is out of fashion—it will be worn out in a fortnight," says the merchant. "It is of the best quality, and will last two winters," replies the customer. "Very well, sir, to please you, I will add 5 francs—this is all the length that fraternity will allow me to go." "It is against my Socialist principles to pay less than 20 francs, but we must learn to make sacrifices, and I agree." Thus this whimsical transaction will just arrive at the ordinary result, and our system-makers will regret to see accursed liberty still surviving, although turned upside down and engendering a new antagonism.

That is not what we want, say the organisateurs; what we desire is liberty. Then what would you be at? for services must still be exchanged, and conditions adjusted. We expect that the care of adjusting them should be left to us. I suspected as much.

Fraternity! bond of brotherhood, sacred flame kindled by heaven in man's soul, how has thy name been abused! In thy name all freedom has been stifled. In thy name a new despotism, such as the world had never before seen, has been erected; and we are at length driven to fear that the very name of fraternity, after being thus sullied, and having served as the rallying cry of so many incapables, the mask of so much ambition, and proud contempt of human dignity, should end by losing altogether its grand and noble significance.

Let us no longer, then, aim at overturning everything, domineering over everything and everybody, and withdrawing all—men and things—from the operation of natural laws. Let us leave the world as God has made it. Let us, poor scribblers, not imagine ourselves anything else than observers, more or less exact, of what is passing around us. Let us no longer render ourselves ridiculous by pretending to change human nature, as if we were ourselves beyond humanity and its errors and weaknesses. Let us leave producers and consumers to take care of their own interests, and to arrange and adjust these interests by honest and peaceful conventions. Let us confine ourselves to the observation of relations, and the effects to which they give rise. This is precisely what I am about to do, keeping always in view this general law, which I apprehend to be the law of human society, namely, the gradual equalization of individuals and of classes, combined with general progress.

A line no more resembles a force or a velocity than it does a value or a utility. Mathematicians, nevertheless, make use of diagrams; and why should not the economist do the same?

We have values that are equal, values the mutual relations of which are known as the half, the quarter, double, triple, etc. There is nothing to prevent our representing these differences by lines of various lengths.

But the same thing does not hold with reference to utility. General utility, as we have seen, may be resolved into gratuitous utility and onerous utility, the former due to the action of nature, the latter the result of human labor. This last being capable of being estimated and measured, may be represented by a line of determinate length; but the other is not susceptible of estimation or of measurement. No doubt in the production of a measure of wheat, of a cask of wine, of an ox, of a stone of wool, a ton of coals, a bundle of faggots, nature does much. But we have no means of measuring this natural co-operation of forces, most of which are unknown to us, and which have been in operation since the beginning of time. Nor have we any interest in doing so. We may represent gratuitous utility, then, by an indefinite line.

Now, let there be two items, the value of the one being double that of the other, they may be represented by these lines:

```
I                              A                          B
. . . . . . . . . . . . . . . . . _____

I                              C              D
. . . . . . . . . . . . . . . . . _____
```

IB, ID, represent the total items, general utility, what satisfies man's wants, absolute wealth.

IA, IC, the co-operation of nature, gratuitous utility, the part that belongs to the domain of community.

AB, CD, human service, onerous utility, value, relative wealth, the part that belongs to the domain of property.

I need not say that AB, which you may suppose, if you will, to represent a house, a piece of furniture, a book, a song sung by Jenny Lind, a horse, a bale of cloth, a consultation of physicians, etc., will exchange for twice CD, and that the two men who effect the exchange will give into the bargain, and without even being aware of it, the one, once IA, the other twice IC.

Man is so constituted that his constant endeavor is to diminish the proportion of effort to result, to substitute the action of nature for his own action; in a word, to accomplish more with less. This is the constant aim of his skill, his intelligence, and his energy.

Let us suppose then that John, the producer of IB, discovers a process by means of which he accomplishes his work with one-half the labor it formerly cost him, taking everything into account, even the construction of the instrument by means of which he avails himself the co-operation of nature.

As long as he preserves his secret, we shall have no change in the figures we have given above; AB and CD will represent the same values, the same relations; for John alone of all the world being acquainted with the improved process, he will turn it exclusively to his own profit and advantage. He will take his ease for half the day, or else he will make, each day, twice the quantity of IB, and his labor will be better remunerated. The discovery he has made is for the good of mankind, but mankind in this case is represented by one man.

And here let us remark, in passing, how fallacious is the axiom of the English Economists that value comes from labor, if thereby it is intended to represent value and labor as proportionate. Here we have the labor diminished by one-half, and yet no change in the value. This is what constantly happens, and why? Because the service is the same. Before as after the discovery, as long as it is a secret, he who gives or transfers IB renders the same service. But things will no longer be in the same position when Peter, the producer of ID, is enabled to say, "You ask me for two hours of my labor in exchange for one hour of yours; but I have found out your process, and if you set so high a price on your service, I shall serve myself."

Now this day must necessarily come. A process once realized is not long a mystery. Then the value of the product IB will fall by one-half, and we shall have these two figures:

I	A	A′	B
. . . .		_____	

I		C	D
. . . .		_____	

AA′ represents value annihilated, relative wealth that has disappeared, property become common, utility formerly onerous, now gratuitous.

For, as regards John, who here represents the producer, he is reinstated in his former condition. With the same effort it cost him formerly to produce IB, he can now produce twice as much. In order to obtain twice ID, we see him constrained to give twice IB, or what IB represents, be it furniture, books, houses, or what it may.

Who profits by all this? Clearly Peter, the producer of ID, who here represents consumers in general, including John himself. If, in fact, John desires to consume his own product, he profits by the saving of time represented by the suppression of AA′. As regards Peter, that is to say as regards consumers in general, they can now purchase IB with half the expenditure of time, effort, labor, value, compared with what it would have cost them before the intervention of natural forces. These forces, then, are gratuitous and, moreover, held in common.

Since I have ventured to illustrate my argument by geometrical figures, perhaps I may be permitted to give another example, and I shall be happy if by this method—somewhat whimsical, I allow, as applied to Political Economy—I can render more intelligible to the reader the phenomena I wish to describe.

As a producer, or as a consumer, every man may be considered as a center, from whence radiate the services he renders, and to which tend the services he receives in exchange.

Suppose then that there is placed at A (Fig. 1) a producer, a copyist, for example, or transcriber of manuscripts, who here represents all producers, or production in general. He furnishes to society four manuscripts. If at the present moment the value of each of these manuscripts is equal to 15, he renders services equal to 60, and receives an equal value, variously spread over a multitude of services. To simplify the demonstration, I suppose only four of them, proceeding from four points of the circumference BCDE.

This man, we now suppose, discovers the art of printing. He can thenceforth produce in 40 hours what formerly would have cost him 60. Admit that competition forces him to reduce proportionally the price of his books, and that in place of being worth 15, they are now worth only 10. But then in place of four our workman can now produce six books. On the other hand, the fund of remuneration proceeding from the circumference,

Figure 1

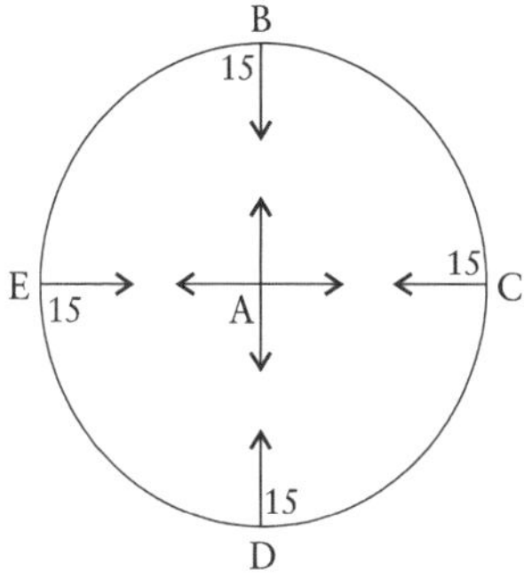

Figure 2

Value produced	=	60
Value received	=	60
Utility produced	=	4

Value produced	=	60
Value received	=	60
Utility produced	=	6

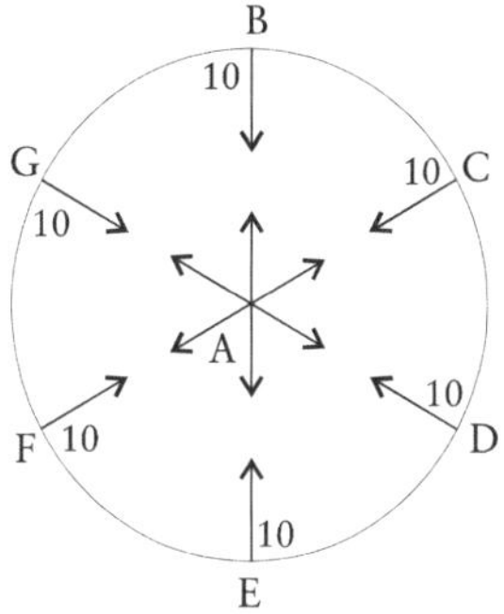

amounting to 60, has not changed. There is remuneration for six books, worth 10 each, just as there was formerly remuneration for four manuscripts, each worth 15.

This, let me remark briefly, is what is always lost sight of in discussing the question of machinery, of free trade, and of progress in general. Men see the labor set free and rendered disposable by the expeditive process, and they become alarmed. They do not see that a corresponding proportion of remuneration is rendered disposable also by the same circumstance.

The new transactions we have supposed are represented by Fig. 2, where we see radiate from the center A a total value of 60 spread over six books, in place of four manuscripts. From the circumference still proceeds a value equal to 60, necessary now as formerly to make up the balance.

Who then has gained by the change? As regards value, no one. As regards real wealth, positive satisfactions, the countless body of consumers ranged around the circumference. Each of them can now purchase a book with an amount of labor reduced by one-third. But the consumers are the human race. For observe that A himself, if he gains nothing in his capacity of producer—if he is obliged, as formerly, to perform 60 hours' labor in order to obtain the old remuneration—nevertheless, in so far as he is a consumer of books, gains exactly as others do. Like them, if he desires to read, he can procure this enjoyment with an economy of labor equal to one-third.

But if, in his character of producer, he finds himself at length deprived of the profit of his own inventions by competition, where in that case is his compensation?

His compensation consists, first, in this, that as long as he was able to preserve his secret, he continued to sell for 15 what he produced at the cost of 10; second, in this, that he obtains books for his own use at a smaller cost, and thus participates in the advantages he has procured for society. But, third, his compensation consists above all in this, that just in the same way as he has been forced to impart to his fellow-men the benefit of his own progress, he benefits by the progress of his fellow-men.

Just as the progress accomplished by A (Fig. 3) has profited B, C, D, and E, the progress realized by B, C, D, and E has profited A. By turns A finds himself at the center and at the circumference of universal industry, for he is by turns producer and consumer. If B, for example, is a cotton-spinner who has introduced improved machinery, the profit will redound to A as well as to C and D. If C is a mariner who has replaced the oar by the sail, the economy of labor will profit B, A, and E.

In short, the whole mechanism reposes on this law:

Progress benefits the producer, as such, only during the time necessary to recompense his skill. It soon produces a fall of value, and leaves to the first imitators a fair, but small, recompense. At length value becomes proportioned to the diminished labor, and the whole saving accrues to society at large.

Thus all profit by the progress of each, and each profits by the progress of all. The principle, each for all, all for each, put forward by the Socialists, and which they would have us receive

Figure 3

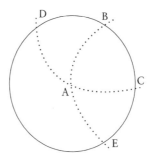

as a novelty, the germ of which is to be discovered in their organizations founded on oppression and constraint, God Himself has given us; and He has educed it from liberty.

God, I say, has given us this principle, and He has not established it in a model community presided over by Mr. Considerant, or in a Phalanstere of six hundred "harmoniens," or in a tentative Icaria, on condition that a few fanatics should submit themselves to the arbitrary power of a monomaniac, and that the faithless should pay for the true believers. No, God has established the principle each for all and all for each, generally, universally, by a marvelous mechanism, in which justice, liberty, utility, and sociability are mingled and reconciled in such a degree as ought to discourage these manufacturers of social organizations.

Observe that this great law of each for all and all for each is much more universal than my demonstration supposes it. Words are dull and heavy, and the pen still more so. The writer is obliged to exhibit successively, and one after the other, with despairing slowness, phenomena that recommend themselves to our admiration only in the aggregate.

Thus, I have just spoken of inventions. You might conclude that this was the only case in which progress, once attained, escapes from the producer, and goes to enlarge the common fund of mankind. It is not so. It is a general law that every advantage of whatever kind, proceeding from local situation, climate, or any other liberality of nature, slips rapidly from the hands of the person who first discovered and appropriated it—not on that account to be lost, but to go to feed the vast reservoir from which the enjoyments of mankind are derived. One condition alone is attached, which is that labor and transactions should be free. To run counter to liberty is to run counter to the designs of Providence; it is to suspend the operation of God's law, and limit progress in a double sense.

What I have just said with reference to the transfer of advantages holds equally true of evils and disadvantages. Nothing remains permanently with the producer—neither advantages nor inconveniences. Both tend to disseminate themselves through society at large.

We have just seen with what avidity the producer seeks to avail himself of whatever may facilitate his work; and we have seen, too, in how short a time the profit arising from inventions and discoveries slips from the inventor's hands. It seems as if that profit were not in the hands of a superior intelligence, but of a blind and obedient instrument of general progress.

With the same ardor he shuns all that can shackle his action; and this is a happy thing for the human race, for it is to mankind at large that in the long run obstacles are prejudicial. Suppose for example that A, the producer of books, is subjected to a heavy tax. He must add the amount of that tax to the price of his books. It will enter into the value of the books as a constituent part, the effect of which will be that B, C, D, and E must give more labor in exchange for the same satisfaction. Their compensation will consist in the purpose to which Government applies the tax. If the use to which it is applied is beneficial, they may gain instead of losing by the arrangement. If it is employed to oppress them, they will suffer in a double sense. But as far as A is concerned, he is relieved of the tax, although he pays it in the first instance.

I do not mean to say that the producer does not frequently suffer from obstacles of various kinds, and from taxes among others.

Sometimes he suffers most seriously from the operation of taxes, and it is precisely on that account that taxes tend to shift their incidence, and to fall ultimately on the masses.

Thus, in France, wine has been subjected to a multitude of exactions. And then a system has been introduced that restricts its sale abroad.

It is curious to observe what skips and bounds such burdens make in passing from the producer to the consumer. No sooner has the tax or restriction begun to operate than the producer endeavors to indemnify himself. But the demand of the consumers, as well as the supply of wine, remaining the same, the price cannot rise. The producer gets no more for his wine after, than he did before, the imposition of the tax. And as before the tax he received no more than an ordinary and adequate price, determined by services freely exchanged, he finds himself a loser by the whole amount of the tax. To cause the price to rise, he is obliged to diminish the quantity of wine produced.

The consumer, then—the public—is relative to the loss or profit that affects in the first instance certain classes of producers, what the earth is to electricity—the great common reservoir. All proceeds from it, and after some detours, longer or shorter as the case may be, and after having given rise to certain phenomena more or less varied, all returns to it again.

We have just shown that the economic effects only glance upon the producer, so to speak, on their way to the consumer, and that consequently all great and important questions of this kind must be regarded from the consumer's point of view if we wish to make ourselves masters of their general and permanent consequences.

This subordination of the interests of the producer to those of the consumer, which we have deduced from the consideration of utility, is fully confirmed when we advert to the consideration of morality.

Responsibility, in fact, always rests with the initiative. Now where is the initiative? In demand.

Demand (which implies the means of remuneration) determines all—the direction of capital and of labor, the distribution of population, the morality of professions, etc. Demand answers to Desire, while Supply answers to Effort. Desire is reasonable or unreasonable, moral or immoral. Effort, which is only an effect, is morally neutral, or has only a reflected morality.

Demand or Consumption says to the producer, "Make that for me." The producer obeys. And this would be evident in every case if the producer always and everywhere waited for the demand.

But in practice this is not the case.

Is it exchange that has led to the division of labor, or the division of labor that has given rise to exchange? This is a subtle and thorny question. Let us say that man makes exchanges because, being intelligent and sociable, he comprehends that this is one means of increasing the proportion of result to effort. That which results exclusively from the division of labor and from foresight, is that a man does not wait for a specific request to work for another. Experience teaches him tacitly that demand exists.

He makes the effort beforehand which is to satisfy the demand, and this gives rise to trades and professions. Beforehand he makes shoes, hats, etc., or prepares himself to sing, to teach, to plead, to fight, etc. But is it really the supply that precedes the demand, and determines it?

No. It is because there is a sufficient certainty that these different services will be demanded that men prepare to render them, although they do not always know precisely from what quarter the demand may come. And the proof of it is that the relation between these different services is sufficiently well known, that their value has been so widely tested that one may devote himself with some security to a particular manufacture, or embrace a particular career.

The impulse of demand is then pre-existent, seeing that one may calculate the intensity of it with so much precision.

Moreover, when a man betakes himself to a particular trade or profession, and sets himself to produce commodities, about what is he solicitous? Is it about the utility of the article he manufactures, or its results, good or bad, moral or immoral? Not at all; he thinks only of its value. It is the demander who looks to the utility. Utility answers to his want, his desire, his caprice. Value, on the contrary, has relation only to the effort made, to the service transferred. It is only when, by means of exchange, the producer in his turn becomes the demander that utility is looked to. When I resolve to manufacture hats rather than shoes, I do not ask myself the question whether men have a greater interest in protecting their heads or their heels. No, that concerns the demander, and determines the demand. The demand in its turn determines the value, or the degree of esteem in which the public holds the service. Value, in short, determines the effort or the supply.

Hence result some very remarkable consequences in a moral point of view. Two nations may be equally furnished with values, that is to say, with relative wealth (see part 1, chapter 6), and very unequally provided with real utilities, or absolute wealth; and this happens when one of them forms desires that are more unreasonable than those of the other—when the one considers its real wants, and the other creates for itself wants that are factitious or immoral.

Among one people a taste for education may predominate; among another a taste for good living. In such circumstances we render a service to the first when we have something to teach them; to the other, when we please their palate.

Now, services are remunerated according to the degree of importance we attach to them. If we do not exchange, if we render these services to ourselves, what should determine us if not the nature and intensity of our desires?

In one of the countries we have supposed, professors and teachers will abound; in the other, cooks.

In both, the services exchanged may be equal in the aggregate, and may consequently represent equal values, or equal relative wealth, but not the same absolute wealth. In other words, the one employs its labor well, and the other employs it ill.

And as regards satisfactions the result will be this: that the one people will have much instruction, and the other good dinners. The ultimate consequences of this diversity of tastes will have considerable influence not only upon real, but upon relative wealth; for education may develop new means of rendering services, which good dinners never can.

We remark among nations a prodigious diversity of tastes, arising from their antecedents, their character, their opinions, their vanity, etc.

No doubt there are some wants so imperious (hunger and thirst, for example) that we regard them as determinate quantities. And yet it is not uncommon to see a man scrimp himself of food in order to have good clothes, while another never thinks of his dress until his appetite is satisfied. The same thing holds of nations.

But these imperious wants once satisfied, everything else depends greatly on the will. It becomes an affair of taste, and in that region morality and good sense have much influence.

The intensity of the various national desires determines always the quantity of labor that each people subtracts from the aggregate of its efforts in order to satisfy each of its desires. An Englishman must, above all things, be well fed. For this reason he devotes an enormous amount of his labor to the production of food, and if he produces any other commodities, it is with the intention of exchanging them abroad for alimentary substances. The quantity of wheat, meat, butter, milk, sugar, etc., consumed in England is frightful. A Frenchman desires to be amused. He delights in what pleases his eye, and in frequent changes. His labors are in accordance with his tastes. Hence we have in France multitudes of singers, mountebanks, milliners, elegant shops, coffee-rooms, etc. In China, the natives dream away life agreeably under the influence of opium, and this is the reason why so great an amount of their national labor is devoted to procuring this precious narcotic, either by direct production or indirectly by means of exchange. In Spain, where the pomp of religious worship is carried to so great a height, the exertions of the people are bestowed on the decoration of churches, etc.

I shall not go to the length of asserting that there is no immorality in services that pander to immoral and depraved desires. But the immoral principle is obviously in the desire itself.

That would be beyond doubt were man living in a state of isolation; and it is equally true as regards man in society, for society is only individuality enlarged.

Who then would think of blaming our laborers in the south of France for producing brandy? They satisfy a demand. They dig their vineyards, dress their vines, gather and distill the grapes, without concerning themselves about the use that will be made of the product. It is for the man who seeks the enjoyment to consider whether it is proper, moral, rational, or productive of good. The responsibility rests with him. The business of the world could be conducted on no other footing. Is the tailor to tell his customer that he cannot make him a coat of the fashion he wants because it is extravagant, or because it prevents his breathing freely, etc., etc.?

Then what concern is it of our poor vintners if rich diners-out in London indulge too freely in claret? Or can we seriously accuse the English of raising opium in India with the deliberate intention of poisoning the Chinese?

A frivolous people requires frivolous manufactures, just as a serious people requires industry of a more serious kind. If the human race is to be improved, it must be by the improved morality of the consumer, not of the producer.

This is the design of religion in addressing the rich—the great consumers—so seriously on their immense responsibility. From another point of view, and employing a different language, Political Economy arrives at the same conclusion, when she affirms that we cannot check the supply of any commodity that is in demand; that as regards the producer, the commodity is simply a value, a sort of current coin that represents nothing either good or evil, while it is in the intention of the consumer that utility, or moral or immoral enjoyment, is to be discovered; consequently, that it is incumbent on the man who manifests the desire or makes the demand for the commodity to weigh the consequences, whether useful or hurtful, and to answer before God and man for the good or bad direction he impresses upon industry.

Thus from whatever point of view we regard the subject, we see clearly that consumption is the great end of Political Economy; and that good and evil, morality and immorality, harmonies and dissonances, all come to center in the consumer, for he represents mankind at large.

12

THE TWO APHORISMS

Modern moralists who contrast the maxim *Chacun pour tous, tous pour chacun*, to the old proverb *Chacun pour soi, chacun chez soi*, have formed a very incomplete, and for that reason a very false, and, I would add, a very melancholy idea of Society.

Let us eliminate, in the first place, from these two celebrated sayings what is superfluous. All for each is a redundancy, introduced from love of antithesis, for it is expressly included in each for all. As regards the saying *chacun chez soi*, the idea has no direct relation with the others; but, as it is of great importance in Political Economy, we shall make it hereafter the subject of inquiry.

It remains for us to consider the assumed opposition between these two members of the adages we have quoted, namely, each for all—each for himself. The one, it is said, expresses the sympathetic principle, the other the individualist or selfish principle. The first unites, the second divides.

Now, if we refer exclusively to the motive that determines the effort, the opposition is incontestable. But I maintain that if we consider the aggregate of human efforts in their results, the case is different. Examine Society, as it actually exists, obeying, as regards services that are capable of remuneration, the individualist or selfish principle; and you will be at once convinced that every man in working for himself is in fact working for all. This is beyond doubt. If the reader of these lines exercises a profession or trade, I entreat him for a moment to turn his regards upon himself; and I would ask him whether all his labors have not the satisfaction of others for their object, and, on the other hand, whether it is not to the exertions of others that he himself owes all his satisfactions.

It is evident that they who assert that each for himself and each for all are contradictory, conceive that an incompatibility exists between individualism and association. They think that each for himself implies isolation, or a tendency to isolation; that personal interest divides men, in place of uniting them, and that this principle tends to that of each by himself, that is to say, to the absence of all social relations.

In taking this view, I repeat, they form a false, because incomplete, idea of society. Even when moved only by personal interest, men seek to draw nearer each other, to combine their efforts, to unite their forces, to work for one another, to render reciprocal services, to associate. It would not be correct to say that they act in this way in spite of self-interest; they do so in obedience to self-interest. They associate because they find their benefit in it. If they did not find it to their advantage, they would not associate. Individualism, then, or a regard to personal interest, performs the work that the sentimentalists of our day would confide to Fraternity, to self-sacrifice, or some other motive opposed to self-love. And this just establishes the conclusion at which we never fail to arrive—that Providence has provided for the social state much better than the men can who call themselves its prophets. For of two things, choose only one; either union is injurious to individuality, or it is advantageous to it. If it injures it, what are the Socialist gentlemen to do, how can they manage, and what rational motive can they have to bring about a state of things that is hurtful to everybody? If, on the contrary, union is advantageous, it will be brought about by the action of personal interest, which is the strongest, the most permanent, the most uniform, the most universal, of all motives, let men say what they will.

Just look at how the thing actually works in practice. A squatter goes away to clear a field in the Far West. Not a day passes without his experiencing the difficulties isolation creates. A second squatter now makes his way to the desert. Where does he pitch his tent? Does he retire naturally to a distance from the first? No; he draws near to him naturally—and why? Because he knows all the advantages that men derive, with equal exertion, from the very circumstance of proximity. He knows that on various occasions they can accommodate each other by lending and borrowing tools and instruments, by uniting their action, by conquering difficulties insurmountable by individual exertion, by creating reciprocally a market for produce, by interchanging their views and opinions, and by providing for their common safety. A third, a fourth, a fifth squatter penetrates into the desert, and is invariably attracted by the smoke of the first settlements. Other people will then step in with larger capital, knowing that they will find hands there ready to be set to work. A colony is formed. They change somewhat the mode of culture; they form a path to the highway, by which the mail passes; they import and export; construct a church, a school-house, etc., etc. In a word, the power of the colonists is augmented by the very fact of their proximity, and to such a degree as to exceed, to an incalculable extent, the sum of their isolated and individual forces; and this is the motive that has attracted them toward each other.

But it may be said that every man for himself is a frigid maxim, which all the reasoning and paradoxes in the world cannot render otherwise than repugnant; that it smells of greed a mile off, and that greed is more than an evil in society, being itself the source of most other evils.

Now, listen a little, if you please.

If the maxim every man for himself is understood in this sense, that it is to regulate all our thoughts, acts, and relations, that we are to find it at the root of all our family and domestic affections, as fathers, sons, brothers, husbands, friends, citizens, or rather that it is to repress and to extinguish these affections, then I admit that it is frightful, horrible, and such, that were there one man upon the earth heartless enough to make it the rule of his conduct, that man dared not even proclaim it in theory.

But will the Socialists, in the teeth of fact and experience, always refuse to admit that there are two orders of human relations—one dependent on the sympathetic principle, and which we leave to the domain of morals—another springing from self-interest, and regulating transactions between men who know nothing of each other, and owe each other nothing but justice,—transactions regulated by voluntary covenants freely adjusted? Covenants of this last species are precisely those which come within the domain of Political Economy. It is, in truth, no more possible to base commercial transactions on the principle of sympathy, than it is to base family and friendly relations on self-interest. To the Socialists I shall never cease to address this remonstrance: You wish to mix up two things that cannot be confounded. If you were fools enough to wish to confound them, you have not the power to do it. The blacksmith, the carpenter, and the laborer, who exhaust their strength in rude avocations, may be excellent fathers, admirable sons; they may have the moral sense thoroughly developed, and carry in their breasts hearts of large and expansive sympathy. In spite of all that, you will never persuade them to labor from morning to night with the sweat of their brow, and impose upon themselves the hardest privations, upon a mere principle of devotion to their fellow-men. Your sentimental lectures on this subject are, and always will be, powerless. If, unfortunately, they could mislead a few operatives, they would just make so many dupes. Let a merchant set to work to sell his wares on the principle of Fraternity, and I venture to predict that, in less than a month, he will see himself and his children reduced to beggary.

Providence has done well, then, in giving to the social state very different guarantees. Taking man as we find him—sensibility and individuality, benevolence and self-love being inseparable—we cannot hope, we cannot desire to see the motive of personal interest universally eradicated—nor can we understand how it could be. And yet nothing short of this would be necessary in order to restore the equilibrium of human relations; for if you break this mainspring of action only in certain chosen spirits, you create two classes—scoundrels whom you thus tempt to make victims of their fellow-men—and the virtuous, for whom the part of victims is reserved.

Seeing, then, that as regards labor and exchanges, the principle each for himself must inevitably have the predominance as a motive of action, the marvelous and admirable thing is that the Author of all should have made use of that principle in order to realize in the social order the maxim of the advocates of Fraternity, each for all. In His skillful hand, the obstacle has become the instrument. The general interest has been entrusted to personal interest, and the one has become infallible because the other is indestructible. To me it would seem that, in presence of these wondrous results, the constructors of artificial societies might, without any excess of humility, acknowledge that, as regards organization, the Divine Architect has far surpassed them.

Remark, too, that in the natural order of society, the principle of each for all, based upon the principle of each for himself, is much more complete, much more absolute, much more personal, than it would be in the Socialist and Communist point of view. Not only do we work for all, but we cannot realize a single step of progress without its being profitable to the Community at large. (See part 1, chapters 10 and 11.) The order of things has been so marvelously arranged, that when we have invented a new process, or discovered the liberality of nature in any department—some new source of fertility in the soil, or some new mode of action in one of the laws of the physical world—the profit is ours temporarily, transiently, so long as to prove just as a recompense, and useful as an encouragement—after which the advantage escapes from our grasp, in spite of all our efforts to retain it. From individual it becomes social, and falls forever into the domain of the common and gratuitous. And while we thus impart the fruits of our progress to our fellow-men, we ourselves become participators in the progress that other men have achieved.

In short, by the rule each for himself, individual efforts, reinforced and invigorated, act in the direction of each for all, and every partial step of progress brings a thousand times more to society, in gratuitous utility, than it has brought to its inventor in direct profits.

With the maxim each for all no one would act exclusively for himself. What producer would take it into his head to double his labor in order to add a thirty-millionth part to his wages?

It may be said, then, why refute the Socialist aphorism? What harm can it do? Undoubtedly it will not introduce into workshops, counting-rooms, warehouses, nor establish in fairs and markets, the principle of self-sacrifice. But then it will either tend to nothing, and then we may let it sleep in peace, or it will bend somewhat that stiffness of the egotistical principle, that, excluding all sympathy, has scarcely right to claim any.

What is false is always dangerous. It is always a dangerous thing to represent as detestable and pernicious an eternal and universal principle that God has evidently destined to the conservation and advancement of the human race; a principle, I allow, as far as motive is concerned, that does not come home to our heart, but that, when viewed with reference to its results, astonishes and satisfies the mind; a principle, moreover, that leaves the field perfectly free to the action of those more elevated motives God has implanted in the heart of man.

But, then, what happens? The Socialist public adopts only one-half the Socialist maxim—the last half, all for each. They continue as before to work each for himself, but they require, over and above, that all should work for them.

It must be so. When dreamers desired to change the grand mainspring of human exertion by substituting fraternity for individualism, they found it necessary to invent a hypocritical contradiction. They set themselves to call out to the masses, "Stifle self-love in your hearts and follow us; you will be rewarded for it by unbounded wealth and enjoyment." When men try to parody the Gospel, they should come to a Gospel conclusion. Self-denial implies sacrifice and pain—self-devotion means "Take the lowest seat, be poor, and suffer voluntarily." But under pretense of abnegation to promise enjoyment; to exhibit wealth and prosperity behind the pretended sacrifice; to combat a passion they brand with the name of greed by addressing themselves to the grossest and most material tendencies; this is not only to render homage to the indestructible vitality of the principle they desire to overthrow, but to exalt it to the highest point while declaiming against it; it is to double the forces of the enemy, instead of conquering him; to substitute unjust covetousness for legitimate individualism; and, in spite of all the artifice of a mystical jargon, to excite the grossest sensualism. Let avarice answer this appeal.[1]

And is that not the position in which we now are? What is the universal cry among all ranks and classes? All for each. In pronouncing the word each, we are thinking of ourselves, and what we ask is to have a share that we have not merited in the fruits of other men's labor. In other words, we systematize spoliation. No doubt spoliation simple and naked is so unjust that we repudiate it; but by dint of the maxim, all for each, we allay the scruples of conscience. We impose upon others the duty of working for us, and we arrogate to ourselves the right to enjoy the fruits of other men's labor. We summon the State, the law, to impose the pretended duty, to protect the pretended right, and we arrive at the whimsical result of robbing one another in the sacred name of

---

[1] When the vanguard of the Icarian expedition left Havre, I questioned some of these visionaries with a view to discover their real thoughts. Competence easily obtained, such was their hope and their motive. One of them said to me, "I am going, and my brother follows with the second expedition. He has eight children, and you see what a great thing it will be for him to have no longer to educate and maintain them." "I see it at once," I replied, "but that heavy charge must fall on some other body." To rid oneself of a burden and transfer it to the shoulders of another, such was the sense in which these unfortunate people understood the apothegm of fraternity—all for each.

Fraternity. We live at other men's expense, and attribute heroism to the sacrifice. What an odd, strange thing the human mind is! and how subtle is covetousness! It is not enough that each of us should endeavor to increase his share at the expense of his fellows, it is not enough that we should desire to profit by labor that we have not performed; we persuade ourselves that in acting thus we are displaying a sublime example of self-sacrifice. We almost go the length of comparing ourselves to the primitive Christians, and yet we blind ourselves so far as not to see that the sacrifices that make us weep in fond admiration of our own virtue are sacrifices we do not make, but which, on the contrary, we exact.

It is worth observing the manner in which this mystification is effected.

Steal! Horrors, that is mean—besides it leads to jail, for the law forbids it. But if the law authorized it, and lent its aid, would not that be very convenient? . . . What a happy thought!

No time is lost in soliciting from the law some trifling privilege, a small monopoly, and as it may cost some pains to protect it, the State is asked to take it under its charge. The State and the law come to an understanding to realize exactly that which it was their business to prevent or to punish. By degrees the taste for monopolies gains ground. There is no class but desires a monopoly. All for each, they cry; we desire also to appear as philanthropists, and show that we understand solidarity.

It happens that the privileged classes, in thus robbing each other, lose at least as much by the exactions to which they are subject as they gain by the contributions they levy. Besides, the great body of the working classes, to whom no monopolies can be accorded, suffer from them until they can endure it no longer. They rise up, and cover the streets with barricades and blood; and then we must come to a reckoning with them.

What is their demand? Do they require the abolition of the abuses, privileges, monopolies, and restrictions under which they suffer? Not at all. They also are imbued with philanthropy. They have been told that the celebrated apothegm, all for each, is the solution to the social problem. They have had it demonstrated to them over and over again that monopoly (which in reality is only a theft) is nevertheless quite moral if sanctioned by law. Then they demand. . . . What? . . . Monopolies! They also summon the State to supply them with education, employment, credit, assistance, at the expense of the people. What a strange illusion! and how long will it last? We can very well conceive how all the higher classes, beginning with the highest, can come to demand favors and privileges. Below them there is a great popular mass upon whom the burden falls. But that the people, when once conquerors, should take it into their heads to enter into the privileged class, and create monopolies for themselves at their own expense; that they should enlarge the area of abuses in order to live upon them; that they should not see that there is nothing below them to support those acts of injustice: this is one of the most astonishing phenomena of our age, or of any age.

What has been the consequence? By pursuing this course, Society has been brought to the verge of shipwreck. Men became alarmed, and with reason. The people soon lost their power, and the old spread of abuses has been provisionally resumed.

The lesson, however, has not been quite lost upon the higher classes. They find that it is necessary to do justice to the working class. They ardently desire to succeed in this, not only because their own security depends upon it, but impelled, as we must acknowledge, by a spirit of equity. Of this I am thoroughly convinced, that the wealthier classes desire nothing more than to discover the solution of the great problem. I am satisfied that if we were to ask the greater part of our wealthy citizens to give up a considerable portion of their fortune in order to secure the future happiness and contentment of the people, they would cheerfully make the sacrifice. They anxiously seek the means of coming (according to the consecrated phrase) to the assistance of the laboring classes. But for that end on what plan have they fallen? . . . Still the communism of monopolies; a mitigated communism, however, and which they hope to subject to prudential regulation. That is all—they go no farther.

13

RENT

If, with an increase in the value of land, a corresponding augmentation took place in the value of the products of the soil, I could understand the opposition that the theory I have explained in the present work (part 1, chapter 9) has encountered. It might be argued, "that in proportion as civilization is developed the condition of the laborer becomes worse in comparison with that of the proprietor. This may be an inevitable necessity, but assuredly it is not a law of harmony."

Happily it is not so. In general those circumstances that cause an augmentation of the value of land diminish at the same time the price of landed produce. . . . Let me explain this by an example.

Suppose a field worth £100 situated ten leagues from a town. A road is made that passes near this field, and opens up a market for its produce. The field immediately becomes worth £150. The proprietor having by this means acquired facilities for improvement and for a more varied culture, then increases the value of the land, and it comes to be worth £200.

The value of the field is now doubled. Let us examine this added value—both as regards the question of justice and as regards the utility that accrues, not to the proprietor, but to the consumers of the neighboring town.

As far as concerns the increase of value arising from ameliorations the proprietor has made at his own cost, there can be no question. The capital he has expended follows the law of all capital.

I venture to say the same thing of the capital expended in forming the road. The operation is more circuitous, but the result is the same.

In point of fact, the proprietor has contributed to the public expenditure in proportion to the value of his field. For many years he contributed to works of general utility executed in more remote parts of the country, and at length a road has been made in a direction that is profitable to him. The gross amount of taxes which he has paid may be compared to shares taken in a Government enterprise, and the annual augmentation of rent he derives from the formation of this new road may be compared to dividends upon these shares.

Will it be said that a proprietor may pay taxes forever, without receiving anything in return? . . . But this just comes back to the case we have already put. The amelioration, although effected by the complex and somewhat questionable process of taxation, may be considered as made by the proprietor at his own cost, in proportion to the partial advantage he derives from it.

I have put the case of a road. I might have cited any other instance of Government intervention. Security, for example, contributes to give value to land, like capital, or labor. But who pays for this security? The proprietor, the capitalist, the laborer.

If the State expends its revenue judiciously, the value expended will reappear and be replaced, in some form or other, in the hands of the proprietor, the capitalist, or the laborer. In the case of the proprietor, it must take the form of an increase in the value of his land. If, on the other hand, the State expends its revenue injudiciously, it is a misfortune. The tax is lost; and that is the taxpayer's risk. In that case, there is no augmentation of the value of the land, but that is no fault of the proprietor.

But for the produce of the soil thus augmented in value, by the action of Government and by individual industry, do the consumers of the neighboring town pay an enhanced price? In other words, does the interest of the £100 become a charge on each quarter of wheat the field produces? If we paid formerly £15 for it, shall we now be obliged to pay more than £15? That is an interesting question, seeing that justice and the universal harmony of interests depend on its solution.

I answer boldly, No.

No doubt the proprietor will get £5 more (I assume the rate of interest to be 5 percent); but he gets this addition at the expense of nobody. On the contrary, the purchaser will derive a still greater profit.

The field we have supposed having been formerly at a distance from the market, was made to produce little, and on account of the difficulty of transit what was sent to market sold at a high price. Now, production is stimulated, and transport made cheaper, a greater quantity of wheat comes to market, and comes there at less cost, and is sold cheaper. While yielding the proprietor a total profit of £5, its purchaser, as we have already said, may realize a still greater profit.

In short, an economy of power has been realized. For whose benefit? For the benefit of both of the contracting parties. According to what law is this gain distributed? According to the law we have described in the case of capital, seeing that this augmentation of value is itself capital.

When capital increases, the portion falling to the proprietor or capitalist increases in absolute value and diminishes in relative value, while the portion falling to the laborer (or consumer) increases both in absolute and relative value

Observe how this takes place. In proportion as civilization advances, lands that are situated near populous centers rise in value. Productions of an inferior kind in such places give way to productions of a superior description. First of all, pasture gives way to cereal crops, then cereal crops give way to market gardening. Products are brought from a greater distance at less cost, so that (and this in point of fact is incontestable) meat, bread, vegetables, even flowers, are sold in such places cheaper than in neighborhoods less advanced, although manual labor costs more.

Le Clos-Vougeot[1]

Services are exchanged for services. Frequently services prepared beforehand are exchanged for present or future services.

The value of services is determined not by the labor they exact or have exacted, but by the labor they save.

Now, in point of fact, human labor goes on constantly improving in efficiency.

From these premises we may deduce a phenomenon that is very important in social economy, which is that in general anterior labor loses in exchange with present labor.

Twenty years ago I manufactured a commodity that cost me 100 days' labor. I propose an exchange, and I say to the purchaser, Give me in exchange a thing that cost you also 100 days' labor. Probably he will be in a situation to make this reply, That great progress has been made in twenty years. What you ask 100 days' labor for can be made now in 70 days. I don't measure your service by the time it has cost you, but by the service it renders me. That service is equal only to 70 days' labor, for in that time I can render it to myself, or find one who will render it to me.

The consequence is that the value of capital goes on continually deteriorating, and that anterior labor and capital are not so much favored as superficial economists believe.

Apart from wear and tear, there is no machine a little old but loses value, for the single reason that better machines of the same kind are made nowadays.

The same thing holds in regard to land. There are few soils, to bring which into their present state of culture and fertility, has

---

[1]Celebrated vineyard of Burgundy.

not cost more labor than would be necessary now with our more effective modern appliances.

This is what happens in the usual case, but not necessarily so.

Anterior labor may, at the present day, render greater services than it did formerly. This is rare, but it sometimes happens. For example, I store up wine which cost me twenty days' labor to produce. Had I sold it immediately, my labor would have yielded me a certain remuneration. I have preserved my wine; it has improved; the succeeding vintage has failed; in short, the price has risen, and my remuneration is greater. Why? Because I render a greater amount of service—my customers would have greater difficulty in procuring themselves such wine than I myself experienced—I satisfy a want that has become greater, more felt, etc This is a consideration that must always be looked to.

There are a thousand of us. Each has his piece of land, and clears it. Some time elapses, and we sell it. Now it so happens that out of the 1,000 there are 998 who never receive as many days' present labor in exchange for their land as it cost them formerly; and this just because the anterior labor, which was of a ruder and less efficient description, does not render as great an amount of service comparatively as present labor. But there are two of the proprietors whose labor has been more intelligent, or, if you will, more successful. When they bring their land to market, they find that it is capable of rendering service that cannot be rivaled. Every man says to himself, It would cost me a great deal to render this service to myself, therefore I must pay well for it, for I am quite certain that it would cost me more to obtain what I am in quest of by my own exertions.

This is just the case of the celebrated vineyard, the Clos Vougeot, and it is the same case as that of the man who finds a diamond, or possesses a fine voice, or other personal advantages or peculiarities, etc.

In my neighborhood there is much uncultivated land. A stranger asks, Why not cultivate this field? Because the soil is bad. But here, alongside of it you have another of the same quality that is cultivated. To this objection the native has no answer.

Was he wrong in the first answer he gave, namely, It is bad?

No. The reason that induces him not to clear new fields is not that they are bad, for there are excellent fields that also remain uncultivated. His reason is that it would cost him more to bring this field into the same state of cultivation as the adjoining field that is cultivated, than to buy the latter.

Now, to any thinking man this proves incontestably that the field has no intrinsic value.

14

WAGES

Men are always anxiously on the lookout for something fixed. We meet sometimes with restless and unquiet spirits who have a craving for risk and adventure. But, taking mankind in the gross, we may safely affirm that what men desire is to be tranquil as regards their future, to know what they have to count upon, and be enabled to make their arrangements beforehand. To be convinced how precious fixity is in their eyes, we have only to observe how very anxious men are to obtain for themselves government employments. Nor is this on account of the honor that such places confer, for there are many of these situations where the work is not of a very elevated description, consisting in watching and vexing their fellow citizens, and prying into their affairs. Such places, however, are not the less sought after—and why? Because they confer an assured position. Who has not heard a father speak thus of his son: "I am soliciting for him a place as a candidate or supernumerary in such or such a government office. It is a pity, no doubt, that so costly an education is required—an education that might have ensured his success in a more brilliant career. As a public functionary he will not get rich, but he is certain to live. He will always have bread. Four or five years hence he will begin to receive a salary of thirty pounds a year, which will rise by degrees to a hundred and twenty or a hundred and sixty. After thirty years' service, he will be entitled to retire. His livelihood then is secured, and he must learn to live upon a small income," etc.

Fixity, then, has for most men an irresistible attraction.

And yet, when we consider the nature of man, and of his occupations, fixity would seem to be incompatible with them.

Go back in imagination to the origin of human society, and you will have difficulty in comprehending how men can ever succeed in obtaining from the community a fixed, assured, and constant quantity of the means of subsistence. Yet this is one of those phenomena that strike us less because we have them constantly before our eyes. We have public functionaries who receive fixed salaries; proprietors who can count beforehand on their revenues; men of fortune who can calculate on their dividends; workmen who earn every day the same wages. Apart from the consideration of money, which is only employed to facilitate exchanges and estimates of value, we perceive that what is fixed is the quantity of the means of subsistence, the value of the satisfactions received by the various classes of workmen. Now, I maintain that this fixity, which by degrees extends to all men and all departments of industry, is a miracle of civilization, and a marvelous effect of that social state which, in our day, is so madly decried.

For, let us go back to a primitive social state, and suppose a nation of hunters, or fishers, or shepherds, or warriors, or agriculturists, to be told, "In proportion as you advance on the road of progress, you will know more and more beforehand what amount of enjoyment will be secured to you for each year," they would not believe us. They would reply, "That must always depend on something that eludes calculation—the inconstancy of the seasons, etc." The truth is, they could form no idea of the ingenious efforts by means of which men have succeeded in establishing a sort of mutual assurance between all places and all times.

Now, this mutual assurance against all the risks and chances of the future is entirely dependent on a branch of human science I shall denominate experimental statistics. This department of science, depending as it does upon experience, admits of indefinite progress, and consequently the fixity of which we have spoken also admits of indefinite progress. That fixity is favored by two circumstances that are permanent in their operation: First, Men desire it. Second, they acquire every day greater facilities for realizing it.

Before showing how this fixity is established in human transactions, in which it is little thought of, let us first of all see how it operates in a transaction of which it is the special object. The reader will, in this way, comprehend what I mean by experimental statistics.

A number of men have each a house. One of these houses happens to be burnt down and its owner is ruined. All the rest immediately take alarm, and each says to himself, "The same thing may happen to me." We cannot be surprised, then, that these proprietors should unite and divide the risk of such accidents as much as possible, by establishing a mutual assurance against fire. The bargain is very simple—here is its formula: "If the house of one of us is burnt down, the rest will club to make good the loss to the man who is burnt out."

By this means each proprietor acquires a double security; in the first instance he must take a small share in all losses of this nature; but then he is assured that he will never himself be obliged to suffer the whole loss arising from any such misfortune.

In reality, and if we extend the calculation over a great number of years, we see that the proprietor makes, so to speak, a bargain with himself. He sets aside a sufficient fund to repair the misfortunes that may afterwards befall him.

This is association. Indeed it is to arrangements of this nature that the Socialists give exclusively the name of association. Whenever speculation intervenes, association, as they think, disappears.

It is improved and perfected, as I think, and as we shall afterwards see.

What has led the proprietors to associate, to enter into this mutual assurance, is the love of fixity, of security. They prefer known risks to risks that are unknown, a multitude of small risks to one great one.

Their design, however, has not yet been completely attained, and there is still much uncertainty in their position. Each of them may say, "If accidents are multiplied, my quota will become insupportable. In any case, I should like to know beforehand, and to have insured in the same way my furniture, my merchandise, etc."

It would seem that such inconveniences belong to the nature of things, and that it is impossible for men to get rid of them. After each step of progress we are tempted to think that all has been accomplished. How, indeed, can we elude this uncertainty, which depends upon accidents still unknown to us?

But mutual assurance has developed in the social state an experimental knowledge, namely, the average annual proportion between the values lost by accident and the values assured.

Having made all the necessary calculations, a company or an individual says to the proprietors, "In entering into a mutual assurance, you have wished to purchase freedom from anxiety, and the indeterminate quota you reserve annually to cover accidents is the price you pay for this immunity. But if you do not know what this price is beforehand, your tranquillity is never perfect. I now propose to you, therefore, another expedient. In consideration of a fixed annual premium which you shall pay me, I take upon myself all your chances of accidents. I will insure you all, and here is the capital that will guarantee the fulfillment of my engagement."

The proprietors accept the proposal, even though this fixed premium should amount to somewhat more than the sum their mutual assurance cost them; for their object is not so much to save a few shillings as to obtain perfect repose and freedom from anxiety.

At this point the Socialists pretend that the principle of association is destroyed. For my part, I think it is improved, and on the road to other improvements to which I can see no limits.

But, say the Socialists, the assured have no longer any mutual tie. They no longer see each other and come to a common understanding. Intermediary parasites have come among them, and the proof that the proprietors are now paying more than is required to cover accidents is to be found in the fact that the insurers obtain large profits.

It is not difficult to answer this objection.

First of all, association exists, but under another form. The premium contributed by the assured is still the fund that is to make good the losses. The assured have found the means of remaining in the association without taking part in its business. This is evidently an advantage to each of them, seeing that the design they have in view is nevertheless attained; and the possibility of remaining in the association while they have their independence of movement and free use of their faculties restored to them is just the characteristic of social progress.

As regards the profit obtained by the intermediate party, it is easily explained and justified. The assured remain associated for the purpose of repairing accidents and making good what is lost. But a company has stepped in that offers them the following advantages: first, it takes away whatever of uncertainty remained in the position of the assured; secondly, it frees them from all care and trouble in connection with accidents. These are services, and the rule is, service for service. The proof that the intervention of the company is a service possessed of value is to be found in the fact that it is freely accepted and paid for. The Socialists only make themselves ridiculous when they declaim against such middlemen. Do they intrude themselves into commercial transactions by force? Have they any other means of introducing themselves and their services than by saying to the parties with whom they deal, "I will cost you some trouble, but I will save you more"? How, then, can they be called parasites or even intermediaries?

I affirm, moreover, that association thus transformed is on the direct road of progress in every sense.

In fact, companies that expect to realize profits proportioned to the extent of their business, promote insurance. To aid them in this they have agents in all quarters, they establish credits, they devise a thousand combinations to increase the number of the assured—in other words, of the associated parties. They undertake a multitude of risks that were unknown to the primitive mutual insurance associations. In short, association is extended progressively to a greater number of men and things. In proportion as this development takes place, the companies find they can lower their prices; they are even forced by competition to do so. And here we again get a glimpse of the great law, that profit soon escapes from the hands of the producer to settle in those of the consumer.

Nor is this all: companies insure each other by reassurances, so that, with a view to providing for losses, which is the principal object in view, a thousand associations scattered over England, France, Germany, and America, are melted into one grand and unique association. And what is the result? If a house is burnt down at Bordeaux, Paris, or elsewhere, the proprietors of the whole world, English, Belgians, Germans, Spaniards, club together and repair the disaster.

This is an example of the degree of power, universality, and perfection, that may be reached by means of free and voluntary association. But to attain this they must be left free to manage their own business. Now, what happened when the Socialists, those great partisans of association, were in power? Their chief business was to threaten association in every form, and principally association for insurance. And why? Just because, in order to render itself more universal, it adopted those expedients that left each of its members in a state of independence. How little these unfortunate Socialists understand the social mechanism! They would bring us back to the rude and primitive forms that association assumed when society was in its infancy, and they would suppress all progress under the pretext that it has departed from these forms.

We shall see by-and-by that from the same prejudices, the same ignorance, arise their incessant declamations against interest. The interest and wages are fixed, and, consequently, improved forms of remuneration for the use of labor and capital.

The wages-system (salariat) has been peculiarly the butt of the Socialists. They have almost gone the length of representing it as a modified, and not greatly modified, system of slavery and thralldom. At all events, they see in it only a bargain which is one-sided and predatory, founded on liberty merely in appearance, an oppression of the weak by the strong, or the tyranny of capital over labor.

Continually wrangling about new institutions to be founded, the Socialists display in their common hatred of existing institutions, and especially of the system of remuneration by wages, a striking unanimity. If they cannot attain unity as to the new social organization to be established, they are at least marvelously united in calumniating, decrying, running down, hating, and making hated, everything that actually exists. I have assigned the reason for this elsewhere.[1]

Much unfortunately takes place that is beyond the domain of philosophical discussion; and the Socialist propaganda, seconded by an ignorant and cowardly press, that, without avowing Socialism, seeks for popularity in fashionable declamations, has succeeded in instilling hatred of the wages system into the minds of the very people who live by wages. Workmen have become disgusted with this form of remuneration. It appears to them unjust, humiliating, and odious. They think it brands them with the mark of servitude. They desire to participate on another principle in the distribution of wealth. Hence they have fallen passionately in love with the most extravagant Utopias. They had but one step to take, and they have taken it. When the revolution of February

---

[1]See part I, chaps. 1 and 2.

broke out, the grand object of the working classes was to get rid of wages. Upon the means of accomplishing this they consulted their oracles; but when these oracles did not remain mute, they followed the usual mode by giving obscure utterances, in which the word that predominated was association, as if association and wages were incompatible. Then the workmen would try all the forms of this liberty-giving association; and, to impart to it greater attraction, they were pleased to invest it with all the charms of Solidarity, and attributed to it all the merits of Fraternity. For the moment, one would have been led to believe that the human heart itself had been about to undergo a grand transformation, and to throw off the yoke of self-interest, in order to give place to the principle of sympathy. By a singular contradiction, they hoped from association to reap at once all the glory of self-sacrifice, and material profits of hitherto unheard-of amount. They fell down before the statue of Fortune, prayed, and decreed to themselves the glory of martyrdom. It seemed as if these workmen, thus misled, and on the point of being seduced into a career of injustice, felt it necessary to shut their eyes to their true position, to glorify the methods of spoliation that had been taught them by their apostles, and place them covered with a veil in the sanctuary of a new revelation. Never, perhaps, had so many and such dangerous errors, so many and such gross contradictions, found their way before into the human brain.

Let us inquire, then, what wages really are, and consider their origin, form, and effects. Let us trace the subject to its foundation, and make sure whether, in the development of humanity, wages constitute retrogression or progress—whether in receiving wages there be anything humiliating or degrading, or which can in any degree be allied with slavery.

Services are exchanged for services, labor, efforts, pains, cares, natural or acquired ability—these are what we give and receive. What we confer on one another is satisfaction or enjoyment. What determines the exchange is the common advantage, and its measure is the free evaluation of reciprocal services. The various combinations to which human transactions give rise have necessitated a voluminous economic vocabulary; but the words Profits, Interest, Wages, although indicating shades of difference, do not change the nature and foundation of things. We have still the do ut des, or rather the *facio ut facias*, that constitutes the basis of the whole economic evolution.

The class that lives by wages forms no exception to this law. Examine the subject attentively. Do these men render services? Unquestionably they do. Are services rendered to them? Undoubtedly they are. Are these services exchanged freely and voluntarily? Do we perceive in this kind of transaction any appearance of fraud or violence? It is at this point, perhaps, that the grievances of the workman begin. They don't go to the length of pretending that they are deprived of their liberty, but they assert that this liberty is merely nominal and a mockery, because the man whose necessities force the determination is not really free. It remains for us to inquire, then, whether the defect of liberty thus understood does not belong to the situation of the workman rather than to the mode of his remuneration.

When one man enters into the service of another, his remuneration may consist in a part of the work produced, or in a determinate wage. In either case he must bargain for this part of the product—for it may be greater or less; or for this wage—for it may be higher or lower. If the man is in a state of absolute destitution, if he cannot wait, if he acts on the spur of urgent necessity, he must submit, and cannot get rid of the other's exactions. But you will observe that it is not the form of remuneration that gives rise to this dependence. Whether he runs the risk of the enterprise by stipulating for a share of the product, or bargains for a fixed remuneration whether the other gain or lose, it is his precarious situation that gives him an inferior position in the discussion which precedes the arrangement. Those innovators who have represented association to the working classes as an infallible remedy have misled them, and are themselves mistaken. They can convince themselves of this by observing attentively the circumstances in cases where the indigent workman receives part of the product in place of wages. There are assuredly no men in the country worse off than fishermen or vinedressers, although they have the satisfaction of enjoying all the benefits the Socialists denominate, exclusively, association.

But before proceeding to inquire into the circumstances that influence the quota of wages, I must define, or rather describe, the nature of the transaction.

Men have a tendency—which is natural, and advantageous, moral, universal, indestructible—to desire security with reference to the means of subsistence, to seek fixity, and avoid uncertainty.

However, in the early stages of society uncertainty reigns supreme, and it has frequently astonished me that Political Economy has failed to mark the great and happy efforts that have been made to restrain this uncertainty within narrower and narrower limits.

Take the case of a tribe of hunters, or a nomad people, or a colony newly founded—is there a single man who can say with certainty what tomorrow's labor will be worth? Would there not even seem to be an incompatibility between the two ideas, and that nothing can be of a more casual nature than the result of labor, whether applied to hunting, to fishing, or to agriculture?

It will be difficult, then, to find, in an infant society, anything that resembles stipends, salaries, wages, revenues, rents, interest, assurance, etc., which are all things that have been invented in order to give more and more fixity to personal situations, to escape, to a greater and greater degree, that feeling so painful to men of uncertainty with reference to the means of subsistence.

The progress that has been made in this direction is indeed admirable, although custom has so familiarized us with this phenomenon that we fail to attend to it. In fact, since the results of labor, and consequently the enjoyments of mankind, may be so profoundly modified by events, by unforeseen circumstances, by the caprices of nature, the uncertainty of the seasons, and accidents of every kind, we may ask how it comes to pass that so great a number of men find themselves set free for a time, and some of them for life, by means of rents, salaries, and retiring pensions, from this species of eventuality, of uncertainty, which would seem to be essentially part of our nature.

The efficient cause, the motive power of this beautiful evolution of the human race, is the tendency of all men toward competency and material prosperity, of which Fixity is so essential a part. The means consist in the substitution of a fixed unconditional bargain for one dependent merely on appreciable chances, or the gradual abandonment of that primitive form of association that consists in committing all the parties concerned irrevocably to all the risks and chances of the enterprise; in other words, the improvement of association. It is singular at least that all our great modern reformers exhibit association to us as destroyed by the very element that improves and perfects it.

In order that men should consent to take upon themselves, unconditionally, risks that fall naturally on others, it is necessary that a species of knowledge, which I have called experimental statistics, should have made some progress; for experience alone can place them in a situation to appreciate these risks, at least approximately, and consequently to appreciate the value of the service rendered in securing them against such risks. This is the reason why the bargains and transactions of rude and ignorant nations admit no stipulations of this nature, and hence, as I have said, uncertainty exercises over such people uncontrolled power. Were a savage, grown old and having laid up some stock of game, to take a young hunter into his service, he would not give him fixed wages, but a share in the produce of the chase. How, indeed, could either of them, from the known infer the unknown? The teachings of past experience do not permit them to insure the future beforehand.

In times of barbarism and inexperience, men no doubt associate, for we have demonstrated that otherwise they could not exist; but association can assume among them only that primitive and elementary form that the Socialists represent as the only one that can secure our future safety.

When two men have long worked on together, encountering equal risks, there at length comes a time when, from experience, they can estimate and appreciate the value of these risks, and one of them consents to take the entire risk upon his own shoulders, in consideration of a fixed recompense.

This arrangement is undoubtedly a step of progress, and it is shown to be so by the very fact that it has been effected freely and voluntarily by the two parties, who would not have entered into it had it not been felt to be for their mutual benefit. It is easy to see in what the benefit consists. The one party gains by obtaining the exclusive management of an undertaking of which he takes all the risks upon himself; the other by attaining that fixity of position that is so much desired. And society at large must be benefited by having an enterprise, formerly subjected to two minds and two wills, henceforth conducted with unity of views and unity of action.

But although association is modified in this way, it by no means follows that it is dissolved. The co-operation of the two men is continued, although the mode of dividing the product of their enterprise has been changed. Association is not vitiated by an innovation voluntarily agreed to, and which satisfies all parties.

The co-operation of anterior labor and present labor is always, or almost always, required in order to realize new means of satisfaction and enjoyment. Capital and labor, in uniting in a common undertaking, are, in the first instance, forced to undertake each its share of the risk; and this continues until the value of the risk can be experimentally estimated. Then two tendencies, which are alike natural to the human heart, manifest themselves— I mean the tendencies toward unity of direction and fixity of situation. Capital then says to labor: "Experience has taught us that your eventual profit amounts, on an average, to so much. If you wish it, I will ensure you this amount, and take charge of the operation, taking upon myself the chances of profit or loss."

Labor may possibly answer: "This proposal suits me very well. Sometimes I earn twenty pounds a year; sometimes I earn sixty. These fluctuations are very inconvenient, for they hinder me from regulating uniformly my own expenditure and that of my family.

It is an advantage to me to get rid of this uncertainty, and to receive a fixed recompense of forty pounds."

By this arrangement the terms of the contract will be changed. They will continue to unite their efforts, and to share the proceeds, and consequently the association will not be dissolved; but it will be modified in this way, that the capitalist will take all the risks with the compensation of all the extraordinary profits, while the laborer will be secured the advantages of fixity. Such is the origin of Wages.

The agreement may take place in the reverse way. Frequently the person who undertakes a commercial enterprise says to the capitalist: "Hitherto we have worked together, sharing the risks. Now that we are in a situation to appreciate these risks, I propose to make a fixed bargain. You have invested a thousand pounds in the undertaking, for which one year you receive twenty-five pounds, another year seventy-five. If you agree to it, I will give you fifty pounds, or 5 percent per annum, and free you from all risk, on condition that I have henceforth the entire management of the concern."

The capitalist will probably answer: "Since, with great and troublesome fluctuations, I receive on an average, only fifty pounds per annum, I should much prefer to have that sum regularly assured to me. I shall, therefore, allow my capital to remain in the concern, but I am to be exempted from all risk. My activity and intelligence will now be free to engage in some other undertaking."

This is an advantage in a social as well as in an individual point of view.

We see that men are constantly in quest of a fixed and stable position, and that there is an incessant effort to diminish and circumscribe on all sides the element of uncertainty. Where two men participate in a common risk, this risk, having a substantive existence, cannot be annihilated; but the tendency is for one of them to take that risk upon himself. If the capitalist undertakes the risk, the laborer's remuneration is fixed under the name of wages. If the laborer runs the chances of profit or loss, then the remuneration of the capitalist is fixed under the name of interest.

And as capital is nothing else than human services, we may say that capital and labor are two words that in reality express one and the same idea; and consequently, the same thing may be said of interest and wages. Thus, where false science never fails to find antagonism, true science ever finds identity.

Considered, then, with reference to their origin, nature, and form, wages have in them nothing degrading or humiliating any more than interest has. Both constitute the return for present and anterior labor derived from the results of a common enterprise. Only it almost always happens that one of the two associates agrees to take upon himself the risk. If it be the present labor which claims a uniform remuneration, the chances of profit are given up in consideration of wages. If it be the anterior labor that claims a fixed return, the capitalist gives up his eventual chance of profits for a determinate rate of interest.

For my own part, I am convinced that this new stipulation that is added to the primitive form of association, far from destroying it, improves and perfects it. I have no doubt of this, when I consider that such a stipulation takes its rise from a felt want, from the natural desire of all men for stability, and, moreover, that it satisfies all parties, without injury but, on the contrary, by serving the interests of the public.

Modern reformers who, under pretense of having invented association, desire to bring it back to its primitive and rudimentary forms, ought to tell us in what respect these fixed bargains are opposed to justice or equity, in what respect they are prejudicial to progress, and on what principle they wish to interdict them. They ought also to tell us why, if such stipulations bear the stamp of barbarism, they are constantly and more and more mixed up with that association which is represented as the perfection of human society.

In my opinion, such stipulations are among the most marvelous manifestations, as they are among the most powerful springs, of progress. They are at once the perfection and reward of a past and very ancient civilization, and the starting point of a new and unlimited career of future civilization. Had society adhered to that primitive form of association which saddles all the parties interested with a share of the risks of an enterprise, ninety-nine out of every hundred such enterprises never would have been undertaken. The man who at the present day participates in a score of enterprises would have been tied down for ever to one. Unity of design and of will would have been wanting in all commercial operations; and mankind would never have tasted that precious good that is perhaps the source of genius—stability.

The wages system (*salariat*), then, takes its rise in a natural and indestructible tendency. Observe, however, that it satisfies men's desires but imperfectly. It renders the remuneration of workmen more uniform, more equal, and brings it nearer to an average; but there is one thing it cannot do, and which their admission to a participation in profits and risks could not accomplish, namely, to ensure them employment.

And here I cannot help remarking how powerful the feeling is to which I have made reference throughout the whole of this chapter, and the very existence of which our modern reformers do not seem even to suspect—I mean men's aversion to uncertainty. It is exactly this very feeling that has made it so easy for Socialist declaimers to create such a hatred on the part of the working classes to receive their remuneration in the shape of wages.

We can conceive three phases in the condition of the laborer: the predominance of uncertainty; the predominance of stability; and an intermediate state, from which uncertainty is partly excluded, but not sufficiently so to give place to fixity and stability.

What the working classes do not sufficiently understand is that the association the Socialists preach up to them is the infancy of society, the period when men are groping their way, the time of quick transitions and fluctuations, of alternations of plethora and atrophy—in a word, the period when absolute uncertainty reigns supreme. The wages system, on the contrary, forms the intermediate link between uncertainty and fixity.

Now, the working classes, being far as yet from feeling themselves in a state of stability, place their hopes—like all men ill at ease—on a certain change of position. This is the reason why it has been an easy task for Socialism to impose upon them by the use of the grand term association. The working classes fancy themselves pushed forward, when they are in reality falling behind.

Yes, these unfortunate people are falling back to the primitive and rudimentary stage of the social movement; for what is the association now so loudly preached up to them but the subjection of all to all risks and contingencies? This is inevitable in times of ignorance, since fixed bargains presuppose some progress at least in experimental statistics. But the doctrine now inculcated is nothing else than a pure and simple revival of the reign of uncertainty.

The workmen who were enthusiasts for association when they knew it only in theory, were enchanted when the revolution of February seemed to render possible its practical adoption.

At that period many employers of labor, either infected with the universal infatuation, or giving way to their fears, offered to substitute a participation in the returns for payment by wages. But the workmen did not much fancy this solidarity of risk. They understood very well what was offered them; for in case the enterprise turned out a losing concern, they would have had no remuneration of any kind—which to them was death.

We saw then what would not have been to the credit of our working classes, had the blame not lain with the pretended reformers, in whom, unhappily, they placed confidence. The working classes demanded a sort of bastard association in which the rate of wages was to be maintained, and in which they were to be entitled to a share of the profits without being subject to any of the losses.

The workmen would probably never of themselves have thought of putting forward such pretensions. There is in human nature a fund of good sense and a feeling of justice to which such bare-faced iniquity is repugnant. To corrupt man's heart, you must begin by depraving his intellect.

This is what the leaders of the Socialist school did not fail to do; and with this fact before us, I am frequently asked whether their intentions were not perverse. I am always inclined to respect men's motives; but it is exceedingly difficult, under such circumstances, to exculpate the Socialist chiefs.

After having, by the unjust and persevering declamations with which their books are filled, irritated the working classes against their employers, after having persuaded them that they were in a state of war, in which everything is fair against the enemy, they enveloped the ultimatum of the workmen in scientific subtleties, and even in clouds of mysticism. They postulated an abstract being called Society that owed to each of its members a minimum, that is to say, an assured means of subsistence. "You have, then, a right," they told the workmen, "to demand a fixed wage." In this way they began by satisfying the natural desire of men for stability. Then they proceeded to teach them that, independently of wages, the workman should have a share in the profits; and when asked whether he was also to bear his share of the losses, their answer was that in virtue of State intervention and the guarantee of the taxpayer, they had invented a system of universal industry, protected from all loss. By this means they removed all the remaining scruples of the unfortunate workmen; and when the revolution of February broke out, we saw them, as I have said, disposed to make three stipulations:

1. Continuance of wages,
2. Participation in profits,
3. Immunity from losses.

It may be said, perhaps, that these stipulations were neither so unjust nor so impossible as they appeared, seeing that they are introduced in many enterprises, having reference to newspapers, railways, etc.

I answer that there is something truly puerile in allowing oneself to be duped by high-sounding names applied to very trivial things. A little candor will at once convince us that this participation in profits, which some concerns allow to their workmen receiving wages, does not constitute association, or merit that title, nor is it a great revolution introduced into the relations of two classes of society. It is only an ingenious and useful encouragement given to workmen receiving wages under a form that is not exactly new, although it has been represented as an adhesion to Socialism. Employers who, in adopting this custom, devote a tenth, a twentieth, or a hundredth part of their profits, when they have any, to this largess bestowed on their workmen, may make a great noise about it, and proclaim themselves the generous renovators of the social order; but it is really unworthy of occupying more of our time at present, and I return to my argument.

The system of payment by wages, then, was a step of progress. In the first instance, anterior labor and present labor were associated together with common risks, in common enterprises, the circle of which, in such circumstances, must have been very limited. If society had not discovered other combinations, no important work could ever have been undertaken. Men would have remained hunters and fishers, and there might have been perhaps some rude attempts at agriculture.

Afterwards, in obedience to the double feeling that prompts us to seek stability, and, at the same time, retain the direction of those operations of which we must encounter the risks, the two associates, without putting an end to the association, seek to supersede the joint hazard by a fixed bargain, and agree that one of them should give the other a fixed remuneration, and take upon himself the whole risk, along with the exclusive direction of the enterprise. When this fixity applies to the anterior labor, or capital, it is called interest; when it applies to the present labor, it is called wages.

But, as I have already said, wages serve only imperfectly to constitute a state of stability for a certain class of men, or of security in regard to the means of subsistence. It is one step, and a very marked one, toward the realization of this benefit, and so difficult that at first sight we should have thought it impossible; but it does not effect its entire realization.

And it is perhaps worthy of remark in passing that fixity of situation, stability, resembles in one respect all the great results of which mankind is in pursuit. We are always approximating to such results, but we never fully attain them. For the very reason that stability is a good, a benefit, we must always be making efforts more and more to extend its domain; but it is not in our nature ever to obtain complete possession of it. We may even go to the length of saying that to obtain such possession would not be desirable for man in his present state. Absolute good of whatever kind would put an end to all desire, all effort, all combination, all thought, all foresight, all virtue. Perfection excludes the notion of perfectibility.

The working classes having then, with the lapse of time, and the progress of civilization, reached the improved system of payment by wages, have not stopped short at that point, or relaxed their efforts to realize stability.

No doubt wages come in with certainty at the conclusion of the day's work; but when circumstances—as, for example, an industrial crisis, or a protracted illness—have interrupted work, the wages are interrupted also. What, then, is the workman to do? Are he and his wife and children to be deprived of food?

He has but one resource, and that is to save, while employed, the means of supplying his wants in sickness and old age.

But, in the individual case, who can estimate beforehand the comparative length of time in which he has to assist, or be assisted?

What cannot be done in the individual case may be found more practicable with reference to the masses in virtue of the law of averages. The tribute paid by the workman while employed to provide for his support in periods of stoppage answers the purpose much more effectually, and with much more regularity and certainty, when it is centralized by association, than when it is abandoned to individual chances.

Hence the origin of Friendly Societies—admirable institutions that benevolence had given birth to long before the name of Socialism was ever heard of. It would be difficult to say who was their inventor. The true inventor, I believe, was the felt want of some such institutions—the desire of men for something fixed, the restless active instinct that leads us to remove the obstacles that mankind encounters in its progress toward stability.

I have myself seen friendly societies rise up spontaneously, more than five-and-twenty years ago, among the most destitute laborers and artisans of the poorest villages in the department of the Landes.

The obvious design of these societies is to equalize enjoyments, and to spread and distribute over all periods of life the wages earned in days of health and prosperity. In all localities in which they exist, these societies have conferred immense benefits. The contributors are sustained by a feeling of security, a feeling the most precious and consolatory that can enter the heart of man in his pilgrimage here below. Moreover, they feel their reciprocal dependence and their usefulness to each other. They see at what point the prosperity or adversity of each individual, or of each profession, becomes the prosperity or adversity of all.

They meet together on certain occasions for religious worship, as provided by their rules; and then they are called to exercise over each other that vigilant surveillance so proper to inspire self-respect, which is the first and most difficult step in the march of civilization.

What has hitherto ensured the success of these societies—a success that has been slow, indeed, like everything that concerns the masses—is liberty: of this there can be no doubt.

The natural danger they encounter is the removal of the sense of responsibility. It is never without creating great dangers and great difficulties for the future that we set an individual free from the consequences of his own acts.

Were all our citizens to say, "We will club together to assist those who cannot work, or who cannot find employment," we should fear to see developed to a dangerous extent man's natural tendency to idleness; we should fear that the laborious would soon become the dupes of the slothful. Mutual assistance, then, implies mutual surveillance, without which the common fund would soon be exhausted. This reciprocal surveillance is for such association a necessary guarantee of existence—a security for each contributor that he shall not be made to play the part of dupe; and it constitutes besides the true morality of the institution. By this means, we see drunkenness and debauchery gradually disappear; for what right could that man have to assistance from the common fund who has brought disease and want of employment upon himself by his own vicious habits? It is this surveillance that re-establishes that responsibility the association might otherwise tend to enfeeble.

Now, in order that this surveillance should operate beneficially, friendly societies must be free and select, and have the control of their own rules, as well as of their own funds. It is necessary also that they should be able to suit their rules to the requirements of each locality.

If Government were to interfere, it is easy to see the part it would play. Its first business would be to lay hold of all these funds, under the pretense of centralizing them; and to give a color to the proceeding, it would promise to enlarge the funds from resources taken from the taxpayer. "Is it not," it would be said, "very natural and very just that the State should contribute to so great, so generous, so philanthropic, so humane a work?" This is the first injustice—to introduce the element of force into the society, and, along with the contributions, to obtrude citizens who have no right to a share of the fund. And then, under pretense of unity, of solidarity, the State would set itself to fuse all these associations into one, subject to the same rules.

But, I would ask, what will become of the morality of the institution when its funds are augmented by taxation; when no one except a government official has an interest to defend the common stock; when everyone, instead of feeling it his duty to prevent abuses, will take pleasure in favoring them; when all mutual surveillance has ceased; and when to feign disease would only be to play off a good trick on the Government? The Government, to do it justice, is well disposed to defend itself; but being no longer able to avail itself of private action, it must necessarily substitute official action. It will name examiners, controllers, inspectors. Countless formalities will be interposed between want and assistance. In short, what was originally an admirable institution will be transformed into a mere department of police.

The State will, in the first instance, perceive only the advantage of swelling the mob of its creatures, of multiplying the places at its disposal, and of extending its patronage and electioneering influence. It will not remark that in arrogating to itself a new function, it has assumed a new responsibility—a responsibility that I venture to designate as fearful. For what must the immediate consequence be? The working classes will no longer regard the common fund as a property that they administer and keep up, and the limits of which are the limits of their rights. They will soon accustom themselves to regard assistance in cases of sickness or want of employment not as proceeding from a limited fund, prepared by their own foresight, but as a debt due to them by society. Its resources will appear to them unbounded, and they will never be contented with their share. The State will find itself under the necessity of demanding constant additions to the budget. Encountering opposition in that, the Government will find itself involved in inextricable difficulties. Abuses will go on increasing, which, year after year, they will shrink from reforming, until an explosion comes at last. And then it will be found that we have to deal with a population that can no longer act for itself, that expects everything from a minister to a prefect, even subsistence, and whose ideas are so far perverted as to have lost all rational notions of Right, Property, Liberty, or Justice.

Such are some of the reasons that alarmed me, I confess, when I saw lately that a Commission of the Legislative Assembly had been charged to prepare a project of law on friendly societies. It struck me that the hour of their destruction was approaching, and it afflicted me the more that I had thought a great future was in store for them, could we only preserve them in the bracing air of liberty. Is it then, I would ask, so very difficult a thing to leave men to make a trial, to feel their way, to make a choice, to find themselves mistaken, to rectify their mistakes, to inform themselves, to act in concert, to manage their own property and their own interests, to act for themselves on their own proper risk and peril, and on their own responsibility? Is it not evident that this is the way to make them really men? Shall we never cease to begin with the fatal hypothesis that all governors are guardians, and the governed only children?

I maintain that, left to the vigilance of the parties interested, our Friendly Societies have before them a great future, and I require no other proof of this than what has taken place on the other side of the Channel.

"In England, individual foresight has not waited for Government impulse to organize a powerful and reciprocal association between the working classes. For a long period, free associations, administering their own affairs, have been founded in all the principal towns of Great Britain," etc.

"The total number of these associations for the United Kingdom amounts to 33,223, including not less than 3,052,000 individuals—one half the adult population of Great Britain."

"This great confederation of the working classes, this institution of effective and practical fraternity, rests on the most solid basis. Their revenue is five millions sterling, and their accumulated capital amounts to eleven millions and two hundred thousand pounds."

"It is upon this fund that the contributors draw when out of employment. We are astonished to see how England rallies from the immense and profound perturbations which her gigantic industry experiences from time to time and almost periodically—and the explanation of the phenomenon is, to a great extent, to be found in the facts now stated."

"Mr. Roebuck wished, on account of the great importance of the question, that the Government would assume the initiative by taking the question into its own hands. . . . This was opposed by the Chancellor of the Exchequer."

"Where individual interests are sufficient for their own free government, power, in England, judges it useless to interpose its action. It watches from above to see that all goes on regularly; but it leaves to every man the merit of his exertions, and the care of administering his affairs, according to his own notions and convenience. It is to this independence of her citizens that England assuredly owes a portion of her greatness as a nation."[2]

It might have been added that it is to that independence also that the citizens owe their experience and personal worth. To that independence, too, the English Government owes its relative freedom from responsibility, and consequently its stability.

Among the institutions that may take their rise from Friendly Societies, when they shall have made that advance which has scarcely yet been begun, I should give the first place, on account of their social importance, to the laborer Caisse de Retraite.[3]

There are persons who treat such an institution as a chimera. Such people, no doubt, pretend to be acquainted with the extreme limits, as regards Stability, beyond which the human race is not permitted to go. I would ask them a few simple questions: If they had never known anything beyond the social state of those barbarous tribes who live by hunting and fishing, would they have been able to anticipate the existence, I do not say of our present land revenues, of Government funds, and fixed salaries, but even of the system of payment by wages, which is the first step toward fixity in the condition of the poorest classes? And then, if they had never seen anything beyond this wages system, as it exists in countries that have not yet displayed the spirit of association, would they have ventured to predict the destinies reserved for Friendly Societies as we find them at work in our own day in England? Do they imagine that these first steps of progress were more easy than it is for us to establish Caisses de Retraite? Is this third step more difficult to take than the other two?

For myself, I see clearly that mankind thirsts after stability. I see men, century after century, adding to their incomplete conquests, for the benefit of one class or another, and this by marvelous processes, which would seem to be much above individual invention, and I confess that I dare not venture to predict at what point men will stop short on the road of progress.

---

[2]Extract from *La Presse*, 22nd June 1850.

[3]A charity organization that provides for the laborer in his old age.

One thing is certain, that these Caisses de Retraite are universally, unanimously, ardently desired by all our workmen; and very naturally so.

I have frequently interrogated them, and I have always found that the great pain and grief of their existence is not the severity of their work, nor the smallness of their wages, nor even the irritation that the spectacle of inequality is supposed to excite. No, what affects them, discourages them, pains them, tortures them, is their uncertainty as regards the future. Whatever profession we may belong to, whether we are public functionaries, or men of independent fortune, or landed proprietors, or merchants, physicians, lawyers, soldiers, magistrates, we enjoy without perceiving it, consequently without acknowledging it, the progress that has been realized by Society—so that we cannot comprehend the torture of uncertainty. Let us place ourselves, then, in the situation of a workman, of an artisan who, on getting up every morning, is haunted by such thoughts as these: "I am young and robust; I work on, and sometimes harder than my neighbors, and have less leisure than they. And yet I have difficulty in providing for the modest wants of myself and of my wife and children. But what will become of me, what will become of them, when old age or disease shall have palsied my arm? To provide for those days of helplessness by saving from my wages would require self-control and prudence almost superhuman. Yet in spite of sickness, I have the prospect of enjoying happiness by means of a Friendly Society. Old age, however, is not an eventuality; it will come inevitably and without fail. Every day I feel its approach; it will soon overtake me; and then, after a life of honest labor, what prospect have I before me? For myself the garret, the hospital, or the jail; for my wife, beggary; for my daughter, worse still. Oh for some social institution which would compel me even by force, while still young, to secure a provision for old age!"

Such are the thoughts, feebly as I have expressed them, that every day, and every night, and every hour, haunt the terror-stricken imaginations of vast numbers of our fellow men. And when a problem presents itself under such conditions, you may be very sure that it is not insoluble.

If in their efforts to impart more stability to their future, the working classes have disseminated alarm among the other classes of society, it has arisen from their having given to these efforts a false, dangerous, and unjust direction. Their first idea, according to French custom, has been to attack the treasury; to found the Caisses de Retraite on the contributions of the taxpayer, and to bring into play the State and the Law, that is to say, to secure all the profits of spoliation without incurring the dangers, or bearing the shame of it.

It is not from this quarter of the social horizon that the institution so much desired by the working classes may be expected to come. The Caisse de Retraite, in order that its origin may be in keeping with its end and design, and to ensure its being useful, solid, and respectable, must proceed from the working classes themselves, must be the fruit of their exertions, their energy, their sagacity, their experience, their foresight. It must be supported by their contributions, and fed and nourished by their sacrifices. All they have to ask from Government is liberty of action and repression of fraud.

But has the time come when a Caisse de Retraite for the working classes is possible? I think it has. In order that an institution that brings new stability to the interests of a class should be established, a certain amount of anterior progress is necessary. It is necessary that a certain stage of civilization should have been reached by the Society in the midst of which such an institution is to be established, a healthful atmosphere must be prepared for it. If I am not mistaken, it is to friendly societies, with the material resources they create, and the spirit of association, the experience, the foresight, and the sense of dignity they infuse into the working classes, that we are to owe the establishment of those kindred institutions that provide for the old age of the workman.

For if you observe what is going on in England, you will be satisfied that all such things are bound up together and depend upon each other, and that one step of progress, in order to be attainable, must be preceded by another step of progress.

In England all the adults to whom it is an object to join benefit societies have done so of their own accord; and that is a point of very great importance, seeing that operations of this kind require to be conducted on a great scale, and according to the law of averages.

These societies are possessed of large accumulated capitals, and have, besides, considerable annual revenues.

We cannot help thinking that, with the advance of civilization, the prodigious sums that these societies now require to pay to their members will become proportionally smaller and smaller.

Good health is one of the benefits that civilization develops. The healing art makes progress; machinery performs the harder and more painful part of labor; longevity increases. All these causes tend to lessen the calls on such associations.

A still more decisive and infallible symptom is the disappearance of great commercial crises in England. Such convulsions have had their origin sometimes in sudden manias with which the English are now and then seized for enterprises that are more than hazardous, and that entail a great loss of capital; sometimes they arise from great fluctuations in the price of food, the consequence of restrictive laws, for it is evident that when the price of bread and butcher's meat is very high, all the resources of the people are absorbed in the purchase of necessities, and other branches of trade languish, and a stoppage of manufactures is the inevitable result.

The first of these causes is now disappearing under the teachings of experience and public discussion; and we can already foresee that the English nation, which in former days threw itself into American loans, Mexican mines, and railway schemes with such sheep-like credulity, will now be much less a dupe than others to Californian illusions.

What shall I say of Free Trade, the triumph of which is due to Mr. Cobden, not to Sir Robert Peel—for the apostle would always have called forth a statesman, but the statesman could not have dispensed with the apostle. Here, then, we have a new power ushered into the world, which I hope will go far to do away with commercial stoppages and convulsions. Restriction has the admitted tendency and effect of placing many of the manufactures of the country, and, consequently, part of its population, in a precarious situation. As those piled-up waves that a transient force keeps for a moment above the level of the sea have a constant tendency to descend, so factitious industries, surrounded on every side by victorious competition, have a constant tendency to collapse. A modification in a single article of a single home or foreign tariff may bring ruin to them; and then comes a crisis. The variations in the price of a commodity, moreover, are much greater when you limit the field of competition. Surround a department, or a district, with custom-houses, and you render the fluctuation of prices much more marked. Liberty acts on the principle of insurance. In different countries, and in successive years, it compensates bad harvests by good ones. It sustains prices thus brought back to the average. It is a levelling and equalizing force. It contributes to stability, and it combats instability, which is the great source of convulsions and stoppages. There is no exaggeration in asserting that the first fruit of Mr. Cobden's work will be to lessen many of those dangers that gave rise in England to friendly societies.

Mr. Cobden has undertaken another task that will have a not less beneficial influence on the stability of the laborer's lot, and I doubt not he will succeed in it; for good service in the cause of truth is always triumphant. I refer to his efforts for the suppression of war, or, what is the same thing, for the infusion of the spirit of peace into that public opinion by which the question of peace or war comes always to be decided. War constitutes always the greatest disturbing force to which a nation can be subjected in its industry, in its commerce, in the disposal of its capital, even in its tastes. Consequently, it is a powerful cause of derangement and uneasiness to those classes who have difficulty in changing their employment. The more, of course, this disturbing force is lessened, the less onerous will the burdens be that fall upon benefit societies.

On the other hand, by dint of progress, by the mere lapse of time, the resources of these societies will be extended; and a day will come when they can undertake something more decisive—with a view to lessen the instability that is inherent in human affairs. These societies might then be transformed into Caisses de Retraite, or institutions for the aged, and this will undoubtedly happen, since it is the ardent and universal desire of the working classes that it should be so.

And it is worthy of remark that while material circumstances thus pave the way for such a transformation, moral circumstances arising from the influence of these very societies tend in the same direction. Those societies develop among the working classes habits, qualities, and virtues, the possession and diffusion of which are in this respect an essential preliminary. When we examine the matter closely, we must be convinced that the creation of such societies presupposes a very advanced stage of civilization. They are at once its effect and its reward. They could, in fact, have no existence if men had not been previously in the habit of meeting, of acting in concert, and of managing in common their own affairs; they could not exist if men were prone to vices which induce premature old age; nor could they exist were the working classes brought to think that everything is fair as against the public, and that a common fund is the object at which everyone intent on fraud may legitimately take aim.

In order that the establishment of Caisses de Retraite should not give rise to discord and misunderstanding, the working classes should be made to feel that they must depend upon nobody but themselves; that the common fund must be voluntarily created by those who are to have the benefit of it; and that it is supremely unjust and anti-social to call for co-operation from other classes, who are to have no share in the advantage, and who can only be made to concur by means of the tax-gatherer, that is to say, by means of force. Now, we have not yet got to that length—but the frequent appeals to the State show us but too plainly what are the hopes and pretensions of the working classes. They think that their benefit society should be fed and alimented by State subventions like that for public functionaries. And thus it is that one abuse always gives rise to another.

But if these Caisses de Retraite are to be maintained exclusively by the parties interested, may it not be said that they exist already, seeing that life assurance companies present combinations that enable every workman to provide for the future by the sacrifice of the present?

I have dwelled at great length upon friendly societies and Caisses de Retraite, although these institutions are only indirectly connected with the subject of this chapter. I have given way to the desire to exhibit mankind marching gradually on to the conquest of stability, or rather (for stability implies something stationary), emerging victorious from its struggle with uncertainty—uncertainty, that standing menace that mars all the enjoyments of life, that sword of Damocles that seems so fatally suspended over the human destinies. That this menace may be progressively and indefinitely rendered less formidable by reducing to an average the risks and chances of all times, of all places, and of all men, is certainly one of the most admirable social harmonies that can be presented to the view of the philosophic economist.

We must not, however, conclude that this victory depends upon these two institutions, the establishment of which may be more or less accidental. No; experience demonstrated these institutions to be impracticable, the human race would not the less find its way to fixity. It is enough to know that uncertainty is an evil in order to be assured that it will be incessantly, and sooner or later successfully, combated; for such is the law of our nature.

If, as we have seen, the system of remunerating labor by wages is, as regards stability, a more advanced form of association between capital and labor, it still leaves too much room for the uncertain. As long as he continues to work, the laborer knows on what he has to depend. But how long will he have employment, and how long will he be fit for work? This is what he is ignorant of and, as regards his future, it places before him a fearful problem for solution. The uncertainty that affects the capitalist is different. With him it is not a question of life or death. "I shall always derive an interest from my means; but will that interest be higher or lower?" That is the question that affects capital or anterior labor.

Sentimental philanthropists who see in this a frightful inequality that they desire to get rid of by artificial, sometimes by unjust and violent, means, do not consider that after all we cannot change the nature of things. Anterior labor must necessarily provide more security than present labor, simply for this reason, that products already created must always present more certain resources than products that are yet to be created; that services already rendered, received, and estimated, present a more solid foundation for the future than services that are still in the state of supply. If you are not surprised that of two fishermen, the one who, having long labored and saved, possesses lines, nets, boats, and some previous supply of fish, is more at ease as regards his future than the other who has absolutely nothing but his willingness to take part in the work, why should you be astonished that the social order presents to a certain extent the same differences? In order to justify the envy, the jealousy, the absolute spitefulness with which the laborer regards the capitalist, it would be necessary to conclude that the relative stability of the one is caused by the instability of the other. But it is the reverse which is true. It is precisely the capital that pre-exists in the hands of one man that is the guarantee of the wages of another, however insufficient that guarantee may appear. But for that capital, the uncertainty of the laborer would be still greater and more striking. Would the increase, and the extension to all, of that uncertainty be any advantage to the laborer?

Two men run equal risks, which we may represent, for each, as equal to 40. One of them succeeds so well by his labor and his foresight that he reduces the risks that affect him to 10. Those of his companion from the same cause, and in consequence of a mysterious solidarity, are reduced not to 10, but to 20. What can be more just than that the man who has the greater merit should reap the greater reward? What more admirable than that the other should profit by the virtues of his neighbor? Now, this is just what philanthropy repudiates under the pretext that such an order of things is opposed to equality.

Suppose that one fine day the old fisherman should thus address his companion: "You have neither boat, nor nets, nor any instrument to fish with, except your hands, and you are likely to make but a poor business of it. You have no stock of provisions, and it is poor work to fish with an empty stomach. Come along with me—it is your interest as well as mine. It is yours, for I will give you a share of the fish we take, and, whatever the quantity be, it will at least be greater than the produce of your isolated exertions. It is my interest also, for the additional quantity caught with your assistance will be greater than the share I will have to give you. In short, the union of your labor with my labor and capital, as compared with their isolated action, will produce a surplus, and it is the division of this surplus that explains how association may be of advantage to both of us."

They proceed in this way in the first instance; but afterwards the young fisher will prefer to receive every day a fixed quantity of fish. His uncertain and fluctuating profits are thus converted into wages, without the advantages of association being destroyed, and, by stronger reason, without the association itself being dissolved.

And it is in such circumstances as these that the pretended philanthropy of the Socialists comes to declaim against the tyranny of boats and nets, against the situation, naturally less uncertain, of him who possesses them, and who has come to possess them just because he has constructed them in order to obviate this uncertainty! It is in such circumstances that they endeavor to persuade the destitute young fisherman that he is the victim of his voluntary arrangement with the old fisherman, and that he ought instantly to return to his state of isolation!

To assert that the future of the capitalist is less uncertain than that of the workman, is just to assert that the man who already possesses is in a better situation than the man who does not yet possess. It is so, and it must be so, for it is for this very reason that men aspire to possess.

The tendency, then, is for men to cease being workmen in receipt of wages in order to become capitalists. This progress is in conformity with human nature. What workman does not desire to have tools of his own, a stock of his own, a warehouse, a workshop, a field, a dwelling-house, of his own? What workman but aspires to become an employer? Who is not delighted to command after having long obeyed? Do the great laws of the economic world, does the natural play of the social organs, favor or oppose this tendency? This is the last question we shall examine in connection with the subject of wages.

Can its solution be attended with any doubt?

Let us revert once more to the necessary evolution of production: gratuitous utility substituting itself incessantly for onerous utility; human efforts constantly diminishing in relation to each result and, when rendered disposable, embarking in new enterprises; every hour's labor corresponding to an always increasing amount of enjoyment. How, from these premises, can we fail to deduce a progressive increase of useful effects to be distributed, consequently a sustained amelioration of the laborer's condition, consequently, also, an endless increase and progression of that amelioration?

For here the effect having become a cause, we see progress not only advance, but become accelerated by its advance; *vires acquirere eundo*. In point of fact, from century to century accumulation becomes more easy, as the remuneration of labor becomes more ample. Then accumulation increases capital, increases the demand for labor, and causes an elevation of wages. This rise of wages, in its turn, facilitates accumulation and the transformation of the paid laborer into a capitalist. Between the remuneration of labor and the accumulation of capital, then, there is a constant action and reaction, which is always favorable to the laboring class, always tending to relieve that class from the yoke of urgent necessity.

It may be said, perhaps, that I have brought together here all that can dazzle the hopes of the working classes, and that I have concealed all that could cause them discouragement. If there are tendencies toward equality, it may be said, there are also tendencies toward inequality. Why do you not analyze the whole, in order to explain the true situation of the laboring classes, and thus bring science into accord with the melancholy facts to which it seems to shut its eyes? You show us gratuitous utility substituted for onerous utility, the gifts of God falling more and more into the domain of community, and, by that very fact, human labor obtaining a continually increasing recompense. From this increase of remuneration you deduce an increased facility of accumulation, and from this facility of accumulation a new increase of remuneration, leading to new and still more abundant accumulations, and so on *ad infinitum*. It may be that this system is as logical as it is optimistic; it may be that we are not in a situation to oppose to it a scientific refutation. But where are the facts that confirm it? Where do we find realized this emancipation from paid labor? Is it in the great centers of manufactures? Is is among the agricultural laborers? And if your theoretical predictions are not accomplished, is not this the reason, that alongside the economic laws you invoke, there are other laws which act in an opposite direction, and of which you say nothing? For instance, why do you tell us nothing of that competition which takes place among workmen, and which forces them to accept lower wages; of that urgent want of the necessities of life that presses upon the laborer, and obliges him to submit to the conditions of the capitalist, so that, in fact, it is the most destitute, famished, isolated, and consequently the loudest and most demanding workman who fixes the rate of wages for all? And if, in spite of so many obstacles, the condition of our unfortunate fellow citizens comes to be improved, why do you not show us that law of population that steps in with its fatal action, multiplying the multitude, stirring up competition, increasing the supply of labor, deciding the controversy in favor of the capitalist, and reducing the workman to receive, for twelve or sixteen hours' labor, only what is indispensable (that, indeed, is the consecrated phrase) to the maintenance of life?

If I have not touched upon all these phases of the question, the reason is that it is scarcely possible to include everything within the limits of a single chapter. I have already explained the general law of Competition, and we have seen that that law is far from furnishing any class, especially the poorer class, with serious reasons for discouragement. I shall by-and-by explain the law of Population, which will be found, I hope, in its general effects, not more severe. It is not my fault if each great solution—such, for example, as the future of a whole class of men—cannot be educed from one isolated economic law, and consequently from one chapter of this work, but must be educed from the aggregate of these laws, or from the work taken as a whole.

And here I must remind the reader of a distinction, which is by no means a subtlety, that when we have to do with an effect, we must take good care not to attribute it to the action of general and providential laws if, on the contrary, it be found to proceed from a violation of these very laws.

I by no means ignore the calamities that, under all forms—excessive labor, insufficient wages, uncertainty as to the future, a feeling of inferiority—bear hard upon those of our fellow citizens who have not yet been able, by the acquisition of Property, to raise themselves to a higher and more comfortable condition. But then, we must acknowledge that uncertainty, destitution, and ignorance constitute the starting point of the whole human race; and this being so, the question, it seems to me, is to discover—first, if the general providential laws do not tend to relieve all classes from the weight of this triple yoke; secondly, if the conquests already secured by the more advanced classes do not constitute a facility prepared beforehand for the classes that yet lag behind. If the answer to these questions be in the affirmative, we may conclude that the social harmony is established, and that the ways of Providence are vindicated if, indeed, they needed vindication.

Man being endowed with discretion and free will, the beneficent laws of Providence can profit him only while he conforms himself to their operation; and although I affirm that man's nature is perfectible, I must not be understood to assert that he makes progress when he misunderstands or violates these laws. Thus, I maintain that transactions that are natural, free, voluntary, and exempt from fraud or violence, have in themselves a principle of progress for all. But that is not to affirm that progress is inevitable, and must spring from war, monopoly, or imposture. I maintain that wages have a tendency to rise, that this rise facilitates saving, and that saving, in its turn, raises wages. But if the class that lives by wages, in consequence of habits of dissipation and debauchery, neutralize at the outset this cause of progressive effects, I do not say that these effects will exhibit themselves in the same way, for the contrary is implied in my affirmation.

In order to bring the scientific deduction to the test of facts, we must take two epochs; for example, 1750 and 1850.

We must first of all establish what, at these two periods, was the proportion of proletaires to proprietaires—of the men who live by wages without having any realized property, to the men in the actual possession of property. We shall find, I presume, that for a century the number of people who possess some resources has much increased relatively to the number of those who are in possession of no resources whatever.

We must then discover the specific situation of each of these two classes, which we cannot do otherwise than by observing the enjoyments and satisfactions they possess; and very probably we shall find in our day they derive a greater amount of real satisfaction and enjoyment, the one from accumulated labor, the other from present labor, than was possible in the middle of the last century.

If the respective and relative progress of these classes, especially of the working class, has not been what we could wish, we must then inquire whether it has not been more or less retarded by acts of injustice and violence, by errors, by passions—in a word, by faults incident to mankind, by contingent causes that we cannot confound with what are called the great and constant laws of the social economy. Have we not, for example, had wars and revolutions that might have been avoided? And have not these atrocities, in the first instance, absorbed and afterwards dissipated an incalculable amount of capital, consequently diminished the funds for the payment of wages, and retarded the emancipation of the working classes? Have they not diverted capital from its legitimate employment, seeking to derive from it, not enjoyment, but destruction? Have we not had monopolies, privileges, and unequal taxation? Have we not had absurd expenditure, ridiculous fashions, and a loss of vitality, which can be attributed only to puerile tastes and prejudices?

And what has been the consequence?

There are general laws to which man may conform himself, or which he may violate.

If it be incontestable that Frenchmen, during the last hundred years, have frequently run counter to the natural order of social development; if we cannot forbear to attribute to incessant wars, to periodical revolutions, to acts of injustice, to monopolies, to dissipation, to follies of all kinds, a fearful sacrifice of the power of capital and of labor.

And if, on the other hand, in spite of all this, which is undeniable, we can establish another fact—namely, that during this same period of a hundred years the class possessed of property has been recruited from the laboring class, and that both have at the same time had at their command a greater amount of satisfaction and enjoyment—do we not, by rigorous deduction, arrive at this conclusion, namely, that:

The general laws of the social world are in harmony, and that they tend in all respects to the improvement of the human race?

For since, after a period of a hundred years during which these laws have been so frequently and so deeply violated, men find themselves in a more advanced state of comfort and well-being, the action of these laws must be beneficent, and sufficiently so even to compensate the action of disturbing causes.

How indeed could it be otherwise? Is there not something equivocal, or rather redundant, in the expression, beneficent general laws? How can general laws be other than beneficent? When God placed in man's heart an irresistible impulse to what is good, and, to enable him to discern it, imparted to him sufficient light to enable him to rectify his errors, from that moment He decreed that the human race was perfectible, and that, in spite of many errors, difficulties, deceptions, oppressions, and oscillations, mankind should still march onwards on the road of progress. This onward march, while error, deception and oppression are absent, is precisely what we denominate the general laws of the social order. Errors and oppressions are what I call the violation of these laws, or disturbing causes. It is not possible, then, to doubt that the one should be beneficent, and the other the reverse, unless we go to the length of doubting whether disturbing causes may not act in a manner more regular and permanent than general laws. Now that conclusion would contradict the premises. Our intelligence, which may be deceived, can rectify its errors, and it is evident that, the social world being constituted as it is, error might sooner or later be checked by Responsibility, and that, sooner or later, oppression must be destroyed by Solidarity. Whence it follows that disturbing causes are not in their nature permanent, and it is for that reason that the laws that countervail the action of such disturbances merit the name of General Laws.

In order to conform ourselves to general laws, it is necessary to be acquainted with them. Allow me then to enlarge a little on the relations, so ill understood, of the capitalist and the laborer.

Capital and labor are indispensable to one another. Perpetually confronting each other, their adjustment constitutes one of the most important and most interesting subjects that can come under the observation of the economist. And it is a solemn consideration that erroneous notions and superficial observations on this subject, if they become popular, may give rise to inveterate enmities, struggles, and bloodshed.

Now, I express my deliberate conviction when I say that for some years the public mind has been saturated with the falsest theories on this subject. We have been told that free and voluntary transactions between the capitalist and the laborer lead, not accidentally, but necessarily, to monopoly for the capitalist, and oppression for the laborer; from which the obvious conclusion is that liberty ought everywhere to be put down and stifled; for, I repeat, that when men have accused liberty of engendering monopoly, they have pretended not only to assert a fact but to establish a law. In support of this thesis they have appealed to the action of machinery and of competition. Mr. de Sismondi was, I believe, the founder and Mr. Buret the propagator, of these unhappy doctrines, although the latter has stated his conclusions very timidly, and the former has not ventured to state any conclusion at all. But bolder spirits have succeeded them who, after trumpeting their hatred to capitalists and men of property, after having got the masses to accept as an incontestable axiom the discovery that liberty leads inevitably to monopoly have, whether designedly or not, induced the people to raise their hands against this accursed liberty.[4] Four days of a sanguinary struggle brought emancipation, without restoring confidence; for do we not constantly discover the hand of the State (obedient in this to vulgar prejudices) ever ready to interpose in the relations of capital and labor?

We have already deduced the action of competition from our theory of value, and we shall do the same thing as regards the effects of machinery. We must limit ourselves in this place to an exposition of some general ideas upon the subject of the reciprocal relations of the capitalist and the laborer.

The fact with which our pessimist reformers are much struck in the outset is that the capitalists are richer than the workmen, and obtain a greater amount of satisfactions and enjoyments; whence it results that they appropriate to themselves a greater, and consequently an unjust, share of the product elaborated by their joint exertions. It is in this direction that their statistics, more or less impartial, professing to explain the condition of the working classes, tend.

---

[4]Riots of June 1848.

These gentlemen forget that absolute poverty and destitution is the inevitable starting point of the human race, and that men continue inevitably in this state until they have acquired something for themselves, or have had something acquired for them by others. To remark, in the gross, that capitalists are better off than mere workmen, is simply to assert that those who have something have more than those who have nothing.

The questions the workman ought to ask himself are not, "Does my labor give me much? Does it give me little? Does it give me as much as it gives to another? Does it give me what I desire?" The questions he should ask himself are these: "Does my labor give me less because I employ it in the service of the capitalist? Would it give me more if I worked in a state of isolation, or if I associated my labor with that of other workmen as destitute as myself? I am ill situated, but would I be better off were there no such thing as capital in the world? If the part I obtain in consequence of my arrangement with capital is greater than what I would obtain without that arrangement, what reason have I to complain? And then, according to what laws would our respective shares go on increasing or diminishing were transactions free? If it be of the nature of these transactions to allow me, in proportion as the total product to be divided increases, to obtain a continually increasing proportion of the excess (part 1, chapter 7), then in place of breathing hatred against capital, ought I not to treat it as a friend? If it be indisputably established that the presence of capital is favorable to my interests, and that its absence would be death to me, am I very prudent or well-advised in calumniating it, frightening it away, and forcing its dissipation or flight?" In the discussion that precedes the bargain, an inequality of situation is constantly alleged, because capital can afford to wait, but labor cannot. The one upon which the greatest pressure bears must give way to the other, so that the capitalist in reality fixes the rate of wages.

Undoubtedly, looking at the surface of things, he who has created a stock, and who in consequence of this foresight can wait on, has the advantage in the bargain. Taking even an isolated transaction, the man who says, *Do ut facias* (commodity against service), is not in such a hurry to come to a conclusion as the man who replies, *Facio ut des* (service against commodity). For, when a man can say "Do," he possesses something to give; and when he possesses something to give, he can wait.

We must not, however, lose sight of this, that value has the same principle, whether it reside in the service or in the product. If one of the parties says, "*do*," in place of "*facio*," it is because he has had the foresight to execute the *facio* beforehand. In reality, it is the service on both sides that is the measure of the value. Now, if delay for present labor is a suffering, for anterior labor it is a loss. We must not then suppose that the man who says "do," the capitalist, will amuse himself (above all if we consider the aggregate of his transactions) by deferring the bargain. In point of fact, do we see much capital idle for this reason? Do many manufacturers stop their mills, or shipowners delay their voyages, or agriculturists defer their harvests, on purpose to depreciate wages, and get hold of their workmen by means of famine?

But without denying that the position of the capitalist in relation to the workman is favorable in this respect, is there not something else to be considered with reference to their arrangements? For instance, is it not a circumstance quite in favor of present labor that accumulated labor loses value by mere lapse of time? I have elsewhere alluded to this phenomenon. But it is important to solicit the reader's attention again to it in this place, seeing how great an influence it has upon the remuneration of present labor.

That which in my opinion renders Adam Smith's theory, that value comes from labor, false, or at least incomplete, is that this theory assigns to value only one element, while, being a relation, it has necessarily two. Besides, if value springs exclusively from labor, and represents it, it would be proportionate to that labor, which is contrary to all observed facts.

No; value comes from service received and rendered; and the service depends as much, if not more, on the pains saved to the man who receives it, as upon the pains taken by the man who renders it.

In this respect the most common facts confirm our reasoning. When I purchase a product, I may indeed ask myself, "How long time has it taken to make it?" And this undoubtedly is one of the elements of my estimate of its value. But again, and above all, I ask, "How long time would it take me to make it? How long time have I taken to make the thing which is asked from me in exchange?" When I purchase a service, I not only ask how much it will cost another to render that service to me, but how much it would cost me to render that service to myself.

These personal questions and the answers they call forth are such essential elements in every estimate of value, that they most frequently determine it.

Try to purchase a diamond that has been found by chance. The seller will transfer to you very little labor, but he will ask from you a great deal. Why, then, should you consent to this? Because you take into account the labor it saves you, the labor you would be obliged to undergo in order to satisfy by any other means your desire to possess a diamond.

When an exchange, then, takes place between anterior labor and present labor, it is not at all on the footing of their intensity or duration, but on that of their value, that is to say, of the service which they render, and their relative utility. If the capitalist shall say, "Here is a product that cost me formerly ten hours' labor," and if the laborer be in a situation to reply, "I can produce the same thing in five hours," the capitalist would be forced to give up the difference; for I repeat, that it does not concern the present acquirer of a commodity to ask how much labor it formerly cost to produce it. What concerns him is to know what labor it will save him now, what service he is to expect from it.

A capitalist, in a general sense, is a man who, having foreseen that such or such a service would be in demand, has prepared beforehand to satisfy this demand by incorporating the value in a commodity.

When labor has been thus expended by anticipation, in expectation of future remuneration, we cannot tell whether, on a definite future day, it will render exactly the same service, or save the same pains, or preserve, consequently, a uniform value. We cannot even hazard a probable conjecture as to this. The commodity may be very "*recherché*," very difficult to procure in any other way; it may come to render services that will be better appreciated, or appreciated by more people; it may acquire an increasing value with time—in other words, it may exchange for a continually increasing proportion of present labor. Thus it is not impossible that such a product, a diamond for example, a violin of Stradivarius, a picture of Raphael, a vine-plant from the Chateau-Laffitte, may come to exchange for a thousand times more labor than they cost. In fact it just comes to this, that the anterior labor is well remunerated in these cases, because it renders a great amount of service.

The contrary may also happen. A commodity that has cost four hours' labor may come to exchange for one that has cost only three hours' labor of equal intensity.

But—and this appears to me extremely important as regards the interests of the working classes, of those classes who aspire so ardently to get rid of their present state of uncertainty—although the two alternatives we have stated are both possible, and each may be realized in its turn, although accumulated labor may sometimes gain, and sometimes lose value, in relation to present labor, the first alternative, nevertheless, is so rare as to be considered accidental and exceptional; while the second is the result of a general law that is inherent in the very organization of man. That man, with all his intellectual and experimental acquisitions, is of a progressive nature, is, at least industrially speaking (for, in a moral point of view, the assertion might be disputed), beyond doubt. It is beyond doubt that the greater part of those commodities that exacted formerly a given amount of labor, exact at the present day a less amount, in consequence of improvements in machinery, and the gratuitous intervention of natural forces; and we may assert without hesitation, that in each period of ten years, for example, a given quantity of labor will accomplish, in the majority of cases, greater results than the same quantity of labor could have accomplished in the preceding decennial period.

What is the conclusion to be drawn from this? Obviously, that anterior labor goes on constantly deteriorating in value relatively to present labor; that in every act of exchange it becomes necessary to give, of the first, a greater number of hours than you receive of the second; and this without any injustice, but simply to maintain the equivalence of services. This is a consequence that progress forces upon us.

You say to me, "Here is a machine; it was made ten years ago but it is still new. It cost 1,000 days' work to make it. I will give it to you in exchange for an equal number of days' labor." To this I reply, "Within the last ten years so many new tools have been invented, and so many new processes discovered, that I can now construct, or, what comes to the same thing, get constructed for me, an equally good machine, with an expenditure of only 600 days' labor. I will not, therefore, give you more than 600 for yours." "But I should in this way lose 400 days' labor." "No," I reply; "for 6 days' work now are worth 10 formerly. At all events, what you offer me for 1,000 I can now procure for 600." This ends the debate; if the lapse of time has deteriorated the value of your labor, there is no reason why I should bear the loss.

Again you say to me, "Here is a field. In order to bring it to its present state of productiveness, I and my ancestors have expended 1,000 days' labor. They were unacquainted, no doubt, with the use of axe, and saw, and spade, and did all by muscular exertion. But no matter; give me first of all 1,000 of your days' work, as an equivalent for the 1,000 I give to you, and then add 300 as the value of the productive power of the soil, and you shall have the field." I answer, "I will not give you 1,300, or even 1,000, days' labor for it; and here are my reasons: There are on the surface of the globe an indefinite number of productive powers that are destitute of value. We are now accustomed to handle spade, and axe, and saw, and plough, and employ many other means of abridging labor, and rendering it more productive; so that, with 600 days' work, I can either bring an uncultivated field into the state in which yours is, or (which comes absolutely to the same thing, as far as I am concerned) I can procure myself, by an act of exchange, all the advantages you reap from your field. I will give you, then, 600 days, and no more." "In that case, not only should I have no profit from the pretended value of the productive powers of the soil; I should not even be reimbursed for the actual labor that I and my ancestors have devoted to the cultivation of this field. Is it not strange that I should be accused by Ricardo of selling the powers of nature; by Senior of intercepting the gifts of God; by all the Economists of being a monopolist; by Proudhon of being a robber; while in reality I am only a dupe?" You are no more a dupe than a monopolist. You receive the equivalent of what you give; and it is neither natural nor just, nor possible, that rude labor performed with the hand centuries ago should exchange, day for day against the more intelligent and productive labor of the present time.

Thus we see that by an admirable effect of the social mechanism, when anterior and present labor are brought into juxtaposition, and when the business is to know in what proportion the joint product of both is to be divided, the specific superiority of the one and of the other is taken into account; and they participate in the distribution according to the relative services they render. In exceptional cases, it may happen that this superiority is on the side of anterior labor. But in the great majority of cases, it is otherwise; and the nature of man and the law of progress cause the superiority to be manifested on the side of present labor. Progress is advanced by the latter; and the deterioration falls upon capital.

Independently of this result, which shows how vain and hollow the declamations of our modern reformers on the pretended tyranny of capital are, there is another consideration still more fitted to extinguish in the hearts of the working classes that factitious hatred of other classes, which it has been attempted but with too much success to light up.

The consideration I refer to is this:

Capital, however far it may carry its pretensions, and however successful it may be in its endeavors to ensure the triumph of these pretensions, can never place labor in a worse situation than it would occupy in a state of isolation. In other words, capital is always more favorable to labor by its presence than by its absence.

Let us revert to the example I gave a little ago.

Two men live by fishing. One of them has nets, lines, a boat, and some provisions to enable him to wait for the fruit of his labor. The other has nothing but his personal exertions. It is their interest to associate. Whatever may be the terms on which they agree to share the produce, the condition of either of these two fishermen, whether the rich one or the poor one, never can be made worse, and for this obvious reason, that the moment either of them finds association disadvantageous as compared with isolation, he may return to isolation.

In savage as in pastoral, in agricultural as in industrial life, the relations of capital and labor are always represented by this example.

The absence of capital is a limit that is always within the power of labor. If the pretensions of capital go the length of rendering joint action less profitable for labor than isolated action, labor can take refuge in isolation, an asylum always open (except in a state of slavery) to voluntary association found to be disadvantageous. Labor can always say to capital, Rather than work jointly on the conditions you offer me, I prefer to work alone.

It may be objected that this resource is illusory and ridiculous, that to labor isolated action is forbidden by a radical impossibility, and that to dispense with tools and instruments would be fatal to it.

This is no doubt true; but it just confirms the truth of my assertion that even if capital carries its exactions to an extreme limit, it still benefits labor by the very fact of its being associated with it. Labor can be brought into a worse condition than the worst association only when all association ceases and capital retires. Cease, then, apostles of misfortune, to cry out against the tyranny of capital, since you allow that its action is always—in a greater or less degree, no doubt, but always—beneficent. Some tyranny this is, whose power is beneficial to all those who desire to feel its effects, and is hurtful only when withdrawn.

But the objector may still insist that although this might be so in the earlier stages of society, capital has at the present day invaded everything. It occupies every post, it lays hold of every field. The working man has no longer either air, or space, or soil to put his foot on, or stone to lay his head on, without the permission of capital. He is subject to its inexorable law, and you would afford him no refuge but isolation, which you admit is death!

All this displays a deplorable confusion of ideas, and a total ignorance of the social economy.

If, as has been said, capital has possessed itself of all the forces of nature, of all lands, of all space, I would ask for whose profit? For the profit of the capitalist, no doubt. But then, how does it happen that a simple workman, who has nothing but his muscular powers, can obtain in France, in England, in Belgium, a thousand, a million times greater amount of satisfaction and enjoyment than he could have reaped in a state of isolation—not on the social hypothesis that you repudiate, but on that other hypothesis that you cherish and cling to, that which presupposes capital to have been guilty of no usurpation.

I shall continue to entertain this view of the subject until your new science can give a better account of it; for I am convinced I have assigned valid reasons for the conclusion at which I have arrived—(part 1, chapter 7).

Take the first workman you meet with on the streets of Paris. Find out the amount of his earnings and the amount of enjoyments he can procure himself, and when you have both finished complaining about that monster, capital, I will step in, and thus address the workman:

We are about to annihilate capital and all its works; and I am going to place you in the midst of a hundred thousand acres of the most fertile land, which I shall give you in full property and possession, with everything above and below ground. You will not be elbowed by any capitalist. You will have the full employment of the four natural rights of hunting, fishing, reaping the fruits, and pasturing the land. True, you will have no capital; for if you had, you would be in precisely the situation you censure in the case of others. But you will no longer have reason to complain of landlordism, capitalism, individualism, usurers, stockjobbers, bankers, monopolists. The land will be absolutely and entirely yours. Think if you would like to accept this position.

This workman would, no doubt, imagine at first that he had obtained the fortune of a monarch. On reflection, how ever, he would probably say: Well, let us calculate. Even when a man possesses a hundred thousand acres of land, he must live. Now, how does the bread account stand in the two situations? At present I earn half-a-crown a day. At the present price of wheat I can have three bushels a week, just as if I myself sowed and reaped. Were I proprietor of a hundred thousands acres of land, at the utmost I could not, without capital, produce three bushels of wheat in two years, and in the interim I might die of famine. . . . I shall, therefore, stick to my wages.

The truth is, we do not consider sufficiently the progress which the human race must have made, to be able even to maintain the wretched existence of our workmen.[4]

Amelioration of the laborer's lot is to be found in wages themselves and in the natural laws by which wages are regulated.

First, the laborer tends to rise to the rank of a capitalist and employer.

Second, wages tend to rise.

Corollary—The transition from the state of a paid workman to that of an employer becomes constantly less desirable, and more easy.

---

[4]The manuscript brought from Rome stops here. What is subjoined was found among the papers left by the author in Paris. It indicates how he intended to terminate and sum up this chapter.—Editor.

15

SAVING

To save is not to accumulate quantities of wheat, of game, or of crown-pieces. This hoarding-up of material and consumable commodities, which must necessarily from its nature be restrained within narrow bounds, represents only the saving of man in a state of isolation. All that we have hitherto said of value, of services, of relative wealth, shows us that, socially, saving, although it proceeds from the same source, develops itself differently and assumes another character.

To save is to interpose voluntarily an interval between the time when we render services to society and the time when we receive back from society equivalent services. A man, for example, may every day from the time he is twenty until he is sixty, render to his neighbors professional services equal to four, and demand from them services only equal to three. In that case he reserves the power of drawing upon society in his old age and when he can no longer work, for payment of the remaining fourth of his forty years' labor.

The circumstance that he has received and accumulated through a succession of years notes of acknowledgment consisting of bills of exchange, promissory notes, bank notes, money, is quite secondary, and belongs only to the form of the transaction. It has relation only to the means of execution. It changes neither the nature nor the consequences of saving. The illusion to which the intervention of money gives rise in this respect is not the less an illusion, although we are almost always the dupes of it.

In fact, it is with difficulty that we can avoid believing that the man who saves withdraws from circulation a certain amount of value, and, in consequence, does a certain amount of harm to society.

And here we encounter one of those apparent contradictions that are at war with logic, one of those barriers that would seem to oppose an insurmountable obstacle to progress, one of those dissonances that gives us pain by appearing to call in question the Divine power and will.

On the one hand, we know that the human race can only extend itself, raise itself, improve itself, acquire leisure, stability, and, by consequence, intellectual development and moral culture, by the abundant creation and persevering accumulation of capital. It is this rapid augmentation of capital on which depends the demand for labor, the elevation of wages, and, consequently, the progress of men toward equality.

But, on the other hand, to save is not the opposite of to spend, and if the man who spends gives a fillip to industry and additional employment to labor, does the man who saves not do exactly the reverse? If everyone set himself to economize as much as possible, we should see labor languish in the same proportion, and if all could be saved, we should have no fund for the employment of labor.

In such circumstances, what advice can we give? And what solid basis can political economy offer to morals, when we appear to be able to educe from the former only this contradictory and melancholy alternative:

If you do not save, capital will not be replaced, but dissipated, the laboring class will be multiplied, while the fund for their remuneration will remain stationary; they will enter into competition with each other, and offer their services at a lower rate; wages will be depressed, and society will, in this respect, be on the decline. It will be on the decline also in another respect, for unless you save you will be without bread in your old age; you can no longer set your son out in the world, give a portion to your daughter, or enlarge your trade," etc.

"If you do save, you diminish the fund for wages, you injure a great number of your fellow-citizens, you strike a blow at labor, which is the universal creator of human satisfactions, and you lower, consequently, the general level of humanity."

Now these frightful contradictions disappear before the explanation that we have given of saving—an explanation founded upon the ideas to which our inquiries on the subject of value conducted us.

Services are exchanged for services.

Value is the appreciation of two services compared with each other.

In this view, to save is to have rendered a service and to allow time for receiving the equivalent service, or, in other words, to interpose an interval of time between the service rendered, and the service received.

Now, in what respect can a man do injury to society or to labor who merely abstains from drawing upon society for a service to which he has right? I can exact the value that is due to me upon the instant, or I may delay exacting it for a year. In that case, I give society a year's respite. During that interval, labor is carried on and services are exchanged just as if I did not exist. I have not by this means caused any disturbance. On the contrary, I have added one satisfaction more to the enjoyments of my fellow-citizens, and they possess it for a year gratuitously.

Gratuitously is not the word, for I must go on to describe the phenomenon.

The interval of time that separates the two services exchanged is itself the subject of a bargain, of an exchange, for it is possessed of value. It is the origin and explanation of interest.

A man, for instance, renders a present service. His wish is to receive the equivalent service only ten years hence. Here, then, is a value of which he refuses himself the immediate enjoyment. Now, it is of the nature of value to be able to assume all possible forms. With a determinate value, we are sure to obtain any imaginable service, whether productive or unproductive, of an equal value. He who delays for ten years to call in a debt not only delays an enjoyment, but he delays the possibility of further production. It is on this account that he will meet with people in the world who are disposed to bargain for this delay. They will say to him: "You are entitled to receive immediately a certain value. It suits you to delay receiving it for ten years. Now, for these ten years, make over your right to me, place me in your room and stead. I shall receive for you the amount for which you are a creditor. I will employ it during these ten years in a productive enterprise, and repay you at the end of that time. By this means you will render me a service, and as every service has a value, which we estimate by comparing it with another service, we have only to estimate this service which I solicit from you, and so fix its value. This point being discussed and arranged, I shall have to repay you at the end of the ten years, not only the value of the service for which you are a creditor, but the value likewise of the service you are about to render me."

It is the value of this temporary transference of values saved that we denominate interest.

For the same reason that a third party may desire that we should transfer to him for an onerous consideration the enjoyment of a value saved, the original debtor may also desire to enter into the same bargain. In both cases this is called asking for credit. To give credit is to give time for the acquittance of a debt, of a value; it is to deprive oneself of the enjoyment of that value in favor of another, it is to render a service, it is to acquire a title to an equivalent service.

But to revert to the economic effects of saving, now that we are acquainted with all the details of the phenomenon, it is very evident that it does no injury to general activity or to labor. Even when the man who economizes realizes his economy, and, in exchange for services rendered, receives hard cash and hoards it, he does no harm to society, seeing that he has not been able to withdraw that amount of value from society without restoring to it equivalent values. I must add, however, that such hoarding is improbable and exceptional, inasmuch as it is detrimental to the personal interests of the man who would practice it. Money in the hands of such a man may be supposed to say this: "He who possesses me has rendered services to society, and has not been paid for them. I have been put into his hands to serve him as a warrant; I am at once an acknowledgment, a promise, and a guarantee. The moment he wills it, he can, by exhibiting and restoring me, receive back from society the services for which he is a creditor."

Now this man is in no hurry. Does it follow that he will continue to hoard his money? No; for we have seen that the lapse of time that separates two services exchanged becomes itself the subject of a commercial transaction. If the man who saves intends to remain ten years without drawing upon society for the services that are owing to him, his interest is to substitute a representative in order to add to the value for which he is a creditor the value of this special service. Saving, then, implies in no shape actual hoarding.

Let moralists be no longer arrested by this consideration.

16

POPULATION

I have been longing to enter upon the subject of this chapter, were it for no other purpose than to have an opportunity of vindicating Malthus from the violent attacks that have been made upon him. It is scarcely credible that a set of writers of no reputation or ability, and whose ignorance is transparent in every page of their works, should, by echoing one another's opinions, have succeeded in lowering in public estimation a grave, conscientious, and philanthropic author; representing as absurd a theory that at all events deserves to be studied with serious attention.

It may be that I do not myself adopt all the opinions of Malthus. Every question has two phases; and I believe that Malthus may have fixed his regards too exclusively upon the somber side. In my own economical studies and inquiries, I have been so frequently led to the conclusion that whatever is the work of Providence is good that when logic has seemed to force me to a different conclusion, I have been inclined to distrust my logic. I am aware that this faith in final causes is not unattended with danger to the mind of an inquirer. But this will not prevent me from acknowledging that there is a vast amount of truth in the admirable work of this economist, or from rendering homage to that ardent love of mankind by which every line of it is inspired.

Malthus, whose knowledge of the social economy was profound, had a clear view of all the ingenious mechanisms with which nature has provided the human race to assure its onward march on the road of progress. And yet he believed that human progress might find itself entirely paralyzed by one principle, namely, the principle of Population. In contemplating the world, he gave way to the melancholy reflection that "God appears to have taken great care of the species, and very little of the individual. In fact, as regards a certain class of animated beings, we see them endowed with a fecundity so prolific, a power of multiplication so extraordinary, a profusion of spawn so superabundant, that the destiny of the species would seem undoubtedly well assured, while that of the individuals of the species appears very precarious; for the whole of these spawn cannot be brought to life and maturity. They must either fail to live, or must die prematurely."

"Man makes no exception to this law." (It is surprising that this should shock the Socialists, who never cease telling us that the collective must take precedence over individual right.) "This much is certain, that God has secured the continuance of the human race by providing it with a great power of reproduction. The numbers of mankind, then, would come naturally, but for prudence and foresight, to exceed what the earth could maintain. But man is endowed with foresight, and it is his reason and his will alone that can alone interpose a check to this fatal progression."

Setting out from these premises, which you may dispute if you will, but which Malthus regarded as incontestable, he attached necessarily the highest value to the exercise of foresight. For there was no alternative; man must either restrain voluntarily this excessive multiplication, or else he must become subject, like all the other species of living creatures, to the operation of positive or repressive checks.

Malthus, then, believed that he could never urge men too strongly to the exercise of foresight. His very philanthropy engaged him to exhibit in strong relief the fatal consequences of imprudent reproduction, in order to put men upon their guard. He said to them: If you multiply inconsiderately, you cannot avoid the chastisement that awaits you in some form or other, and always in a hideous form—famine, war, pestilence, etc. Benevolence, charity, poor-laws, and all other expedients, are but ineffectual remedies.

In his ardor, Malthus allowed an expression to escape him that, when separated from the rest of his system, and from the sentiment that dictated it, may appear harsh. It occurred in the first edition of his work, which was then only a brochure, and has since become a book of four volumes. It was represented to him that his meaning in this objectionable passage might give rise to erroneous interpretations. He immediately suppressed it, and it has never since reappeared in any of the numerous editions of his *Essay on Population*.

But Mr. Godwin, one of his opponents, had quoted this suppressed passage, and the consequence was that Mr. de Sismondi (a man who, with the best intentions in the world, has done much mischief) reproduced this unlucky sentence. The Socialists instantly laid hold of it, and on this they proceeded to try, condemn, and execute Malthus. Truly, they were much indebted to Sismondi's learning, for they had never themselves read either Malthus or Godwin.

The Socialists have thus represented an unguarded passage, which Malthus himself had suppressed, as the basis of his system. They repeat it ad nauseam. In a little volume, Mr. Pierre Leroux reproduced it at least forty times, and it forms the stock-in-trade of all our declamatory second-rate reformers.

The most celebrated and the most vigorous of that school of writers having written an article against Malthus, I happened one day to converse with him, and cited some opinions expressed in the *Essay on Population*. I thought I perceived that he was not acquainted with the work. I remarked to him, "You who have refuted Malthus, have you not read his book from beginning to end?" "I have not read it at all," he replied. "His whole system is to be found in one page, and is condensed in the famous 'arithmetical and geometrical progressions'—that is enough for me." "It seems to me," I said, "that you are jesting with the public, with Malthus, with truth, with conscience, and with yourself."

This is the way that opinions obtain currency with us. Fifty ignorant people repeat in chorus something spiteful and absurd, put forward by one more ignorant than themselves, and if it happens to have the least connection with the fashionable opinions or passions of the hour, it is at once received as an axiom.

Science, however, it must be allowed, cannot enter on the solution of a problem with the settled intention of establishing a foregone conclusion, however consolatory. What should we think of a man who should sit down to the study of physiology, resolved beforehand to demonstrate that God has not willed that mankind should be afflicted with diseases? Were one physiologist to found a system on such a basis as this, and another to controvert it by an appeal to facts, the former would most likely fly into a rage, and accuse his opponent of impiety; but it is difficult to believe that he would go to the length of accusing his opponent himself of being the author of diseases.

This, however, is what has happened to Malthus. In a work founded on facts and figures, he explained a law that has given great offense to our optimists; and in their anxiety to ignore the existence of this law, they have attacked Malthus with rancorous virulence and flagrant bad faith, as if he had himself deliberately thrown in the way of mankind those obstacles that flowed, as he thought, from the principle of population. It would surely have been more philosophical to have proved simply that Malthus was mistaken, and that his pretended law had in reality no existence.

Population, we must allow, is one of a numerous class of subjects that serve to remind us that man has frequently left him only a choice of evils. Whatever may have been its design, suffering has entered into the plan of Providence. Let us not, then, seek for harmony in the absence of evil, but in the tendency of evil to bring us back to what is good, and in the gradual contraction of its own domain. God has endowed us with free will. It is necessary that we should learn—which is a long and difficult process—and then it is necessary that we should act on the knowledge thus acquired, which is not much less difficult. In this way we shall gradually emancipate ourselves from suffering, but without ever altogether escaping from it; for even when we succeed completely in eluding chastisement, we have still to exercise the painful effort of foresight. In freeing ourselves from the one, we must submit ourselves to the other.

It is of no use to rebel against this order of things; for it envelops us; it is the atmosphere in which we live and breathe; and it is with this alternative of restriction or prevention before us, which we cannot get rid of, and cannot lose sight of, that we proceed, with Malthus to enter upon the problem of population. On this great question I shall first of all assume the function of a mere reporter, and then give you my own views. If the laws of population can be comprised in a short aphorism, it will be a happy thing for the advancement and diffusion of the science. But if, from the number and the shifting nature of the postulates, we find that these laws refuse to be shut up in a brief and rigorous formula, we must acquiesce. Prolix exactitude is better than delusive brevity.

We have seen that progress consists in causing natural forces to co-operate more and more toward the satisfaction of our wants so that at each successive epoch, the same amount of utility is obtained, while to society is left either more leisure or a greater amount of disposable labor to be applied to the acquisition of new enjoyments.

On the other hand, we have demonstrated that every fresh conquest we thus gain over nature, after having for a time brought additional profit to the inventor, never fails to become, by the operation of the law of competition, the common and gratuitous patrimony of mankind at large.

From these premises we should conclude that human happiness must be enlarged and, at the same time, rapidly equalized.

That it has not been so in reality, however, is a point beyond all dispute. There are in the world multitudes of unfortunate people whose wretchedness has not been caused by their own misdeeds.

How are we to account for this?

I believe it is owing to a multiplicity of causes. One of them is called spoliation, or, if you will, exploitation. Economists have referred to it only incidentally, as implying some error, some false scientific notion. Engaged in the explanation of general laws, it is not their business, they think, to concern themselves with those laws when they are not in operation, or are violated. Spoliation, however, has borne, and still bears, too prominent a share in human affairs to permit even economists to throw it aside as a consideration unworthy of being taken into account. What we have to do with here is not accidental thefts, petty larcenies, or isolated crimes. War, slavery, priestly impostures, privileges, monopolies, restrictions, abuses of taxation—these are the more salient manifestations of spoliation. It is easy to see what influence disturbing forces of such magnitude must have exercised, and must still exercise by their presence, or the deep traces they have left behind them, on the inequality of conditions; and it will be our business hereafter to estimate the vast extent of their effects.

But another cause that retards progress and above all, that hinders its extension to all classes, is, as some authors think, the principle of population.

And no doubt, if in proportion as wealth increases, the number of people among whom that wealth is to be divided increases also and more rapidly, absolute wealth may be greater, and individual wealth less.

If, moreover, there be one species of services that everybody can render, like the services that require only muscular exertion, and if it be just the class whose business it is to render such services, the worst paid of all, that multiplies with the greatest rapidity, we must conclude that labor creates for itself a fatal competition. The lowest class will never benefit by progress, if that class increases faster than it can spread and distribute itself.

You see, then, how important the principle of population is.

Malthus has reduced the principle to this formula:

Population has a tendency to keep on a level with the means of subsistence.

I cannot help remarking in passing that it is surprising that the honor and responsibility of enunciating this principle, be it true or false, should have been ascribed to Malthus. Every writer on such subjects since the days of Aristotle has proclaimed it, and frequently in the very same words.

It is impossible to look around us on the aggregate of animated beings without being convinced beyond doubt that nature has been more engrossed with the care of species than of individuals.

The precautions that nature has taken to ensure the perpetuity of races are remarkable; and among these precautions, a very noticeable one is the profusion of spawn or seeds. This superabundance appears to be calculated in an inverse ratio to the sensibility, intelligence, and power with which each species is endowed, to enable it to resist destruction.

Thus, in the vegetable kingdom, the means of reproduction, by seeds, cuttings, etc., that a single plant can furnish are countless. One elm (were all its seeds to take root) might give birth in a single year to a million trees. Why should this not actually happen? Because all the seeds have not the benefit of the conditions that vegetable life requires namely, space and nourishment. They are destroyed; and as plants are destitute of sensibility, nature has spared neither the means of reproduction nor those of destruction.

Animals too, whose life is of a type akin to vegetable life, reproduce themselves in immense numbers. Who has not wondered that oysters, for instance, could multiply sufficiently to supply the enormous consumption of them?

As we advance in the scale of animal life, we find that the means of reproduction has been bestowed by nature with greater parsimony.

Vertebrated animals, especially the larger species, do not multiply so quickly as others. The cow goes nine months, produces only one calf, and must suckle it for some time. Yet even among cattle the reproductive power surpasses what might be thought absolutely necessary. In rich countries, such as England, France, and Switzerland, the number of animals of this description increases notwithstanding the enormous destruction of them; and had we boundless pastures and prairies, there can be no doubt that we might have both a still greater destruction and more rapid reproduction of them. I should say that if nourishment and space were not limited, we might have in a few years ten times more oxen and cows, even if we consumed ten times more meat. The reproductive power of cattle, then, even laying aside the extraneous consideration of the limitation of space and nourishment, is far from being fully developed.

It is certain that the reproductive faculty in the human species is less powerful than in any other, and it ought to be so. Man, in the superior situation in which nature has placed him, as regards intelligence and sympathy, ought not to be exposed to destruction in the same degree as the inferior animals. But we are not to suppose that physically he escapes from that law in virtue of which all species have the faculty of multiplying to a greater extent than space and nourishment permit.

I say physically, because I am speaking here only of the physiological law.

There is a wide difference between the physiological power of multiplying and actual multiplication.

The one is an absolute organic power when freed from all obstacle and all limitation *ab extra*—the other is the effective resulting force of this power combined with the aggregate of all the resistance that limits and restrains it. Thus the power of multiplication of the poppy may be a million a year, perhaps; but in a field of poppies the actual reproduction may be stationary or even decrease.

It is this physiological law that Malthus essayed to reduce to a formula. He inquired in what period of time a given number of men would double, if their space and food were unlimited.

We can see beforehand that as this hypothesis of the complete satisfaction of all wants is never realized in practice, the theoretic period must necessarily be shorter than any period of actual doubling which has ever been observed.

Observation, in fact, gives very different results for different countries. According to the results obtained by Mr. Moreau de Jonnes, taking for basis the actual increase of population, the period of doubling would require—in Turkey, 555 years; in Switzerland, 227; in France, 138; in Spain, 106; in Holland, 100; in Germany, 76; in Russia and in England, 43; and in the United States of America, 25 years, deducting the contingent furnished by immigration.

Now, what is the reason of such enormous differences? We have no reason to think that they are the result of physiological causes. Swiss women are as well formed and as prolific as American women.

We must conclude, then, that the absolute generative power is restrained by external obstacles. And what proves this beyond doubt is that it is manifested as soon as circumstances occur to remove these obstacles. Thus an improved agriculture, new manufactures, some new source of local wealth, leads invariably in that locality to an increase of population. In the same way, when a scourge like the plague, or a famine, or war, destroys a great part of the population, we immediately find that multiplication is more rapidly developed.

When an increase of population, then, is retarded, or stops, we find that space and nourishment are awanting, or likely to be so; that it has encountered an obstacle, or is scared by one.

This phenomenon, the announcement of which has brought down so much abuse on Malthus, appears in truth beyond the reach of doubt.

If you put a thousand mice into a cage, with only as much provision as is necessary for their daily sustenance, their number, in spite of the acknowledged fecundity of the species, can never exceed a thousand, or if it do, there will be privation and there will be suffering—both tending to reduce the number. In this case it would be correct to say that an external cause limits, not the power of fecundity but the result of fecundity. There would assuredly be an antagonism between the physiological tendency and the restraining force, and the result would be that the number would be stationary. To prove this, increase gradually the provision until you double it, and you will very soon find two thousand mice in the cage.

And what is the answer that is made to Malthus? He is met with the very fact upon which his theory is founded. The proof, it is said, that the power of reproduction in man is not indefinite, is that in certain countries the population is stationary. If the law of progression were true, if population doubled every twenty-five years, France, which had thirty million inhabitants in 1820, would now have more than sixty million.

Is this logical?

I begin by proving that the population of France has increased only a fifth in twenty-five years, while in other countries it has doubled. I seek for the cause of this; and I find it in the deficiency of space and sustenance. I find that in the existing state of cultivation, population, and national manners and habits, there is a difficulty in creating with sufficient rapidity subsistence for generations that might be born, or for maintaining those that are actually born. I assert that the means of subsistence cannot be doubled—at least that they are not doubled—in France every twenty-five years. This is exactly the aggregate of those negative forces that restrain, as I think, the physiological power—and you bring forward this slowness of multiplication in order to prove that this physiological power has no existence. Such a mode of discussing the question is mere trifling.

Is the argument against the geometrical progression of Malthus more conclusive? Malthus has nowhere asserted that, in point of fact, population increases according to a geometrical progression. He alleges, on the contrary, that the fact is not so, and the subject of his inquiry has reference to the obstacles that hinder it. The progression is brought forward merely as a formula of the organic power of multiplication.

Seeking to discover in what time a given population can double itself on the assumption that all its wants are supplied, he fixed this period at twenty-five years. He so fixed it, because direct observation had shown him that this state of things actually existed among a people who, although very far from fulfilling all the conditions of his hypothesis, came nearer the conditions he had assumed than any other—namely, the people of America. This period once found, and the question having always reference to the virtual power of propagation, he lays it down that population has a tendency to increase in a geometrical progression.

This is denied; but the denial is in the teeth of evidence. It may be said, indeed, that the period of doubling may not be everywhere twenty-five years; that it may be thirty, forty, or fifty years; that it varies in different countries and races. All this is fair subject of discussion; but granting this, it certainly cannot be said that, on the hypothesis assumed, the progression is not geometrical. If, in fact, a hundred couples produce two hundred in a given time, why may not two hundred produce four hundred in an equal time?

Because, say the opponents of the theory, multiplication will be restrained.

This is just what Malthus has said.

But by what means will multiplication be restrained?

Malthus points out two general obstacles to indefinite multiplication, which he has denominated the preventive and repressive checks.

As population can be kept down below the level of its physiological tendency only by a diminution of the number of births, or an increase of the number of deaths, the nomenclature of Malthus is undoubtedly correct.

Moreover, when the conditions, as regards space and nourishment are such that population cannot go beyond a certain figure, it is evident that the destructive check has more power, in proportion as the preventive check has less. To allege that the number of births may increase without an increase in the number of deaths, while the means of subsistence are stationary, would be to fall into a manifest contradiction.

Nor is it less evident, a priori, and independently of other grave economic considerations, that in such a situation voluntary self-restraint is preferable to forced repression.

As far as we have yet gone, then, the theory of Malthus is in all respects incontestable.

He was wrong, perhaps, in adopting this period of twenty-five years as the limit of human fecundity, although it holds good in the United States. I am convinced that in assuming this period he wished to avoid the imputation of exaggeration, or of dealing in pure abstractions. "How can they pretend," he may have thought, "that I give too much latitude to the possible if I found my principle on what actually takes place?" He did not consider that by mixing up in this way the virtual and the real, and representing as the measure of the law of multiplication, without reference to the law of limitation, a period that is the result of facts governed by both laws, he should expose himself to be misunderstood. This is what has actually happened. His geometrical and arithmetical progressions have been laughed at; he has been reproached for taking the United States as a type of the rest of the world; in a word, the confusion he has given rise to by mixing up these two distinct laws has been seized upon to confute the one by the other.

When we seek to discover the abstract power of propagation, we must put aside for the moment all consideration of the physical and moral checks arising from deficiency of space, food, or comfortable circumstances. But the question once proposed in these terms, it is quite superfluous to attempt an exact solution. This power, in the human race, as in all organized existences, surpasses in an enormous proportion all the phenomena of rapid multiplication that we have observed in the past, or can ever observe in the future. Take wheat, for example: allowing five stalks for every seed, and five grains for every stalk, one grain has the virtual power of producing four hundred million grains in five years. Or take the canine race, and suppose four puppies to each litter, and six years of fecundity, we shall find that one couple may in twelve years produce eight million cubs.

As regards the human race, assuming sixteen as the age of puberty and fecundity to cease at thirty, each couple might give birth to eight children. It is making a large deduction to reduce this number to one-half on account of premature deaths, since we are reasoning on the supposition of absolute comfort and all wants satisfied, which greatly limits the amount of mortality. However, let us state the premises in this way, and they give us in twenty-five years 2—4—8—16—32—64—128—256—512, etc.; in short, two million in two centuries.

If we make the calculation on the basis adopted by Euler, the period of doubling will be twelve years and a half. Eight such periods will make exactly a century, and the increase in that space of time will be as 512:2.

At no era, and in no country, have we ever observed the numbers of the human race increase with this frightful rapidity. According to the book of Genesis, the Hebrews who entered Egypt amounted to seventy couples; and we find from the book of Numbers that when Moses numbered the people two centuries afterwards, they amounted to six hundred thousand men above twenty-one years of age, which supposes a population of two million at least. From this we may infer that the period of doubling was fourteen years. Statistical tables can scarcely be admitted to control Biblical facts. Shall we say that six hundred thousand men "able to go to war" supposes a population larger than two million, and infer from that a period of doubling less than Euler has calculated? In that case, we should cast doubt either on the census of Moses or on the calculations of Euler. All that we contend for is that it should not be pretended that the Hebrews multiplied with greater rapidity than it is possible to multiply.

After this example, which is probably that in which actual fecundity approximates most nearly to virtual fecundity, we have the case of the United States of America, where we know that the population doubles in less than twenty-five years.

It is unnecessary to pursue such researches further. It is sufficient to know that in our species, as in all, the organic power of multiplication is superior to the actual multiplication. Moreover, it would involve a contradiction to assert that the actual surpasses the virtual.

Alongside of this absolute power, which it is unnecessary to determine more exactly, and which we may safely regard as uniform, there exists, as we have said, another force, which limits, compresses, and suspends to a certain extent the action of the first, and opposes to it obstacles of different kinds, varying with times and places, with the occupations, the manners, the laws, or the religion of different nations.

I denominate this second force the law of limitation; and it is evident that the progress of population in each country, and in each class, is the result of the combined action of these two laws.

But in what does this law of limitation consist? We may say in a very general way that the propagation of life is restrained or prevented by the difficulty of sustaining life. This idea, which we have already expressed in the terms of the formula of Malthus, it is of importance to develop further, for it is the essential part of our subject.[1]

Organized existences, that are imbued with life but without feeling are entirely passive in this struggle between the two principles. As regards vegetables, it is strictly true that the number of each species is limited by the means of subsistence. The profusion of germs is infinite, but the resources of space and territorial fertility are not so. These germs injure or destroy one another; they fail to grow, or they take root and come to maturity only to the extent that the soil allows of. Animals are induced with feeling, but they would seem in general to be destitute of foresight. They breed, increase, and multiply without regard to the fate of their offspring. Death, premature death, alone limits their multiplication, and maintains the equilibrium between their numbers and their means of subsistence.

---

[1]What follows was written in 1846.—Editor.

Mr. de Lamennais, in his inimitable language, thus addresses the people:

"There is room enough in the world for all, and God has made it fertile enough to supply the wants of all." And, further on, he says, "The Author of the universe has not assigned a worse condition to man than to the inferior animals. Are not all invited to the rich banquet of nature? Is one alone excluded?" And again he adds, "Plants extend their roots from one field to another, in a soil which nourishes them all, and all grow there in peace; none of them absorbs the sap of another."

In all this we see only fallacious declamation, which serves as the basis of dangerous conclusions; and we cannot help regretting that an eloquence so admirable should be devoted to giving popular currency to the most fatal of errors.

It is not true that no plant robs another of its sap, and that all extend their roots in the soil without injury. Hundreds of millions of vegetable germs fall every year upon the ground, derive from it a beginning of vitality, and then die stifled by plants stronger, ranker, hardier than themselves. It is not true that all animals that are born are invited to the banquet of nature, and that none of them is excluded. Wild beasts devour one another; and of domestic animals, man destroys a countless number. Nothing in fact is better calculated than this to show the existence and relations of these two principles—that of multiplication and that of limitation. Why have we in this country so many oxen and sheep, notwithstanding the havoc we make? Why are there so few bears and wolves, although we slaughter far fewer of them, and they are so organized as to be capable of multiplying much faster? The reason is that man prepares subsistence for the one class of animals, and takes it away from the other class. As regards each, he so arranges the law of limitation as to leave more or less latitude to the law of increase.

Thus, as regards both vegetables and animals, the limiting force appears only in one form, that of destruction. But man is endowed with reason and foresight, and this new element modifies, and even changes the mode of action of this force, so far as he is concerned.

Undoubtedly, in so far as he is a being provided with material organs, or, to speak plainly, in so far as he is an animal, the law of limitation, in the form of destruction, applies to him. It is impossible that the numbers of men can exceed their means of subsistence; for to assert that more men existed than had the means of existing, would imply a contradiction. If, then, his reason and foresight are lulled asleep, he becomes a vegetable, he becomes a brute. In that case, he will inevitably multiply in virtue of the great physiological law that governs all organized nature; and in that case, it is equally inevitable that he should perish in virtue of that law of limitation the action of which he has ignored.

But if he exercises foresight, this second law comes within the sphere of his will. He modifies and directs it. It is in fact no longer the same law. It is no longer a blind, but an intelligent force; it is no longer a mere natural, it has become a social law. Man is the center in which these two principles, matter and intelligence, meet, unite, and are blended; he belongs exclusively neither to the one nor to the other. As regards the human race, the law of limitation is manifested in both its aspects, and maintains population at the necessary level by the double action of foresight and destruction.

These two actions are not of uniform intensity. On the contrary, the one is enlarged in proportion as the other is restrained. The thing to be accomplished, the point to be reached, is limitation; and it is so more or less by means of repression, or by means of prevention, according as man is brutish or spiritual, according as he is more allied to matter or to mind, according as he has in him more of vegetative or of moral life. The law may be external to him or internal, but it must exist somewhere.

We do not form a just idea of the vast domain of foresight, which the translator of Malthus has much circumscribed by giving currency to that vague and inadequate expression, moral restraint (*contrainte morale*), which he has still further limited by the definition he has given of it, namely, "The virtue which consists in not marrying, when one has not the means of maintaining a family, and yet living in chastity." The obstacles that intelligent human society opposes to possible multiplication take many other forms besides that of moral restraint thus defined. What means, for example, the pure and holy ignorance of early life, the only ignorance that it is criminal to dissipate, that everyone respects, and over which the timid mother watches as over hidden treasure? What means the modesty that succeeds that ignorance, that mysterious defense of the young female, which intimidates while it enchants her lover, and prolongs, while it embellishes, the innocent season of courtship? The veil that is thus interposed at first between ignorance and truth, and then between truth and happiness, is a marvelous thing, and in anything but this would be absurd. What means that power of opinion which imposes such severe laws on the relations of the sexes, stigmatizes the slightest transgression of those laws, and visits it not only on the erring feebleness that succumbs, but, from generation to generation, on the unhappy offspring? What means that sensitive honor, that rigid reserve, so generally admired even by those who have cast it off, those institutions, those restraints of etiquette, those precautions of all sorts—if they are not the action of that law of limitation manifested in an intelligent, moral, and preventive shape—in a shape, consequently, that is peculiar to man?

Let these barriers be once overturned—let mankind, in what regards the sexes, be no longer concerned either with etiquette or with fortune, or with the future, or with opinion, or with manners—let men lower themselves to the rank of vegetables or animals—can we doubt that for the former, as for the latter, the power of multiplication would act with a force to necessitate the instant intervention of the law of limitation, manifested under such circumstances in a physical, brutal, and repressive shape; that is to say, by the action of indigence, disease, and death?

It is impossible to deny that, but for foresight and moral considerations, marriage would, in most cases, be contracted at an early age, or immediately after puberty. If we fix this age at sixteen, and if the registers of a given country show that marriages, on an average, do not take place before four-and-twenty, we have then eight years deducted by the law of limitation, in its moral and preventive form, from the action of the law of multiplication; and if we add to this figure the necessary allowance for those who never marry, we shall be convinced that the Creator has not degraded man to the level of the beasts that perish, but, on the contrary, has given him the power to transform the repressive into the preventive limitation.

It is singular enough that the spiritualist school and the materialist school should have, as it were, changed sides on this great question: the former fulminating against foresight, and endeavoring to set up the principle of animal nature; the latter exalting the moral part of man, and enforcing the dominion of reason over passion and appetite.

The truth is, the subject is not rightly understood. Let a father consult the most orthodox clergyman he can find as to the management of his family, the counsels he will receive are just those which science has exalted into principles, and which, as such, the clergyman might probably repudiate. "Keep your daughter in strict seclusion," the old minister will say; "conceal from her as much as you can the seductions of the world; cultivate, as you would a precious flower, that holy ignorance, that heavenly modesty, which are at once her charm and her defense. Wait until an eligible match presents itself; and labor in the meantime to secure her an adequate fortune. Consider that a poor and improvident marriage brings along with it much suffering and many dangers. Recall those old proverbs which embody the wisdom of nations, and which assure us that comfortable circumstances constitute the surest guarantee of union and domestic peace. Why be in a hurry? Would you have your daughter at five-and-twenty burdened with a family which she cannot maintain and educate suitably to your rank in life? Would you have her husband, feeling the inadequacy of his income to support his family, fall into affliction and despair, and finally, perhaps, betake himself to riot and debauchery? The subject which now occupies you is the most important which can come under your consideration. Weigh it well and maturely; and avoid precipitation," etc.

Suppose that the father, borrowing the language of Mr. de Lamennais, should reply: "In the beginning God addressed to all men the command to increase and multiply, and replenish the earth and subdue it. And yet you would persuade a young woman to live single, renounce family ties, and give up and abandon the chaste happiness of married life, and the holy joys of maternity; and all this for no better reason than a sordid fear of poverty." Think you the old clergyman would have no reply to this?

God, he might say, has not commanded man to increase and multiply without discretion and without prudence; to act with as little regard to the future as the inferior animals. He has not endowed man with reason in order that he may cease to use it in the most solemn and important circumstances. He has commanded man, no doubt, to increase, but in order to increase he must live, and in order to live he must have the means of living. In the command to increase, therefore, there is implied another command, namely, to prepare for his offspring the means of subsistence. Religion has not placed celibacy in the catalogue of crimes. So far from that, she has ranked it as a virtue, which she honors and sanctifies. We must not think that we violate the commandment of God when we are preparing to fulfill it with prudence, and with a view to the future good, happiness, and dignity of our family.

Now this reasoning, or reasoning of a similar kind, which we hear repeated every day, and which regulates the conduct of every moral and enlightened family, what is it but the application of a general doctrine to particular cases? Or rather, what is that doctrine, but the generalization of reasoning that applies to every particular case? The spiritualist who repudiates on principle the intervention of preventive limitation, is like the natural philosopher who should say to us, "Act in every case as if gravity existed, but don't admit gravitation in theory."

In our observations hitherto we have followed the theory of Malthus; but there is one attribute of humanity to which it seems to me that most of our authors have not assigned the importance it merits, and which plays an important part in the phenomena relative to population, resolves many of the problems to which this great question has given rise, and gives birth in the mind of the philanthropist to a confidence and serenity that false science had banished; this attribute, which is comprised, indeed, in the notions of reason and foresight, is man's perfectibility. Man is perfectible; he is susceptible of improvement and of deterioration; and if, in a strict sense, he can remain stationary, he can also mount and descend without limit the endless ladder of civilization. This holds true not only of individuals, but of families, nations, and races.

It is from not having taken into account all the power of this progressive principle that Malthus has landed us in those discouraging consequences that have rendered his theory generally repulsive.

For, regarding the preventive check, in a somewhat ascetic and not very attractive light, he could hardly attribute much force to it. Hence he concludes that it is the repressive check that generally operates; in other words, vice, poverty, war, crime, etc.

This, as I think, is an error; and we are about to see that the limitative force presents itself not only in the shape of an effort of chastity, an act of self-control, but also, and above all, as a condition of happiness, an instructive movement that prevents men from degrading themselves and their families.

Population, it has been said, tends to keep on a level with the means of subsistence. I should say that for this expression, means of subsistence, formerly in universal use, J.B. Say has substituted another that is much more nearly correct, namely, means of existence. At first sight it would seem that subsistence alone enters into the question, but it is not so. Man does not live by bread alone, and a reference to facts shows us clearly that population is arrested or retarded when the aggregate of all the means of existence, including clothing, lodging, and other things that climate or even habit renders necessary, come to be awanting.

We should say, then, that population tends to keep on a level with the means of existence.

But do these means constitute something that is fixed, absolute, and uniform? Certainly not. In proportion as civilization advances, the range of man's wants is enlarged, having regard even to simple subsistence. Regarded as a perfectible being, the means of existence, among which we comprehend the satisfaction of moral and intellectual as well as physical wants, admit of as many degrees as there are degrees in civilization itself, in other words, of infinite degrees. Undoubtedly, there is a lower limit— to appease hunger, to shelter oneself from cold to some extent, is one condition of life, and this limit we may perceive among American savages or European paupers. But an upper limit I know not—in fact there is none. Natural wants satisfied, others spring up, which are factitious at first, if you will, but which habit renders natural in their turn and, after these, others still, and so on without assignable limit.

At each step, then, that man takes on the road of civilization, his wants embrace a wider and more extended circle, and the means of existence, the point where the laws of multiplication and limitation meet, is displaced and elevated. For although man is susceptible of deterioration as well as of improvement, he aspires after the one and shuns the other. His efforts all tend to maintain the rank he has gained, and to rise still higher; and habit, which has been so well called a second nature, performs the part of valves of our arterial system, by checking every retrograde tendency. It is very natural, then, that the intelligent and moral control that man exercises over his own multiplication should partake of the nature of these efforts to rise, and be combined and mixed up with his progressive tendencies.

The consequences that result from this constitution are numerous. We shall confine ourselves to pointing out a few of them. First of all, we admit with the Economists that population and the means of existence come to an equilibrium; but the last of these terms being infinitely flexible, and varying with civilization and habits, we cannot admit that in comparing nations and classes, population is proportionate to production, as J.B. Say[2] affirms, or to income, as is represented by Mr. de Sismondi. And then every advancing step of culture implies greater foresight, and the moral and preventive check comes to neutralize the repressive one more and more as civilization is realized in society at large, or in one or other of its sections. Hence it follows that each step of progress tends to a new step in the same direction, *vires acquirit eundo*; seeing that better circumstances and greater foresight engender one another in indefinite succession. For the same reason, when men, from whatever cause, follow a retrograde course, narrower circumstances and want of foresight become reciprocally cause and effect, and retrogression and decay would have no limit had society not been imbued with that curative force, that vis medicatrix, which Providence has vouchsafed to all organized bodies. Observe, too, that at each step of this retrograde movement, the action of the law of limitation in its destructive form becomes at once more painful and more apparent. At first, it is only deterioration and sinking in the social scale; then it is poverty, famine, disorder, war, death; painful but infallible teachers.

I should like to pause here to show how well this theory explains facts, and how well facts in their turn justify the theory. When, in the case of a nation or a class, the means of existence have descended to that inferior limit at which they come to be confounded with the means of pure subsistence, as in China, in Ireland, and among the lowest and poorest class of every country, the smallest oscillations of population, or of the supply of food, are tantamount to death. In this respect, facts confirm the scientific induction. Famine has not for a long period visited Europe, and we attribute the absence of this scourge to a multitude of causes. The most general of these causes undoubtedly is that the means of existence, by reason of social progress, have risen far above the means of mere subsistence. When years of scarcity

---

[2]It is fair to mention that J.B. Say represents the means of existence as a variable quantity.

come, we are thus enabled to give up many enjoyments before encroaching on the first necessaries of life. Not so in such countries as China or Ireland, where men have nothing in the world but a little rice or a few potatoes. When the rice or potato crops fail, they have absolutely no means of purchasing other food.

A third consequence of human perfectibility we must notice here, because it tends to modify the doctrine of Malthus in its most afflicting phase. The formula we have attributed to that economist is, that "Population tends to keep on a level with the means of subsistence." We should say that he has gone much farther, and that his true formula, that from which he has drawn his most distressing conclusions, is this: "Population tends to go beyond the means of subsistence." Had Malthus by this simply meant to say that in the human race the power of propagating life is superior to the power of sustaining life, there could have been no controversy. But this is not what he means. He affirms that, taking into account absolute fecundity on the one hand, and on the other, limitation as manifested in the two forms, repressive and preventive, the result is still the tendency of population to go beyond the means of subsistence.[3] This holds true of every species of living creatures except the human race. Man is an intelligent being, and can make an unlimited use of the preventive check. He is perfectible, seeks after improvement, and shuns deterioration. Progress is his normal state, and progress presupposes a more and more enlightened exercise of the preventive check; and then the means of existence increase more rapidly than population. This effect not only flows from the principle of perfectibility, but is confirmed by fact, since on all sides the range of satisfactions is

---

[3]"There are few states in which there is not a constant effort in the population to increase beyond the means of subsistence. This constant effort as constantly tends to subject the lower classes of society to distress, and to prevent any great permanent melioration of their condition. . . . The constant effort toward population . . . increases the number of people before the means of subsistence are increased," etc.—*Malthus on Population*, 6th edition, vol. 1, pp. 17, 18.

extended. Were it true, as Malthus asserts, that along with every addition to the means of subsistence there is a still greater addition to the population, the misery of our race would be fatally—inevitably—progressive; society would begin with civilization and end with barbarism. The contrary is the fact; and we must conclude that the law of limitation has had sufficient force to restrain the multiplication of men, and keep it below the multiplication of products.

It may be seen from what has been said how vast and how difficult the question of population is. We may regret, no doubt, that a precise formula has not been given to it, and we regret still more that we find ourselves unable to propose one. But we may see how repugnant the narrow limits of a dogmatic axiom are to such a subject. It is a vain endeavor to try to express in the form of an inflexible equation the relations of data so essentially variable. Allow me to recapitulate these data.

(1) The law of increase or multiplication. The absolute, virtual, physiological power that resides in the human race to propagate life, apart from the consideration of the difficulty of sustaining life. This first datum, the only one susceptible of anything like precision, is the only one in which precision is superfluous; for what matters it where the superior limit of multiplication is placed in the hypothesis, if it can never be attained in the actual condition of man, which is to sustain life with the sweat of his brow?

(2) There is a limit, then, to the law of multiplication. What is that limit? The means of existence, it is replied. But what are the means of existence? The aggregate of satisfactions or enjoyments, which cannot be exactly defined. They vary with times, places, races, ranks, manners, opinions, habits, and consequently the limit we are in search of is shifted or displaced.

(3) Last of all, it may be asked, in what consists the force that restrains population within this limit, which is itself movable? As far as man is concerned, it is twofold: a force that represses, and a force that prevents. Now, the action of the first, incapable as it is in itself of being accurately measured, is, moreover, entirely

subordinated to the action of the second, which depends on the degree of civilization, on the power and prevalence of habits, on the tendency of political and religious institutions, on the organization of property, of labor, of family relations, etc. Between the law of multiplication and the law of limitation, then, it is impossible to establish an equation from which could be deduced the actual population. In algebra a and b represent determinate quantities that are numbered and measured, and of which we can fix the proportions; but means of existence, moral government of the will, inevitable action of mortality, these are the three data of the problem of population, data that are flexible in themselves, and that partake somewhat, moreover, of the astonishing flexibility of the subject to which they have reference—man—that being whom Montaigne describes as so fluctuating and so variable. It is not surprising, then, that in desiring to give to this equation a precision of which it is incapable, economists have rather divided men's minds than brought them into unison, and this because there is not one of the terms of their formulas that is not open to a multitude of objections, both in reasoning and in fact.

We shall now proceed to say something on the practical application of the doctrine of population, for application not only elucidates doctrine, but is the true fruit of the tree of science.

Labor, as we have said, is the only subject of exchange. In order to obtain utility (unless the utility that nature gives us gratuitously), we must be at the pains to produce it, or remunerate another who takes the pains for us. Man creates, and can create, nothing; he arranges, disposes, or transports things for a useful purpose; he cannot do this without exertion, and the result of this exertion becomes his property. If he gives away his property, he has right to recompense in the shape of a service that is judged equivalent after free discussion. Such is the principle of value, of remuneration, of exchange—a principle that is not the less true because it is simple. Into what we denominate products, there enter various degrees of natural utility, and various degrees of artificial utility; the latter, which alone implies labor, is alone the subject of human bargains and transactions; and without questioning in the least the celebrated and suggestive formula of J.B. Say, that "products are exchanged for products," I esteem it more rigorously scientific to say that labor is exchanged for labor, or better still, that services are exchanged for services.

It must not be inferred from this, however, that quantities of labor are exchanged for each other in the ratio of their duration or of their intensity; or that the man who transfers to another an hour's labor, or even the man who labors with the greatest intensity, who, as it were, pushes the needle of the dynamometer up to 100 degrees, can always stipulate for an equal effort in return. Duration and intensity are, no doubt, two of the elements taken into account in the evaluation of labor; but they are not the only ones; for we must consider, besides, that labor may be more or less repugnant, dangerous, difficult, intelligent, that it may imply more or less foresight, and may even be more or less successful. When transactions are free and property completely secured, each has entire control over his own labor, and, consequently need only dispose of it at his own price. The limit to his compliance is the point at which it is more advantageous to reserve his labor than to exchange it; the limit to his demands is the point at which the other party to the bargain finds it his interest not to make the exchange.

There are in society as many strata, if I may use the expression, as there are degrees in the scale of remuneration. The worst remunerated of all labor is that which approximates most nearly to brute force. This is an arrangement of Providence that is just, useful, and inevitable. The mere manual laborer soon reaches that limit to his demands of which I have just spoken, for everybody can perform this kind of muscular automatic labor; and the limit to his compliance is also soon reached, for he is incapable of the intelligent labor that his own wants require. Duration and intensity, which are attributes of matter, are the sole elements of the remuneration of this species of unskilled material labor; and that is the reason why it is usually paid by the day. All industrial progress consists in this, namely, in replacing in each product a certain amount of artificial, and consequently onerous utility by the same amount of natural, and, therefore, gratuitous utility. Hence it follows that if there be one class of society more interested than another in free competition, it is the laboring class. What would be the fate of these men if natural agents, and new processes and instruments of production, were not brought continually by means of competition to confer gratuitously on all the results of their co-operation? The mere day-laborer knows not how to make available in the production of the commodities he has occasion for, heat, gravitation, or elasticity; nor can he discover the processes, nor does he possess the instruments, by which these forces are rendered useful. When such discoveries are new, the labor of inventors, who are men of the highest intelligence, is well remunerated; in other words, that labor is the equivalent of a large amount of rude unskilled labor; or again, to change the expression, his product is dear. But competition interposes, the product falls in price, the co-operation of natural agents is no longer profitable to the producer, but to the consumer, and the labor that has made them available approximates as regards remuneration, to that labor which is estimated by mere duration. Thus, the common fund of gratuitous wealth goes on constantly increasing. Products of every kind tend day after day to become again invested—and they are in reality invested—with that condition of gratuitousness which characterizes our supply of air, and light, and water. The general level of humanity thus continues to rise, and to equalize itself; and, apart from the operation of the law of population, the lowest class of society is that whose advancement is virtually the most rapid. We have said, apart from the operation of the law of population; and this brings us back to the subject we are now examining.

Figure to yourself a basin into which an orifice that is constantly enlarging admits a constantly increasing supply of water. If we look only to this circumstance we conclude that the level of the water in the basin is continually rising. But if the sides of the basin are flexible, and capable of contracting and expanding, it is evident that the height of the water will depend on the manner in which this new circumstance is combined with the other. The level of the water will sink, however great may be the supply running into the basin, if the capacity of the basin itself is enlarged still more rapidly. It will rise if the circle of the reservoir is enlarged only proportionally and very slowly, higher still if it remain fixed, and highest of all if it is narrowed or contracted.

This is a picture of the social class whose destinies we are now considering and which constitutes, it must be allowed, the great mass of mankind. The water that comes into the basin through the elastic orifice represents their remuneration, or the objects fitted to supply their wants and to sustain life. The flexibility of the sides of the basin represents the movement of population. It is certain[4] that the means of existence overtake our population in a constantly increasing progression, but then it is equally certain that their numbers may increase in a still superior progression. The life of this class, then, will be more or less happy, more or less comfortable, according as the law of limitation in its moral, intelligent, and preventive form, shall circumscribe, to a greater or less extent, the absolute law of multiplication. There is a limit to the increase of the numbers of the working class. That limit is the point at which the progressive fund of remuneration becomes insufficient for their maintenance. But there is no limit to their possible advancement, because of the two elements that constitute it, the one, wealth, is constantly increasing and the other, population, is under their own control.

What we have just said with reference to the lowest social grade, the class of mere manual laborers, is applicable also to each of the superior grades when classified in relation to one another in an inverse proportion, so to speak, to the rudeness and materiality of their occupations. Taking each class simply by itself, all are subjected to the same general laws. In all there is a struggle between the physiological power of multiplication and the moral power of limitation. The only respect in which one class differs from another is with reference to the point where these two

---

[4]See chapter 11, "Producer—Consumer," above.

forces meet, the height to which the limit between the two laws may be raised by remuneration or be fixed by the habits of the laborers—this limit we have denominated the means of existence.

But if we consider the various classes no longer each by itself, but in their reciprocal relations, I think we can discern the influence of two principles acting in an inverse sense, and this without doubt is the explanation of the actual condition of mankind. We have shown how all the economic phenomena, and especially the law of competition, tend to an equality of conditions. Theoretically this appears to us incontestable. Seeing that no natural advantage, no ingenious process, none of the instruments by which such processes are made available, can remain permanently with producers as such; and seeing that the results of such natural advantages or discoveries, by an irresistible law of Providence, tend to become the common, gratuitous, and, consequently equal, patrimony of all men, it is evident that the poorest class is the one which derives the greatest relative profit from this admirable arrangement of the laws of the social economy. Just as the poor man is as liberally treated as the rich man with reference to the air he breathes, in the same way he becomes equal to the rich man as regards all that portion of the value of commodities that progress is constantly annihilating. Essentially, then, the human race has a very marked tendency toward equality. I do not speak of a tendency of aspiration, but a tendency of realization. And yet equality is not realized, or is realized so slowly that in comparing two distant epochs we are scarcely sensible of the progress. Indeed we are so little sensible of it that many able men deny it altogether, although in this they are certainly mistaken. Now, what is the cause that retards this fusion of classes on a common and progressive level?

In searching for the cause we need not, I think, look farther than the various degrees of foresight that each class exercises as regards the increase of population. The law of limitation, as has been already said, in so far as it is moral and preventive, we have under our own control. Man, as we have also said, is perfectible, and in proportion to his progress in improvement, he pays a more intelligent regard to this law. The superior classes, then, in proportion as they are more enlightened, are led to make greater exertions, and submit to greater sacrifices, in order to maintain their respective numbers on a level with the means of existence that their position in society demands.

Were we sufficiently far advanced in statistics, we should probably have this theoretical deduction converted into certainty, and have it proved by fact that marriages are less hasty and precocious among the higher than among the lower classes of society. If it be so, it is easy to see that in the general market, to which all classes bring their respective services, and in which labor of every kind is the subject of exchange, unskilled labor will be supplied in greater abundance than skilled labor; and this explains the continuance of that inequality of conditions, that so many, and such powerful causes of another kind tend constantly to efface.

The theory which we have now briefly explained leads us to the practical conclusion that the best forms of philanthropy, the best social institutions, are those which, while acting in accordance with the Providential plan as revealed to us by the social harmonies—I mean the plan of progressive equality—shall cause to descend among all ranks of society, and especially the lowest ranks, knowledge, discretion, morality, and foresight.

I say institutions because, in fact, foresight results as much from the necessities of position as from resolutions purely intellectual. There are certain organizations of property, or I should rather say of industry, that are more favorable than others to what economists call a knowledge of the market, and, consequently, to foresight. It seems certain, for example, that metayage is much more efficacious than *fermage*[5] (the latter necessitating the

---

[5] "Although we might describe fermage, in a general way, as the letting or leasing of land, in whatever form it is done, we must distinguish two forms of letting, equally common in various parts of Europe, and very different in their effects. In the one form, the land is let for a fixed rent, payable in money annually. In the other, it is let under the condition of the

employment of day-laborers) in interposing a preventive obstacle to the exuberance of population among the lower classes. A family of metayers is in a much more likely situation than a family of day-laborers to experience the inconveniences of hasty marriages and improvident multiplication.

I have also used the expression, "forms of philanthropy." In fact, almsgiving may effect a local and present good, but its influence must be limited even where it is not prejudicial to the happiness of the laboring classes; for it does not develop, but on the contrary may paralyze, that virtue which is most fitted to elevate the condition of the laborer, namely, foresight. To disseminate sound ideas and above all, to induce those habits that mark a certain degree of self-respect, is the greatest and most permanent good that we can confer upon the lower orders.

The means of existence, we cannot too often repeat, do not constitute a fixed quantity; they depend upon the state of manners, of opinion, and of habits. Whatever rank a man holds in the social scale, he has as much repugnance to descend from the position to which he has been accustomed as can be felt by men of an inferior grade. Perhaps there is even greater suffering in the mind of the aristocrat, the noble scions of whose house are lost among the bourgeoisie, than in that of the citizen whose sons become manual laborers, or in that of manual laborers whose children are reduced to pauperism. The habit, then, of enjoying a certain amount of material prosperity and a certain rank in life is the strongest stimulant to the exercise of foresight; and if the working classes shall once raise themselves to the possession of a higher amount of enjoyment, and be unwilling again to descend in the social scale, then, in order to maintain themselves in that position and preserve wages in keeping with their new habits, they must employ the infallible means of preventive limitation.

---

produce being divided between the proprietor and the cultivator. It is to the first of these two modes of leasing land that we give more particularly the name of fermage, the other is generally designated in France as metayage." *Dictionnaire de l' Economie Politique*, vol. 1, p. 759.

It is for this reason that I regard as one of the finest manifestations of philanthropy the resolution that appears to have been taken in England by many of the proprietors and manufacturers, to pull down cottages of mud and thatch, and substitute for them brick houses, neat, spacious, well lighted, well aired, and conveniently furnished. Were such a measure to become general, it would elevate the tone of the working classes. It would convert into real wants what are nowadays regarded as comparative luxuries; it would raise that limit we have denominated the means of existence and by consequence the standard of remuneration, from its present low rate. And why not? The lower orders in civilized countries are much above the lower orders among savages. They have raised themselves so far; and why should they not raise themselves still more?

We must not, however, deceive ourselves on this subject; progress can be but very slow, since to some extent it must be general. In certain parts of the world it might perhaps be realized rapidly if the people exercised no influence over each other; but this is not so. There is a great law of solidarity for the human race, in progress as well as in deterioration. If in England, for example, the condition of the working classes were sensibly improved, in consequence of a general rise of wages, French industry would have more chances of surpassing its rival, and by its advance would moderate the progressive movement manifested on the other side of the Channel. It would seem that, beyond certain limits, Providence has not designed that one people should rise above another. And thus, in the great aggregate of human society, as in its most minute details, we always find that admirable and inflexible forces tend to confer, in the long run, on the masses, individual or collective advantages, and to bring back all temporary manifestations of superiority to a common level, which, like that of the ocean when the tide flows, is always equalizing itself and always advancing.

To conclude, perfectibility, which is the distinctive characteristic of man, being given, and the action of competition and the law of limitation being known, the fate of the human race, as regards its worldly destinies, may be thus summed up: First, Simultaneous elevation of all the social ranks, or of the general level of humanity; Second, Indefinite approximation of conditions, and successive annihilation of the distances which separate classes, as far as consistent with absolute justice; Third, Relative diminution of the numbers of the lowest and highest orders, and extension of intermediate classes. It may be said that these laws must lead to absolute equality. No more than the constant approximation of asymptotical lines can finally lead to their junction.

17

PRIVATE AND PUBLIC SERVICES

Services are exchanged for services. The equivalence of services results from voluntary exchange, and the free bargaining and discussion that precede it.

In other words, each service rendered to society is worth as much as any other service of which it constitutes the equivalent, provided supply and demand are in all respects perfectly free.

It is in vain to carp and refine upon it; it is impossible to conceive the idea of value without associating with it the idea of liberty.

When the equivalence of services is not impaired by violence, restriction, or fraud, we may pronounce that justice prevails.

I do not mean to say that the human race will then have reached the extreme limit of improvement, for liberty does not exclude the errors of individual appreciations—man is frequently the dupe of his judgments and passions; nor are his desires always arranged in the most rational order. We have seen that the value of a service may be appreciated without there being any reasonable proportion between its value and its utility; and this arises from our giving certain desires precedence over others. It is the progress of intelligence, of good sense, and of manners that establishes this fair and just proportion by putting each service, if I may so express myself, in its right moral place. A frivolous object, a puerile show, an immoral pleasure, may have much value in one country and may be despised or repudiated in another. The equivalence of services, then, is a different thing from a just appreciation of their utility. But still, as regards this, it is liberty and the sense of responsibility which correct and improve our tastes, our desires, our satisfactions, and our appreciations.

In all countries of the world, there exists one class of services, which, as regards the manner in which they are distributed and remunerated, accomplishes an evolution quite different from that of private or free services. I allude to public services.

When a want assumes a character so universal and so uniform that one can describe it as a public want, it may be convenient for those people who form part of the same agglomeration (be it district, province, or country) to provide for the satisfaction of that want by collective action, or a collective delegation of power. In that case, they name functionaries whose duty it is to render to the community and distribute among them the service in question, and whose remuneration they provide for by a contribution that is, at least in principle, proportionate to the means of each member of the society.

In reality, the primordial elements of the social economy are not necessarily impaired or set aside by this peculiar form of exchange—above all, when the consent of all parties is assumed. It still resolves itself into a transmission of efforts, a transmission of services. These functionaries labor to satisfy the wants of the taxpayers, and the taxpayers labor to satisfy the wants of the functionaries. The relative value of their reciprocal services is determined by a method that we shall have afterwards to examine; but the essential principles of the exchange, speaking in the abstract at least, remain intact.

Those authors, then, are wrong who, influenced by their dislike of unjust and oppressive taxes, regard as lost all values devoted to the public service.[1] This unqualified condemnation will not bear examination. In so far as loss or gain is concerned, the public service, scientifically considered, differs in nothing from private service. Whether I protect my field myself, or pay a man for protecting it, or pay the State for causing it to be protected, there is always a sacrifice with a corresponding benefit. In both ways, no doubt, I lose this amount of labor, but I gain security. It is not a loss, but an exchange.

Will it be said that I give a material object, and receive in return a thing without body or form? This is just to fall back upon the erroneous theory of value. As long as we attribute value to matter, not to services, we must regard every public service as being without value, or lost. Afterwards, when we begin to shift about between what is true and what is false on the subject of value, we shift about between what is true and what is false on the subject of taxation.

If taxation is not necessarily a loss, still less is it necessarily spoliation.[2] No doubt, in modern societies, spoliation by means

---

[1] "The moment this value is handed over by the taxpayer, it is lost to him; the moment it is consumed by the Government, it is lost to everybody, and does not return to society." J.B. Say, *Traite d' Economie Politique*, p. iii, chap. 9.

Unquestionably; but society gains in return the service that is rendered to it—security, for example. Moreover, Say returns to the correct doctrine almost immediately afterwards, when he says, "To levy a tax is do a wrong to society—a wrong which is compensated by no advantage, when no service is rendered to society in exchange." Ibid.

[2] "Public contributions, even when they are consented to by the nation, are a violation of property, seeing they can be levied only on values which have been produced by the land, capital, and industry of individuals. Thus, whenever they exceed the amount indispensable for the preservation of society, we must regard them as spoliation." Ibid.

Here again, the subsequent qualification corrects the absolute judgment previously pronounced. The doctrine that services are exchanged for services simplifies much both the problem and its solution.

of taxation is perpetrated on a great scale. We shall afterwards see
that it is one of the most active of those causes which disturb the
equivalence of services and the harmony of interests. But the best
way of combating and eradicating the abuses of taxation, is to
steer clear of that exaggeration that would represent all taxation
as being essentially and in itself, spoliation.

Thus, considered in themselves, in their own nature, in their
normal state, and apart from abuses, public services, like private
services, resolve themselves into pure exchanges.

But the modes in which, in these two forms of exchange, services are compared, bargained for, and transmitted, the modes in
which they are brought to an equilibrium or equivalence, and in
which their relative value is manifested, are so different in themselves and in their effects that the reader will bear with me if I
dwell at some length on this difficult subject, one of the most
interesting that can be presented to the consideration of the economist and the statesman. It is here, in truth, that we have the connecting link between politics and social economy. It is here that
we discover the origin and tendency of the most fatal error that
has ever infected the science, the error of confounding society
with Government: society being the grand whole, which includes
both private and public services, and Government, the fraction
that includes public services alone.

Unfortunately, when, by following the teaching of Rousseau,
and his apt scholars the French republicans, we employ indiscriminately the words Government and Society, we pronounce implicitly, beforehand and without examination, that the State can and
ought to absorb private exertion altogether, along with individual
liberty and responsibility. We conclude that all private services
ought to be converted into public services. We conclude that the
social order is a conventional and contingent fact that owes its
existence to the law. We pronounce the law-giver omnipotent,
and mankind powerless, as having forfeited its rights.

In fact, we see public services, or governmental action,
extended or restrained according to circumstances of time and
place, from the Communism of Sparta or the Missions of

Paraguay, to the individualism of the United States and the centralization of France.

The question that presents itself on the threshold of Politics, as a science, then, is this:

What are the services that should remain in the domain of private activity? And what are the services that should fall within that of public or collective activity?

The problem, then, is this:

In the great circle called society, to trace accurately the inscribed circle called government.

It is evident that this problem belongs to Political Economy, since it implies the comparative examination of two very different forms of exchange.

This problem once solved, there remains another, namely, what is the best organization of public services? This last belongs to pure Politics, and we shall not enter upon it.

Let us examine, then, first of all, the essential differences by which public and private services are characterized, which is a preliminary inquiry necessary to enable us to fix accurately the line that should divide them.

The whole of the preceding portion of this work has been devoted to exhibit the evolution of private services. We have had a glimpse of it in this formal or tacit proposition: Do this for me, and I shall do that for you; which implies, whether as regards what we give away or what we receive, a double and reciprocal consent. We can form no correct notion, then, of barter, exchange, appreciation, or value apart from the consideration of liberty, nor of liberty apart from responsibility. In having recourse to exchange, each party consults, on his own responsibility, his wants, his tastes, his desires, his faculties, his affections, his convenience, his entire situation; and we have nowhere denied that to the exercise of free will is attached the possibility of error, the possibility of a foolish and irrational choice. The error belongs not to exchange, but to human imperfection; and the remedy can only reside in responsibility itself (that is to say, in liberty), seeing that liberty is the source of all experience. To establish restraint in the business of exchange, to destroy free will under the pretext that man may err would be no improvement unless it were first proved to us that the agent who organizes the restraint does not himself participate in the imperfection of our nature, and is subject neither to the passions nor to the errors of other men. On the contrary, is it not evident that this would be not only to displace responsibility but to annihilate it, at least as regards all that is valuable in its remunerative, retributive, experimental, corrective, and consequently, progressive character? Again, we have seen that free exchanges, or services voluntarily rendered and received, are, under the action of competition, continually extending the cooperation of gratuitous forces, as compared with that of onerous forces, the domain of community as compared with the domain of property, and thus we have come to recognize in liberty that power which promotes progressive equality, or social harmony. We have no need to describe the form that exchanges assume when thus left free. Restraint takes a thousand shapes; liberty has but one. I repeat once more, that the free and voluntary transmission of private services is defined by the simple words: "Give me this, and I will give you that; do this for me, and I shall do that for you"—*Do ut des; facio ut facias.*[3]

The same thing does not hold with reference to the exchange of public services. Here constraint is to a certain extent inevitable, and we encounter an infinite number of different forms, from absolute despotism, down to the universal and direct intervention of all the citizens.

Although this ideal order of things has never been anywhere actually realized, and perhaps may never be so, except in a very elusory shape, we may nevertheless assume its existence. What is the object of our inquiry? We are seeking to discover the modifications that services undergo when they enter the public domain; and for the purposes of science we must discard the consideration of individual and local acts of violence, and regard the public

---

[3]Civil law terms. See part 1.

service simply as such, and as existing under the most legitimate circumstances. In a word, we must investigate the transformation it undergoes from the single circumstance of its having become public, apart from the causes that have made it so, and of the abuses that may mingle with the means of execution.

The process is this:

The citizens name representatives. These representatives meet, and decide by a majority that a certain class of wants—the want of education, for example—can no longer be supplied by free exertions and free exchanges made by the citizens themselves, and they decree that education shall be provided by functionaries specially delegated and entrusted with the work of instruction. So much for the service rendered. As regards the services received, as the State has secured the time and abilities of these new functionaries for the benefit of the citizens, it must also take from the citizens a part of their means for the benefit of the functionaries. This is effected by an assessment or general contribution.

In all civilized communities such contributions are paid in money. It is scarcely necessary to say that behind this money there is labor. In reality, it is a payment in kind. In reality, the citizens work for the functionaries, and the functionaries work for the citizens, just as in free and private transactions the transactors work for one another.

We set down this observation here, in order to elude a very widely spread sophism that springs from the consideration of money. We hear it frequently said that money received by public functionaries falls back like refreshing rain on the citizens. And we are led to infer that this rain is a second benefit added to that which results from the service. Reasoning in this way, people have come to justify the existence of the most parasitical functions. They do not consider that if this service had remained in the domain of private activity, the money (which, in place of going to the treasury, and from the treasury to the functionaries) would have gone directly to men who voluntarily undertook the duty, and in the same way would have fallen back like rain upon the masses. This sophism will not stand examination when we extend our regards beyond the mere circulation of money and see that at the bottom it is labor exchanged for labor, services for services. In public life, it may happen that functionaries receive services without rendering any in return; and then there is a loss entailed on the taxpayer, however we may delude ourselves with reference to this circulation of specie.

Be this as it may, let us resume our analysis:

We have here, then, an exchange under a new form. Exchange includes two terms—to give, and to receive. Let us inquire then how this transaction, which from being private has become public, is affected in the double point of view of services rendered and services received.

In the first place, it is proved beyond doubt that public services always, or nearly always, extinguish, in law or in fact, private services of the same nature. The State, when it undertakes a service, generally takes care to decree that no other body shall render it, more especially if one of its objects be to derive a revenue from it. Witness the cases of postage, tobacco, gunpowder, etc. If the State did not take this precaution, the result would be the same. What manufacturer would engage to render to the public a service which the State renders for nothing? We scarcely meet with anyone who seeks a livelihood by teaching law or medicine privately, by the formation of highways, by rearing thorough-bred horses, by founding schools of arts and design, by clearing lands in Algeria, by establishing museums, etc. And the reason is this, that the public will not go to purchase what the State gives it for nothing. As Mr. de Cormenin has said, the trade of the shoemakers would soon be put an end to, even were it declared inviolable by the first article of the constitution, if Government took it into its head to furnish shoes to everybody gratuitously.

In truth, in the word gratuitous as applied to public services, there lurks the grossest and most puerile of sophisms.

For my own part, I wonder at the extreme gullibility of the public in allowing itself to be taken in with this word. What! it is said, do you not wish gratuitous education? gratuitous studs?

Certainly I wish them, and I should also wish to have gratuitous food and gratuitous lodging—if it were possible.

But there is nothing really gratuitous but what costs nothing to anyone. Now public services cost something to everybody; and it is just because everybody has paid for them beforehand that they no longer cost anything to the man who receives the benefit. The man who has paid his share of the general contribution will take good care not to pay for the service a second time by calling in the aid of private industry.

Public service is thus substituted for private service. It adds nothing either to the general labor of the nation or to its wealth. It accomplishes by means of functionaries what would have been effected by private industry. The question, then, is, Which of these arrangements entails the greatest amount of inconvenience? and the solution of that question is the object of the present chapter.

The moment the satisfaction of a want becomes the subject of a public service, it is withdrawn, to a great extent, from the domain of individual liberty and responsibility. The individual is no longer free to procure that satisfaction in his own way, to purchase what he chooses and when he chooses, consulting only his own situation and resources, his means, and his moral appreciations, nor can he any longer exercise his discretion in regard to the order in which he may judge it reasonable to provide for his various wants. Whether he will or not, his wants are now supplied by the public, and he obtains from society, not that measure of service he judges useful, as he did in the case of private services, but the amount of service the Government thinks it proper to furnish, whatever be its quantity and quality. Perhaps he is in want of bread to satisfy his hunger, and part of the bread of which he has such urgent need is withheld from him in order to furnish him with education or with theatrical entertainments, which he does not want. He ceases to exercise free control over the satisfaction of his own wants, and having no longer any feeling of responsibility, he no longer exerts his intelligence. Foresight has become as useless to him as experience. He is less his own master; he is deprived, to some extent, of free will, he is less progressive, he is less a man. Not only does he no longer judge for himself in a particular case; he has got out of the habit of judging for himself in any case. The moral torpor which thus gains upon him gains, for the same reason, on all his fellow-citizens, and in this way we have seen whole nations abandon themselves to a fatal inaction.[4]

As long as a certain class of wants and of corresponding satisfactions remains in the domain of liberty, each, in so far as this class is concerned, lays down a rule for himself, which he can modify at pleasure. This would seem to be both natural and fair, seeing that no two men find themselves in exactly the same situation; nor is there any one man whose circumstances do not vary from day to day. In this way, all the human faculties remain in exercise, comparison, judgment, foresight. In this way, too, every good and judicious resolution brings its recompense and every error its chastisement; and experience, that rude substitute for

---

[4]The effects of such a transformation are strikingly exemplified in an instance given by Mr. d'Hautpoul, the Minister of War: "Each soldier," he says, "receives 16 centimes a day for his maintenance. The Government takes these 16 centimes, and undertakes to support him. The consequence is that all have the same rations, and of the same kind, whether it suits them or not. One has too much bread, and throws it away. Another has not enough of butcher's meat, and so on. We have, therefore, made an experiment. We leave to the soldiers the free disposal of these 16 centimes, and we are happy to find that this has been attended with a great improvement in their condition. Each now consults his own tastes and likings, and studies the market prices of what they want to purchase. Generally they have, of their own accord, substituted a portion of butcher's meat for bread. In some instances they buy more bread, in others more meat, in others more vegetables, in others more fish. Their health is improved; they are better pleased; and the State is relieved from a great responsibility."

The reader will understand that it is not as bearing on military affairs that I cite this experiment. I refer to it as calculated to illustrate a radical difference between public and private service, between official regulations and liberty. Would it be better for the State to take from us our means of support, and undertake to feed us, or to leave us both our means of support and the care of feeding ourselves? The same question may be asked with reference to all our wants.

foresight, so far at least fulfills its mission that society goes on improving.

But when the service becomes public, all individual rules of conduct and action disappear, and are mixed up and generalized in a written, coercive, and inflexible law, which is the same for all, which makes no allowance for particular situations and strikes the noblest faculties of human nature with numbness and torpor.

If State intervention deprive us of all self-government with reference to the services we receive from the public, it deprives us in a still more marked degree of all control with reference to the services we render in return. This counterpart, this supplementary element in the exchange, is likewise a deduction from our liberty, and is regulated by uniform inflexible rules, by a law passed beforehand, made operative by force, and of which we cannot get rid. In a word, as the services the State renders us are imposed upon us, those it demands in return are also imposed upon us, and in all languages take the name of imposts.

And here a multitude of theoretical difficulties and inconveniences present themselves; for practically the State surmounts all obstacles by means of an armed force, which is the necessary sequence of every law. But, to confine ourselves to the theory, the transformation of a private into a public service gives rise to these grave questions:

Will the State under all circumstances demand from each citizen an amount of taxation equivalent to the services rendered? This were but fair; and this equivalence is exactly the result that we almost infallibly obtain from free and voluntary transactions, and the bargaining that precedes them. If the design of the State, then, is to realize this equivalence (which is only justice), it is not worth while taking this class of services out of the domain of private activity. But equivalence is never thought of, nor can it be. We do not stand higgling and chaffering with public functionaries. The law proceeds on general rules, and cannot make conditions applicable to each individual case. At best, and when it is conceived in a spirit of justice, it aims at a sort of average equivalence, an approximate equivalence, between the two services exchanged. Two principles—namely, the proportionality and the progression of taxation—have appeared in many respects to carry this approximation to its utmost limit. But the slightest reflection will convince us that proportional taxation cannot, any more than progressive taxation, realize the exact equivalence of services exchanged. Public services, after having forcibly deprived the citizens of their liberty as regards services both rendered and received have, then, this further fault of unsettling the value of these services.

Another, and not less grave, inconvenience is that they destroy, or at least displace, responsibility. To man responsibility is all-important. It is his mover and teacher, his rewarder and avenger. Without it man is no longer a free agent, he is no longer perfectible, no longer a moral being, he learns nothing, he is nothing. He abandons himself to inaction, and becomes a mere unit of the herd.

If it be a misfortune that the sense of responsibility should be extinguished in the individual, it is no less a misfortune that it should be developed in the State in an exaggerated form. Man, however degraded, has always as much light left him as to see the quarter from whence good or evil comes to him; and when the State assumes the charge of all, it becomes responsible for all. Under the dominion of such artificial arrangements, a people that suffers can only lay the blame on its Government, and its only remedy, its only policy, is to overturn it. Hence an inevitable succession of revolutions. I say inevitable, for under such a regime the people must necessarily suffer; and the reason of it is that public services, besides disturbing and unsettling values, which is injustice, lead also to the destruction of wealth, which is ruin; ruin and injustice, suffering and discontent—four fatal causes of effervescence in society, that, combined with the displacement of responsibility, cannot fail to bring out political convulsions like those from which we have been suffering for more than half a century.

Without desiring to indulge in digressions, I cannot help remarking that when things are organized in this fashion, when Government has assumed gigantic proportions by the successive transformation of free and voluntary transactions into public services, it is to be feared that revolutions, which constitute in themselves so great an evil, have not even the advantage of being a remedy, unless the remedy is forced upon us by experience. The displacement of responsibility has perverted public opinion. The people, accustomed to expect everything from the State, never accuse Government of doing too much, but of not doing enough. They overturn it, and replace it by another, to which they do not say, "Do less," but "Do more"; so that, having fallen into one ditch, they set to work to dig another.

At length the moment comes when their eyes are opened, and it is felt to be necessary to curtail the prerogatives and responsibilities of Government. Here we are stopped by difficulties of another kind. Functionaries alleging vested rights rise up and coalesce, and we are averse to bear hard on numerous interests to which we have given an artificial existence. On the other hand, the people have forgotten how to act for themselves. At the moment they have succeeded in reconquering the liberty of which they were in quest, they are afraid of it, and repudiate it. Offer them a free and voluntary system of education: they believe that all science is about to be extinguished. Offer them religious liberty: they believe that atheism is about to invade us—so often has it been dinned into their ears that all religion, all wisdom, all science, all learning, all morality, resides in the State or flows from it.

But we shall find a place for such reflections elsewhere, and must now return to the argument.

We set ourselves to discover the true part that competition plays in the development of wealth, and we found that it consisted in giving an advantage in the first instance to the producer; then turning this advantage to the profit of the community; and constantly enlarging the domain of the gratuitous and consequently the domain of equality.

But when private services become public services, they escape competition, and this fine harmony is suspended. In fact, the functionary is divested of that stimulant which urges on to progress, and how can progress turn to the public advantage

when it no longer exists? A public functionary does not act under
the spur of self-interest, but under the influence of the law. The
law says to him, "You will render to the public such or such a
determinate service, and you will receive from it in return a determinate recompense." A little more or a little less zeal has no effect
in changing these two fixed terms. On the contrary, private interest whispers in the ear of the free laborer, "The more you do for
others, the more others will do for you." In this case, the recompense depends entirely on the efforts of the workman being more
or less intense, and more or less skillful. No doubt esprit de corps,
the desire for advancement, devotion to duty, may prove active
stimulants with the functionary; but they never can supply the
place of the irresistible incitement of personal interest. All experience confirms this reasoning. Everything that has fallen within
the domain of Government routine has remained almost stationary. It is doubtful whether our system of education now is better
than it was in the reign of Francis the First; and no one would
think of comparing the activity of a government office with the
activity of a manufactory.

In proportion, then, as private services enter into the class of
public services, they become, at least to a certain extent, sterile and
motionless, not to the injury of those who render these services
(their salaries are fixed), but to the detriment of the public at large.

Along with these inconveniences, which are immense, not
only in a moral and political, but in an economical point of
view—inconveniences that, trusting to the sagacity of the reader,
I have only sketched—there is sometimes an advantage in substituting collective for individual action. In some kinds of services,
the chief merit is regularity and uniformity. It may happen that,
under certain circumstances, such a substitution gives rise to
economy, and saves, in relation to a given satisfaction, a certain
amount of exertion to the community. The question to be
resolved, then, is this: What services should remain in the domain
of private exertion? What services should pertain to collective or
public exertion? The inquiry, which we have just finished, into the

essential differences that characterize these two kinds of services, will facilitate the solution of this important problem.

And first of all, it may be asked, is there any principle to enable us to distinguish what may legitimately enter the circle of collective action, and what should remain in the circle of private action?

I begin by intimating that what I denominate here public action is that great organization which has for rule the law, and for means of execution, force; in other words, the Government. Let it not be said that free and voluntary associations display likewise collective exertion. Let it not be supposed that I use the term private action as synonymous with isolated action. What I say is that free and voluntary association belongs still to the domain of private action, for it is one of the forms of exchange, and the most powerful form of all. It does not impair the equivalence of services, it does not affect the appreciation of values, it does not displace responsibilities, it does not exclude free will, it does not destroy competition nor its effects; in a word, it has not constraint for its principle.

But the action of Government is made general by constraint. It necessarily proceeds on the *compelle intrare*. It acts in form of law, and everyone must submit to it, because a law implies a sanction. No one, I think, will dispute these premises; which are supported by the best of all authorities, the testimony of universal fact. On all sides we have laws, and force to restrain the refractory.

Hence, no doubt, has come the saying that "men, in uniting in society, have sacrificed part of their liberty in order to preserve the remainder," a saying in great vogue with those who, confounding government with society, conclude that the latter is artificial and legalistic like the former.

It is evident that this saying does not hold true in the region of free and voluntary transactions. Let two men, animated by the prospect of greater profit and advantage, exchange their services, or unite their efforts, in place of continuing their isolated exertions—is there in this any sacrifice of liberty? Is it to sacrifice liberty to make a better use of it?

The most that can be said is this, that men sacrifice part of their liberty to preserve the remainder not when they unite in society, but when they subject themselves to a Government, since the necessary mode of action of every Government is force.

Now even with this modification, the pretended principle is erroneous, as long as Government confines itself to its legitimate functions.

But what are these functions?

It is precisely this special character of having force for their necessary auxiliary that marks out to us their extent and their limits. I affirm that as Government acts only by the intervention of force, its action is legitimate only where the intervention of force is itself legitimate.

Now, where force interposes legitimately, it is not to sacrifice liberty, but to make it more respected. So that this pretended axiom, which has been represented as the basis of political science, and which has been shown to be false as far as society is concerned, is equally false as regards Government. It is always gratifying to me to see these melancholy theoretical discordances disappear before a closer and more searching examination.

In what cases is the employment of force legitimate? In one case, and, I believe, in only one—the case of legitimate defense. If this be so, the foundation of Government is fully established, as well as its legitimate limits.

What is individual right?

The right an individual possesses to enter freely and voluntarily into bargains and transactions with his fellow-citizens, that give rise, as far as they are concerned, to a reciprocal right. When is this right violated? When one of the parties encroaches on the liberty of the other. In that case, it is incorrect to say, as is frequently done, "There is an excess, an abuse of liberty." We should say, "There is a want, a destruction of liberty." An excess of liberty, no doubt, if we regard only the aggressor, but a destruction of liberty, if we regard the victim, or even if we regard the phenomenon as a whole as we ought to do.

The right of the man whose liberty is attacked, or, which comes to the same thing, whose property, faculties, or labor is attacked, is to defend them even by force; and this is in fact what men do everywhere, and always, when they can.

Hence may be deduced the right of a number of men of any sort to take counsel together, and associate, in order to defend, even by their joint force, individual liberty and property.

But an individual has no right to employ force for any other purpose. I cannot legitimately force my neighbors to be industrious, sober, economical, generous, learned, devout; but I can legitimately force them to be just.

For the same reason the collective force cannot be legitimately applied to develop the love of industry, of sobriety, of economy, of generosity, of science, of religious belief; but it may be legitimately applied to ensure the predominance of justice, and vindicate each man's right.

For where can we seek for the origin of collective right but in individual right?

The deplorable mania of our times is the desire to give an independent existence to pure abstractions, to imagine a city without citizens, a human nature without human beings, a whole without parts, an aggregate without the individuals who compose it. They might as well say, "Here is a man, suppose him without members, viscera, organs, body, soul, or any of the elements of which he is composed—still here is a man."

If a right does not exist in any of the individuals of what for brevity's sake we call a nation, how should it exist in the nation itself? How, above all, should it exist in that fraction of a nation which exercises delegated rights of government? How could individuals delegate rights they do not themselves possess?

We must, then, regard as a fundamental principle in politics this incontestable truth, that between individuals the intervention of force is legitimate only in the case of legitimate defense; and that a collective body of men cannot have recourse to force legally but within the same limit.

Now, it is of the very essence of Government to act upon individuals by way of constraint. Then it can have no other rational functions than the legitimate defense of individual rights, it can have no delegated authority except to secure respect to the lives and property of all.

Observe that when a Government goes beyond these bounds, it enters on an unlimited career, and cannot escape this consequence, not only that it goes beyond its mission, but annihilates it, which constitutes the most monstrous of contradictions.

In truth, when the State has caused to be respected this fixed and invariable line that separates the rights of the citizens, when it has maintained among them justice, what could it do more without itself breaking through that barrier, the guardianship of which has been entrusted to it—in other words, without destroying with its own hands, and by force, that very liberty and property which had been placed under its safeguard? Beyond the administration and enforcement of justice, I defy you to imagine an intervention of Government that is not an injustice. Allege, as long as you choose, acts inspired by the purest philanthropy, encouragements held out to virtue and to industry, premiums, favor, and direct protection, gifts said to be gratuitous, initiatives styled generous; behind all these fair appearances, or, if you will, these fair realities, I will show you other realities less gratifying; the rights of some persons violated for the benefit of others, liberties sacrificed, rights of property usurped, faculties limited, spoliations consummated. And can the people possibly behold a spectacle more melancholy, more painful, than that of the collective force employed in perpetrating crimes that it is its special duty to repress?

In principle, it is enough that the Government has at its disposal as a necessary instrument, force, in order to enable us to discover what the private services are which can legitimately be converted into public services. They are those that have for their object the maintenance of liberty, property, and individual right, the prevention of crime—in a word, everything that involves the public security.

Governments have yet another mission.

There are in all countries a certain amount of common property, enjoyed by the citizens jointly—rivers, forests, roads. On the other hand, unfortunately, there are also debts. It is the duty of Government to administer this active and passive portion of the public domain.

Finally, from these two functions there flows another—that of levying the contributions that are necessary for the public service.

Thus:

To watch over the public security.

To administer common property.

To levy taxes.

Such I believe to be the legitimate circle within which Government functions ought to be circumscribed, and to which they should be brought back if they have gone beyond it.

This opinion, I know, runs counter to received opinions. "What!" it will be said, "you wish to reduce Government to play the part of a judge and a police-officer! You would take away from it all initiative! You would restrain it from giving a lively impulse to learning, to arts, to commerce, to navigation, to agriculture, to moral and religious ideas; you would despoil it of its fairest attribute, that of opening to the people the road of progress!"

To people who talk in this way, I should like to put a few questions.

Where has God placed the motive spring of human conduct, and the aspiration after progress? Is it in all men? or is it exclusively in those among them who have received, or usurped, the delegated authority of a legislator, or the patent of a bureaucrat? Does every one of us not carry in his makeup, in his whole being, that boundless, restless principle of action called desire? When our first and most urgent wants are supplied, are there not formed within us concentric and expansive circles of desires of an order more and more elevated? Does the love of arts, of letters, of science, of moral and religious truth, does a thirst for the solution of those problems that concern our present and future existence, descend from collective bodies of men to individuals, from abstractions to realities, from mere words to living and sentient beings?

If you set out with this assumption—absurd upon the face of it—that moral energy resides in the State, and that the nation is passive, do you not place morals, doctrines, opinions, wealth, all that constitutes individual life, at the mercy of men in power?

Then, in order to enable it to discharge the formidable duty that you would entrust to it, has the State any resources of its own? Is it not obliged to take everything of which it disposes, down to the last penny, from the citizens themselves? If it be from individuals that it demands the means of execution, individuals have realized these means. It is a contradiction then to pretend that individuality is passive and inert. And why have individuals created these resources? To minister to their own satisfactions. What does the State do when it seizes on these resources? It does not bring satisfactions into existence, it displaces them. It deprives the man who earned them in order to endow a man who has no right to them. Charged to chastise injustice, it perpetrates it.

Will it be said that in displacing satisfactions it purifies them, and renders them more moral?—that the wealth that individuals had devoted to gross and sensual wants, the State has devoted to moral purposes? Who dare affirm that it is advantageous to invert violently, by force, by means of spoliation, the natural order according to which the wants and desires of men are developed?— that it is moral to take a morsel of bread from the hungry peasant, in order to bring within the reach of the inhabitants of our large towns the doubtful morality of theatrical entertainments?

And then it must be remembered that you cannot displace wealth without displacing labor and population. Any arrangement you can make will be artificial and precarious when it is thus substituted for a solid and regular order of things reposing on the immutable laws of nature.

There are people who believe that by circumscribing the province of Government you enfeeble it. Numerous functions, and numerous agents, they think, give the State the solidity of a broader basis. But this is pure illusion. If the State cannot overstep the limits of its proper and determinate functions without becoming an instrument of injustice, of destruction, and of spoliation—without unsettling the natural distribution of labor, of enjoyments, of capital, and of population—without creating commercial stoppages, industrial crises, and pauperism—without enlarging the proportion of crimes and offenses—without recurring to more and more energetic means of repression—without exciting discontent and disaffection—how is it possible to discover a guarantee for stability in these accumulated elements of disorder?

You complain of the revolutionary tendencies of men, but without sufficient reflection. When in a great country we see private services invaded and converted into public services, the Government laying hold of one-third of the wealth produced by the citizens, the law converted into an engine of spoliation by the citizens themselves, thus impairing, under pretense of establishing, the equivalence of services—when we see population and labor displaced by legislation, a deeper and deeper gulf interposed between wealth and poverty, capital, which should give employment to an increasing population, prevented from accumulating, entire classes ground down by the hardest privations—when we see Governments taking to themselves credit for any prosperity that may be observable, proclaiming themselves the movers and originators of everything, and thus accepting responsibility for all the evils that afflict society—we are only astonished that revolutions do not occur more frequently, and we admire the sacrifices that are made by the people to the cause of public order and tranquillity.

But if laws and the Governments that enact laws confined themselves within the limits I have indicated, how could revolutions occur? If each citizen were free, he would doubtless be less exposed to suffering, and if, at the same time, the feeling of responsibility were brought to bear on him from all sides, how should he ever take it into his head to attribute his sufferings to a law, to a Government that concerned itself no further with him than to repress his acts of injustice and protect him from the injustice of others? Do we ever find a village rising against the authority of the local magistrate?

The influence of liberty on the cause of order is sensibly felt in the United States. There, all, save the administration of justice and of public property, is left to the free and voluntary transactions of the citizens; and there, accordingly, we find fewer of the elements and chances of revolution than in any other country of the world. What semblance of interest could the citizens of such a country have in changing the established order of things by violence when, on the one hand, this order of things clashes with no man's interests and, on the other, may be legally and readily modified if necessary?

But I am wrong. There are two active causes of revolution at work in the United States—slavery and commercial restriction. It is notorious that these two questions are constantly placing in jeopardy the public peace and the federal union. Now, is it possible to conceive a more decisive argument in support of the thesis I am now maintaining? Have we not here an instance of the law acting in direct antagonism to what ought to be the design and aim of all laws? Is not this a case of law and public force sanctioning, strengthening, perpetuating, systematizing, and protecting oppression and spoliation, in place of fulfilling its legitimate mission of protecting liberty and property? As regards slavery, the law says, "I shall create a force at the expense of the citizens, not to maintain each in his rights, but to annihilate altogether the rights of a portion of the inhabitants." As regards tariffs, the law says, "I shall create a force, at the expense of the citizens, not to ensure the freedom of their bargains and transactions, but to destroy that freedom, to impair the equivalence of services, to give to one citizen the liberty of two, and to deprive another of liberty altogether. My function is to commit injustice, which I nevertheless visit with the severest punishment when committed by the citizens themselves without my interposition."

It is not, then, because we have few laws and few functionaries or, in other words, because we have few public services, that revolutions are to be feared; but on the contrary, because we have many laws, many functionaries, and many public services. Public services, the law that regulates them, the force that establishes them, are, from their nature, never neutral. They may be enlarged without danger, on the contrary with advantage, when they are necessary to the vigorous enforcement of justice; but carried beyond this point, they are so many instruments of legal oppression and spoliation, so many causes of disorder and revolutionary ferment.

Shall I venture to describe the poisonous immorality that is infused into all the veins of the body politic when the law thus sets itself, upon principle, to indulge the plundering propensities of the citizens? Attend a meeting of the national representatives when the question happens to turn on bounties, encouragements, favors, or restrictions. See with what shameless rapacity all endeavor to secure a share of the spoil—spoil that, as individuals, they would blush to touch. The very man who would regard himself as a highway robber if, meeting me on the frontier and clapping a pistol to my head, he prevented me from concluding a bargain that was for my advantage, makes no scruple whatever in proposing and voting a law that substitutes the public force for his own and subjects me to the very same restriction at my own expense. In this respect, what a melancholy spectacle France presents at this very moment! All classes are suffering, and in place of demanding the abolition for ever of all legal spoliation, each turns to the law and says, "You who can do everything, you who have the public force at your disposal, you who can bring good out of evil, be pleased to rob and plunder all other classes to put money in my pocket. Force them to come to my shop, or pay me bounties and premiums, give my family gratuitous education, lend me money without interest," etc.

It is in this way that the law becomes a source of demoralization, and if anything ought to surprise us, it is that the propensity to individual plunder does not make more progress, when the moral sense of the nation is thus perverted by legislation itself.

The deplorable thing is, that spoliation when thus sanctioned by law, and opposed by no individual scruple, ends by becoming quite a learned theory with an attendant train of professors, journals, doctors, legislators, sophisms, and subtleties. Among the traditional quibbles that are brought forward in its support we may note this one, namely, that *ceteris paribus*, an enlargement of demand is of advantage to those by whom labor is supplied, seeing that the new relation between a more active demand and a supply that is stationary is what increases the value of the service. From these premises the conclusion follows that spoliation is of advantage to everybody: to the plundering class, which it enriches directly; to the plundered class, by its reflex influence. The plundering class having become richer finds itself in a situation to enlarge the circle of its enjoyments, and this it cannot do without creating a larger demand for the services of the class that has been robbed. Now, as regards each service, an enlargement of demand is an increase of value. The classes, then, who are legally plundered are too happy to be robbed, since the profit arising from the theft thus redounds to them, and helps to find them employment.

As long as the law confined itself to robbing the many for the benefit of the few, this quibble appeared specious, and was always invoked with success. "Let us hand over to the rich," it was said, "the taxes levied from the poor, and we shall thus augment the capital of the wealthy classes. The rich will indulge in luxury, and luxury will give employment to the poor." And all, poor included, regarded this recipe as infallible; and for having exposed its hollowness, I have been long regarded, and am still regarded, as an enemy of the working classes.

But since the revolution of February the poor have had a voice in the making of our laws. Have they required that the law should cease to sanction spoliation? Not at all. The sophism of the rebound, of the reflex influence, has got too firmly into their heads. What is it they have asked for? That the law should become impartial, and consent to rob all classes in their turn. They have asked for gratis education, gratis advances of capital, friendly societies founded by the State, progressive taxation, etc.

And then the rich have set themselves to cry out, "How scandalous! All is over with us! New barbarians threaten society with an invasion!" To the pretensions of the poor they have opposed a desperate resistance, first with the bayonet, and then with the ballot box. But for all this, have the rich given up spoliation? They have not even dreamt of that; and the argument of the rebound still serves as the pretext.

Were this system of spoliation carried on by them directly, and without the intervention of the law, the sophism would become transparent. Were you to take from the pocket of the workman a franc to pay your ticket to the theatre, would you have the gall to say to him, "My good friend, this franc will circulate and give employment to you and others of your class"? Or if you did, would he not be justified in answering, "The franc will circulate just as well if you do not steal it from me. It will go to the baker instead of the scene-painter. It will procure me bread in place of procuring you amusement."

We may remark also that the sophism of the rebound may be invoked by the poor in their turn. They may say in their turn to the rich, "Let the law assist us in robbing you. We shall consume more cloth, and that will benefit your manufactures; more meat, and that will benefit your land estates; more sugar, and that will benefit your shipping."

Unhappy, thrice unhappy, nation in which such questions are raised, in which no one thinks of making the law the rule of equity, but an instrument of plunder to fill his own pockets, and applies the whole power of his intellect to try to find excuses among the more remote and complicated effects of spoliation. In support of these reflections it may not be out of place to add here an extract from the debate that took place at a meeting of the Conseil general des Manufactures, de l'Agriculture, et du Commerce, on Saturday the 27th of April, 1850.[5]

---

[5] Here ends the manuscript. We refer the reader to the author's pamphlet entitled *Spoliation et Loi*, in the second part of which he has exposed the sophisms which were given utterance to at this meeting of the Conseil general.

18

DISTURBING CAUSES

In what state would human society have been had the transactions of mankind never been in any shape infected with force or fraud, oppression or deceit?

Would Justice and Liberty have given rise inevitably to Inequality and Monopoly?

To find an answer to these questions it would seem to me to be necessary to study the nature of human transactions in their essence, in their origin, in their consequences, and in the consequences of these consequences, down to the final result; and this apart from the consideration of contingent disturbances which might engender injustice; for it will be readily granted that injustice is not of the essence of free and voluntary transactions.

That the entry of Injustice into the world was inevitable and that society cannot get rid of it may be argued plausibly, and I think even conclusively, if we take man as he exists, with his passions, his greed, his ignorance, and his original improvidence. We must also, therefore, direct our attention to the origin and effects of Injustice.

But it is not the less true that economical science must set out by explaining the theory of human transactions, assuming them to be free and voluntary, just as physiology explains the nature and relations of our organs, apart from the consideration of the disturbing causes that modify these relations.

Services, as we have seen, are exchanged for services, and the great desideratum is the equivalence of the services thus exchanged.

The best chance, it would seem, of arriving at this equivalence, is that it should be produced under the influence of Liberty, and that every man should be allowed to judge for himself.

We know that men may be mistaken; but we know also that they have the power given them of rectifying their mistakes; and the longer, as it appears to us, that error is persisted in, the nearer we approximate to its rectification.

Everything that restrains liberty would seem to disturb the equivalence of services, and everything that disturbs the equivalence of services engenders inequality in an exaggerated degree, endowing some with unmerited opulence, entailing on others poverty equally unmerited, together with the destruction of national wealth and an attendant train of evils, animosities, disturbances, convulsions, and revolutions.

We shall not go to the length of saying that Liberty—or the equivalence of services—produces absolute equality; for we believe in nothing absolute in what concerns man. But we think that Liberty tends to make men approximate toward a common level, which is movable and always rising.

We think also that the inequality that may still remain under a free regime is either the result of accidental circumstances, or the chastisement of faults and vices, or the compensation of other advantages set opposite to those of wealth; and, consequently, that this inequality ought not to introduce among men any feeling of irritation.

In a word, we believe that Liberty is Harmony.

But in order to discover whether this harmony exists in reality, or only in our own imagination, whether it be in us a perception or only an aspiration, we must subject free transactions to the test of scientific inquiry; we must study facts, with their relations and consequences.

This is what we have endeavored to do.

We have seen that although countless obstacles are interposed between the wants of man and his satisfactions, so that in a state of isolation he could not exist—yet by the union of forces, the separation of occupations, in a word, by exchange, his faculties are developed to such an extent as to enable him gradually to overcome the first obstacles, to encounter the second and overcome them also, and so on in a progression as much more rapid as exchange is rendered more easy by the increasing density of population.

We have seen that his intelligence places at his disposal means of action more and more numerous, energetic, and perfect, that in proportion as capital increases, his absolute share in the produce increases, and his relative share diminishes, while both the absolute and relative share falling to the laborer goes on constantly increasing. This is the primary and most powerful cause of equality.

We have seen that that admirable instrument of production called land, that marvelous laboratory in which are prepared all things necessary for the food, clothing, and shelter of man, has been given him gratuitously by the Creator; that although the land is nominally appropriated, its productive action cannot be so, but remains gratuitous throughout the whole range of human transactions.

We have seen that Property has not only this negative effect of not encroaching on community; but that it works directly and constantly in enlarging its domain; and this is a second cause of equality, seeing that the more abundant the common fund becomes, the more is the inequality of property reduced.

We have seen that under the influence of liberty services tend to acquire their normal value, that is to say, a value proportionate to the labor. This is a third cause of equality.

For these reasons we conclude that there is a tendency to the establishment among men of a natural level, not by bringing them back to a retrograde position, or allowing them to remain stationary, but urging them on to a state that is constantly progressive.

Finally, we have seen that it is not the tendency of the laws of Value, of Interest, of Rent, of Population, or any other great natural law, to introduce dissonance into the beautiful order of society, as crude science has endeavored to persuade us, but, on the contrary, that all these laws lead to harmony.

Having reached this point, I think I hear the reader cry out, "The Economists are optimists with a vengeance! It is in vain that suffering, poverty, inadequate wages, pauperism, the desertion of children, starvation, crime, rebellion, inequality, are before their eyes; they chant complacently about the harmony of the social laws, and turn away from a hideous spectacle that mars their enjoyment of the theory in which they are wrapped up. They shun the region of realities, in order to take refuge, like the Utopian dreamers whom they blame, in a region of chimeras. More illogical than the Socialists or the Communists themselves—who confess the existence of suffering, feel it, describe it, abhor it, and only commit the error of prescribing ineffectual, impracticable, and empirical remedies—the Economists either deny the existence of suffering, or are insensible to it if, indeed, they do not engender it, calling out to diseased and distempered society, '*Laissez faire, laissez passer*; all is for the best in this best of all possible worlds.'"

In the name of science, I repel, I repudiate with all my might, such reproaches and such interpretations of our words. We see the existence of suffering as clearly as our opponents. Like them, we deplore it, like them we endeavor to discover its causes, like them we are ready to combat them. But we state the question differently. "Society," say they, "as liberty of labor and commercial transactions (that is to say, the free play of natural laws) has made it, is detestable. Break, then, the wheels of this ill-going machine, liberty (which they take care to nickname competition, or oftener anarchic competition), and substitute for them, by force, new wheels of our invention." No sooner said than done. Millions of inventions are paraded; and this we might naturally expect, for to imaginary space there are no limits.

As for us, after having studied the natural and providential laws of society, we affirm that these laws are harmonious. These laws admit the existence of evil, for they are brought into play by men—by beings subject to error and to suffering. But in this mechanism evil has itself a function to perform, which is to circumscribe more and more its own limits and ultimately to check its own action, by preparing for man warnings, corrections, experience, knowledge; all things that are comprehended and summed up in the word, Improvement.

We add that it is not true that liberty prevails among men, nor is it true that the providential laws exert all their action. If they do act, at least, it is to repair slowly and painfully the disturbing action of ignorance and error. Don't arraign us, then, for using the words *laissez faire*, let alone; for we do not mean by that, let man alone when he is doing wrong. What we mean is this: Study the providential laws, admire them, and allow them to operate. Remove the obstacles they encounter from abuses arising from force and fraud, and you will see accomplished in human society this double manifestation of progress—equalization in advancement.

For, in short, of two things only one can be true: either the interests of men are, in their own nature, concordant, or they are in their nature discordant. When we talk of one's Interest, we talk of a thing toward which a man gravitates necessarily, unavoidably; otherwise it would cease to be called interest. If men gravitated toward something else, that other thing would be termed their interest. If men's interests, then, are concordant, all that is necessary for the realization of harmony and happiness is that these interests should be understood, since men naturally pursue their interest. This is all we contend for; and this is the reason why we say, *Eclairez et laissez faire*, Enlighten men, and let them alone. If men's interests are in their nature and essence discordant, then you are right, and there is no other way of producing harmony, but by forcing, thwarting, and running counter to these interests. A perverse harmony, it truly would be, that can result only from an external and despotic action directed against the interests of all! For you can easily understand that men will not tamely allow themselves to be thwarted; and in order to obtain their acquiescence in your inventions, you must either begin by being stronger than the whole human family, or else you must be able to succeed in deceiving them with reference to their true interests. In short, on the hypothesis that men's interests are naturally discordant, the best thing that could happen would be their being all deceived in this respect.

Force and imposture, these are your sole resources. I defy you to find another, unless you admit that men's interests are harmonious—and if you grant that, you are with us, and will say, as we say, Allow the providential laws to act.

Now, this you will not do; and, therefore, I must repeat that your starting-point is the antagonism of interests. This is the reason why you will not allow these interests to come to a mutual arrangement and understanding freely and voluntarily; this is the reason why you advocate arbitrary measures, and repudiate liberty; and you are consistent.

But take care. The struggle that is approaching will not be exclusively between you and society. Such a struggle you lay your account with, the thwarting of men's interests being the very object you have in view. The battle will also rage among you, the inventors and organizers of artificial societies, yourselves; for there are thousands of you, and there will soon be tens of thousands, all entertaining and advocating different views. What will you do? I see very clearly what you will do—you will endeavor to get possession of the Government. That is the only force capable of overcoming all resistance. Will someone among you succeed? While he is engaged in thwarting and opposing the Government, he will find himself set upon by all the other inventors, equally desirous to seize upon the Government; and their chances of success will be so much the greater, seeing that they will be aided by that public disaffection that has been stirred up by the previous opposition to their interests. Here, then, we are launched into a stormy sea of eternal revolutions, and with no other object than the solution of this question. How, and by whom, can the interests of mankind be most effectually thwarted?

Let me not be accused of exaggeration. All this is forced upon us if men's interests are naturally discordant, for on this hypothesis you never can get out of the dilemma, that either these interests will be left to themselves, and then disorder will follow, or someone must be strong enough to run counter to them, and in that case we shall still have disorder.

It is true that there is a third course, as I have already indicated. It consists in deceiving men with reference to their true interests; and this course being above the power of a mere mortal, the shortest way is for the organisateur to erect himself into an oracle. This is a part that these Utopian dreamers, when they dare, never fail to play, until they become Ministers of State. They fill their writings with mystical cant; and it is with these paper kites that they find out how the wind sits, and make their first experiments on public credulity. But, unfortunately for them, success in such experiments is not very easily achieved in the nineteenth century.

We confess, then, frankly that, in order to get rid of these inextricable difficulties, it is much to be desired that, having studied human interests, we should find them harmonious. The duty of writers and that of governments become in that case rational and easy.

As mankind frequently mistakes its true interests, our duty as writers ought to be to explain these interests, to describe them, to make them understood, for we may be quite certain that if men once see their interest, they will follow it. As a man who is mistaken with reference to his own interests injures those of the public (this results from their harmony), the duty of Government will be to bring back the small body of dissenters and violators of the providential laws into the path of justice, which is identical with that of utility. In other words, the single mission of Government will be to establish the dominion of justice; and it will no longer have to embarrass itself with the painful endeavor to produce, at great cost, and by encroaching on individual liberty, a Harmony that is self-created, and that Government action never fails to destroy.

After what has been said, we shall not be regarded as such fanatical advocates of social harmony as to deny that it may be, and frequently is, disturbed. I will even add that in my opinion the disturbances of the social order, which are caused by blind passions, ignorance, and error, are infinitely greater and more prolonged than are generally supposed; and it is these disturbing causes that we are about to make the subject of our inquiry.

Man comes into the world having implanted in him ineradicably the desire of happiness and aversion from pain. Seeing that he acts in obedience to this impulse, we cannot deny that personal interest is the moving spring of the individual, of all individuals, and, consequently, of society. And seeing that personal interest, in the economic sphere, is the motive of human actions and the mainspring of society, Evil must proceed from it as well as Good; and it is in this motive power that we must seek to discover harmony and the causes by which that harmony is disturbed.

The constant aspiration of self-interest is to silence want or, to speak more generally, desire, by satisfaction.

Between these two terms, which are essentially personal and intransmissible, want and satisfaction, there is interposed a mean term that is transmissible and exchangeable—effort.

Over all this mechanism we have placed the faculty of comparing, of judging—mind, intelligence. But human intelligence is fallible. We may be mistaken. That is beyond dispute; for were anyone to assert that man cannot err, we should at once conclude that it was unnecessary to hold any further argument with him.

We may be mistaken in many ways. We may, for instance, form a wrong appreciation of the relative importance of our wants. In this case, were we living in a state of isolation, we should give to our efforts a direction not in accordance with our true interests. In a state of society, and under the operation of the law of exchange, the effect would be the same; for then we should

direct demand and remuneration to services of a kind either frivolous or hurtful, and so give a wrong direction to labor.

We may also err, from being ignorant that a satisfaction we
ardently seek for can only remove a suffering by becoming the
source of still greater sufferings. There is scarcely any effect that
may not in its turn become a cause. Foresight has been given us
to enable us to observe the concatenation of effects, so that we
may not sacrifice the future to the present; but we are frequently
deficient in foresight.

Here, then, is the first source of evil, error arising from the
feebleness of our judgment or the force of our passions; and it
belongs principally to the domain of morals. In this case, as the
error and the passion are individual, the resulting evil must, to a
certain extent, be individual also; and reflection, experience, and
the feeling of responsibility are its proper correctives.

Errors of this class, however, may assume a social character
and, when erected into a system, may give rise to widespread suffering. There are countries, for example, in which the governing
power is strongly convinced that the prosperity of nations is
measured not by the amount of wants that are satisfied, but by the
amount of efforts, whatever may be their results. The division of
labor assists powerfully this illusion. When we observe that each
profession sets itself to overcome a certain species of obstacle, we
imagine that the existence of that obstacle is the source of wealth.
In such countries, when vanity, frivolity, or a false love of glory
are predominant passions, and provoke corresponding desires,
and determine a portion of the national industry in that direction,
Governments believe that all will be over with them if their subjects come to be reformed and rendered more moral. What will
become now, they say, of milliners, cooks, grooms, embroiderers,
dancers, lace-manufacturers, etc.? They do not reflect that the
human heart is always large enough to contain enough of honest,
reasonable, and legitimate desires to afford employment and support to labor; that the business is not to suppress desires, but to
rectify and purify them; and that labor, consequently, following
the same evolution, may have its direction changed and still be

carried on to the same extent as before. In countries where these melancholy doctrines prevail, we hear it frequently said, "It is unfortunate that morals and industry cannot march side by side. We should desire, indeed, that the citizens should be moral, but we cannot allow them to become idle and poor. This is the reason why we must continue to make laws that are favorable to luxury. If necessary, we impose taxes on the people; and for the sake of the people, and to ensure them employment, we charge Kings, Presidents, Ambassadors, and Ministers with the duty of representing them." All this is said and done in the best possible faith; and the people themselves acquiesce in it with a good grace. It is very clear that when luxury and frivolity thus become a legislative affair, regulated, decreed, imposed, systematized, by public force, the law of Responsibility loses all its moral power.

19

WAR

Of all the circumstances that contribute to impart to nations their distinctive character and aspect, and to form and modify their genius, their moral condition, their customs, and their laws, the one that exerts a far more powerful influence than all the rest, because it includes all the rest, is the manner in which they provide for their subsistence. For this observation we are indebted to Charles Comte, and we have reason to be surprised that it has not had a more prominent place given to it in the moral and political sciences.

This circumstance, in fact, acts upon the human race in two ways, and with equal power in both—by its continuity, and by its universality. To subsist, to better one's condition, to bring up a family, are not affairs of time, or place, or taste, or opinion, or choice; they are the daily, constant, and unavoidable concern of all men, at all times, and in all countries.

Everywhere, the greater part of their moral, intellectual, and physical force is devoted directly or indirectly to create and replace the means of subsistence. The hunter, the fisher, the shepherd, the agriculturist, the manufacturer, the merchant, the laborer, the artisan, the capitalist—all think first of how they are to live (prosaic as the avowal may seem), and then how to live better and better, if they can. The proof of it is that it is only for this end that they are hunters, fishers, manufacturers, agriculturists, etc. In the same way, the public functionary, the soldier, the magistrate, enter upon their careers in order to ensure the supply of their wants. We do not necessarily charge a man with want of devotion or disinterestedness when we quote the proverb, The priest lives by the altar, for before he belonged to the priesthood he belonged to humanity; and if at this moment he sits down to write a book against this vulgar view of human nature, the sale of his book will demolish his argument.

God forbid that I should seek to deny the existence of self-denial and disinterestedness. But it must be granted that they are exceptional, and it is because they are so that they merit and call forth our admiration. If we consider human nature in its entirety, without having made a previous covenant with the demon of sentimentalism, we must allow that disinterested efforts bear no comparison, as respects their number, with those that are called forth by the hard necessities of our condition. And it is because those efforts, which constitute the aggregate of our employments, engross so large a portion of each man's life, that they cannot fail to exert a powerful influence on national character.

Mr. Saint-Marc Girardin says somewhere or other that he has been led to acknowledge the relative insignificance of political forms in comparison with those great general laws that their employments and their wants impose upon nations. "Do you desire to know the condition of a people?" says he. "Ask not how they are governed, but how they are employed."

As a general view, this is just; but the author hastens to falsify it by converting it into a system. The importance of political forms has been exaggerated; and what does he do? He denies their importance altogether, or acknowledges it only to laugh at it. Forms of government, he says, do not interest us but on the day of an election, or when we are reading the newspapers. Monarchy or

Republic, Aristocracy or Democracy, what matters it? And what conclusion does he arrive at? In maintaining that infant nations resemble each other, whatever their political constitution happens to be, he compares the United States to ancient Egypt, because in both countries gigantic works have been executed. Americans clear lands, dig canals, construct railways, and they do all this for themselves, because they are a democracy, and their own masters. The Egyptians raised temples, pyramids, obelisks, and palaces for their kings and their priests, because they were slaves. And yet we are told that the difference is a mere affair of form, not worth regarding, or which we should regard merely to laugh at. Alas! how the contagion of classical lore corrupts and misleads its superstitious votaries!

Mr. Saint-Marc Girardin, still proceeding on his general proposition that the prevailing occupations of a nation determine its genius, soon after remarks that formerly we were occupied with war and religion, but nowadays with commerce and manufactures. This is the reason why former generations bore a warlike and religious impress.

Rousseau had long before remarked that the care for subsistence was the prevailing occupation only of some nations, and those the most prosaic; and that other nations, more worthy of the name, had devoted themselves to nobler exertions.

Now, in this have not both Mr. Saint-Marc Girardin and Rousseau been the dupes of an historical illusion? Have they not mistaken the amusements, the diversions, or the pretexts and instruments of despotism, which give employment to some of the people, for the occupations of all? And has the illusion not arisen from this, that historians are always telling us about the class that does not work, never about the class that does; and in this way we come to regard the first of these classes as the entire nation.

I cannot help thinking that among the Greeks, among the Romans, among the people of the Middle Ages, men just did what they do now, and were subject to wants so pressing and so constantly recurring, that they were obliged to provide for them under pain of death. Hence I cannot help concluding that such employments then, as at present, formed the principal and absorbing occupation of the great bulk of the human race.

This much is certain, that very few people succeeded in living without work, on the labor of the subject masses. The small number of idlers who did so caused their slaves to construct for them sumptuous palaces, magnificent castles, and somber fortresses. They loved to surround themselves with all the sensual enjoyments of life, and with all the monuments of art. They amused themselves by descanting on philosophy and cosmogony; and, above all, they cultivated assiduously the two sciences to which they owed their supremacy and their enjoyments—the science of force, and the science of fraud.

Although below this aristocracy there existed countless multitudes engaged in creating for themselves the means of sustaining life, and for their oppressors the means of reveling in pleasures, yet as historians have never made the slightest allusion to those multitudes, we have come to forget their existence, and never taken them into account. Our regards are exclusively fixed on the aristocracy. To it we give the name of Old or Feudal Families; and we imagine that the men of those times maintained themselves without having recourse to commerce, to manufactures, to labor, to vulgar occupations. We admire their disinterestedness, their generosity, their taste for the arts, their spirituality, their disdain of servile employments, their elevation of mind and sentiment; and, in high-sounding language, we assert that at one epoch nations cared only for military glory, at another for the arts, at another for philosophy, at another for religion, at another for virtue. We sincerely lament our own condition, and give utterance to all sorts of sarcastic observations to the effect that, in spite of these sublime models, we are unable to attain the same elevation, but are reduced to assign to labor and its vulgar merits a prominent place in the system of modern life.

Let us console ourselves with the reflection that it occupied a no less important place among the ancients. Only, the drudgery of labor, from which a limited number of people had succeeded in freeing themselves, fell with redoubled weight upon the enslaved masses, to the great detriment of justice, of liberty, of property, of wealth, of equality, and of progress. This is the first of those disturbing causes to which I propose to solicit the attention of the reader.

The means, then, to which men have recourse in order to obtain the means of subsistence cannot fail to exert a powerful influence on their condition, physical, moral, intellectual, economical, and political. Who can doubt that if we were in a situation to observe different tribes of men, one of which had devoted itself exclusively to the chase, another to fishing, a third to agriculture, a fourth to navigation, we should discover very considerable differences in their ideas, in their opinions, in their habits, their manners, their customs, their laws, and their religion? No doubt we should find human nature everywhere essentially the same; these various laws, customs, and religions would have many points in common; and such points we designate as the general laws of human society.

Be this as it may, there can be no doubt that in our great modern societies, we find at work all, or nearly all, the various means of providing subsistence—fisheries, agriculture, manufactures, commerce, arts, and sciences, although in different proportions in different countries. This is the reason why we do not discover among nations so situated such marked and striking differences as would be apparent if each devoted itself to one of these occupations exclusively.

But if the nature of the occupations in which a people is engaged exercises a powerful influence on its morality, its desires, and its tastes—its morality in its turn exercises a great influence upon its occupations, at least upon the proportion that obtains between these occupations. But I shall not dwell on this observation, which I have presented in another part of this work, but hasten to the principal subject of the present chapter.

A man (and the same thing may be said of a people) may procure the means of existence in two ways—by creating them, or by stealing them.

Each of these two great sources of acquisition presents a variety of methods.

We may create the means of existence by the chase, by fishing, by agriculture, etc.

We may steal them by breach of trust, by violence, by force, fraud, war, etc.

If, confining ourselves to the circle of one or other of these two categories, we find that the predominance of one of these methods establishes so marked a difference in the character of nations, how much greater must the difference be between a nation that lives by production and a nation that lives by spoliation?

For it is not one of our faculties only, but all of them, that the necessity of providing for our subsistence brings into exercise; and what can be more fitted to modify the social condition of nations than what thus modifies all the human faculties?

This consideration, important as it is, has been so little regarded that I must dwell upon it for an instant.

The realization of an enjoyment or satisfaction presupposes labor; whence it follows that spoliation, far from excluding production, presupposes it and takes it for granted.

This consideration, it seems to me, ought to modify the partiality that historians, poets, and novel-writers have displayed for those heroic epochs that were not distinguished by what they sneer at under the epithet of industrialism. In these days, as in our own, men lived, subsisted; and labor must have done its office then as now. Only there was this difference, that nations, classes, and individuals succeeded in laying their share of the labor and toil on the shoulders of other nations, other classes, and other individuals.

The characteristic of production is to bring out of nothing, if I may so speak, the satisfactions and enjoyments that sustain and embellish life; so that a man, or a nation, may multiply *ad infinitum* these enjoyments without inflicting privation on any other man, or any other nation. So much is this the case, that a profound study of the economic mechanism shows us that the success of one man's labor opens up a field for the success of another's exertions.

The characteristic of spoliation, on the contrary, is this, that it cannot confer a satisfaction on one without inflicting a corresponding privation on another; for spoliation creates nothing, but displaces what labor has created. It entails an absolute loss of the exertions of both parties. So far, then, from adding to the enjoyments of mankind, it diminishes these enjoyments, and confers them, moreover, on those who have not merited them.

In order to produce, man must direct all his powers and faculties to obtain the mastery over natural laws; for it is by this means that he accomplishes his object. Hence, iron converted into a ploughshare is the emblem of production.

To steal, on the other hand, man must direct all his powers and faculties to obtain the mastery over his fellow-man; for it is by this means that he attains his end. Hence, iron converted into a sword is the emblem of spoliation.

Between the ploughshare, which brings plenty, and the sword, which brings destruction and death, there is no greater difference than between a nation of industrious workmen and a nation of spoliators. They have, and can have, nothing whatever in common. They have neither the same ideas, nor the same rules of appreciation, nor the same tastes, manners, character, laws, morals, or religion.

No more melancholy spectacle can present itself to the eye of philanthropy than to see an industrial age putting forth all its efforts, in the way of education, to get inoculated with the ideas, the sentiments, the errors, the prejudices, the vices, of an era of spoliation. Our own era is frequently accused of wanting consistency, of displaying little accordance between the judgments that are formed and the conduct that is pursued; and I believe that this arises principally from the cause I have just pointed out.

Spoliation, in the shape of War—that is to say, pure, simple, barefaced spoliation—has its root deep in the human heart, in the makeup of man, in the universal motives that actuate the social world, namely, desire of happiness and repugnance to pain—in short, in that principle of our nature called self-interest.

I am not sorry to find myself arraigning that principle, for I have been accused of devoting to it an idolatrous worship, of representing its effects as productive only of happiness to mankind, and even of elevating it above the principle of sympathy, of disinterestedness, and of self-sacrifice. In truth, I have not so esteemed it; I have only proved beyond the possibility of doubt its existence and its omnipotence. I should ill appreciate that omnipotence, and I should do violence to my own convictions, in representing personal interest as the universal actuating motive of the human race, did I fail now to point out the disturbing causes to which it gives rise, just as I formerly pointed out the harmonious laws of the social order spring from it.

Man, as we have already said, has an invincible desire to support himself, to improve his condition, and to attain happiness, or what he conceives to be happiness, at least to approximate toward it. For the same reason he shuns pain and toil.

Now labor, or the exertion we make in order to cause nature to co-operate in production, is in itself toil or fatigue. For this reason, it is repugnant to man, and he does not submit to it, except for the sake of avoiding a still greater evil.

Some have maintained philosophically that labor is not an evil but a good, and they are right if we take into account its results. It is a comparative good; or if it be an evil, it is an evil that saves us from greater evils. This is precisely the reason why men have so great a tendency to shun labor when they think that without having recourse to it, they may be able to reap its results.

Others maintain that labor is in itself a good; and that, independently of its productive results, it elevates, strengthens, and purifies man's character, and is to him a source of health and enjoyment. All this is strictly true; and it is an additional evidence to us of the marvelous fertility of those final intentions which the Creator has displayed in all parts of His works. Apart altogether from the productions that are its direct results, labor promises to man as a supplementary recompense a sound mind in a sound body; and it is not more true that idleness is the parent of every vice than that labor is the parent of many virtues.

But this does not at all interfere with the natural and unconquerable inclinations of the human heart, or with that feeling which prompts us not to desire labor for its own sake, but to compare it constantly with its results; not to desire to expend a great effort on what can be accomplished with a smaller effort; not of two efforts to choose the more severe. Nor is our endeavor to diminish the relation that the effort bears to the result inconsistent with our desire, when we have once acquired some leisure, to devote that leisure to new labors suited to our tastes, with the prospect of thus securing a new and additional recompense.

With reference to all this, universal facts are decisive. At all times and everywhere, we find man regarding labor as undesirable and satisfaction as the thing in his condition that makes him compensation for his labor. At all times and everywhere, we find him endeavoring to lighten his toil by calling in the aid, whenever he can obtain it, of animals, of the wind, of water-power, of steam, of natural forces, or, alas! of his fellow-creature, when he succeeds in enslaving him. In this last case—I repeat, for it is too apt to be forgotten—labor is not diminished, but displaced.[1]

Man, being thus placed between two evils, want or labor, and urged on by self-interest, seeks to discover whether, by some means or other, he cannot get rid of both. It is then that spoliation presents itself to him as a solution of the problem.

He says to himself: "I have not, it is true, any means of procuring the things necessary for my subsistence and enjoyments—food, clothing, and lodging—unless these things are previously produced by labor. But it is by no means indispensable that this should be my own labor. It is enough that they should be produced by the labor of someone, provided I can get the mastery."

---

[1] We forget this, when we propose the question: Is slave labor dearer or cheaper than free labor?

Such is the origin of war.

I shall not dwell upon its consequences.

When things come to this, that one man, or one nation, devotes itself to labor, and another man, or another nation, waits on till that labor is accomplished, in order to devote itself to rapine, we can see at a glance how much human power is thrown away.

On the one hand, the spoliator has not succeeded as he desired in avoiding every kind of labor. Armed robbery exacts efforts, and sometimes very severe efforts. While the producer devotes his time to the creation of products fitted to yield satisfactions, the spoliator employs his time in devising the means of robbing him. But when the work of violence has been accomplished, or attempted, the objects calculated to yield satisfaction are neither more nor less abundant than before. They may minister to the wants of a different set of people, but not of more wants. Thus all the exertions the spoliator has made with a view to spoliation, and the exertions also that he has failed to make with a view to production, are entirely lost, if not for him, at least for society.

Nor is this all. In most cases an analogous loss takes place on the side of the producer. It is not likely that he will wait for the violence with which he is menaced without taking some precaution for his own protection; and all precautions of this kind— arms, fortifications, munitions, drill—are labor, and labor lost forever, not to him who expects security from this labor, but to mankind at large.

But should the producer, after undergoing this double labor, not esteem himself able to resist the threatened violence, it is still worse for society, and power is thrown away on a much greater scale; for, in that case, labor will be given up altogether, no one being disposed to produce in order to be plundered.

If we regard the manner in which the human faculties are affected on both sides, the moral consequences of spoliation will be seen to be no less disastrous.

Providence has designed that man should devote himself to pacific combats with natural agents, and should reap directly from nature the fruits of his victory. When he obtains this mastery over natural agents only by obtaining a mastery over his fellow-creatures, his mission is changed, and quite another direction is given to his faculties. It is seen how great the difference is between the producer and the spoliator as regards foresight—foresight that becomes assimilated in some degree to providence, for to foresee is also to provide against (*prevoir c'est aussi pourvoir*).

The producer sets himself to learn the relation between cause and effect. For this purpose, he studies the laws of the physical world, and seeks to make them more and more useful auxiliaries. If he turns his regards on his fellow-men, it is to foresee their wants, and to provide for them, on condition of reciprocity.

The spoliator does not study nature. If he turns his regards on his fellow-men, it is to watch them as the eagle watches his prey, for the purpose of enfeebling and surprising them.

The same differences are observable in the other faculties, and extend to men's ideas.

Spoliation by means of war is not an accidental, isolated, and transient fact; it is a fact so general and so constant as not to give place, as regards permanence, to labor itself.

Point me out any country of the world where of two races, conquerors and conquered, the one does not domineer over the other. Show me in Europe, in Asia, or among the islands of the sea, a favored spot still occupied by the primitive inhabitants. If migrations of population have spared no country, war has been equally widespread.

Its traces are universal. Apart from rapine and bloodshed, public opinion outraged, and faculties and talents perverted, war has everywhere left other traces behind it, among which we must reckon slavery and aristocracy. Not only has the march of spoliation kept pace with the creation of wealth, but the spoliators have seized upon accumulated riches, upon capital in all its forms; and, in particular, they have fixed their regards upon capital in the shape of landed property. The last step was taking possession of man himself. For human powers and faculties being the instruments of labor, they found it a shorter method to lay hold of these powers and faculties than to seize upon their products.

It is impossible to calculate to what extent these great events have acted as disturbing causes and as trammels on the natural progress of the human race. If we take into account the sacrifice of industrial power that war occasions and the extent to which the diminished results of that power are concentrated in the hands of a limited number of conquerors, we may form to ourselves an idea of the causes of the destitution of the masses—a destitution that in our days it is impossible to explain on the hypothesis of liberty.

How the warlike spirit is propagated.

Aggressive nations are subject to reprisals. They often attack others; sometimes they defend themselves. When they act on the defensive, they have on their side the feeling of justice, and the sacredness of the cause in which they are engaged. They may then exult in their courage, devotion, and patriotism. But, alas! they carry these same sentiments into their offensive wars—and where is their patriotism then?

When two races, the one victorious and idle, the other vanquished and humiliated, occupy the same territory, everything calculated to awaken desire or arouse popular sympathies falls to the lot of the conquerors. Theirs are leisure, fetes, taste for the arts, wealth, military parade, tournaments, grace, elegance, literature, poetry. For the conquered race nothing remains but ruined huts, squalid garments, the hard hand of labor, or the cold hand of charity.

The consequence is that the ideas and prejudices of the dominant race, always associated with military force, come to constitute public opinion. Men, women, and children all unite in extolling the soldier's life in preference to that of the laborer, in preferring war to industry, and spoliation to production. The vanquished race shares the same sentiments, and when, at periods of transition, it succeeds in getting the better of its oppressors, it shows itself disposed to imitate them. What is this imitation but madness?

How war ends.

Spoliation, like Production, having its source in the human heart, the laws of the social world would not be harmonious, even to the limited extent for which I contend, if the latter did not succeed in the long run in overcoming the former.

20

RESPONSIBILITY

There is a leading idea which runs through the whole of this work, which pervades and animates every page and every line of it; and that idea is embodied in the opening words of the Christian Creed—I believe in God.

Yes, if this work differs from those of some other Economists, it is in this, that the latter appear to say, "We have but little faith in Providence, for we see that the natural laws lead to an abyss. And yet we say *laissez faire* merely because we have still less faith in ourselves, and because we see clearly that all human efforts designed to arrest the action of these natural laws tend only to hasten the catastrophe."

Again, if this work differs from the writings of the Socialists, it is in this, that the latter say, "We pretend to believe in God, but in reality we believe only in ourselves; seeing that we have no faith in the maxim, *laissez faire*, and that we all give forth our social nostrums as infinitely superior to the plans of Providence."

For my part, I say, *laissez faire*; in other words, respect liberty, and the human initiative.[1] Responsibility, solidarity; mysterious

---

[1]Because I believe that it is under the direction of a superior impulse, because, Providence being unable to act in the social order except through the intervention of men's interests and men's wills, it is impossible that the natural resulting force of these interests, the common tendency of these wills, should be toward ultimate evil; for then we must conclude that it is not only man or the human race, which proceeds onward toward error; but that God himself, being powerless or malevolent, urges on to evil His abortive creation. We believe, then, in liberty, because we believe in universal harmony, because we believe in God. Proclaiming in the name of faith, and formulating in the name of science, the Divine laws of the moral movement, living and pliant as these laws are, we spurn the narrow, sinister, unbending, and unalterable institutions which the blind leaders of the ignorant would substitute for this admirable mechanism. It would be absurd in the atheist to say, *laissez faire le hasard!*—seek not to control chance, or blind destiny. But, as believers, we have a right to say, seek not to control the order and justice of God—seek not to control the free action of the sovereign and infallible mover of all, or of that machinery of transmission which we call the human initiative. Liberty thus understood is no longer the anarchical deification of individualism. What we adore is above and beyond man who struggles; it is God who leads him.

We acknowledge, indeed, that man may err; yes, by the whole interval which separates a truth realized and established from one which is merely guessed at or suspected. But since man's nature is to seek, his destiny is to find. Truth, be it observed, has harmonious relations, necessary affinities, not only with the constitution of the understanding and the instincts of the heart, but also with the whole physical and moral conditions of our existence; so that even when we fail to grasp it as absolute truth, even when it fails to recommend itself to our innate sympathies as just, or to our ideal aspirations as beautiful, it nevertheless at length contrives to find acceptance in its practical and unobjectionable aspect as useful.

Liberty, we know, may lead to evil. But evil has itself its mission. Assuredly God has not thrown it across our path as a stumbling block. He has placed it, as it were, on each side of the path as a warning—as a means of keeping us in the right road, or bringing us back to it.

Man's will and inclinations, like inert molecules, have their law of gravitation. But, while things inanimate obey blindly their pre-existent and inevitable tendencies, in the case of beings endowed with free will, the force of attraction and repulsion does not precede action; it springs from the voluntary determination which it seems to be waiting for, it is developed by the laws, of which, apart from Revelation, it is impossible to appreciate the cause, but the effects and infallible action of which, on the progress of society, it is given us to appreciate—laws that, for the very reason that man is sociable, are linked together and act together, although they appear sometimes to run counter to each other; and that would require to be viewed in their ensemble, and in their common action if science, with its feeble optics and uncertain steps, were not reduced to method—that melancholy crutch that constitutes its strength while it reveals its weakness.

———————

Nosce te ipsum—know thyself: this, according to the oracle, is the beginning, the middle, and the end of the moral and political sciences.

As we have elsewhere remarked, in what concerns man or human society, Harmony can never mean Perfection, but only

———————

very act itself, and it reacts for or against the agent, by a progressive exertion of co-operation or resistance, which we term recompense or chastisement, pleasure or pain. If the direction of the will coincides with that of the general laws, if the act is good, happiness is the result. If it takes an opposite direction, if it is bad, something opposes or repels it; error gives rise to suffering, which is its remedy and its end. Thus, Evil is constantly opposed by Evil, and Good as constantly gives rise to Good. And we venture to say that, when seen from a higher point of view, the errors of free will are limited to certain oscillations, of a determinate extent, around a superior and necessary orbit; all persistent resistance, which would force this limit, tending only to destroy itself, without at all succeeding in disturbing the order of the sphere in which it moves.

This reactive force of co-operation or repulsion, which, by means of recompense and suffering, governs the orbit, at once voluntary and necessary, of the human race, this law of gravitation of free beings (of which Evil is only a necessary part) is distinguished by the terms Responsibility and Solidarity; the one brings back upon the individual; the other reflects and sends back on the social body the good or bad consequences of the act; the one applies to a man as a solitary and self-governing individual; the other envelops him in an inevitable community of good and evil as a partial element, a dependent member, of a collective and imperishable being—man. Responsibility is the sanction of individual liberty, the foundation of the rights of man. Solidarity is the evidence of his social subordination, and his principle of duty.

Improvement. Now improvement or perfectibility implies always, to a certain extent, imperfection in the future as well as in the past. If man could ever find his way into the promised land of absolute Good, he would no longer have occasion to use his understanding and his senses—he would be no longer man.

Evil exists. It is inherent in human infirmity. It manifests itself in the moral as in the material world; in the masses, as in the individual; in the whole as in the part. But because the eye may suffer and be lost, does the physiologist overlook the harmonious mechanism of that admirable organ? Does he deny the ingenious structure of the human body, because that body is subject to pain, to disease, and to death—to such extremity of suffering as caused Job in the depth of his despair, "to say to corruption, Thou art my father; and to the worm, Thou art my mother and my sister"? In the same way, because the social order will never bring mankind to the fancied haven of absolute good, is the economist to refuse to recognize all that is marvelous in the organization of the social order—an organization prepared with a view to the constantly-increasing diffusion of knowledge, of morality, and of happiness?

Strange! that we should deny to economic science the same right to admire the natural order of things that we concede to physiology. For, after all, what difference is there between the individual and the collective being as regards the harmony displayed by final causes? The individual, no doubt, comes into existence, grows and is developed, educates and improves himself as life advances, until the time comes when his light and life are to be communicated to others. At that moment everything about him is clothed in the hues of beauty; all breathes grace and joy; all is expansion, affection, benevolence, love, and harmony. For a while, his intelligence continues to be enlarged and confirmed, as if to qualify him to be the guide of those whom he has just called to tread the crooked paths of human existence. But soon his beauty fades, his grace disappears, his senses are blunted, his body becomes feeble, his memory clouded, his thoughts less bright; his affections even (except in the case of some choice spirits) get clogged with selfishness, and lose that charm, that freshness, that sincerity and simplicity, that depth and disinterestedness, that distinguished his earlier days—the poetry of life has fled. In spite of all the ingenious precautions that nature has taken to retard his dissolution—precautions that physiology sums up in the phrase *vis medicatrix*—he treads back the path of improvement, and loses, one after another, all his acquisitions by the way; he goes on from privation to privation until he reaches that which is the greatest of all, because it includes all. The genius of optimism itself can discover nothing consolatory, nothing harmonious in this slow but unavoidable decadence—in seeing that being once so proud and so beautiful descending sadly into the tomb. The tomb!

But is not that the door of another habitation? It is thus, when science stops short, that religion[2] renews, even for the individual, in another region, the concordant harmonies that have been interrupted here.[3]

Despite this fatal denouement, does physiology cease to see in the human body the most perfect masterpiece that ever proceeded from its Creator's hands?

But if the social body is liable to suffering, if it may suffer even to death, it is not for that reason finally condemned. Let men say what they will, it has not, in perspective, after having been elevated to its apogee, an inevitable decline. The crash of empires even is not the retrogradation of humanity, and the ancient models of civilization have only been dissolved in order to make room

---

[2]Religion (*religare*, to bind), that which connects the present life with the future, the living with the dead, time with eternity, the finite with the infinite, man with God.

[3]May we not say that Divine Justice, which is so incomprehensible when we consider the lot of individuals, becomes striking when we reflect on the destinies of nations? Each man's life is a drama which is begun on one theatre and completed on another. But the same thing cannot be said of the life of nations. That instructive tragedy begins and ends upon earth. This is the reason why history becomes a holy lesson; it is the justice of Providence. De Custine's *La Russie*.

for a civilization still more advanced. Dynasties may be extinguished; the forms of government may be changed; yet the progress of the human race may not the less be continued. The fall of States is like the fall of leaves in autumn. It fertilizes the soil; contributes to the return of spring; and promises to future generations a richer vegetation, and more abundant harvests. Nay, even in a purely national point of view, this theory of necessary decadence is as false as it is antiquated. In the life of no one people can we possibly perceive any cause of inevitable decline. The analogy that has so frequently given rise to a comparison between a nation and an individual, and led men to attribute to the one as to the other an infancy and an old age, is nothing better than a false metaphor. A community is being incessantly renewed. Let its institutions be elastic and flexible, so that in place of coming in collision with those new powers to which the human mind gives birth, they shall be so organized as to admit of this expansion of intellectual energy and accommodate themselves to it; and we see no reason why such institutions should not flourish in eternal youth. But whatever may be thought of the fragility and fall of empires, it must never be forgotten that society, which in its aggregate represents the human race, is constituted upon more solid bases. The more we study it, the more we shall be convinced that it too, like the human body, is provided with a curative force, a *vis medicatrix*, which delivers it from the evils that afflict it; and that it carries in its bosom, moreover, a progressive force; and is by the latter urged on to improvements to which we can assign no limits.

If individual evil, then, does not weaken or invalidate physiological harmony, still less does collective evil weaken or invalidate social harmony.

But how are we to reconcile the existence of evil with the infinite goodness of God? I cannot explain what I do not understand.

All I shall say is that this solution can no more be exacted from Political Economy than from Anatomy. These sciences, which are alike sciences of observation, study man as he is, without asking the Creator to reveal His impenetrable secrets.

Thus I again repeat, harmony does not correspond with the idea of absolute perfection, but with that of indefinite improvement. It has pleased God to attach suffering to our nature, seeing that He has designed that in us feebleness should be anterior to force, ignorance to science, want to satisfaction, effort to result, acquisition to possession, destitution to wealth, error to truth, experience to foresight. I submit without murmuring to this ordinance, being able, moreover, to imagine no other combination. But if, by a mechanism as simple as it is ingenious, He has provided that all men should approximate to a common level, which is continually rising, if He assures them—by the very action of what we denominate evil—both of the duration and the diffusion of progress, then am I not only content to bow myself under His bountiful and almighty hand—I bless that hand, I worship it, I adore it.

We have seen certain schools arise that have taken advantage of the insolubility (humanly speaking) of this question to embroil all others, as if it were given to our finite intelligence to comprehend and reconcile things that are infinite. Placing over the portal of social science this sentence, God cannot desire evil, they arrive at the following series of conclusions: "Evil exists in society; then society is not organized according to the designs of God. Let us change, and change again, and change continually this organization. Let us try about, and make experiments, until we have effaced all trace of suffering from the world. By that sign we shall know that the kingdom of God has come."

Nor is this all. These schools have been led to exclude from their social plans liberty as well as suffering, for liberty implies the possibility of error, and consequently the possibility of evil. Addressing their fellow-men, they say, "'Allow us to organize you—don't you interfere—cease to compare, to judge, to decide anything by yourselves and for yourselves. We abhor the *laissez faire*; but we ask you to let things alone, and to let us alone. If we succeed in conducting you to perfect happiness, the infinite goodness of God will be vindicated."

Contradiction, inconsistency, presumption—we ask which is most apparent in such language?

One sect among others, not very philosophical, but very noisy, promises to mankind unmixed felicity. Only deliver over to that sect the government of the human race, and in virtue of certain formulas, it makes bold to rid men of every painful sensation.

But if you do not accord a blind faith to the promises of that sect, then, bringing forward that formidable and insoluble problem that has vexed philosophy since the beginning of the world, they summon you to reconcile the existence of evil with the infinite goodness of God. Do you hesitate? they accuse you of impiety.

Fourier rings the changes on this theme till he exhausts all its combinations.

"Either God has not been able to give us a social code of attraction, of justice, of truth, and of unity; in which case He has been unjust in giving us wants without the means of satisfying them;"

"Or He has not desired to give it us; and in that case He has deliberately persecuted us by creating designedly wants which it is impossible to satisfy;"

"Or He is able, and has not desired; in which case the principle of good would rival the principle of evil, having the power to establish good, and preferring to establish evil;"

"Or He has desired, and has not been able; in which case He is incapable of governing us, acknowledging and desiring good, but not having the power to establish it;"

"Or He has been neither able nor willing; in which case the principle of good is below the principle of evil, etc.;"

"Or He has been both able and willing; in which case the code exists, and it is for us to promulgate it, etc."

And Fourier is the prophet of this new revelation. Let us deliver ourselves up to him and to his disciples: Providence will then be justified, sensibility will change its nature, and suffering will disappear from the earth.

But how, I would ask, do these apostles of absolute good, these hardy logicians, who exclaim continually that "God being perfect, His work must be perfect also;" and who accuse us of impiety because we resign ourselves to human imperfection—how, I say, do these men not perceive that, on the most favorable hypothesis, they are as impious as we are? I should like, indeed, that, under the reign of Misters Considerant, Hennequin, etc., no one in the world should ever lose his mother, or suffer from the toothache—in which case he also might chant the litany, Either God has not been able or has not been willing—I should like much that evil were to take flight to the infernal regions, retreating before the broad daylight of the Socialist revelation—that one of their plans, phalanstere, credit gratuit, anarchie, triade, atelier social, and so forth, had the power to rid us of all future evils. But would it annihilate suffering in the past? The infinite, observe, has no limits; and if there has existed on the earth since the beginning of the world a single sufferer, that is enough to render the problem of the infinite goodness of God insoluble in their point of view.

Let us beware, then, of linking the science of the finite to the mysteries of the infinite. Let us apply to the one reason and observation, and leave the other in the domain of revelation and of faith.

In all respects, and in every aspect, man is imperfect. In this world, at least, he encounters limits in all directions, and touches the finite at every point. His forces, his intelligence, his affections, his life, have in them nothing absolute, and belong to a material mechanism that is subject to fatigue, to decay, and to death.

Not only is this so, but our imperfection is so great that we cannot even imagine perfection as existing either in ourselves or in the external world. Our minds are so much out of proportion to this idea of perfection that all our efforts to seize it are vain. The oftener we try to grasp it, the oftener it escapes us, and is lost in inextricable contradictions. Show me a perfect man, and you will show me a man who is exempt from suffering, and who has consequently neither wants, nor desires, nor sensations, nor sensibility, nor nerves, nor muscles; who can be ignorant of nothing, and consequently has neither the faculty of attention, nor judgment, nor reasoning, nor memory, nor imagination, nor brains; in short, you will show me a being who does not exist.

Thus, in whatever aspect we regard man, we must regard him as being subject to suffering. We must admit that evil has entered as one spring of action into the providential plan; and in place of seeking by chimerical means to annihilate it, our business is to study the part it has to play, and the mission on which it is sent.

When it pleased God to create a being made up of wants, and of faculties to supply these wants, it was at the same time decreed that this being should be subject to suffering; for, apart from suffering, we could form no idea of wants, and, apart from wants, we could form no idea of utility, or of the use and object of any of our faculties. All that constitutes our greatness has its root in what constitutes our weakness.

Urged on by innumerable impulses, and endowed with an intelligence that enlightens our exertions, and enables us to appreciate their results, we have free will to guide and direct us.

But free will implies error as possible, and error in its turn implies suffering as its inevitable effect. I defy any one to tell me what it is to choose freely, if it be not to run the risk of making a bad choice, and what it is to make a bad choice if it be not to prepare the way for suffering.

And this is no doubt the reason why those schools who are content with nothing less than absolute good are all materialist and fatalist. They are unable to admit free will. They see that liberty of acting proceeds from liberty of choosing; that liberty of choosing supposes the possibility of error; and that the possibility of error is the possibility of evil. Now, in an artificial society such as our organisateurs invent, evil cannot make its appearance. For that reason, men must be exempted from the possibility of error; and the surest means to accomplish that is to deprive them of the faculty of acting and choosing—in other words, of free will. It has been truly said that Socialism is despotism incarnate.

In presence of these fooleries, it may be asked, By what right does the organizer of artificial systems venture to think, act, and choose, not only for himself, but for everyone else? for, after all, he belongs to the human race, and in that respect is fallible; and he is so much the more fallible in proportion as he pretends to extend the range of his science and his will.

No doubt the organizer finds this objection radically unfounded, inasmuch as it confounds him with the rest of mankind. But he who professes to discover the defects of the Divine workmanship and has undertaken to recast it is more than a man; he is an oracle, and more than an oracle

Socialism has two elements: the frenzy of contradiction, and the madness of pride!

But when free will, which is the foundation of the whole argument, is denied, is not this the proper place to demonstrate its existence? I shall take good care not to enter upon any such demonstration. Everyone feels that his will is free, and that is enough. I feel this, not vaguely, but a hundred times more intensely than if it had been demonstrated to me by Aristotle or by Euclid. I feel it with conscious joy when I have made a choice that does me honor; with remorse when I have made a choice that degrades me. I find, moreover, that all men by their conduct affirm their belief in free will, although some deny it in their writings. All men compare motives, deliberate, determine, retract, try to foresee; all give advice, are indignant at injustice, admire acts of devotion. Then all acknowledge in themselves and in others the existence of free will, without which, choice, advice, foresight, morality, and virtue, are impossible. Let us take care how we seek to demonstrate what is admitted by universal practice. Absolute fatalists are no more to be found, even at Constantinople, than absolute skeptics are to be met with at Alexandria. Those who proclaim themselves such may be fools enough to try to persuade others, but they are powerless to convince themselves. They prove with much subtlety that they have no will of their own; but when we see that they act as if they had it, we need not dispute with them.

Here, then, we are placed in the midst of nature and of our fellow-men—urged on by impulses, wants, appetites, desires—provided with various faculties enabling us to operate on man and on things—determined to action by our free will—endowed with intelligence, which is perfectible and therefore imperfect, and that, if it enlightens us, may also deceive us with reference to the consequences of our actions.

Every human action—giving rise to a series of good or bad consequences, of which some fall back on the agent, and others affect his family, his neighbors, his fellow-citizens, and sometimes mankind at large—every such action causes the vibration of two chords, the sounds of which are oracular utterances—Responsibility and Solidarity.

As regards the man who acts, Responsibility is the natural link that exists between the act and its consequences. It is a complete system of inevitable Rewards and Punishments that no man has invented, that acts with all the regularity of the great natural laws, and that may, consequently, be regarded as of Divine institution. The evident object of Responsibility is to restrain the number of hurtful actions, and increase the number of such as are useful.

This mechanism, which is at once corrective and progressive, remunerative and retributive, is so simple, so near us, so identified with our whole being, so perpetually in action, that not only can we not ignore it, but we see that, like Evil, it is one of those phenomena without which our whole life would be to us unintelligible.

The book of Genesis tells us that, the first man having been driven from the terrestrial paradise because he had learned to distinguish between good and evil, *sciens bonum et malum*, God pronounced this sentence on him: *In laboribus comedes ex terra cunctis diebus vitae tuae. Spinas et tribulos germinabit tibi. In sudore vultus tui vesceris pane, donec revertaris in terram de qua sumptus es: quia pulvis es, et in pulverem reverteris.*[4]

---

[4]"Cursed is the ground for thy sake; in sorrow shalt thou eat of it all the days of thy life: Thorns also and thistles shall it bring forth to thee. . . . In the sweat of thy face shalt thou eat bread, until thou return unto the ground; for out of it wast thou taken: for dust thou art, and unto dust shalt thou return." Genesis 3: 17, 18, 19.

Here, then, we have good and evil—or human nature. Here we have acts and habits producing good or bad consequences—or human nature. Here we have labor, sweat, thorns, tribulation, and death—or human nature.

Human nature, I say; for to choose, to be mistaken, to suffer, to rectify our errors—in a word, all the elements that make up the idea of Responsibility—are so inherent in our sensitive, rational, and free nature, they are so much of the essence of that nature itself, that I defy the most fertile imagination to conceive for man another mode of existence.

That man might have lived in an Eden, in *paradiso voluptatis*, ignorant of good and evil, we can indeed believe, but we cannot comprehend it, so profoundly has our nature been transformed.

We find it impossible to separate the idea of life from that of sensibility; that of sensibility from that of pleasure and pain; that of pleasure and pain from that of reward and punishment; that of intelligence from that of liberty and choice, and all these ideas from the idea of Responsibility; for it is the aggregate of all these ideas that gives us the idea of Being or Existence, so that when we think upon God, our reason, which tells us that He is incapable of suffering, remains confounded—so inseparable are our notions of sensibility and existence.

It is this undoubtedly which renders Faith the necessary complement of our destinies. It is the only bond that is possible between the creature and the Creator, seeing that God is, and always will be, to our reason incomprehensible, *Deus absconditus*.

In order to be convinced how hard Responsibility presses us, and shuts us in on every side, we have only to attend to the most simple facts.

Fire burns us; the collision of bodies bruises us. If we were not endowed with sensibility, or if our sensibility were not painfully affected by the approach of fire, and by rude contact with other bodies, we should be exposed to death every moment.

From earliest infancy to extreme old age, our life is only a long apprenticeship. By frequently falling, we learn to walk. By rude and reiterated experiments, we are taught to avoid heat, cold, hunger, thirst, excess. Do not let us complain of the roughness of this experience. If it were not so, it would teach us nothing.

The same thing holds in the social order. From the unhappy consequences of cruelty, of injustice, of fear, of violence, of deceit, of idleness, we learn to be gentle, just, brave, moderate, truthful, and industrious. Experience is protracted; it will never come to an end; but it will never cease to be efficacious.

Man being so constituted, it is impossible that we should not recognize in responsibility the mainspring to which social progress is specially confided. It is the crucible in which experience is elaborated. They, then, who believe in the superiority of times past, like those who despair of the future, fall into the most manifest contradiction. Without being aware of it, they extol error, and calumniate knowledge. It is as if they said, "The more I have learned, the less I know. The more clearly I discern what is hurtful, the more I shall be exposed to it." Were humanity constituted on such a basis as this, it would in a short time cease to exist.

Man's starting-point is ignorance and inexperience. The farther we trace back the chain of time, the more destitute we find men of that knowledge which is fitted to direct their choice—of knowledge that can be acquired only in one of two ways; by reflection or by experience.

Now it so happens that man's every action includes, not one consequence only, but a series of consequences. Sometimes the first is good, and the others bad; sometimes the first is bad, and the others good. From one of our undertakings there may proceed good and bad consequences, combined in variable proportions. We may venture to term vicious those actions that produce more bad than good effects, and virtuous those that produce a greater amount of good than of evil.

When one of our actions produces a first consequence that we approve, followed by many other consequences that are hurtful, so that the aggregate of bad predominates over the aggregate of good, such an action tends to limit and restrain itself, and to be abandoned in proportion as we acquire more foresight.

Men naturally perceive the immediate consequences of their actions before they perceive those consequences that are more remote. Whence it follows that what we have denominated vicious acts are more multiplied in times of ignorance. Now the repetition of the same acts constitutes habit. Ages of ignorance, then, are ages of bad habits.

Consequently, they are ages of bad laws, for acts that are repeated, habits that are general, constitute manners, upon which laws are modeled, and of which, so to speak, they are the official expression.

How is this ignorance to be put an end to? How can men be taught to know the second, the third, and all the subsequent consequences of their acts and their habits?

The first means is the exercise of that faculty of discerning and reasoning that Providence has vouchsafed them.

But there is another still more sure and efficacious—experience. When the act is once done, the consequences follow inevitably. The first effect is good; for it is precisely to obtain that result that the act is done. But the second may inflict suffering, the third still greater suffering, and so on.

Then men's eyes are opened, and light begins to appear. That action is not repeated; we sacrifice the good produced by the first and immediate consequence, for fear of the still greater evil that the subsequent consequences entail. If the act has become a habit, and if we have not power to give it up, we at least give way to it with hesitation and repugnance, and after an inward conflict. We do not recommend it; on the contrary, we blame it, and persuade our children against it; and we are certainly on the road of progress.

If, on the other hand, the act is one that is useful, but from which we refrain, because its first, and only known, consequence is painful, and we are ignorant of the favorable ulterior consequences, experience teaches us the effects of abstaining from it. A savage, for instance, has had enough to eat. He does not foresee that he will be hungry tomorrow. Why should he labor today? To work is present pain—no need of foresight to know that. He therefore continues idle. But the day passes, another succeeds, and as it brings hunger, he must then work under the spur of necessity. This is a lesson that, frequently repeated, cannot fail to develop foresight. By degrees idleness is regarded in its true light. We brand it; we warn the young against it. Public opinion is now on the side of industry.

But in order that experience should afford us this lesson, in order that it should fulfill its mission, develop foresight, explain the series of consequences that flow from our actions, pave the way to good habits, and restrain bad ones—in a word, in order that experience should become an effective instrument of progress and moral improvement—the law of Responsibility must come into operation. The bad consequences must make themselves felt, and evil must for the moment chastise us.

Undoubtedly it would be better that evil had no existence; and it might perhaps be so if man was constituted differently from what he is. But taking man as he is, with his wants, his desires, his sensibility, his free will, his power of choosing and erring, his faculty of bringing into play a cause that necessarily entails consequences that it is not in our power to elude as long as the cause exists; in such circumstances, the only way of removing the cause is to enlighten the will, rectify the choice, abandon the vicious act or the vicious habit; and nothing can effect this but the law of Responsibility.

We may affirm, then, that man being constituted as he is, evil is not only necessary but useful. It has a mission, and enters into the universal harmony. Its mission is to destroy its own cause, to limit its own operation, to concur in the realization of good, and to stimulate progress.

We may elucidate this by some examples that the subject that now engages us—Political Economy—presents. Frugality. Prodigality. Monopolies. Population.[5]

Responsibility guards itself by three sanctions:

First, The natural sanction; which is that of which I have just been speaking—the necessary suffering or recompense which certain acts and habits entail.

Second, The religious sanction; or the punishments and rewards of another life, which are annexed to acts and habits according as they are vicious or virtuous.

Third, The legal sanction; or the punishments and rewards decreed beforehand by society.

Of these three sanctions, I confess that the one that appears to me fundamental is the first. In saying this I cannot fail to run counter to sentiments I respect; but I must be permitted to declare my opinion.

Is an act vicious because a revelation from above has declared it to be so? Or has revelation declared it vicious because it produces consequences that are bad? These questions will probably always form a subject of controversy between the philosophical and the religious mind.

I believe that Christianity can range itself on the side of those who answer the last of these two questions in the affirmative. Christianity itself tells us that it has not come to oppose the natural law, but to confirm it.[6] We can scarcely admit that God, who

---

[5] The interesting developments which the author intended to present here by way of illustrations, and of which he indicated beforehand the character, he unfortunately did not live to write. The reader may supply the want by referring to chapter 16 of this work, and likewise to chapters 7 and 9 of Bastiat's pamphlet, *Ce qu'on voit et Ce qu'on ne voit pas.*—Editor.

[6] "For when the Gentiles, which have not the law, do by nature the things contained in the law, these, having not the law, are a law unto themselves; which show the work of the law written in their hearts, their conscience also bearing witness, and their thoughts the meanwhile accusing or else excusing one another." Romans 14, 15. See also Bishop Butler's 3rd

is the supreme principle of order, should have made an arbitrary classification of human actions, that He should have denounced punishment on some, and promised reward to others, and this without any regard to the effects of these actions, that is to say, to their discordance, or concordance, in the universal harmony.

When He said, "Thou shalt not kill—thou shalt not steal," no doubt He had in view to prohibit certain acts because they were hurtful to man and to society, which are His work.

Regard to consequences is so powerful a consideration with man that if he belonged to a religion that forbade acts that universal experience proved to be useful, or that sanctioned the observance of habits palpably hurtful, I believe that such a religion could not be maintained, but that it would at length give way before the progress of knowledge. Men could not long suppose that the deliberate design of God was to cause evil and to interdict good.

The question I broach here has perhaps no very important bearing on Christianity, since it ordains only what is good in itself, and forbids only what is bad.

But the question I am now examining is this, whether in principle the religious sanction goes to confirm the natural sanction, or whether the natural sanction goes for nothing in presence of the religious sanction, and should give way to the latter when they come into collision.

Now, if I am not mistaken, the tendency of ministers of religion is to pay little attention to the natural sanction. For this they have an unanswerable reason: "God has ordained this; God has forbidden that." There is no longer any room left for reasoning,

---

Sermon, on Human Nature: "Nothing," says he, "can be more evident than that, exclusive of revelation, man cannot be considered as a creature left by his Maker to act at random, and live at large up to the extent of his natural power, as passion, humor, willfulness, happen to carry him; which is the condition brute creatures are in. But that, from his make, constitution, or nature, he is in the strictest and most proper sense a law to himself. He hath the rule of right within. What is wanting is only that he honestly attend to it." Butler's *Works*, vol. 2, p. 65.—Translator.

for God is infallible and omnipotent. Although the act should lead to the destruction of the world, we must march on like blind men, just as we would do if God addressed us personally, and showed us heaven and hell.

It may happen, even in the true religion, that actions in themselves innocent are forbidden by Divine authority. To exact interest for money, for example, has been pronounced sinful. Had mankind given obedience to that prohibition, the race would long since have disappeared from the face of the earth. For without interest the accumulation of capital is impossible; without capital there can be no cooperation of anterior and present labor; without this cooperation there can be no society; and without society man cannot exist.

On the other hand, on examining the subject of interest more nearly, we are convinced that not only is it useful in its general effects, but that there is in it nothing contrary to charity and truth—certainly not more than there is in the stipend of a minister of religion, and less than in certain perquisites belonging to his office.

Thus, all the power of the Church has not been able for an instant to supersede, in this respect, the nature of things. The most that has been accomplished is to cause to be disguised one of the forms, and that the least usual form, of exacting interest, in a number of very trifling transactions.

In the same way, as regards precepts; when the Gospel says, "Unto him who smiteth thee on the one cheek, offer also the other," it gives a precept that, if taken literally, would destroy the right of legitimate defense in the individual, and consequently in society. Now, without this right, the existence of the human race is impossible.

And what has happened? For eighteen hundred years this saying has been repeated as a mere conventionalism.

But there is a still graver consideration. There are false religions in the world. These necessarily admit precepts and prohibitions that are in antagonism with the natural sanctions attached to certain acts. Now, of all the means that have been given us to distinguish in a matter so important the true from the false, that which emanates from God from that which proceeds from imposture, none is more certain, more decisive, than an examination of the good or bad consequences a doctrine is calculated to have on the advancement and progress of mankind—*a fructibus eorum cognoscetis eos.*

Legal sanction. Nature having prepared a system of punishments and rewards, the shape of the effects that necessarily proceed from each act and from each habit, what is the province of human law? There are only three courses it can take—to allow Responsibility to act, to chime in with it, or to oppose it.

It seems to me beyond doubt that when a legal sanction is brought into play, it ought only to be to give more force, regularity, certainty, and efficacy to the natural sanction. These two powers should co-operate, and not run counter to each other.

For example, if fraud is in the first instance profitable to him who has recourse to it, in the long run it is more frequently fatal to him; for it injures his credit, his honor, and his reputation. It creates around him distrust and suspicion. It is, besides, always hurtful to the man who is the victim of it. Finally, it alarms society, and obliges it to employ part of its force in expensive precautions. The sum of evil, then, far exceeds the sum of good. This is what constitutes natural Responsibility, which acts constantly as a preventive and repressive check. We can understand, however, that the community does not choose to depend altogether on the slow action of necessary responsibility, and judges it fit to add a legal sanction to the natural sanction. In that case, we may say that the legal sanction is only the natural sanction organized and reduced to rule. It renders punishment more immediate and more certain; it gives more publicity and authenticity to facts; it surrounds the suspected party with guarantees, and affords him a regular opportunity to exculpate himself if there be room for it; it rectifies the errors of public opinion, and calms down individual vengeance by substituting for it public retribution. Finally—and this perhaps is the essential thing—it does not destroy the lessons of experience.

We cannot, then, say that the legal sanction is illogical in principle when it advances alongside the natural sanction and concurs in the same result. It does not follow, however, that the legal sanction ought in every case to be substituted for the natural sanction, and that human law is justified by the consideration alone that it acts in the sense of Responsibility.

The artificial distribution of punishments and rewards includes in itself, and at the expense of the community, an amount of inconvenience that it is necessary to take into account. The machinery of the legal sanction comes from men, is worked by men, and is costly.

Before submitting an action or a habit to organized repression, there is always this question to be asked:

Does the excess of good that is obtained by the addition of legal repression to natural repression compensate the evil that is inherent in the repressive machinery?

In other words, is the evil of artificial repression greater or less than the evil of impunity?

In the case of theft, of murder, of the greater part of crimes and delicts, the question admits of no doubt. Every nation of the earth represses these crimes by public force.

But when we have to do with a habit that it is difficult to account for, and which may spring from moral causes of delicate appreciation, the question is different, and it may very well be that although this habit is universally esteemed hurtful and vicious, the law should remain neutral, and hand it over to natural responsibility.

In the first place, this is the course the law ought to take in the case of an action or a habit that is doubtful, that one part of the population thinks good and another part bad. You think me wrong in following the Catholic ritual; I think you wrong in adopting the Lutheran faith. Let God judge of that. Why should I aim a blow at you, or why should you aim a blow at me? If it is not right that we should strike at each other, how can it be right that we should delegate a third party, the depository of the public force, to chastise one of us for the satisfaction of the other?

You allege that I am wrong in teaching my child the moral and natural sciences; I believe that you are wrong in teaching your child Greek and Latin exclusively. Let us act on both sides according to our feeling of what is right. Let our families be acted on by the law of Responsibility. That law will punish the one who is wrong. Do not invoke human law, which may punish the one who is right.

You assert that I would do better to pursue such and such a career, to work according to your process, to employ an iron in place of a wooden plough, to sow thin in place of sowing thick, to purchase in the East rather than in the West. I maintain just the contrary. I have made all my calculations; and surely I am more interested than you in not falling into any mistake in matters upon the right ordering of which my welfare, my existence, and the happiness of my family depend, while in your case they interest only your amour-propre and the credit of your systems. Give me as much advice as you please, but constrain me to nothing. I decide upon my own proper risk and peril, and surely that is enough without the tyrannical intervention of law.

We see that, in almost all the important actions of life, it is necessary to respect free will, to rely on the individual judgment of men, on that inward light that God has given them for their guidance, and after that to leave Responsibility to do its own work.

The intervention of law in analogous cases, over and above the very great inconvenience of opening the way equally to error and to truth, has the still greater inconvenience of paralyzing intelligence itself, of extinguishing that light which is the inheritance of humanity and the pledge of progress.

But even when an action, a habit, a practice is acknowledged by public good sense to be bad, vicious, and immoral, when it is so beyond doubt; when those who give themselves up to it are the first to blame themselves, that is not enough to justify the intervention of law. As I have already said, it is necessary also to know if, in adding to the bad consequences of this vice the bad consequences inherent in all legal repression, we do not produce, in the long run, a sum of evil that exceeds the good that the legal sanction adds to the natural sanction.

We might examine, for instance, the evils that would result from the application of the legal sanction to the repression of idleness, prodigality, avarice, greed, cupidity, ambition.

Let us take the case of idleness.

This is a very natural inclination, and there are not wanting men who join the chorus of the Italians when they celebrate the *dolce far niente*, and of Rousseau, when he says, *Je suis paresseux avec delices*. We cannot doubt, then, that idleness is attended with a certain amount of enjoyment. Were it not so, in fact, there would be no idleness in the world.

And yet there flows from this inclination a host of evils, so much so that the wisdom of nations has embodied itself in the proverb that Idleness is the parent of every vice.

The evils of idleness infinitely surpass the good; and it is necessary that the law of Responsibility should act in this matter with some energy, either as a lesson or as a spur, seeing that it is in fact by labor that the world has reached the state of civilization that it has now attained.

Now, considered either as a lesson or as a spur to action, what would a legal sanction add to the providential sanction? Suppose we had a law to punish idleness. In what precise degree would such a law quicken the national activity?

If we could find this out, we should have an exact measure of the benefit resulting from the law. I confess I can form no idea of this part of the problem. But we must ask, at what price would this benefit, whatever it were, be purchased; and surely little reflection is needed in order to see that the certain inconveniences of legal repression would far exceed its problematical advantages.

In the first place, there are in France thirty-six million inhabitants. It would be necessary to exercise over them all a rigorous surveillance, to follow them into their fields, their workshops, to their domestic circles. Think of the number of functionaries, the increase of taxes, etc., that would be the result.

Then, those who are now industrious—and the number, thank God, is great—would be, no less than the idle, subjected to this intolerable inquisition. It is surely an immense inconvenience to subject a hundred innocent people to degrading measures in order to punish one guilty person whom nature has herself taken it in hand to chastise.

And then, when does idleness begin? In the case of each man brought to justice, the most minute and delicate inquiries would be necessary. Was the accused really idle, or did he merely take necessary repose? Was he sick, or was he meditating, or was he saying his prayers, etc.? How could we appreciate all those shades of difference? Did he work harder and longer in the morning in order to have a little more time at his disposal in the evening? How many witnesses, judges, juries, policemen, would be needed, how much resistance, espionage, and hatred would be engendered!

Next we should have the chapter of judicial blunders. How great an amount of idleness would escape! and, in return, how many industrious people would go to redeem in prison the inactivity of a day by the inactivity of a month!

With these consequences and many others before our eyes, we say, Let natural Responsibility do its own work. And we do well in saying so.

The Socialists, who never decline to have recourse to despotism in order to accomplish their ends—for the end is everything with them—have branded Responsibility with the name of individualism—and have then tried to annihilate it, and absorb it in the sphere of action of a solidarity extended beyond all natural bounds.

The consequences of this perversion of the two great springs of human perfectibility are fatal. There is no longer any dignity, any liberty, for man. For from the moment that the man who acts is not personally answerable for the good or bad consequences of his actions, his right to act singly and individually no longer exists. If each movement of the individual is to reflect back the series of its effects on society at large, the initiative of each movement can no longer be left to the individual—it belongs to society. The community alone must decide all, and regulate all—education, food, wages, amusements, locomotion, affections, families, etc. Now, the law is the voice of society; the law is the legislator. Here, then, we have a flock and a shepherd—less than that even, inert matter, and a workman. We see, then, to what point the suppression of Responsibility and of individualism would lead us.

To conceal this frightful design from the eyes of the vulgar, it was necessary to flatter their selfish passions by declaiming against greed. To the suffering classes Socialism says, "Do not trouble yourselves to examine whether your sufferings are to be ascribed to the law of Responsibility. There are fortunate people in the world, and in virtue of the law of Solidarity they ought to share their prosperity with you." And for the purpose of paving the way to the degrading level of a factitious, official, legal, constrained, and unnatural Solidarity, they erect spoliation into a system, they twist all our notions of justice, and they exalt that individualist sentiment, which they were thought to have proscribed, up to the highest point of power and perversity. Their whole system is thus of a piece—negation of the harmonies that spring from liberty in the principle—despotism and slavery in the result—immorality in the means.

Every effort to divert the natural course of responsibility is a blow aimed at justice, at liberty, at order, at civilization, and at progress.

At justice. An act or a habit being assumed to exist, its good or bad consequences must follow necessarily. Were it possible, indeed, to suppress these consequences, there would doubtless be some advantage in suspending the action of the natural law of responsibility. But the only result to which a written law could lead would be that the good effects of a bad action would be reaped by the author of that action, and that its bad effects would fall back on a third party, or upon the community; which has certainly the special aspect of injustice.

Thus, modern societies are constituted on the principle that the father of a family should rear and educate his children. And it is this principle that restrains within just limits the increase and distribution of population; each man acting under a sense of responsibility. Men are not all endowed with the same amount of foresight; and in large towns improvidence is allied with immorality. We have nowadays a regular budget, and an administration, for the purpose of collecting children abandoned by their parents; no inquiry discourages this shameful desertion, and a constantly-increasing number of destitute children inundates our poorer districts.

Here, then, we have a peasant who marries late in life, in order not to be overburdened with a family, obliged to bring up the children of others. He will not inculcate foresight on his son. Another lives in continence, and we see him taxed to bring up a set of bastards. In a religious point of view, his conscience is tranquil, but in a human point of view he must call himself a fool.

We do not pretend here to enter on the grave question of public charity, we wish only to make this essential observation, that the more a State is centralized, the more that it turns natural responsibility into factitious solidarity, the more it takes away from consequences (which thenceforth affect those who have no connection with their cause) their providential character of justice, chastisement, and preventive restraint.

When Government cannot avoid charging itself with a service that ought to remain within the domain of private activity, it ought at least to allow the responsibility to rest as nearly as possible where it would naturally fall. Thus, in the question of foundling hospitals, the principle being that the father and mother should bring up the child, the law should exhaust every means of endeavoring to enforce this. Failing the parents, this burden should fall on the commune; and failing the commune, on the department. Do you desire to multiply foundlings *ad infinitum*? Declare that the State will take charge of them. It would be still worse if France should undertake to maintain the children of the Chinese, and vice versa.

It is, in truth, a singular thing that we should be always endeavoring to make laws to check the evils of responsibility! Will it never be understood that we do not annihilate these evils—we only turn them into a new channel? The result is one injustice the more, and one lesson the less.

How is the world to be improved if it be not by every man learning to discharge his duty better? And will each man not discharge his duties better in proportion as he has more to suffer by neglecting or violating them? If social action is to be mixed up in the work of responsibility, it ought to be in order to reinforce it, not to thwart it, to concentrate its effects, not to abandon them to chance.

It has been said that opinion is the mistress of the world. Assuredly, in order that opinion should have its proper sway it is necessary that it should be enlightened; and opinion is so much more enlightened in proportion as each man who contributes to form it perceives more clearly the connection of causes and effects. Now nothing leads us to perceive this connection better than experience, and experience, as we know, is personal, and the fruit of responsibility.

In the natural play, then, of this great law of responsibility we have a system of valuable teaching with which it is very imprudent to tamper.

If, by ill-considered combinations, you relieve men from responsibility for their actions, they may still be taught by theory—but no longer by experience. And I think instruction that has never been sanctioned and confirmed by experience may be more dangerous than ignorance itself.

The sense of responsibility is eminently capable of improvement.

This is one of the most beautiful moral phenomena. There is nothing we admire more in a man, in a class, in a nation, than the feeling of responsibility. It indicates superior moral culture, and an exquisite sensibility to the awards of public opinion. It may be, however, that the sense of responsibility is highly developed in one thing and very little in another. In France, among the educated classes, one would die of shame to be caught cheating at cards or addicting oneself to solitary drinking. These things are laughed at among the peasants. But to traffic in political rights, to make merchandise of his vote, to be guilty of inconsistency, to cry out by turns *Vive le Roi! Vive la Ligue!* as the interest of the moment may prompt, these are things that our manners do not brand with shame.

The development of the sense of responsibility may be much aided by female intervention.

Females are themselves extremely sensible of the feeling of responsibility.

It rests with them to create this force moralisatrice among the other sex; for it is their province to distribute praise and blame effectively. Why, then, do they not do so? Because they are not sufficiently acquainted with the connection between causes and effects in the moral world.

The science of morals is the science of all, but especially of the female sex, for they form the manners of a nation.

21

SOLIDARITY

If man were perfect, if he were infallible, society would present a very different harmony from that which is the subject of our inquiries. Ours is not the society of Fourier. It does not exclude evil; it admits dissonances; only we assert that it does not cease to be harmony if these dissonances pave the way to concord, and bring us back to it.

Our point of departure is that man is fallible, and that God has given him free will; and with the faculty of choosing, that of erring, of mistaking what is false for what is true, of sacrificing the future to the present, of giving way to unreasonable desires, etc.

Man errs. But every act, every habit has its consequences.

By means of Responsibility, as we have seen, these consequences fall back on the author of the act. A natural concatenation of rewards or punishments, then, attracts him toward good, or repels him from evil.

Had man been destined to a solitary life, and to solitary labor, Responsibility would have been his only law.

But he is differently placed; he is sociable by destination. It is not true, as Rousseau has said, that man is naturally a perfect and solitary whole, and that the will of the lawgiver has transformed him into a fraction of a greater whole. The family, the province, the nation, the human race, are aggregates with which man has necessary relations. Hence it follows that the actions and the habits of the individual produce, besides the consequences that fall back upon himself, other good or bad consequences that extend themselves to his fellow-men. This is what we term the law of Solidarity, which is a sort of collective Responsibility.

This idea of Rousseau that the legislator has invented society—an idea false in itself—has been injurious in this respect, that it has led men to think that Solidarity is of legislative creation, and we shall immediately see that modern legislators have based upon this doctrine their efforts to subject society to an artificial solidarity, acting in an inverse sense to natural solidarity. In everything, the principle of these great manipulators of the human race is to set up their own work in room of the work of God, which they disown.

Our first task is to prove undeniably the natural existence of the law of Solidarity.

In the eighteenth century, they did not believe in it. They adhered to the doctrine of the personalness of faults. The philosophers of the last century, engaged above all in the reaction against Catholicism, would have feared, by admitting the principle of Solidarity, to open a door to the doctrine of original sin. Every time Voltaire found in the Scriptures a man bearing the punishment of another, he said ironically, "This is frightful, but the justice of God is not that of man."

We are not concerned here to discuss original sin. But what Voltaire laughed at is nevertheless a fact, which is not less incontestable than it is mysterious. The law of Solidarity makes its appearance so frequently and so strikingly, in the individual and in the masses, in details and in the aggregate, in particular and in general facts, that to fail to recognize it implies either the blindness of sectarianism or the zeal of embittered controversy.

The first rule of all human justice is to concentrate the punishment of an action on its author, in virtue of the principle that faults are personal. But this law, sacred as regards individuals, is not the law of God, or even the law of society.

Why is this man rich? Because his father was active, honest, industrious, and economical. The father practiced virtue; the son reaps the rewards.

Why is this other man always suffering, sick, feeble, timorous, and wretched? Because his father, endowed with a powerful constitution, abused it by debauchery and excess. To the guilty fall the agreeable consequences of vice, to the innocent fall its fatal consequences.

There exists not a man upon this earth whose condition has not been determined by thousands of millions of facts in which his own determinations have had no part. What I complain of today was perhaps caused by the caprice of my great-grandfather, etc.

Solidarity manifests itself on a greater scale still, and at distances that are still more inexplicable, when we consider the relations of diverse nations, or of different generations of the same people.

Is it not strange that the eighteenth century was so occupied with intellectual or material works of which we are now enjoying the benefit? Is it not marvellous that we ourselves should make such efforts to cover the country with railways, on which none of us perhaps will ever travel? Who can fail to recognize the profound influence of our old revolutions on the events of our own time? Who can foresee what an inheritance of peace or of discord our present discussions may bequeath to our children?

Look at the public loans. We make war—we obey savage passions—we throw away by these means valuable vitality; and we find means of laying the scourge of all this destruction on our children, who may haply hold war in abhorrence, and be unable to understand our passions and hatreds.

Cast your eyes upon Europe; contemplate the events that agitate France, Germany, Italy, and Poland, and say if the law of Solidarity is a chimerical law.

There is no need to carry this enumeration farther. In order to prove undeniably the existence of the law, it is enough that the action of one man, of one people, of one generation, exerts a certain influence upon another man, another people, or another generation. Society at large is only an aggregate of solidarities that cross and overlap one another. This results from the communicable nature of human intelligence. Conversation, literature, discoveries, sciences, morals, etc., are all examples of this. All these unperceived currents by which one mind corresponds with another, all these efforts without visible connection, the resulting force of which nevertheless pushes on the human race toward an equilibrium, toward an average level that is always rising—all that vast treasury of utilities and of acquired knowledge, which each may draw upon without diminishing it, or augment without being aware of it—all this interchange of thoughts, of productions, of services, and of labor, of good and evil, of virtue and vice, which makes the human family one grand whole, and imparts to thousands of millions of ephemeral existences a common, a universal, a continuous life—all this is Solidarity.

Naturally, then, and to a certain extent, there is an incontestable Solidarity among men. In other words, Responsibility is not exclusively personal, but is shared and divided. Action emanates from individuality; consequences are spread over the community.

We must remark that it is in the nature of every man to desire to be happy. You may say that I am extolling egocentrism if you will; I extol nothing; I show, I prove undeniably, the existence of an innate universal sentiment, which can never cease to exist—personal interest, the desire for happiness, and the repugnance to pain.

Hence it follows that the individual is led so to order his conduct that the good consequences of his actions accrue to himself, while the bad effects fall upon others. He endeavors to spread these bad consequences over the greatest possible number of men, in order that they may be less perceived, and call forth less reaction.

But opinion, that mistress of the world, the daughter of solidarity, brings together all those scattered grievances, and collects all aggrieved interests into a formidable resisting mass. When a man's habits become injurious to those who live around him, they call forth a feeling of repulsion. We judge such habits severely. We denounce them, we brand them; and the man who gives himself up to them becomes an object of distrust, of contempt, and of abhorrence. If he reap some advantages, they are soon far more than compensated by the sufferings that public aversion accumulates on his head. To the troublesome consequences that a bad habit always entails in virtue of the law of Responsibility, there come to be added other consequences still more grievous in virtue of the law of Solidarity.

Our contempt for the man soon extends to the habit, to the vice; and as the want of consideration is one of our most powerful springs of action, it is clear that solidarity, by the reaction that it brings to bear against vicious acts, tends to restrain and to prevent them.

Solidarity, then, like Responsibility, is a progressive force; and we see that, in relation to the author of the act, it resolves itself, if I may so speak, into repercussive or reflected responsibility; that it is still a system of reciprocal rewards and punishments, admirably fitted to circumscribe evil, to extend good, and to urge on mankind on the road of progress.

But in order that it should operate in this way, in order that those who benefit or suffer from an action that is not their own should react upon its author by approbation or disapprobation, by gratitude or resistance, by esteem, affection, praise, or blame, hatred or vengeance—one condition is indispensable; and that condition is that the connecting link between the act and all its effects should be known and appreciated.

When the public is mistaken in this respect, the law fails in its design.

An act is hurtful to the masses; but the masses are convinced that this act is advantageous to them. What is the consequence? The consequence is that instead of reacting against it, in place of condemning it, and by that means restraining it, the public exalt it, honor it, extol it, and repeat it.

Nothing is more frequent, and here is the reason of it: An act produces on the masses not only an effect, but a series of effects. Now it frequently happens that the primary effect is a local good, visible and tangible, while the ulterior effects set a-filtering through the body politic evils that are difficult to discover or to connect with their cause.

War is an example of this. In the infancy of society, we do not perceive all the consequences of war. And, to say truth, in a state of civilization in which there is a less amount of anterior labor (capital) exposed to destruction, less science and money devoted to the machinery of war, etc., these consequences are less prejudicial than they afterwards become. We see only the first campaign, the booty that follows victory, the intoxication of triumph. At that stage, war and warriors are very popular. Then we see the enemy, having become conqueror in his turn, burning down houses and harvests, levying contributions, and imposing laws. In these alternations of success and misfortune, we see generations of men annihilated, agriculture crushed, and two nations impoverished. We see the most important portion of the people spurning the arts of peace, turning their arms against the institutions of their country, serving as the tools of despotism, employing their restless energy in sedition and civil discord, and creating barbarism and solitude at home, as they had formerly done among their neighbors. Do we then pronounce war to be plunder upon a great scale? . . . No; we see its effects without desiring to understand its cause; and when this people, in a state of decadence, shall be invaded in its turn by a swarm of conquerors, centuries after the catastrophe, grave historians will relate that the nation fell because the people had become enervated by peace, because they had forgotten the art of war and the austere virtues of their ancestors.

I could point out the same illusions in connection with the system of slavery.

The same thing is true of religious errors.

In our day, the regime of prohibition gives rise to the same fallacy.

To bring back public opinion, by the diffusion of knowledge and the profound appreciation of causes and effects, into that intelligent state in which bad tendencies come to be branded, and prejudicial measures opposed, is to render a great service to one's country. When public opinion, deceived and misled, honors what is worthy of contempt, spurns what is honorable, punishes virtue and rewards vice, encourages what is hurtful and discourages what is useful, applauds a lie and smothers truth under indifference or insult, a nation turns its back upon progress, and can only be reclaimed by terrible lessons and catastrophes.

We have indicated elsewhere the gross misuse that certain Socialist schools have made of the word Solidarity.

Let us now see in what spirit human laws should be framed.

It seems to me that here there can be no room for doubt. Human law should coincide with the natural law. It should facilitate and ensure the just retribution of men's acts; in other words, it should circumscribe solidarity, and organize reaction in order to enforce responsibility. The law can have no other object than to restrain vicious actions and to multiply virtuous ones, and for that purpose it should favor the just distribution of rewards and punishments, so that the bad effects of an act should be concentrated as much as possible on the person who commits it.

In acting thus, the law conforms itself to the nature of things; solidarity induces a reaction against a vicious act, and the law only regulates that reaction.

The law thus contributes to progress: The more rapidly it brings back the bad effect of the act upon the agent, the more surely it restrains the act itself.

To give an example: Violence is attended with pernicious consequences. Among savages the repression of violence is left to the natural course of things; and what happens? It provokes a terrible reaction. When a man has committed an act of violence against another man, an inextinguishable desire of vengeance is lighted up in the family of the injured party, and is transmitted from generation to generation. The law interferes; and what ought it to do? Should it limit itself to stifle the desire for vengeance, to repress it, to punish it? It is clear that this would be to encourage violence, by sheltering it from reprisals. This is not, then, what the law should do. It ought to substitute itself, so to speak, for the spirit of vengeance, by organizing in its place a reaction against the violence. It should say to the injured family, "I charge myself with the repression of the act you complain of." When the whole tribe considers itself as injured and menaced, the law inquires into the grievance, interrogates the guilty party, makes sure that there is no error as to the fact and as to the person, and thus represses with regularity and certainty an act that would have been punished irregularly.

22

SOCIAL MOTIVE FORCE

It belongs to no human science to assign the ultimate reason of things.

Man suffers; society suffers. We ask why? This is to ask why God has been pleased to endow man with sensibility and free will. As regards this, no one knows more than the revelation in which he has faith has taught him.

But whatever may have been the designs of God, what human science can take as its point of departure is a positive fact, namely, that man has been created free and endowed with feeling.

This is so true that I defy those who are astonished at it to conceive a living, thinking, acting being, endowed with volition and affections—such a being, in short, as man—yet destitute of sensibility and free will.

Could God have ordered things otherwise? Reason undoubtedly answers yes, but imagination says eternally no, so radically impossible is it for us to separate in thought humanity from this double attribute. Now, to be endowed with feeling is to be capable of experiencing sensations that are agreeable or painful.

Hence comfort or uneasiness. From the moment, then, that God gave existence to sensibility, He permitted evil, or the possibility of evil.

In giving us free will, He has endowed us with the faculty, at least in a certain measure, of shunning evil and seeking after good. Free will supposes and accompanies intelligence—what would the faculty of choosing signify if it were not allied with the faculty of examining, of comparing, of judging? Thus, every man who comes into the world brings with him mind and a motive force.

The motive force is that personal irresistible impulse, the essence of all our forces, which leads us to shun Evil and seek after Good. We term it the instinct of preservation, personal or private interest.

This sentiment has been sometimes decried, sometimes misunderstood, but as regards its existence there can be no doubt. Irresistibly we seek after all that, according to our notions, can enhance our destiny, and we avoid all that is likely to deteriorate it. This is at least as certain as it is that every material molecule possesses centripetal and centrifugal force. And just as the double movement of attraction and repulsion is the grand spring of the physical world, we may affirm that the double force of human attraction toward happiness and human repulsion from pain is the mainspring of the social mechanism.

But it is not enough that man is irresistibly led to prefer good to evil; he must also be able to discern what is good and what is evil. This is what God has provided for in giving him that marvelous and complex mechanism called intelligence. To fix his attention, to compare, judge, reason, connect effects with causes, to remember, to foresee; such are—if I may use the expression—the wheels of that admirable machine.

The impulsive force that is possessed by each of us moves under the direction of our intelligence. But our intelligence is imperfect. It is liable to error. We compare, we judge, we act in consequence; but we may err, we may make a bad choice, we may tend toward evil, mistaking it for good, or we may shun good, mistaking it for evil. This is the first source of social dissonances; and it is inevitable, for this reason, that the great motive spring of humanity—personal interest—is not, like material attraction, a blind force, but a force guided by an imperfect intelligence. Let us be very sure, then, that we shall not see Harmony except under this restriction. God has not seen proper to found social order or Harmony upon perfection, but upon human perfectibility, our capacity for improvement. If our intelligence is imperfect, it is improvable. It develops, enlarges, and rectifies itself. It begins of new and verifies its operations. Experience at each moment puts us right, and Responsibility suspends over our heads a complete system of punishments and rewards. Every step that we take on the road of error plunges us into increased suffering, and in such a way that the warning cannot fail to be heard, and the rectification of our determinations, and consequently of our actions, follows, sooner or later, with infallible certainty.

Under the impulse that urges him on, ardent to pursue happiness, prompt to seize it, man may be seeking his own good in the misery of others. This is a second and an abundant source of discordant social combinations. But the limit of such disturbances is marked; and they find their inevitable doom in the law of Solidarity. Individual force thus misapplied calls forth opposition from all the analogous forces, which, antagonistic to evil by their nature, repel injustice and chastise it.

It is thus that progress is realized, and it is not the less progress from being dearly bought. It springs from a native impulse, which is universal, and inherent in our nature, directed by an intelligence that is frequently misled, and subjected to a will that is frequently depraved. Arrested on its march by Error and Injustice, it receives the all-powerful assistance of Responsibility and Solidarity to enable it to surmount these obstacles, and it cannot fail to receive that assistance since it springs from these obstacles themselves.

This internal, universal, and imperishable motive power, which resides in each individual and constitutes him an active being, this tendency of every man to pursue happiness and shun misery, this product, this effect, this necessary complement of sensibility, without which sensibility would be only an inexplicable scourge, this primordial phenomenon that is at the bottom of all human actions, this attractive and repulsive force we have denominated the mainspring of the social mechanism, has had for detractors the greater part of our publicists; and this is one of the strangest aberrations the annals of science present.

It is true that self-interest is the cause of all the evils, as it is of all the good, incident to man. It cannot fail to be so, since it determines all our acts. Seeing this, some publicists can imagine no better means of eradicating evil than by stifling self-interest. But as by this means they would destroy the very spring and motive of our activity, they have thought proper to endow us with a different motive force, namely, devotion, self-sacrifice. They hope that henceforth all transactions and social combinations will take place at their bidding, upon the principle of self-abandonment. We are no longer to pursue our own happiness, but the happiness of others; the warnings of sensibility are to go for nothing, like the rewards and punishments of Responsibility. All the laws of our nature are to be reversed; the spirit of sacrifice is to be substituted for the instinct of preservation; in a word, no one is to think longer on his own personality, but for the purpose of hastening to sacrifice it to the public good. It is from such a universal transformation of the human heart that certain publicists, who think themselves very religious, expect to realize perfect social harmony. They have forgotten to tell us how they hope to effect this indispensable preliminary, the transformation of the human heart.

If they are foolish enough to undertake this, they will find that they lack the power to accomplish it. Do they desire the proof of what I say? Let them try the experiment on themselves; let them endeavor to stifle in their own hearts all feeling of self-interest, so that it shall no longer make its appearance in the most ordinary actions of life. They will not be long in finding out their powerlessness. Why, then, pretend to impose upon all men, without exception, a doctrine to which they themselves cannot submit?

I confess myself unable to see anything religious, unless it be in intention and appearance, in these affected theories, in these impracticable maxims that they affect so earnestly to preach, while they continue to act just as the vulgar act. Is it, I would ask, true and genuine religion that inspires these Catholic economists with the presumptuous thought that God has done His work ill, and that it is their mission to repair it? Bossuet did not think so when he said, "Man aspires to happiness, and he cannot help aspiring to it."

Declamations against personal interest never can have much scientific significance; for self-interest is part of man's indestructible nature—at least, we cannot destroy it without destroying man himself. All that religion, morals, and political economy can do is to give an enlightened direction to this impulsive force—to point out not only the primary, but the ulterior consequences of those acts to which it urges us. A superior and progressive satisfaction consequent on a transient suffering, long continued and constantly increased suffering following on a momentary gratification; such after all are moral good and evil. That which determines the choice of men toward virtue is an elevated and enlightened interest, but it is always primarily a personal interest.

If it is strange that personal interest should be decried, when considered not with reference to its immoral abuse, but as the providential moving spring of all human activity, it is still stranger that it should have been put aside altogether, and that men should have imagined themselves in a situation to frame a system of social science without taking it into account.

It is an inexplicable instance of folly that publicists in general should regard themselves as the depositaries and the arbiters of this motive spring. Each starts from this point of departure. Assuming that mankind is a flock, and that I am the shepherd, how am I to manage in order to make mankind happy? Or this: Given on the one hand a certain quantity of clay, and on the other a potter, what should the potter do in order to turn that clay to the best account?

Our publicists may differ when the question comes to be which is the best potter, who forms and moulds the clay most advantageously? but they are all at one upon this, that their function is to knead the human clay, and what the clay has to do is simply to be kneaded by them. Under the title of legislators, they establish between themselves and the human race relations analogous to those of guardian and ward. The idea never occurs to them that the human race is a living sentient body, endowed with volition and acting according to laws that it is not their business to invent, since they already exist, nor to impose, but to study; that humanity is an aggregate of beings in all respects like themselves, and in no way inferior or subordinate; endowed both with an impulse to act, and with intelligence to choose; which feels on all sides the stimulus of Responsibility and Solidarity; and that, in short, from all these phenomena there results an aggregate of self-existing relations, which it is not the business of science to create, as they imagine, but to observe.

Rousseau, I think, is the publicist who has most naively exhumed from antiquity this omnipotence of the resuscitated legislator of the Greeks. Convinced that the social order is a human invention, he compares it to a machine; men are the wheels of that machine, the ruler sets it in motion; the lawgiver invents it, under the impulse given him by the publicist, who thus finds himself definitively the mainspring and regulator of the human species. This is the reason why the publicist never fails to address himself to the legislator in the imperative style; he decrees him to decree: "Found your society upon such or such a principle; give it good manners and customs; bend it to the yoke of religion; direct its aims and energies toward arms, or commerce, or agriculture, or virtue," etc. Others more modest speak in this way: "Idlers will not be tolerated in the republic; you will distribute the population conveniently between the towns and the country; you will take order that there shall be neither rich nor poor," etc.

These formulas attest the unmeasured presumption of those who employ them. They imply a doctrine that does not leave one atom of dignity to the human race.

I know not whether they are more false in theory or pernicious in practice. In both views, they lead to deplorable results.

They would lead us to believe that the social economy is an artificial arrangement coined in the brain of an inventor. Hence every publicist constitutes himself an inventor. His greatest desire is to find acceptance for his mechanism; his greatest care is to create abhorrence of all others, and principally of that which springs spontaneously from the organization of man and from the nature of things. The books conceived and written on this plan are, and can only be, prolix declamations against Society.

This false science does not study the concatenation of effects and causes. It does not inquire into the good and evil produced by men's actions, and trust afterwards to the motive force of Society in choosing the road it is to follow. No; it enjoins, it constrains, it imposes, or, if it cannot do that, it counsels; like a natural philosopher who should say to the stone, "Thou art not supported; I order thee to fall, or at least I advise it." It is upon this footing that Mr. Droz has said that "the design of political economy is to render easy circumstances as general as possible"— a definition that has been welcomed with great favor by the Socialists, because it opens a door to every Utopia, and leads to artificial regulation. What should we say if Mr. Arago were to open his course in this way, "The object of astronomy is to render gravitation as general as possible?" It is true that men are animated beings, endowed with volition, and acting under the influence of free will. But there also resides in them an internal force, a sort of gravitation: and the question is to know toward what they gravitate. If it be fatally, inevitably, toward evil, there is no remedy, and assuredly the remedy will not come to us from a publicist subject like other men to the common tendency. If it be toward good, here we have the motive force already found; science has no need to substitute for it constraint or advice. Its part is to enlighten our free will, to display effects as flowing from causes, well assured that, under the influence of truth, "ease and material prosperity tend to become as general as possible."

Practically, the doctrine that would place the motive force of society not in mankind at large, nor in its peculiar organization, but in legislators and governments, is attended with consequences still more deplorable. It tends to draw down upon Governments a crushing responsibility, from which they never recover. If there are sufferings, it is the fault of Government; if there are poor, it is the fault of Government. Is not Government the prime mover? If the mainspring is bad or inoperative, break it, and choose another. Or else they lay the blame on science itself; and in our days we have it repeated ad nauseam that "all social sufferings are imputable to political economy."[1] Why not, when Political Economy presents herself as having for design to realize the happiness of men without their co-operation? When such notions prevail, the last thing men take it into their heads to do is to turn their regards upon themselves, and inquire whether the true cause of their sufferings is not their own ignorance and injustice; their ignorance that brings them under the discipline of Responsibility, and their injustice that draws down upon them the reaction of Solidarity. How should mankind ever dream of seeking in their errors the cause of their sufferings when the human race is persuaded that it is inert by nature, and that the principle of all activity, consequently of all responsibility, is external, and resides in the will of the lawgiver and the governing power?

Were I called upon to mark the feature that distinguishes Socialism from Political Economy, I should find it here. Socialism boasts of a vast number of sects. Each sect has its Utopia, and so far are they from any mutual understanding that they declare against each other war to the knife. The atelier social organize of Mr. Blanc, and the anarchie of Mr. Proudhon—the association of

---

[1]"Poverty is the fruit of Political Economy. . . . Political Economy requires death to come to its aid; . . . it is the theory of instability and theft." Proudhon, *Contradictions Economiques,* t. xi. p. 214. "If the people want bread, it is the fault of Political Economy." Ibid.

Fourier, and the communism of Mr. Cabet—are as different from each other as night is from day. Why do these sectarian leaders, then, range themselves under the common denomination of Socialists, and what is the bond that unites them against natural or providential society? They have no other bond than this, they all repudiate natural society. What they wish is an artificial society springing ready made from the brain of the inventor. No doubt each of them wishes to be the Jupiter of this Minerva—no doubt each of them hugs his own contrivance and dreams of his own social order. But they have this in common, that they recognize in humanity neither the motive force, which urges mankind on to good, nor the curative force, which delivers it from evil. They fight among themselves as to what form they are to mold the human clay into, but they are all agreed that humanity is clay to be molded. Humanity is not in their eyes a living harmonious being that God himself has provided with progressive and self-sustaining forces, but rather a mass of inert matter that has been waiting for them to impart to it sentiment and life; it is not a subject to be studied, but a subject to be experimented on.

Political Economy, on the other hand, after having clearly shown that there are in each man forces of impulse and repulsion, the aggregate of which constitutes the social impellent, and after being convinced that this motive force tends toward good, never dreams of annihilating it in order to substitute another of its own creation, but studies the varied and complicated social phenomena to which it gives birth.

Is this to say that Political Economy is as much a stranger to social progress as astronomy is to the motion of the heavenly bodies? Certainly not. Political Economy has to do with beings that are intelligent and free—and, as such, let us never forget, subject to error. Their tendency is toward good; but they may err. Science, then, interferes usefully, not to create causes and effects, not to change the tendencies of man, not to subject him to organizations, to injunctions, or even to advice, but to point out to him the good and the evil that result from his decisions.

Political Economy is thus quite a science of observation and exposition. She does not say to men, "I enjoin you, I counsel you, not to go too near the fire;" she does not say, "I have invented a social organization; the gods have taught me institutions that will keep you at a respectful distance from the fire." No, Political Economy only shows men clearly that fire will burn them, proclaims it, proves it, and does the same thing as regards all other social or moral phenomena, convinced that this is enough. The repugnance to die by fire is considered as a primordial pre-existent fact, which Political Economy has not created, and which she cannot alter or change.

Economists cannot be always at one; but it is easy to see that their differences are quite of another kind from those that divide the Socialists. Two men who devote their whole attention to observe one and the same phenomenon and its effects—rent, for example, exchange, competition—may not arrive at the same conclusion, and this proves nothing more than that one of the two has observed the phenomenon inaccurately or imperfectly. It is an operation to be repeated. With the aid of other observers, the probability is that truth in the end will be discovered. It is for this reason, that if each economist were, like each astronomer, to make himself fully acquainted with what his predecessors have done, as far as they have gone, the science would be progressive, and for that reason more and more useful, rectifying constantly observations inaccurately made, and adding indefinitely new observations to those which had been made before.

But the Socialists—each pursuing his own road, and coining artificial combinations in the mint of his own brain—may pursue their inquiries in this way to all eternity without coming to any common understanding, and without the labors of one aiding to any extent the labors of another. Say profited by the labors of Adam Smith; Rossi by those of Say; Blanqui and Joseph Garnier by those of all their predecessors. But Plato, Sir Thomas More, Harrington, Fenelon, Fourier, might amuse themselves with organizing according to their own fancy a Republic, an Utopia, an Oceana, a Salente, a Phalanstere, and no one would ever discover the slightest affinity between their chimerical creations. These dreamers spin all out of their own imaginations, men as well as things. They invent a social order without respect to the human heart, and then they invent a human heart to suit their social order.

23

EXISTENCE OF EVIL

In these last days science has retrograded and been driven back. It has been bent and twisted under the obligation imposed upon it, if I may so speak, of denying the existence of Evil under pain of being convicted of denying the existence of God.

Writers whose business it is to display exquisite sensibility, unbounded philanthropy, and unrivaled devotion to religion, have got into the way of saying, "Evil cannot enter into the providential plan. Suffering is no ordinance of God and nature, but comes from human institutions."

As this doctrine falls in with the passions that they desire to cherish, it soon becomes popular. Books and journals have been filled with declamations against society. Science is no longer permitted to study facts impartially. Whoever dares to warn men that a certain vice, a certain habit, leads necessarily to certain hurtful consequences is marked down as a man devoid of human feelings, without religion, an Atheist, a Malthusian, an Economist.

Socialism has carried its folly so far as to announce the termination of all social suffering, but not of all individual suffering. It has not ventured to predict that a day will come when man will no longer suffer, grow old, and die.

Now, I would ask, is it easier to reconcile with the infinite goodness of God, evil that assails individually every man who comes into the world, than evil that is extended over society at large? And then is it not a contradiction so transparent as to be puerile to deny the existence of suffering in the masses, when we admit its existence in individuals?

Man suffers, and will always suffer. Society, then, also suffers, and will always suffer. Those who address mankind should have the courage to tell it this. Humanity is not a fine lady, with delicate nerves, and an irritable temperament, from whom we must conceal the coming storm, more especially when to foresee it is the only way to ensure our getting out of it safely. In this respect, all the books with which France has been inundated, from Sismondi and Buret downward, appear to me to be wanting in virility. Their authors dare not tell the truth; nay, they dare not investigate it, for fear of discovering that absolute poverty is the necessary starting point of the human race, and that, consequently, so far are we from being in a position to attribute that poverty to the social order, it is to the social order that we must attribute all the triumphs we have already achieved over our original destitution. But, then, after such an avowal, they could no longer constitute themselves tribunes of the people, and the avengers of the masses oppressed by civilization.

After all, science merely establishes, combines, and deduces facts; she does not create them; she does not produce them, nor is she responsible for them. Is it not strange that men should have gone to the length of announcing and disseminating the paradox that if mankind suffers, its sufferings are due to Political Economy? Thus, after being blamed for investigating the sufferings of society, Political Economy is accused of engendering those sufferings by that same investigation.

I assert that science can do nothing more than observe and establish facts. Prove to us that humanity, instead of being progressive, is retrograde; and that inevitable and insurmountable laws urge mankind on to irremediable deterioration. Show us that the law of Malthus and that of Ricardo are true in their worst and most pernicious sense, and that it is impossible to deny the tyranny of capital, or the incompatibility between machinery and labor, or any of the other contradictory alternatives in which Chateaubriand and Tocqueville have placed the human race; then I maintain that science ought to proclaim this, and proclaim it aloud.

Why should we shut our eyes to a gulf that is gaping before us? Do we require the naturalist or the physiologist to reason upon individual man on the assumption that his organs are exempt from pain or not liable to destruction? *Pulvis es, et in pulverem reverteris*; such is the declaration of anatomical science backed by universal experience. No doubt this is a hard truth for us to receive—not less hard than the contested propositions of Malthus and Ricardo. But are we for this reason to spare the delicate sensibility that has sprung up all at once among our modern publicists, and has given existence to Socialism? Is medical science for the same reason, to affirm audaciously that we are constantly renewing our youth and are immortal? Or if medical science refuse to stoop to such juggling, are we to foam at the mouth and cry out, as has been done in the case of the social sciences— "Medical science admits the existence of pain and death; it is misanthropical; it is cruel; it accuses God of being malevolent or powerless; it is impious; it is atheistical; nay, more, it creates the evil the existence of which it refuses to deny"?

I have never doubted that the Socialist schools have led away many generous hearts and earnest minds, and I have no wish to humiliate anyone. But the general character of Socialism is very whimsical, and I cannot help asking myself how long such a tissue of puerilities can continue in vogue.

In Socialism all is affectation.

It affects scientific forms and scientific language, and we have seen what sort of science it teaches.

In its writings it affects a delicacy of nerve so feminine as to be unable to listen to a tale of social sufferings; and while it has introduced into literature this insipid and mawkish sensibility, it has established in the arts a taste for the trivial and the horrible; in ordinary life, a sort of scarecrow fashion in dress, appearance, and deportment—the long beard, the grim and sullen countenance, the vulgar airs of a village Titan or Prometheus. In politics (where such puerilities are less innocent), Socialism has introduced the doctrine of energetic means of transition, the violence of revolutionary practices, life and material interests sacrificed en masse to what is ideal and chimerical. But what Socialism affects, above all, is a certain show and appearance of religion! This is only one of the Socialist tactics, it is true—such tactics are always disgraceful to a school when they lead to hypocrisy.

These Socialists are perpetually talking to us of Christ; but I would ask them, how it is that while they acknowledge that Christ, the innocent par excellence, prayed in His agony that "the cup might pass from Him," adding, "Nevertheless, not my will but Thine be done," they should think it strange that mankind at large should be called upon to exercise resignation also.

No doubt, had God willed it, He might have so arranged His almighty plans that just as the individual advances toward inevitable death, the human race might have advanced toward inevitable destruction. In that case, we should have had no choice but to submit, and science, whether she liked it or not, would have to have admitted the somber social denouement, just as she now admits the melancholy individual denouement.

But happily it is not so.

There is redemption for man, and for humanity.

The one is endowed with an immortal soul; the other with indefinite perfectibility.

24

PERFECTIBILITY

That the human race is perfectible; that it progresses towards a higher and higher level; that its wealth is increasing and becoming more equalized; that its ideas are being enlarged and purified; that its errors, and the oppressions these errors support, are disappearing; that its knowledge shines with brighter and brighter effulgence; that its morality is improving; that it is learning, by reason or by experience, in the domain of responsibility, the art of earning a constantly larger amount of recompense, and a constantly smaller amount of chastisement; that, consequently, evil is continually lessening, and good continually increasing—these are conclusions that it is impossible to doubt when we scrutinize the nature of man and that intelligent principle, which is his essence, which was breathed into him with the breath of life, and warrants the scriptural declaration that man is made in the image of God.

We know too well that man is not a perfect being. Were he perfect, he would not reflect a vague resemblance of God; he would be God himself. He is imperfect, then—subject to error and to suffering—but, on the other hand, were he stationary, what title could he have to claim the unspeakable privilege of bearing in himself the image of a perfect being?

Moreover, if intelligence, which is the faculty of comparing, of judging, of rectifying errors, of learning, does not constitute individual perfectibility, what can constitute it?

And if the union of all individual perfectibilities, especially among beings capable of communicating to each other their acquisitions, does not afford a guarantee for collective perfectibility, we must renounce all philosophy and all moral and political science.

What constitutes man's perfectibility is his intelligence, or the faculty that has been given to him of passing from error, which is the parent of evil, to truth, which is the generating principle of good.

It is science and experience that cause man to abandon in his mind, error for truth, and afterwards, in his conduct, evil for good; it is the discovery he makes, in phenomena and in acts, of effects he had not suspected.

But to enable him to acquire this science, he must have an interest in acquiring it. In order that he should profit by this experience, he must have an interest in profiting by it. It is in the law of responsibility, then, that we must search for the means of realizing human perfectibility.

And as we can form no idea of responsibility apart from liberty; as acts that are not voluntary can afford neither instruction nor available experience; as beings capable of being improved or deteriorated by the exclusive action of external causes without the participation of choice, reflection, or free will (although this happens in the case of unconscious organized matter), could not be called perfectible, in the moral acceptation of the word, we must conclude that liberty is the very essence of progress. To impair man's liberty is not only to hurt and degrade him; it is to change his nature; it is (in the measure and proportion in which such oppression is exercised) to render him incapable of improvement; it is to despoil him of his resemblance to the Creator; it is to dim and deaden in his noble nature that vital spark that glowed there from the beginning.

But in thus proclaiming aloud our fixed and unalterable belief in human perfectibility, and in progress, which is necessary in every sense, and that, by a marvelous correspondence, is as much more active in one direction as it is more active in all others, we must not be regarded as indulging in Utopianism, or be considered as optimists, believing "all to be for the best, in the best of worlds," and expecting the immediate arrival of the millennium.

Alas! when we turn our regards on the world as it is, and see around us the enormous amount of mud and meanness, suffering and complaint, vice and crime, that still exist—when we reflect on the moral action exerted on society by the classes who ought to point out to the lagging multitude the Way to the New Jerusalem—when we ask ourselves what use the rich make of their fortune, the poets of their genius, philosophers of their scientific lucubrations, journalists of the ministry with which they are invested, high functionaries, ministers of state, representatives of the people, kings, of the power fate has placed in their hands—when we witness revolutions like that which has recently agitated Europe, and in which each man seems to be in search of what must in the long-run prove fatal to himself and to society at large—when we see cupidity in all shapes and among all ranks, the constant sacrifice of the interests of others to our own selfish interest, and of the future to the present—when we see that great and inevitable moving spring of the human race, personal interest, still making its appearance only in manifestations the most material and the most improvident—when we see the working classes, preyed upon by the parasitism of public functionaries, rise up in revolutionary convulsions, not against this withering parasitism, but against wealth legitimately acquired, that is to say, against the very element of their own deliverance and the principle of their own right and force—when such spectacles present themselves to us on all sides, we get afraid of ourselves, we tremble for our faith in human perfectibility, the light would seem to waver, and be on the eve of extinction, leaving us in the fearful darkness of Pessimism.

But no—there is no ground for despair. Whatever be the impressions that too recent circumstances have made upon us, humanity still moves onward. What causes the illusion is that we measure the life of nations by the short span of our own individual lives; and because a few years are a long period for us, we imagine them also a long period for them. But even adopting this inadequate measure, the progress of society on all sides is visible. I need scarcely remind you of the marvels that have already been accomplished in what concerns material advantages, the improved salubrity of towns, and in the means of locomotion and communication, etc.

In a political point of view, has the French nation gained no experience? Who dares affirm that had all the difficulties through which we have just passed presented themselves half a century ago, or sooner, France would have overcome them with as much ability, prudence, and wisdom, and with so few sacrifices? I write these lines in a country that has been fertile in revolutions. Florence used to have a rising every five years, and at each rising one half of her citizens robbed and murdered the other half. Had we only a little more imagination—not that which creates, invents, and assumes facts, but that which recalls them and brings them to mind—we should be more just to our times and to our contemporaries! What remains true, and it is a truth no one can know better than an Economist, is this, that human progress, especially in its dawn, is excessively slow, so very slow as to give rise to despair in the heart of the philanthropist.

Men whose genius invests them with the power of the press ought, it seems to me, to regard things more nearly, before scattering amidst the social fermentation discouraging speculations that imply for humanity the alternative of two modes of degradation.

We have already seen some examples of this when treating of population, of rent, of machinery, of the division of inheritance, etc.

Here is another, taken from Mr. de Chateaubriand, who merely formulates a fashionable conventionalism: "The corruption of morals and the civilization of nations march abreast. If the last present means of liberty, the first is an inexhaustible source of slavery."

It is beyond doubt that civilization presents means of liberty, and it is equally beyond doubt that corruption is a source of slavery. That which is doubtful, more than doubtful—and what for my own part I deny solemnly and formally—is this, that civilization and corruption march abreast. If it were so, a fatal equilibrium would be established between the means of liberty and the sources of slavery; and immobility would be the fate of the human race.

There cannot, moreover, enter into the human heart a thought more melancholy, more discouraging, more desolating, a thought more fitted to urge us to despair, to irreligion, to impiety, to blasphemy, than this, that every human being, whether he wills it or not, whether he doubts it or not, proceeds on the road of civilization—and civilization is corruption!

Then, if all civilization be corruption, wherein consists its advantages? It is impossible to pretend that civilization is unattended with moral, intellectual, and material advantages, for then it would cease to be civilization. As Chateaubriand employs the term, civilization signifies material progress, an increase of population, of wealth, of prosperity, the development of intelligence, the advancement of the sciences; and all these steps of progress imply, according to him, a corresponding retrogression of the moral sense.

This would be enough to tempt men to a wholesale suicide; for I repeat that material and intellectual progress is not of our preparation and ordination. God himself has decreed it, in giving us expansible desires and improvable faculties. We are urged on to it without wishing it, without knowing it—Chateaubriand and his equals, if he has any, more than any one else. And this progress is to sink us deeper and deeper into immorality and slavery, by means of corruption!

I thought at first that Chateaubriand had let slip an unguarded phrase, as poets frequently do, without examining it too narrowly. With that class of writers, sound sometimes runs away with sense. Provided the antithesis is symmetrical, what matters it that the thought be false or objectionable? Provided the metaphor produces its intended effect, that it has an air of inspiration and depth, that it secures the applause of the public, and enables the author to pass for an oracle, of what importance are exactitude and truth?

I had thought, then, that Chateaubriand, giving way to a momentary excess of misanthropy, had allowed himself to formulate a conventionalism, a vulgarism dragged from the kennel. "Civilization and corruption march abreast" is a phrase that has been repeated since the days of Heraclitus, but it is not more true on that account.

At a distance of several years, however, the same great writer has reproduced the same thought, and in a more didactic form; which shows that it expressed his deliberate opinion. It is proper to combat it, not because it comes from Chateaubriand, but because it has got abroad, and so generally prevails.

"The material condition is ameliorated," he says,

> intellectual progress advances, and nations, in place of profiting, decay. Here is the explanation of the decay of society and the growth of the individual. Had the moral sense been developed in proportion to the development of intelligence, there would have been a counter weight, and the human race would have grown greater without danger. But it is just the contrary which happens. The perception of good and evil is obscured in proportion as intelligence is enlightened; conscience becomes narrowed in proportion as ideas are enlarged. *Memoires d' Outre-Tombe*, vol. 11.

25

RELATIONSHIP OF POLITICAL
ECONOMY AND RELIGION

A phenomenon is always found placed between two other phenomena, one of which is its efficient, and the other its final cause; and science has not done with that phenomenon as long as either of these relations remains undeveloped.

The human mind generally begins, I think, with the discovery of final causes, because they are more immediately interesting to us. No species of knowledge, besides, leads us with more force toward religious ideas, or is more fitted to make us feel in all the fibers of our heart a lively sense of gratitude for the inexhaustible goodness of God.

Habit, it is true, has so familiarized us with a great number of these providential intentions, that we enjoy them without thought. We see, and we hear, without thinking of the ingenious mechanism of the eye and of the ear. The sun, the dew, the rain, lavish upon us their useful effects, or their gentle sensations, without awakening our surprise or our gratitude. This is solely owing to the continued action upon us of these admirable phenomena. For let a final cause, although comparatively insignificant, come to be disclosed to us for the first time, let the botanist explain to us why this plant affects such or such a form, or why that other is clothed in such or such a color, we immediately feel in our heart the unspeakable enchantment with which new proofs of the power, the goodness, and the wisdom of God never fail to penetrate us.

The region of final intentions, then, is for man's imagination as an atmosphere impregnated with religious ideas.

But after we have perceived, or had a glimpse of the phenomenon in this aspect, we have still to study it in another relation, that is to say, to seek for its efficient cause.

It is strange, but it sometimes happens that after having obtained the full knowledge of that cause, we find that it carries with it so necessarily the effect we had admired at first, that we refuse to recognize in it any longer the character of a final cause; and we say: "I was very simple to believe that God had provided such an arrangement with such a design; I see now that the cause I have discovered being given (and it is inevitable), this arrangement must follow necessarily, apart from any pretended providential intention."

It is thus that defective and superficial science, with its scalpel and its analyses, comes sometimes to destroy in our souls the religious sentiment to which the simple aspect of nature had given rise.

This is the case frequently with the anatomist and the astronomer. What a strange thing it is, exclaims the ignorant man, that when an extraneous substance penetrates into a tissue, where its presence does great injury, an inflammation and a suppuration take place, which tend to expel it! No, says the anatomist, there it nothing intentional in that expulsion. It is a necessary effect of the suppuration; and the suppuration itself is a necessary effect of the presence of an extraneous substance in our tissues. If you wish it, I shall explain to you the mechanism, and you will acknowledge yourself that the effect follows the cause, but that the cause has not been arranged intentionally to produce that effect, since it is itself the necessary effect of an anterior cause.

How I admire, says the ignorant man, the foresight of God who has willed that the rain should not descend on the soil in a sheet, but should fall in drops, as if it came from the gardener's watering-pot! Were it not so, vegetation would be impossible. You throw away your admiration, answers the learned naturalist; the cloud is not a sheet of water; if it were, it could not be supported by the atmosphere. It is a collection of microscopic vesicles, or minute bladders like soap-bubbles. When their density increases, or when they burst by compression, these thousands of millions of infinitesimal drops fall, growing larger in their descent by the vapor of the water which they precipitate, etc. If vegetation is benefited in consequence, it is by accident; but we must not think that the Creator amuses himself in sending us down water through the sieve of a monster watering-pot.

Ignorance, we must confess, very often imparts a certain plausibility to science when the connection of causes and effects is regarded in this way, by attributing a phenomenon to a final intention that does not exist, and that is dissipated before the light of superior knowledge.

Thus, in former days, before men had any knowledge of electricity, they were frightened by the noise of thunder, being able to recognize in that astounding voice, bellowing amid the storm, nothing less than a manifestation of Divine wrath. This is an association of ideas that, like many others, has disappeared before the progress of physical science. Man is so constituted that when a phenomenon affects him, he searches for the cause of it; and if he finds out that cause, he gives it a name. Then he sets himself to find out the cause of that cause, and so he goes on until he can mount no higher, when he stops, and exclaims, "It is God; it is the will of God." This is his ultimate ratio. He is arrested, however, only for the moment. Science advances, and soon this second, third, or fourth cause, which had remained unperceived, is revealed to his eyes. Then science says, This effect is not due, as we believed, to the immediate will of God, but to that natural

cause I have just discovered. And man, after having taken possession of this discovery, after having gained this step in the region
of science, finds himself, so to speak, one step farther removed
from the region of Faith, and again asks, What is the cause of that
cause? And not finding it, he persists in the ever-recurring explanation, "It is the will of God." And so he proceeds onwards for
indefinite ages, through a countless succession of scientific reve-
lations and exercises of faith.

This procedure on the part of mankind must appear to superficial minds to be destructive of every religious idea; for is the
result of it not this, that as science advances, God recedes? Do we
not see clearly that the domain of final intentions is narrowed in
proportion as the domain of natural causes is enlarged?

Unhappy are they who give to this fine problem so narrow a
solution. No, it is not true that as science advances, the idea of
God recedes. On the contrary, what is true is that, as our intelligence increases, this idea is enlarged, and broadened, and elevated. When we discover a natural cause for what we had imagined an immediate, spontaneous, supernatural act of the Divine
will, are we to conclude that His will is absent or indifferent? No,
indeed; all that it proves is that that will acts by processes different from those it had pleased us to imagine. All that it proves is,
that the phenomenon we regarded as an accident in creation
occupies its place in the universal frame; and that everything,
even the most special effects, have been foreseen from all eternity
by the divine prescience. What! Is the idea we form of the power
of God lessened when we come to see that each of the countless
results which we discover, or that escape our investigations, not
only has its natural cause, but is bound up in an infinite circle of
causes; so that there is not a detail of movement, of force, of
form, of life, that is not the product of the great whole, or that
can be explained apart from that whole.

But why this dissertation, which is foreign, as it would seem,
to the main object of our inquiries? The phenomena of the social
economy have likewise their efficient cause, and their providential intention. In this department, as in natural science, as in

anatomy, or in astronomy, men have frequently denied the final cause precisely because the efficient cause assumes the character of an absolute necessity.

The social world abounds in harmonies, of which we can form no adequate or complete conception until the mind has traced back to causes, in order to seek their explanation, and descended to effects, to discover the destination of the phenomena.

INDEX

The Mises Institute, founded in 1982, is a teaching and research center for the study of Austrian economics, libertarian and classical liberal political theory, and peaceful international relations. In support of the school of thought represented by Ludwig von Mises, Murray N. Rothbard, Henry Hazlitt, and F.A. Hayek, we publish books and journals, sponsor student and professional conferences, and provide online education. Mises.org is a vast resource of free material for anyone in the world interested in these ideas. For we seek a radical shift in the intellectual climate, away from statism and toward a private property order.

For more information, see Mises.org, write us at info@mises.org, or phone us at 1.800.OF.MISES.

Mises Institute
518 West Magnolia Avenue
Auburn, Alabama 36832